SOLDIERS OF THE PÁTRIA

Soldiers of the Pátria

A History of the Brazilian Army, 1889-1937

FRANK D. McCANN

Stanford University Press, Stanford, California 2004

Stanford University Press
Stanford, California
© 2004 by the Board of Trustees of the
Leland Stanford Junior University.
All rights reserved.

Publication assistance for this book was provided by the
University of New Hampshire.

Printed in the United States of America
on acid-free, archival-quality paper

Library of Congress Cataloging-in-Publication Data
McCann, Frank D.
  Soldiers of the Pátria : a history of the Brazilian Army,
1889-1937 / Frank D. McCann.
      p. cm.
  Includes bibliographical references and index.
  ISBN 0-8047-3222-1 (alk. paper)
  1. Brazil. Exército—History—19th century. 2. Brazil.
Exército—History—20th century. I. Title.
UA619.M387 2004
355'.00981—dc21   2003007567

Original Printing 2004
Last figure below indicates year of this printing:

13   12   11   10   09   08   07   06   05   04

Typeset by Classic Typography in 10.5/12 Bembo

To my *netinhas*, Cassidy Clare and Samantha Katherine,
with confidence that they will make their dreams come true
and never lose their love of books. And to the memory
of my friends Newton Bonuma and John Wirth.

Contents

Maps

Tables

Recife, October 1930. The sergeant came to attention and saluted the commanding colonel, saying that he was under arrest. The colonel unsnapped his holster, stating, "[Y]ou should take my pistol because a prisoner should not be armed." The sergeant replied, "Colonel, keep your pistol." Officers within earshot applauded. The sergeant then asked the arrested colonel for permission to order the changing of the guard. The colonel refused, saying that he was no longer in charge, that he was nobody. Hearing that, the sergeant snapped to attention and said, "To me you are a colonel in the army. . . . [O]nly momentarily are we in opposing camps." The colonel then told him to order the guard changed.[1]

That this scene actually happened during the Revolution of 1930 challenges common ideas about military rebellions. Brazilian military lore included unwritten norms that guided behavior in extralegal situations. Although discipline as conventionally understood in other armies was disrupted in Brazilian rebellions, certain attitudes were maintained. Disruption of discipline was transitory; as the sergeant told his colonel, "[O]nly momentarily are we in opposing camps." The history of the Brazilian army is best understood as a reflection of the complex, complicated, and sometimes contradictory national culture.

The military, particularly the army, has had a significant part in Brazilian social and political history; indeed, the armed forces oversaw the government from 1964 to 1985. When I set out to understand the how and why of military behavior, my path continually returned to the 1889–1937 period, which I came to see as the seedbed of later developments. I am particularly confident in asserting this because I carried my research on the history of the army down to the early 1990s. Moreover, my earlier work had given me a familiarity with the army during the *Estado Novo* of 1937 to 1945. In a series of articles and conference papers, some of which were published in Brazil as a book entitled *A Nação Armada* (1982), whose topics took me back and forth across the twentieth century, I examined various aspects of the army's role in Brazilian society and politics. That project convinced me that a history of the army itself was necessary. My original goal was to take the story up to the 1990s, but the Old Republic and the 1930s proved too rich in documentation and literature to be dealt with briefly, so I decided to end with what I see as the crucial event in Brazil's twentieth-century army history, namely the establishment of the Estado Novo in November 1937. The experiences of the Old Republic and the 1930s explain the preoccupation of the officer corps in later decades with institutional unity during political crises.

Many of the fine studies of post-1930 Brazil miss fundamental aspects of the military's role in society. Even when portions of the army rose up, as in the *tenente* rebellions of the 1920s and in the Revolution of 1930, the tendency of the literature has been to explain behavior in relation to civilian politics and society, making the military rebels instruments of, spokesmen for, or symbols of urban middle-class desires. Yet to do so ignored powerful influences within the army itself that molded the conduct of both individuals and the institution of which they were a part. In 1916 the army's new procedures for recruiting its rank-and-file soldiers changed the relationship between the army and society, altered civilian penal practices, and injected the army and the *Pátria* [motherland] it espoused and the State that it defended, into the private realm of the family and into the far corners of Brazil.

In the period with which this book is concerned the army was the *only national institution,* the core of the developing Brazilian State. It was a position that the army assumed fitfully, almost haphazardly, filling the vacuum left by the collapse of the monarchy and gradually acquiring doctrine and vision to support its de facto role. Although it had more units and men in Rio de Janeiro and Rio Grande do Sul than elsewhere, its presence was felt throughout the country, and its personnel, its interests, its ideology, its vision, and its commitments were national. The *Pátria Brasileira* stood above Constitution, cabinet, emperor, or president.

Exceptional or extralegal behavior would ultimately be justified as acts of loyalty to the Pátria. Alone among the various Brazilian elites, the officer corps of the armed forces were nationalists by definition and constitutionally mandated at that. The political parties of the 1889–1930 period were not national but regional and/or personalist. The Catholic Church, although present throughout the country, was international in its personnel, ideology, liturgy, and purposes. Although Catholicism certainly was, as Gilberto Freyre noted, the cement of Brazilian *culture,* neither the church nor political parties held Brazil's territory together; the army did that.

It is startling that Brazil, alone among the continental countries of Latin America, not only still embraces the area claimed in colonial times but extends beyond it in the west and north. The only significant piece of colonial terrain that Brazil lost was the *Banda Oriental,* now Uruguay. In contrast, all of the Spanish-American viceroyalties were torn apart by regionalist forces. The Brazilian army stood, and still stands, as a bulwark against regionalist, centrifugal forces.

Interpretations of post-1930 Brazil often lack an understanding of what the army and its role was prior to that watershed year that opened the important Getúlio Vargas era (1930–54). This book is a history of the core institution of the expanding Brazilian state that examines how the army developed, how it was co-opted by the civilian elites, how the processes of professionalization and Europeanization disrupted the bonds of co-optation, and how the stress of rebellion and social change in the 1920s led to its unraveling in 1930, as well as how it reinvented itself in the 1930s, eventually becoming the backbone of the Estado Novo dictatorship after 1937. At the same time army recruitment; expansion of its postings; suppression of internal rebellions; road, railroad, and telegraph line construction; and mapping of the interior injected the army and Pátria that it represented into the vastness of its claimed, but poorly controlled, territory. In the 1930s the rebuilding of the state and the army went on apace of one another, and by 1940 both were different from what they had been a decade earlier. The events and struggles of the turbulent 1930s, and the subsequent trends that culminated three decades later in the military regime of 1964 to 1985, are more clearly understood against the backdrop of the army's experience in the Old Republic. That experience explains why civil war broke out in 1932 and why the army became the core of the dictatorial Estado Novo—the country's first rational and nationalist government that laid the foundations for post–World War II Brazil.

The attitudes of officers who directed the destinies of Brazil from 1964 to 1985 were shaped to a good extent by their experiences as junior officers, or as the sons of major actors, in the Old Republic. Presidents (Generals) Humberto Castelo Branco, Arthur Costa e Silva, Emilio Garrastazú Medice, and Ernesto Geisel were only the most prominent; there were literally hundreds of others. João Batista Figueiredo, the last general president, was heavily influenced by his father, Euclydes, whom the reader will meet in these pages.

It is easy to forget that every army's mission is to be ready to wage war, to exercise controlled violence in the name of a state. An army's structure, doctrine, equipment, and training exist for the paramount test of the battlefield. A history of an army that does not deal with its ultimate mission would be partial at best. The book takes the reader into battle because I believe that we should not separate the army's barracks life, internal politics, and relations with society from its exercise of violence, from its war making. Without examining what it did at Canudos in 1897, in the Contestado from 1912 to 1915, in the tenente revolts of the 1920s, in the Revolution of 1930, and in the paulista revolt of 1932, we would be left with an incomplete understanding of the army and the men who constituted it.

I emphasize the officer corps because, especially after obligatory service was instituted in 1916, the officers were the only permanent element in the army. The Brazilian army did not develop a strong tradition of leadership by sergeants, as did the American, British, German, and French armies; from top to bottom it was an organization controlled by officers.

Although the officers are the main actors in this story, however, I have called the reader's attention at several points to the common soldiers who marched in the army's columns. Throughout its history the army has been plagued with recruitment policies that were shaped by the protective mechanisms of a class society bent on keeping the mass of the population relatively ignorant and subservient. The officer corps' modernizing ideology collided with the tenacity of the land-based regional oligarchies determined to maintain their supply of cheap labor. That determination explains why recruitment prior to 1916 was frequently forced and why after that date its results often fell short of projected goals; it also explains why the army was small, relative to the rapidly expanding Brazilian population.

Although it has not been possible here to do more than give passing reference to military family life, I have provided career sketches of officers to highlight their friendships and family ties and to show how such social linkages affected behavior. I have stressed bonds of friendship, of loyalty to classmates and to certain commanders, and the importance of trusting colleagues, having what the Brazilians call *gente de confiança* (someone you trust). On an individual level such personal loyalties, which are so much a part of the Brazilian culture, could be linked to idealized loyalty to the Pátria. After the closure of the Rio de Janeiro military school in 1904, the officer corps lacked a single, shared common educational tradition. As a result officers felt affinity with those who had common backgrounds and shades of alienation from those who did not, and as the various schools were opened and closed, the results of alienation turned explosive. Put another way, the men who passed through the military school at Realengo had a different introduction to their careers from the men who studied in the schools at Porto Alegre or Praia Vermelha. Efforts to shape a standard educational program in the 1920s gave the army permanent schools, but in the short run intensified intracorps and intergeneration alienation. Only after 1944 with the creation of the Academia Militar das Agulhas Negras would the army get the curricular and experiential commonalty that provided later generations of officers a bonding tradition.

Why does the navy only appear at the margins of this story? Because that was its role and stature during the era. Especially after the naval rebellions of 1893 and 1910, the generals and politicians did not trust the admirals or the sailors and deliberately kept their service weak and marginal. The air force came into being as a separate service in 1941, but I give some attention to the early development of military aviation under army aegis.

Because revolutions, popular and military rebellions, and armed state interventions play such an important part in the era, it may be useful to the reader to have some explanation as to how I view such phenomena. I agree with Alain Rouquié that regimes that begin in a coup d'état are marked with an "original sin" that "affects everything that they do, for conspiracy and surprise are at the opposite end of the spectrum from social progress. Plotters, far from mobilizing politically the social forces interested in change, exclude or ignore them. From the outset radical praetorianism appears like enlightened despotism: everything for the people, nothing by the people."[2]

Military intervention in politics and society is a sign of weakness of both the state and society. But to apply that statement to Brazil is to say the obvious. During the nineteenth century the monarchy and the army were the sole national institutions in a remarkably weak state and society. The coup of 1889 left the army as the republic's core institution but without the ideology, structure, experience, personnel, political mandate, or will to embrace fully such a role. During the Old Republic the prime mission of the officer corps evolved into building the infrastructure of the state and the human "fiber" of the society. In the early 1960s the pathbreaking studies of Edwin Lieuwen and John J. Johnson depicted military intervention as flowing from social class and interest group demands. One result of their books was the scholarly norm, at least in the United States, that equated the study of the "military" with analysis of civil-military relations. It was widely accepted among American intellectuals and government officials that increased "professionalization" of the Latin American military would reduce intervention. However, the reality of the 1964 to 1985 military regime's being supported by the most professional military in Brazilian history called that idea into question.

Much of the social science literature on the military in Brazil, and elsewhere in Latin America, rests on a precarious foundation that consists more of conjecture and assumption than historical research. In his influential book, *The Military in Politics: Changing Patterns in Brazil* (1971), Alfred Stepan assumed that the moderator model of military political behavior that he observed in the 1960s could be extrapolated backward into the Old Republic. He supposed that after overthrowing the empire, the military had taken over the moderating power from the emperor. He later added that the military regime born in 1964 displayed an internal nationally focused "new professionalism" that contrasted with the external, foreign-defense focus of the previous decades.[3] But my research does not bear out such assumptions.

The army did not become the moderator in the 1890s; its power was too shaky and too co-opted. Prior to the 1930s it did not have the institutional will, doctrine, or capability for such a role. This is not to say that some officers, such as the 1890s Jacobins, did not want to play moderator; rather, the institution could not do so. Nor was the officer corps the nonpolitical, externally oriented force that Stepan pictured; rather, officers were politically involved in securing their promotions, assignments, and benefits. Some used their military status to propel them into political position. Throughout the 1889–1930 period many officers held congressional, state, and municipal posts. The kind of involvements that I once assumed had grown out of the Estado Novo dictatorship of 1937 to 1945 had in fact been the norm throughout the Old Republic.[4] Officers ran the frontier strategic towns, mapped the country, demarcated the borders, constructed roads and telegraph and railroad lines, built barracks, commanded police forces and firemen in Rio de Janeiro and elsewhere, intervened in local politics on federal order, and otherwise enforced court orders. They also ran arsenals, a steel mill, prisons, and apprentice orphanage programs, and they supervised the Indian Protective Service and taught in and administered the army's educational system. In short, the old professionals were much like Stepan's new professionals. Understanding that historical perspectives shape thinking about the present, I came to believe that studies of Brazilian civil-military relations would continue to be marred by inaccuracies until the military's institutional history became clearer.

Happily, I was not the only one to reach such a conclusion. José Murilo de Carvalho argued that it was necessary to understand the army institution in order to understand its relations with state and society. The army, he noted, was not merely an instrument of political and social forces; rather, its internal structure, mission, and ideology shaped its relationships with the political and social spheres. He held that the behavior of military institutions could not be reduced to mere reactions to external influences. But that is not to say that the army would refuse to enforce the political and social norms set by the political elite; it was, after all, the strong arm of the state. He also emphasized the interpretative importance of some of the army's structural characteristics: recruitment; size, function, and distribution of personnel; formation and makeup of the officer corps; military training and education; and development of ideologies.

Recruitment policies reflected the institution's relative openness or closedness, its social roles, its missions, its self-image, and its most basic interaction with the society. Size and distribution tell much about the institution's real power and ability to act, whereas analysis of training and education sheds light on internal cohesion and professionalism. The army's increased capacity in the 1930s for political intervention on the national level rested on the transformations it experienced, not on the demands of social classes or interest groups.[5]

In a similar vein Edmundo Campos Coelho rejected analyses of the army's role in society and politics that were based on the idea that it was the instrument of the oligarchy, the "dominant" or middle classes, or even that it was the moderator that arbitrated disputes among classes and groups, because if the army were merely an instrument, then researchers could "concentrate on the play of the antagonistic interests of the social classes" and could ignore the study of the military organization itself. He argued in favor of research on the organization, noting that three related processes had marked the historical evolution of the army: that the institution's own needs and interests were factors in its political behavior, that it increasingly became more autonomous in relation to the social system, and that it was progressively more closed to the influences of civil society.[6] Yet in this book we see the army suppressing social movements on the orders of a national government controlled by the "dominant classes," thereby suggesting that the army's evolution followed a path from instrumentality to autonomy. Hopefully, this book will sharpen our understanding of the army's roles and of its place in Brazilian history.

By its very nature an army is different from other social institutions. As the principal agency of state violence it is set apart and has its own special characteristics as a social organization. An army is a *total institution,* in the sense that Erving Goffman used the term, whose members distinguish themselves from others who follow different, less embracing lifestyles. A "central feature of total institutions" is that they breakdown the barriers separating the three spheres of life—sleep, play, and work—by controlling where, when, and how they take place. Total institutions tend to separate their members from the surrounding society and to press them into a closely managed routine in "a single rational plan purportedly designed to fulfill the official aims of the institution." Such institutions are composed of people divided into a large managed group and a small supervisory group, with little social mobility between them and with specified ways of dealing with each other. Total institutions socialize their members in particular ways that shape their thinking, self-image, and behavior.[7] Of course, we should expect that a total institution in Brazil will reflect aspects of Brazilian culture that will distinguish it from similar institutions in other countries.

Regarding revolution, social movements, and state violence, I have found helpful ethnohistorian Anthony F. C. Wallace's suggestions toward a theory of revolution for Latin America. He specified two types of revolutions: those based on the "politics of the appetites" and those related to the "politics of identity." It might be objected that he is not a Latin Americanist and that he did not deal specifically with Brazil, but I think that applying his appetites/identity model provides a useful way to look at seemingly familiar events. In the 1889 overthrow of the empire the officers and their civilian republican allies wanted to seize power in an essentially intact social and economic system to exercise influence within it; they wanted to change the political trappings but not the underlying structures. They avoided expanding and extending the two requisites of effective political participation by the citizenry, namely public education and the vote. Theirs was the politics of the appetites. Their successors often experienced conflict between the legacy of those politics and the goal of a professionally efficient army.

The politics of identity applies neatly to the popular rebellions of Canudos (1897) and the Contestado (1912–15). In the pursuit of new and better identities the people of those places were swept up in revitalization movements. Wallace defined such movements as deliberate, organized efforts "by some members of a society to construct a more satisfying culture." The persons involved were likely to have had "an intense religious experience, a moment of revelation, after some prolonged period of personal dissatisfaction and disillusionment, and see as their combined task the salvation of their own souls and the salvation of the world around them." Collectively the people of Canudos and the Contestado were seeking salvation in an earthly, as well as a heavenly, sense. In the process they designed what Wallace called a "transfer culture" that was to reshape the flawed society into an ideal one. The demands of "transfer culture" adherents for change were not "fundamentally hostile to the personnel of the Establishment." Rather they wanted to convert the rest of the world by words, not by force. However, when the Establishment itself responded with force, the movement's participants defended themselves accordingly.[8]

In Brazil the establishment historically responded violently to demands for change because to acknowledge the validity of the politics of identity would threaten the foundations of the politics of the appetites. In crushing the Canudos and Contestado movements, and the 1904 Vaccination Revolt in Rio de Janeiro, the army was the instrument of the politics of the appetites, and in the 1911–1913 salvationist *(salvações)* interventions a number of senior officers were active practitioners of those politics. The appetites/identity framework can*not* be applied so neatly to the tenentes of the 1920s or to the Liberal Alliance of 1930; however, in their desire to reshape Brazil the tenentes shared some identity attributes. But their goal, and that of the Liberal Alliance, was to take over an intact political, social, and economic system. The revolutionaries of 1930 were, to continue with Wallace's terms, an appetites/identity mix, which is one reason why the decade of the 1930s was so violent as the contending political and social forces struggled for dominance. It also helps explain the many contradictions of the dictatorial Estado Novo that ended that decade's conflicts.

Violence was the common response to demands for change because Brazil, the nation-state, was still being formed. The break with Portugal in 1822 had not provided a crucible to blend the many regional Pátrias or homelands into a Brazilian nation, much less a nation-state. During the empire the government had relied on political alliances in the provinces (Pátrias) to deliver victories in highly restricted elections. That electoral system obligated the ruling party so deeply to provincial interests that it severely curtailed, as Roderick Barman has written, "the capacity of the national government to undertake bold, independent action in internal affairs," and it precluded the formation of a strong national party system. The Pátrias, dominated by *parentelas* (kinship networks), resisted external influences and control, and throughout the nineteenth century monarchs had difficulty extending their authority into them.[9] The monarchy repeatedly used the army to hold the country together by suppressing regional revolts between 1817 and 1848. The formation of Brazil, as a political entity, required that the central government weaken the independence of the Pátrias. The process of state formation had not been completed under the empire and continued on into the republic. Indeed, the republic expanded the power of the Pátrias, the former provinces now called states, and at the same time searched for a formula that would hold the country together. The often contrary trends of decentralization and centralization placed physical, psychological, and emotional pressures on the army, whose sole reason for existence was to serve the national Pátria. The crushing of the naval rebellion and suppressing the civil war in the south in the 1890s and the salvationist interventions (1911–13) can be seen as part of the state formation or nation-building process.

Those actions were aimed at the political elites; however, as mentioned above, the army was also used to keep the common people or masses in line. The political history of republican Brazil is the story of the growth of the Brazilian nation-state. The army, as the one national institution, was a central actor in that story. By extending the power of the central government into the Pátrias, the army contributed to political change, to the formation of the nation-state, and to the aggrandizement of the national Pátria. As the strong arm of the state, the army's role was, to borrow Alain Rouquié's phrase, the "intervention of the state within itself."[10]

One of my goals in writing this book was to tell the army's story in terms of the interaction between the institution and the men who shaped it and who were shaped by it. I introduce the reader to a large number of officers whose beliefs, emotions, strengths, and weaknesses molded the institution and through it affected the history of Brazil. This subtheme of mutual influence of institution, membership, and society runs throughout the book.

In these pages the reader will follow the Brazilian army through civil war, rebellions, and conspiracies, moving back and forth from ministerial offices to the firing lines. Armies are instruments of organized violence, and their histories should reflect that fact. I have sketched the careers of key officers; sought to show the institutional, national, and international pressures involved in decision making; and tried to keep the reader abreast of the army's relationships to society and politics. I have also called attention to the networks of friendships, *turmas,* families, *parentelas,* and patronage that interlaced the army and linked it here and there to civilian society.

The narrative runs from the fall of the empire through the end of the Old or First Republic in 1930 to the onset of the dictatorial Estado Novo in 1937. It is the period in which the army established itself as the one national institution, the strong arm of the state. Indeed, during those decades the army extended the reach of the central state throughout the vastness of Brazil.

There is a wide range of labels applied to the various regime changes in Brazil. *Revolution* particularly is thrown about with abandon in Brazilian historiography. Were the events leading to the overthrow of the empire in 1889 or the "Old" republic in 1930 revolutions or coups d'etat? The question may well have relevance only for those who regard revolution positively and coup negatively. Historians have the choice of using the terminology employed by the actors of the time or an established definition rooted in accepted social science usage. In the period of this book there were three regime changes: in 1889, in 1930, and in 1937. In my view *revolution* should only be used to label popular upheavals that change the nature of government and society; I do not believe that such an event or set of events has yet occurred in Brazil. The changes resulting from each of the three were important and, after the latter two, far-reaching, but they were not revolutionary in the sense of being deliberately sought by policies of the newly imposed popular regime. Of the three, 1930 came closest to a popular revolution, but the resulting government lost that quality; oddly, the dictatorship established in 1937 gradually took on some qualities of a populist, if not a popular, regime.

What has interested me here is not the descriptive label but the process behind the events. For example, I do not see 1930 as an army seizure of power but rather as a prolonged crisis during which the army's chain of command disintegrated. The central command in Rio de Janeiro struggled to maintain control over units in the capital. In effect, if not in the historiography, the army fell apart in the rebellion, and the events in Rio de Janeiro, such as taking President Washington Luís into custody, were a cosmetic attempt by a small group of senior officers to maintain some influence in the new order that was being born. They had no choice about passing authority to Getúlio

Vargas because they had lost effective control of everything save the tiny federal district.

The years 1889, 1930, and 1937 were years of "regime change." In each case the initial violence was limited but followed by extended periods of violent adjustment. The relatively pacific nature of the coups themselves gave the appearance of compromise, but invariably turmoil burst forth afterward. The periods of adjustment in the three cases were protracted and involved some authoritarian rule. This book is a study of the army during the first two periods of adjustment to regime change. That which followed 1889, the Old Republic, ultimately failed and resulted in the "Revolution" of 1930 and the opening of the more profound adjustment process of the Vargas era.

In doing the research I followed a well-marked trail. Edwin Lieuwen's landmark study *Arms and Politics in Latin America* (1960) was the first book I read about the military in Latin America, so it was an honor to have his comments on earlier versions of some of these chapters before his untimely death. Another historian who encouraged me was John J. Johnson, whose *The Military and Society in Latin America* (1964) suggested that the Brazilian military was different from its Spanish-American counterparts, that militarism in Brazil derived "from the uncertainties arising from the abolition of slavery in 1888 and the overthrow of the empire in 1889" (244). Although I agree on both counts, these pages tell a considerably more violent story than he thought was the case back in the early 1960s. I have benefited from the work of Robert A. Potash on Argentina, Frederick M. Nunn, Karen Remmer, and Brian Loveman on Chile and Latin America generally, Roderic A. Camp on Mexico, and Ronald M. Schneider and Alfred Stepan on Brazil. The tack that I have taken is somewhat different from theirs. They focus primarily on the interaction between military institutions and politics, whereas I have concentrated more on the military institution itself. Clearly, the army is not totally separate from society, but it has developed a special status that has influenced its interactions with society and politics. I concur with the above authors that social science theory should seek to explain how the various segments of society contribute to the functioning of the whole. However, I think that history is more than the testing ground for theory and models; it is a process of research and writing that gives people the stories that shape their self-images and identities. The stories that they know about the past influence the way they think and act in the present and thereby shape the future.

Armies are closed institutions, anxious about security, and suspicious of outsiders. As a foreigner studying the Brazilian army I have been a double outsider, both to the society and to the institution, so to do this study I had to become intellectually an insider. As a U.S. Army reserve officer during the Vietnam War I was ordered to active duty and sent to teach at the United

States Military Academy. During those years, in attempting to explain West Point and the United States Army to my civilian friends and academic colleagues, I was impressed with how different the view from inside the army was from that outside it. This awareness led me to consider more carefully the problems related to studying closed institutions and to look more critically at the literature on the Latin American militaries, particularly the Brazilian. The difficulties that scholars in the United States face in interpreting other societies and their institutions are magnified when dealing with military organizations. Moreover, from 1964 to 1985 the military dominated the Brazilian government, so in that period to be doing research on the army invited suspicion from all sides. Many Brazilian intellectuals were so alienated that they could not understand why anyone would or how anyone could study the military.

Establishing credibility was a major problem. The key army research facilities are run directly by active-duty officers. The army's historical archives and library are located in the regional headquarters in Rio de Janeiro, and its documentation center is in the General Staff building, known in the army as "Fort Apache," in Brasília. Armed guards abound, leaving no doubt that these are serious places. Obtaining access to collections and individual officers is time consuming and frustrating, especially in the absence of clear rules and procedures. On several occasions officials ran security checks to assure themselves that I was not working for United States intelligence agencies. My patience, willingness to listen, and frequent returns convinced officers that I was an independent scholar. I made clear that although I did not favor military regimes, my purpose was to understand the history that had given the military such a significant role in contemporary Brazil.

At times my research was obstructed. Documents that I read one day disappeared mysteriously the next. Once some officers tried to have me ejected, and on one memorable occasion a general threatened arrest if I used a 1930s intelligence report "injudiciously." In retrospect, however, such incidents provided an atmosphere of creative tension that helped me to understand the social pressures within the army officer corps that molded thinking and behavior. I should say that eventually toleration turned into acceptance, and I was invited to give talks on my research to groups of officers; and my writings have been used in classes at the command and general staff school and at the military academy.

Whatever measure of success I have had in capturing the tone and substance of Brazilian army history is a result in no small part of the interest, advice, assistance, hospitality, and patience of a large number of army officers who welcomed me into their offices, barracks, schools, and homes. They took me inside the institution and reduced my handicap of being an outsider. There is not enough space to list them all, but I would be remiss if I did not mention several who have been continuously helpful even to the extent of reading and commenting on various pieces of writing. Colonel Newton C. de Andrade Mello was the first Brazilian officer I met when he was a military attaché in Washington in the early 1960s, and years later he sponsored my membership in the Instituto de Geografia e História Militar do Brasil. Colonel Luiz Paulo Macedo Carvalho has been my counselor, teacher, critic, commentator, translator, sponsor, publisher, host, and friend. General Carlos de Meira Mattos has opened many doors, has been a genial host, has explained things that are written nowhere, and has read and critiqued my writing. Brigadier General Newton Bonumá dos Santos helped me understand the nuances and functioning of the military educational system and ran interference for me. And Colonel Sérgio Paulo Muniz Costa has shown me how today's younger officers view their army's history. These men have been my mentors, sponsors, and friends. However, although they may see some of their ideas in these pages, I alone am responsible for errors of fact and interpretation.

No one produces a book alone. Thomas Skidmore convinced me to put aside administration to complete this "owed" book. Michael Corniff commented on various versions with helpful insight. John Dulles provided valuable British sources. Sonny Davis debated evolving interpretations. Although I invested my time, energy, and money, the project could not have been done without the encouragement and financial assistance of the American Philosophical Society, the Fulbright program, the Social Sciences Research Council and the American Council of Learned Societies, the Heinz Endowment, the Woodrow Wilson International Center for Scholars, and numerous grants, fellowships, and leaves from the University of New Hampshire. I am grateful to my history department colleagues for their critiques and boosting, and to Provost David R. Hiley for crucial support.

Great thanks to Norris Pope, Director of Scholarly Publishing at Stanford University Press, for his unfailing encouragement and extraordinary patience. Kimberly L. Brown took the manuscript through the initial stages, while Mariana Raykov guided it through production. Joe Abbott skillfully handled the copyediting.

I am saddened that my friends of the pioneering Brazilian turma John Wirth and Bob Levine did not live to know how much they had influenced this work. John's unfailing support and confidence helped me through some low points.

My daughters Teresa Bernadette and Katherine Diane, and my son-in-law Eric Jensen have been steadfast cheerleaders. When I complained that the project was too big, they were always confident that I would get it done.

No words are sufficient thanks to my loving companion on the long journey from my discovery of Brazil at Indiana University through various residencies in Rio and Brasilia, and so many research trips. It has been a continuous Brazilian adventure that has given a distinct texture to our lives. Diane Marie Sankis McCann has kept me focused on getting the writing done, preventing me from taking myself too seriously, and convincing me that it was all great fun. She endured far more than was reasonable to expect. I really did drive her across rickety plank bridges, through cattle drives and antiguerrilla operations, into mud holes, and once on a breathless dash through a forest fire. She has been a congenial hostess to academics, diplomats, politicians, army officers, journalists, and many, many students. So in a very special sense this book is hers as much as mine.

A thousand thanks to all.

Frank D. McCann
Durham, New Hampshire
June 2003

SOLDIERS OF THE PÁTRIA

CHAPTER 1

Republican Turmoil

They went and meddled with the Army which in the days
of the Empire stayed quiet in its corner. We're running
now the risk of a military dictatorship. And henceforth no
one will ever do anything more without first hearing and
sniffing round the generals.
—Erico Verissimo, *Time and the Wind*

I tried to establish a dictatorship of peace and harmony.
—Deodoro da Fonseca, *Deodoro: A Espada contra o Império*

History would have no time for this crude slaughter pen.
—Euclydes da Cunha, *Rebellion in the Backlands*

The Coming of the Republic

In the *Academia Militar das Agulhas Negras* there is a large, dramatic portrait of Field Marshal Manoel Deodoro da Fonseca mounted on a bay horse
in the patio of the army's general headquarters, his right arm raised, waving
his cap in acknowledgment of the *Vivas* of the troops, who had just adhered
to the rebellion against the imperial government on the morning of November 15, 1889. It is a painting frequently reproduced in Brazilian schoolbooks,
whose captions usually associate the scene with the proclamation of the republic. The painting exalts the role and position of the marshal relative to the
other actors in the event, who appear in the background. He was, at the moment captured in the painting, asserting his personal control over the only
troops then standing with the cabinet of the Visconde de Ouro Preto, which
Deodoro, the army's senior officer, was determined to force from power. Beginning the day after this scene there has been a controversy over the recipient of his first Viva, which reportedly was directed at His Majesty Pedro II.
Ardent republicans argued that was impossible. Like the dubious Viva, other
aspects of the plot against the monarchy remain in shadowy vagueness. Was

Deodoro fully aware that the objective was to topple the imperial dynasty and not just His Imperial Majesty's cabinet? Whose role was more important: Deodoro's or Lt. Col. Benjamin Constant, republican propagandist in the army's schools? Was the army's commander, Adjutant General Field Marshal Floriano Peixoto, sincerely trying to defend the regime in its last days, or was he a double agent? Such uncertainty creates historical space that myth makers happily fill. The historiographical gap surrounding 1889 is more than curious; it is one of the bizarre aspects of modern Brazilian history, itself worthy of study. The objective here is the broader history of the army in the republic, but it cannot ignore the beginning point even if it raises still more questions. There is no doubt, however, that the imperial cabinet had met all night of November 14–15 at the Naval Ministry, seeking ways to save itself, and at dawn it had moved to a supposedly safer refuge in the army headquarters only to be soon confronted by units of the garrison of Rio de Janeiro.[1]

During the 1880s the imperial government had become increasingly nervous about the loyalty of the army. The distance between the two widened steadily—philosophically, emotionally, and materially. The officers of the era tended to be better educated than earlier military generations and had spent much of their careers in urban areas, even if some of these were small garrison towns. The senior ranks were filled with veterans of the war with Paraguay who felt depreciated by the regime and by society—even military school students and junior officers made fun of their war medals. Most officers lived on their salaries and so felt the slow promotion rate in both their economic well-being and their professional pride. They had little in common with the great landowners who produced the coffee and sugar displayed on the empire's coat-of-arms. Promotion was ideally linked to merit, yet political influence and patronage of senior officers often determined who was favored. Captains might wait ten to fifteen years to became majors, which encouraged bureaucratic routine instead of hard training and study. The generals of 1895 averaged thirty-nine years of age when they were promoted to major.

As officers looked at the imperial cabinet and the various ministries, they saw fewer and fewer senior officers in high positions and instead saw graduates of the law schools of São Paulo and Recife, who they derisively called "frocked coats" (*casacos*). The lack of officers in high political positions created a feeling of distance and disconnection from the government. The gap between the civilian and military elites grew. The mission of the army was not clearly defined, so military education took directions contrary to the development of a professional force. Recent military school graduates had been bathed in a curriculum that had more to do with liberal arts and theoretical science than with the military arts and practice. Upon receiving their bachelor of mathematics or of natural and physical Sciences they styled themselves *Doutor* and were addressed as "Lieutenants Doctors." The army's rank and file were much less pretentious, being filled with many ex-slaves and the dregs of society that had been rounded up by impressment squads. An 1874 law proclaimed universal enlistment for a draft lottery, but it was never put into operation, much to the officer corps's loudly professed frustration. In truth army service was part of the empire's penitentiary system, and the officers resented it and the negative impact it had on their social standing and the image of their institution.[2]

Particularly younger officers had been attracted to the Republican Party after its formation in 1870, and one, Captain Dr. Luiz Vieira Ferreira, had helped draft the famous republican manifesto of that year and had participated in editing the newspaper *A República*. The military school became a rich source of republican discussion and conversion. In 1880 many officers sympathized with the instigators of the so-called Vintém (twenty réis) tax demonstrations and riots that followed the imposition of a tax on streetcar fares. Their attitude was interesting because the tax was felt mostly by the lower classes. Several junior officers provided republicans with information on an arms deposit at a Rio fortification and promised to delay reinforcements until the plotters could seize the weapons. Because there are no references to its outcome, the raid appears to have been aborted or to have failed, but it should also be noted that other officers commanded troops who helped police suppress the rioters.[3] Officer attitudes and certainly behavior were not monolithic.

In October 1883 a Rio newspaper, *O Corsário,* criticized the misuse of conscription for political purposes and belittled officers demanding freedom to dispute publicly government policy. In response a group of cavalry officers and troopers invaded and destroyed the paper's printing office. The police did not intervene or pursue. Later that month the editor, Apulcro de Castro, fearing for his life, went to police headquarters asking for protection. Meanwhile, a suspicious-looking crowd gathered outside the building. The police chief recognized officers of the First Cavalry regiment and requested help from the adjutant general, who sent his aide, a captain. This officer spoke with men in the street and then convinced Castro that he would be safe under his escort. Barely had their carriage started to move away when men in civilian clothes wearing fake beards attacked, shooting and stabbing the poor editor. He died in the lobby of the police headquarters. The captain took sick leave for several weeks, and the police chief was dismissed. A formal inquiry named eleven officers, but none were arrested or tried. Among the assailants was Captain Antônio Moreira César, who later would have major roles in the civil war and the Canudos campaign. Debate over the case in the Parliament led to the fall of the governing cabinet.[4]

Also in 1883 Major Frederico Sólon Sampaio Ribeiro and a large number of other officers met with Quintino Bocaiuva, Saldanha Marinha, Aristides Lobo and other republicans to develop a plan to proclaim a republic.
As the abolition movement grew more heated, it became linked to discontent in the army. In the Chamber of Deputies Joaquim Nabuco declared
that the "highest and most honorable" profession of the soldier should not be
confused with "the lowest and most degrading" profession of slave catcher.
Abolition also got mixed into a debate over national security when reports
from the south warned that war with Argentina was possible over the disputed boundary between Missiones (Arg.) and Santa Catarina. The Conservative Party cabinet then in office wanted to increase military expenditures,
but the army and its parliamentary allies argued that it could not go to war,
as it had in 1865, with slaves in its ranks.[5] Officers envisioned an army of
citizen soldiers defending their Pátria. Abolition in their eyes was a national
defense measure. In 1884 the adjutant general, the marquis of Gavea, who
held many slaves on his lands above Angra dos Reis, reprimanded Colonel
Antonio de Sena Madureira, commandant of the artillery school, for hosting a visit of one of the *jangadeiros* who had been active in the struggle to
end slavery in Ceará. Colonel Sena was Brazil's expert on European military
affairs, one of the most respected officers in the army, and a friend of the
emperor and his son-in-law the Conde d'Eu. His refusal to accept the aged
Gavea's rebuke on the grounds that he was subject solely to the artillery chief
Conde d'Eu raised tensions considerably. Gavea refused officers requests to
be excused from slave-chasing duty.[6]

Officers, and even whole units, throughout the empire had associated
themselves with the abolitionist movement, in some instances refusing to
follow orders to pursue groups of runaways. As early as 1881 the Fifteenth
Battalion was transferred from Fortaleza (Ceará) to Belém (Pará) because it
had declared itself an abolitionist society. Identifying with such a reform
movement and deciding to obey or refuse orders according to extramilitary
standards contributed to distancing officers from established social and political norms, and accustomed them to setting their own standards of obedience.[7] By the time the princess regent decreed abolition in May 1888, the
officers had absorbed so much republican propaganda in their studies at the
military school and the Superior War School that they were ready to substitute abolitionist sentiments with republican ones as necessary to make Brazil
a free Pátria.

In the shadows behind all of this, secret groups of officers and military
students talked, argued, and plotted. The idea of a third reign often came to
the fore after Pedro's health declined as a result of diabetes. His heir, Isabel,
was married to a French noble, Conde d'Eu, who, in spite of his service in
Paraguay and his commitment to the army's interests, aroused misgivings

among the officer corps. The notion of Isabel's renouncing in favor of her son likewise was unappealing. Private and public discussion among the officers regarding the future finally would undermine their increasingly unsteady loyalties to the Bragança dynasty.

They also believed rumors that the government planned to disband the army. Certainly, the cabinet sought to weaken the army's ability to pressure the Imperial Court by sending units away from Rio and by considering reinvigoration of the National Guard, which had been in decline since an 1873 law reduced the number of its officers and limited its call up to national crises caused by foreign war or internal rebellion. Before long its annual training exercise consisted of strutting politicians dressed in fancy uniforms with no soldiers to command.

Sergio Buarque de Holanda criticized the substitution idea as the resurrection of a myth from the 1830s arguing that the historical memory regarding the National Guard had been distorted; back then, he asserted the guard had *not* been created to substitute the early imperial army as was often asserted; rather, its purpose had been to help the army maintain order. To substantiate his argument, he noted that a key organizer of the National Guard was none other than Luis Alves de Lima e Silva, the future duke of Caxias and modern "patron" of the army.[8] In the midst of the 1889 crisis the cabinet did discuss moving some units away from the capital and possibly rebuilding the guard, but talk had not become action. Indeed, in 1889, rather than cutting the army's size, the government increased the authorized strength over the previous year by more than three thousand.[9] Reality was not as important as what officers believed to be true.

In analyzing the military crisis of the 1880s historians may not have given sufficient attention to tables of organization and chains of command. It is well known that after the Paraguayan War (1865–70) the army went through a variety of adjustments, one of which was to restore the peacetime chain of command. The army was divided into provincial garrisons, each headed by a commander *(comandante das armas)* subject to the president of the province, who oversaw troops in his province. Such presidents were usually civilians who rated military honors in the tradition of the colonial Portuguese governors-general. The commander's decisions were subject to the approval of the civilian provincial president.[10] It is true that sometimes a commander might hold both positions, or that the president might be an officer, but normally the command structure placed civilians in control. At the top of the chain of command was the emperor, who was the "generalíssimo" of the armed forces; as king he was *ipso facto* a soldier, among whose titles was the "perpetual defender of Brazil." During the war the civilian wedge into the peacetime structure was removed as the field forces organized themselves into a combat army far from civilian politicians at home. Pedro II kept up

his image by using the plain uniform of a *Voluntário da Pátria* and stubbornly demanding total victory. After the war, resubmitting to the old system of provincial garrisons was onerous to the combat veterans. At the national level the emperor generalíssimo was declining in health and was more
distant from the affairs of state, which meant that the top officers no longer
dealt with their "natural" leader, a soldier like themselves, but with elected
politicians tainted with partisan allegiances.[11]

The army's estrangement from the reigning political system was stimulated by the so-called military question of the 1880s, which saw officers being punished for their public criticism of the government. In 1886 and 1887
officers of different political affiliations had joined to defend the army's interests, which they saw as threatened by the penalties imposed on their vocal
comrades. Their unity and public opposition had forced the government to
cancel the objectionable penalties. In June 1887, in the flush of victory, they
formed the Military Club, an organization for discussion completely outside
of the army's structure, and in October of that year they disassociated themselves from the landed oligarchies by petitioning the princess regent "in the
name of humanity and of the honor of the very flag that it defends" to re-
lieve the army of the distasteful duty of hunting runaway slaves. The officer
corps thereby got more in step with the opinion of the urban middle sectors, from which many of its members came. But note that now they were
stepping outside the normal chain of command to express their grievances
directly to the throne. In the process the officer corps became an even more
powerful actor on the national stage. The Military Club sponsored Deodoro's
unsuccessful campaign for imperial senator, and its members joined the constant political discussions in the restaurants, tailor shops, and bordellos with
which it shared the fashionable Rua do Ouvidor in Rio de Janeiro.

In effect, but not according to a defined plan, the officers were gradually
distancing themselves emotionally and politically from the empire's basic institutions. Their stance on slavery drew a line between themselves and the
most stubborn members of the slave-owning, landed oligarchy. They also
became more secular. From 1881 until the formation of the Military Club
the principal vehicle for officers to meet and to organize had been the religious Brotherhood of Santa Cruz dos Militares that had gathered in the
church of that name on Rua 1 de Março. The most decisive step, however,
would be severing the army's bonds of loyalty to the emperor, and because
this involved the violation of oaths, it was a grave matter for a military organization in which lives depended on fulfilling one's word.

Deodoro's state of mind and that of many officers appears to have been
affected by the ministry's nonenforcement of the emperor's instruction of
November 1888 to implement the decision of the Supreme Military Council to wipe clean the records of officers punished for speaking out. Deodoro

wrote twice to the emperor asking him to make the ministry act; otherwise, he said, the officers would see continued nonenforcement as approbation of the "insults" to the army's pride, honor, and dignity. "The soldier's obedience does not extend to self-abasement; the soldier," Deodoro wrote, "is obedient, but not servile; and whoever does not rebut acts of indignity and servileness is not worthy to wear the uniform, the same uniform that Your Imperial Majesty honors by wearing." Instead of a response from the emperor, Deodoro was dismissed as quarter-master general, the second-ranked post in the army. He wrote again, more heatedly, to His Imperial Majesty: "Consider, Senhor! What the military asks is as just and as small . . . as it is grave. . . . This thing is very serious, Senhor. . . . [Y]our ministry betrays you in this!" He threatened that, if his petition was denied, he would have to resign from the service. The minister of war wanted to retire him, but the emperor refused, so the minister himself resigned, and his replacement ordered the records to be wiped clean, upon the request of the officers involved. But instead of the crisis fading, the officers refused to make the request. Wouldn't that be admitting that they had done wrong? Tempers flared anew. The government forbade officers to use the telegraph lines to prevent those in the provinces from expressing solidarity with their offended brethren in Rio. Brevet Marshal of the Army and Viscount of Pelotas José Antônio Corrêa da Câmara wrote to Deodoro that "we can not stop before the question is resolved honorably, because retreat would bring our moral annihilation."[12] Clearly, if this attitude was widespread in the officer corps, this was a group of men feeling harassed, threatened, and cornered. Officers frequently complained that civilians, especially the "frocked coats," their pejorative name for politicians, many of whom had law school degrees, did not understand military matters and were prone to selling out the Pátria.

Such civilian ignorance must have been frustrating, but did it justify overthrowing the government? Heitor Lyra, in his masterful study of the fall of the empire, observed that the officers were normally just as ignorant of civilian affairs as the civilians were of military matters and that civil-military disputes never centered on strictly military matters. "They occurred," he said, "when officers stepped beyond the limits of their profession and injected themselves into the civilian life of the country." It was as if officers believed that might made right, that their will should prevail over civil authority rather than the reverse. Lyra noted that using the arms that the nation had entrusted to them, they justified themselves by saying that they were defending the honor of their class, which they identified with the honor of the Pátria. Lyra thought that their definition of honor was hazy and overly elastic.[13]

Theoretically and internationally one can say that a soldier's individual identity and feelings of self-worth and contentment are bound up in his sense of participation in and belonging to a larger collective identity. A shared sense of honor serves as the link between the individual soldier and the collective or corporate identity. The formation of personal identity takes place through socialization, which involves continuous revision of the individual's self-image. Army training aims directly at changing an independent-minded civilian into a disciplined soldier whose self-worth comes from fusing his individuality with the collective goals and demands of his unit.[14]

Honor, duty, country, and discipline are watchwords of military vocabulary worldwide. The Russian Tsarist army of the 1880s and 1890s maintained regimental courts of honor that determined how offended officers were to respond to insults. In Russia "defense of honor was a major feature of the collective identity of the officer corps. An insult to the officer's person, his regiment, the army as a whole, or the tsar required instantaneous response."[15] Honor duels were common in many nineteenth-century societies. In the United States the most famous such duel was that between Aaron Burr and Alexander Hamilton, two former officers. American army officers dueled even though regulations outlawed such behavior from early in the century; even General Winfield Scott, who wrote the regulation, issued challenges. In the American army honor was linked to the proper fulfillment of one's duty, which was to carry out lawful orders. Of course, the American army had its own peculiar honor and obedience problems, as shown by its division into contending forces in the Civil War; but generally obedience was considered honorable, and breeches of it were punished.

Obedience in Brazil was complicated by the long and widespread existence of slavery. A man could not be overly submissive to another without suffering loss of status or damaged ego, unless the other was without doubt of superior status. Obedience in that society and military was more complex than the idea of simply fulfilling one's self-assumed obligation to obey or of complying with a consensual decision. In Brazil obedience meant submitting to another's will, accepting a lower status, something that was undesirable. Differing notions of equality need to be understood as well. Equality in the American military was possible only among officers of the same rank and date of promotion; among such peers they could be different, not conforming to anyone else of their rank. Of course, the outer limits of difference and conformity were generally understood and set by the officers' academy experience. Equality *(igualdade)* in Brazilian society, according to Roberto Kant de Lima, implied a "similarity of status, . . . [and] an assumed similarity of perspective on the established order, given not by individual opinion but by the mandatory perspective resulting from the same social position in the hierarchy."[16] These differing definitions affected the way command was exercised in the two armies; consensus was more important in the Brazilian system, where an officer could not afford to be too independent or too different from the norm. The relatively closed military life and the small numbers involved encouraged the social endogamy of the officer corps that helped to preserve and to intensify such attitudes and behaviors.[17]

The republic was born of a contradiction. How could an illegal, treasonous act create a legal, secure political order? Article 15 of the army's articles of war prescribed hanging as punishment for mutiny or treason or for even knowing about it and not preventing it. So the officers and troops who took part in the events of November 15, 1889, had decided to break the law that governed their lives. Much testimony indicates that the initial intention, certainly that of Deodoro da Fonseca, was to replace the empire's governing cabinet but that before the day was out, Deodoro was manipulated into proclaiming a republic. The usual account has him vacillating until the last moment. And historians have been fond of quoting statements such as that from a September 1888 letter to a nephew then in the military school in Rio Grande do Sul warning that he should keep away from republican matters because a "Republic in Brazil and complete disaster are the same thing"—Brazilians would never have the education and respect to make it work.[18]

Such an approach has Deodoro overturning a monarchy to which he had devoted his life, to give Brazil a form of government in which he had no faith. Such a line of reasoning places a matter of great import on the level of whimsy. Something profound must have motivated Deodoro and the conspiring officers to cast aside their solemn oaths to uphold emperor and empire. Every officer had sworn on the New Testament to be a "good and loyal subject of His Imperial Majesty, and to obey with the most exact promptness and respect, the Articles of War, Military Regulations and Ordinances, and all orders of my superiors related to Imperial Service . . . even to shedding all my blood in his defense, [and in defense] of the Independence of the Empire, of its Constitutional system and of the Imperial Dynasty." Of course, one phrase seemed to provide a convenient dodge; the oath applied "as far as it is possible for me" [quanto me for possível].[19] By breaking their word of honor, the officers were setting themselves above the law, claiming a special status that gave them a direct supragovernmental connection to the motherland (Pátria). To establish a new order, the old had to be betrayed, but in the process the new was born with the stain of treachery.

Or a more culturally sensitive way to analyze it might be that the officers had developed a new common perspective on the way the Pátria should be ordered. According to the new perspective the old rules had ceased to function. The law and the need to obey it no longer applied; it no longer compelled their obedience.

On that November morning, as the troops marched through Rio de Janeiro to the general headquarters fronting the Campo Santana, Deodoro may have considered his oath intact because he was moving to replace the cabinet, which, although a violation of the articles of war, was a somewhat lesser crime than breaking the parts of the oath regarding the emperor and dynasty. But whether his intent involved minor or major violations, they all carried the death penalty. In practice the army was subordinate to the civilian cabinet rather than to the emperor, who maintained some aloofness from the day-to-day management of the government. Confronting the cabinet in the army headquarters, Deodoro had announced that it was deposed and that names for a new one would be submitted to the emperor. At that moment it appears that his intentions were limited, if technically insubordinate.

Although large structural forces were at work in this change of system, the actual participants were real people moved by emotions and sentiments that shaped their actions and thereby the destinies of the nation. In the early hours of November 15 Deodoro had refused to go to the summer palace in Petrópolis to meet with the emperor for fear that he would lose his composure and his determination. Later in the afternoon in Rio, in the midst of hurried discussions among the conspirators on the one side and the emperor and monarchists on the other, Pedro II indicated that he would invite Senator Gaspar Silveira Martins, Deodoro's archenemy, to form a new cabinet. The republicans, who had been pressuring the sick, exhausted, and now offended general for hours, told Deodoro that toppling the empire was the only way to prevent his enemy from assuming power.[20] So in a fit of irritation Deodoro, a monarchist, signed the empire into oblivion and made Brazil a republic.

This first chapter examines the army of 1889, the turmoil of the 1890s, and the disaster of Canudos. It shows that rather than experiencing a peaceful transition from monarchy to republic Brazil passed through a decade of pain and bloodshed that contributed to the formation of the conservative Old Republic, narrowed subsequent political and social reforms, and kept the army in a repressive role.

The Army of 1889

A portrait of the army at the end of the empire will provide a basis for examining the changes and continuities of the following decades. This was a small army of about 13,500 spread over the map of Brazil in fifty regiments and battalions that averaged fewer than three hundred men each; these units, plus a transportation unit and the garrisons of frontier and Amazonian forts, were controlled by three brigade headquarters, two of which were in Rio de Janeiro and one of which was in Curitiba, Paraná. The officer corps had an authorized size of 1,595. Table 1.1 gives an idea of what the unit distribution was like; the largest concentrations were in Rio Grande do

TABLE I.I.

Distribution of Brazilian Army in 1889

Units	RGS	PA	RJ	MT	SC	SP	MG	PE	BA	NEB[a]	GO	PARÁ	AM[b]	Totals[c]
Infantry	8	1	6	3	1	—	—	2	2	4	1	1	3	32
Cavalry	5	1	1	1	—	1	1	—	—	—	—	—	—	10
Transport	1	—	—	—	—	—	—	—	—	—	—	—	—	1
Artillery	3	1	2	1	—	—	—	—	—	—	—	1	—	8
Engineers	1	—	1	—	—	—	—	—	—	—	—	—	—	2
Totals	18	3	10	5	1	1	1	2	2	4	1	2	3	53

SOURCE: Ministerio da Guerra, Almanak do Ministerio da Guerra no anno de 1889 (Oranizado na Repartição de Ajudante General sendo chefe interino desta repartição O Exm. Sr. Marechal de Campo Floriano Peixoto) (Rio de Janeiro: Imprensa Nacional, 1889), xii.

NOTE: The infantry and engineer units were called battalions, the cavalry were regiments, and the artillery were divided into four regiments of field artillery and four battalions of fixed position in port defenses.

[a]Northeast Brazil: 1 São Luís, Ma.; 1 Fortaleza, Ce.; 1 Maceió, Al.; 1 Paraíba, Pb.

[b]Amazonia: Types and size of units unspecified in garrisons of forts at Rio Branco, Rio Negro, and Rio Madeira.

[c]Total units = 50 plus the transport unit and garrisons of Amazonia forts.

Sul and Rio de Janeiro, a situation that would continue for another century. There were more infantry units (29) than the more expensive cavalry and artillery units (18). Although this reflected the conventional battlefield distribution of arms, it also was related to low military funding, to a defensive external posture, and to internal control missions.

The commanding officer of the army was the adjutant general. This position, which had been created in 1857, was doubly powerful because its holder directly commanded the garrison of the Imperial Court and province of Rio de Janeiro, whose troops acted as a mainstay of the government in moments of crisis. Thus, the adjutant general necessarily had political importance. His duties ranged from personnel administration to planning and carrying out operations. Since the minister of war during the empire was usually a civilian, the structure simultaneously recognized civilian authority and military responsibility. In 1889 three officers held the post, the last being Field Marshal Floriano Peixoto (beginning June 8, 1889). After the general staff replaced the adjutant general's office in 1899, there would be continuous struggle between the minister of war, with one exception a general officer, and the chief of the general staff, both perhaps trying to recapture the earlier power of the adjutant general.

The army also administered military colonies in Rio Grande do Sul, Santa Catarina, São Paulo, Mato Grosso, Goiás, Pará, and Amazonas that involved officers in a host of activities related to infrastructural development and provided the army with institutional awareness of conditions in frontier areas. These colonies, which had their origins in the 1850s, were populated mostly by foreign immigrants, particularly in the southern provinces. The idea behind the colonies was to shore up claims to disputed borderlands and to extend population into the internal frontier regions.[21]

The officer corps was drawn largely from coastal urban areas, mostly from families who could not provide alternative careers for their sons. Many of these families, perhaps a majority, were from the middle sectors of the society. Educational opportunities in late-nineteenth-century Brazil were extremely limited because of the lack of public education in general and universities in particular. Families that could not bear the costs of the law and medical schools advised their sons to seek admittance to one of the three military schools in Rio de Janeiro, Porto Alegre (Rio Grande do Sul), or Fortaleza (Ceará). These schools, especially that of Praia Vermelha in Rio, prepared many of the leaders and intellectuals who influenced Brazilian thinking and institutions.

Early in the nineteenth century to become a cadet a young man had to be born of a noble or military family, but as such prerequisites faded at mid-century the army schools attracted ambitious men seeking inexpensive ways to improve themselves. Although there were courses in military engineering and in the art of war, philosophy and literature competed successfully for cadet attention alongside offerings in mathematics, physics, and other sciences. Indeed the separation between science and the humanities was vague, with Colonel Benjamin Constant Botelho de Magalhães, professor of mathematics, acting as the principal exponent of positivist philosophy. Positivism's emphasis on science and authority, on progress and order, provided a vision of state activism directed by technocrats, which appealed to men who were not choosing a military career out of love for the profession of arms but as a vehicle for personal advancement. Positivism also provided a critique of the existing order that served to weaken the officer corps's commitment to the empire. Indeed, some of its proponents thought that the military no longer had a purpose, that soon enlightenment would spread to all civilized nations, who would eliminate their armies and navies and would pursue scientific progress in an orderly and peaceful world. Such a utopian attitude was hardly conducive to military preparedness. Even so, a number of those educated in the military school would play a major role in developing the elite's image of itself and of the Brazilian nation. In 1890, in a national population estimated at about fourteen million, of which 85 percent was illiterate, the few hundreds of officers who graduated from the military schools in the last years of the empire influenced the society disproportionately to their numbers. Graduates such as Alfred d'Escragnolle Taunay and Euclides da Cunha wrote books that shaped Brazilian national identity.[22]

The problem was that the school's curriculum "looked more toward the construction of Brazil than its defense."[23] It had more the feel of a civilian program of study than a military one, a phenomenon called *bacharelismo.*

Military education was slighted. The army itself had not conducted field maneuvers since 1880, and troops and officers rarely had marksmanship training. It was the type of education that produced writers, bureaucrats, and politicians but not competent military field commanders. Even so, officers dedicated to the military profession turned out articles on a wide range of subjects in the principal military journal of the era, the *Revista do Exército Brasileiro* (1882–89).[24]

Officers sent to serve in units in the interior experienced conditions and people that few of their civilian counterparts in the Europeanized coastal cities had occasion to observe. For most of these latter "the interior" began at the city limits and was fearsome, wild, and inhabited by uncivilized people. Army ministerial reports frequently referred to the United States and the European nations as "civilized countries," as if Brazil were not. Such images of Brazil would lead, in the period examined in this book, to policy decisions that made the Brazilian army a vehicle of social control with a supposed civilizing mission. The army would also extend the reach of the expanding Brazilian state into the far corners of national territory.

Army life was not comfortable. In 1889 the barracks throughout the country were in poor condition. Many were in rented buildings crudely adapted for army use. The food served to the troops depended on the dubious skill of the cooks, the commander's access to funds, and his willingness to allot them to the kitchens. The troops were mostly "volunteers," persons who were physically coerced into the service from among the least educated and poorest people. And given that most dark-skinned people were poor, the ranks were predominately black and mulatto. Well-behaved soldiers might receive their commander's permission to marry or cohabitate and thereby escape having to live in the barracks, although in some places the couple might be given a room in the building or space to build a shack within the compound. In many places soldiers' families lived in shacks adjacent to the barracks. Most officers were white, although the term *white* was not as rigorous as it was in North America and Europe. The battalion or regimental colonel controlled all aspects of the lives of his subordinates, including their pay. He frequently lived with other officers in a local pension or small hotel that provided lodging and meals. Many officers married women either from Rio Grande do Sul or from the environs of Rio de Janeiro because most of them served in those places when they were of marriageable age. Their wives tended not to accompany them to the more remote areas that were devoid of comfort, social life, schools for children, and health care. So it is not surprising that officers strove to be assigned to Rio de Janeiro, with Porto Alegre being a second choice. Above the rank of captain officers enjoyed the services of ever-present orderlies. Training was scanty, consisting of a manual of arms, close-order drills, and basic familiarization with weapons, and was usually administered by a corporal or sergeant. The troops guarded public buildings, patrolled streets, and, on occasion, chased bandits, none of which duties contributed much to the army's operational readiness.

The army, like the empire, was officially Catholic. Each day at the 9 P.M. assembly, the soldiers recited the Rosary and the litany of Our Lady of the Immaculate Conception. Sunday and holy day Masses were obligatory. The spiritual needs of the soldiers were ministered to by an ecclesiastic corps of some fifty priests. The Republic's sudden abolition of this corps and the various mandatory religious practices indicated that influential officers disliked the army's relationship with the church.

The officers and troops dressed in uniforms modeled on those of the French and Prussian armies. The predominate color was dark blue, sometimes with white trousers, although there was a white uniform as well. As elsewhere, the idea of a practical khaki field uniform was off in the future. Rank was worn on the lower sleeve. As a rule the Brazilian army kept itself abreast of uniform fashions as they developed "in the more advanced nations," as ministerial reports would phrase it. Officers and men wore their hair long, and handlebar mustaches were common.

The infantry soldiers of 1889 were armed with Comblain breech-loading rifles, although some units still used midcentury muzzle loaders, known as Miniés. Comblains used black powder to fire a 12 mm round a maximum of 1,200 meters. The cavalry used Winchester (1872–76 models) repeating carbines, adapted to fire Comblain cartridges, and carried Nagant revolvers. Officers used 8 mm Gerard pistols. Weaponry was a touchy issue. The rumors about imperial government plans to weaken the army included giving the National Guard and police the army's Comblains and replacing them with the old Miniés. The infantry used bayonets, of course, whereas the cavalry wore sabers, and half the mounted regiments carried lances. The field artillery consisted of a mix of La Hitte, Paixahans, Whitworth, and Krupp pieces of various calibers; some of the first were front loaders, and the latter two brands were heavy 130 mm, 80 mm, and 75 mm. The coastal forts were armed with Parrot, Whitworth, Armstrong, and Krupp cannon and Congrève rockets, none of which could reach beyond three miles. The listing, of course, indicates the heavy dependence on imported foreign arms.

The tactical use of these weapons was based on Paraguayan War experience (1865–70), which emphasized small-unit fire and maneuver. In theory offensive action consisted of four steps: artillery bombardment, establishing contact with the enemy, attack, and pursuit. Defensive theory stressed maintaining advanced observers, a secure line of resistance, a strong central position, rear guard, and mounting counterattacks. Bugles controlled the various movements for which the regulations specified 203 different calls![25]

Those officers who won their commissions on the battlefields of Paraguay, and had not subsequently gone to military school, were known as *tarimbeiros,* after the crude wooden sleeping racks in the old colonial forts. Such men had a commonsense approach to military life based on their experience but were out of place in the army of the *bacheleis.* They may have joined the school graduates in acquiring a proper understanding of military art via reading the manual of the French general Ildefonse Favé, which appeared in a Brazilian edition in 1882.[26] It was intended for the *tarimbeiros,* especially senior officers, including generals, who earned their ranks on their personal merit and services without knowing the doctrinal reasons for the various maneuvers and weapons that they employed in combat. Both groups contributed to the army bureaucracy that applied the enormous and complex military legislation that today fills many volumes on the shelves of the army archives.

The Turbulent 1890s

The overthrow of the empire was a coup d'etat rather than a popular revolution; the republic was the product of an officer corps defending its particular interests and allying itself to a political minority. In fact, only a portion of the corps was directly involved; some officers were motivated by fears for their institution and for their own welfare, some by republican ideology or the desire to be up-to-date with international trends, but no officer displayed his willingness to die for the empire. However, at least one sailor did do so. Aboard the warship *Parnaíba* an officer shot and killed a seaman who refused his order to strike the imperial flag. This Brazilian republic was not an heir of either the American or French Revolutions, even though the republican government would do its best to associate itself symbolically with both.[27] The republican regime survived by force and delayed seeking a popular mandate because it did not have enough legitimacy to risk elections. Denied the vote, the vast majority of the Brazilian people continued to be bystanders to events that shaped their lives and history. The imperial government had not represented them, nor would the republic that was born so abruptly. In the last quarter of the nineteenth century, while the United States, Argentina, and much of Europe were expanding the franchise and with it popular participation in government, Brazil had moved in the opposite direction, restricting the right to vote. In 1874, out of a population of about ten million, Brazil had 1,114,066 voters, and worse, in 1881 an electoral "reform" law reduced the electorate to 145,296! This restriction weakened the legitimacy of the imperial system and allowed the military's organized political voice to have an importance out of proportion to its size.[28]

The republic did not change this situation. The electorate expanded because of economic growth that gave more men the income qualifications necessary to obtain the franchise. Women would not get to vote until 1934. The creeping growth in numbers of voters to about 627,000 in 1910, was infinitesimal in a population of twenty-two million! The political and military instability and violence of the 1890s resulted in part from the lack of consensus among civilian elites over how the country was to be governed, and likewise military officers could not reach consensus regarding their status, relationship to the political regime, or their institutional goals. Moreover, they were divided by personal rivalries and conflicting visions of the future of the army and the nation. Their lack of unity and the civilian elite's lack of agreement as to the military's role in society provides a partial explanation for why they did not establish a long-term military dictatorship as some positivist officers desired.

The overthrow of the empire quickly led to removal of imperial provincial governors by officers and local republican allies who imposed officers in their stead. For the most part such initial changes were carried out peacefully, but afterward violent struggles for control of state governments became the norm. There was little agreement about the meaning of republicanism. Without parties or ideologies to structure the new political order the old one disintegrated into messy conflicts rooted in local feuds and jealousies. Officers criticized Deodoro's government in the press, as discipline and respect for the chain of command dissolved under a torrent of personal ambition. So, too, did respect for freedom of expression. Now in power, partly as the result of a struggle to secure the right of officers to express their opinions in the press, the regime curtailed the opposition press by threats and arrests. A "law of suspects" of December 23 aimed at those who "promote by words, writing, or actions civil revolt or military indiscipline."[29] The politics of the appetites spread like a fever; this was not to be the republic of which its proponents had dreamed.

Indiscipline was encouraged by the prestige that the new government showered on the military, stimulating the officers' self-importance and ambition. The republican government raised salaries less than a month after the coup, and beginning in early January 1890 wholesale promotions moved some officers up two or three grades in a matter of weeks or months, whereas others with less favorable connections were retired. Deodoro was upset by, but could not prevent, promotions of many men who had nothing to do with the events of November 15, whom he labeled "patriots of the streets and bars" *(ruas e botequins)*. In fact, his own promotions set a tone of exaggeration. Before the coup he had been due to be promoted from field marshal to marshal of the army, so this occurred in the January round of promotions. An elaborate "palace conspiracy," orchestrated by the minister of war's secretary, Major Inocêncio Serzedelo Correia co-opted Deodoro into agreeing to further promotions. Because the promotion of Minister of War Benjamin Constant Botelho de Magalhães from lieutenant colonel to brigadier general did not fit the established rules, his ironically named secretary proposed linking it to the desire of some naval officers to increase the prestige of the navy in the new regime by promoting the minister of the navy, Eduardo Wandenkolk, from rear admiral to vice admiral. And if Major Inocêncio could persuade Deodoro to accept another honor, he would be less inclined to resist these and other promotions. On January 15, 1890, to mark the second month of the republic, the navy paraded the crews of its vessels anchored in the harbor through the streets of Rio, where they were joined by army units in a show of interservice cordiality. The sailors and soldiers ended their march in front of the Itamarati Palace, then seat of government where Deodoro was honoring the minister of the navy at a formal luncheon. Major Inocêncio entered, as the men began to relax after the meal, to tell Deodoro that the army wished to proclaim him generalíssimo of the Brazilian forces. With some reluctance he agreed to accept the emperor's former title, perhaps unaware that the other two names would be added to the acclamation. Back in the street the major called on the waiting paraders to assent to the three new titles, which reportedly they did with enthusiastic *Vivas.* The assembled bands broke into the *Marseillaise,* and then, responding to the true demands of the crowd, the old national anthem that had not been played since November. It was a moment never to be repeated in Brazilian military history—promotions pseudoproclaimed in the street. The three accepted and rapidly grew accustomed to their new dignities. Later in 1890 the major received his own reward, promotion to lieutenant colonel and the governorship of the state of Paraná.[30]

In May 1890 the government handed out honorary military titles to civilian members of the cabinet and other distinguished figures, as if to replace the imperial nobility with a republican one. Deodoro's first minister of war, the newly acclaimed Brigadier General Benjamin Constant, the intellectual leader in the officer corps of positivism, of republicanism, and of the coup, turned out to be too tolerant of disruptive officer behavior; so the president replaced him with General Floriano Peixoto in March 1890. Floriano was the man of the hour as he moved firmly to reassert central authority over the army. When civilian Rui Barbosa resigned as first vice president of the regime, Deodoro appointed Floriano to that post as well, in effect making him his heir.[31]

Generals and colonels moved in and out of governorships, and at one point half of the twenty states were ruled by officers. Using the military with varying degrees of control, the central government intervened in the states to cleanse them of monarchists but with limited success. In São Paulo, for example, the historic republicans were less adept at political maneuvering than were the ex-monarchists, who by the end of 1890 were in control. In a number of states the proclamation of the republic had been a complete surprise. In Bahia the initial reaction of the provincial president, Salvador's municipal council, and the local army commander, who happened to be Deodoro's brother, General Hermes da Fonseca, was to resist. But before the next year was out, General Hermes was state president and was appointing officers (Adm. José Custódio de Mello, Gen. Dionísio de Castro Cerqueira, and Col. Francisco de Paulo Argolo) to the constitutional convention. In Rio Grande do Sul the ex-imperial liberals fell into such a tumultuous competition for power with republicans that between November 1889 and November 1890 eighteen men sat in the governor's chair. The ascension there of Júlio de Castilhos, rather than bringing peace, led to increased radicalization that finally exploded into civil war in 1894.

The unhappiness in the states was mirrored in the struggle in Rio de Janeiro over the nature of the new regime. Deodoro, Rui Barbosa, Benjamin Constant, and others in the cabinet repeatedly threatened resignation as they argued over how to rule Brazil. One meeting became so acrimonious that Deodoro drew his sword in anger. Irritated with press criticism, he ordered, then rescinded, the arrest of the head of *A Tribuna Liberal* (Rio) and closed his eyes to an assault by officers and soldiers on the newspaper's offices. Military men, reflecting positivist attitudes, called on the Constituent Assembly, which began work on a new constitution in November 1890, to concentrate power in the hands of one man. The government should be dictatorial rather than parliamentary. Young Lieutenant Augusto Tasso Fragoso, who would later play important roles in army history, called for a strong, responsible government.[32]

The constituent assembly was a battleground between those seeking to limit the executive's existing dictatorial power and the so-called Jacobins (the term being adopted from the French Revolution) who wanted to maintain and enhance it. Naval officers, perhaps feeling their declining status under the army-controlled regime, and civilian politicians, particularly those from São Paulo, believing that only legislative sovereignty would protect their interests, opposed the Jacobin position. From this point to the end of the decade there would be a strong Jacobin element in the army officer corps. But even after extreme Jacobinism faded, belief in a strong central government would be an undercurrent in military thinking that would reassert itself in the Estado Novo (1937–45) and in the military republic (1964–85).

The constitutional assembly was handpicked, many of the delegates being unknown in the very provinces they supposedly represented, and about a quarter were military officers. Their task was to write a constitution, elect the executive, and then become the national congress. A majority had pledged to elect Deodoro president. But before that occurred a cabinet crisis at the end of January 1891 led to its mass resignation and the formation of a cabinet that had few historic republicans, driving many civilian politicians, such as future president Manuel Ferraz de Campo Sales, into opposition. Meanwhile, military supporters exerted their own pressure; for example, they circulated a petition in the garrisons of Rio Grande do Sul declaring that Deodoro should be imposed as president because no one else merited the position.

The majority of the Rio de Janeiro garrison appeared ready to proclaim him dictator if the assembly elected someone else. But naval officers such as Admiral José Custódio de Mello supported the paulista politician Prudente José de Morais Barros and planned to raise the fleet in rebellion to defend him if he were elected. Even General Floriano Peixoto flirted with anti-Deodoro plotters but seemingly did not take a firm position. In the election itself, on February 25, 1891, Deodoro carried the day with 129 votes to 79 for Prudente, and Floriano was elected vice president, with 153 to 57 for Admiral Eduardo Wandenkolk. Because he was elected with more votes than Deodoro, and because he was wildly cheered at the swearing-in ceremony, when the president was received in near silence, the election signaled that Floriano's star would soon overwhelm Deodoro's.[33]

The new constitution was prepared by the cabinet and presented as a package for approval. The section on the military was particularly important for the future. Article 14 declared the army and navy to be permanent national institutions responsible for maintaining law and order and for guaranteeing the continuance of the three constitutional powers (executive, legislative, judicial). The article made the officer corps the only constitutionally mandated elite among Brazil's elite groups. The article also required that the military be obedient to the president but "within the limits of the law." As Alfred Stepan observed: "This in effect authorized the military to give only discretionary obedience to the president, since obedience was dependent upon their decision regarding the legality of the presidential order."[34]

While the declaration of institutional permanency mollified officer fears that the civilian elites might one day abolish the armed forces, the discretionary obedience troubled some officers, including Deodoro, who saw it as subversive of discipline. In a society where men already had difficulty following orders, it was an invitation to potential chaos, as the early 1890s showed only too well. Interestingly, the later constitutions of 1934 and 1946 kept the discretionary provision intact, but that of the dictatorial Estado Novo of 1937, which some see as a military regime in civilian dress, placed the military firmly under obedience to the president.

Almost immediately Deodoro, who had ruled as a dictator for the better part of fifteen months, had difficulty adjusting to sharing power with the Congress. Questionable government actions such as emitting so much paper currency that the money supply doubled by 1891, giving unsecured loans to weak railroad companies, easing access to credit, and selling off accumulated gold stocks, accompanied by swirling speculation, fraud, and rapid inflation undermined the aged generalíssimo's popularity and stiffened the backs of the growing opposition. In November 1890 Deodoro added another potentially disruptive element to the political mix by decreeing an end to the banishment of the monarchists. His frustration with the Congress caused Deodoro to dissolve it in November 1891, only to see a revolt depose his ally Júlio de Castilhos in Rio Grande do Sul, and Admiral Custódio de Mello led much of the fleet in Guanabara Bay in a protest rebellion against the closure of Congress. Rather than face defeat or civil war, he resigned, leaving Floriano Peixoto to clean up the mess. This succession was at first glance constitutional, but the recently adopted charter required new elections if the president died or stepped down during the first two years of the term.

The first and major issue for Floriano was the legality of his presidency. He kept the title of vice president (but referred to his "presidency" in correspondence) to deflate demands that he call new elections. Throughout Brazil state governments that favored elections fell to local coups that produced a kaleidoscope of faces, parties, and factions fighting over governors' chairs and assembly halls. If anything should have given the lie to the fiction of peaceful transition from empire to republic, the near chaos of this period was it. The historiography's focus on Rio de Janeiro made the story seem much simpler than it really was. The events in Rio appear as the final boiling over after the states had reached maximum temperatures. Voices inside and outside the armed forces called for new elections to legitimize the regime. However, there was a strong dose of self-interest in the campaign for elections; Edgard Carone concluded after a minute examination that it was led by civilians and officers who had lost their positions when Deodoro was forced to resign.

A coup d'etat planned for April 1 did not materialize but thirteen flag officers of the army and navy issued a manifesto appealing to Floriano that elections would "reestablish . . . tranquility in the Brazilian family, and thus the reputation of the Republic abroad." Floriano accused the signers of violating their duty to "defend the honor of the Pátria," of inciting disorder, and of discrediting the country abroad. Floriano's police arrested generals, high-ranking officers, members of Congress, journalists, and other adversaries and sent them into "internal" exile at Tabatinga, "the waiting room of Hell," and other such spots in the far Amazon.[35] He stubbornly faced one of the most turbulent situations in Brazilian history and forcibly maintained the new regime at the price of a civil war that all but destroyed the navy and left the southern states bloodstained. Floriano's iron-fisted tactics factionalized and embittered republican ranks. His insistence on ousting all the state presidents, who had supported Deodoro in the November crisis, stirred regional violence in many parts of Brazil.

In Rio Grande do Sul it pitted the ex-monarchist liberals, led by Gaspar da Silveira Martins, concentrated in the new Federalist Party, against Julio de Castilhos's republicans. At the outbreak of fighting, army units were on both sides, although most followed Vice President Floriano's lead and aided Castilhos. The gaúcho conflict, which spilled over into Santa Catarina and Paraná, saw families, towns, and military units divided according to monarchist or republican sentiments, personal grudges, and ambitions.

In 1893–94 the army and part of the fleet in Rio's harbor engaged in a frustrating conflict that became linked to the civil war in the south. Unlike the interregional nature of the American Civil War, which contributed to the professionalization of the opposing forces, the Brazilian civil war of 1893–95, embracing both the fighting in the south and in Rio's Guanabara Bay, had more the appearance of a massive feud than of a conventional war. The intensity of feelings, particularly in Rio Grande, caused both sides to look on each other as unpatriotic traitors who deserved the slit throat that often awaited prisoners.[36]

In the last two months of 1891 the events that led to the navy revolt and the fighting in the south—Deodoro's dissolution of Congress, his resignation, and Floriano Peixoto's assumption of power—produced divisions in the army. Some officers such as Colonels Arthur Oscar de Andrada Guimarães, Thomaz Thompson Flores, Carlos Eugênio de Andrada Guimarães, João César Sampaio, and Fernando Setembrino de Carvalho had not only opposed Deodoro's attack on the constitution but had been ready to march on Rio de Janeiro to depose him. They had supported Floriano's assumption of power, whereas others such as Major Generals Antônio M. Coelho, Cândido José da Costa, Brigadier Generals José Cerqueira de Aguiar Lima, and João Nepomuceno de Medeiros Mallet had backed Deodoro.[37]

Although Floriano ordered these latter arrested and expelled from the army, others, like Colonel Antonio Carlos da Silva Piragibe, fought with the rebel Federalists.[38] The regional issue of which political grouping would govern Rio Grande do Sul became a national issue once Floriano threw the weight of the national government behind Julio de Castilhos. The gaúcho rebels may have argued that they were against Castilhos and not Floriano, that they accepted the republic and were not seeking to restore the monarchy, but whatever their personal reasons, they were taking to the field against regular army units.

The savage nature of the fighting did not contribute to a smooth transition to peace or to the subsequent building of a cohesive officer corps. The internal dissension of these years would plague the army in the first decades of the new century. The rebel Federalists' sieges of Bagé in Rio Grande do

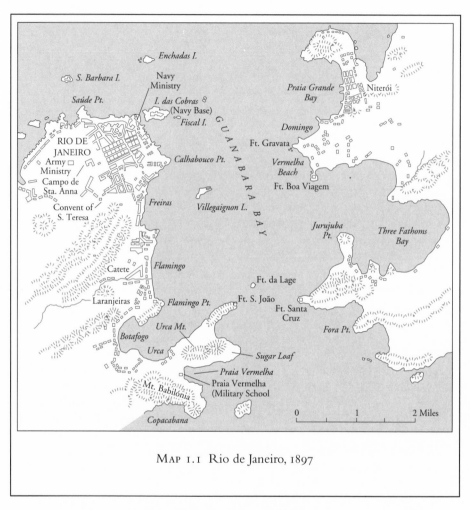

MAP 1.1 Rio de Janeiro, 1897

SOURCE: From *Century Atlas South America*, Eastern Part, Map 71. NY: Century Co., 1897. From author's map collection. Redrawn by Bill Nelson.

Sul and Lapa in Paraná were not soon forgotten or forgiven. In a eulogy to the determined, but defeated, defender of Lapa, the Federalists were called shameful enemies of the republic who hired foreign mercenaries to invade the Pátria under the guise of civil war.[39] But in what historian José Maria Bello called the "cruellest of Brazil's civil wars," there was shame enough for both sides, as the mutilation of the bodies of rebel commanders Gumercindo Saraiva and Saldanha da Gama and the summary executions of captives amply demonstrated. In November 1893 near besieged Bagé, three hundred captured Castilhistas and federal soldiers went under the knife. And the following April the other side repaid the atrocity with a like number of *degola*s at Boi Prêto. This ferocity gave the defenders of Bagé incentive to withstand a thirty-day siege during which they consumed the town's horses, dogs, and cats.[40]

Floriano was no Lincoln. Generosity in victory marked neither him nor his commanders. His followers, to whom he was the Iron Marshal, were "drunk with victory, [and] saw monarchic plotters in every corner." And because they believed themselves the "only republicans and the only patriots," they afflicted the nation with "a ferocious intransigence."[41]

Floriano gained a reputation as a nationalist, determined to fight tooth and nail for the Pátria; his name became synonymous with Brazilian nationalism. That image includes holding the line against foreign interests. Yet in truth Floriano owed the survival of his government partly to the United States government and to private American citizens who provided crucial naval support against the rebel fleet. Brazil's minister in Washington, Salvador de Mendonça, had lived in the United States for fifteen years, was married to an American, and had close ties with businessman Charles R. Flint and Secretaries of State James G. Blaine and Walter G. Gresham. In a major revision of the history of the naval and economic aspects of this crisis, Steven C. Topik uncovered the depth of American involvement. At the outset of the naval rebellion at Rio de Janeiro Washington's stance was similar to that of the Europeans, namely that foreign citizens, property, and trade should not be endangered and that the foreign ships should stay "neutral." Initially the United States had no war vessels at Rio, so its voice was somewhat muted. The foreign commanders, particularly the British, told rebel commander Admiral Custódio de Mello that they would oppose any attack on the capital city, and they convinced Floriano to remove batteries from the heights of several hills from which guns could threaten the rebel ships. They also refused entry of Floriano's supply ships into the bay. However, in response to their suggestion that they might have to land marines to protect their citizens on land, Floriano was firm: if they tried it, he asserted that they would be met with gunfire *(a bala)*. He and his supporters concluded that the foreign officers, particularly the British, favored the rebels.

The United States was different. President Benjamin Harrison, following Secretary Blaine's advice, had immediately recognized the republican regime, despite the high regard Pedro II was accorded in the United States, where memories of his extensive 1876 tour were still vivid. Harrison had grumbled that Deodoro's salary was higher than his and that the lack of elections and of a free constitutional convention raised serious doubts about the democratic nature of the regime. But there was no mistake that the republicans, no matter how shallow their democratic roots, were more inclined toward the North American republic and the Americas generally than their imperial predecessors had been.

Moreover, Deodoro and Floriano agreed to the Blaine-Mendonça Reciprocity Treaty as part of a strategy to establish closer ties, even alliance, with the United States. Two-thirds of all Brazilian coffee and four-fifths of its natural rubber went to the American market, but most of Brazil's manufactured imports came from Europe. In the early 1890s the United States was the only power that Brazilians did not accuse of sabotaging the republic and frustrating its economic development. Even extreme Jacobins saw the United States as a kindred spirit. It, too, was an ex-colony, suspicious of monarchies. It was the world's senior republic and, from the Brazilian perspective, a more secure model than the French one because it had achieved stability without the widespread violence and social upheaval represented by the guillotine. The Brazilians made Pan-Americanism an element of their nationalism. The masthead of the main Jacobin newspaper, *O Jacobino* (Rio), proclaimed: "Brazil for the Brazilians & America for Americans." Alone among the countries of the Americas, Brazil saw the Monroe Doctrine as a positive gesture of goodwill. For all Washington's expressed need for overseas markets opened by reciprocal trade agreements, American industry exported little to Brazil because it did not bother to explore the needs of that market, to develop credit practices that could make their high prices more competitive; moreover, in the 1890s there were no American bank branches in Brazil, and direct steamship service consisted of one line with three vessels that made round trips every three weeks. Mail and telegraph went by way of Europe; in fact London was the clearinghouse for Brazil–United States trade. American investment, too, was very small. So it is understandable that Steven Topik concluded that "Florianistas looked on their northern neighbor as a fellow ex-colony rather than as an imperialist threat."[42]

The Brazilian navy, which had enjoyed prestige since the early empire, felt neglected and resentful of its inferior position in the republic. Promotions, pay, and political positions went to army officers to a greater degree than to naval officers. Floriano's election over Admiral Eduardo Wandenkolk was an outward sign of the divisions between the two services. Deodoro's resignation had been forced largely by the naval revolt led by Admiral Custódio de

Mello, but Floriano had not rewarded him, had not given him any share of the power he craved. The 1880s had seen the United States initiate its new navy of steel vessels, and the importance of naval power was emphasized in confrontations among the great powers. Naval power would soon be the new measure of power status and the guarantee that national commerce and property abroad would not be disturbed. Expansion of industry, trade, and naval power would become elements of United States imperialism according to the writ of Alfred T. Mahan, whose highly influential book *The Influence of Sea Power upon History* appeared in 1890. Awareness of these events and trends frustrated Brazilian naval officers, even though they sailed some of the most modern vessels afloat; the U.S. Navy had only four more steel-protected vessels than Brazil's nine. *Jane's Fighting Ships* listed Brazil among the countries having modern navies.[43]

On September 6, 1893, the eve of independence day, Admiral de Mello's conspirators seized fifteen warships and nine commercial vessels and tried unsuccessfully to cut the Central Railway's access to Rio. The warships and the harbor forts put on a great pyrotechnic display of sloppy marksmanship, which visiting actress Sarah Bernhardt thought "a marvel—a scene of a lifetime,"[44] but it did little damage to either side. Floriano, who had avoided bloodshed in 1889 and in securing power in 1891, now showed his mettle. His troops held the harbor forts, which, although their guns were outmoded, could still damage vessels attempting to leave or enter Guanabara Bay. He had lost his fleet, an important munitions depot, and the bay's largest island, *Governador*. Worse, the lack of road or rail connections along Brazil's 4,600-mile coastline meant that with de Mello's ships potentially in command of the sea-lanes, troops outside Rio who were not guarding seaports could not be transported to the capital. Foreign commentators gave the advantage to the admiral and made sport of the affair.

Admiral de Mello justified his rebellion as a defense of the Constitution and civilian government against militarism. He claimed that he acted in response to Floriano's veto of a congressional bill that would have required him to end his term in November 1894 without possibility of reelection. For the admiral the veto was proof that Floriano intended to impose a dictatorship. Floriano defended his veto by saying that the Constitution already forbade reelection, so that portion of the bill was redundant. If the admiral truly intended to forestall dictatorship and to defend the Constitution with his cruisers, he failed. Floriano declared martial law, and police arrested hundreds of suspected enemies, imposed strict censorship of press and telegraph, controlled internal movement with special passports, and suspended the congressional elections set for October. The regime may not have been a dictatorship at the outset of the fighting, but the emergency soon made it one.[45]

The various republican clubs of Rio formed patriotic battalions, which were given regular officers as trainers and leaders. Jacobins helped to whip up patriotic sentiments by linking immigrant Portuguese to the revolt. Floriano pointed to a vague "cosmopolitanism" (usually connected with the Portuguese) as a threat to national unity. His followers accused the conservative Portuguese colony of financing the fleet's rebellion. Who did provide the money? Floriano had infuriated some important financiers with his stock market and banking reforms. He was in a difficult spot as soaring prices replaced the stability of the 1880s; prices increased by 20 percent a year; and the government tried to keep pace by printing money to the point that by 1894 money in circulation had tripled over the 1889 level. Exchange rates deteriorated as foreign lenders grew weary of Brazilian ventures. Leading financial figures such as Francisco de Paula Mayrink, the Visconde de Figueiredo, and the Conde de Leopoldina supplied money, munitions, and merchant ships to the rebels.

Admirals Saldanha da Gama, de Mello, and Wandenkolk had friendship and business ties to those financiers. They not only lent their own money to the insurrectionists but sailed to Europe in search of funds. The ties among Brazilian and Portuguese financiers and the European money marts bound the naval revolt to European capitalists. And the Rio government's citing the European linkage was a useful propaganda ploy to stir popular indignation and to gain support in Washington, which was sensitive to European machinations in the Americas.[46]

It is not clear how much popular sentiment was manipulated, but the fleet rebellion contributed to the rapid rise in food prices, and, perhaps to help finance its defense, the government chose this moment to impose a sales tax that further inflamed emotions and stimulated street demonstrations. On September 11 hundreds of protesters seeking redress in front of government buildings were dispersed by mounted troops. The stifled citizenry returned home, likely feeling even more unhappy about paying the Portuguese green grocer his price or landlord his rent and perhaps even willing to blame the Portuguese rather than Floriano for their problems.[47] The degree of popular support for Floriano is impossible to measure. The lack of onshore support for the rebels may have been the result of police efficiency or of street wisdom that identified the rebels with elite and foreign speculators; or it may have been that Floriano's denunciations of profiteering, his expansion of government jobs, and his own simple lifestyle won him sympathy. He wore civilian clothes and often used the streetcars between his office in the Itamarati Palace and his home in Cosme Velho. He avoided the limelight to a fault. Whereas others gave grand public speeches, he acted quietly. On his death in 1895 the *Jornal do Brasil* (Rio), pointed out that his predecessors as leader of Brazil—João VI, Pedro I, Pedro II, and

Deodoro—had all buckled under pressure of rebellion but that Floriano had broken that tradition of weakness; he had resisted and won. The newspaper reports were uniform in their astonishment at the thousands of people who lined the streets and hung from trees, lampposts, and windows along the route to the cemetery.[48]

At the outset of the naval revolt the United States had no vessels at Rio and so was untainted by the first European moves restricting the terms of engagement between the two sides. Washington was cautious because two years before, it had chosen the losing side in a revolt in Chile backed by the British. This time President Grover Cleveland and Secretary of State Walter Gresham wanted to be with the winner. They rejected de Mello's request for belligerency status, in spite of rebel control of a large area in the south and a provisional government in place on Santa Catarina Island. Slowly the United States steamed its new warships down to Rio. Given the tensions between Great Britain and the United States in the 1890s, British favoritism toward the rebels pushed the Americans closer to Floriano. American investor and importer Charles Flint and Brazilian minister Salvador de Mendonça orchestrated a press campaign in the United States favorable to the Rio regime. And Flint outfitted and armed a twelve-ship flotilla, crewed and officered by Americans, some of whom were commissioned naval officers. As Topik has demonstrated, this aspect of the affair slipped below the historical horizon for a century.

Flint was one of those characters who easily disappear when historians focus on the presidents and ministers. He was powerful and influential, but as a New York newspaper observed, he was "little known except in Washington and the capitals of the countries situated around the equator."[49] He had long experience in shipping and arms sales; he had helped Peru obtain ships for its conflict with Chile, had sold munitions to Brazil in the 1880s, had partnerships with W. R. Grace, held a large block of stock in the U.S. and Brazil Mail Steamship Company, and led a syndicate that bought the *New York Times* in 1893. Flint was so adept and well connected that with the United States in severe depression he was able to secure credit for his Brazilian fleet from the British Rothchilds (who it seems also supplied funds to the rebels in Rio harbor).

Although the outfitting and arming of Flint's fleet violated U.S. neutrality laws, the Cleveland administration encouraged the effort. Flint bought a dozen rapid-fire Hotchkiss guns from the company's display at Chicago's Colombian Exposition. He also acquired a new Thomas Edison invention, the Sims-Edison submarine electrical fish torpedo, and a few Howell torpedoes. Most sensationally, he bought the highly feared weapon of the era, the pneumatic or dynamite gun, which fired 980-pound projectiles over a three-mile range. These were experimental weapons that governments were reluctant to share, yet Flint had free reign. As Topik noted, "by rapidly converting merchantmen to gunboats and fitting out the ships with the most advanced experimental weapons, Flint was providing the U.S. Navy with combat trials."[50]

But the Cleveland administration went beyond facilitating Flint's Fleet to show its support of Floriano. It dispatched to Rio, in the words of Assistant Secretary of the Navy William McAdoo, "the most powerful fleet which ever represented our flag abroad."[51] The five big cruisers outgunned and outmaneuvered the rebel and foreign vessels in Guanabara Bay. The American commander Admiral Andrew Benham acted as mediator between Floriano and the rebel officers, who promised that they would give up the fight if Floriano left office and a civilian was elected president. In fact, Floriano set elections for March 1 and São Paulo's Prudente J. de Morais was elected. The combination of supposed super weapons on the Flint Fleet and the gunships of the American navy took the steam out of the rebels at Rio and exposed the provisional authorities on Santa Catarina Island to seaward attack and capture. In celebration Floriano made the fourth of July a national holiday, Congress had a medal struck with Cleveland and Floriano's images, and frontier towns in Santa Catarina and in Amazonas (later Amapá) were christened "*Clevelandia.*"[52] The foundation of the "unwritten alliance" of the next decade was firmly laid.

Although a worn-down Floriano was succeeded by civilian Prudente de Morais and soon died in June 1895, his name became a banner for fanatical Jacobins. His parting advice to a group of young republicans set the tone for the next years: "They say . . . that the Republic is consolidated and in no danger. Don't depend on it, and don't let yourselves be taken by surprise. The ferment of restoration works quietly but constantly and relentlessly. So be on your guard."[53]

That advice added fuel to the emotional atmosphere that encouraged students at the military school in Rio de Janeiro to join in street disorders, provoke fights during Carnaval celebrations, and to jeer and publicly insult their anti-Florianista commander. After Floriano's death the military school's students took on themselves the guardianship of the Florianista political spirit.[54] The military students—cadets and officers attending the school to complete their education—saw themselves as the purest of the pure, the most patriotic of the patriotic, who had the double duty of saving the Pátria while preserving the integrity of the army, the vehicle of national salvation. In February 1891, when Congress elected the president and overzealous uniformed officers had crowded the galleries to intimidate the representatives in favor of Deodoro, the military students had taken a different tack, affirming that they would take to the field to guarantee congressional freedom of choice. The students regarded shielding the Congress as defense of the republic that their school had helped to create. In November 1891, with the collapse of Deodoro's dictatorship after his armed dissolution of Congress and Floriano Peixoto's assumption of power, the military reshuffled into new groupings for or against the vice president.[55]

Where Deodoro had been impulsive and politically ingenuous, Floriano was a calculating skeptic who maneuvered carefully to impose his will. For Deodoro the republic was a challenge, a form of revenge for slights to the army's honor; for Floriano it was the embodiment of new governing techniques to be imposed energetically on Brazil. He favored a strong, if not dictatorial, presidency and seemed inclined toward the interests of the middle classes.[56]

For the military students, Floriano Peixoto personified the republican cause. When the fleet rebelled in 1893, the military school provided the government with combatants, messengers, escorts for political prisoners, and training cadres for the rapidly raised citizen battalions. Having stood four-square with the government, the students believed that the victory was particularly theirs. They took to heart Floriano's charge that "we have to put Brazil in such condition as to be respected as it should and to claim its position in the American hemisphere."[57] The future of Brazil, the republic, and the army became as one in their minds.

In November 1894 the accession of Prudente J. de Morais Barros to the presidency returned the agrarian elite to power with the consequent fading of urban middle-class influence. The new president's republicanism was suspect in military student eyes. Moreover, the return to normal military school routine was rather dull after the excitement of the previous year. Indeed, as Jehovah Motta, an analyst of military education, observed, for years the institution at Praia Vermelha "had been functioning as a mixture of school and center of political activism. Routine, pure and simple—classes, examinations, exercises—would necessarily have for the students the flavor of frustration, if not defeat."[58]

So in January 1895, when classes reopened, the commandant, General Joaquim Mendes Ourique Jacques, a sixty-year-old veteran of the Paraguayan War, who was reputedly anti-Florianista, dealt with the rising wave of insubordination and lack of discipline by expelling a number of student officers. This action led to a student manifesto in the press censoring the authorities and to a demonstration in which students filled the school's windows booing and shouting against the commandant and the government and giving *vivas* for Floriano. Some sixty students were dismissed, producing renewed demonstrations and forceful occupation of the school by loyal government troops. The commandant discharged from the army students with soldier ratings *(alunos praças)* and arrested the student officers, who were sent to units throughout the country. No classes had been held in 1894, and by the end of March 1895 the student body was scattered. For his services General Mendes Ourique Jacques was promoted to brevet marshal and retired. A new commandant welcomed a newly matriculated corps of student officers and soldiers, as well as several new faculty members. Even with this apparent cleansing, if the subsequent revolts of 1897 and 1904 are an indication, it seems that the students preserved the school's Florianista, hard-line republican tradition. The public outpouring that attended the elaborate funeral rites when Floriano Peixoto died, in June 1895, also contributed to republican emotionalism. The presence of the former students in the commemorations did not go unnoticed.[59]

The Prudente de Morais administration sought to quiet passions by bringing the war in the south to a negotiated end, with amnesty for the rebels. Even the general officers, who Floriano had expelled, were allowed to return to active duty. Moreover, Prudente weakened the army's archrepublican faction by furthering the careers of anti-Florianistas.[60]

The president's intention of lessening the army's political weight found acceptance among officers who, with Minister of War General Bernardo Vasques, viewed the army as representing the nation's collective strength, "sustaining the great principles on which it is based." Reduction of political involvement would be accomplished by "maintaining order and defending national rights and sovereignty." National institutions, laws, and methods were subject to the "law of progress" and had to be altered now and again to harmonize with social realities.[61] Officers who held this view saw their task as building a professional force that would be at the disposal of the national authorities, who would determine when and where order was to be maintained and rights and sovereignty defended. They might be termed apolitical professionals, but one suspects that they tended to be conservative politically, comfortable with Brazil's social realities, and not overly concerned whether the country lived under a constitutional monarch or a parliamentary or presidential republic. Florianista officers rejected such soft-headedness. For Florianista General Francisco de Paula Argollo, who was wounded commanding the government forces at Niterói during the navy rebellion, the army's mission was "to sustain the institutions conquered by the patriotic movement of the 15th of November 1889."[62] Although such an attitude quickly caused Prudente to become disenchanted with Argollo as war minister and to dismiss him, both Argollo and Vasques believed that the army had to be modernized if it were to be effective.[63]

The linchpin of this reorganization was to be a general staff modeled on that of the Germans. In 1895 General Vasques had complained about the antiquated organization and disconnected functioning of the various sections of the army's administration. And in October 1895 he had named a commission to propose regulations for a general staff and a quartermaster section. The need for the latter would shortly be made disastrously clear at Canudos. And it was time, Vasques argued, to make the army compatible with the "present democratic regime" and to convince the population that every citizen had a duty to give military service to his Pátria. Although a small army was sufficient for Brazil's peacetime needs, it had to be well organized, trained, and equipped, and it must be capable of mobilizing rapidly while expanding its effectiveness without the embarrassments it had commonly encountered in the past, when "the *Pátria* required the effort and sacrifice of all its sons." This meant that military service should become obligatory, that reserve forces should be organized, and that the National Guard should be restructured to parallel "the permanent Army."[64]

Military education was decadent. None of the several schools produced desired results because Vasques said there were too many of them, duplicating each other's programs and offering studies that were overly theoretical, speculative, and philosophical, with little or no relationship to military instruction. The "superabundance of subjects in a course of military studies" lengthened the time spent in the schools at the expense of time spent with the troops. Reform was sorely needed, and to insure that the coming reforms would be modeled on the latest foreign innovations, the government sent Brigadier General João Vicente Leite de Castro to Europe to examine the newest armament, to visit installations, and to witness maneuvers. The resulting modifications would even include new uniforms and a refurbished transportation corps.[65]

Canudos Looms

When Canudos emerged before the national consciousness, the army was attempting to reorganize itself after the disorder of the first years of the republic. The combat experience of the era did not produce a more professional army; rather it disrupted it. The nervous political atmosphere of the 1890s allowed a harmless religious colony, deep in the backlands of Bahia, to be portrayed as a monarchist horde poised to march. Screams out of the flames of Canudos would disturb the sleep of many a soldier for years to come and would leave a scar on the institutional psyche. There are no monuments in Brazil's cities to the army's dead and wounded at Canudos, although five thousand soldiers fell there in less than a year.

The story of Canudos is well known in its general outlines. The religiously based community in the dry interior of north central Bahia became involved in a dispute with the authorities of a nearby town, who called down the military power of the state only to have three successively larger expeditions inexplicably defeated. In Rio de Janeiro nervous republicans attributed the defeats to an extensive monarchist plot of which Canudos was

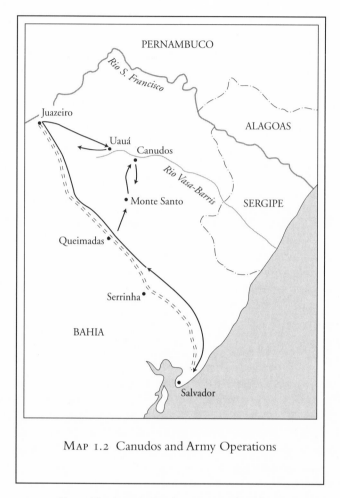

MAP 1.2 Canudos and Army Operations

SOURCE: From *The Army in Brazilian History*, edited by Luiz Paulo Macedo Cavalho. Rio de Janeiro & Salvador, Ba.: Biblioteca do Exército & Odebrecht, 1998. 4 vols. Redrawn by Bill Nelson. Used with permission of Biblioteca do Exército, Rio de Janeiro.

the supposed center. From there monarchist forces would supposedly march on Salvador and then on down to Rio de Janeiro. To save the republic, a fourth powerful expedition pulverized the backlands "citadel" into the earth. It was not the finest hour of the Brazilian army.[66] Just as it was on the verge of a massive restructuring, of lessening its active political role, and of healing the wounds of the civil war, almost accidentally, and certainly unnecessarily, Brazil's mystical and political worlds collided in a deadly struggle.

In his after-action report Lieutenant Manoel da Silva Pires Ferreira of the Ninth Infantry Battalion wrote that at dawn, on November 21, 1896, in the Bahian backlands hamlet of Uauá, his one hundred soldiers had been awakened by an exchange of gunfire as the outlying sentries were "attacked by an enormous multitude of fanatic bandits." The soldiers had arrived at that place two days before to intercept people from Canudos reportedly en route to the São Francisco River town of Juazeiro, some 119 miles distant, to collect forcibly a quantity of undelivered, prepaid supplies. The approximately five hundred *sertanejos* (backlanders), armed with old muskets, pikes, scythes, and poles, and reportedly carrying saints' images, rosaries, and a large wooden cross, approached the settlement. Drowsy soldiers bounded out of doors and windows to set up a defense line. Knives and scythes against Comblain rifles and revolvers hardly made for even-matched combat, but the battle supposedly raged for about four hours before the sertanejos broke it off and headed back to Canudos. The troops buried their ten dead, looted and burned Uauá, then retreated to Juazeiro.

It is possible that this report is not fully honest and that the soldiers provoked the fight or fired on an innocent assembly. It is odd that they looted and burned the hamlet, especially since its people had fled and seem to have been innocent bystanders. Bahian governor Luiz Vianna later cited the troop behavior in arguing that a new expedition was "entirely unnecessary and perhaps more dangerous to the public order and to the well being of the zone that it was to help" than were the people of Canudos. However it started, this engagement began a series of campaigns that disrupted the army's plans as it faced trials for which it was not prepared.[67]

Canudos was a religiously-based settlement in the northern *sertão* of Bahia. Its population may have been as high as thirty thousand drawn together by the hope that Antonio Maciel, the "Counselor," would give them a better life. His community was so wrapped up in its own world that it is amazing that Brazilian officials could have viewed it as a threat to the republic. They perceived Antonio Conselheiro as a fanatic who threatened national institutions by somehow casting a spell on the backward, ignorant people of the region. In the imagery of Euclides da Cunha, who wrote what is considered the classic book of twentieth-century Brazilian literature about the destruction of Canudos, the entire drama pitted the civilized coast against the isolated, savage interior.[68] It was a facile literary device that perhaps eased the troubled consciences of his generation but was not true to life.

Conselheiro was a *beato,* a layman, who devoted himself to personal asceticism and to good works. Since 1871 he had roamed the backlands, often in the company of foreign missionaries, organizing local people to rebuild abandoned churches, chapels, and cemeteries. The parish priests, then attempting to spark religious revival, as was the whole northeastern Church from the 1860s onward, were pleased with his efforts, as were labor-poor local colonels (as local political bosses were called), who "appreciated the dams and roads that the *beato* constructed for them, and above all, the free labor provided by workers whom the Counselor kept well disciplined."[69] Rather than being an isolated, hermetic holy man, he was an activist tied to the backlands' religious, economic, and political life. And through that triad he was linked to the state, regional, and national political and economic structures.

Although the parish priests were happy to support his work, indeed his status as *beato* depended on their recognition, his efforts irritated the archbishop of the Bahia, who wished to concentrate religious leadership in a disciplined clergy. In 1887 he had the imperial authorities expel the counselor from the province on the grounds that his teaching was subversive to church and state.[70] In a religious sense it is likely that Conselheiro was caught in the grips of an ancient Episcopal prejudice against lay preachers, especially ones that attracted large numbers of followers, because his teachings were conservative, traditional Catholicism, and, although vulgarized, were a precise reflection of the then current Scholastic Theology. As Duglas Teixeira Monteiro observed, he was a "mystic, spiritual director, *beato*. Nothing more than this, however." His surviving writings show no sign of "messianism or of prophetism; no new or renewed form of millenarianism." For him history was an interval in which one accumulated, "particularly by suffering, the merits which flow to us from the Passion of Christ." Rather than a religious subversive or a messiah pointing to a new path to salvation, "Antonio Conselheiro was, in the religious sense, a herald" of an already founded and established order."[71]

Although he may not have differed with Church doctrine, there is evidence that he differed with the social doctrines of nineteenth-century Brazil. He knew of Thomas More's *Utopia,* and Belo Monte, as Conselheiro called Canudos, can be seen as a utopian community where all worked for the common good and shared equally in the fruits of their labor. Contemporary observers remarked that the settlement's communism attracted the sertão's *camponeses* whom labor laws and landowners' gunslingers *(jagunços)* kept tied to the great properties. The republic, based as it was on alliance between the urban middle class and the great landowners, avoided revolutionizing the social-economic structure of the countryside. So for the poor backlander, Antonio Conselheiro represented an alternative, whereas for the great landowners, such as the baron of Geremoabo, he represented a potential threat. Far from being a demented, isolated holy man, Antonio Conselheiro was very much involved in the principal issues of 1890s Brazilian society.[72]

Indeed, it appears that his ties with the greater political world, rather than isolation from it, caused the disaster. The steady outward migration from the northeast, spurred by the severe droughts and pulled by the coffee boom in

the south and the rubber boom in the Amazon, made the capacity "to attract" pilgrims "to the labor-shy region of Bahia . . . (where they remained
as workers) . . . tantamount to political power." Because workers represented "potential wealth and votes," the local colonels-*fazendeiros* courted
Conselheiro.[73] He became a pawn in the struggle for control of Bahia's political machinery, which in the interior involved competing colonels.

It is ironic that, in 1893, he was allied to Luis Vianna, who would be governor when Canudos was attacked four years later. In fact, Conselheiro's famous burning of the tax decrees at Bom Conselho in 1893 was merely one
of several incidents in which Vianna's supporters made bonfires of tax
edicts. And a subsequent skirmish with the state police, which resulted in
the flight to Canudos, was instigated by the baron of Geremoabo, the big
landowner of the area and Vianna's political opponent. In May 1896, after
Vianna became governor, accusations mounted that he was exploiting the
growing Canudos movement and that his hesitation to disperse what his
opponents saw as a force that could be used to harass local landowners was
due to his intention to use Conselheiro in the upcoming December 1896
elections. The intense republicanism of the era made it possible to raise
charges of monarchism, which Vianna could not ignore lest zealous army
officers in Salvador throw in with his opponents.[74]

Vianna's opponents spread rumors that Conselheiro was set to attack nearby
towns and demanded that the governor act. He responded by requesting
that one hundred federal troops be placed under his direction to disperse
Conselheiro's settlement. The Third Military District commander, General
Frederico Sólon, was unhappy with the arrangement because he believed
that federal troops could be used constitutionally only if the president of
Brazil ordered an intervention in the state. He believed that there was no
provision in the law for federal forces to be placed at the disposal of state
authorities. But he did what he was told and sent Lt. Manoel da Silva Pires
Ferreira with three officers and 104 soldiers by train to Juazeiro and overland to the encounter at Uauá described above.[75]

If superior officers had taken the time to read Lieutenant Pires Ferreira's
after-action report and had taken steps to prepare for the problems he reported, much suffering could have been avoided. The dust, the ruggedness
of the trails, the blistering sun made control on the march extremely difficult. The men marched and slept in their uniforms, which were soon in tatters from the stress of heat, rain, thorns, and combat. Their shoes wore out
on the rough trails, leaving most barefoot. They had no tents and so suffered
whatever the night would bring. Their Mannlicher rifles had been used in
the fighting in the south in 1894, and most showed signs of repair. Although
accurate and powerful under test conditions, the rifles were undependable
in combat because they overheated, their shell ejectors were not reliable,

and the least dirt or sand in the chamber rendered them useless. Hardly the weapon for a campaign in the sertão![76]

District Commander General Sólon continued to object to placing army troops at the disposal of the state government, but on the expressed order of the minister of war he charged army Major Febrônio de Brito of the Ninth Infantry Battalion to command a new attack force. They still thought that a few hundred troops would do the trick. And because all of the army's units were under strength, they scrapped together soldiers from units in Salvador, Aracajú, and Maceio; and later, en route, he received about 250 Bahian state police, bringing his total command to some 560. The process of assembling this force produced a struggle for control between Governor Vianna and District Commander Sólon that led to the latter's removal. Vianna complained to fellow Baianos, Acting President Manuel Vitoriano and Minister of War Dionísio Cerqueira, that General Sólon's continuation as district chief would be "prejudicial to Bahia"; so they replaced him with Colonel Saturnino Ribeiro da Costa Jr. The general had argued in favor of sending multiple columns from different directions and not attacking until the units were properly deployed and provisioned. Unhappily his caution was borne out. After considerable delay, with two Krupp 7.5 field guns and Nordenfeldt machine guns in tow, they moved from their base camp in the town of Queimadas toward Monte Santo (a distance of 47.2 miles) through countryside whose soil blossomed with rocks and cacti. Local civilian leaders were confident; a judge and some fifty inhabitants of Monte Santo telegraphed the governor that the major's force could approach Canudos "advantageously," that "the bandits . . . are panicked and depressed." A police officer asserted that Conselheiro did not have more than a thousand poorly armed combatants. All seemed to believe that Canudos would just fade before their advance.[77]

By mid-January 1897 the column would be facing very different opponents. As they marched from Monte Santo, their security was nonexistent, and they were accompanied on the trail by watchful eyes. Major Febrônio, unable to find sufficient mules and drivers, left precious supplies behind in each hamlet, only to find himself a few miles from Canudos without food. Even the remaining two oxen had to be slaughtered, and among so many, they did not go far. If the soldiers were to survive, they would have to take Canudos. They were understandably nervous.

This barren, bone-dry land, with its jagged rock formations, worn-down quartz-speckled mountains, and hills cut by narrow gullies that here and there widened into passes, was awesome, especially under a blazing, unforgiving sun. The thick, scrubby vegetation along the trail bristled with thorns that reached out from tough irregular branches, looking all the world like angry trees in a nightmare. Here and there the *joaz* fruit tree, *umbú* palm, *mandacarú* fig tree, and the *chique-chique* cactus offered variety.[78] But this was no place for the unwary or the citified; here survival depended on knowing where the water holes were, which plants contained moisture, and which had edible roots. In such a setting the Brazilian soldier, "who is courageous enough when facing an enemy, becomes a coward, a prey to fears, when that enemy is a hidden one, who shows his presence without being seen as he lies in ambush."[79] A sudden attack on the point of the column might cause those behind to break ranks and flee. But hunger held the major's troops together as they moved close to their objective.

They were on the Cambaio road, named after the rocky mount to the southwest of Canudos. To reach the settlement, they would have to cross the mountain "along a steep path hemmed in by cliffs, to come out finally in a narrow, tunnel-like pass."[80] It was there that the sertanejos attacked the sweaty, straggling soldiers. Major Febrônio held his startled troops firm and brought the Krupps into action. After much irregular, helter-skelter fighting, the sertanejos tried a desperate heroic attack on the thundering artillery. Their cries of "Viva ao Conselheiro!" and "Viva a Bom Jesus!" suddenly turned to howls of pain as a shell fired at point-blank range exploded in their midst. The survivors turned heel with the troops in pursuit. A five-hour battle secured the mountain, opened the road to Canudos, and exhausted both sides. The military casualties totaled four dead and twenty-three wounded, whereas the sertanejos left 115 corpses scattered over the battlefield.[81]

The troops, hungry and exhausted, had such an illusion of victory that they did not press their advantage. The sudden darkness of the backlands night was descending. Major Febrônio had his men encamp beside the small lake Cipó; the coup de grâce could wait for morning.

Canudos lay before them, little more than a mile away. It sat in a basin through which ran the meandering Vasa-Barris River, which curved in such a way as to brace the settlement in moatlike fashion on its southern, eastern, and western sides. The town was on a rise above the river, whose banks rose steeply to meet it. Beyond the town there were rolling hills to the north and across the Vasa-Barris on the other three sides was an elliptical circle of mountains, with Cambaio to the southwest and Mount Favela to the southeast. All the trails leading into the tight basin passed through narrow gorges and defiles or over rough, rutted terrain. Even the flatter land on the open side of the settlement was so cut with gullies that the orderly movement of troops there would be extremely difficult. To Euclydes da Cunha, it seemed "a colossal armed field, indeed it was impossible to descry any point" at which the settlement "was wholly accessible."[82]

The town itself mirrored the mazelike quality of the surrounding terrain. There were no streets; rather alleyways ran without noticeable pattern in all directions. On the southeastern side there was a *praça* with a large cross and two churches, one of which was still under construction, providing the only relief to the confusion of dwellings. Aside from a few better houses on the *praça,* belonging to the elite of the place, the nearby five thousand structures were mostly typical northeastern mud-and-wattle construction, divided into cooking and sleeping chambers, most with no windows and an open door-way covered with a woven straw mat.[83]

As the day lightened on January 19, the settlement was quiet; no ser-tanejo could be seen. At the cannons' first discharge the sertanejos, who had silently surrounded the soldiers during the night, leaped from their hiding places and raced at the drawn up ranks shouting and brandishing iron bars, scythes, pitchforks, and broad-blade knives. A corporal and a sertanejo fell, having impaled each other on cattle prong and bayonet. The startled artillery battery was momentarily overwhelmed, the attackers wheeling away a can-non before the soldiers retook it in fierce hand-to-hand struggle. The ser-tanejos fell back to continue the action from a distance—crossbows, flintlock muskets, and culverins (hurling pebbles and nail heads) against army rifles. Their objective was to prolong the fight indefinitely to wear down the troops, forcing them to expend their ammunition. The settlement lay in view, but suddenly the mile and a quarter that separated them from it seemed a life span away. The soldiers were weak from hunger, not having eaten in two days, and the surprise attack had shaken their resolve. What if they pressed on and ran out of their now diminished ammunition? What if the weakened, famished horses died, forcing abandonment of the artillery? Febrônio and his staff decided on retreat. In his report of the action he claimed to have been attacked by nearly four thousand "bandidos," who died clawing at the artillery. "I never saw such ferociousness," he said.[84] He had more than seventy men wounded and ten dead. But, although some three hundred sertanejo bodies were strewn about, there were hundreds more reinforcements in Canudos.

In a constant rearguard action, the troops reentered the defile of Mt. Cambaio, now fighting their way in the opposite direction. Amid catcalls, laughter, and insults the sertanejos sent avalanches of stone down on the hapless soldiers. Hours later, having escaped the pass and having reached a flat stretch of trail, the troops threw back with deadly machine-gun fire a fi-nal assault on the artillery. They stumbled into Monte Santo the next day. "There was not an able-bodied man among them. . . . The population re-ceived them in silence."[85] The messages that raced over the telegraph lines shocked the government in Rio de Janeiro.

The Moreira César Expedition

This "rebellion" clearly called for a hand experienced at repression. The in-terim minister of war, General Dionísio Cerqueira, ordered Colonel Antonio Moreira César, ardent Florianista and suppressor of the Federalists in Santa

Catarina, who had just arrived in Rio de Janeiro from the south, to proceed to Salvador. He took command of a reinforced brigade, plus Bahian state police, in all about thirteen hundred men. The impatient, overly confident colonel refused to be briefed by Major Febrônio; instead, he accepted the view of the state bosses that all that was needed was a determined show of force. There is also some suspicion that he may have been conspiring with officers and politicians interested in seeing that the sick leave of President Prudente de Morais, which he began in November 1896, be made permanent and that Vice President Manuel Vitoriano finish out the term. The colonel may have feared that Prudente would allow an inquiry into his questionable actions in the south and so had considerable reason to support his removal. With a rapid victory the Florianistas would be strengthened, and he would return to Rio the conquering hero and the iron hand of the regime.[86]

Moreira César was approaching his forty-seventh birthday and had served in the army since 1869. He was the army's expert on infantry tactics; his book on the subject had served as the basis for army doctrine since 1894.[87] He had a reputation for violence and was feared in Bahia, where in 1891 he had helped depose Governor José Gonçalves, who mistakenly had supported Deodoro's dissolution of Congress, and where, as chief of police, he had ordered street demonstrators shot down. Indeed, the sertanejos called him the head-hunter (*corta-cabeça*)! That earlier era had found him at odds with Luis Vianna, the present governor, who apparently attempted to have someone else named to head the new expedition. Soldiers in the Bahian garrison were saying Moreira César would depose Vianna, seemingly at the behest of Francisco Glicério, government leader in the Congress, who was unhappy that Bahians Rui Barbosa and José Joaquim Seabra had been elected to that body.[88]

Three incidents after his arrival in Salvador indicated that his violent reputation was deserved. In the first, as his troops were disembarking, they forced onlookers to carry their baggage to the railroad station. In the second, noticing some of his soldiers unloading a harbor launch, he brusquely ordered the civilian crew, who happened to be foreigners, to do the work instead. When they refused, saying it was not their job, he changed their minds with the flat of his sword on their backs. In the third incident, a number of the Fifth Battalion of Bahian police announced they would not be able to march because of illness. Moreira César had the unit formed up, ordering that the sick ones step forward to be examined by medical officers. Those found healthy would be shot on the spot. No one moved. Moreira César turned to the captain: "See? There aren't any sick. Move out." In the army he had a reputation for refusing to accept material obstacles; his orders were to be instantly fulfilled, regardless of the cost.[89]

Within twenty-seven days of his departure from Rio he and 1,281 troops were at Mt. Favela overlooking Canudos but not without personal cost. He suffered from epilepsy, and since leaving Santa Catarina he had been on the go constantly; and, although he claimed to be nerveless, the strain was visible. En route he telegraphed the minister of war that "I only fear that Antonio Conselheiro won't wait for us." But the medical officers worried that the seizures he suffered on the trip would worsen, and if he were incapacitated in combat, "it could be fatal for us." He reassured them that "I don't fear death and I won't die without going to Canudos."[90] To avoid being ambushed, as his predecessor had been, he left the Cambaio road to approach Canudos from the less mountainous southeast. But that meant slowly cutting a trail through the thick, thorny *caatinga* under a withering sun.

To guard against a lack of water, Moreira César's troops had brought along an artesian pump. But when they arrived at Serra Branca exhausted, suffering from eight hours of scorching heat, and attempted to put it into operation, they found to their chagrin that instead of a pile driver to sink the well, they had packed a jack! The necessity of a good quartermaster service would be learned the hard way. They had to struggle along another fifteen miles into the night before reaching the next water hole. So instead of a difficult day's march, they staggered more than twenty hours merely to survive. And with their suffering they forgot that they were in the heart of their opponents' country. Their noisy progress was easily tracked.[91]

Not surprisingly their fatigue and tension produced a number of false alarms that did nothing to improve morale. Meanwhile sertanejos had been flocking into Canudos since Febrônio's defeat and were carefully preparing the town's defenses—digging trenches, making gunpowder, sharpening knives and cattle prongs, and planning.

On March 2 Moreira César said that the next day they would advance six miles and then rest for a day before attacking. However, the next morning he changed his mind and proposed to his officers that they advance immediately. Perhaps he was convinced that because their adversaries had let them advance this far with only scattered resistance that a rapid show of force would disperse them. At a distance of about three miles the colonel announced their coming with a salvo of two artillery grenades.[92]

At 10 A.M. they sighted the settlement. After an initial defensive attack from the Canudos side, the colonel carefully arranged his units. Seeking to scare the defenders he ordered the artillery moved to within 430 yards of the nearest houses, from whence the Krupp guns fired six opening rounds. Bugle calls directed the blue-uniformed troopers forward, while the church bell tolled the alarm, and Moreira César, resplendent in a white uniform, observed the scene. He called for a bayonet charge, assuming that a rout was imminent, unable to believe that the people would hold their ground. The troops plunged forward, and shortly whole battalions disintegrated in the narrow maze of alleys among the huts. Curses and cries mingled with gunfire. The artillery was so close to its targets that it had to hold its fire from time to time for fear of getting hit by fragments of its own exploding shells or of hitting the advancing soldiers. It also had to stop periodically to cool its cannons, which grew hot from firing about three hundred rounds between noon and 5 P.M. The colonel threw his Bahian police reserve into the far right, where the Geremoabo road entered the town, and then ordered the cavalry to charge the plaza in front of the churches. The horsemen set fire to shacks and cut down defenders with their sabers. Impetuously, in the late afternoon, Moreira César rode forward to a point beside the artillery to observe the action. He dropped his binoculars when a bullet hit him in the abdomen. A lieutenant kept him in the saddle as his staff led him back to their observation point, where he took a second bullet. The staff officers did their best to keep secret the fact that he was wounded.[93]

Colonel Pedro Nunes Batista Ferreira Tamarindo took command as next senior officer, but he could do nothing to stop what was becoming a disaster. As night began to descend, the buglers sounded withdrawal. Military precepts of the era limited combat to daylight hours; if an attack was not successful by dark, it was customary to fall back and try again the next day. Of course, this allowed the enemy to recompose their lines, and as word gradually spread that Moreira César was dying, the soldiers lost their nerve. They formed a large square with the fading colonel's tent at its center, so it was impossible to keep the truth from running from man to man. What began with a few slipping away in the darkness was confirmed by the officers who decided during the night to fall back to Rosário to regroup. They had an unknown number of soldiers killed and some two hundred wounded, on whom the doctors worked throughout the night. They lacked food and water, and having given up the river to the enemy, they were cut off from that source. But they were still a thousand strong in the infantry units, the artillery battery was intact, and they had fifty thousand cartridges and sixty artillery shells. And they occupied the high ground.

Certainly, disciplined troops could have held on, but this throng of forced and ill-trained recruits, who were suffering from weariness, shock, and hunger, was not up to the challenge and succumbed to panic and terror. Many were credulous sertanejos themselves, who had heard reverent tales of Antonio Conselheiro since childhood and were ready to believe that there was an element of the supernatural in what they had just experienced. How could they battle against, let alone defeat, God's messenger? Moreira César died between 4 A.M. and 5 A.M.; at 6 A.M. the units began a disorderly retreat that rapidly turned into wholesale flight.[94]

Dejected, Colonel Tamarindo, according to Euclides da Cunha, replied to an officer seeking instructions by quoting a phrase from a northeaster song: "It is time to die, every man for himself."[95] Officers, even with revolvers drawn, were powerless to bring order to the chaos, as the running soldiers threw their equipment away. Stretcher bearers abandoned the wounded, who soon felt the knives of the advancing enemy, as did the body of Moreira César, which was mutilated and burned. Captain Joaquim Quirino Villarim fought to the end alone; Captain José Agostinho Salomão da Rocha, with a half-dozen men, died defending his four Krupps that were providing the only cover to the fleeing soldiers; Colonel Tamarindo took a bullet that knocked him from his horse. A few officers and men carried the colonel into a nearby house, only to be overwhelmed soon thereafter.

Bodies, Mannlicher carbines and Comblain rifles, knapsacks, trousers, coats, caps, and cartridge boxes littered the countryside for miles in all directions. Terrified survivors stumbled on into Monte Santo, where many had left their extra gear and personal effects with a detachment guarding supplies only to find the place looted and empty. Many died of wounds, hunger, or thirst before they reached the next outpost at Queimadas. The lack of solidarity among the troops and between officers and soldiers is evident in the after-action reports and memoirs. Truly, it was every man for himself as the strong abandoned the weak and wounded. Meanwhile, the sertanejos collected the discarded armament, which increased their ability to defend themselves a hundredfold, and arranged the dead soldiers' severed heads along the road as a warning.[96]

The Response to the Moreira César Disaster

On March 4, without knowledge of what was occurring in the Bahian backlands, Prudente de Morais returned unannounced to resume the presidency after a four-month absence. Three days later word of the disaster reached Rio de Janeiro, where a mob, inflamed by speeches of republicans, such as Nilo Peçanha, took possession of the streets, "destroying monarchist newspapers to shouts of "Viva a República" and "Viva Floriano." Gentil José de Castro, monarchist editor of *Gazeta da Tarde* (Rio), was murdered by radical officers. Street violence and attacks on newspapers and publishers also occurred in São Paulo, Minas Gerais, and Rio Grande do Sul. Vice President Manuel Vitoriano, who had approved the expedition, wrote to the Military Club to excuse himself from responsibility for the disaster by making clear that he had offered the dead hero all the support he wanted but that Moreira César had refused to take more troops so as not to weaken the garrisons of the capital and other key cities, in face of the supposed monarchist threat. Republican newspapers such as *O Estado de S. Paulo* avowed a connection between Canudos and forces supposedly gathering in Uruguay to invade Rio Grande do Sul. The paulista paper declared, "The insurrection in the sertão of Bahia is monarchist. . . . For monarchists and republicans the move-ment of Antonio Conselheiro's fanatics is today restorationist. . . . Whether or not it was monarchist at its birth, it is certain that today it is, and that, as such . . . it has to be combated." Its editors reported that monarchist con-tingents from throughout the country were moving toward Canudos, that they had chosen Bahia to be the center of the restoration movement.[97]

The Florianistas took advantage of the unrest to threaten liberal republi-cans, such as Senator Rui Barbosa and Deputy Arthur Rios, who opposed their extremism. It may be that Florianistas used the monarchist threat as an excuse for actions aimed at demoralizing the government as a prelude to imposing a Bonapartist dictatorship. Chamber of Deputies president Arthur Rios was beaten on Rua Ouvidor in Rio, and in Bahia a plot to assassinate Governor Luis Vianna was barely foiled. The conspirators may have been chance, rather than ideological, bedfellows, but they included company grade officers, the army adjutant general, General of Division Dr. Bibiano S. Macedo de Fontoura Costallat, and the baron of Geremoabo. Perhaps the tie with regional landowners, such as the baron, is what led Florianistas to involve the army's honor in this struggle "between the *camponeses* and the landed proprietors." During the empire, the army had refused to hunt slaves; why should it now bring the rural masses to heel for the ex-slave masters?[98] Cer-tainly Lt. Henrique Macedo Soares was correct in seeing "occult and igno-ble" political maneuvering behind the scenes. But to accuse the Florianistas of "trying to involve the army in an inglorious struggle" that had the explicit purpose of destroying the "civil and constitutional order" is to imagine too much organization in what was a chaotic situation. Edmundo Moniz was closer to the truth when he observed that "it was not ideas that were in play but rather individual opportunism."[99] One could go farther and say that civil-ian and military leaders were being swept along on a wave of irrationality.

The situation worked to President Prudente de Morais's advantage be-cause although some began to blame the government for the defeat, he could point out that he had nothing to do with the ill-fated expedition, and he could appease his army critics by using Florianista officers. Shortly after re-turning to office, he invited General Francisco de Paula Argollo to be war minister and agreed that another ardent Florianista, General Arthur Oscar de Andrade Guimarães, should head a new expedition that would "destroy those that are shaming our civilization."[100]

But the president's relationship with the new minister proved difficult. On May 17, in the midst of a cabinet meeting, Prudente complained that the press received news bulletins before he did. He immediately accepted Gen-eral Argollo's resignation and sent an aide to find Marshal Carlos Machado Bittencourt, a fellow paulista and old adversary of Florianismo, who was

TABLE I.2.

High Command, 1894–1897

Rank	Dates of Tenure
Minister of War	
Bernardo Vasques	Nov. 15, 1894–Nov. 23, 1896
Dionisio de Castro Cerqueira	Nov. 23, 1896–Jan. 4, 1897
Francisco de Paulo Argollo	Jan. 4, 1897–May 17, 1897
Carlos Machado de Bittencourt	May 17, 1897–Nov. 5, 1897
João Thomaz Cantuaria	Nov. 7, 1897–Nov. 15, 1898
Adjutant General	
Argollo	Mar. 1896–Jan. 1897
Bibiano de Fontoura Costallat	Jan. 1897–May 1897
Cantuaria	May 1897–May 1897
Conrad Jacob de Niemeyer	Nov. 1897-
J. N. de Medeiros Mallet	Nov. 1897-
Quartermaster General	
Argollo	Nov. 1895–Mar. 1896
Mallet	Mar. 1896–Nov. 1897

currently a judge on the Supreme Military Tribunal and who took his seat as minister before the meeting ended. To secure control over the army's central administration Bittencourt transferred General Costallat from the important adjutant general post back to his former position as professor at the *Escola Superior de Guerra* and called General João Thomaz Cantuaria from command of the Third Military Region (Bahia), where he had been sent in March to replace Sólon. He also counted on the support of General J. N. de Medeiros Mallet, the quartermaster general, whom Floriano had expelled and whom Prudente had amnestied in October 1895. It was an indication of the extreme turbulence of 1897 that in eleven months there would be four ministers of war and three adjutant generals (see Table 1.2).[101]

Gripped with nervousness, Bittencourt and Cantuaria took preventative measures, the most important of which was disarming the military school. Under the pretext that a revolt in Uruguay was endangering the frontier in Rio Grande do Sul and that the army depots in the south lacked ammunition, they ordered the school to turn over the more than fifty thousand Mauser cartridges in its stores. Although most of the units in the new expedition were armed with Mannlicher carbines and Comblain rifles, the war ministry was determined to have the few units with Mausers adequately munitioned. On March 18 it had telegraphed to Germany for fifteen tons of smokeless powder for use in Mauser cartridges. It could be that the delay in receipt of the powder was a factor in the decision to requisition the military school stocks. More than likely the frontier situation was merely an excuse.[102]

On May 27 the students rejected the order, imprisoned their commandant, and prepared to resist. A tremor went through the government, while military and naval units in and around Rio stood ready. Colonel Hermes da Fonseca, nephew of Deodoro, commander of the Second Artillery Regiment and ex-chief of Manuel Vitoriano's military staff, who was widely respected for his professional attitudes, helped convince the students that it was foolish to resist the superior forces arrayed against them. Fourteen insubordinate officers and 321 with soldier ratings *(praça de pret)* were dismissed, as were 356 at the military school of Ceará in Fortaleza, who had declared solidarity with their colleagues in Rio.[103] It is not certain whether unrest at about the same time at the sergeants school was related to that in the military school, but "acts of indiscipline" there resulted in dismissal of 117 of the 245 enrolled. The school was closed later that year, supposedly because it did not meet the government's expectations and could not justify its "financial sacrifices."[104] The incidents helped to strengthen the president because they undermined the power in the Congress of Deputy Francisco Glicério, who had defended the military school rebels in 1895 and whose links with Florianistas made Prudente distrust him.

They also provided "volunteers" for the units assigned to the force Arthur Oscar was preparing in Bahia. *Folha da Tarde* (Rio) protested against punishing the disorderly students in this fashion with a triplet addressed to General Bittencourt: "Either the children learn or they go to die in Canudos."[105] The Constitution of 1891 (Art. 87) prohibited forced recruitment, but, since it provided no other way to fill the ranks, police dragnets still swept the streets and plazas of their "vagrant and ruffian riffraff" and tossed them into the army. Thanks to police sabers, such recruits were transformed into "volunteers." According to a well-informed officer of the era, every Brazilian soldier, regardless of how he entered the army, was "always considered a volunteer."[106] Although a number of the civilian Patriotic Battalions from the civil war had again offered their services, some even taking up residence in barracks, the president did not trust them, and the army did not want to appear dependent, so they had been mustered out late in March.[107] The army preferred to avenge Moreira César itself and to resort to impressment to fill gaps in the ranks.

The army personnel structure at the time was peculiar. During the civil war nearly two thousand soldiers had been promoted to *alferes,* the lowest rung on the commissioned officer's ladder, and as a result units were topheavy with junior officers. The army's table of organization called for 1,959 officers in staff and unit positions, but the actual total in December 1897 was 3,082, and although the same table called for 28,160 soldiers there were only 20,035. That meant that there was one officer for every 6.5 enlisted men. Moreover, because funding did not allow for the officer surplus, troop strength appears to have been kept 8,125 below the authorized level in order to pay the officers. Table 1.3 illustrates the surplus of officers and the deficiency of common soldiers in the units sent to Canudos, which was similar to the situation throughout the army.[108]

Most units had too many officers and too few soldiers and had to turn to local police, judges, and jails to meet their needs. Indeed, as Peter M. Beattie has shown, this was an old practice that provided the army with troops and saved state and federal authorities from the need to build more civilian prisons. The army acted as a "quasi-penal system."[109] The public resented and

TABLE 1.3.

Strength of Units Sent to Canudos

Unit	Location	Authorized[a]		Actual[a]		Surplus[a]		Deficiency[a]	
		Off	EM	Off	EM	Off	EM	Off	EM
9 Cav	Rio	25	405	50	354	25			51
5 Arty	Rio	25	402	24	287			1	115
4 Inf	RGS	21	425	31	195	10			230
5 Inf	Mar.	21	425	30	221	9			204
7 Inf	Rio	21	425	31	488	10	63		
9 Inf	Bahia	21	425	52	335	31			90
12 Inf	Rio	21	425	33	270	12			155
14 Inf	Pernambuco	21	425	53	478	32	53		
15 Inf	Pará	21	425	32	246	11			179
16 Inf	Bahia	21	425	47	260	26			165
22 Inf	Rio	21	425	43	358	22			167
25 Inf	RGS	21	425	37	309	16			116
26 Inf	Sergipe	21	425	38	412	17			13
27 Inf	Paraíba	21	425	67	489	46	64		
28 Inf	Minas G.	21	425	38	238	17			187
29 Inf	RGS	21	425	43	325	22			100
30 Inf	RGS	21	425	35	330	14			95
31 Inf	RGS	21	425	22	309	1			116
32 Inf	RGS	21	425	39	240	18			185
33 Inf	Alagoas	21	425	30	501	9			76
34 Inf	RGN	21	425	40	322	19			103
35 Inf	Piauí	21	425	48	353	27			72
37 Inf	SC	21	425	28	242	7			183
38 Inf	Rio	21	425	49	371	28			54
39 Inf	Paraná	21	425	43	311	22			114
40 Inf	Pernambuco	21	425	33	282	12		143	
TOTALS		554	10,200	1,016	8,526	463	256	1	2,737
Whole Army		1,959	28,160	3,082	20,035	1,128			8,125

[a]Off = Officers; EM = enlisted men.

feared the forced recruitment, and the press satirized it bitterly, often in verse. Four lines in *Folha da Tarde* (Rio) expressed the mood:

I walk about distrustful,
Eyes down, lips silent,
In fear of being taken
To the slaughterhouse of Canudos![110]

A Bahia (Salvador) published a short dramatic piece in which a common citizen *(popular)* made the mistake of talking with a sailor and ended up impressed, while a chorus of "volunteers" sang in the background:

We are the quarrelsome
The dregs, the small change:
Which to the grandees aren't but trash
To send to Canudos!
We will return from the tempest
Twisted, one-eyed, scrawny
If we aren't beaten
Yet again in Canudos![111]

A new slang word became immediately popular when *O País* (Rio) combined terms for the decade's two enemies into one. The southern Federalist rebels had been called *maragatos* (after a Spanish province), and the people of Canudos were referred to as *jagunços* (gunslingers); thus, *maragunço* was born. As forced recruitment spread, some wag took *maragunço* and joined it to the nickname for Prudente de Morais (*biribas*: native of São Paulo, but also used for a hick and someone with whom you had to be very careful) to create *maragabirigunço*, which was applied to any representative of the regime, then bent on crushing all opposition. The *maragabirigunço* became the bogeyman "who devoured indifferently *maragatos, biribos, jagunços,* and the unprotected of every type, via forced recruitment."[112]

Units from throughout Brazil converged on the assembly points in April and May. General Arthur Oscar, who set up his headquarters in Queimadas, divided his forces into columns of three brigades each, the first under Brigadier General João da Silva Barbosa, which was to advance by way of Monte Santo, while the second under Brigadier General Cláudio do Amaral Savaget was to group in Sergipe and move on Canudos from the east by way of Geremoabo. In Brazilian army parlance of the era, brigades were composed of battalions of infantry, supported by regiments of artillery and cavalry. Here most designating numbers have been relegated to the notes to smooth out the narrative. From Rio the Fifth Field Artillery regiment took ship for Bahia, as did infantry battalions from Pernambuco, Maranhão, Paraíba, and Rio Grande do Sul. At Queimadas they joined two battalions from Bahia and Moreira César's Seventh Infantry, which had been reorganized and augmented. Meanwhile, an infantry battalion and an artillery battery from Rio and two battalions from Rio Grande do Sul sailed for Sergipe, where they met the local battalion, plus battalions from Alagoas, Rio Grande do Norte, and Piauí.[113] With ten of the battalions coming from the northeast the affair took on the coloration of a civil war: northeasterners in soldier-blue against northeasterners in vaqueiro leather.[114]

Preparations were difficult. The army had no centralized supply systems for foodstuffs or transportation; both were obtained from local contractors. Without a quartermaster corps the quality of logistical support depended on the commander's talent and energy and the local market. The area around the Queimadas, where Arthur Oscar had his headquarters, was already short on supplies, but at least he was linked to Salvador by railroad. General Savaget, perhaps because he would not have a supply line during his march inland, gave more attention to provisions, forage, and transport than did Generals Arthur Oscar and Barbosa. Savaget commented that he faced three serious difficulties: Aracaju's "modest" facilities; distrustful sertanejos, who stayed away from the city market so that the army could not get their mules and oxen; and the local businessmen, whose "major interest was in delaying the force as long as possible."[115] He contracted with a local National Guard colonel to furnish all foodstuffs and transport. Sacks of rice, beans, farinha, salt, cases of cachaça, and herds of cattle made up the list.

Between May 22 and June 7 the various units of the Savaget column marched in echelon from Aracaju to Geremoabo (116 miles), where the 2,480 men in eight infantry battalions, one battery of Krupp 7.5's, and an engineer detachment awaited Arthur Oscar's orders to advance. The encampments and the march provided the only training the large number of green "volunteers" received before entering combat. During daily marches of twelve to fourteen miles the troops suffered, struggling over the poor roads in their bare feet. At least since the Paraguayan War, and probably before, it had been the custom for the infantry to march barefoot. For the hardy sertanejos, who often went without footwear, this represented no novelty, but for the stray city boys it was a painful introduction to campaigning. There were many cases of temporarily maimed soldiers.[116]

Although the official reports are silent about it, the various memoirs make clear that the column's impedimenta included three hundred women and eighty children. Francisco de Paula Cidade, one of the most knowledgeable students of army history, observed that "it had always been that way"; when the troops marched to war, so did their families. It had been so during the Paraguayan War, as well as in the civil war of 1893 to 1895; it would occur during the fighting over the Acre (1903), and women would accompany the tenente columns in the 1920s.[117]

Arthur Oscar's orders instructed Savaget to be in position for a pincer attack on Canudos on June 27, apparently with the idea of being able to announce victory on June 28, the anniversary of Floriano's death. Having moved rapidly to the forward assembly point, Savaget now had time to spare. Although it would have been best to use the pause for training, malaria struck a "great number" of his troops, which made him afraid to remain in one spot; so he decided to move forward in short marches. As they did so their surroundings became increasingly arid, with long stretches of the Vasa-Barris River, whose course they followed, being bone dry, and the widely spaced muddy pools of water were inadequate for such a large number of people and animals.[118]

On June 25, some five miles from Canudos, at the Fazenda Cocorobó, the sertanejos held rocky heights that dominated the road. A battle was soon joined. On the left was the Vasa-Barris, bordered by thick-growth *caatinga*, from where the Fifth Brigade, made up entirely of northeastern units, provided a covering fire for the rest of the column as it arrived on the scene. To the right, below the heights, was a plain where the approaching units took up positions 874 yards from the well-placed sertanejos, whom General Savaget described as "daring and tenacious."[119] Unable to dislodge them after more than two hours of rifle and artillery fire, Savaget ordered a bayonet charge. In his report he described the troops as "electrified," "crazy with enthusiasm," rushing forward to the "strident blare of the bugles" into a "veritable downpour of iron."[120]

Some women joined the attacking soldiers. An eyewitness, Manuel Benicio, who covered the campaign for Rio de Janeiro's *Jornal de Comércio*, reported that a young, attractive girl named Maria Rita, who had accompanied the advance, on seeing a soldier fall, bound his wound, then picked up his carbine and ran forward.[121] That such an action may not have been uncommon is suggested in another journalist's conversation with a woman in the Barbosa column who, when asked why she was following her man to Canudos, replied: "Why not follow him? I was his wife [companheira] in peace; I should also accompany him even in death."[122] And many women did just that!

Although the bayonet charge successfully drove off the sertanejos and opened the trail, it was not without cost. One officer and 26 soldiers lay dead, and 10 officers, including General Savaget, and 141 soldiers were wounded.[123] There had been no provision made to return the wounded to Sergipe, so the rear guard transported them in hammocks to an uncertain fate in Canudos. Their eventual evacuation route lay on the far side of Canudos via Monte Santo and Queimadas.

The sertanejos deliberately sought to disable officers as a way of disorienting their opponents. Poorly trained, ill-motivated "volunteers" would not likely make a determined fight without their officers. That the sertanejos

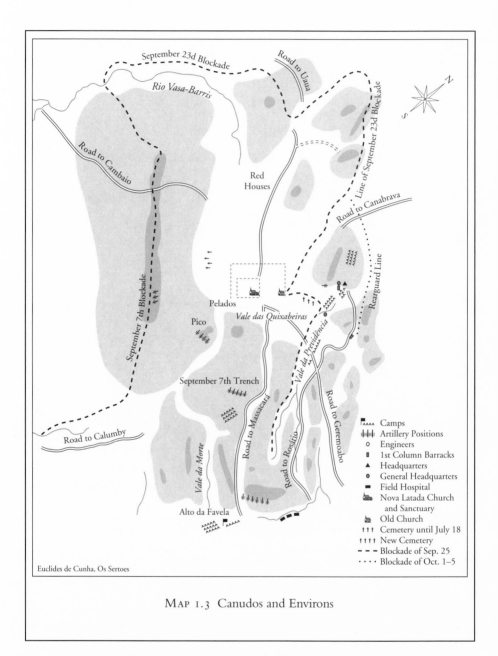

Map legend:

- ▰▴ᴀᴀᴀ Camps
- ᛁᛁᛁᛁ Artillery Positions
- o Engineers
- ▯ 1st Column Barracks
- ▲ Headquarters
- ◉ General Headquarters
- ▬ Field Hospital
- 🏛 Nova Latada Church and Sanctuary
- 🏛 Old Church
- ✝✝✝ Cemetery until July 18
- ✝✝✝✝ New Cemetery
- – – – Blockade of Sep. 25
- · · · · Blockade of Oct. 1–5

Labels on map:

September 23d Blockade

Road to Uaua

Rio Vasa-Barris

Road to Cambaio

Red Houses

Line of September 23d Blockade

Road to Canabrava

Rearguard Line

September 7th Blockade

Pelados

Pico

Vale das Quixabeiras

Vale da Providência

September 7th Trench

Road to Calumby

Road to Massacará

Road to Rosario

Road to Geremoabo

Vale da Morte

Alto da Favela

Euclides de Cunha, Os Sertoes

MAP 1.3 Canudos and Environs

SOURCE: From *The Army in Brazilian History*, edited by Luiz Paulo Macedo Cavalho. Rio de Janeiro & Salvador, Ba.: Biblioteca do Exército & Odebrecht, 1998. 4 vols. Redrawn by Bill Nelson. Used with permission of Biblioteca do Exército, Rio de Janeiro.

understood the army's social structure and lack of cohesiveness was suggested when some soldiers encountered an isolated sniper firing at the officers around the wounded General Savaget. On seeing the soldiers approach, he said calmly, "Don't kill me, comrades, I am one of you. I only shoot at officers."[124] Whether they agreed with his logic is not recorded, but continued officer casualties indicate that the idea was pervasive among the sertanejos. From the first engagement on June 25 until their arrival overlooking Canudos on June 27, continuous engagements cost six officers and thirty-four soldiers killed, and eight officers and one hundred soldiers wounded.[125]

Manuel Benício described the three days of fighting as "the most dangerous and terrible that the Brazilian army had yet had in its campaigns." It was so intense that the troops could only eat at night, and many of the wounded were left to die where they fell because their comrades could not reach them. It was a much worse experience than the bombardment of Niterói during the fleet revolt. The effect of bullets whizzing through the foliage, seemingly from all sides, and being attacked from directions they had thought cleared, was terrifying. Sertanejo resistance was especially fierce because Savaget was unwittingly advancing over the principal supply route into Canudos. For this reason his column was feared more than that under the command of General Barbosa.[126]

Late on the twenty-seventh, with Canudos in his sights, Savaget ordered the artillery to begin bombardment. And while he prepared for an all-out attack in the morning, he and his men could hear firing from the other side of the town where Barbosa's column was heatedly engaged. Brigadier General João da Silva Barbosa, with expedition commander Brigadier General Arthur Oscar accompanying, had moved from Queimadas via Monte Santo toward Canudos. Whereas the Savaget column had suffered skirmishes and firefights since the twenty-fifth, Barbosa's troops went unopposed until the twenty-seventh, when they advanced on Mount Favela overlooking the town. There they were hit with such a violent and heavy crossfire that the general was moved to report that he had not seen its equal in the five years of the Paraguayan War. They eventually were able to take the high ground but only after a startling expenditure of lives and ammunition. Here, too, the sertanejos aimed at the officers. The Seventh Infantry Battalion lost its commander, Col. Thomaz Thompson Flores, who was shot off his horse; the major who succeeded him was immediately wounded, as was a second major who assumed command briefly before passing it to a captain. The toll was severe. In its first half-hour Moreira César's fated old battalion lost 9 officers and 114 men. The experience of other units was similar.[127]

On the morning of June 28 the sertanejos were caught between the two columns, and even though they were inflicting heavy casualties, their own unrecorded losses were high. Given the army's superior armament, its victory should not have been far off. But Generals Arthur Oscar and Barbosa had not anticipated the tremendous rate at which their untrained troops would expend their ammunition and had left cases of it behind at the base camps and had allowed the units to engage the enemy without first bringing up the supply train. As a result the sertanejos were able to keep it isolated and penned down while the entire Barbosa column, with steadily dwindling ammunition, fought to survive. The sertanejo onslaught on the main force was fierce. The combat began at 5 a.m. and by 7 a.m. the twenty-one cannon, extended in a line high on the hill, had lost nearly all their gun crews and fell silent. One was brought bravely back into action by a wounded gunnery sergeant and a makeshift gun crew. Colonel Olímpio da Silveira, with his Girard revolver in hand, went along the line telling his men to stand firm and to shoot any comrade, including himself, who turned to run.[128] Relief detachments sent to retrieve the supply train were beaten back. Once again disaster threatened. The only recourse was to call on Savaget for assistance.

Savaget's report does not say that Arthur Oscar ordered him to give up his hard-won position completely but that the messengers requested aid because the Barbosa column's "munitions were exhausted and its position desperate." He apparently decided that he could not both hold his position and send aid, so under fire he marched around Canudos with his entire column to join up with his trapped colleagues.[129] When his units filed into the Barbosa/Oscar lines, they saw complete disorder and confusion. Hundreds of saddled horses and harnessed mules stood or lay next to vague-eyed men who seemed shocked and dejected, some hugging the earth while others appeared oblivious to the bullets buzzing by. Equipment was scattered here and there, the dead were unburied, the wounded huddled together, and all were covered with a fine dust and suffered from thirst in the shimmering heat.[130] Now, although the Savaget column shared its food supplies and ammunition, the entire expedition was trapped. The next weeks were hellish.

What started as an elaborate pincer attack had ended with the attackers surrounded and cut off. General Arthur Oscar's cavalier underestimation of the capabilities of his opponents had led his force into a double siege, a "siege of hunger, siege of *jagunços*." By July 5, as Manuel Benício scribbled in his notes, "our position is horrible. We don't attack and the longer we wait the worse it becomes."[131] Arthur Oscar had advanced without securing his supply of munitions, food, or water and for twelve crucial hours had doggedly held his position, expending ammunition—*more than a million rounds*—and suffering frightful casualties instead of sensibly falling back to the supply train. Why? Euclydes da Cunha thought the general was "displaying his one most striking quality as a military leader, namely his tendency to establish himself firmly in any position he had won."[132] Or had he plunged forward and then held on in fear that General Savaget would take Canudos alone and get all the glory?[133]

Whatever the reason, instead of attacking once the juncture was made, he waited. Although the supply train eventually got through, half its contents were gone; some four hundred thousand to five hundred thousand cartridges were in sertanejo hands. The next days saw the sertanejos attack time and again with frightful effects on the soldiers' morale. There had been nearly a thousand casualties since the initial encounters, and the five thousand troops began to feel more like a hodgepodge of survivors than part of organized military units. Discipline declined with the steadily dwindling food. Escort units went out in search of a nonexistent supply column that the deputy quartermaster at the Monte Santo base camp had promised but never sent. One search unit, under Colonels Joaquim Manoel de Medeiros and Antonio Tupy Ferreira Caldas, finding nothing in Monte Santo went on rounding up cattle and foodstuffs that would arrive back at Mount Favela in time to prevent wholesale starvation. That two full colonels led that operation says a lot about the weakness of the army's command structure.

But in the meantime the army suffered. It was impossible to wash because the Vasa-Barris was beyond the lines. The troops' uniforms, issued in March and April, were in filthy tatters. The last of the rations from the Savaget column ran out on July 5. Soldiers' wives set up a lively commerce in food: an ear of dried corn going for 5$000, a cup of *farinha* for 12$000, a bit of tobacco for 8$000, and sugar for any price asked. Foraging parties searched the countryside for wild cattle and goats and raided the sertanejos' gardens. Many were led into traps and died because of their hunger. The successful would gorge themselves and carry the rest back to sell or to dry for the future. Even selling could be dangerous. One couple prepared their tapioca cakes only to have the husband killed by a stray bullet when he began to sell them. Strangely, none of the accounts tell what happened to the widowed women or orphaned children. Did they move on to other men as John Reed observed with Pancho Villa's forces in the Mexican Revolution?[134] Were they still entitled to rations?

The officers suffered with their troops. Battalion commanders were reduced to asking humbly for a handful of *farinha*. They, too, paid the vendors' prices and passed occasional cigarettes from hand to hand. Manuel Benício noted that "when hunger enters the officers' tent, it must already be sleeping in those of the soldiers."[135] General Arthur Oscar appeared oblivious to all this. When some commanders pointed out the condition of the troops, he replied that he was unaware that there was hunger in the camp. With such a superior, no wonder General Savaget, nursing his wound, sunk into depression and held to his tent.[136]

As the privations increased, so did the number of deserters. On July 9 twenty privates of the Thirty-third from Alagoas left the lines. Others from various units followed their example, but total figures are lacking. Da Cunha assumed that deserters preferred "a merciful bullet at the hands of the *jagunço* to this slow and agonizing death."[137] But since the unit he mentioned was from the northeast, it is possible that a number of the deserters were ser-tanejos who knew how to survive in the sertão and were troubled about the campaign or had been "volunteered" in the first place. Some may have joined the Conselheiro's forces, as Lieutenant Macedo Soares suggested. He said that members of military police units that had rebelled in Sergipe and Alagoas, and other deserters from military units elsewhere, had fled to Canudos and had trained the sertanejos in the use of the captured rifles, "whose use re-quired certain practice." He noted that Pajeú, a key leader, was a "bold and cunning, long-time deserter."[138] Certainly, believers among the soldiers must have been unnerved by the daily Angeles bells, the voices singing the *Ave Maria* and reciting the Rosary.

The army's position on Favela was unhealthy in every sense. Body lice did not respect rank or sex. Animals were slaughtered in the center, the inedible parts being strewn about causing a stench and attracting clouds of flies. One woman was shot while grinding corn, another while she crossed the camp, and a third while lying in a tent. An *alferes*, sharing a tent with reporter Manuel Benício, was hit in the head while he slept. Daily, between six and eight per-sons died of wounds even when there was no combat. And there were peri-ods when the bodies went unburied for days.[139]

On July 13 Colonels Medeiros and Caldos finally returned with supplies. They entered a cheering camp, and the next day, Bastille Day, a national holi-day in republican Brazil, the officers gathered to plan the first major assault that would seek to break the encirclement, to lay siege instead of being besieged. On the fifteenth the sertanejos drove a large herd of cattle into Canudos, and the following day their forces attacked the army positions. Clearly they were determined to continue the struggle. The officers prepared their assault for the eighteenth.

It was to be a mass attack of 3,349 men arrayed in five brigades, com-plete with a cavalry wing and an artillery detachment of two Krupp 7.5s. General Barbosa estimated that they faced four thousand dug-in sertanejos. It was already light when the artillery began its preparatory bombardment while the troops marched to the southeast and then swung around to come at Canudos from the northeast, on its open side. But formations were im-possible to hold in the rolling, gully-rutted terrain. The units mixed and changed their alignment as they struggled forward against the land and its determined defenders. In a matter of minutes hundreds of soldiers were cut down; ammunition burros tumbled over on their backs, pinning their cargoes beneath them; and officers' horses were shot out from under them. Repeatedly the bugles sounded "charge" and "no quarter" *(degola)* while the artillery finally silenced the effective flanking fire from the towers of the new church. The losses mounted as the troops reached the first shacks and plunged into them helter-skelter. Whatever bravery their morning ration of *cachaça* had provided was by now superseded by the will to survive. Not a few famished attackers were distracted into pursuing chickens and eating and drinking whatever they encountered in the vacated dwellings. Fearing that his forces would be swallowed up in the maze, General Barbosa ordered a halt after they had advanced to within almost one hundred yards of the old church. There the lines firmed. Although it was far from clear for weeks, it was the beginning of the end for Antonio Conselheiro's holy city.[140]

Although the battle marked the breakout of the beleaguered army units and a turning point in the campaign, it also permanently damaged the reputation of General Arthur Oscar. The advance had cost 1,014 casualties, or nearly every third man of the attacking forces. The wounded lay parching in the sun for hours before the few men assigned to their recovery began their work. Many died of thirst or bled to death from fly-covered wounds. The nine hundred shacks taken and the somewhat more than a hundred sertanejo cadavers were not sufficient to label the day a victory. The army would not be able to mount another such effort without reinforcements. On July 19 General Arthur Oscar sent a message to the war ministry asking for five thousand more men and settled down to wait.

Now it was the sertanejos who were the besieged, but the soldiers could not move about safely during daylight because their lines were open to clear fields of fire from the opposing trenches and the church tower. In the advanced posts food could not be prepared so precooked meat had to be distributed at night. Likewise, water could be obtained and the wounded removed only under cover of darkness. If the army's position had improved, it was more a morale improvement than a physical one. After July 18 the two lines carried on a constant fire, broken by short, spontaneous truces at night during which both camps gathered their wounded and buried their dead. Each dawn the church bell tolled six times, while army sentinels fired on the tower without apparently weakening the sexton's determination. At night the troops could hear the barking of dogs, the crying of children, and the scolding of parents. Frequently between 9:00 and 10:00 P.M. voices praying the Rosary would rise from the church. While exchanging fire, the two lines would trade insults, curses, and threats all night long, week after week.[141]

On July 24 the sertanejos made two fierce attacks attempting to breach the weakest point in the army's line, at the same time sweeping around the extreme right. They were beaten back, leaving some fifty dead, including their "renowned and daring chieftain, Pajeú." It was, Lieutenant Macedo

Soares recalled, the last time that the sertanejos staged a serious offensive. Henceforth they "maintained a desperate defense until the day on which the last one died fighting."[142] Some slipped out of the settlement in the dark and many women surrendered. Antonio Conselheiro reportedly sent out emissaries to try to mobilize new sertanejos favorable to Canudos to attack the expedition from the flanks and rear. But what became of them is unknown.[143] The army waited and ran low on food once again.

An unknown soldier's diary expressed the desperation, frustration, and degeneration that afflicted the troops:

August 5 "I feel very hungry."

August 6 "I woke up so weak that I don't have courage for anything. . . . "

August 7 "More wounded left for Monte Santo. Barros and Armeiros are now considered deserters. . . . Squadron Corporal Antônio Francisco died."

August 8 " . . . Geraldo, Nicolau, Floriano and Bento, scoundrels all, have gone too far, they robbed. Geraldo refused me a spoon of sugar!!"

August 9 "Bombardment and hunger continue. Only received a cup of chow, full of *farinha* (manioc flour) and salt: nothing more. The convoy is expected."

August 11 (Dreamed of food.) "I awoke missing the family and delirious with hunger! What horror!"

August 12 "The ration was the same or worse. The convoy left for Monte Santo with some sick."

August 13 "The bombardment continues. Nicolau kept the larger portion of the *farinha* and meat rations. He stole it. . . . "

August 15 "It is impossible to describe the impatience that we feel. . . . "

August 17 "The lack of *farinha* continues, in spite of the many shipments that arrived. It's shameful. It's infamy!"

Shortly thereafter, this soldier was sent to Monte Santo with a convoy. Reporter Manuel Benício found the notebook with the above entries in the infirmary at Queimadas.[144]

Although the sertanejos were still capable in mid-August of staging night attacks, during the daylight hours they were rarely seen, many days firing only ten to twenty rounds. One journalist observed that the soldiers were so weakened that "presently we fear hunger more than the *jagunços.*"[145] Throughout August and into September the weather was dry, with clear, hot days and cool, pleasant nights. Ritualistically, every morning at daybreak, one of the cannons would fire a wakening round into the *Conselheirista* fortifications, which would be responded to with rifle and shotgun blasts. At dusk, the Angelus bell would slowly toll six times, while a carefully aimed cannon would fire a grenade at the tower as the last vibration faded away.[146]

The situation of the wounded was horrible. The army doctors did what they could, but the ambulances were not equipped or stocked for the volume of wounded. When the first group of six hundred was evacuated,[147] there were still more than a thousand in the crude field hospital. The antiseptic ran out, and doctors were reduced to using *cachaça* to wash wounds. Surgical instruments were kept busy amputating limbs to stop the spread of gangrene, but there was little they could do to check internal hemorrhaging, fevers, and hunger. Some wounded went crazy, broken by the suffering. Until September evacuation likely meant death on the trail. Nothing had been prepared in Monte Santo and until the arrival of Dr. Carlos Autran de Mata e Albuquerque, the infirmary at Queimadas was an unsanitary pesthole. Indeed, the army medical corps was overwhelmed, and hundreds more would have died if citizens' committees in Salvador and medical students from the school there had not offered their services.[148] If such was the case on the army side, the imagination recoils at the horrors the wounded in Canudos must have suffered before death released them.

The war correspondents had difficulty reporting the disorganization and suffering because General Arthur Oscar imposed censorship on their dispatches to prevent "inconvenient and alarming" news. Some hired their own couriers after the appropriate "visa" had been given and their dispatches put on the wire, but these still failed to reach their destinations. On July 13 General Arthur Oscar called Manuel Benício, who was an honorary captain and had been praised in official reports for his bravery in action with the Savaget column, to his tent to tell him that one of his cables had produced "a bad effect down in Rio." Benício asked the general's tolerance, saying that "if I don't report what I see to the newspaper that I represent, what should I do here? I am fulfilling my mission, nothing more. I don't invent or exaggerate." Shortly thereafter, he was "invited" to leave the combat zone.[149]

Arthur Oscar telegraphed to Minister Bittencourt that Benício's stories in the *Jornal do Comércio* were not to be believed, that the reporter was "indiscreet," "perfidious," and "invented and adulterated facts." Interestingly, he based these accusations on a telegram that the office at Monte Santo had sent to the general asking if it could be sent.[150] Arthur Oscar must have been stung by Benício's commentary. In one paragraph the reporter compared Savaget's ability to travel from Aracajú with more than two thousand well-fed men and arrive with rations to spare on an allotment of 500$000 to Arthur Oscar's performance. The latter, with considerably less distance from the railhead to the objective and a war chest of 1,500$000, was out of food and ammunition almost immediately.[151]

Straightforward reporting would quickly reveal the horror that was Canudos, give the lie to the myth of its being a monarchist conspiracy, display the true abilities of the commanding general, and damage the affair's political utility. The censorship was also intended to cover up profiteering on the part of General Arthur Oscar and other officers. While troops went without in Canudos, the store rooms in Monte Santo were reportedly over-flowing.[152] Judging from the language employed in their reports, officers were trying to convince one another that these rough sertanejos were in-deed "enemies of the Republic," "partisans of the Bragança monarchy" de-fending a "monarchist citadel."[153]

The soldiers' frustration, anger, fear, and suffering were vented on help-less prisoners. For a man to surrender meant death. The journalists gener-ally were silent until the town was crushed, but the minister of war and the president knew and did nothing to prevent the disembowelments and throat cuttings that were the entertainment of the blood-crazed. Indeed Marshal Bittencourt reportedly advised Arthur Oscar that in the rear areas, there was no place to hold prisoners.[154] But the *degolado* was established practice long before Bittencourt came on the scene. Lieutenant Macedo Soares spoke of the "beastly slaughter" of nearly two thousand captives, including the wounded.[155] Whether prisoners felt cold steel at their throats because of custom (certainly wars in the south suggest as much), convenience (there was no food to feed them), or control (it provided the vengeful an outlet) is uncertain. But that such merciless savagery stained the army's honor in blood and made a mockery of the "holy cause" for which it fought there can be no doubt.

Some collective psychosis must have gripped the minds of all concerned for officers to imagine themselves on a crusade in the "cause of civilization" against the "monster called Canudos" and to imagine "our dear *Pátria*, cry-ing for its sons, martyrs of civilization, who fell on this barren earth, where at the cost of much blood today waves our glorious banner of Order and Progress."[156] In his memoir participant Lieutenant Macedo Soares first said that pity could not be shown because the salvation of each of the con-tenders depended on the rapid and complete "extermination of the other"; later, he commented that "if some unworthy excess, if some unjust reprisal was practiced, it should not be thrown up to those responsible for the com-batant forces, but to a certain few who were wild with hate."[157] Perhaps they all came to believe, as Euclydes da Cunha suggested, that Canudos was a hiatus, a vacuum, that "once having crossed that cordon of mountains, no one sinned any more."[158] Eventually the national consciousness understood the enormity of the wrongs done but the subsequent contrition came too late for the people of Canudos.

In July, when Colonels Medeiros and Tupi Caldas were scouring the rear areas for desperately needed supplies, they must have realized that Arthur Oscar's supply arrangement with a local contractor named Aníbal Galvão was geared more to personal profit than to getting food and munitions to the troops. Stepping outside the chain of command, they notified the minister of war about the situation. Minister Bittencourt ordered the Twenty-second,

Twenty-fourth, and Thirtieth Infantry Battalions of the federal district's garrison to proceed to Bahia under the command of General Miguel Maria Girard, director of the military school. He asked Girard to inform him of what was happening in Bahia because up to then he had received no useful news.[159]

Disembarking at Salvador on July 18–19, Girard's troops entrained for Queimadas. There they found that their predecessors had so terrorized the inhabitants that the town was nearly abandoned. Worse, the irregularities in the supply system were so scandalous and General Arthur Oscar's handling of the campaign so distasteful that Girard and two battalion commanders withdrew from their commands, pleading illness. A third battalion commander retired from the army on the spot. Because of their previous service records, there is no reason to suspect that fear motivated their actions. The brigade, made up largely of new "volunteers," suffered from the march and from sertanejo attacks before finally reaching the Canudos lines on August 15 under the command of a captain.

After the battle of July 18 Arthur Oscar had pleaded for reinforcements. Initially, Minister Bittencourt may have believed that the Girard brigade was sufficient, or for political reasons he may have hesitated to place more troops under Arthur Oscar, but the latter's July 26 telegram, citing casualties of 155 officers and 1,583 soldiers, convinced him that the frightful situation was not being exaggerated.[160] He ordered up infantry battalions from their posts in Minas Gerais, Paraná, Santa Catarina, and two from Rio Grande do Sul; he also asked São Paulo, Pará, and Amazonas to send police detachments and placed them under Brigadier General Carlos Eugênio de Andrade Guimarães, the brother of Arthur Oscar.[161] And to insure the smooth conclusion of the campaign, the minister himself set out for the war zone.[162] There he purchased mules by the score and, stationing himself in Monte Santo, saw to it that two or three supply convoys went to the lines around Canudos each day. Knowing that "a thousand domesticated burros in this emergency were worth ten thousand heroes," Bittencourt "transformed a huge, unplanned conflict into a regular campaign."[163]

The military police from São Paulo, Pará, and Amazonas, well armed, equipped, and uniformed, began to arrive at the end of August. By September 11 the siege lines reached around the town save for 875 yards on the Uauá road entrance, through which the last supply pack mules were seen passing to Canudos on September 21. How, who, and from where the sertanejo supply system functioned is unknown. The next day, unknown to the soldiers, Antonio Conselheiro died of natural causes before the altar of the church. On the twenty-fourth the soldiers closed the last gap in the siege line, trapping, Lieutenant Macedo Soares estimated, eight thousand in the ruins of the town.[164] The captured houses were set ablaze, and the smell of burning flesh filled the air for days. Although the fifteen cannons in the expedition's batteries pounded away at point-blank range, the sertanejos seemed determined to fight to the end.[165]

Brigadier General Carlos Eugênio's brigade arrived September 27, eager to join in the kill. The newcomers' enthusiasm for battle seems to have contributed to the decision to launch another all-out assault. Although veteran officers were inclined to continue the siege until a surrender that could not be long off, recently arrived Colonel João César Sampaio argued (incorrectly) that there could not be more than a hundred armed men left, that a projected daily average of twenty casualties for thirty more days would be higher than those produced in one last attack, that the hundreds of unburied bodies could produce an epidemic, that the constant firefights could cause another shortage of ammunition, that the onset of the rainy season in late October and early November would weaken the line along the Vasa-Barris and interfere with supplies when the roads became muddy, and that the seizure of the sertanejos' last water holes would more likely force a surrender. Finally, it was not entirely impossible that the sertanejos would receive powerful reinforcements from the sertão if the army delayed attacking.[166]

At daybreak on October 1 the artillery bombarded the sertanejo-held area, some thirty-three yards distant, with three hundred rounds in twenty minutes, for an average of fifteen shells per minute. This was probably the most intense bombardment ever directed at Brazilian combatants! Then nine battalions, including the newcomers, rushed forward to take the defenders by storm. Suddenly, "a cloud of *jagunços*" seemingly "rose from the ground" to offer an "invincible resistance." There were over a thousand and not the mere hundred estimated.[167] In the afternoon, at General Barbosa's insistence, another attempt was made. The Thirty-fourth, of Rio Grande do Norte, had two companies decimated in minutes; the Fifth, of Maranhão, lost nearly all of its officers as mounds of bodies began to block the narrow alleys. Surrealistically, two sertanejos "danced and sang" while demolishing a part of the Fifth Battalion before being killed.[168] The results included an estimated four hundred sertanejo fighters, and probably more noncombatants, dead, another one hundred men and an uncertain number of women and children, all terribly wounded, taken prisoner. And 587 officers and men were dead or wounded. At twenty casualties a day for thirty days, the army would have lost 600. Macedo Soares wrote that there were still two thousand men, women, and children in the ruined town.[169] If his earlier estimate of eight thousand when the siege was closed on the twenty-fourth, was correct, then excluding a couple of hundred taken prisoner, at least fifty-five hundred either died or slipped through the lines.

On October 2 a parley, strangely the first between the combatants, led to the surrender of several hundred sertanejos, mostly women and children.

The following day, upwards of five hundred, including sixty men, crossed into the army lines. Two days later, with resistance continuing, General Arthur Oscar ordered that dynamite bombs and kerosene be used. Reporter Favila Nunes commented that "further delay was impossible and the sentiments of humanity must be banished." Flaming balls of kerosene-soaked cloth and dynamite were tossed into the sertanejo-held areas. The fire spared nothing. "The nauseous stench of burning human flesh was unbearable for . . . us, at 20 meters [22 yards] distance." Finally an *alferes* ran to verify the results. "It's all over! There isn't one *jagunço* left!" he yelled back. General Arthur Oscar ordered the units to form up, the green, gold, and blue flag was raised while the bands played the national anthem, and the generals reviewed the troops to "enthusiastic and delirious" *vivas*. "Canudos was a vast pyre, the streets carpeted with thousands of cadavers!" General Arthur Oscar, amidst *abraços* and congratulations, ordered a search for the body of the sertanejo saint.[170]

The next day, leaving behind a number of soldiers to burn the remaining structures and to dispose of the dead, the conquerors' columns began the journey to the coast. The surviving children were prized war souvenirs, especially, it seems, little girls. General Arthur Oscar took one with him, and General Barbosa took two. Other officers, journalists, army contractors, and less well-meaning individuals scrambled to take one or more of the "poor things" home. One artillery officer coming on two abandoned, sick, and skinny, four-year-old black girls hoisted them up on his saddle, pledging to care for them. However, some went so far as to yank children from the arms of their mothers, and many, like twelve-year-old Maria Domingas de Jesus, were raped. The Patriotic Committee of Bahia, which had formed to care for the wounded during the fighting, sought to protect the unclaimed children, to reunite mothers and children, and to gain custody of those who ended up in taverns and houses of prostitution. For some the nightmare they had survived was only a prelude to further tragedy. There was at least one happy ending—an eighteen-year-old girl whose parents had died in the fighting fell in love with, and accepted the marriage proposal of, a captain in the Fifth Bahian police.[171]

The army was victorious but in tatters. Of its 20,035 soldiers and 3,082 officers, about 8,526 soldiers (42 percent) and 1,016 officers (32 percent) had seen service in the campaign. Of these, 4,193 were wounded between July and October 1897. The actual number of soldier deaths is not clear. Lieutenant Macedo Soares wrote that five thousand died, but it may be that he used total casualty figures and some poetic license. Regardless of his accuracy, the losses sustained on both sides have not been matched since in Brazilian history.[172]

A Bloody Decade Ends

On November 5 President Prudente de Morais, Vice President Manuel Vitoriano, Minister Bittencourt, many generals, and members of the Congress
gathered at the army arsenal in Rio de Janeiro to welcome returning units
under General Barbosa. A soldier who had been wounded, Marcelino Bispo
dos Santos, leapt at the president with pistol in hand. Prudente knocked it
aside with his top hat and the chief of the president's military staff, Col. Luís
Mendes de Morais, knocked the assailant down with his sword. In the struggle to disarm him, the assailant pulled out a knife with which he mortally
wounded Marshal Bittencourt, who was yelling "Don't kill him," and he also
managed to cut Colonel Mendes severely. The assassin had been encouraged
by a group of conspirators who wished to remove Prudente and to establish a
radical, Jacobin regime. The editor of the republican newspaper *O Jacobino*
was the key instigator, and at the moment of the assault he was awaiting word
with officer conspirators at the First Cavalry barracks in Rio.[173]

The president's prestige soared as he attended unguarded the war minister's burial and was acclaimed in the streets for his bravery. The Congress
voted a state of siege in the federal district and in the area around Niterói.
The assassination attempt was the fruit of a high-level conspiracy. The vice
president was implicated and former government leader in the Congress
Francisco Glicério fled to São Paulo. The assassin told police, apparently under torture, that he was "fanatically devoted to the memory of Marshal Floriano Peixoto" and believed editor Deocleciano Martyr, who had provided
the weapons, when he told him that "the Canudos affair was created by the
government for the purpose of bringing back the monarch." Anger at having been wounded at Canudos may also have motivated him. The conspirators included a group of officers who had been involved in the May 1897
military school uprising and who had secretly plotted in the Military Club.[174]

Congressmen and officers were imprisoned, the Military Club was closed,
and politicians rallied around the president. The support and cohesion that
had been lacking in his administration was suddenly abundant. The attempt
on his life not only miscarried—it backfired. If there had lingered any possibility that Florianistas might use the victory over Canudos to seek to
weaken the president or overthrow him, the tainting of their cause with the
murder of Bittencourt and the attempt on Prudente de Morais undermined
their civilian and military support.

The assassination attempt strengthened Prudente and made possible the
holding of elections in March 1898 and the orderly transfer of the presidency to Campos Sales in November. In the army high command it consolidated the hold of anti-Florianista generals, such as João Nepomuceno de
Medeiros Mallet as adjutant general, the equivalent at the time of the later

chief of staff. They took advantage of the nation's near bankruptcy to eliminate some inconvenient officers supposedly for financial reasons. Brigadier General Arthur Oscar waited in vain at his Second Military Region headquarters in Recife for the republic to reward his efforts. He was passed over in the November 15, 1897, promotions to general of division, the coveted third star going to anti-Florianista Mallet instead. The freeze was permanent.[175] In the next administration Mallet would be minister of war and would begin the slow rebuilding of the Brazilian army.

The empire may have been overturned in a bloodless coup, but the bloodshed of the succeeding decade more than made up for it. If some hoped that Canudos would launch a military-dominated republic, the result was the opposite. The disaster strengthened the control of officers who wanted to reform and professionalize the officer corps and of civilian politicians who wanted to lessen military influence on the government. The army ended the decade in a state of near collapse. The next years would be devoted to rebuilding and to establishing the army's proper role in Brazilian society and politics.

CHAPTER 2

Reform and Construction

An army that cannot mobilize becomes inert and inspires
neither fear nor hope.
—João Nepomuceno de Medeiros Mallet, *Relatório*, 1902

[T]o be an officer and to care for the well-being of the
soldier, it is necessary to have experienced his way of life.
—Hermes da Fonseca, *Relatório*, 1907

After Canudos the army lay in ruins. The woeful reports of its leaders complained of problems and lamented the lack of money for even simple repairs.
Civilian society seemed unconcerned and content to let the army decay. But
the Acre crisis, fear of United States intervention, the *Panther* incident, and
the sense of weakness in the face of the militarism abroad in the world produced demands for reform.[1] The process was slow; indeed, some of those
who proposed changes grew old waiting for their fulfillment. Lack of continuity from one ministry to the next was characteristic of the army's history
during the Old Republic.

This dangerous feature resulted from frequent leadership changes, the
army's weak traditions, and its inadequate administrative procedures. But the
lack of continuity also reflected the nation's political economy. There was
no integrated national economy; instead, Brazil had a grouping of regional
economies that each exported its own key products to European and North
American markets. The lack of overland transportation systems hindered internal economic integration, political cohesion, and military efficiency. Each
region moved to its own rhythms.

The northeast's political influence declined as its sugar lost foreign markets
to Caribbean producers. The Amazonian rubber boom was at its zenith, but
it would collapse after 1912. The far south was an exception. The nationally
oriented economies of the southern states were less spectacular but steady gen-
erators of growth that would permit Rio Grande do Sul to increase steadily its

political leverage. The Maté tea exports of Paraná and Santa Catarina largely went to the Rio de La Plata and west-coast republics. The coffee-growing states of the center south produced most of Brazil's exports. São Paulo, Minas Gerais, Rio de Janeiro (including the Federal District), and Rio Grande do Sul harvested 60 percent of the nation's crops, turned out 75 percent of the industrial and meat products, and owned 80 percent of Brazil's banking assets. The period from 1898 to 1910 witnessed the peaking of the São Paulo coffee elite's control of the national government and the shift toward diffusion of political power among the above states, plus Bahia.

The civil war of 1893–95 and especially the Canudos disaster of 1897 eliminated the military's ability to play a moderating role that some believed it had inherited when it overthrew the monarchy. By the end of Rodrigues Alves's term (1898) the rural-based regional oligarchies had reestablished their dominance over the political system. The rural landowners were so powerful that they prevented the obligatory service law, which will be discussed in this chapter, from being applied to their peons. They shaped fiscal policies that supported their view of Brazil as an agricultural country whose major role was to supply Europe and North America with coffee, rubber, and sundry natural resources. At the turn-of-the-century, Brazil was producing more than 75 percent of the world's coffee, but it struggled to maintain market share as Central American and Colombian production increased; worse, as world supply had risen in the mid-1890s, prices had entered a continuous fall. To stay price competitive, the Brazilian government responded with frequent devaluations of the exchange rate of the *milreis* against the British pound sterling. But devaluation raised the cost of imported manufactured products, lowered their consumption, and, at the same time, decreased government revenues because import taxes were the federal government's major source of income. The government and the economy were further restricted by a heavy foreign debt, which resulted in most of the trade surplus being used to pay interest on foreign loans down to 1898. In that year the government arranged a thirteen-year suspension of debt payments (until 1911), with the understanding that it would balance the budget and reduce the amount of currency in circulation. In 1900 the national economic situation was so perilous that half of the banks failed. The oligarchy responded to the situation by restricting its vision of Brazil to maintaining its own status and to limiting development of national industry and infrastructure to what was needed to service the agricultural economy.[2]

The society that this economy shaped was one in which the elites saw the majority of the population as existing to provide cheap labor for agricultural enterprises. Elite interest in immigration was primarily to keep labor plentiful and inexpensive, although secondarily they wanted to "whiten" the population. And the elites continued to show little interest in public education.

The various military reform plans discussed below would be frustrated by the limited vision of the state-based oligarchies, which eventually, as will be seen in later chapters, transformed the more impatient officers from reformists into revolutionaries.

The Brazilian political system functioned on two levels, the apparent and the real. There was the Constitution of 1891, with its provisions for a president, legislature, balance of powers, and so forth, but the real system was based on the unwritten agreements that allowed state autonomy in return for support of the president's national policies. What appeared to be a constitutional, representative democracy was actually rule by oligarchic alliance. The system functioned because it was rooted in limited political participation. The military's role, as we saw at Canudos and will see again in the Contestado in Chapter 3, was to maintain order. But that role sat awkwardly with the ideals of professionalism that the officers imported from Europe, and the gap between role and ideals would eventually contribute to rebellion.

The twelve years between 1898 and 1910 saw four presidents and six ministers of war. In November 1898 Prudente de Morais passed the presidency to the president (as state chiefs were then called) of São Paulo, Manoel Ferraz de Campos Sales (1898–1902), who had served as justice minister under Deodoro before breaking with him in the crisis of 1891. Campos Sales established the "politics of the governors" system of state autonomy referred

TABLE 2.1.

Presidents, Ministers of War, and Chiefs of Staff, 1898–1910

Presidents	Ministers	Chiefs of Staff
Manoel Campos Salles Nov. 15, 1898–Nov. 15, 1902	João de Medeiros Mallet Nov. 15, 1898–Nov. 15, 1902	João Thomaz Cantuária Jan. 23, 1899–Dec. 9, 1902
Rodrigues Alves Nov. 15, 1902–Nov. 15, 1906	Francisco de P. Argollo Nov. 15, 1902–Nov. 15, 1906	B. da Fontoura Costallat Dec. 19, 1902–Dec. 8, 1904
Afonso A. Moreira Pena Nov. 15, 1906–June 14, 1909	Hermes R. da Fonseca Nov. 15, 1906–May 27, 1909	Francisco A. Rodrigues de Salles Jan. 24, 1905–Nov. 19, 1906
Nilo Peçanha June 14, 1909–Nov. 15, 1910	Luis Mendes de Morais May 27, 1909–June 18, 1909	João P. Xavier da Câmara Nov. 19, 1906–May 29, 1909
	Carlos Eugênio de Andrade Guimarães June 18, 1909–Oct. 16, 1909	Carlos Eugênio de Andrade Guimarães May 29, 1909–June 18, 1909
	José Bernardino Borman Oct. 16, 1909–Nov. 15, 1910	José Bernardino Borman July 9, 1909–Oct. 16, 1909
		Marciano A. Botelho de Guimarães Oct. 23, 1909–Nov. 16, 1910

NOTE: During the gaps in the dates in office the position was filled with an interim officer whose identity is unimportant for the purposes of this table.

to above, consolidated Brazil's foreign debts, and kept the army loyal despite minor revolts. Another paulista president, Francisco de Paula Rodrigues Alves (1902–6) succeeded him, dealt with the Acre Crisis and the 1904 military school rebellion, and encouraged modest military reforms. The 1906 succession brought the chief executive of Minas Gerais, Afonso Augusto Moreira Pena (1906–9), to the Catete Palace thanks to the insistence of Rio Grande do Sul king maker José Gomes Pinheiro Machado on breaking São Paulo's lock on the presidency. It seemed fitting that Minas, with the largest population, have its turn in power. Afonso Pena's death on June 14, 1909, brought Vice President Nilo Peçanha of Rio de Janeiro to power. Table 2.1 shows the names and dates of the ministers of war and the chiefs of staff who served under these presidents.

In the midst of a tight-money era the army leadership did what it could to reform the institution, to bring it abreast of international developments in warfare, to modernize it. This chapter stresses the ministries of Generals Mallet, Argollo, and Hermes, set against the backdrop of an examination of army life, officer education, and attempts to secure foreign training and advisers. We will first turn to the ministry of General João Nepomuceno de Medeiros Mallet, who in 1899 and 1900 proposed a series of changes that shaped the reform debate over the next decade.

The Mallet Ministry

Mallet, who assumed the minister of war's portfolio at age fifty-nine, was in many ways typical of the generation of officers who commanded the army as it entered the new century. Born into a military family in Rio Grande do Sul, he had joined the army at seventeen and by the end of 1863 was a first lieutenant. He earned his captaincy for bravery in the war with Paraguay, experienced the advancement slowdown of the 1870s and 1880s, and reached full colonel during the orgy of promotions in the weeks following the overthrow of the empire. One of the officers immediately placed in a political position, he was installed as governor of Ceará. His return to Fortaleza was ironic because it had been his removal as commandant of the military school there that had precipitated the crisis that ended with the overthrow of the monarchy. As I noted in the previous chapter, although he was a historic republican, his opposition to Floriano's assumption of power resulted in Mallet's expulsion from the army. Amnestied in 1895, he supervised the preparation of regulations for the new general staff and quartermaster service, and between 1896 and 1899 in rapid succession served as quarter-master general, adjutant general, and minister of war. He reached the top post, having avoided both the civil war and Canudos. To the extent that his reputation was not associated with those events, his ministry was a fresh start.

Mallet wanted to change the composition of army units, centralize their posting, reorganize military education, emphasize the importance of target practice, hold regular field maneuvers, regularize planning, improve promotion procedures, and raise the intellectual level of the officer corps. In addition the army's barracks and other installations needed remodeling and its units lacked up-to-date weaponry. He appointed his predecessor as minister of war, General João Thomaz Cantuaria, the chief of the newly created general staff and set him and his subchief, Brigadier General Luis Mendes de Morais, to work fleshing out his ideas. Unhappily, reasonable as the resulting plans were, the tight money policies of the Campo Sales administration (1898–1902), formulated in response to Brazil's heavy foreign indebtedness, made immediate implementation impossible. Still, "Project Mallet," as it was known, provided the intellectual basis for reform efforts down to World War I.

Armies use what are called "principles of war" as the basis of their operational doctrine; that doctrine in turn affects structure, size, armament, and training. In 1900 Mallet wrote that armament advances abroad were making warfare increasingly destructive and, consequently, had reduced the main principles of war to (1) shooting without exposure to the enemy's return fire and (2) applying maximum pressure with the smallest force possible to secure the objective.[3]

The recent experience at Canudos, he noted, had shown that with sure aim even groups lacking "the simplest notions of ballistics" and the "subtleties of tactics" could produce "formidable and fearful" fire. He further remarked that "the losses that our troops suffered on that occasion speak with irrefutable eloquence."[4] He stressed that marksmanship had been integral to the recent Boer victories over the British and to American successes in the war with Spain. The army had to provide more and better marksmanship training; it had to give closer attention to discipline and to instruction. That the minister of war had to argue such basic points, citing domestic and foreign evidence, says a great deal about the army of the turn of the century.

Mallet also criticized other aspects of army training. Arguing that theoretical instruction was insufficient, he accentuated the need for practical field experience that gave officers and soldiers opportunities to commit and to correct errors.[5] He understood that the army's traditions of command stifled initiative, which made it difficult for platoon leaders to apply rationally the orders they received from above. The army needed well-prepared lieutenants as much as it did talented generals. But improvement, he declared, would be impossible unless the army's widely dispersed units were concentrated to allow for low-cost training. Only by concentrating forces could Brazil's generals obtain the command experience they would need in wartime.

Certainly Mallet was correct in thinking that isolated units scattered across the map of Brazil contributed little to national defense and that grouping them would reduce the cost of training, health care, rations, and supplies. He believed that once concentrated, the whole army could be reorganized.

Mallet ordered the new general staff to draw up a reorganization plan, "adapting to our situation the precepts and improvements sanctioned by the experience of more advanced nations,"[6] but he cautioned that Brazil's "political and geographic situation, the lack of manpower for industrial and agricultural development, impeded modeling our army completely on those of the European powers."[7] Staff officers quickly showed their inexperience with planning and lack of agreement both among themselves and with Mallet's ideas. To resolve the impasse, he appointed a committee of two colonels, Chief of Staff Cantuaria, and a captain who would leave his own mark on the army, Augusto Tasso Fragoso, to meet with him to formulate a plan, within the budgetary restraints of the Campo Sales administration, for early submission to the Congress.[8] The underlying rationale of the charge that he gave to the committee was that, unable to afford a large army, Brazil should develop a small one that could be easily mobilized and deployed. A limited, efficient, rapidly expandable cadre army was the goal of this and nearly every later reform effort.

The situation exemplified some of the army's characteristics for decades to come: the general staff's inability to fulfill its planning function; the tendency to become bogged down in debate over untested theory; the necessity for the leader to involve himself with minutiae and to depend on a few trusted officers *(gente de confiança);* the undue importance attributed to "the plan," which took on aspects of holy writ; and the attempt to complete highly complex tasks hastily. In this and similar later situations leaders spent so much energy on paperwork that they had little left for execution. Worse still, the officer corps that would have to turn any plan into reality had too few capable officers who were truly interested in the military as a profession. The majority were inured to a bureaucratic routine that had next to nothing to do with preparing troops for combat. Indeed, according to military historian General Francisco de Paula Cidade, there were officers who had risen from recruit to colonel to general "without ever having fired a regulation rifle!"[9]

Mallet was a flawed visionary; some of his ideas were ahead of their time, but others were mired in the past. His 1901 *Relatório,* full of minute advice, including suggestions for conducting combat reconnaissance, read like a treatise on army organization and operations instead of an annual report on the ministry's affairs. He urged that the combat arms and services (infantry, cavalry, artillery, and engineers) be organized on a three-echelon pattern, as were the German, French, Portuguese, Italian, and Argentine armies, rather than on the four-echelon model that some officers preferred. His design would mean three platoons per company, three companies per battalion, three battalions per regiment, three regiments per brigade, and three brigades per division. Tactically this organization would allow one unit on the front, one on the flank, and one in reserve. However, because of budgetary restraints, the peacetime organization would limit the number of battalions to two, which would make it impossible for regiments to practice three-echelon tactics.[10]

To this built-in defect was added another. Although Mallet recognized that one of the lessons of Canudos was the necessity for an efficient transportation-and-supply service, lack of funds allowed creation of only two transport companies for the whole army! He himself designed two light wagons for munitions, baggage, or wounded based on his "observations in the Paraguayan War." He wrongly thought that in wartime additional units could be organized "with facility" by summoning volunteers or reserve personnel[11]—two elements that were always lacking. He admitted that the army did not have enough animals and wagons to go on campaign and if war occurred the usual "friendly purchase and contract" process would give way quickly to requisition. The procedure could be streamlined, he thought, by having each unit take a census of local horses, oxen, and wagons so that in time of necessity they could be seized and their owners properly indemnified. He saw requisition of private, civilian property as normal and was only concerned with making it acceptable by eliminating its "odious character of depredation and violence."[12] He failed to see that with such a precarious, last minute transportation system mobilization would be uncertain. It could not even be tested because no government would expend the necessary compensation funds or risk widespread civilian animosity.

Probably Mallet's greatest contribution to Brazilian military thinking was his insistence that constant training maneuvers were necessary to create a real army. "Our generals are obliged," he wrote, "to limit themselves . . . , to administration . . . which . . . makes them excellent peacetime administrators, however, with little aptitude for command functions, [or] for maneuver in war. Save for theoretical studies, absorbed from excellent treatises by the masters of war and on the history of European and American campaigns, they are generally unfamiliar with command for lack of practice." Peacetime preparation of general officers should, he argued, correspond to their wartime functions. But until units were concentrated, he lamented, the army would not be able to hold the joint exercises that would prepare generals for command in war.[13]

Army Life for Common Soldiers

If the Brazilian generals of 1900 were not prepared to lead, the soldiers were likewise unfit to follow. The troops barely knew a manual of arms and rudiments of close-order drill. Garrison duty consisted mostly of standing guard before public buildings or participating in parades and funerals rather than physical development, training in small unit tactics, marksmanship, or camping.[14]

The obligatory service law of 1874 had failed because of widespread resistance. The civilian selection boards simply did not work, partly because the citizenry ignored the civil registers established in 1888, making it impossible to compile draft lists. The white bourgeoisie regarded barracks life with horror, and the powerful land owners did not want to lose their peons. Forced recruitment during the nineteenth century had left disturbing memories. Ministerial reports constantly complained of the people's aversion to service in the ranks. Interestingly, the antipathy was not as great to becoming an officer or serving in the National Guard. Mallet suggested altering the useless obligatory service law to apply only to the National Guard and then to transfer the guard from the Ministry of Justice to the Ministry of War, thereby providing the army with a true reserve. Argentina had dealt with the same problem in that fashion.[15] The guard would become the "territorial army," whose instructors would be drawn from the "ranks of the active army," creating a force that would be "an integral part of the nation in arms" *(nação armada).*[16] This was one of the army's many attempts to gain control over the National Guard, which functioned mostly as a social-political organization that provided some muscle for local oligarchies. The Ministry of Justice's control of the guard indicated that its purpose was internal control rather than national defense. In any case army officers saw it as a competitor that they wished to eliminate.

A sketch of the enlisted man's army will help the reader understand civilian aversion to army service. The conditions described below changed slowly in the first two decades of the century. So-called volunteers, most of the common soldiers entered the army from the ranks of the unemployed. Some joined willingly, seeking meals and shelter, but many others, perhaps even a majority, had been seized by the police in sweeps, called *canoas,* and sent under guard into the barracks. In this fashion large numbers were sent from the north and northeast to the central and southern states. Illiteracy was typical, and many suffered from malaria, parasites, and inadequate diet; discipline was harsh, even brutal. In 1901 Mallet warned that "cruelty was counter-productive. In many cases excessive punishments worsened that depravity of character, the corruption of weak and degenerate types." He argued that the time was past when terror could produce "subordination." "Irons, the lash, degrading prisons, the death penalty, gave way to milder, persuasive methods; to simple imprisonment or with hard labor." He wrote that superiors no longer spoke to subordinates in insulting fashion; rather, they "persuaded them with reason, regenerated them with example."[17] What a flight of wishful thinking! Most likely, Mallet's claim that harsh discipline no longer existed was an attempt to discourage its use.

Custom and the commander's whim, rather than a set code, determined army discipline. Until 1899 the military code in force was a mixture of the 1710 code, the 1763 regulations of the Conde de Lippe, the *ordenanças* of

1805, and the Imperial Criminal Code. Despite Mallet's rosy view, the 1899 code, which was actually the navy code applied to the army on a supposedly temporary basis, was only slightly more moderate than its predecessors, and attempts to revise it in 1907 and 1916 failed.[18]

Regardless of what the regulations prescribed, punishments were applied capriciously. One retired officer, who served in the enlisted ranks at the beginning of the century, observed that the "dosage of disciplinary punishments" usually depended on the "passing humor" of the commanders, who were not always governed by a desire to correct or to teach. They confused the "duty to punish" with the "right to castigate."[19] When the commander believed that some infraction of discipline required lowering the boom, he did not bother calling together a tribunal or writing a report. He formed the troops in a rectangle in the barracks patio, had the offender stripped to the waist, and, with the unit band playing marches to cover the screams, had the man beaten with a flexible saber or switches. In 1909 the Eighth Infantry Regiment in Cruz Alta, Rio Grande do Sul, kept on permanent display hundreds of switches in the officer-of-the-day's room as an incentive to discipline. And because such discipline was handled at the unit level, the statistics on discipline that appear in ministerial reports only represent the most serious cases, which reached the Supreme Military Tribunal.[20]

Among the punishments were lashings, marching for hours in a courtyard with a pack loaded with roofing tiles, solitary confinement on a bread-and-water diet in a damp, dark, tomblike cell for up to twenty-five days, and using the so-called *palmatória* to beat the unfortunate soldier on the hands and feet; in the field troublemakers would be spread-eagled on their backs and staked to the ground in front of the tents.[21] Sometimes soldiers held in solitary were taken out for marches or beatings and then returned to their dank cubicles. Given an opportunity, some imprisoned soldiers committed suicide as the only way to end their suffering. In one case two prisoners, being held for murder in Fort Santa Cruz at the entrance to Guanabara Bay, jumped from the wall onto the surf-pounded rocks rather than submit to a lashing. There were instances of whole garrisons mutinying against brutal treatment.[22]

Rough treatment was the only way that officers could imagine making soldiers out of such poor human specimens. They protested that they had to accept all who came their way or face gaps in the ranks. As one officer expressed it, "[T]o reject them would leave the unit ineffective. The solution was, then, to take them and discipline them with a strong hand."[23]

The troops were poorly housed. The barracks were often makeshift, with inadequate sanitary facilities. In 1902 some units, such as those in Curitiba, were in rented quarters, whereas those in Recife were awaiting funds so that they could build their own barracks. The problem of adequate barracks would continue for years to come, with major efforts to improve quarters coming with the slow construction of Vila Militar in the Federal District beginning in 1909 and in a vast program in the early 1920s.

Units acquired foodstuffs locally, and the quality, not surprisingly, was often a cause for complaint. Although the American military attaché recommended to his own army adoption of some of the German appliances and methods that he saw in the kitchens at Vila Militar in 1912, the following year troops quartered in nearby Deodoro rebelled over bad food and *O Estado de São Paulo* reported that the army served "wormy beans and rancid dried meat."[24]

Pay and allowances were never more than enough to preserve the barest existence. Table 2.2 shows enlisted pay (in *milreis*) in 1897. Officers did better, to be sure, receiving allowances, travel expenses, rations allotments, and so forth (see Table 2.3).

TABLE 2.2.

Soldiers' Pay (in milreis), 1897

Rank	Monthly	Annual Pay
Private (Praças de Pret)	$360	4$320
Private First Class (Anspeçada)	$400	4$800
Corporal (Cabo)	$500	6$000
Clerk (Furriel)	$750	9$000
2d Sergeant	1$000	12$000
First Sergeant	1$250	15$000
Sgt.-Major or Quartermaster Sgt.	2$000	24$000

SOURCE: José Feliciano Lobo Vianna, *Guia Militar Para o Anno de 1898* (Rio de Janeiro: Imprensa Nacional, 1897), 336.

TABLE 2.3.

Officers' Base Pay (in milreis), 1897

Rank	Monthly Pay	Annual Pay
Ensign (Alferes)	120$000	1:440$000
Lieutenant	140$000	1:680$000
Captain	200$000	2:400$000
Major	280$000	3:360$000
Lieutenant Colonel	320$000	3:840$000
Colonel	400$000	4:800$000
Brigadier General	600$000	7:200$000
Major General (Divisão)	800$000	9:600$000
Marshal	1:000$000	12:000$000

SOURCE: José Feliciano Lobo Vianna, *Guia Militar Para o Anno de 1898* (Rio de Janeiro: Imprensa Nacional, 1897), 336.
NOTE: In 1897 1:000$000 equaled U.S. $143.90. For a conversion table by years see Robert M. Levine, *Pernambuco in the Brazilian Federation* (Stanford, Calif.: Stanford University Press, 1978), 189.

Allowances for officers were determined by their assignment. The listing is too long and varied to be reproduced here, but a sampling indicates that command brought some financial as well as other privileges (see Table 2.4).

Heads of engineering or general staff commissions and commanders of forts all received special allowances. An individual officer's income, then, could vary considerably, depending on his assignment; and, not surprisingly, he stood a better chance of picking up extra allowances if he were assigned in or close to army headquarters in Rio de Janeiro. It seems that an inordinate amount of the war ministry's budget went for salaries, allowances, rations payments, and travel pay. In 1900 out of a total budget of 48.375:684$375 some 32.367:481$700 (66.9 percent) went for those items alone, whereas war material was allotted 8.901:690$642 (18.4 percent), and the military hospitals and infirmaries were run on 366:250$000 (.75 percent).[25] The relative cost of maintaining officers and common soldiers can be seen by comparing totals for base pay. Using the 1897 pay figures five thousand privates received

TABLE 2.4.

Annual Allowances (Gratificações de exercicios) for 1902

Positions	Annual Allowances
Commander in chief (Marshal)	12:000$000
Chief of staff (Gen. Div.)	8:760$000
Asst. chief of staff (Brig. Gen.)	5:400$000
Corps commander (Gen. Div.)	7:200$000
Division commander (Gen. Div.)	5:400$000
Brigade commander (Brig. Gen.)	4:440$000
Regimental commander (Col. or Lt. Col.)	3:000$000
Battalion commander (Major)	3:000$000
Company commander (Capt.)	840$000
Commander of 1st-class garrison	2:400$000
Commander of 2d-class garrison	1:560$000
Commander of military school	5:400$000
Commander of preparatory school	5:400$000
Quartermaster General (Intendente)	7:200$000
Member of promotions commission	5:400$000
Director of an arsenal	3:120$000
Regimental or battalion executive officer	1:920$000
Regimental or battalion adjutant	1:140$000
Regimental or battalion quartermaster	780$000
Lieutenants	660$000

SOURCE: Ministerio da Guerra, *Relatório apresentado ao Presidente da República dos Estados Unidos do Brasil pelo General de Divis[til]ao João Nepomuceno de Medeiros Mallet, Ministro de Estado dos Negocios da Guerra em Maio de 1902* (Rio de Janeiro: Imprensa Nacional, 1902), 13–15.

21:600$000, whereas one hundred top officers (four marshals, nine major generals, eighteen brigadiers, and sixty-nine colonels) received 595:200$000, and 372 lieutenants were paid 624:960$000. To maintain the upper ranks in comfort, it seems that enlistments were deliberately kept *below* the authorized limits. In the period 1900 to 1910 the army's annual authorized strength was about thirty thousand officers and soldiers, but contemporary testimony indicates that effective troop strength rarely reached fifteen thousand, and, in 1904, one officer commented that there were less than ten thousand effectives. It appears that the money not spent on soldiers went into extra allowances and into maintaining an inflated officer corps. For example, in 1901 by law the army was to comprise 1,914 officers and 28,160 soldiers, when in reality it had 2,917 officers and 15,000 soldiers.[26] In 1902 there were 668 ensigns *(alféres)* and six second lieutenants beyond the legal limit who were left over from emergency promotions during the civil war. Their salaries absorbed 961:920$000.[27] It should also be noted that this surplus in the lowest officer rank was a barrier to the aspirations of enlisted men wishing to enter the military school and for students already in the school. Upward movement would not be possible until space appeared among the lieutenants.

By comparison civilian workers in army employ were paid according to skill and status; an electrician might make 4:800$000 a year, a first-class worker 2:400$000, whereas a fifth-class apprentice might receive 150$000.[28] Because Brazil did not have a minimum wage, workers in private employ were paid according to their status and their employer's goodwill. Field hands' daily wages in Pernambuco between 1900 and 1910 ranged between $800 to 1$100.[29] Toward the end of the decade laborers in Rio de Janeiro averaged about three milreis (3$000) a day or, assuming full employment, 936$000 a year; a civil policeman or a junior clerk earned about 1:200$000 to 2:400$000 per year; a household servant got by on 180$000 to 600$000 plus room and board. What that money could buy is difficult to determine with accuracy. From 1895 to 1899 Brazil experienced inflation that turned into deflation and very nearly depression from 1900 to 1902 thanks to Campo Sales's tight money policies, and from then until 1914 price fluctuation averaged six points a year.[30] In 1913 the *Jornal do Comercio* (Rio de Janeiro) estimated that the cost of living had risen 940 percent between 1887 and 1912.[31] While prices were constantly changing, salaries held comparatively steady. As a result there were periodic protests, riots, and street demonstrations in Rio de Janeiro over prices of food and transportation. Both the inflation and resulting unrest undoubtedly affected the army and formed the backdrop against which the various military revolts and conspiracies should be seen.

Many married soldiers reenlisted repeatedly, clinging to the security that the army provided for ten to twenty years. Every post had its old soldiers who formed the core of its personnel. One officer, who knew firsthand the

1910 army and who became an authority on the history of the last years of the empire and first years of the republic, noted that most of the sergeants were single, lived in the barracks, and had a reputation for leading wild lives. Of course, because most officers were married, the reputation of the single sergeants may have been more fancy than fact. The married privates, privates first-class, and corporals would seek housing in the streets and alleys near the barracks, or if they were stationed outside the city, they would build shacks on land assigned by the commander. In some places they obtained space within the post itself. They formed a tight society in which excessive alcohol, immoderate gambling, and family violence disrupted periodically. To some extent the army encouraged drinking by providing a *cachaça* ration, which had been customary since the Paraguayan War.[32] Family heads, perhaps passing on their own frustrations, sometimes beat wives and children. Usually the officers avoided interfering in this subworld, but post jails held more than one husband until tempers cooled.

The soldiers and their families lived in "a closed circle" of dependency and obligations among themselves and the officers. The mental outlook was one of "dedication to the chiefs in an ambience closed to the surrounding civilian society."[33] The army reflected the patriarchal nature of Brazilian society. The soldiers lived in a relationship to their officers, who frequently spent long years in the same post, not unlike that between the rural landowner and his peons. The officers might be called on to mediate family disputes, and some sought to provide schooling for post children. But, considering the underdeveloped nature of public education, it is hardly surprising that this was rare. What efforts the officers made in education were aimed at teaching the soldiers basic literacy skills and simple mathematics.[34]

Dependents had access to army medical facilities, at least to the extent of receiving medicines, but health care for dependents had a low priority. As in civilian society, the quality of army medical care varied with time and place. But even so, the eight hospitals and nineteen infirmaries existing in 1902 treated 16,123 patients when the total effective force of the army was no more than 16,000. At some posts it would seem that whole units marched through the infirmaries en masse. In 1900 Mallet noted that the high treatment figure was a result of troops seeking attention for "the slightest infirmities," to which practice he attributed a lower death rate than in the United States Army. According to him, in the United States 565 out of every 1000 soldiers sought treatment and of these, 5 to 6 percent died, whereas in Brazil the figures were 813.7 per 1000 with a 2.29 percent death rate. However, at that time the United States was engaged in combat operations in the Philippines and China. And it should be recalled that the state of medicine was such that of the 5,462 deaths resulting from the Spanish-American War (1898), fully 3,443 or 63 percent resulted from illness or accidents, not combat wounds. In

1902, without combat, the Brazilian army had a death rate of 2.2 percent for sixteen thousand effectives, or looked at another way, one out of every forty-two of the 14,380 army patients died (see Table 2.5).

The most common killers of the era were tuberculosis and beriberi, the latter being endemic in army units. But smallpox, bubonic plague, yellow fever, and malaria were also common, as were a host of parasites. That the death rates were not higher may have been partly a result of traditional military concern for neatness and cleanliness. It may also have resulted from the work of the army's sanitary police commission, established in 1900, which was responsible for hygiene in military facilities.[35]

It should be noted that the army participated in turn-of-the-century efforts to bring modern analysis and research methods to Brazil. In 1896 it established a clinical microscopy and bacteriological laboratory in Rio de Janeiro. Although the lab's utility had been questioned at the outset, it proved its worth in 1900, during the outbreak of immigrant-carried bubonic plague, when it examined and verified suspected cases. In addition to providing analysis of urine and other specimens for the Central Army Hospital, its staff did x-ray examinations. And interestingly, considering the state of the art in Brazil at the time, its staff conducted research regarding yellow fever, tuberculosis, beriberi, malaria, bubonic plague, and other diseases.[36]

Despite this modern laboratory's existence, the medical personnel of the era left much to be desired. In 1900 the army's "Health Corps" was composed of 180 medical doctors and 87 pharmacists, of whom 120 doctors and

TABLE 2.5.

Patients and Death Rates in Army Facilities, 1900–1908

Year	Number of Patients	Number of Dead	Death Rate (%)
1900	14,683	337	2.3
1901	14,380	346	2.4
1902	16,123	369	2.2
1903	17,191	426	2.4
1904	20,119	456	2.2
1905	25,587	633	2.5
1906	20,790	476	2.3
1907	15,894	410	2.6
1908	19,807	375	1.9
TOTALS	164,574	3,828	2.3

NOTE: This table is based on figures in medical sections of Ministerio da Guerra, *Relatórios,* 1900–1908. For health in the American army in the 1890s see Edward M. Coffman, *The Old Army: A Portrait of the American Army in Peacetime, 1784–1898* (New York: Oxford University Press, 1986), esp. 381–82. The average annual sick rate in the U.S. Army in the year before the Spanish-American War (1898) was 1,186, with a mortality rate of 5.1 percent.

43 pharmacists were officers; the remaining 60 doctors and 44 pharmacists were contracted civilians. There was a constant turnover among the latter who, with a monthly salary of 260$, only stayed if they could not obtain a better position or if they were allowed to do as they pleased. The contracted doctors could not be transferred from one region to another and so could not be counted on in an emergency. And since some of the army doctors held permanent positions, were in politics, taught in army schools, or owned civilian clinics, headquarters had difficulty staffing facilities around the country. Also there were no regular nursing, stretcher-bearer, or ambulance services, which, Mallet admitted, created a situation that "would be fatal in case of a campaign."[37]

Although the army's health profile reflected that of the population as a whole, soldiers and their families were undoubtedly better off medically speaking than the majority of Brazilians; at least they had health facilities and practitioners available to them. The quality of the medical doctors gradually improved between 1900 and 1920, both in and outside the army. It was a slow struggle. In 1904, at the Rio de Janeiro medical school, one of two in Brazil, the professor of microbiology was attempting to teach 150 students with a single microscope. In the traditionalist medical education of the era the laboratory approach to medicine was not routine.[38] But then, the same could be said of military education.

Officer Career at the Turn of the Century

Although the white, urban middle and upper classes were opposed to their sons serving as common soldiers in the environment described above, they had more enthusiasm for an officer's career. Novelist Afonso Henriques Lima Barreto, describing the middle-class functionaries who lived in the Rio suburbs in 1904, wrote that "the Brazilian is vain and fond of empty titles and hollow honors. His ideal is to have the marks of distinction—rings, decorations, citations—to go about bedecked with gold braid."[39] Politicians seemed to enjoy the honorary officer titles the army bestowed. As Gilberto Freyre observed, the insecurity of republican politicians produced an itch for status-laden military honors that would make them appear to the populace as princes of the Republic equal to the professional generals.[40] It was suggestive of the era's atmosphere that the Academy of Letters, founded in 1896, chose to bedeck its members with braided uniforms, plumes, and swords. This did not mean that Brazilians had developed a martial spirit or a liking for military life but rather that they enjoyed display, pageantry, and parades. Perhaps civilian men donned uniforms and titles as a disguise to project the appearance of machismo without the discomforts or risks of military life? And some carried the delusion to the extreme of actually becoming career officers.

Despite the public's lack of enthusiasm for army life, the opportunity for a free education attracted young men to the officer corps. For those without resources the army offered the possibility of upward social mobility. The officers who began their careers between 1900 and 1911 would command the army at midcentury. They entered a military educational system that was in a constant state of flux without any governing tradition.

At the end of the empire there were three military schools—at Fortaleza, Porto Alegre, and Rio de Janeiro. Shortly after the declaration of the republic two "practical schools" were added at Realengo, outside Rio, and at Rio Pardo, in Grande do Sul, to serve as preparatory schools. In 1898 the army closed the Fortaleza and Porto Alegre institutions, making the military school of Brazil at Praia Vermelha in Rio its sole source of officers. Rio Pardo and Realengo continued as preparatory schools for Praia Vermelha. The former appears to have placed more importance on field exercises and target practice than did Realengo, but at both institutions students studied Portuguese, French, English, geography, history, arithmetic algebra, geometry, natural history, cavalry, and artillery. The emphasis given to military training over general education depended on the whim of the commanding colonel rather than on the regulation curriculum. Indeed, after the 1897 rebellion Realengo remained disarmed for some years.[41]

The treatment accorded the student rebels indicated that the Brazilian army did not treat potential officers with the same severity that it disciplined its troops. Initially, the 1897 rebels were dismissed from the service or sent to serve as ordinary soldiers, but in 1899 the Congress conceded an amnesty that included reentry into the military schools. At Realengo this created a heterogeneous student body ranging from fifteen to forty-five years, some of whom had been top sergeants and presented a hardened appearance by comparison to the young boys away from home for the first time. The custom of amnesty and reincorporation was also followed after the 1904 rebellion and contributed to the willingness of military students to risk involvement in later rebellions such as in 1922. Indeed, the unwillingness of the government to concede an amnesty after the latter episode led to further uprisings in 1924 and thereby contributed to the unrest that led to the Revolution of 1930.

Historians have not noticed the wide range of ages of the students at Realengo or Praia Vermelha and have given the impression that they were all teenagers or men in their early twenties. But the figures for Realengo show that in 1901 some 41 out of 438 students were between twenty-four and thirty-four years of age, and in 1902 fully 149 out of 527 (28 percent) were between twenty-four and forty-five. I did not find figures for 1904, but contemporary testimony indicates that the student body that rebelled in that year contained a number of older men, amnestied veterans of the 1897 rebellion, who perhaps incited the younger ones. This suggests that the term *cadet* should not universally call up images of naive young men.[42]

The foregoing discussion of the army at the opening of the century shows an institution badly in need of reform. Much of its leaders' attention in the next years would be devoted to various reform projects. A crisis brewing on the far western Amazonian frontier stimulated their growing sense of insecurity.

The Acre Crisis

The demand for rubber products, particularly tires for automobiles, focused manufacturers on the world's sole source of natural rubber, the vast Amazon. The turn of the century was the heyday of Amazonian rubber production. And although all of it passed through Brazilian ports en route to world markets, some of the highest quality rubber came from the Bolivian Acre. In 1867 a Brazilian-Bolivian treaty had recognized the latter's sovereignty over the Acre, a region between the Madeira and Javarí Rivers that embraced the upper reaches of the Juruá, Purus, Acre, and Abuña Rivers, but the document had left the actual delimitation in doubt, giving rise to disputes. By 1900 about sixty thousand Brazilians, especially large numbers of unemployed and land-hungry Cearenses, had entered the Acre. Bolivia was rapidly losing the richest rubber-producing region in the world.[43]

In January 1899 Bolivia belatedly sought to secure its position by placing a customhouse at Puerto Alonso (Pôrto Acre) that levied a 30 percent export tax on rubber heading downriver. The governor of Amazonas and Brazilian rubber barons in the Acre supported a Spaniard, Luis Galvez Rodrigues, in an uprising that led to a declaration of independence in July 1899. The independent "State of Acre's" flag was done in Brazilian national colors, green and gold; its civil, criminal, and commercial codes and customs tariffs were the same as Brazil's; the official language was Portuguese; and Brazilian currency was its legal tender. Yet Galvez was more than a melodramatic foreign adventurer or a stalking horse for Brazilian expansion. If his Amazonian republic had succeeded it would have taken territories claimed by both Bolivia and Brazil.[44]

Initially Brazilian press opinion and the Rio government seemed inclined to help Bolivia put down the insurrection. Galvez did not endear himself to the commercial houses of Manaus or Belém with his intention of pooling Acre's rubber production to force better prices. Without telegraph communications to the region all manner of wild rumors circulated along the steamboat grapevine. Some of these stories had the United States preparing to support Bolivia in return for customs and territorial concessions. The mysterious and, as it turned out, unauthorized voyage of the USS *Wilmington* up the Amazon to Accedes, Peru, lent credibility to such suspicions. Intense press coverage of the Acre affair agitated public opinion with the idea that the government was giving away valuable Brazilian territory by upholding Bolivian claims. In March 1900 a Brazilian naval force's seizure of Galvez gave the impression that the Brazilian government was intervening on Bolivia's behalf.[45]

But even as this occurred, the awareness that Bolivian forces were marching to the Acre hardened the Brazilian position. A Bolivian proposal to trade the Acre for a similar extension of Brazilian land along the Madeira River was a tacit admission of La Paz's uncertainty that it could restore control. The Belém newspaper, *Folha do Norte,* termed the naval expedition that deposed Galvez "deceitful' and "disgraceful," saying it was "an expedition against Brazilians, not an expedition in favor of the rights and duties of Brazilians."[46] In late September 1900, after an overland trek of some five months, a Bolivian military expedition retook Puerto Alonso (Pôrto Acre) without serious opposition. But that did not end the matter. Press accounts of the expedition and agitation by members of the Amazonas state government and members of Congress awakened the Brazilian government to the plight of its citizens "who had fallen under Bolivian dominion" after years of believing that they had settled in Brazil. The Rio government refused the Bolivian request to allow an armed expedition to steam up the Amazon to the Acre.[47]

The subsequent maneuverings included the Acreanos' renewed determination to hold themselves independent from Bolivia until the Brazilian flag waved over the territory and until Bolivia's desperate search for foreign assistance had ended. In January 1900 the American consul at Belém had recommended that an American syndicate purchase rubber lands on the banks of the Purus and its tributaries to secure "the key to the [rubber] situation, and dictate terms to the rest of the world."[48] Rumors circulated about a German syndicate leasing the Acre and about a French proposal to build a railway in northern Bolivia to free that country of dependence on the Madeira route through Brazil. By mid-1900 Bolivian authorities had sought great power protection by offering to cede rubber lands to the United States and England.[49] Although the two governments did not get directly involved, Bolivia signed a contract with an Anglo-American syndicate that all but transferred to it sovereignty over the region. If it had been carried out, the arrangement would have created a seventy-five-thousand-square-mile private empire in the heart of South America.[50]

Throughout 1900 the Brazilian press attacked the government for failing to back the Acreanos against Bolivia.[51] And when word about the syndicate leaked out, the press began to clamor for action, raising the specter of the powers subdividing South America as they had Africa.

At the end of 1900 the Amazonian state authorities took matters into their own hands, outfitting an expedition to attack Puerto Alonso. Later

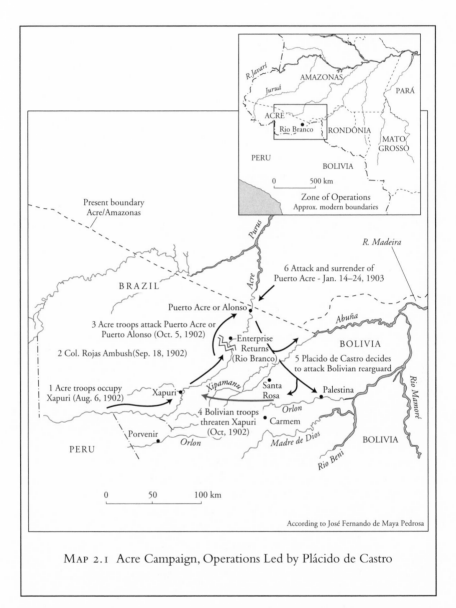

MAP 2.1 Acre Campaign, Operations Led by Plácido de Castro

SOURCE: From *The Army in Brazilian History*, edited by Luiz Paulo Macedo Cavalho. Rio de Janeiro & Salvador, Ba.: Biblioteca do Exército & Odebrecht, 1998. 4 vols. Redrawn by Bill Nelson. Used with permission of Biblioteca do Exército, Rio de Janeiro.

dubbed the "Poets' Expedition," its failure awakened the leaders of Brazilian Amazonia to the need for professionally trained military leadership, careful planning, and better arms to dislodge the Bolivians. That awareness eventually led them to entrust command of a renewed insurrection to José Plácido de Castro, a gaúcho surveyor with military training. He roused the Acreanos once again and with Amazonas state military police and so-called volunteers, pressed into service off the streets of Manaus, moved against the Bolivians (see Map 2.1).

Meanwhile, the Baron of Rio Branco had become foreign minister with the idea that Brazil should change its policy of recognizing Bolivian sovereignty as set forth in the Treaty of 1867 and extend its claim to the sources of the rivers whose lower reaches and mouths the Brazilians occupied. He argued that Brazil should take everything up to the line of the 10°20′ parallel, pointing out that if the area in dispute was not Brazilian, "what right have we of seeking to block the operations of the American syndicate?"[52] He notified the Bolivian government that the Amazon was closed to its commerce and cautioned that the military expedition that President José Maria Pando was leading toward the disputed zone should not cross the 10°20′ line. To back up this warning the army reinforced Corumbá, opposite Bolivia in Mato Grosso, and sent four infantry regiments and three artillery batteries to the Acre.

Was it to be war? No, Rio Branco was orchestrating a bluff. As he had admitted to a friend, to secure the Acre without great bloodshed, "it is necessary that we appear strong and resolute to all. God deliver us from a war, unequipped and impoverished as we are."[53]

The government's financial condition had forced a troop reduction from 28,170 to 15,000, making movement to Mato Grosso and the Acre a painful affair. Many units in the north were already short of officers and soldiers because so many were suffering from the beriberi endemic to the region and had been transferred south.[54] The infantry regiments involved in the mobilization had to borrow soldiers to fill out their ranks, in the process leaving gaps in the regiments from which the troops came. The navy was so ill-prepared for river transport that the army had to contract with civilian companies to move its troops. Several battalions embarked short of officers because they had been elected to municipal councils (*camaras*) or state assemblies, which freed them from their military obligations. One battalion left without any of its captains because all of them had been elected to office—some *after* receiving their orders—and another departed Belém for the Alto Purus commanded by a major because the colonel had been elected state senator.[55]

Among the soldiers who answered the call to the colors was a twenty-one-year-old sergeant of the Twenty-fifth Infantry Battalion of Porto Alegre, Getúlio Dornelles Vargas, who would a few decades later become the major political figure of twentieth-century Brazil. His father, Manoel do Nascimento Vargas, had gone off to the war with Paraguay as a corporal and had returned a lieutenant colonel. In the 1870s he became a fazendeiro in the area of São Borja on the Uruguay River across from Missiones, Argentina. In the civil war of 1893–95 he fought on the winning Julio de Castilhos-Florianista side, even though it meant fighting against troops led by his brother-in-law. As with other gaúcho families the war split the Dornelles-Vargas clans into republicans *(chimangos)* and federalists *(maragatos)*. Floriano promoted Manoel Vargas to colonel, and Prudente de Morais made him a brigadier general. With this background in 1898 Getúlio decided on a military career and sought admission to the army's preparatory school in Rio Prado, RGS. Put on a waiting list and wishing to improve his chances, in February 1899 he enlisted in the Sixth Infantry Battalion in São Borja, from which he moved the next year to the school in Rio Prado. In 1902 a disciplinary incident led to the expulsion of several students, and Vargas resigned from the school in solidarity with them and resolved to forgo a career as an officer, but as a result he returned to the ranks as a common soldier. In that category he joined the troops sent to reinforce Corumbá, on the Bolivian border, and thereby took his place on Rio Branco's chessboard. His initial dreams of military glory, of returning a hero like his father, quickly faded before the "apathy, disorder, and indiscipline" of the frontier. Years later he told his daughter that "it was there that I learned to understand men. . . . It is in the difficult and uncertain moments that we can perceive them best."[56]

Minister of War (Marechal) Francisco de Paula Argollo (1837–1930) complained that the army's units were so under strength that instruction, training exercises, and maneuvers had become impossible, not the least because most officers used every pretext to avoid spending time with the troops. They reduced their participation in regimental life to being present at the reading of the orders of the day and at the changing of the guard.[57] Moreover, the army lacked maps of the areas of operations, and both Corumbá, Mato Grosso, and the Acre were beyond the telegraph lines. They could only be reached via river steamer.[58] It was indeed fortunate for the Brazilians that Bolivia was worse off than they.

In March 1902 the two sides signed a modus vivendi by which Brazilian troops occupied the contested area and crossed the 10°20' line to prevent clashes between the Bolivian troops and the Acreano rebels. The negotiations leading to the 1903 Treaty of Petrópolis recognizing Brazil's possession of the Acre are beyond the scope of this study. It should be observed, however, that Rio Branco sought to lessen Bolivia's financial loss by paying it two million pounds sterling and by promising to build the Madeira-Mamoré railroad around the Madeira rapids to transport Bolivian rubber.[59]

The Acre affair was not so much a story of military conquest as it was a story of migration and economic expansion. The army had a decisive weight only because the United States and England chose to look on while Brazil bought out the Anglo-American syndicate and because Bolivia was so weak. The irony is that within a decade the Amazonian rubber boom turned to bust as the colonial plantations of Southeast Asia reached full production of a cheaper, more dependable product.

The crisis on the Bolivian border and the perceived great power threat convinced the Rio government that it had to improve communications with the far west of Mato Grosso and the Rio Madeira and Acre areas. From 1896 Belém and Manaus had been connected by underwater cable to Britain but not to the rest of Brazil. Cable communications with the rubber-rich north by way of London contributed to official Rio's insecurity regarding the Amazon. In 1890–91 army engineers had extended telegraph lines to Cuiabá, Mato Grosso, and by 1906 they had reached points on the borders of Paraguay and Bolivia. An active participant, and then commander of these efforts (1892), was Candido Mariano da Silva Rondon, who would spend his long career (1889–1939) and longer life (1865–1958) in projects linked to telegraph construction, mapping, opening of frontier areas, and pacification of newly contacted native peoples. In 1907, as head of the Commission for Strategic Telegraph Lines from Cuiabá to Acre, he led his handpicked energetic lieutenants into unmapped jungle for months at a time, cutting trail and stringing wire to the new railhead town of Porto Velho on the Madeira (see Map 2.2). When they were done, the line stretched 1,406 miles through twenty-five telegraph stations, linking north and south by Morse Code, and they had filled in 20,005 square miles of previously blank space on the national map with fifteen new rivers, exact locations of headwaters of major rivers, mountain ranges, and extensive savanna. In addition they contacted and "pacified" thirteen native tribes. Rondon's men photographed and produced motion pictures of all this activity, the latter being shown in the popular urban cinemas to spur interest in the army and the frontier and to show Brazilians that the natives were "fine-looking, well-developed, sturdy people, very well worth saving among the world's races." The films were also to encourage the idea that the unknown northwest was "no terrible jungle, but an open, honest country awaiting the plough."[60] The films were part of a debate among the elites that contributed to a Rondon-led service for the "Protection of Indians and the Settlement of National Workers." Although this service is often attributed to the army, it was located under the Ministry of Agriculture, and its purpose was not to preserve the native cultures but to remove the natives from the path of progress and to assimilate them into the Brazilian nation.[61]

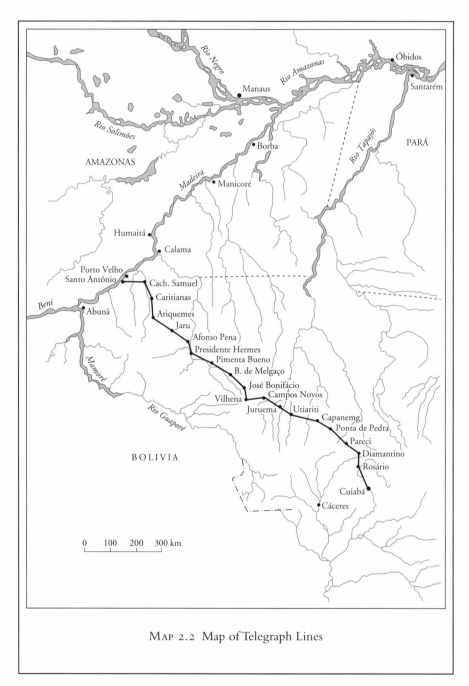

MAP 2.2 Map of Telegraph Lines

SOURCE: From *The Army in Brazilian History*, edited by Luiz Paulo Macedo Cavalho. Rio de Janeiro & Salvador, Ba.: Biblioteca do Exército & Odebrecht, 1998. 4 vols. Redrawn by Bill Nelson. Used with permission of Biblioteca do Exército, Rio de Janeiro.

Both the telegraph and the Indian services ended sadly. In February 1913 the wire was superseded by radio-telegraphy that was already in use by foreign companies in the Amazon when the Acre line was being built. This new "wireless" service established stations whose signals blanketed Brazil and reached neighboring countries and those around the Atlantic basin. The telegraph had been introduced into Brazil in 1852 and over the next sixty years more than thirty-three million meters of wire connected 658 stations, but this impressive network was concentrated in the narrow band of coastal settlement.[62]

As with the railroads in the same era, this technology was not used to open the vast interior of Brazil until the technology itself was on the verge of obsolescence. Instead of stimulating a wave of immigration into and development of what Theodore Roosevelt, who explored part of it with Rondon in 1913, called the world's "last frontier," the rubber boom burst, and ants and rain undermined Farquhar's "mad Mary" railroad around the Madeira rapids. As for the telegraph line and its stations, in 1938 the French anthropologist Claude Lévi-Strauss described this forgotten wonder of the Amazon: "When I reached them, it was several years since they had been sent any provisions. Nobody quite dared to shut the line down; but nobody thought of using it, either. The poles were left to tumble down, the wire to go rusty; as for the last survivors of the staff, they had neither the courage nor the means to leave, and so, slowly, one after another, eaten away by sickness, hunger, and solitude, they were dying off."[63]

Argollo Ministry and Reform Efforts

Brazil's muscle flexing in the Amazon produced some patriotic euphoria, but while civilians celebrated the victory, military leaders were more realistic. "The recent successes on the frontiers of Amazonas," Minister of War Argollo wrote, "once more manifest the evident necessity to organize our army."[64] Unhappily, he observed, Brazilians still did not understand the danger to which their territory was exposed. They could not trust solely in "the principles of international jurisprudence and the efficacy of diplomatic notes" because as long as the diplomat lacked military force to make the logic of his arguments prevail—ultima ratio—their success would depend on the willingness of the great powers to recognize Brazilian rights. "The weak countries," the minister lamented, "lived condemned to the degrading tutelage of the strong, who feel that they possess the right to counsel them, direct them and even to admonish them, transforming, de facto, their independence and autonomy into a true fiction." He pointed to Japan as an example of a formerly backward country that the great powers now treated with respect, even admiration, because of its demonstrated military prowess. He raised the specter of the great powers remaking and reinterpreting international law to crush Brazilian national interests in "the superior interest of humanity." In this nightmare the powers would justify their seizure of Brazilian territory with the argument that all people had the right to the fruits of the planet and that Brazilians had demonstrated their incapacity to exploit and to utilize their land's riches for the benefit of all. Only armed force would prevent such a situation.

Minister Argollo went on to discuss why the army was in such lamentable condition. In moments of crisis the voices of patriotism, he said, protested against the deplorable state of things:

"They organize plans of reform, conceive the most varied projects, but the moment passes, enthusiasm fades, prudence and consideration appear, the doctrinaire humanists emerge discussing universal peace, the barbarism of the military regimen, the destroyer of the nation's vital forces, nothing is done; everything remains as it was. . . . The army is in the condition it finds itself, not because we ignore its necessities . . . but only because of the lack of firmness, resolution and courage on our part to fulfill that which we recommend and avow to be indispensable."[65]

What the high command viewed as indispensable was obligatory military service. Military ideology held that the army was the people in arms. The 1889 proclamation ending the empire declared that the people, the army, and the navy had decreed the "dethronement of the Imperial dynasty."[66] Generalíssimo Manoel Deodoro da Fonseca, head of the provisional government, had declared that "the soldier . . . ought to be from today forward the armed citizen," supporting and furthering "republican institutions."[67] Year after year ministerial reports touted the importance of obligatory service to no avail. The 1874 draft law was never put into effect. Even though the Constitution of 1891 (Article 86) declared that "every Brazilian is obligated to military service, in defense of the *Pátria* and of the Constitution," the requisite enabling act, which stipulated one year of service with selection by lottery, languished until 1908. Its eventual implementation resulted from the combined efforts of military officers and the urban middle class. As more sons of middle-class families entered the officer corps, military and middle-class views of national goals and means became increasingly similar.[68]

The Brazilian middle class saw the country controlled by rural landowners, or *coroneis,* who with their armed hangers-on constituted irregular military forces that limited the central government's ability to enforce national law. And worse, from the middle-class point of view the coroneis, through an elaborate alliance system, actually controlled the central government. A strong military under middle-class control might be able to impose their vision of Brazil. The middle class did not, however, desire to provoke conflict but rather to avoid it. The economic dislocations resulting from the civil war of 1893–95 showed that they would suffer in such struggles. Because they seemed to have little basis, or perhaps taste, for unified political action, they subordinated themselves to the prevailing system: in historian Edgard Carone's phrase, "instead of struggle, collaboration; in place of its own ideology, the vague glorification of citizenship *(civismo)*."[69]

The ill-fated 1904 Escola Militar uprising, with its feeble rumblings of monarchical restoration, may also have contributed to middle-class interest in improving the army. Certainly the events of 1904 deeply disturbed the already worried high command. The generals feared dissension, insubordination, and political partisanship in the ranks; and, as would happen in like situations in the future, they moved to protect the cohesion and unity of the institution while seeking to strengthen the army's ties to the people. Minister Argollo complained that "no one knew the difficult art of obeying," yet all were only too ready to command. "One of the deadly consequences" of slavery, he said, was the association of "submission and obedience with the condition of the slave," leading Brazilians to have "an extravagant notion of liberty . . . a morbid predisposition to discuss and criticize all orders . . . undermine all laws."[70] Brazilians, he lamented, lacked "the fundamental qualities which characterize the spirit of the true soldiers." The struggle to form that spirit was aggravated by the vocation of "our intelligentsia for theoretical studies, for purely abstract speculations from which results a lamentable lack of aptitude for practical work, for the professional occupations and open aversion to the military regimen, although enthusiastically impassioned by all of its brilliant externals."[71]

Even before the military school erupted in rebellion in November 1904, army leaders were coupling reform of the military education system with establishment of obligatory military service. General Luiz Mendes de Morais, director-general of artillery, proposed educational reforms to improve "our obsolete military institutions" not only because a solid military organization was needed for defense but also because it would be "a regenerating agent" for society. The "generalization of military duty" would strengthen the people physically and morally; virility, discipline, and civic virtues would become widespread. Quoting General Colmar Von der Goltz, the German adviser to the Turkish army, to the effect that a people's military organization is "the image of its social condition," Mendes de Morais linked the "strengthening" of society to the consolidation of Brazil's "power and prestige." And with Teddy Roosevelt he argued that "preparation for war" was the best "guarantee of peace." Roosevelt had noted that peace was always portrayed as a goddess with a sword at her side.[72]

According to Mendes de Morais the most important element in the army's "great work of regeneration" was professional instruction, which he termed the "nerves of the system."[73] The task of education and of military instruction,

Minister of War Argollo declared, was the "radical moral and intellectual transformation of the individual" so that soldiers would be characterized by more than their uniforms. Brazil's "military problem" went far beyond mere reform, organization, and regulations. The military education system, the minister went on, was incapable of transforming civilians into officers. Even if the most intelligent, educated, and brave men were well armed and organized into an army modeled on those of the "most advanced countries," once they went into action, he said that they proved that they were fundamentally civilians—lacking solidarity, unity of effort, cohesion, and discipline.[74]

The same national defect that made it impossible to organize an army likewise prevented formation of strong, disciplined political parties in whose absence misguided political chieftains were only too willing to try to "transform the army into a dangerous instrument for their disorderly ambitions."[75] It was absolutely essential, he argued, that civilians and military men keep the army out of partisan struggles, restricting it to the role specified in the constitution, seeking "to conquer public veneration" by the correctness of their behavior, the inflexibility of their fulfillment of duty, and their indifference to the "lying and ephemeral applause of exploitative politicians." Otherwise the army would lose the confidence of, and become an object of fear for, "the conservative classes of society, of whose interests it ought to be the best and most solid guarantee."[76]

This painfully blunt analysis of the relationship between the army and Brazilian society showed how alarmed the top officers were. Some lower-ranking officers were also reform minded. In the January 1904 issue of the *Revista Academia Militar,* "Captain Doctor" Liberato Bittencourt called for more humane disciplining of the soldiers. Once the "black whip" *(chibata negra)* was banned from the barracks, behavior in the ranks would improve, he argued. The soldiers should be provided with education and treated with respect rather than being kept "anti-patriotically in the most damnable ignorance," requiring things of them that they did not understand. On the day military men "only differentiate themselves by insignias and not by culture, the customary indiscipline of our barracks and fortresses will be a thing of the past."[77]

But it was not just a question of discipline. The education offered at Praia Vermelha was overly theoretical and had little military content. Of the eighteen subjects that constituted the curriculum, five could be classified as military: military art (i.e., military history), fortifications, artillery, military administration, and military hygiene. There was nothing taught about ballistics. The course on fortifications concentrated on old styles, and students of artillery learned the minutiae of black powder in an era when other armies had replaced it with smokeless powder. Thus, in a school intended to prepare officers, candidates learned nothing of weapons or their use. In the other disciplines, such as physics, chemistry, law, and astronomy, each professor was free to design and to teach his course as he saw fit. The emphasis was on oral exposition, with little attention to experimentation or application. There were no laboratories; chemistry and physics were studied abstractly via chalk and blackboards, and political economy was taught by rote class repetition of the professor's phrases. Although some professors distinguished themselves with their learned lectures and publications, their style of teaching and the content of their courses did not lend themselves to the development of officers capable of leading a modern army in warfare.[78] Given this intellectual environment it is not surprising that the students found politics more interesting.

Military School Revolt, 1904

In 1904 the Escola Militar do Brasil at Praia Vermelha became a focal point of the unrest that gripped the capital. The inflation and the government's program of sanitizing and modernizing Rio de Janeiro weighed most heavily on the backs of the working class. As their housing was torn down to create the wide Avenida Central, Rua Carioca, and other center city streets, they were squeezed into even less desirable quarters at higher rents or forced to seek shelter further away from downtown and dock area working places. Dispossessed home owners, shopkeepers, barkeeps, and kiosk operators joined the ranks of the discontented, which were further swelled by the commercial crisis of May 1904, which wiped out many businessmen, throwing more workers into the streets. The cost of living and foreign-exchange rates soared in tandem. In the midst of this agitated scene the government forced through a compulsory vaccination law that was the final straw. Street disorders began on November 10. Positivists, Jacobin politicians, monarchists, labor leaders, military officers, and students at the military school formed a de facto alliance. During the next four days mounted police with drawn sabers scattered and arrested demonstrators. Some of those arrested were military school students. By late on the fourteenth, mobs had barricaded numerous downtown streets, seized two police stations, and expanded the fighting into suburbs such as Vila Isabel and Santa Teresa. Because the police could not control the situation, President Rodrigues Alves called out the army.[79]

At the same time conspirators met at the Military Club. Two generals, Sylvestre Rodrigues da Silva Travassos and Antonio Olympio da Silveira, Lieutenant Colonel and Senator Lauro Sodré, and a number of lower-ranked officers had been plotting for months. Their earlier efforts had come to naught owing to police vigilance. And it should be noted that the plot was related to the military school rebellions of 1895 and 1897. Veterans of the latter were members of the class that entered Praia Vermelha from the preparatory school at Realengo in 1901. They had been sent to serve with the troops after the rebellion and were readmitted after the Congress approved an amnesty. Undoubtedly some of these were the agitators who, Leitão de Carvalho said, tried to convince students to seize the then president Campos Sales during a visit to the school in 1902. Apparently the plotters hoped to set up a military dictatorship with the support of the positivist movement. The 1904 affair had roots deeper than the current crisis.[80]

Now, because the street disorders appeared to have depleted the government's moral and military strength, the conspirators decided to strike. Indeed, they may have been involved in press and word-of-mouth efforts to stimulate the violence. They failed to incite the students of the Escola Preparatoria e de Tactica do Realengo thanks to the timely interception of the conspirators' agent by the school's commander, Brigadier General Hermes da Fonseca.[81] But at the Escola Militar do Brasil (Praia Vermelha) they had better luck. Some three hundred students adhered to the cause and marched on the Catete Palace to depose President Rodrigues Alves. But they were alone in revolt. Their contacts in the Fortress São João failed to win over that garrison. And loyalist troops under Rio's chief of police, Brigadier General Antonio Carlos da Silva Piragibe, blocked their way. With the gas streetlights destroyed in the previous day's rioting, the two sides confronted each other in the dark. After wild, directionless firing both sides retreated in disorder. The rebel leaders, General Travassos and Senator Sodré, were wounded, Travassos mortally. During the night naval vessels turned their searchlights on the school and fired a couple of rounds into the patio to demonstrate the futility of further resistance. At dawn troops under Colonel José Caetano de Faria found the students in formation in front of the school ready to surrender.[82]

With the suppression of military revolt the street violence lasted only another day. Far from being a quixotic rebellion against compulsory vaccination, the 1904 rising was aimed, in conspirator Colonel Innocencio Serzedello Correa's words, at the "complete renovation of the nation" via "the destruction of the present order and a complete change of the political scenario."[83] Its purpose was the destruction of the oligarchy that had regained control during the 1890s turmoil and maintained itself in power via the "politics of the governors" system. It was, according to Robert G. Nachman, "the first sign of united opposition to oligarchical control of Republican Brazil."[84] As a protest against that control it was part of a series of outbursts that would lead through the "salvationist" movement and Contestado rebellion of the next decade and the tenente revolts of the 1920s to the Revolution of 1930.[85]

Attempted Reform of Officer Education

The revolt's most immediate effect was the permanent closing of the military school at Praia Vermelha, marking the end of an era in the preparation of officers. The lingering academic debate over military education was suddenly given purpose and the reformers had less institutional inertia to overcome. Mallet had wanted to abolish the school and to separate the combat arms courses in order to eliminate the overly academic nature of the curriculum and to give it a more practical orientation. Although the financial problems of the Campos Sales administration had made implementation of his ideas impossible, the revolt of 1904 made action mandatory. The students were sent to various Rio Grande do Sul garrisons and there summarily dismissed from the army without pay or uniforms. Many had to borrow clothes and money to return home. Still, they fared better than civilian prisoners who were loaded on ships headed for the Acre.

It tells a great deal about Brazilian society and the problem of military discipline that in 1905 the rebel students received an amnesty and were allowed to take final examinations covering work done during 1904. Of the 569 who took either the general or special course tests, 59 qualified for promotion to *alferes-alumno* (student ensign), the first officer rank of the era, and 184 were given passing grades. Only 19 were awarded bachelors degrees in "mathematics and physical sciences."[86]

With the closing of Praia Vermelha and the preparatory school at Realengo in February 1906, the war ministry created a School of War *(Escola de Guerra)* in Porto Alegre that provided officer candidates with two years of cavalry and infantry training and a third of "application." Instruction was based on the new military school regulations of 1905 that had their inspiration in Mallet's 1900 proposals. Teaching was supposed to emphasize practical experience, and theoretical studies were to be limited to nonmilitary subjects. The intention was to put an end to the "Doctor Lieutenants" or "Doctor Colonels," to end *bacharelismo militar* [military academism]. Officer candidates were to learn to shoot, to ride, to function in the field, and to be "troopers." Severe discipline would be reinforced by the elimination of student officers, limiting admission to the student body to candidates with enlisted soldier status.[87] And to prepare instructors who would carry out the intended reform, the war minister sent six junior officers to serve in the German Imperial Army for two years' training, thereby beginning a practice that would have major repercussions in the future.[88]

Unfortunately, the regulations were not put into practice. Inertia won out over reform. Senior officers continued to teach and to train as they had before—theory still dominated.[89] Close-order drill, extension of skirmish lines, and tactical notions dating from the Paraguayan War were the instructional elements that stood out in the memory of General Francisco de Paula Cidade.[90] Improvement of military education was still some years off, but reform was in the wind, as middle- and upper-class civilians took an interest in national defense.

Hermes da Fonseca's Reforms

Shortly after the 1904 revolt, President Rodrigues Alves rewarded General Hermes da Fonseca (1855–1922) for his role in suppressing it by making him commander of the Fourth Military District, which included the capital city.[91] Hermes launched a campaign to invigorate the forces of his district, which made up nearly half the army. With considerable fanfare and press coverage, he held annual combined arms field exercises that created such a stir as to be remembered for decades.

Hermes da Fonseca was of the officer generation that spanned the period from just after the Paraguayan War to the First World War. Born into a distinguished military family in São Gabriel, Rio Grande do Sul, in 1855, he grew up hearing stories of family exploits in the Farroupilha (1835–45) and Paraguayan campaigns. In 1871, at age sixteen, he received a bachelor of letters from the Imperial Colégio Dom Pedro II in Rio de Janeiro and entered the army. Concluding the infantry and cavalry arms course at Praia Vermelha in 1876 and the artillery course two years later, he spent much of his career serving with the artillery. In the late 1870s he was aide to his father, who was commanding general in the Province of Pará; and after an interval as a battery commander he acted as aide to the Conde D'Eu, husband of Princess Isabel and commanding general of the imperial army's artillery, during an inspection tour of the northern provinces. In the 1880s he taught at the imperial military school (Escola Militar da Corte) and in 1888 went as aide with his uncle Marshal Deodoro da Fonseca when the imperial government assigned him to Mato Grosso to remove him from the political scene in Rio. The next year he was with Deodoro in the *praça* before the war ministry on November 15. Indeed, he was a key figure in the republican conspiracy, acting as a filter for those pressing Deodoro to act. He benefited from the republic, rising from captain to lieutenant colonel in ten months. During the naval revolt of 1893 he distinguished himself in the defense of Niterói and stood by Floriano despite antipathy for him.

Promoted to colonel in 1894, from then until 1896 he commanded the Second Mounted Artillery Regiment (Rio de Janeiro), turning it into a model unit. In 1896, with Prudente de Morais's leave of absence and Vice President Manuel Vitoriano's assumption of the government, Hermes became head of the military staff of the presidency *(Casa Militar de Presidência),* a post that brought him into regular contact with civilian leaders, giving him increased political visibility. Over the years he gained a reputation in the army for his studies of organization and training. He was a member of the commission that drew up regulations for the new general staff and was identified with Mallet's reformist ideas. That President Campos Sales regarded him as a secure supporter of the regime was indicated by his appointment as commander of the Federal District's Police Brigade in 1899, a post he held until he took over the Realengo preparatory school in August 1904.

Hermes was a prototype of the twentieth-century Brazilian officer. As a captain he conspired to overthrow the monarchy, and as a retired marshal he would plot against President Epitácio Pessôa. His wearing of military uniforms during his presidency (1910–14), even for ministerial meetings, suggests that his most intimate self-image was that of an officer. His career mixed together soldiering, politics, and institutional and social reform. His example of concern for military proficiency, and of his willingness to see both individual officers and the army as a whole meddle in politics, would be a powerful one for years to come. And like the rest of the officer corps in this century, except for those who served in World War II, his combat experience was against other Brazilians.[92]

Under his leadership, with martial music setting the cadence, the garrison of Rio de Janeiro marched out to the Campo dos Cajueiros, in Santa Cruz, State of Rio, where for eighteen days in September and October 1905 they lived in tents, staged simulated attacks, marched, and posed for photographers, doing their best to look like soldiers. The army had not attempted anything similar since the early days of the republic, and it showed. Although the Sunday trains running out from Pedro II station might have been packed with sightseers, and although the newspapers gave the military activities major space, there was little reason for satisfaction. General Hermes' report was more a listing of shortcomings and problems than of demonstrated martial prowess. Despite an issue of new boots just prior to the march, these were so poorly made that "the majority of the troops . . . arrived at Santa Cruz barefoot." Once there, they found their tents too small, their food supply tenuous because of the lack of transportation, their arms old and ineffective, their packs excessively heavy and with a strap system that cut off circulation in the arms, belts that tended to snap open, and leather cartridge pouches that came apart at the seams from the weight of the shells. The cavalry complained about the quality of its saddles and harnesses and reported that it lacked wagons to carry forage. Clearly, the Brazilian army was not prepared to wage a campaign. Although the 1905 maneuvers roused civilian enthusiasm, they demonstrated to the army high command that reform had to be thoroughgoing.[93]

Civilians exhibited ardor, at least for military display, in the formation of shooting clubs *(tiros),* in the volunteers that signed up for the annual field exercises, and in congressional support for an obligatory military service law.[94] However, the enthusiasm was limited to the urban middle and upper classes and was an outgrowth of their heightened sense of nationalism. Brazil in the first decade of the twentieth century had modernized Rio de Janeiro and eliminated yellow fever from the capital; it also received the first cardinal's hat to be bestowed on a Latin American, hosted the third Pan American conference, raised its legation in Washington to an embassy, sent a distinguished delegation to the second Hague Peace Conference (1907), successfully arbitrated possession of hundreds of thousands of square miles of disputed territory, founded the humanitarian Indian Protective Service, and purchased two of the world's largest dreadnoughts for its navy. Behind these events, both quickening them and feeding on them, was a rising wave of nationalism. Many intellectuals agreed with Alfonso Celso when he hailed, "The dawn of our greatness. We will arrive inevitably at the brilliance and full heat of its mid-day. . . . We will be the second or first power of the world."[95]

Brazilians, accustomed to thinking of themselves as cultural and economic appendages of Europe, were turning inward and discovering the true Brazil. The Canudos disaster had the positive effect of forcing urban coastal dwellers to look on the face of the nation, which, as Euclydes da Cunha declared, was that of "sturdy *caboclos.*" There, in the people of sertão, where "shadings tend to disappear," was "the hardy nucleus" of Brazil's future, "the bedrock of our race."[96]

Somehow the fierce energy that the sertanejo displayed at Canudos and the emerging patriotism of the urban middle class had to be harnessed to a military machine that would support the diplomacy and vision of the Baron of Rio Branco and the presidents that he served. A weak nation would not be respected. Brazil's international policy would be pacific, but it was to be an armed pacifism.[97]

The nationalist enthusiasm pushed a new obligatory service law through the Congress in 1908. To avoid actual barracks duty, many civilians took the more pleasant expedient of joining the so-called *linhas de tiro,* or shooting clubs, which came to form the army's reserve. The army was relatively static in size and had no process for expanding in time of war. It had displayed its inability to mobilize in the Acre crisis. Obligatory military service was intended to transform the army into a training cadre that would turn annual levies of raw recruits into soldiers, who would then pass into a steadily growing reserve that could be summoned in periods of crisis.

As noted earlier, the Canudos campaign had revealed the troops' weak marksmanship, so in 1898 the Rio garrison had built a rifle range but soon found that it had more attraction for civilian shooters than it did for soldiers and officers.[98] A civilian-organized shooting federation was chartered by Congress in 1906, and a group in Rio got Hermes to loan them Mauser rifles for practice sessions. The Carioca shooters formed "Tiro 7" and in 1908 joined ten clubs in other parts of Brazil in creating a battalion that eventually expanded into a corps of marksmen, the country's first organized reserve. The Tiros were living propaganda for the armed Brazil that Hermes and Foreign Minister Rio Branco wanted. They were spectacular on parade in their khaki uniforms, with yellow leggings, bandoliers over their shoulders, and jaunty plumed, gray Australian-style bush hats.[99] Their display made good press copy, even if it was only a marginal contribution to national defense.

But the Tiros were a factor in getting the obligatory service bill through the Congress. From the time the bill was introduced in October 1906, until it was signed into law in January 1908, the Tiros and the lieutenants who advised and instructed them waged a public relations campaign in its favor.[100] In 1906 and 1907 newspapers filled their pages with photos of army field maneuvers; of 37–mile endurance races, called "raids," that were part of the army's new physical education program; and of Tiro parades and shooting contests.[101]

However, public acclaim was not universal; these exhibitions of middle-class patriotism made workers suspicious. They formed the Anti-Militarist League in a fit of what President Afonso Augusto Moreira Pena (1906–9) labeled "repugnance" for the proposed law.[102] The Rio newspapers *Correio da Manhã, O Século,* and *Gazeta de Notícias* attacked the measure as bellicose and anti-individualist. Although congressional opponents delayed passage with constant changes in the bill, and positivists and workers attacked the measure, the middle class's enthusiastic support and governmental pressure carried the bill into law.[103] But in Brazil a law on the books did not necessarily mean it would be implemented. It would take eight years and World War I to put obligatory service into operation.

The ambience of enthusiasm described above centered on Hermes da Fonseca, who as minister of war (1906–9) under President Afonso Pena sought to extend to the whole army the reforms he had pursued in the Fourth Military District. He was blunt in his 1907 report to the president. The army was "deficient in personnel, war materiel, organization and command." Obligatory service would require new barracks because existing ones did not meet the requirements of "comfort and sociability" necessary for the proper mixing of conscripts, "among whom will be found the most uneducated peasant with the most cultured intellectual." Each state should have a training area; the *Vila Militar* to be built on the fazenda *Sapopemba* outside Rio was to serve as the model. He urged refurbishing of arsenals and powder and shell factories. Despite past administrations having been aware of the need to reorganize the army, it was, according to Hermes, "reduced to units scattered over the vast national territory with extremely diminished effectives, without ability to mobilize, some even without armament, and existing independently, without the slightest tie of solidarity, save for common subordination to the district commanders." But because the district commanders were absorbed in administrative trivia, they did not actually command; rather, the battalions and regiments went their separate ways, organized more for "pacific and indolent barracks life, than for the intense labors of a campaign." They suffered an absolute lack of equipment—not enough weapons, munitions wagons, or tents. Worse still, their officers did not know how to command field operations. Frankly, he said, in spite of the "great sums spent annually on its maintenance, the army is not prepared for war."[104]

He urged reform of army administration, which was top-heavy and deficient. The artillery, engineering, health, and accounting directories should be trimmed to more modest size and annexed to the war secretariat, which would also take over much of the administrative work that was clogging up the general staff. The latter should be left free to oversee troop training, to study the country's defense, and to plan future campaigns.[105]

He worried, too, about the production of officers beyond the army's ability to absorb them. The blockage in the lower ranks had been a serious problem since the rapid promotion of noncommissioned officers during the civil war in the 1890s. By 1907 it could take up to a dozen years for promotion to first lieutenant or captain, which was depressing morale and efficiency among lower officers. The solution would be to increase the number of slots for those ranks. Hermes thought that "our small army" had too many schools and urged closings until sufficient spaces in the officer corps opened again. Moreover, only those candidates with more than a year of service as a common soldier should be selected for the military schools because "in order to be an officer and to care for the well-being of the soldier it is necessary to have experienced his way of life."[106]

Since much of what he wished to do depended on government expenditures, congressional opposition to military spending would prevent full-scale reform. Perhaps the most important change Hermes achieved was in the general staff. Created in 1899 to replace the old adjutant general's office, the army's previous administrative center, the general staff took over most of its functions. Its officers were from the old general staff corps and were more comfortable with pushing paper and creating meaningless tasks than with planning troop training exercises, mobilization procedures, weapons procurement, and campaigns. Some officers spent their whole careers in the bureaucracy, never setting foot in a unit. Hermes blamed the "defective education" provided in the military school system, which linked the general staff course to the engineering course. Over time, he said, that linkage combined with the staff's "bureaucratic mold" to produce an "army general staff solely composed of skilled engineers and scrupulous public functionaries." In 1908 the closed general staff corps was abolished and staff duty opened to officers of any branch. The model was the German system that emphasized that staff officers should have firsthand knowledge of conditions in the line units. Hermes hoped that the Brazilian general staff, like the German and Japanese staffs, would become "the very brain of the army, the organizer of victory."[107]

To achieve that goal the army reorganization of August 1909 relieved the general staff of many administrative tasks, such as codifying military legislation; supervising transfers, retirements, and military justice; and registering whether officers were single or married. Its remaining everyday administrative jobs were given over to sergeants and civilians to allow the officers to concentrate on overseeing officer education and troop training. This was the beginning of a real general staff, but it would be a decade or more before it would take the form and substance that its proponents desired. Change would come slowly because of officers' and civilian bureaucrats' resistance to new ways, to the almost continual lack of financial resources, and to the tendency of each administration, minister, or chief of staff to seek to impose his own ideas and methods. The lack of continuity, of new reforms being proposed before the old ones had taken effect, was a characteristic of the Brazilian army.[108]

For example, the structural changes that Hermes' ministry produced endured only to the end of his presidency (1910–14). Many of the alterations produced overlapping lines of authority within the ministry, which would prove cumbersome later in the Contestado operations (1912–15). In summary, the ministry was given the following structure: the Central Department under a colonel maintained personnel records, prepared data for the promotion board, supervised preparation of lists of men eligible for the draft, and oversaw the Military Press publications; the Department of War, under a brigadier general, was the command center of the army and was divided into six divisions—the first handled the business of the high command and the troops in general; the second, third, fourth, and fifth supervised the infantry, cavalry, artillery, and engineers respectively; and the sixth managed the health and veterinary services; the Department of Administration, headed by a colonel, was the quartermaster service.[109] Moreover, an attempt to lessen unit isolation and to increase effectiveness by creating five strategic brigades and thirteen regional inspectorates only complicated matters. The brigades—two in Rio Grande do Sul and one each in Paraná-Santa Catarina, Rio de Janeiro, and Mato Grosso—were directly under the war ministry, whereas other units in the thirteen regions were subject to the local inspectors-general. This was especially a problem in Rio Grande (Twelfth Region) and Rio de Janeiro (Ninth Region), where the duality of command resulted in conflicting instructions even regarding such small details as the proper uniform of the day.[110]

Probably the most durable of Hermes' creations was Vila Militar, located at Deodoro, about ten miles from Rio proper. Reviving Mallet's notion of concentrating scattered army units, Hermes proposed construction of specially designed posts to replace the haphazard collection of barracks then in use. Specifically, his intention was to quarter each strategic brigade on its own base. Rio would receive its vila militar first, which would serve as a model for others to be built around the country. Each regiment had its own barracks, offices, infirmary, and shops, and individual houses were provided for officers and sergeants. They were so well designed and constructed that they are still in use. Unfortunately, lack of government revenue made it impossible until after World War I to carry the construction program beyond Rio.

Foreign Military Instruction

Foreign Minister Rio Branco encouraged Hermes' reorganization efforts because he feared that Argentine Foreign Minister Estanislau S. Zeballos's hostility toward Brazil might lead to war. He arranged for Kaiser Wilhelm II to invite Hermes and General Luis Mendes de Morais, then commander of the Fourth Military District (Rio), to attend German army maneuvers in 1908. The invitation and the trip netted considerable publicity for Hermes and enhanced his popularity. The Germans wined and dined the Brazilians, gave them a flight over Frankfurt in a military dirigible, staged a parade in Hermes' honor, and impressed them with maneuvers in Alsace-Lorraine. The Brazilian generals had the benefit of the explanations of Captain Constantino Deschamps Cavalcante, one of the officers Minister of War Argollo had sent to Germany for training in 1906. Hermes negotiated with Germany to send a mission to Brazil to oversee the army's reorganization.[111]

The Germans had gained a considerable advantage in their competition with the French for influence in the Brazilian army. In 1909 a second contingent of six officers went to serve two years in German regiments, and Krupp solidified its position as supplier of artillery. By the time the third contingent of twenty-two officers sailed in 1910, the Germans had selected the members of the mission to go to Brazil and could look forward to working with a dedicated nucleus of German-trained officers. Arrangements for the German mission were so far advanced that Lieutenant Amaro de Azambuja Villanova, who had completed his training with the 1909 group, was ordered to remain in Germany as aide to the mission's designated chief.[112]

That the German mission never became a reality puzzled the officers sent to Germany, such as Estevão Leitão de Carvalho, and subsequent students of Brazilian history. It was primarily the victim of French influence with the Brazilian elite and of skillful French diplomacy. The paulistas had contracted a French military mission in 1906 to turn São Paulo's *Força Pública* into a small army to protect the state against federal intervention. Key paulista politicians, such as Governor Jorge Tibiriçá and Rodolfo Miranda, were pro-French. Tibiriçá, who led São Paulo twice, in 1890–91 and 1904–8, and did more than any other man to shape the state's future, had been born in Paris to a French mother and a paulista aristocrat and had lived in both France and Germany. He is credited with hiring the French trainers for the state police and with interesting French banks in paulista agriculture. Miranda had studied in Paris, had been federal deputy from 1897 to 1909, had served as Nilo Peçanha's minister of agriculture in 1909–10, and had broken with the paulista political establishment to back Hermes da Fonseca in 1910. As a result, during the administrations of those two presidents he acted as a conduit for his state's interests.[113] He and Tibiriçá were two of the voices that pressured Hermes to withdraw from his commitments to Berlin. Elected president in 1910, Hermes was faced with considerable political turmoil, and withdrawal from the German arrangements could earn some political capital in São Paulo, most of whose leaders had backed Senator Rui Barbosa. Moreover, the French, British, and Americans were unhappy about the seeming German success. At stake was not only their prestige but arms sales, which each of the foreign powers related to increased trade with Brazil.

For example, the American military attaché, Capt. LeVert Coleman, and Ambassador Edwin V. Morgan worked to secure a lucrative contract for Bethlehem Steel to supply the guns for Brazil's planned new coastal defenses, only to have it go to Germany's Krupp. American officials complained that both the English and the Germans were using bribery to influence the study commissions, whose officers showed a lively interest in such graft, and the newspapers, whose journalists produced articles criticizing the American products and representatives. At stake were future profits and political influence.[114]

The French contract with the paulista Força Pública was to expire in 1910, and the French feared that Hermes, whom they regarded as pro-German, would somehow prevent the paulistas from renewing the agreement. They brought pressure on their Brazilian allies by saying that even if it were renewed, they could not serve in the same country with the Germans. They also invited Hermes to France so that he could see for himself that the French army had been rebuilt and was not shot through with anarchist indiscipline as German propaganda said. The French outdid the Germans in their efforts to win Hermes to their side. In addition to visits to military units, schools, and arms factories, he was presented to intellectuals such as Madame Curie and Anatole France, honored by a reception at the Sorbonne, and received by the president of France. Moreover, the French general staff orchestrated a clever, eulogistic press campaign, with the collaboration of one of the marshal's entourage, Major Alfredo Oscar Fleury de Barros, designed to appeal to Hermes' self-esteem. For example, French officers had a short passage describing Hermes appear in the Parisian newspaper *Le Matin* on August 23, 1910, in which his silhouette on horseback was said to recall that of Napoleon I.[115] Thanks to Major Fleury de Barros's translations and rewriting, such articles appeared almost simultaneously in Brazilian newspapers. He did not miss opportunities to insert favorable comments on the French army, arms industry, and culture.[116] Aside from the favorable comments Major Fleury de Barros undoubtedly whispered in his ear, Hermes had at his side the French military attaché to Rio de Janeiro, Captain Salats, who was adept at arranging things to make the best impression.[117]

Hermes was won over. Before departing France he released a statement denying ever having been a Germanophile: "Far from being a blind admirer of Germany, my personal formation is French: I have read your military authors and it was in them that I searched for teachings when as Minister of War I began to reorganize the Brazilian army." Furthermore, he said, "the character of the Brazilian people and the Brazilian soldier are closer to that of the French people and soldier than to any other people and any other soldier."[118] Obviously, he could not suddenly switch to the French without harming relations with Germany, so he followed the tact that the French had been developing among their allies in the Brazilian officer corps: Brazil would receive no foreign mission; its own officers were good enough to train its forces.[119] But the whole affair needs further study because it must have caused a tremendous battle in the government.

In May 1910 President Nilo Peçanha, who had been Afonso Pena's vice president and had succeeded him when Pena died in June 1909, reported to the Congress that he favored bringing "foreign instructors" to Brazil as an economy measure. Although the training in Germany had been valuable, it was "a practice which caused appreciable outlays from the public coffers." He thought that on balance it would be best to dispense with sending so many officers abroad.[120] Between May and August the scales tipped away from Germany and toward France. The process of policy change was part of the hidden but fierce struggle between the two European powers for military influence in Brazil.[121]

The French were determined that their years of work with the paulista troops and of cultivating the elite would not go for naught. Down to World War I they continued to seek a contract to provide a training mission. They kept up a constant propaganda campaign via word of mouth and in the Brazilian press favorable to France and denigrating Germany. The propaganda sought to exploit unpleasant incidents involving the German mission in Turkey, including one in which a Turkish soldier killed a German officer who had struck him. The Germans were painted as racists, as in the case of an officer who demanded extra pay for training Negro troops.[122]

The French military's efforts to sway the Brazilian elite to support their cause can be seen in French general staff reports. It was a matter of French policy to inculcate the Brazilian elite, as they had Marshal Hermes, with "the profound conviction that the French Army is still the Model Army."[123] In October 1911, while Senator Antônio Azeredo of Mato Grosso, who served as President Hermes da Fonseca's spokesman in the Senate, and who had close, clientelistic ties with paulista politicians,[124] visited Paris, French officers, including the minister of war, met with him repeatedly, "with the intention of making him the advocate of a French Military Mission to Rio." In the course of the conversations the French war minister, M. Messimy, formally offered to send a mission. The senator noted that the Congress would discuss the mission question in November and that although it would be a hard battle, he guaranteed that either the mission would be French or that there would be none at all. He promised that four newspapers would back the French—*O Malho* and *A Tribuna,* which he owned, and *O Pais* and *Jornal do Comercio,* in which he had interests.

The French general staff officers developed a list of arguments that they suggested the senator use:

1. German prestige was in decline after the Moroccan crisis;
2. With a German mission Brazil ran the risk of suffering humiliations and being turned into a protectorate, like Turkey;
3. German protection had proven worthless to the Turks;
4. Germany was seeking supply posts for its fleet, and the smallest incident with a German mission would be used as a pretext to seize a base in the southern states;
5. Brazil needed French money for development, and a German mission would cut off such investments;
6. The Brazilian Latin temperament was closer to the French than the German;
7. Strength was on the Franco-British side in the European balance of power rather than the German;
8. The Triple Alliance was dead, and on the horizon was a quadruple alliance of France-England-Italy-Russia;
9. Therefore, it was in Brazil's interest to join the French-British side, matching its affinities with its interests.[125]

The French and their Brazilian allies, such as Azeredo, prevented a German mission but lacked the strength to impose a French one. The Brazilian Congress took up the matter in October 1911. It was "generally understood" that Hermes had promised the German emperor the award of both army and naval mission contracts. And so in addition to the French and the paulistas, the Americans and the English expressed their unhappiness with an outcome that would result in an increase in Germany's already "powerful commercial prestige." The issue divided the officer corps and the government. Some senior officers, including the war minister and general staff personnel, opposed any foreign mission because they were jealous of their authority and did not want to appear less than competent in their profession. There was so much heat on Hermes that it was less costly to stand against the pro-German position of his foreign minister, Rio Branco, and to refuse to honor the commitments made to Berlin or even to send more officers to join those completing their training in Germany. But to back out of the agreements, the government reportedly had to pay Germany a large indemnity. It is altogether possible that to withdraw from the commitment to hire a German military mission, the Hermes administration promised to buy its artillery and other military goods from German suppliers. At any rate, in December 1912 and January 1913 the American military attaché complained that Hermes was "too much entangled with pledges to Germany" and was afraid to purchase military supplies from other sources.[126] The Brazilians may well have felt that they had to be careful with the Germans, because in the process of obtaining bids from Krupp for the country's coastal defenses they had delivered plans of their coastal forts to the Germans, who, in turn may have used some subtle threats of military retaliation. The outbreak of war in August 1914 and Brazil's entry against Germany in 1917 ended the matter. Azeredo's promise that it would be the French or no one was fulfilled. The question of a foreign military mission would lie in abeyance until the end of World War I.

The Army of 1911

Even though the question of foreign advisers had been put aside, the army by 1911 showed signs of change. There were indications that the idea that the army had to modernize and that it should be a force for the modernization of Brazil appealed to a core of officers. Despite the somewhat indifferent success of the educational reform of 1905, the military students at the *Escola de Guerra* in Porto Alegre embraced the idea that the army could be improved only if the troops were, so they supported obligatory military service and better training. Moreover, they understood that change would not occur by itself; they had to commit themselves. In a departure from the behavior of their predecessors, nearly half of the *aspirantes* (as military school graduates were now called) of the class of 1909 volunteered for troop duty. In mid-1910, while Hermes was in France, and while the last group of officers was getting settled in Germany, other officers in Porto Alegre published the first issue of *Revista dos Militares*. It carried a statement explaining its purpose that captured the current mood: "As it is public knowledge that shortly we will have foreign instructors, it seemed the proper moment for us to call our comrades' attention to the technical aspects of their respective arms, *so that we won't cut a poor figure before the foreigner.*"[127] If national security motivated generals, perhaps personal pride would stimulate the lower ranks!

As we have seen, this and other reform proposals of the decade never left the drawing board or were only partially enacted. Internal discipline was difficult to maintain as political factions whispered around the barracks' gates seeking to draw officers into partisan struggles. As in the interference of the state of São Paulo and its French allies, elements of the Brazilian elite and foreign interests interfered with plans to professionalize the officer corps. The army did not have enough institutional freedom to select its own models; it had to function within the political and international framework of the dominant elites. Because it could not achieve autonomy even in such technical matters as training, its reform-minded officers grew frustrated and impatient for change. As a result, some of the junior officers of this decade would later in their careers become involved in revolutionary activities.

In 1911 the army now had its man in the presidency, and, unhappily for its professionalization, it became embroiled in the republican elite's struggle with the resurgent regional oligarchies for control of the state governments. An orgy of intervention, called the salvationist movement, would discredit the army in many Brazilians' eyes and retarded the drive toward obligatory service. The decade of the 1910s opened with a new military school at Realengo in the State of Rio de Janeiro. And shortly, the army would once again find itself being used as an instrument of repression, this time in the interior of Santa Catarina.

CHAPTER 3

Advance of Sabers

From North to South you saw the advance of sabers on
the [governors'] palaces.
—Afonso Arinos de Melo Franco, *Um estadista da república*

We have no land rights[;] everything is for the peoples of
Oropa [Europe]. . . . The government of the Republic
drives out the Brazilian Sons from the lands that belong to
the nation and sells [them] to the foreigner, we now are
disposed to make prevail our right.
—Herculano Teixeira d'Assumpção,
   A Campanha do Contestado

The Constitution of 1891 assigned internal and external defense missions to
the army. Defense against foreign attack was easy to understand, but what
was internal defense; defense of what and against whom? The republic against
the monarchists? The officer corps believed that the army had established
the republic and consequently had the responsibility to protect it. But what
constituted the republic? Even that had changed since Deodoro and Floriano. By the 1910s the "politics of the governors" had facilitated the return
to power in many states of families who had been prominent in the imperial era. Their goals did not include restoration of the monarchy. Monarchists
made their peace with the new regime after Pedro II's death (December 5,
1891). The regional or state oligarchies were much more focused on the
benefits of local control than on national government; indeed, their lack of
such concern came to worry officers committed to keeping the Pátria intact. Nationally, São Paulo and Minas Gerais dominated the economic and
political scenes, and Rio Grande do Sul's Senator José Gomes Pinheiro
Machado acted as political power broker. The larger states maintained sizable militarized police forces capable of holding at bay, if not directly challenging, the national army. In fact, from 1906 to 1914 São Paulo employed

French army officers to train its troops. At least on paper each state had its National Guard units, whose officers were drawn from the local political elite and whose soldiers, where they actually existed, were the hangers-on of the local bosses. Their purpose was to buttress the elite's control. It was significant that nationally the justice ministry, rather than the war ministry, "supervised" the guard. Moreover, and perhaps closer to reality, in times of crisis the local elites would call together their peons and/or their enforcers, hired gunslingers called *capangas,* into "patriotic battalions." The amount of fire power available to local and state politicians allowed them to impose their will on their subordinates and opponents and to defend themselves against the national army. Brazil's military system left the army with a secondary or backup role in internal defense. Whatever situation the state or local forces could not handle fell to the army. It irritated officers that many of the situations into which the army was summoned were the result of local political squabbles in which one side or the other called on the Rio government for help. The number of local and state-level "civil" wars that flared up and burned out throughout Brazil during the Old Republic is startling given the apparent stability of the national government. Such conflicts drained human energy, lives, and wealth into unproductive power struggles. Idealistic officers felt misused in roles they saw as beneath their dignity, whereas politically ambitious ones saw opportunities for advancement.

The Hermes Presidency

The 1910 presidential succession forcefully brought the military and the question of what role officers were to play in national affairs to the foreground. It also exposed the weakness of the "politics of the governors," namely that the system depended on an interstate and intrastate consensus among politicians and oligarchs and no sure mechanism to deal with a lack of agreement. In 1910 the political elites of São Paulo and Minas Gerais disagreed over the choice of president, leading to a situation in which the officer corps, Minas Gerais, and Rio Grande do Sul backed the candidacy of Minister of War Hermes da Fonseca, while the São Paulo establishment supported Bahian senator Rui Barbosa. The senator raised the specter of militarism and of Brazil's credit being shaken if foreign bankers equated the country with military-dominated Spanish-America. Marshal Hermes, asserting that military men enjoyed full citizenship (although he was not a registered voter) and had the right to stand for public office, resigned as war minister to run for the presidency. The tension and public uproar related to these events contributed, it was said, to the death of disillusioned, demoralized President Afonso Pena, who had expected the marshal's steadfast loyalty and support for his chosen replacement, Deputy David Campista of Minas

Gerais. The president's immediate successor, Vice President Nilo Peçanha of Rio de Janeiro, threw the full weight of executive power behind Hermes. The immensely popular Rui Barbosa used his reputation as a historic republican, who had served as Deodoro's finance minister and as Brazil's spokesman at the Second Hague Conference (1907), to project the image of a civilian patriot who questioned the wisdom of turning the presidency over to a general. But as José Murilo de Carvalho has commented, Rui raised the wrong issue by charging "militarism." Hermes' candidacy came out of the failure of the "politics of the governors," not out of an army desire to intervene in the political system. In fact, the oligarchies of Minas and Rio Grande were using Hermes to shield their interests. Curiously, Hermes' personal positions were more in line with Rui's than those of his sponsor, Pinheiro Machado. Hermes agreed with Rui's criticism of the political system and the state oligarchies; indeed, some of the later interventions to overturn them were truly reformist. Hermes was the first candidate to mention workers in his speeches and as president had housing built for workers in Rio and sponsored the Fourth Brazilian Workers Congress in 1912. Note, too, that he invited Rui to join his government. By many accounts Rui won the actual voting, but, of course, the federal government and its allies in the states controlled the ballot boxes. Hermes' victory returned the military to the political stage and created an enduring impression that the military actions of the following years had the backing of the president and the army institution, when in fact they were often actions taken by local commanders with little or no prior consultation with central authorities. Rui's speeches condemning political saber rattling contributed to increased animosity between officers and the state political leaders allied with Pinheiro Machado.[1]

Hermes da Fonseca was not naturally decisive or aggressive, and he probably did not foresee the violence that his presidency would unleash, but once in the Catete Palace he was swept along by events. He presided over the army's repression of the sailors' rebellion of 1910, over the series of interventions that made up the "salvationist" movement, and over the early phases of crushing the popular uprising in the Contestado, a region disputed with Argentina, until arbitration awarded it to Brazil in 1895, and thereafter quarreled over by the states of Santa Catarina and Paraná. The latter movements illustrate the two types of revolutions that, applying Anthony F. C. Wallace's typology, could be labeled the "politics of the appetites" and the "politics of identity." The first label can describe neatly the military salvationists, who wanted to seize power in essentially intact state-level political systems in order to gain influence and power. The second can be applied to the Contestado, which experienced a popular revitalization movement whose underlying motive force was the pursuit of a new and better identity. Collectively the Contestado rebels were seeking salvation in an earthly as well as a heavenly sense.[2]

Hermes's interests were somewhat more mundane. The Constitution did not require him to resign his officer's commission or to retire from the service in order to become president, and he saw no need to project a civilian facade. From 1910 through 1914 he was carried on the list of active officers as marshal, with his assignment reading "President of the Republic." Indeed, one of his ministers of war referred to him in official correspondence as the "*Sr. Marechal presidente.*"[3] He reportedly moved about the capital city, turned out in his dress uniform, in a fancy open carriage pulled by plumed, prancing horses and accompanied by a showy escort of mounted guardsmen.

Hermes set the tone. By 1912 seven senators, six deputies, three governors, and the mayor of the Federal District were active list officers ranging in rank from lieutenant colonel to major general. Not only did most of these men maintain their merit numbers relative to other officers of equal rank, but, instead of being placed in a detached or extended leave category, they also continued to receive promotions. That military service and political position were equal in the eyes of the promotions committee is apparent from an examination of the upward mobility of officers from 1912 to 1914.

In 1912 the third, fourth, and fifth ranked of the eight major generals were José de Sigueira Menezes, governor of Sergipe; José Caetano de Faria, chief of the general staff; and Emygdio Dantas Barreto, governor of Pernambuco. On the 1914 list they appeared in first, second, and third places respectively. Federal District mayor Brigadier General Bento Manoel Ribeiro Carneiro Monteiro's case was even more striking. In 1912 he was number seven (A) on the brigadier list; by the time the 1914 list was published he had leapfrogged seven officers to the eighth position on the major general list. It is significant that some of the men passed over were opposed to military involvement in politics.

Generals were not the only ones who benefited. Colonel Felipe Schmidt, senator from, and later governor (1915) of, Santa Catarina, and Colonel Gabriel Salgado dos Santos, senator from Amazonas, held the ninth and fourteenth positions on the 1912 infantry colonels list. By the time the 1914 list appeared, they had moved up to the third and seventh positions. Perhaps more important were their places on the combat colonels list, which ranked them with all colonels in eligibility for promotion to general. In 1912 they were thirty-seventh and forty-third, but by 1914 they had risen to tenth and seventeenth. Lauro Severiano Müller, lieutenant colonel of engineers, was a senator from Santa Catarina in 1911 and was promoted to full colonel after taking over as Hermes' foreign minister in early 1912. One last example, Eduardo Arthur Socrates, a lieutenant colonel of infantry, was promoted to colonel, for "meritorious service," while federal deputy from Goiás. It seems that these men drew double pay as officers and as deputies, senators, or governors. Colonel Socrates, for example, in addition to being a deputy, was listed

in 1912 as the fiscal (second-ranked officer) of the Fourteenth Infantry Regiment in Aquidauana, Mato Grosso, and in 1914 he was listed with the Fifty-
first Battalion in São João del Rei, Minas Gerais. It was common for officers to be assigned to a particular unit on a more or less permanent basis
while actually serving elsewhere. Although the practice had some justification in the context of army administration, however, it was stretching the
point to apply it to active politicians. All this provides explanation for
Afonso Arinas de Melo Franco's observation that the army had become the
"new dominant political party."[4] Whether it was dominant or not, certainly
the army provided a platform from which a number of officers launched
themselves into politics. Officer involvement in national political and administrative affairs has a long history in Brazil, and the definition of the officer's potential roles in society has long been open ended. If this history
had been clearer at the time of the military seizure of power in 1964, that
event and the subsequent twenty-one years of military government could
have been interpreted more exactly. Indeed, viewed from the perspective
offered in this and subsequent chapters, the "military republic" of 1964–85
appears as the logical outcome of the history of the Brazilian army.[5]

Be that as it may, Hermes' government seemed star-crossed from the outset. Between his selection and his taking office he went to Europe on the
navy's new British-built dreadnought *São Paulo*. The ship was one of the
largest and most modern on the high seas and represented the restoration of
the Brazilian navy from the depths into which it had sunk in the civil war
of 1893–95. On October 3, 1910, during a stopover at Lisbon, while Hermes
entertained King Manuel II at an onboard banquet, Portuguese republicans
began the revolution that overthrew the Bragança monarchy. From the
decks of the *São Paulo,* Brazilian sailors watched Portuguese vessels shell the
royal palace. This successful challenge to authority and to the status quo in
Portugal must have impressed them. Discipline in the navy was abominable,
even though whippings had been banned by the Imperial Constitution of
1824, and by the republic's third decree on November 16, 1889, the lash was
still common. Naval regulations listed numbers such as ten, fifteen, or twenty-
five for various offenses, but two hundred to three hundred were reported
in various cases. A few years before this rebellion, on a cruise to Chile, the
288 seamen of the cruiser *Bahia* committed 911 disciplinary infractions, the
lash being applied liberally. That most officers were white and the sailors
black kept images of master and slave vivid. As a protest note to the commander of one vessel signed by the "Black Hand" put it, "No one is the
officers' slave so enough of the lash." There had been a number of mutinies
in protest. But the naval officers could not conceive of less brutal and more
effective ways of keeping their crews in line.[6]

Hermes took office in Rio on November 15, and on the twenty-second sailors on the twin dreadnoughts *São Paulo* and *Minas Gerais,* and on some smaller vessels, rebelled, threatening to bombard the capital unless their demands for better treatment were met. Shortly before this occurred a sailor had been unmercifully given 250 lashes with the flesh-tearing cat-o'-nine-tails, a punishment that continued even after he had lapsed into unconsciousness! Two of the most modern warships on the high seas were being run with eighteenth-century discipline. Brazil was presenting a facade of modernity with its massive warships, whose boilers and engines were kept running by contracted foreigners. The navy was a classic example of the expression "para ingles ver [for the English to see]." In its first days the new government was compelled to give in to rebellious forces and to grant an amnesty to boot. Despite Hermes' good intentions, his government was born in an atmosphere of tension and violence that would characterize the following years.[7]

The Salvationist Movement

The drama of the salvationist movement should be seen against a backdrop of political ambition, indiscipline, and an expanding definition of the military profession. A small incident during Hermes' inaugural procession gives some idea of the independent mindedness of officers. As the car bearing the new president moved into line, Lt. Col. Joaquim Ignacio Baptista Cardoso motioned his Thirteenth Cavalry Regiment forward to form an honor guard around it. Suddenly an arrogant voice boomed from the second vehicle: "Colonel! Pull back the regiment, don't go in front of my car!" It was the new minister of war, General Emygdio Dantas Barreto. Without perceptible indication that he had heard what was clearly audible to bystanders, the colonel raised his saber in the signal to trot and left the general in the regiment's dust.[8] Although in most organizations such behavior would not be the way to get ahead, the lieutenant colonel was promoted to colonel for merit in 1912 and would eventually make general.[9]

The discipline system was capricious. Some of the rebel sailors of 1910 who got caught up in a second, but quickly snuffed out, rebellion at Rio's Ilha das Cobras naval base were joined with bums and prostitutes swept off the city's streets and shipped to the Acre in the hold of the SS *Satélite.* En route eleven of the sailors were shot and thrown into the sea. However, in 1912 Manuel Gregorio do Nascimento, who had led the revolt on the *São Paulo,* approached Hermes at the entrance to the Catete Palace, asking help in finding a job. He had been amnestied, thrown out of the navy, and unemployed ever since. Hermes responded, "Come work here with us in the Palace. We will arrange a spot for you." The former rebel became a pantryman in the presidential palace![10] Such diversity of treatment served to encourage indiscipline. Rebels might well succeed, and the uncertain price of failure was not a sufficient deterrent.

Poor discipline is usually a symptom of low morale and shaky self-esteem, as well as a weak command structure, and given the status of the army, improvements were easier to plan than to put into effect. Despite the reforms of the previous decade the army was severely understrength. Congress continued to delay legislation that would start obligatory military service, and there simply were not enough volunteers to fill the ranks. The situation of two units in Rio Pardo, Rio Grande do Sul, can serve as examples of how badly understrength the army was. The Ninth Infantry Regiment had 90 soldiers and 2 officers instead of the regulation 590 men and 49 officers; and its companion unit, the Fourth Engineer Battalion, had 50 soldiers under 3 officers rather than the stipulated 235 soldiers and 18 officers! The battalion was cut even more when its commander took sick leave and twenty soldiers were ordered to Rio because of the sailors' revolt. In late 1910 that was the condition in which Captain Alfredo Malan d'Angrogne found the Fourth when he reported for duty. He noted his dismal reaction in a letter to a friend: "how much misery, shame and sadness I encountered. . . . The battalion has no money in the strong-box, no source of revenue, no soldier's mess, no vehicles, no animals." Moreover, it and the Ninth Regiment were quartered in the local hospital instead of in proper barracks. Needless to say, such units were not operational.[11]

Professional frustration and political ambition joined to produce the complicated series of events that made up the salvationist movement. Hermes da Fonseca had come to office with the combined, and somewhat contradictory, support of representatives of the dominant oligarchies of Minas Gerais, Rio Grande do Sul, Pernambuco, Pará, and others, as well as that of the opposing oligarchies of the various states. He also had the backing of key army officers, some with swelling political ambitions. As a result, some supporters expected him to preserve the status quo, whereas others expected change. But the latter did not want structural change, or honest electoral methods, or abolition of the power of rural "colonels." They merely wanted power. It was a classic case of the outs wanting in. The only demands for actual social change would come from the people of the Contestado and would be answered with fire and steel.

In late 1911 and early 1912 elections of state governments found Hermes attempting to fulfill his commitments. There is reason to think that he was not always enthusiastic about using the army as a political instrument. In 1910, even before he took office, some officers had joined with civilian politicians to force shifts in political control in Amazonas and Rio de Janeiro. Now in Sergipe, Pernambuco, Alagoas, Pará, Piauí, Bahia, Rio Grande do

Norte, and Ceará, the Hermes government backed the outs as long as they chose candidates, mostly military officers, who had its blessing. In Alagoas, Rio Grande do Norte, and Bahia relatives of Hermes were involved. The disorderly process of substituting one oligarchic alliance with another often involved the direct use of military force. In some cases the clash between the military and the state oligarchies was clearly delineated; in others it was blurry. The Hermes government, in effect, sponsored coups d'etat against the state governments. In the case of Pernambuco federal troops joined the opposition and street people *(populares)* in attacking the state police barracks and in causing such disorders that the governor had to resign in favor of General Emygdio Dantas Barreto, minister of war.

The case of Bahia was even worse. There the regional commander, Brigadier General José Sotero de Menezes, seeing himself with 882 men facing 5,000 state police and *jagunços,* decided to enforce a habeas corpus in favor of the opposition by bombarding the governor's palace, state police barracks, and other public buildings. He claimed to have received authorization in a telegram from Rio signed vaguely "M. Fonseca." General Antonio Adolpho de Fontoura Mena Barreto, who succeeded Dantas Barreto as minister of war, telegraphed: "Congratulate illustrious comrade for considered, energetic action."[12]

Hermes was less pleased. He sent a trusted general to investigate, ordered the deposed governor reimposed, and recalled General Sotero de Menezes to Rio de Janeiro. Even so, in the end the opposition took over the Bahian government. It tells much about the climate of opinion in the army that, on his arrival in Rio, Sotero de Menezes received a festive reception from such figures as Colonel Fernando Setembrino de Carvalho, chief of the minister of war's personal staff. Obviously enjoying strong backing, the general went so far as to deny that there had been a "bombardment." It was "a lie" *(balela),* he asserted. Being badly outnumbered, he said, he did what any wise tactician would do; he had a "few grenades" fired at the heaviest concentrations of "police and *jagunços*" to disperse them. It was a libel, he declared, that the bombardment caused fires.[13]

Be that as it may, Sotero de Menezes had strong protectors, such as Minister of War Mena Barreto, so Hermes could do little except speed his retirement. However, the minister of war soon overreached himself. In trying to secure the governorship of Rio Grande do Sul for himself, he caused a cabinet crisis that resulted in his forced resignation. But before this occurred at the end of March 1912, the political scene suffered renewed agitation.

In December 1911 federal troops in São Paulo and Rio de Janeiro went on alert in preparation for intervention in São Paulo. Mena Barreto was mentioned as a possible choice for interventor. The paulistas prepared to repel invasion by calling up civilian Patriotic Battalions in major towns and mobilizing the French-trained *Força Pública*. Rather than risk a fight with such strong adversaries, Hermes made an agreement with the governor of São Paulo that left in paulista hands control of the state's politics. However, there were other problems further south, where Mena Barreto's continued mixing in Rio Grandense politics brought him into conflict with Pinheiro Machado, senator from the gaúcho state and kingmaker of the era. The salvationists were deposing the senator's allies in the north, and now the threat was to his own political base. He and his colleagues urged Hermes to condemn any military intervention and to lessen the possibility by removing officers who mixed in politics from federal garrisons throughout the country, that is, those personally loyal to the war minister. Mena Barreto gathered the generals in the war ministry and warned Hermes to keep Pinheiro at arm's length.[14]

On March 29 the test of wills reached a peak at a tempestuous cabinet meeting during which several ministers accused Mena Barreto of interfering in state politics, especially in Rio Grande, to the point of fomenting civil war. Shouts and finally resignations flew about the room, but when the dust cleared Hermes accepted only that of the war minister. Next day the commander of the Ninth Military Region (Federal District), Major General Vespasiano Gonçalves de Albuquerque e Silva, moved into the minister's office to become the third man to occupy it in less than a year and four months. The turbulence at the top undoubtedly furthered the careers of lower-ranked officers, who moved upward into more important positions under the sponsorship of their patron generals. It certainly had an effect on the retirement of senior officers. Between November 1910 and December 1913 at least one hundred colonels and generals were retired, of whom fifty-nine left the active army between Hermes' inaugural and Menna Barreto's departure in 1912.[15] Hermes' struggle to gain control of the army via retirements has been an unnoticed aspect of the salvationist era.

But those pressed into retirement were not simply thrown out into the street. Care was taken to tie their personal interests to the stability of the regime via ample benefits. If they had thirty to thirty-five years of service, they received the full pay of their highest rank and the honors of a brevet promotion to the next highest rank. If they had thirty-five to forty years they were promoted to the next rank at the appropriate pay. This had been the practice since the beginning of the nineteenth century. However, in these years it functioned differently and with clear indications of favoritism. In 1912 and 1913 some lieutenant colonels were retired as brevet or full brigadier generals, whereas some colonels were awarded brevets of major general, others were made marshals, and some brigadiers were breveted marshal, as others were given full marshal rank. Military activist, leader of the

1904 rebellion, and federal senator, Colonel Lauro Sodré, who had not been on active duty in many years, was finally separated as a brigadier general, as were military politicians from Ceará, Minas Gerais, and Piauí. The bombardier of Bahia, Brigadier General Sotero do Menezes, was breveted marshal. Retirement was used both to rid the army of those who were politically undesirable and to co-opt them with honorific and financial benefits into tacit cooperation (see Table 3.1).[16]

TABLE 3.1.

Retirement Promotions, 1912–1913

Retired Rank	Regular Rank (Branch) Name	Retirement Date
Bvt. Brig. Gen.	Lt. Col. (Cav) Frederico Augusto Falção da Frota	1/2/1913
	Lt. Col. (Inf) Manoel Ignacio Domingues	2/21/1912
Brig. Gen.	Lt. Col. (Inf) Alcibiades Cabral	11/20/1913
	Lt. Col. (Inf) Antonio Augusto da Cunha	11/5/1913
	Lt.Col. (Inf) Antonio Froes de Castro Menezes	5/8/1913
	Lt.Col. (Inf) Aristides de Oliveira Goulart	7/10/1912
	Lt. Col. (Inf) Augusto Fabricio Ferreira de Mattos	11/13/1912
	Lt. Col. (Inf) João Nabuco	12/11/1912
	Lt. Col. (Inf) José Ferreira Maciel de Miranda	9/4/1912
	Col. (Inf) João d'Avila França	1/22/1913
	Col. (Inf) Lauro Sodre (Senator/Federal District)	5/21/1913
Bvt. General of Division	Col. (Inf) Antonio Ignacio de Albuquerque Xavier	4/6/1912
	Col. (Art) João Maria de Paiva	12/18/1912
	Col. (Eng) Caetano Manoel de Faria e Albuquerque	9/10/1913
General of Division	Brig. Gen. Innocencio Serzedello Correa	5/2/1912
Bvt. Marshal	Col. (Art) João Candido Jacques	12/11/1912
	Col. (Art) José Freire Bezerril Fontenelle (Federal Deputy/Ceará)	12/11/1912
	Col. (Inf) Rodolpho Gustavo da Paixão (Federal Deputy/Minas Gerais)	4/26/1913
	Brig. Gen. José Sotero de Menezes	10/23/1913
	Brig. Gen. Julio Fernandes de Almeida	7/16/1913
	Brig. Gen. Vicente Osorio de Paiva	12/7/1912
Marshal	Brig. Gen. Alfredo Barbosa	4/20/1912
	Bvt. Gen. Div Pedro Paulo da Fonseca Galvão	12/7/1912
	Gen. Div. Antonio Adolpho da Fontoura Menna Barreto	4/10/1912
	Gen. Div. Antonio Vicente Ribeiro Guimarães	12/3/1912
	Gen. Div. Luiz Antonio de Medeiros	12/24/1912
	Gen. Div. Firmino Pires Ferreira (Senator/Piauí)	1/6/1913

With the retirement of Mena Barreto the tide began to turn away from military intervention aimed at replacing the dominant oligarchies toward neutrality or preserving the status quo. It is true, as Edgard Carone has written, that at that moment the majority of the northern states were in the hands of army officers, but the movement had peaked.[17]

To illustrate how the salvationist process worked and how the oligarchies responded, we will look at the very different cases of Minas Gerais, which avoided intervention, and Ceará, which suffered one but in doing so ended the movement.

Minas Avoided Intervention: Incident in Belo Horizonte

As the most populous state, with the largest congressional delegation, and with a landlocked, mountainous geography, Minas Gerais played a special role in the Brazilian federation. Its strong agricultural and mining economy gave it a degree of independence that was symbolized by the building of its new capital, Belo Horizonte, in 1893–97. Minas, generally regarded as conservative, proudly produced Brazil's first planned modern city. As we saw above, São Paulo and Rio Grande had held off the military saviors through posturing and political maneuver. Minas Gerais obtained the same result in a different fashion. It was an incident in Belo Horizonte involving the Ninth Independent Light-Infantry Company that brought the question of the mineral state's relationship with the federal army, and hence with the government in Rio, to a head. The Ninth had arrived in 1909, the first federal unit to be assigned to the new *mineiro* capital. During its first three years the company had gotten on well with the people of Belo Horizonte. In November 1909 it staged showy maneuvers that included local volunteers. Wenceslau Braz, who was then governor and who would succeed Hermes as president, was moved to say that the Ninth was convincing even "the most reluctant spirits" of the wisdom of Hermes' army reorganization and was giving Minas the opportunity to prove that it had "neither aversion to the uniform nor fear of the sword." He called the army the mainstay of the republic and the defender of "national integrity." People filled the street in front of the barracks, shouting *vivas,* and while a band played the national anthem, women and young girls draped the national flag with flowers. At night animated dances were held in the barracks. When the sailors rebelled in November 1910, the Ninth and civilian Tiro 52 embarked together in a special train for Niterói with Belo Horizonte's cheers ringing in their ears.

In May 1912 this happy relationship ended abruptly. On the twenty-fifth an altercation between a soldier and a policeman *(guarda civil)* resulted in the former's death. At the hospital a doctor reportedly heard the angry company commander say that if his men sought revenge, he would not be able to stop them. The commander and the inspector general of the Eighth Military Region, Brigadier Pedro Paulo da Fonseca Galvão,[18] pressured the mineiro authorities to punish the policeman, asserting that the dead soldier could not have provoked the attack. Although some officers made efforts to calm the troops, tempers flared, and on May 28, armed with revolvers, knives, clubs, and whiplike strands of barbed wire, dozens of soldiers headed toward the police station, where the accused was being held. En route they attacked unwary policemen, whom authorities had disarmed to prevent trouble. The rampaging troops killed two policemen and wounded several others seriously. A cab driver who rushed ahead of them saved other police with timely warnings. Finally, one of the Ninth's lieutenants succeeded in placing the soldiers under arrest and herding them back to the barracks.

Belo Horizonte was in an uproar. Civilians stoned the barracks, shouting "Death to the army!" The newspapers blamed the military for the situation. The governor telegraphed Hermes, demanding that the regiment be withdrawn from his capital. After an army board of inquiry expelled the guilty soldiers from the ranks and turned them over to the state police, the regiment entrained for Niterói in the wee hours of June 4. It would be 1915, with mineiro Wenceslau Braz in the presidency, before the army would again post a unit in Belo Horizonte. Minas had preserved mastery of its own destiny and together with São Paulo and Rio Grande do Sul would continue its dominance of national politics.

The incident in Belo also adversely affected the movement for obligatory military service. Since 1908 the army had been preparing for the draft by setting up municipal registration boards that drew up lists of names from which the draftees would be selected once the Congress gave the go-ahead. By 1912 only 10 of the 178 *municípios* in Minas Gerais had such boards. Mineiros did not care much for the idea of military service. In 1908, when registration was first attempted, there were violent demonstrations. In Sacramento, two hundred women assaulted the building where registration was taking place and destroyed the records. Similar scenes took place elsewhere in the state. After the Ninth Company's rampage the number of boards fell to three in 1913 and two the next year. Only the patriotic campaign of 1916 and Brazil's entry into World War I in 1917 would reverse this trend.[19]

Ceará and the Rise of Setembrino de Carvalho

The forceful mineiro response to the incident in Belo Horizonte headed off the possibility of a salvationist movement, but in the northeastern state of Ceará it would take considerable violence to recover the state's autonomy.

Ceará was the high-water mark of the salvationist movement and an interesting case because the contending forces were clear and the lines separating them sharply drawn.[20]

The case is also important for the history of the army because it brought to the fore Colonel Fernando Setembrino de Carvalho, who would be one of the army's ranking officers for the next decade. Setembrino was thin, pointy-faced, and intense. Born in 1861, he had entered the army in his midteens, receiving the rank of alferes-alumno at the military school of Praia Vermelha in 1882. Like many of his colleagues, he was promoted at the onset of the republic, in his case to captain in 1890. An engineer officer, he participated in the civil war of 1893–95 in Rio Grande do Sul but, even so, spent ten years and nine months as a captain. He was forty when he was promoted to major in 1900 and about to turn fifty when he received his colonelcy in 1911. By then he was clearly upwardly mobile, serving as chief of the minister's personal staff from 1911 through 1914. During the turbulence produced by the coming and going of three ministers, he provided administrative continuity in the minister's office. He also used that time to solidify his friendly relationship with Major General José Caetano de Faria, who headed the general staff from 1910 to 1914 before becoming minister of war.

The army was divided as to its proper role in Ceará, but officers were involved from the first in efforts to end the Accioly family's control. Anti-Accioly forces adopted as their standard bearer a military "savior," Lt. Col. Marcos Franco Rabelo, a Cearense, who had taught at the now defunct military school in Fortaleza and whose father-in-law the Acciolys had deposed from the governorship in 1892. Rabelo's most ardent local backers were Fortaleza merchants, grown prosperous from the state's ties to the booming Amazonian economy, who resented their lack of political power and the oligarch's "nepotistic and peculatory politics."[21] By themselves they were too weak to depose Antonio Pinto Nogueira Accioly, so they formed an alliance with interested officers assuming that these men would have the army high command behind them. In July 1912 Colonel Rabelo won the governorship, but he soon found that he could not control the rich Cariri valley in the sertão, where Padre Cícero Româo Batista held sway. Moreover, after the resignation of War Minister Menna Barreto, top officers either supported Senator Pinheiro Machado, who wanted *Acciolismo* with or without the Acciolys, or favored less army involvement in partisan politics. In any case Hermes had the support of Minister of War Vespasiano de Albuquerque, Chief of Staff Caetano de Faria, and commander of the Ninth Military Region (Federal District), General Antonio Geraldo de Souza Aguiar.[22] Moreover, by October 1913 five of the eight major generals and twenty of the twenty-four brigadier generals owed their promotions to the "Marechal

Presidente."[23] The retirement of politically ambitious officers from the upper ranks made room for Hermes' men.

One of those was Setembrino de Carvalho, who Hermes promoted to brigadier general and sent to Fortaleza in February 1914 to command the combined fourth, fifth, and sixth military regions embracing Ceará, Rio Grande do Norte, Paraíba, Pernambuco, Alagoas, and Sergipe. By having a trusted officer accumulate the three regions, Hermes was seeking to strengthen his own control over the northeast and to lessen the ability of individual commanders to mix independently in local politics. Although the term was not used at the time, Setembrino acted as a viceroy for the northeast.[24] His mission was to bring peace to Ceará and to resolve the state's governmental crisis, that is to say, to remove Rabelo.[25]

Violence was fierce. The state police and allied *capangas* that Rabelo sent against Padre Cicero's stronghold at Juazeiro were repeatedly driven back; worse, the opposition was marching on Fortaleza. The rebellion, which had Pinheiro Machado's blessing, had a legal facade thanks to the rump session of the state assembly that met in Juazeiro and elected Dr. Floro Bartholomeu da Costa as head of a provisional state government.[26] However, protests in the Congress, the press, and from salvationist officers made federal government intervention difficult.

It is clear from his telegrams and final report that Setembrino was anti-Rabelo and followed the advice of both Hermes and Pinheiro Machado. In his report he depicted Rabelo as, a latter-day Brazilian version of Argentine dictator Juan Manuel de Rosas, using gangs of street toughs to terrorize opponents, especially the Accioly family, whose houses and businesses they attacked, sacked, and burned in November 1912. During 1913 the government-sponsored violence forced Rabelo's opponents to flee Fortaleza for safety. "Anarchy" and "dark crimes" enveloped Ceará in mourning. Moreover, Rabelo's administration was implicated "in a complicated tangle of illegalities." Setembrino declared that "in the capital as in the interior, the entire population cursed it, convinced that Ceará never had a government so ruinous to its prosperity" or to the rights of its citizens. The situation, he implied, justified the rebellion. With hyperbole common to such reports he described it as an uprising for "liberty."[27]

However, telegrams in Setembrino's archives reveal his own partisanship. Arriving in Fortaleza on February 18, 1914, he brought in more federal troops, disarmed the state police, and interfered in state business despite Rabelo's protests.[28] But Rabelo was not without support. Rio newspapers such as *Correio da Manhã, O Imparcial, Epoca,* and *A Norte* criticized Setembrino's mission and methods.[29] And some officers in Setembrino's command objected to his refusal to aid Rabelo against what they portrayed as an impending invasion of Fortaleza by a "horde of jagunço assassins." Twenty-eight officers sent a petition to the Military Club in Rio, asking that it declare in favor of Rabelo, and newspapers carried the text. The war ministry wired Setembrino that officers who manifested opposition would be transferred "to the south, Matto Grosso, etc.," and any critics in the noncommissioned or enlisted ranks should be thrown out of the army.[30] Colonel Rabelo also telegraphed the club, asserting that the people had put him in office and that he did not wish to see them "enslaved to the politics of Senator Pinheiro Machado."[31]

A military crisis loomed. Various salvationist officers, including some retired and unassigned active-duty generals, pressured the club directors to convene a meeting for March 4. They drew up a motion urging the garrison of Fortaleza to receive "the *jagunços* with shot" and expressing hope that Rabelo would know how to die at his post like a soldier. The minister of justice issued a statement declaring that agitators were trying to subvert the constitutional order and to undermine discipline in the armed forces. General Souza Aguiar, commander of the Rio garrison, and his subordinates drew up a competing motion that counseled officers to attend to their soldierly professional duties, to stay out of destructive politics, and to maintain public order. It called on the Military Club to instruct the Fortaleza garrison to follow legal orders. Minister of War Vespasiano d'Albuquerque and Chief of Staff Caetano de Faria backed Hermes, who personally visited barracks to hold officers in line. In the senate Rui Barbosa and others attacked the government's partiality. On the night of March 4 the Military Club directorate did not appear for the scheduled meeting, so dissidents from the "saviors" faction attempted to convene the session with retired Marshal Mena Barreto in the chair. Amidst much shouting government agents stormed in and closed the club.[32]

On March 5 Hermes declared a limited state of siege to gain control of the situation in the Federal District, Niterói, and Petrópolis. Dissident officers, including ex-minister Mena Barreto, were arrested, several newspapers and the popular Rio review *Malho* were closed, and the signatories of the Fortaleza petition were detained and sent to Rio. Newspapermen Edmundo Bittencourt of the *Correio da Manhã* (Rio) and José Eduardo de Macedo Soares of *O Imparcial* (Rio) and several federal deputies were imprisoned. Meanwhile Pinheiro Machado, cabinet members, high-ranking army and naval officers, and some deputies and senators buzzed around the Catete Palace to express their solidarity. Strong-arm methods always seem to have had their supporters. Others were less willing to prostrate themselves.[33]

Rui Barbosa fled to São Paulo, as did Macedo Soares when he managed to slip out of jail. It tells much about the extent of presidential power and the nature of the Brazilian federation in 1914 that once in São Paulo Hermes' critics were safe from his grasp! Not that he enjoyed his strongman role, when the chief of police told him of Macedo Soares's flight he reportedly exclaimed, "What a pity they all didn't escape!" Whatever his feelings, he finished all but the last two weeks of his administration under state of siege.[34]

Meanwhile, in Ceará the anti-Rabelo forces were closing on Fortaleza. At first Hermes denied Rabelo help in defending the city unless he requested federal intervention, which he refused to do because it would have meant the end of his government. Then Hermes got nervous about the possible results of turning Fortaleza into a battleground, so he ordered Setembrino to stop the invasion.[35] On March 9 Hermes imposed a state of siege and suspended constitutional guarantees in Ceará. Rabelo, who still had popular support in Fortaleza, refused to heed Hermes' repeated appeals that he step down. So on March 14 Hermes forced the issue and named Setembrino interventor.[36]

In that role Setembrino de Carvalho oversaw the reconstruction of oligarchic control. Senator Pinheiro Machado worked to have the Acciolys make peace with their former competitors. And he advised Setembrino to make use of the Accioly faction because "in the recent political storms they have been loyal, firm companions." He went so far as to suggest names for certain posts.[37] Setembrino set the date for new elections, supervised the reorganization of the *Partido Republicano Conservador* at the municipal level, and oversaw preparation of slates of candidates for state deputy and governor. He even presided over a meeting of elected deputies to work out new ground rules for the state's politics.

After managing the electoral victory of the conservative party, the imposition of the new governor and assembly, and making other political adjustments, such as appointing Padre Cicero intendant of Juazeiro, he ended the intervention and sailed for Rio de Janeiro on June 23, 1914.[38]

The intervention in Ceará was a classic case of how the Brazilian army functioned in the Old Republic to maintain local oligarchic rule. The army's internal debates revealed the fault line, which would grow deeper, between officers who favored apolitical military professionalism and those who saw the army as a political balance wheel that should maintain social order.

The Contestado: Social-Economic Causes of the Rebellion

While Ceará was being brought under control, another crisis had developed in the south. In August 1914 as world attention focused on the outbreak of war in Europe, the Brazilian army was being drawn into its largest field operations since Canudos. In the so-called Serra-Acima (upper mountain range) of Santa Catarina events since the turn of the century had led to a rebellion challenging the "colonel"-dominated social-economic-political system. Whereas the salvationist movement sought merely to replace one oligarchy with another, the Contestado rebels wanted to remake the system,

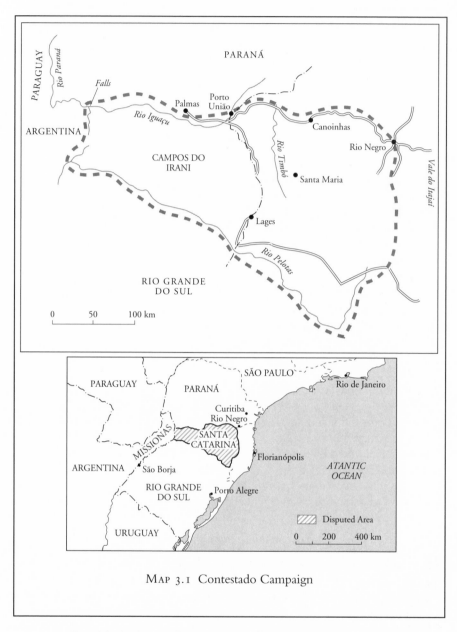

MAP 3.1 Contestado Campaign

SOURCE: From *The Army in Brazilian History*, edited by Luiz Paulo Macedo Cavalho. Rio de Janeiro & Salvador, Ba.: Biblioteca do Exército & Odebrecht, 1998. 4 vols. Redrawn by Bill Nelson. Used with permission of Biblioteca do Exército, Rio de Janeiro.

to change their piece of Brazilian reality. Of course, given their limited horizons and the restricted vision imposed by their messianic beliefs their understanding of what was happening to them was likely not as clear as hindsight and the collective work of contemporary observers and many scholars allows. The affair was a complex mix of economic, political, social, and religious elements brought together by the brusque incorporation of the region into the international capitalist system. The local affected population used messianism as a vehicle to organize their response. The state and federal authorities reacted to their challenge with crushing violence. The army found itself again battling Brazilians in the name of progress, a progress in which foreigners played key roles.[39]

Before plunging the reader into the military aspects of the story some comments on the nature of the crisis are in order. The *Contestado* was so named because it was an area disputed first between Brazil and Argentina, until the 1895 arbitration of American President Grover Cleveland awarded it to Brazil, and then between the states of Santa Catarina and Paraná, who contested jurisdiction over it. The area in which the rebellion occurred was more limited, being bounded on the north by the Negro and Iguaçu Rivers, on the south by the Pelotas and Uruguay Rivers, on the west by a line drawn from the Uruguay through Irani, S.C., to Palmas, Pa., and on the east by a line from Lajes, S.C. to Rio Negro, Pa. (see Map 3.1). The modern traveler will find most of the rebel zone embraced by the rough triangle that highways BR 116, BR 470, and BR 476 form. In the south around Lajes the countryside is relatively open and rolling, becoming increasingly more broken, hilly, and gullied with thick forest covering, streams, and small rivers as you move north and west. It was an area of early European penetration, especially in its eastern portion, being on the livestock route from Rio Grande do Sul to São Paulo and Minas Gerais. Its principal economic activities centered on livestock, *herva mate* collection, and lumbering.

Its social structure was one in which wealth and power were concentrated in the hands of a few "colonels" around whom clustered lesser landowners. Setembrino de Carvalho would later comment that the relations between the top and bottom of the social scale closely resembled those between masters and slaves.[40] Scattered up the gullies and along the rivers were families working the wild *herva* groves, many of whom had tenuous, if any, land titles or existed at the sufferance of a large landowner. The dispute between the two states complicated land titles because sometimes the registry offices *(cartórios)* in both states issued titles for the same land. Possession in such cases was often decided by gunplay. And because of the confused legal jurisdiction the area attracted fugitives from near and far.

The two state governments contributed to an atmosphere of violence. For example, in the valleys of the Timbó and Paciência Rivers, the *herva* groves of the headwaters and courses were in the hands of Catarenses, whereas the Paranenses controlled the junctions with the Iguaçu and the principal town on that river, União da Vitória—the traditional crossing on the livestock trail from Rio Grande do Sul. Between 1905 and 1909 the two governments and competing businessmen backed the formation of informal armed bands whose purpose was to seize territory and erect or remove rival state tax posts on roadways. Federal troops intervened and disarmed such bands in 1905, but for the most part until 1914 the two states were free to have at one another. This officially sponsored violence and the presence of a good number of ex-*Maragatos,* who had migrated from Rio Grande after the civil war of the 1890s, agitated portions of the population and taught them the use of military organization and weapons.

Elements external to the region played roles in the crisis: the building of the São Paulo–Rio Grande do Sul railway brought in construction workers from the northeast and Rio de Janeiro, whom the foreign company abandoned after completion; American capital, which sought to exploit the rich timber; and foreign immigrants, whom the railroad attracted to its land concessions. The federal government had contracted with American Percival Farquhar's Brazil Railway Company to complete the strategically important railway between the north and south. As part of its compensation the railroad was awarded ten miles on either side of its tracks. The Brazil Railway zigzagged its course so as to increase this concession, which overrode existing land titles. As the railroad advanced, it expropriated holdings, leaving behind dispossessed Brazilians, whom it sought to replace with European immigrants. The wisdom of such a policy, enacted in the belief that Europeans would bring a spirit of industry and husbandry that the local Brazilians supposedly lacked, was doubtful without a companion program of schooling and nationalization. In seeking to control movement in and out of rebel areas during this little war, officers found that products of earlier migrations, German-Brazilians born in Brazil still recognized Germany as their Pátria; they spoke only German, and it was difficult to convince them that they were Brazilian citizens. Although this worried nationalist army officers, little would be done about Brazilianizing the "colonial zone" until 1938, when a strong central government moved to stop possible Nazi influence.[41]

When the heightened tension between Argentina and Brazil veered close to war in 1910, the federal government ordered the company to speed completion of the unfinished stretch between Pôrto União and the Uruguay River. To do so it increased its workforce to about eight thousand, which, under tremendous pressure, had the line open by mid-December 1910. Many of these workers had been recruited forcibly in Santos, Rio, Salvador, and Recife and on completion were paid off and abandoned along the rail bed. Farquhar also formed the Southern Brazil Lumber and Colonization Company to work the timber in the northern and western portion of the Contestado. At cheap prices "Lumber," as it was called in the region, acquired over one thousand square miles registered in Paraná but located in the contested area south of the Negro and Iguaçu Rivers. The area reportedly contained nearly four million pine and two million cedar and Brazilian walnut *(imbuia)* trees, many of which towered thirty meters high and were more than a meter in diameter.[42] "Lumber" built a modern, mechanized sawmill at Tres Barras and a railway from União da Vitória to Sao Francisco on the coast below Joinville to export its production. Beginning in 1911 the Brazil Railway began expelling "squatters" from the land. The company's Security Corps killed those who resisted.[43]

There was a rush of land speculators, many of them foreigners. Leaders of the two states, with the help of state officials, legalized seizures and subsequent sales of property. One prominent participant in this wholesale pillage was Afonso de Camargo, political boss and vice governor of Paraná, who just happened to be the lawyer for the Brazil Railway! People whose families had lived in the region for a century suddenly found themselves expelled from their lands and forlornly reading posted notices renting or selling their property to third parties. Social tensions mounted as "a wave of horror swept over all the territory."[44]

It is against this backdrop of violent expulsions, cutting of the forests, sudden predominance of foreigners, and the introduction of modern technology that we need to see the religious movement that gave organization to the rebellion. Moreover, there was social disintegration as the local "colonels" put aside the customary paternalism that linked them to the population in favor of enhancing their own interests via accommodation with the new order of things. The social system lost its pleasant, soothing, tolerable forms of dominance with the region's sudden, violent incorporation into the world capitalist order.[45] The resulting disorientation gave rise to what might be called a collective identity crisis.[46]

In August 1912 the common people of the Contestado gathered for the feast of Bom-Jesus at Taquaruçu. The celebration marked the period between the end of clearing forest and the beginning of burning prior to planting. Usually after such a festival people scattered to their home plots, but that year many stayed because their lands had been seized, and they had no place to go. A curer and supposed lay holy man *(beato* or *monge)* named José Maria led the assembly in prayer, told holy stories, and read from a popular book on Charles the Great of France. Unintentionally, he got drawn into a power struggle between two local "colonels" in nearby Curitibanos. One presented him with his National Guard saber, whereas the other telegraphed the governor of Santa Catarina that religious fanatics had proclaimed a monarchy in Taquaruçu.[47]

The telegram caused alarm in Florianópolis, interest in Curitiba, and was mentioned in the Rio press. The governor of Santa Catarina guaranteed that the "movement" was similar to that of Canudos and ordered the state's military police to the scene. The chief of police, wanting to avoid conflict, sent word to José Maria of his approach, urging him to go to Paraná, probably in the hope that he would cause trouble there! The "monk" and his poor followers regrouped at Irani in the southern portion of the municipality of Palmas, Paraná. Apparently, suspecting that this was an attempt to reinforce Santa Catarina's land claims, the authorities asked for an explanation, and, receiving none, the Paraná military police attacked them on October 22, 1912. José Maria was killed, as was the police commander, one João Gualberto Gomes de Sá Filho, an army captain with the rank of colonel in the Paraná police, who had been graduated from Praia Vermelho in 1902.[48]

Who was José Maria? His real name was Miguel Lucena Boaventura, an ex-soldier in the army railway battalion that was building the link between Guarapuava and Foz do Iguaçu. He also had served in the Paraná state police.[49] In the years prior to the gathering at Taquaruçu he had acted as a healer *(curandeiro)* around Lages, while doing manual labor to earn his bread. And he had lived for a time in Irani. His importance lies in his having attracted a considerable following among the dispossessed, who after his death refused to accept his disappearance and spread the idea that he either was not dead or would rise from the dead. Those who had lost relatives at Irani enlarged on this to the point of saying that no one had died there, that the fallen or disappeared had all gone to join the enchanted army of St. Sebastian. As it happened, St. Sebastian was the patron of the sertão in general but was especially venerated in *Perdizes Grandes,* an area to the east of the Peixe River (Caçador is the principal town today) through which the railroad passed, and from where many of José Maria's followers came. Here, then, was yet another appearance of Sebastianism in Brazilian history. This recurring belief in supernatural assistance in a time of desperation facilitated the transformation of dependent, submissive people, unaccustomed to acting without the patron's sanction, into a determined fighting force.[50]

Various leaders came forward who professed to communicate with the dead José Maria through a series of children, who acted as mediums. The belief spread that he would reappear with the enchanted army in Taquaruçu on the anniversary of his "disappearance." Beginning in December 1913, families from throughout the Contestado began moving to this "Holy City." As their numbers increased, so did the religious rituals that molded them into a cohesive, disciplined group. The men took to wearing white bands on their hats and cutting their beards and hair. Aside from the sanitary value of the latter, both practices facilitated identification and assimilation. Their adversaries called them *pelados,* a term of multiple meaning that was descriptive of their shaved heads and of their poverty. Among gaúchos it referred to those who had lost everything. It is significant that they called their enemies *peludos,* which refers to something (such as mud) from which it is difficult to get free.[51]

Alarmed, the "colonel" of nearby Curitibanos telegraphed the governor, who notified the federal authorities, who sent an army unit. A Franciscan priest tried to convince the people to disperse, but they rejected his advice, saying that they were there "by order of St. Sebastian, the king of glory," that they were seeking "Freedom! Now we are in another century!"[52] Their medium "consulted" with José Maria and advised them not to fear attack for it would not be necessary to fight because the monk and all those who died at Irani would be there to fight the government forces. However, they held military drills every morning under the direction of a black Pernambucano, an army deserter. They were ill-armed with locally made steel or wooden swords, long nail-tipped cattle prods, and a few Winchester rifles.

Contestado: Army Involvement Begins at Taquaruçu

A total of 160 troops from Curitiba arrived by train at assembly points, Caçador to the northwest and Campos Novos to the southwest, while 50 Catarense state police prepared in Curitibanos to the southeast. Their attack on December 29 was a farce! The troops were so credulous of stories of enchanted armies and the skin-head *pelados's* supernatural powers that the detachment moving in from Campos Novos turned in panic before seeing anyone, while the detachment from Caçador held only until the first quick exchange of gunfire. The police did a bit better. Eight rebels led by their eleven-year-old medium came toward them carrying a big banner and shouting *vivas* to José Maria while the rest of the people hid in the tall grass. When the police opened fire with their machine gun, a rebel lassoed it from horseback and rode away pulling it behind. That was it; the police turned and fled, tossing aside their Mauser rifles, supplies, tunics, and caps as they ran. The rebels let them go; indeed, throughout the war they did not run down fleeing opponents. Curiously, although they kept the arms, they considered other supply items impure and burned them.[53]

In early January some of the rebels formed a new "redoubt," as the army termed their settlements, at Caraguatá more to the north. On February 8 a mixed column of seven hundred, composed of troops from five or six different units thrown together for the operation, state police, and civilian "patriots," pounded Taquaruçu with artillery and machine guns. In his campaign report Setembrino dryly commented that they "dispersed the impertinent devotees with shot" and burned the houses while most of the inhabitants fled. Indeed, he said, "innumerable armed bandits escaped" under the cover of the women and children "whose killing it was necessary to avoid."[54] Here, as he would do on other occasions, Setembrino was covering the repugnant reality of a massacre.

Some officers were clearly bothered by the whole affair. The commander of the column, Lt. Col. Duarte de Alleluia Pires, a veteran of some of the worst fighting at Canudos seventeen years before, apparently regarded his assignment with disgust. He delayed the assault while a well-known federal deputy from Paraná, Manoel Correia de Freitas, tried to convince the devotees to disperse, and while the Supreme Federal Tribunal considered but turned down a petition of habeas corpus aimed at preventing the use of force. Throughout this pause the commanding general of the Eleventh Military Region (Paraná and Santa Catarina) Brigadier General Alberto Ferreira de Abreu, peppered Alleluia Pires with telegrams demanding action, suggesting that the officers were cowardly for waiting.[55] The colonel was disposed to surround Taquaruçu and to starve the devotees out to avoid bloodshed. When the negotiations and court appeal failed, he had no choice but to obey his superior officer in Curitiba. But the poor man literally did not have the stomach for it. The day of the attack found him ill in bed and Captain Nester Sezefredo dos Passos directing the artillery fire and marking another step on his rise toward becoming the top general in the next decade.[56]

And what a barrage it was! Incessantly for four hours the two field pieces poured their entire stock of 175 shrapnel shells into the makeshift settlement. The soldiers could hear people in the burning church crying—"Santo José Maria, Santo José Maria"—until it collapsed. When the cannon paused, the besieged tried to respond but most of their rounds fell short of the troops located some six hundred meters away. The *one* Mauser rifle that they possessed managed to kill one soldier and wound three others. During the night the people propped up cadavers as if they were riflemen and slipped away to Caraguatá. In the morning when the soldiers entered what was left of the "holy city," they found between forty and ninety or so bodies mostly in pieces, which made an accurate count impossible. Unlike Setembrino, who was not there, the column's physician was horrified at what he saw, especially the dead women and children.[57] Even army officers recognized that, regardless of its underlying causes, the attack on Taquaruçu was "the torch which ignited the war in the Contestado."[58]

It certainly affected the careers of Lieutenant Colonel Alleluia Pires and Captain Sezefredo dos Passos. The first retired at the end of 1914 to become a "pajama colonel" at the young age of fifty-three, whereas his junior colleague, at forty-two, began a rapid climb upward. He was promoted to major in June 1914, was wounded at Santa Maria in February 1915, and reached brigadier general in August 1922. In 1926 he would succeed Setembrino as minister of war.[59] Following orders and having a strong stomach had their rewards. The affair points up a sad trait in the Brazilian style of resolving social crisis: a lack of patience at the institutional level. The famed Brazilian ability to compromise seemingly was limited to intraelite disputes; common people were allowed less latitude. However, Lieutenant Colonel Alleluia Pires was not the only officer who doubted the wisdom of using force to resolve the problem, as we will see shortly in the actions of Captain João Teixeira de Matos Costa.

Although the Hermes administration, especially the war ministry, was distracted with the Ceará crisis, the minister decided, after the determined sertanejos beat off an army attack on the new Caraguatá redoubt, that piecemeal efforts in the Contestado would resolve little, so he transferred Brigadier General Carlos Frederico de Mesquita, then commander of the Fourth Strategic Brigade, based in São Gabriel, Rio Grande do Sul, to take charge of the repressive operations. At sixty years of age he had an impressive combat record. He had been a fifteen-year-old soldier in the last year of the Paraguayan War, fought in the 1893–95 civil war, and was gravely wounded at Canudos, for which he was rewarded with promotion for bravery to lieutenant colonel.[60] But, although his record might have promised otherwise, Mesquita found that he could do little with the scant resources at his disposal.

His colleague, General Abreu, had described the command's weaknesses in painful detail. There was a tremendous shortage of officers; of the 324 that the table of organization specified, the command had only 172. Field-grade officers were especially lacking, so captains or lieutenants led most units. There were so few army or contracted civilian physicians that there was only one for the Florianópolis garrison and three for the Curitiba units. Indeed, when a company of the Fifth Infantry Regiment was sent to guard the railroad station at Herval (or Erval) the general had to hire a veterinarian to replace the company doctor! Also there was a lack of horses—869 less than the budgeted number—and a shortage of funds to buy feed for the ones they had. The Second Artillery Regiment had discovered that it was less expensive to board its horses at night in a civilian stable than care for them on post. There were barely enough arms and equipment. The infantry was, according to General Abreu, effectively "disarmed" because all of the weapons were "more or less defective." Individual unit commanders reported that their soldiers' rifles were "unusable," old, and in "extremely . . . bad condition." There were not enough tents, and instead of the five hundred wagons that the Second Brigade's mobilization chart called for, there were only thirty-one old and badly maintained vehicles. It was distressing, he wrote, "to see the difficulty with which even a small unit operates in the *sertões*." He complained that without a requisition law they were dependent on hiring transport where they could. The European immigrants, who composed the majority of the population in the interior of Paraná, were reluctant to give the army any assistance and then only at extraordinary prices.

As if all that were not discouraging enough, the picture Abreu sketched of the officers and soldiers was dismal. He divided the officers into two categories: the first were graduates of the army schools who possessed a "half scientific, half literary" education, while the second were untaught *(inculta)*. Although in theory the study of army regulations and rules of war would equalize the two groups, in fact "the regulations are not studied passionately," so an officer of the first group might cite a noted foreign authority and be countered with an old practice from the Paraguayan War. This diversity, which Abreu said existed because of the lack of a durable, required military doctrine, was aggravated when it came to cooperation among the combat arms and the auxiliary services. The lack of unity was such that he feared that "it will be impossible . . . to obtain their regular liaison in combat." Moreover, most officers had almost no familiarity with campaign duty. And, on top of all this, there was the commanders' "disastrous habit" of mixing in their subordinates' areas of responsibility, busying themselves with the tiniest details.

And then there were the troops. In a gentle phrasing he described them as "incorrigibly . . . inelegant." Their basic training on arrival in a regiment was usually given over to the "ineptitude of a sergeant" who rushed them through a program that left them "recruits in the things that are most essential in war; they do not know how to shoot, ride properly, use bayonet or sword." He pointed to Captain João Gualberto's defeat at Irani as a result of such training because the state police that he led were former soldiers who had left the army for the better pay and conditions the state forces provided. As police they displayed the same defects they had as soldiers.[61] He lamented that the only soldiers fully trained by the book were the trumpeters!

Considering the low level of individual preparation, it was not surprising that unit instruction was equally bad. Officers drilled the troops only when maneuvers rolled around. The infantry seemed incapable of moving from a line of march into a skirmish line without first halting, thereby giving their adversaries clear, stationary targets. And the cavalry did not know how to make a reconnaissance or to fight on foot and showed an "exaggerated preference for charges and badly prepared ambushes." The artillery, which employed French techniques and German field guns, lacked mobility because its draft animals were weak and not the proper sort. Finally, the supply train units behaved as if they were cavalry and so could not fulfill their functions.[62]

Faced with taking such a command into combat and with little help from Rio de Janeiro in prospect—the government denied him money, reinforcements, and aircraft—it is not surprising that General Mesquita, after marching his units around a bit and attacking a few weak concentrations that merely melted into the forest, declared the "fanaticos" exterminated and the campaign over.[63] Who knows? Maybe ghosts of Canudos visited his tent at night and he wanted to avoid further bloodshed.

He left behind two hundred men under Captain João Teixeira de Matos Costa to protect the railway. The captain knew the area and developed a certain popularity among the sertanejos. He became convinced that it was the "colonels" who were responsible for the revolt. They sold land on extended payment to sertanejos who, when they had the debt nearly paid, were evicted on some excuse. Since the government stood with the "colonels," the sertanejos had no place to turn. Moreover, the captain discovered that one of the leading "colonels" was involved in the production and passing of counterfeit money. Matos Costa visited redoubts, sometimes in disguise, sometimes with a soldier of Italian origin who performed magic tricks to entertain the people while the captain tried to win them over to less violent means of redress. Perhaps memories of his combat experiences at Canudos persuaded him that discussion would be better than force. Or maybe he had mellowed since his service on the Rio Madeira with Colonel Rondon's Strategic Telegraph Commission, where he reportedly executed as disciplinary examples three prisoners from among those wretches carried there on the infamous ship *Satélite*.[64] Eventually, in August 1914, he took two sertanejos to Rio de Janeiro, where he unsuccessfully attempted to convince the authorities that the Contestado revolt was "only an insurrection of sertanejos despoiled of their lands, their rights, and their security . . . [who in their] ignorance know no other means of defending their rights." He argued that the dispute could be resolved with "a little instruction and adequate justice." The authorities must have wondered at the naivete displayed in the conditions that the sertanejos set for peace: the removal of ten or twelve of the region's leading "colonels" and the return to life of the women and children killed at Taquaruçu![65] It is not surprising that Setembrino observed that no one honestly believed that Matos Costa's way would succeed. "The revolutionary movement that declared itself in the southern parts required," according to Setembrino, "instead of a few hundred badly instructed and badly quartered soldiers, a complete military apparatus, intelligently directed." What was needed, he said, was "the calm energy of the truly strong, the sensible action of real professionals, the lucid understanding of the facts—and troops." Meaning, of course, that he was the man to resolve the problem.[66]

The sertanejos saw General Mesquita's withdrawal as a victory, a view that emboldened many more to join the rebellion. In July and August 1914 rebel leaders such as Francisco Alonso de Souza ordered people in the region either to come into one of the redoubts, or guarded areas, or to be considered enemies. Hundreds came in. Work on the railroad spur from União da Vitória to São Francisco (Santa Catarina) on the coast had halted, leaving more than one thousand foreign and Brazilian laborers unemployed; the majority of them appear to have joined the rebellion either out of frustration or for lack of alternatives.[67]

Beginning in June, Canoinhas, in the north of the zone, suffered frequent attacks by groups of rebels numbering upwards to five hundred. East of there rebels occupied Papanduva and Itaiópolis, destroying land records in the local notary offices *(cartórios)* in the process. This happened whenever rebels seized a town, demonstrating that the affair was not solely a fanatical messianic movement. Although this was an indigenous rebellion, foreigners participated in various ways. There were Americans with the lumber and railroad companies, and a deserter from the German naval vessel *Panther,* Henrique Wolland *(Alemãozinho),* led the attack on Itaiópolis. The Americans staged Fourth of July celebrations and displayed their national flag. On September 5 the rebels attacked and burned Calmon, a stop on the São Paulo–Rio Grande railway, where the first-built of Lumber's sawmills and extensive lumber yards was located. The fire's reflection in the night sky could be seen for miles. Rebels also hit the station and settlement at São João, shot the storekeeper and the railroad repair crew, and left a sign on the store protesting the expulsions from land that was then sold to foreigners. The "Brazilian Sons . . . now are disposed to make prevail our right."[68] In this same vein, in January 1915, army personnel found a pathetic, bloodstained letter in the pocket of a dead rebel. The letter read, "We have no land rights everything is for the peoples of *Oropa* [Europe]."[69]

Panic seized the population in nearby União de Vitória, where trains began shuttling carloads of terrified citizens to Ponta Grossa, which itself prepared for attack. Rumormongers worked overtime, whispering that hordes of *jagunços* were on the way to every settlement! Even in Curitiba it was said that "avalanches of fanatics" were about to pour over the city and that a rebel redoubt had been raised in the suburbs. In Curitibanos, in the south of the zone, families took to sleeping in the woods to avoid surprise attack. The irrational, shoot-first-and-ask-questions-later atmosphere caused one man to kill his own brother, who from a distance he feared was a jagunço!

American railway officials in São Paulo ordered their men in União to inspect the track as far as Calmon. Captain Matos Costa, who had just returned from Rio de Janeiro, and sixty soldiers joined two of Lumber's American bosses to check the line. Some twenty-four miles from União they encountered a man who told them Calmon was in ashes. Matos Costa, the Americans, and forty troopers detrained and walked carefully ahead of the slowly advancing engine. Suddenly, they were attacked. In terror the engineer reversed gears and took off at full steam, not stopping until he was back in União. Matos Costa and his sergeants were killed, and the few soldiers not hit fled into the forest, as did the Americans, who stumbled into União two days later. The rebels, expanding their attacks on fazendas and logging camps, had effective control of the countryside along the left bank of the Iguaçu between União and Canoinhas by the end of September 1914. Because it was widely known that the "fanatics," as they came to be called, spared women, many a brave lad donned a dress and scarf![70]

The movement had reached its peak; it controlled about ten thousand square miles, roughly equal to the state of Alagoas or .3 percent of Brazil's territory. Some twenty thousand people were in the redoubts, of whom somewhat more than eight thousand were male combatants. The redoubts ranged in size from three hundred to five thousand inhabitants. Usually they were located in recently cleared patches of forest amidst the fallen tree trunks. "Streets" and "alleys" ran twisting courses into a large, squared-off plaza where a church would be located. The houses, or better, shacks and huts were improvised from one day to the next, with no indication of permanency. They looked like the commonplace dwelling of the poorest sertanejo: rough-hewn plank or mud-and-wattle walls; roofs of palm or grass thatch, wooden slats, or sometimes leather; floors of either pounded earth or planking. Usually the dwellings were divided into two rooms for cooking, eating, and sleeping. Cooking was done over an open fire on the ground. Beds were crude *tarimbas,* bunks made from bamboo; sheepskins from their saddles doubled as mattresses, and woolen blankets, ponchos, or capes served as covering against the chilly September nights.[71]

Contestado: Setembrino Organized to Avoid Another Canudos

The Brazilian army was hard pressed to respond to the rebel success. In late August Minister of War Vespasiano de Albuquerque named Setembrino de Carvalho acting inspector-general of the Eleventh Region, with instructions to suppress the insurrection. Arriving in Curitiba on September 11, he found the city agitated, the press full of rumors and criticisms.[72] The Eleventh Region and the so-called Fourth Strategic Brigade that official tables of organization located in Curitiba were largely paper fictions that could not actually carry out combat operations. General Mesquita's report had pointed to the lack of men and equipment as deadly hindrances to the command's efficiency, so Setembrino had gone south with the minister's promise that he would receive adequate troops and arms. To keep his word the minister had to order out units from Rio de Janeiro, Minas Gerais, and Rio Grande do Sul. Some of these had been formed only recently, and their green troops had no experience. Moreover, a strike on the Sorocabana railway in São Paulo delayed troops moving south.[73]

As units slowly converged on the Contestado, Setembrino studied the situation. Although the army had maintained several military colonies in

Paraná and Santa Catarina since the middle decades of the previous century,[74] here as elsewhere there were no accurate maps. The army map service was preparing a detailed national map based on field surveys, but it had only completed work on parts of Rio Grande do Sul and the area around Rio de Janeiro. So without maps Setembrino could design only broad plans and would have to depend on civilian scouts and aerial observers to locate rebel strongholds. He knew from the outset that his units would need to move slowly and carefully to escape another Canudos-like disaster. He had to avoid letting his troops be drawn into action until they were in condition to assure victory.

Although Canudos was frequently on his mind, the Contestado contrasted in two ways with the Bahian affair. First, the geography was different. Where the northern sertão was dry and barren, this southern sertão was wet and forested. Numerous swamps, streams, and rivers interspersed the hilly, wooded terrain. Where the baking sun made the soldiers' lives a hell in the Bahian interior, in Santa Catarina heavy rains turned roads and trails into quagmires. Second, at Canudos the fighting had been contained in a restricted locality, but in the Contestado it was a generalized revolt spread over a wide area. Initially, Setembrino spoke of a sertanejo rebellion and not of religious fanatics or bandits, terms he would quickly adopt.[75]

Methodically, Setembrino moved his preparations forward. He saw that he could not put enough troops into the field to snuff out the rebellion and that if he sent his weak forces on ill-designed forays, he would be following "the same disastrous processes of Canudos" that would needlessly give the insurrectionists the illusion of superiority.[76] His strategy was to envelop the rebel area, cutting off food and supplies, letting hunger break the rebels' will to resist while avoiding exposing his troops to demoralizing ambushes. In other words, he was employing Mallet's principles of war (discussed in Chapter 2), limiting exposure to enemy fire while applying maximum pressure with minimum force. The São Francisco–União de Vitória rail line and the Negro River set the zone's northern limit because patrols along both could hinder rebel movement. The São Paulo–Porto Alegre railroad likewise set a western limit, running from the Iguaçu River to the Uruguay River. Setembrino sent troops to reestablish traffic on the railroad and to garrison stations where the line intersected roads leading further west toward Palmas and Chapecó. To the east and south such conveniently clear boundaries were absent, although toward the east the *Serra do Mar* provided an ultimate limit, and the terrain was generally rugged enough to be unattractive to the rebels. But there and in the south it was still a question of placing troops to close off the area.

On September 13 Setembrino laid out his plans for the minister of war and explained that he needed careful organization, supplies, money, and six thousand men. In succeeding days his telegrams repeated requests for more units, doctors, equipment, and credits. General Vespasiano, despite the government's difficult financial situation, produced a 600:000$000 credit, rounded up officers, and sent Brazil's only army aviator to help. The Contestado would see the first military use of aviation in Brazilian history.[77]

Setembrino assembled an operations staff and assigned arriving units to positions along the north-south-east-west box that his four "lines" formed. Amazingly, the army had no regulations for field operations, so he drew up procedures for everything from ration allotments to hospital organization. And he set engineers to making maps and, eventually, building telephone lines and improving roads. They also laid new telegraph lines because the "notorious indiscretion" of civilian operators caused security leaks. Likewise he ordered tight restrictions on journalists and on relations between soldiers and sertanejos. The rebels had been spying on the army camps by mixing with the local sellers of this or that and with curious citizens, who were fascinated with the military display. How carefully this prohibition against fraternization was enforced is not clear. Some commanders issued passes to nearby residents, but the final medical report commented that there were many "fallen women in the encampments," and such prostitutes clearly would have been excellent spies.[78] The cavalry horses and artillery mules were too few and in such poor condition that officers and civilian agents scoured the region's estancias and traveled as far as Rio Grande to buy new mounts. Lacking a requisition law, the army was forced to pay market prices. To provide food, Setembrino contracted with M. Loureiro and Company of Curitiba to set up the supply network. And before the troop units arrived, army doctors and pharmacists set up field hospitals in Rio Negro and União.

Because he needed to pinpoint the location of rebel strongholds, Setembrino was pleased to have Lieutenant Ricardo Kirk, who had recently opened the army's aviation school at Rio de Janeiro, assigned to his command. Kirk, who had learned to fly at his own expense in France, was one of those exceptional characters who had the right ideas but lacked sufficient political influence to put them into practice. When he returned from France with his "wings," the powers could not bring themselves to confide the training of army pilots to a fellow Brazilian and so turned the school over to a contracted Italian pilot, Ernesto Darioli. Sadly, Kirk's mission in the Contestado was star-crossed from the outset. En route from Rio by train, sparks from the engine ignited the fabric bodies of his two aircraft. Before returning to the capital for replacements, he selected landing strips at Rio Negro, Canoinhas, and União and had hangers built at the last.[79]

Abreast of these preparations Setembrino made what he considered an "incisive and hard" gesture toward a peaceful solution with a manifesto inviting rebels to lay down their arms and to present themselves to the nearest commander. They would, he promised, be furnished food "until the government gives them land." But he warned that those who did not come in spontaneously and were found inside the proscribed area would be "considered enemies and as such treated with all the rigors of the laws of war." The message was simple: come in and get land, or stay out and fight the army![80]

Between the last days of September and early November the various units slowly took up their positions on one of the four sides of the rectangle that Setembrino hoped would contain the rebellion. The Tenth Infantry, under Colonel Julio César Gomes da Silva, moved into Rio Negro in the northeast. The Fifty-sixth Light Infantry and attached mountain artillery, under Lt. Col. Manuel Onofre Muniz Ribeiro, set up camp in Canoinhas in the north-central portion of the zone. Lt. Col. Francisco Raul Estillac Leal's Fifty-eighth Light Infantry marched inland from Itajaí on the coast toward Curitibanos in the southeastern corner, and fractions of the Fourth, Fifth, and Sixth Cavalry regiments of Rio Grande do Sul, under Major José Leovegildo Alves de Paiva, took up position in Campos Novos in the southwest. In addition to the regular army there was a "Patriotic Battalion," which Rio Negro political boss "Colonel" Nicolau Bley Netto assembled, the state Security Regiment of Paraná, and some three hundred civilian scouts *(vaqueanos)*. All told, 6,408 men made up the federal forces.[81]

Contestado: Reformist Officers Critique of the Campaign and the Army

The strains this mobilization caused could be seen in the pages of *A Defesa Nacional,* which followed preparations month to month and kept up a steady drumbeat of criticism. Its editors saw no good reason for maintaining "ridiculous units" with the pompous titles of strategic brigade, regiment, battalion, and so forth when they could not function for lack of material, officers, and troops. They argued that instead of preserving the fiction of paper divisions, there ought to be at least one real division. Although this might mean removing garrisons from state capitals and the frontiers, they thought that the police could handle the first, while the "ABC pact" eliminated threats to the second. The so-called ABC pact was a mix of formal and informal understandings among Argentina, Brazil, and Chile. The editors blamed the army's ineffably "complicated bureaucracy" for dangerous supply problems. For example, there was the odd case of the Fifth Infantry Regiment of Ponta Grossa, Paraná, that on requisitioning badly needed new weapons was told that before they could be issued, the regiment would have to turn over its old ones. Knowing how slowly the system worked and fearing that his troops would be left unarmed, the commander refused. It made better sense to exchange the old for the new when the latter arrived. The bureaucracy dug in its heels and won, the regiment kept its unusable rifles![82]

That officers were not pleased with the army's role in the Contestado came through in *Defesa Nacional* editorials. The editors observed that some people were accusing the leaders of Paraná and Santa Catarina of fomenting the rebellion to serve their political interests; others pointed to religious fanaticism; and still others said that the small property holders of the old military colonies, despoiled of their lands by the ruling elites of the two states, were seeking revenge. Regardless of what had touched off the fighting, the editors saw the underlying cause as "the lamentable *ignorance* in which these poor people have been criminally abandoned." That is what had reduced these "fellow countrymen, humble sertanejos to the condition of our enemies." Although it was "lamentable" to have to fight "countrymen" and "brothers," it would be worse in the editors' view "to let our Army slowly die," destroying its morale with "inopportune sentimental considerations." Once the army had been committed, there could be "no more room for palliatives or for concessions, which only serve to weaken troop effectiveness and to discredit the army." As long as the "fanatics" were in arms, there could only be the military objective of "destroying the enemy." "Brazil needs men," the editors declared, "but men who collaborate, within the law *(dentro da ordem),* in the work of its aggrandizement."[83]

The comments of 2d Lt. Francisco de Paula Cidade hint at the thinking of reformist officers. The Contestado was the clash between "the old and the new Brazil." The latter's European ideas and customs had barely penetrated the "hinterland," but somehow their entry into the region had caused the rebellion. He depreciated (and underestimated) rebel military qualities. They used hunting rifles and shotguns, simple bullets, did not have bayonets, and although they were marksmen who were clever at ambushes, their tactics were simple, ferocious attacks or stubborn defenses. In combat they fired at will, preferably at officers. "They do not keep prisoners. They kill them and to save powder, they kill them with knives [arma branca]. Some among them are celebrated as throat slitters [degoladores]."[84] This last remark certainly had some truth to it because throat slitting was a feature of conflicts in the south, but here it has the ring of propaganda because evidence on murder of prisoners, which will be discussed below, points more to the government side than to the rebels. But at least one eyewitness reported rebels cutting the throats of corpses.[85]

Lieutenant Cidade used the Contestado to criticize the army's lack of preparedness. He tossed barbs in all directions: at the dependence on civilian scouts, who frequently passed information to the adversary; at the lack of roads; at the "Exhibitionism" that announced operation plans to the "four winds"; at the state military police, whose function was to maintain internal order but who were all too willing to ask help from the "skeletal battalions of the Army"; and at the infantry, which left "much to be desired." Although the army was better armed than the rebels, its soldiers were notoriously poor shots for lack of practice. Although marksmanship training was based on German methods, it had poor results because, instead of regular practice seeking to reach a minimum skill level, soldiers were given an introductory lesson and then nothing for weeks, during which time they forgot what they had been taught. Instead of training, soldiers spent time guarding military and public buildings, going on fatigue duty or street patrols, or acting as orderlies. And, on top of this, once in combat, soldiers forgot regulation tactics. At all levels, from company to battalion, units entered a fray by extending their lines with no thought to keeping a reserve for moments of crisis. "We do not maneuver in depth," lamented Cidade; "we operate in extension, presenting the enemy with a thin curtain which torn at one point, cannot be mended." The individual soldier was ill-provisioned; he had no first-aid kit nor combat rations, and, worse, he could not depend on proper resupply of ammunition beyond what he could carry in his field bag.

And the Contestado was proving the utter worthlessness of the so-called strategic brigade, which could not be subdivided rationally. Lieutenant Cidade doubted that it really existed. He wondered if it "proved so bad in small operations, what account will it give of itself in a big war?" His response: "God free us from the Strategic Brigade!" He wrapped up his critique with the observation that "if from the study of the present events some profitable lesson results, blessed be the blood that is going to spill."[86]

Contestado: Boxing in the Rebels

And spill it would. Brevet Colonel Eduardo Socrates, commander of the western line from the Iguaçu River to the Uruguay River, restored railway service and occupied ten stations. He and the other commanders set their troops at rifle practice, many, as Setembrino admitted, "for the first time." The overzealous commander of the northern line, Lt. Col. Onofre Ribeiro, could not contain himself after arriving from Rio de Janeiro with his 450–man Fifty-sixth Light Infantry Battalion and requested permission to attack rebel redoubts near Canoinhas. Setembrino, not wanting to dampen his colonel's "military ardor," allowed it. While the attack on October 26 drove the surprised rebels out of a place called Salseiro, advancing troops were beaten back as they attempted to move further into rebel territory. Soon they were bogged down by fierce resistance and heavy rains. By November 10 they had fallen back on Canoinhas and found themselves under nightly attacks from then until Christmas Eve.[87]

Aside from responding to such provocations, the rebels kept their distance from the army. They watched and prepared, gathering in provisions. Some leaders purchased cartridges and food from suppliers in Rio Grande and Paraná; others raided nearby estancias and settlements, such as the Ruthenian colonies of Iracema and Moema in the northeast.

Newspapers criticized the failed northern line offensive and Setembrino's cautious preparations. And when the general injected himself into the jurisdictional dispute between the two states, their politicians demanded his removal. He believed that the interstate dispute, and not religious fanaticism, had caused the rebellion. In early November he wrote Felipe Schmidt, governor of Santa Catarina, demanding an end to the boundary problem. Although admitting that the Supreme Federal Tribunal had ruled in favor of Santa Catarina, he asserted that the court's decision could be enforced only at great cost because the "majority of the inhabitants of the contested region" were opposed. He predicted that enforcement would lead to constant fighting between the two states and to continuous federal occupation to maintain order. It was ridiculous, he thought, in a country with so much land, to fight over a small, underpopulated area. "Little motherlands" (pequenas pátrias) could not be tolerated; "above all we ought to be Brazilians and we all should work for the prosperity and aggrandizement of our dear Brazil. . . . United, we will be able one day soon, to reach a place of prominence among the great civilized nations; disunited and fragmented we will be captive to the unchecked and to a certain point justifiable ambitions of the imperialist peoples." He appealed to Schmidt's patriotism, requesting that he agree to concessions before Setembrino asked the Paranense government to do likewise.[88]

It is likely that Schmidt resented the condescending tone of this letter. He, too, was an army colonel, an infantryman who had outranked Setembrino on the 1914 combat colonel's list by thirty-one places and who had recently represented Santa Catarina in the Federal Senate.[89] Moreover, he could not help but be angry at the proposed limits which would have given Paraná most of the land to the west of the São Paulo–Porto Alegre railroad. Here was Setembrino, who had admitted that maps of the region were not accurate enough for military operations, using imperfect geographical information to propose a definitive boundary solution! Schmidt's reaction and press criticism of the slow preparations led Setembrino to offer his resignation, which the minister of war refused.

Setembrino defended his slowness, saying that "to hurry would be rash." They must not have another Canudos. He instructed his commanders to advance cautiously and to be sure of their ground. He argued that he lacked sufficient troops to execute his plans. On November 20 he had forty-eight hundred men and requested some three thousand more, plus "all sorts of material." Many of the units did not have their full compliment of officers. Setembrino urged that the minister order officers who had not come with their units to join them immediately. It seems that a mysterious "epidemic" had stricken officers of units ordered to the Contestado. The army was paying the price for having created an officer corps of bureaucrats rather than combat leaders. Setembrino said that he was not exaggerating his needs and urged the minister to act "with energy and with rapidity," or later on "the whole Army will be needed to smother a revolution, that is just beginning." In the meantime he had adopted what he termed "the only recourse" of contracting civilians to form small armed bands to patrol roads and trails to interdict the flow of foodstuffs and munitions to the redoubts. This measure, however, led to some robberies and throat slittings that caused foreign governments to protest the mistreatment and murder of their nationals.[90]

Until December 26 Setembrino directed preparations from the relative comfort of his Curitiba headquarters; he then set out to inspect the northern and eastern lines. After meeting in Rio Negro with Lieutenant Colonel Onofre of the northern Line and learning that many rebels in the redoubts were vacillating and awaiting a chance to give up the struggle, he put out a second proclamation. Curiously, this one made no mention of providing land; rather, it promised work. He called for an end to the fighting: "Brazilian blood cannot continue to stain our lands." If the rebels laid down their arms, they would not be killed or jailed but would be allowed to return to work. Among the groups that came in was the German naval deserter Henrique Wolland, leading between two and three hundred men. He was willing to switch sides and showed Setembrino on an army map the locations of various redoubts and made suggestions on how to attack them.[91] Having offered a carrot, the general now used a big stick.

While inspecting troops in Papanduva, Itaiópolis, and Moema, Setembrino learned that Major Atalibio Taurino de Rezende in Iracema had begun to negotiate with rebel leader Antonio Tavares. The latter's motivation for fighting had been his loss of a municipal position in Canoinhas and his unhappiness over the boundary question. Some thought that he enjoyed the secret favor, if not support, of the Santa Catarina government. In a letter of December 18 to Major Taurino de Rezende, Tavares lamented "this fratricidal struggle" but asserted that his people "preferred to give themselves in holocaust rather than endure the unmeasured ambition and continuous persecution of greedy Paraná." The major declared a truce and urged Tavares to accept his guarantees of good treatment in return for surrender. Tavares asked for twenty days, supposedly to meet with other rebel chiefs. He wrote to Setembrino stressing his political motives, his preference for Santa Catarina, and affirming that "we haven't abandoned civilization." This was his way of saying that his millenarianism was only a convenient cover.[92] Army officers later claimed that their spies informed them that, instead of discussing surrender, Tavares sought more men in exchange for supplies. Although possibly true, that story may have been used to justify the unsuccessful ambush that they set up to kill him on his way back to his redoubt. After further exchanges he met Major Taurino de Rezende on neutral ground to consider terms. Apparently he agreed not to press for solution of the land question, but on returning to the redoubt he wrote that he could not lay down his arms until the supreme tribunal's ruling in favor of Santa Catarina was enforced. "I cannot believe that the Government wants to exterminate us . . . for seeking justice." He requested that the truce be extended for twelve days and that the army supply his people with food.[93]

The messenger, one Pedro Nepomuceno, who carried his letter agreed to betray Tavares and helped the officers plan the redoubt's seizure. Nepomuceno returned to the redoubt to subvert it by distributing copies of Setembrino's proclamation. In a complicated envelopment the troops surrounded the rebel position during the early hours of January 8. With artillery and riflemen in place, some hidden in the bush within touching distance of unsuspecting rebels, more than three hundred men and women were taken prisoner when the troops announced their presence. Tavares escaped and survived the war thanks to the benevolence of the Catarense state authorities.[94]

While this had been going on in the east, the army had been busy along the other three lines. The most spectacular combat leader of the campaign, Captain Tertuliano de Albuquerque Potyguara, made his debut on the northern line against the rebels who had been harassing Canoinhas with nightly attacks. He was an exceptionally bold and aggressive man who literally drove the enemy before him. His first assignment (December 20, 1914) was to attack a rebel position at Piedade that was blocking the road between Canoinhas and Paciência. While his colleague Captain Jeremias Froes Nunes led his company in a frontal attack along the road, Potyguara's men made a rapid march through six miles of forest to hit the rebels suddenly from the far side. Instead of firing from cover, he threw his men at the rebels in a "daring bayonet charge" that turned them on their heels.[95]

In the southeast Colonel Estillac Leal's forces moved into fire-blackened Curitibanos and the infamous Taquaruçu, eventually joining up with Major Paiva's units moving along trails leading north out of Campos Novos in the southwestern corner. As these units issued passes to separate loyal sertanejos from rebels and stepped up patrols, rebel caravans withdrew toward the Timbó River in the northwest. With the south and east cleared by mid-January 1915, the eastern, southern, and northern lines began to draw the siege tighter.

Contestado: Treatment of Prisoners

As the pressure built up, more and more rebels began surrendering to the army.[96] Todd Diacon argues that these early surrenders were people less motivated by religious fervor than by political or land issues. Whatever their reasons, by late January between 1,300 and 3,000 had come in. The fate of these people is a bit obscure. The first group of 243 families that came into Canoinhas the army turned over to Santa Catarense authorities for distribution to agricultural colonies throughout the state, "where they could work off the damages" attributed to them. The local caudilho of Rio Negro, National Guard Colonel Bley Netto, supervised concentration camps from which he distributed successive levies of ex-rebels to colonies in Paraná. The destiny of those surrendering depended on the character and attitudes of the officer in charge of the unit to which they surrendered. Some officers accepted prisoners' pledges that they would not take up arms again and let them leave the war zone with safe-conduct passes. Some hired prisoners as scouts, but others tolerated atrocities. At Canoinhas the chief scout, Pedro Ruivo, led prisoners out of the overcrowded jail to an isolated spot and cut their throats. Reportedly more than a hundred unfortunates were left unburied outside of the town to the delight of the pigs and crows.[97]

In a February 18 letter to Governor Schmidt of Santa Catarina, Setembrino vehemently denied that Pedro Ruiva and other civilians with army units had committed "depredations and assassinations of any type." As if it were a testimony of good behavior, he said "they operate jointly with the forces of the Northern Column" in Lieutenant Colonel Onofre's "triumphal march." Admitting that the troops had burned houses and supplies in rebel areas, he justified the destruction as necessary to remove the enemy's life-sustaining resources in order to force surrender. But the tales of murder, Setembrino maintained, were nothing but slander. Schmidt replied that he thought the general would modify his opinion regarding Pedro Ruiva's activities when he heard testimony from some of the officers who served near Canoinhas. Indeed, Ruiva and his scouts murdered noncombatants; rustled a considerable quantity of cattle, horses, and mules; looted and burned houses of the innocent; and in one brutal case shot two men after forcing them to watch their wives being raped. It was indicative of the time and place that when brought to trial in Canoinhas, he and his gunmen were absolved.[98]

Although the available evidence does not show that army officers ordered or participated in these crimes, it is difficult to believe that Colonel Onofre did not know of his scout's murderous behavior. Subsequent army inquiries proved that civilians in army employ had indeed murdered prisoners, but the guilty were not punished. Seemingly the officers accepted such behavior as an unavoidable aspect of a sertanejo war, and their reports imply that they killed rather than took prisoners in combat. And in one documented case Captain Potyguara's men killed and mutilated a prisoner they were escorting to Porto União. Because some of those abused or murdered were foreign nationals, the incidents gave the army "a lot of problems" when foreign diplomats began protesting. Major General José Caetano de Faria, who succeeded Vespasiano de Carvalho as minister when he retired in November 1914, recommended that Setembrino treat the episodes carefully in his after-action report, "if you must refer to these facts."[99]

Contestado: Sealing the Box

By mid-January 1915 a large number of rebels had withdrawn into the Timbó River area, where their principal redoubt was located on the Santa Maria River, a tributary of the upper Timbó. They had outpost redoubts that seemingly shielded access on the north and east. The army's problem was that although officers knew the outer limits of the rebel-held area from a series of probes into it, they did not know where the redoubts themselves were situated. Lt. Ricardo Kirk and, his Italian fellow aviator, Ernesto Davioli, made a reconnaissance flight over the valley. The vast region was covered with giant pines, and they saw no smoke or other signs of life save for a large white flag framed against the dark pines on one of the high hills toward the end of the valley. They thought that from the ground it was likely visible for miles down the Timbó. Although unable to pinpoint the rebel positions, the aviators established that steep *serras* to the northeast, east, and south protected the area where they saw the flag.[100]

On January 21, keeping up the pressure from his temporary command post in Canoinhas, Setembrino issued a new operations order assigning objectives to each Line. Onofre's northern line was to move against the redoubt under rebel Manoel Machado on the left bank of the Timbósinho; Julio César's eastern line was to hit Aleixo Gonçalves's redoubt at Rio da Areia; and Socrates' western line and Estillac Leal's southern line were to assault the redoubts of Tamanduá and Santa Maria. In effect the four sides of the box were to close on one another. Such plans looked marvelous on maps, but in execution the topography, rebel resistance, communications among units, and differences in leadership stalled the southern and western lines, whereas the eastern and northern ones triumphed.

From Rio de Janeiro Minister Faria urged Setembrino to conclude operations before winter to avoid further expenses and sacrifice of troops. "Here," he wrote, "[we] put together money, almost nickel by nickel, to make payment [on the national debt]. It is incredible how much is owed! And I have a budget for this year that is less than the past year, some 800 *contos* more or less." Brazil's financial situation was such that the government could not pay its troops on time. The Curitiba garrison received its September and October 1914 pay in February 1915, and troops in the field received their January 1915 pay in March, while still awaiting their money for November and December 1914! Clearly the funds set aside for soldiers' pay were insufficient, and the minister had to negotiate with the minister of treasury *(fazenda),* various congressional leaders, and the president to obtain supplementary moneys. In its poverty the government even squeezed the troops on campaign for income taxes on their sometime salaries. This was especially noteworthy in a country where few people actually paid income taxes. Faria assured Setembrino that he was trying to satisfy the general's requests for men and material, and he promised not to transfer officers from the Contestado without his consent. He said that he so appreciated the services that the officers were rendering that he had recommended that the president promote several who had distinguished themselves. Two of those who benefited immediately were Estillac Leal, now a full Colonel, and Lt. Col. Leovigildo Paiva, who were then moving toward Santa Maria.[101]

However, their roles in the final phase of the campaign would be less dramatic than those of officers in the northern line.[102] In the south Paiva burned Taquaruçu for a second time, forestalling a sertanejo attempt to relocate there. His line and Estillac Leal's converged on the Serra do Caçador, which separated the streams and rivers that flowed south and southeast toward the Pelotas from those that ran north and northwest to the Iguaçu. Before them unknown numbers of ragged, weary, but determined sertanejo rebels made their way toward the cluster of settlements known as Santa Maria. There, in the rugged fastness of the upper Timbó, they would make their stands. These were diehards; perhaps the army's favorite label—"fanatics"—did fit these embattled souls. Many of the chiefs were gone by February, either dead or surrendered, as had Bonifacio (Papudo) José dos Santos. An army photographer preserved the scene as he rode into Canoinhas, proud and unbroken, at the head of his men. He told Setembrino that he did "not want to fight the government any longer." According to Todd Diacon, "the general recognized that Papudo was not a millenarian rebel and he thus presented little threat to the army." Set free, he sold his lands in the Contestado and moved to the far west of Paraná.[103]

In the east Julio César sent his line against an array of three redoubts along the Rio da Areia during the first week of February. The first two, known as Marcello and Joséphino, after their leaders, fell quickly. In both cases the army used the tactic that had worked so well at Tavares—to stage a "demonstration" assault from the trail and then surprise the rebels with a unit attacking out of the dense forest. Aspirante Heitor Mendes Gonçalves and his improbably named sergeant-major, Argentino Indio do Brasil, led fifty men under cover of night through swamps, with the mud at times reaching their chests, and

thick jungle through which they had to cut their way, to the edge of Marcello's settlement.[104] At 8 A.M. they fell on the surprised rebels. In the rapid
shoot-out, amid screaming, shouting, and crying, and women and children
running for cover, thirty-eight rebels, including Marcello, died, and another
forty were wounded. One soldier was killed. Reconnaissance showed that
Josephino's redoubt was in a better defensive position, so the officers had expected a harder struggle. They used the same tactics; only this time the scout
of the unit sneaking through the jungle got lost. As the enveloping unit
wandered around, the other one approaching frontally along the trail had a
bad time of it from the rebel defenders. The lieutenant commanding the machine guns had part of his head blown away. The leader of the Thirtieth Infantry Battalion took ill and passed his command to a subordinate. Into this
bleak picture stumbled the lost detachment, right into the undefended settlement! The rebels were so stunned that they surrendered without further
ado—158 men, women, and children, this time including the *caudilho*.

Contestado: The Timbó–Santa Maria Phase

The biggest task lay ahead. Aleixo, an old Maragato from the civil war of
the 1890s in Rio Grande do Sul, had some four to five thousand followers
in the principal Rio da Areia redoubt. Colonel César successfully infiltrated
a spy into the encampment and was carefully preparing his attack when a
reconnaissance on January 16 revealed that it was deserted. Aleixo's people
had disappeared into the forests of the Timbó. The defenses of Tamanduá–
Santa Maria now became the army's major objective.

The squeeze continued. During the first days of February, Onofre moved
the northern column through heavy rains and harassing engagements only to
find the settlements—Santo Antônio, Tomazinho and Reichardt—abandoned.
The rebels had been buying time to allow their families to withdraw toward
the Timbó. Meanwhile, Estillac Leal's southern column was conducting reconnaissance probes north from the area known as Perdizes Grandes, east of
the railroad station at Caçador. The probes showed that the rebel positions
were in the thick forests fringing the Santa Maria River about five miles from
the column bivouac.

At six-thirty on the morning of February 8 Estillac Leal's troops marched
out with the main units on the trail and flankers struggling through the jungle alongside. The vanguard made the first contact less than a mile later. The
rebels' tactics were to fire suddenly and heavily from the cover of the thick
growth and then to fall back. The irregular topography favored the rebels because they knew the ground, had prepared barricades, and held the higher
terrain. After advancing for less than three hours the column stalled before a
barricade at a curve in the trail. Withering fire poured down on the soldiers.

Because of the dense jungle there was not room to maneuver. Estillac Leal could not bring the weight of his forces to bear. He ordered the leading Fifty-seventh Battalion to launch a costly bayonet charge. Casualties among officers and soldiers mounted by the minute as the troops rushed at the wall-like jungle that hid their adversaries. Even bringing up a machine-gun section, under Aspirante João Pereira de Oliveira, failed to dislodge their dug-in opponents.[105] A seesaw battle ensued. When the rebel fire slackened, the soldiers would attempt to secure more ground only to be stopped with a murderously effective fire. The commander of the Fifty-seventh, Major Nestor Sezefredo, saw four of his six officers killed or wounded; of the two remaining lieutenants one was lightly wounded, as was the major himself.[106] The killed officers usually were shot in the head as the snipers aimed to panic the troops by eliminating their leaders. Major Nestor sent word to Estillac that it was impossible to turn the flank because of the heights to the one side and of the ground falling away on the other. Stopped dead, Estillac ordered withdrawal to Tapera.

The measure of the rebels' determination and their clever use of the terrain's defensive possibilities is that, according to participants' later testimony, they numbered merely 130. These hungry, besieged sertanejos put six hundred well-armed and provisioned soldiers to rout.[107]

This retreat proved to be almost as painful as the advance had been. The trail was difficult, especially for those straining to carry the dead and wounded in hammocks. At times the soldiers had to widen and smooth the trail to permit passage. Meanwhile, the rebels kept up a harassing fire from the dark forest, but they made no serious counterattack, and after 2 P.M. they gave up the pursuit. Clearly they were defending themselves rather than seeking to destroy the army. As the troops limped away, their losses totaled two officers, one scout, and thirty-seven soldiers killed; three officers, twenty-six soldiers wounded.[108] One veteran of these engagements, Alcibiades Miranda, lamented what he called a sad truth: that soldiers killed in the fighting "almost always remained abandoned in the jungle, unburied in the bosom of the forest! And you could almost say the same about the gravely wounded!" Rather bitterly, he recalled that the wounded first had to strain to reach their comrades and then to live through the difficult journey to the field hospital in Perdizes. The worst means of transport, he thought, was being lashed to the back of a mule or horse. The nerves of medical personnel were often overwhelmed by the suffering that they witnessed and the lack of resources with which to work. He attributed these disastrous shortcomings to the lack of importance the "office warriors" back in Rio de Janeiro attached to this conflict.[109]

Despite their successful defense the rebels were feeling the effects of the north-south vise. Many families had headed east to surrender to Colonel

César, who seems to have gained a reputation for treating prisoners better than the other commanders.[110] Although a certain number gave up, others continued to stream into Santa Maria, escaping the advancing troops. The combination of losing access to outside supplies and accumulating more mouths to feed produced an unprecedented hunger in the redoubt. Each day saw two steers slaughtered, but as the numbers increased the shares got smaller and smaller. Children would crowd around with cups to catch blood as a steer's throat was cut. The lack of salt reduced the people to licking each other's sweat. Dogs and horses disappeared into cooking pots. Walnuts and wild honey fed some, whereas others took to boiling hides, belts, and saddlebags![111] Time was on the army's side. A steadily tightened siege would have ended the affair, slowly and painfully for the rebels. But there is little glory, and fewer promotions, in military operations conducted without death and destruction.

The last dramatic, bloody days would partially determine who was to run the Brazilian army in the following decade. Setembrino ordered his two-man air force aloft to obtain an exact fix on Santa Maria. Unfortunately, on March 1, shortly after takeoff the weather fouled and Lieutenant Ricardo Kirk crashed and was killed.[112] Minister of War Faria telegraphed his condolences to Setembrino (as well he might, for the army had lost its only aviator). Faria ordered the Italian Darioli sent back to Rio along with the aircraft because he thought it improper for the army to depend on a foreign pilot for air support. The incident pointed up a curious contradiction in Brazilian attitudes. The army had hired him in the first place because its decision makers preferred to have a foreigner set up the aviation school rather than give a Brazilian that responsibility. Yet when it came to actual field operations, national pride demanded that aviation be dispensed with rather than rely on that same foreigner. Not without reason *A Defesa Nacional* worried about the future of Brazilian army aviation.[113]

Setembrino had hoped that Estillac would get his renewed attack underway on March 1 to commemorate the forty-fifth anniversary of the conclusion of the Paraguayan War. He sent his aide, First Lieutenant Daltro Filho to Tapera to convey his desire.[114] Estillac, waiting for air support, delayed that attack and then rescheduled it for 2:30 A.M. on March 2. From that hour until 5:30 A.M. his howitzers continuously hurled high-explosive and shrapnel shells in the rebels' direction. To the latter's relief the shells all fell short, and many failed to explode. The artillery was using the wrong range, and the darkness and forest cover prevented discovering and correcting the error. In the daylight, realizing the lengthy bombardment's failure, Estillac ordered scouts to cut a trail to a forward position from which Santa Maria's chapel could be seen. To overcome the barricade that had stopped the column's previous advance, he sent the mountain cannon to blast it away. Why this had not been done on February 8 is not known. With a heavy force of infantry providing cover the civilian scouts hacked away at the thick growth while two teams of heavy oxen pulled a howitzer forward. By 11:30 A.M. all was ready. From their vantage point the soldiers could count three hundred houses and a church in what Setembrino called this "Mecca of Fanaticism."

Down in the settlement a procession could be seen leaving the chapel. The people had assumed that a miracle had prevented the artillery shells from hitting Santa Maria, so they were giving thanks. Their faith and their bodies were shattered when the howitzer's first round exploded in their midst. Horror spread across their faces as parts of bodies flew in all directions. Some ran inside the chapel and shut the door, only to have the building burn and fall on top of them. The howitzer spread fire, destruction, and death until 3 P.M. Curiously, the column did not take advantage of the surprise and shock. The 75-degree slope down to the valley made direct artillery support impossible against rebels who had taken refuge in defiles from which they aimed deadly fire. Sensing that the rebels were maneuvering to get closer shots at the oxen, Estillac ordered the howitzer withdrawn.

And then he made his most basic tactical error, one of the most common in antiguerrilla operations. He withdrew his men to their original lines rather than risk having them surrounded during the night. The inability to hold ground dearly won meant that each day the trail would have to be retaken. There ensued a month of fighting up to the escarpment's edge during daylight and retreating before dark. The column's chief scout, "Colonel" Manoel Fabrício Vieira, told Estillac that he would need five thousand troops, in a combined attack with the northern column, to take Santa Maria.[115] On the southern side the lay of the land gave the defenders the advantage. The troops muttered that from this side taking Santa Maria was impossible.[116]

Morale fell. The skies poured down the rains of March. Supplies of food, clothing, and medicine dwindled. In the Fifty-eighth Battalion some soldiers cut up their blankets to make warmer clothes. Strong winds howled, and the intense, damp cold ate into the shivering soldiers' bones. They could not ease their discomfort with the customary ration of *cachaça* because it had been replaced by coffee for disciplinary reasons. The soldiers cut the forest to improve their lines of defensive fire and covered their tents with warming layers of grass until their encampments looked like so many Indian villages. Their potable water diminished day by day as they fouled the streams. In the coals of their fires they baked *uarube,* a doughy bread made from manioc flour mixed with salt and water. At night they sang and danced the "Mineiro," "Côco," and "Catopé." They waited for better weather and for something to happen.[117]

While they huddled in their camps, General Setembrino enjoyed the relative comfort of Curitiba. He telegraphed Minister Caetano de Faria that he wanted to return to Rio to discuss the situation directly, but the minister replied that his departure from the zone of conflict would look bad in the press and that he should be with his troops.

The decisive action came out of the north. From March 5 to March 7 Setembrino met in Porto União with Colonels Estillac, Onofre, Julio César, and Socrates to devise their final plans. Having witnessed his men dying to little result, Colonel Estillac argued in favor of a siege to let hunger force the sertanejos of Santa Maria into surrender. A siege would save lives on both sides and make it easier to reincorporate the rebels into the Pátria. But Setembrino had his budget and his army and intended to use both. The southern column was to keep up a steady bombardment, and elements of the northern and eastern columns were to rendezvous; then the three were to attack from both sides simultaneously. Having cut the redoubts' lines of communications and retreat, Setembrino believed that the bombardment and harassing attacks, plus a massive assault, would bring victory. He admitted to Minister Faria that the strategy was not original; he was following the counsels of Karl von Clausewitz (1780–1831).[118]

The plan looked great when laid out on the map, but its success required constant communications. These failed completely. Telegraph and telephone lines linked the column's headquarters with Setembrino, but there were no communications where it counted, between the maneuvering units. Overall the combat arms lacked unity of effort and in combat did not keep contact with the auxiliary services. Setembrino complained to Minister Faria that there was a "crisis of command" in the officer corps, that although there were "some competent officers," there were few who had the "moral, intellectual and practical qualities of a true soldier."[119] In his various telegrams and letters during the campaign and in after action reports, the historian looks in vain for word that the general accepted some of the blame for the situation.

Contestado: Potyguara's Attack on Santa Maria

Almost as if he had conjured him up, Setembrino got a soldier after his own heart. The man of the hour was Captain Tertuliano de Albuquerque Potyguara. On March 26 he moved his 400 soldiers and 148 civilian scouts from Canoinhas to Reichardt. He was to meet the eastern column, coming from Colonia Vieira, at a place called Vaca Branca. A mix-up occurred that would have been humorous had lives not been lost as a result. On March 21 the eastern column set out and its scouts reached Vaca Branca on the twenty-third but naturally found no trace of Potyguara's troops, who were still in Canoinhas. In fact, Onofre had changed their rendezvous from Vaca Branca to Tamanduá because rains had muddied the approaches from the north. Although Onofre sent a letter explaining the change to Julio César on the twenty-seventh, it seems likely that he did not receive it in time to act accordingly.[120] As a result, on March 30 the two detachments were miles apart as they searched for each other, Potyguara's men around Tamanduá and Julio César's in the vicinity of Vaca Branca, sounding bugle calls and firing signal shots. Although they failed to link up, they certainly alerted the rebels. With this noisy commotion in the northeast and with the southern column's daily bombardment, hundreds of rebel families sought to escape via the southeast, where some of them found themselves prisoners of the Ninth Cavalry Regiment, whose patrols blocked the routes to Lages.[121] Others fled to São Miguel, a place hidden away in the forested hills, where after the fall of Santa Maria some of the survivors would gather.[122]

Potyguara's attack on Santa Maria had all the earmarks of a gory adventure story. From March 31 until April 4 his detachment crossed flooding rivers and slogged over muddy trails, engaged in nearly constant combat. There was a certain irony or, better, tragedy in that it was Holy Week. On the first of April, Holy Thursday, his men faced the outer edge of the string of settlements or redoubts collectively called Santa Maria. This first section, along the Rio Caçador, was "situated in a beautiful position and arranged in such manner as to offer strong resistance to any regular force." Defense works of walnut and pine trunks protected the houses, and the lay of the land provided many natural foxholes. After forcing the "bandidos," as he termed them, back to these defenses, Potyguara admitted that they staged "one of the bravest and most heroic resistances" he had observed in his twenty-six years of soldiering. Only carefully placed machine guns were able to crack the rebels' one-thousand-meter-long line. Amid shouting and cheers the soldiers burned 1,181 dwellings, counted 109 bodies, and pushed on. Slightly more than a mile later they were hit from the front and flank but fought their way through. That night, with many wounded to care for and fear overcoming bodily demands, none of the detachment slept.[123]

On April 2 the sheer weight of their adversaries' numbers soon stopped their advance. Hand-to-hand combat raged to shouts of *degola!* Bayonets and knives flashed in a "titanic struggle" that even Potyguara saw as "human madness." When it was spent, eighty-five "bandidos" lay on the ground, "completely disfigured."[124] After a brief rest they advanced against old Aleixo's section, where the rebels fired from dug-in positions. This time Potyguara used ten minutes of machine-gun fire to soften up the defenders. Holding his long, machete-like knife, he encouraged, inflamed his men. Six buglers sounded the charge that sent the soldiers racing across twelve hundred meters of terrain toward the defenders. The two sides locked in bloody slaughter. Soldiers, scouts, and rebels fell fighting into the Santa Maria River looking to Potyguara like "wild beasts thirsty for blood and vengeance." An hour after it had begun the rebels had melted into the forest. The troops burned hundreds of dwellings, straw huts, and a chapel. They found a large portrait of Aleixo de Lima, dressed in the uniform of captain of the Fifteenth Cavalry Regiment of the National Guard! For all the drama of the combat only forty-eight rebel bodies were counted.[125]

That afternoon he had the buglers repeatedly sound the "victory call," which he heard echoing through the gullies and forest as "a protest of civilization against barbarism!" Neither the buglers nor the repeated signal shots roused, in Potyguara's sarcastic terms, "the imaginary Southern Column" or the "swift detachment" of the eastern column. He was disillusioned and felt misused. Where were they? The first should have been attacking, and he had thought that the second was a day's march in front of him. Instead, he had fought his way into the center of the rebel "den." The enemy had resisted, but perhaps most had simply gotten out of the way. Now his unit was alone, his scouts were wounded, as were about one-fourth of his force, and most of his officers were dead. They spent Good Friday, April 2, resting, watching, and caring for the wounded.[126]

The next day the troops fought their way into Santa Maria proper. In a three-hour engagement they beat back the rebels, who left ninety-one dead. The soldiers' machine guns gave them a superiority of firepower that overwhelmed the sertanejos' numerical supremacy. But perhaps the latter were only buying time for their families to flee because the troops found no signs of life. Some houses were closed up, others open, all abandoned. As they moved carefully among the deserted buildings only the birds cried out in protest as they took wing. They looted the dwellings for valuables, then set them afire. In the center of the settlement they built a log defense works. Now in the distance, they could hear the many buglers of the southern column encampment at Tapera four miles away. Once again Potyguara ordered his buglers to work, hoping that Estillac's force would respond. There was no food beyond that already distributed. They had misjudged the distance from Reichardt to Tapera (it was eighty-nine miles instead of fifty), and the promised juncture with the other columns proved an illusion. From the tone of his after-action report he obviously felt undone, perhaps betrayed.

It was Holy Saturday, 1915. The last rays of the sun disappeared in a momentarily clear, calm sky. As night fell, huge clouds rolled across it. Potyguara wrote that he thought of God and suffering as he watched. Rifle fire shattered whatever reverie he or his men may have enjoyed. Bit by bit the unseen Winchesters, Comblains, and Mausers barked, cracked, and flashed in the darkness like so many monstrous fireflies filling the air with hissing and whistling death. The "hospital" took heavy fire; the detachment surgeon, Dr. (Lt.) Alexandre de Souto Castagnino, was hit, agonized through the night, and died the next afternoon. The "brave bugler" Marcellino was killed as he sounded signal calls. The night was a "stupefying hell."[127]

Contestado: The Final Fight at Santa Maria

Easter Sunday's dawn brought the notes of the southern column's *reveille* being sounded beyond the *serra,* raising hopes that help would come. Potyguara wrote a plea: "Dear Friend Estillac: I am here in this hell, after ten days of horrendous marches, in day and night combat. I ask that you advance with urgency to help me in the rest of our painful [espinhosa] mission."[128] Under covering machine-gun and rifle fire, thirty select men broke out at a run for the forest cover. By noon rebel pressure eased enough for soldiers to move around, although carefully. An ammunition check revealed that each man had three to five cartridges left. The moans of the wounded soldiers mixed with the neighing and braying horses and mules, who lay slowly bleeding to death with saddles still on their backs. Chief scout Leocádio Pacheco died of a shot in the forehead. Firing slackened still more in the early afternoon, and the weary troops buried their dead. Suddenly at 5 P.M. the reason for the rebels' easing of pressure was clear. Shouts and shots came from the direction of Tapera. Running toward them was Captain Salvador Pinheiro and some of "Colonel" Fabricio's scouts in the vanguard of the Fourteenth Battalion. By nightfall Potyguara's soldiers' salvation was assured. Santa Maria was completely in ashes.[129]

Every day Estillac's troops had repeated the tactic of clearing the trail to the point where rebel resistance halted their advance and then retreating at nightfall. On the morning of April 2 he had telegraphed Setembrino that at 8 A.M. shooting could be heard in the distance, indicating the presence of "friendly forces" to the northeast. "I am already cooperating," he declared, "in joint action which I am confident will give us victory." Setembrino replied immediately that it was "the brave Captain Potyguara," ordering Estillac to "attack with vigor seeking decision." The column's forces engaged the rebels in an intense battle for the trail. But by 1 P.M. the rebels had them pinned down after only a 220-yard advance. Their exact marksmanship had taken twelve soldiers out of action. The rebels did not offer any fixed positions the army could attack but fired from high in the trees, from bamboo thickets, from depressions in the ground. Their invisibility made it impossible to know if the great amount of ammunition the troops expended had any effect. That night, at 7, Estillac pulled his men back, telegraphing Setembrino that the "enemy presented today a resistance equal if not superior to that of the 8th of February." The general questioned the wisdom of this nightly retreat, implying that Estillac ought to reconsider his tactics, but he did not offer a different solution.

On April 3, while Potyguara's men held their ground in the heart of Santa Maria, Estillac wrote a long telegram justifying his tactics and inability to secure a fixed position in the forest or to break through into the valley.

Happily for Potyguara's detachment, the message on Easter morning galva-
nized Estillac's resolve, and he ordered his units "to advance until encounter-
ing Captain Potyguara, regardless of enemy resistance (or) . . . losses that you
suffer!" Much to their surprise on reaching the area of the past days' clashes
they met no resistance; the rebels had either gone to attack Potyguara in the
hope of eliminating his detachment before the column could attack, or,
more likely, they were gradually pulling out altogether. And then the juncture described above took place.[130]

Estillac finally had his men spend a night in the forest, camped at points
along the trail from Tapera to Santa Maria. He did not himself descend into
the valley, so Estillac never set foot in his long-sought objective but awaited
Potyguara on the upper slope. Their meeting was one of the bitterest scenes
in Brazilian military history. Ragged, dirty, his mouth tight with anger, his
oft-used long knife in his belt, Potyguara strode forward vigorously. Behind
him, his men looked exhausted, their clothes torn, their skin scratched and
bruised as they shuffled along slowly. They had lost 2 officers, 32 soldiers,
and 22 scouts killed; and 2 officers, 58 soldiers, and 39 scouts wounded. By
comparison in all the previous fighting the losses had been 8 officers, 110
soldiers, and 22 scouts killed, and 26 officers, 113 soldiers, and 25 scouts
wounded.[131]

With the Fifty-first Light Infantry cheering loudly the two officers faced
each other. Potyguara asked icily why Estillac's "great column" had not
made the juncture much sooner. Estillac replied that for weeks they had
been unable to descend into the valley because of the "great resistance of
the bandidos!" He was not convincing then or later.[132]

Setembrino telegraphed that Estillac should pursue the enemy energetically. "It is necessary," he advised, "that this struggle close as one more significant conquest for the Army and an example of valor for history. It is necessary to win, cost whatever it costs." Estillac replied that they had pursued the
rebels all through the night of April 4, and during the morning of the fifth,
until they ceased to return fire less than two miles from Santa Maria. "I
consider (the enemy) destroyed." From Tamanduá to Santa Maria some five
thousand dwellings were in ashes. Potyguara did not take prisoners and reported killing some six hundred rebels in combat. Although it appears that
most sertanejos either merely got out of the army's path or, desperate and
disillusioned, fled from the region, many regrouped in new redoubts along
the São Miguel River and at Pedro Branca. Even so, Estillac declared the "last
redoubt of banditry" destroyed. "I can not guarantee that all the *bandidos* who
infested the Contestado have disappeared, but the mission given to the Army
is accomplished." Setembrino replied with congratulations and the observation that the "brilliant success" of their forces in taking the redoubts between
Santa Maria and Caçador Rivers would "elevate the name of the Army and

silence the slanderers who heap their sordid contempt on the dignity of soldiers who never refused the fulfillment of their difficult [espinhoso] duty."[133]

Potyguara's detachment rested a day and then marched to Caçador to entrain for Canoinhas. A short distance from the Tapera encampment they killed and mutilated a prisoner entrusted to them for delivery to Porto União.[134] Other surrendering rebels suffered similar fates at the hands of civilian scouts.

It was time to end the campaign. The column's camps were becoming hygienically intolerable. The waters of the streams were contaminated. Cases of typhoid fever were mounting. And from the forests the terrible smell of rotting human and animal flesh made breathing in some places insupportable.

In effect, Setembrino declared the campaign a victory, and the division's units headed back to their home barracks. In a speech in Porto União he gestured toward Potyguara saying: "Captain, you saved the honor of the National Army." A small force was left behind to eliminate those rebels who had avoided the army. Combined harassment and internal dissension led to their defeat or surrender. An unknown, but sizable, number died after being taken prisoner. Surviving prisoners were parceled out as *colonos* to various settlement projects in the region. The mopping-up operation was left in the hands of mixed civilian-military forces and the state police of Paraná and Santa Catarina, under the command of Infantry Colonel Antonio Sebastião Bazilio Pyrrho, a veteran now of both Canudos and the Contestado, whose selection was ironic considering that his family name came from the Greek name that gave rise to the expression "Pyrrhic victory." At the time, some officers feared that their success would turn out to be Pyrrhic. Although Colonel Pyrrho had eliminated the remaining sizable rebel pockets by the end of 1915, a new danger appeared at the end of July 1917 when seditious elements rebelled against the boundary agreement between Santa Catarina and Paraná in favor of a separate state of Missões. This time the army responded promptly and snuffed out the movement by September 1917. Reduced detachments were quartered at Canoinhas and União de Vitória to maintain the national government's presence.[135] The army had made the Contestado safe for progress.

The campaign's effects would be felt for generations. Setembrino declared that it confirmed that the army "needed real organization and training." However, he hesitated to say that the Contestado experience should derail the army's Europeanization. A sertanejo war was not as respectable as a European-style conflict. This "small war," which he compared in his after-action report to the French colonial wars in Asia and Africa, had not "invalidated" the army's regulations based on "magnificent German doctrine," nor had it taught anything new, but "it warned us," Setembrino wrote, "that we must improve intellectually, morally, practically." Despite denying that the campaign had real lessons, he detailed a number of them. Interestingly, the undertone of his report was that future conflicts of this sort on the peripheries of civilized Brazil were likely. Considering that "war is armed politics," he emphasized that future field commanders had to enjoy the "unlimited confidence of the Government" and should be given the "indivisible authority of a dictator" to avoid problems with civil authorities. He criticized the press, which he wanted censored in similar future situations to keep information from the enemy and to prevent negative reports from discouraging the citizenry. He urged that future "expeditionary detachments" consist of mobile columns of predominately infantry troops utilizing civilian scouts *(vaqueanos)*. Later, as minister of war (1922–26), he would deploy such columns against the army's own rebel officers with considerably less success than had been the case in the Contestado. His report detailed the need for proper field uniforms; stronger shoes, tents, and wagons; and better use of telegraph and field telephones; it praised the soldier's Mauser rifle, while urging officer use of Smith and Wesson 38 or 44 side arms. He pointed up the deficiencies of foreign control of the railways, arguing for laws that would give the army authority to run them in emergencies. And calling for improved military training, he admitted that there were large numbers of officers who were innocent of any military theory. And, not intending to be prophetic, he nonetheless pointed ahead to the disciplinary crisis of the 1920s by noting that many junior officers were more critical than in the past of their superiors because they were better trained. During the campaign there had been "truly anomalous situations in which the superiority of the senior officer was due only to rank." Leadership, discipline, and obedience, he warned, were based ultimately on moral authority that came from "real professional capability."[136]

In the next chapter we will see how a remarkable group of officers, who by 1913 had returned from training with the Imperial German Army, produced sparks of reform. They, together with some of the Contestado campaign veterans, worked to give the officer corps the capabilities that Setembrino saw as lacking in the Contestado. Oddly, only a few of the German-prepared officers were sent to Santa Catarina, perhaps because army leaders thought it a war not worthy of their talents or worth the risk of losing the investment made in their European training.[137] But the Contestado experience was certainly of interest to the reformers, who published articles on it in *A Defesa Nacional* during and after the campaign and raised money for the families of those killed in action. Moreover, one of the review's clarion calls—for the majority of officers to end their "criminal," "unpatriotic indifference" and "pernicious inertia" and to join in rebuilding Brazil's war machine—was written by Contestado veteran Second Lieutenant Mario Travassos.[138]

In August 1917 the editors summarized General Setembrino's report and commented that the "loss of precious lives" resulted from a long-standing lack of foresight and decisive action. The army's helter-skelter assembly of an expeditionary force from unrelated units hurled a precarious organization of "irregular troops" into "an inglorious conflict that discredited our arms." The editors issued a severe indictment of the republic declaring that the Contestado was nothing more than the "absence of elevated political norms, the abandonment of thousands of Brazilians, who until today are segregated from national society by the lack of instruction, by the scarcity of easy means of communication, by the want of energy, and by the poverty of initiative that, unhappily, has characterized the administrations generally since the time of the monarchy." They warned "our military chiefs" that "the lesson of the Contestado" was that "the passivity with which the army was accepting all the poorly inspired measures of political origin . . . will only bring it moral damage and [will bring] the most funereal consequences to the country that does not have confidence in its army."[139]

The Contestado remained an important component of the army's institutional memory for years to come. Without clear testimony it is difficult to gauge the impact of the rebellion on the thinking and later behavior of individual officers, but it is noteworthy that officers who played significant roles in the 1920s, and later, participated in the fighting. Three later ministers of war were veterans of the campaign: General Setembrino, Captain Nestor Sezefredo dos Passos, and as a graduate of the first class out of the new military school of Realengo, Aspirante Henrique Batista Duffles Teixeira Lott began his forty-five year career with this campaign. At least two tenente rebels of the 1920s were veterans: 2d Lts. Euclydes Hermes da Fonseca, son of the president and later commander of Ft. Copacabana in the 1922 uprising; and Heitor Mendes Conçalves, who had distinguished himself by conducting long-range reconnaissance in the Contestado. Indeed, at the time of the Revolution of 1930, there were 109 veterans (15 percent) among the 716 active-duty officers who were commissioned in time to have served in the Contestado. Over the next decades at least twenty-six (24 percent) attained generals stars. Six of these were among the thirty-three major and brigadier generals in 1930. If the Contestado experience did not make clear to the officer corps the realities and problems of rural Brazil, it is difficult to imagine what would have done so.[140]

There would be Contestado veterans among the general officers down to the 1960s, most notably General Henrique Lott, who was minister of war from 1954 to 1960. As late as the 1970s, when the army was greatly preoccupied with guerrilla warfare, the study of the Contestado and of Canudos was part of the preparation expected of officers selected for the command and general staff school. Because many of the factors that produced such movements still existed in Brazilian society, army thinkers hoped that the study of history would suggest peaceful solutions. And, perhaps most indicative, modern road maps still show the area of Santa Maria along the Timbó River as empty of roads and towns.[141]

Finally, there is a curious link with the Revolution of 1930. In a ceremony in May 1915 a marble commemorative plaque hailing General Setembrino's victory was affixed to a wall of the army's regional headquarters in Curitiba. During the turmoil of October 1930 someone removed the plaque, which was not seen again.[142]

In this chapter we saw that the army and its officers were deeply involved in two lines of action that immersed the institution and, through it, the national government in the internal affairs of the states: the first, the salvationist movement, which replaced old state oligarchies with groups more acceptable to the national authorities, often to the benefit of individual senior officers; and the second, the Contestado, in which the army acted as the ultimate enforcer of the capitalist development model that the Old Republic was embracing, a model that bent the rural areas to the needs of the coastal cities and foreign capital and markets. The era's dual legacy of political intervention and suppression of dissent would muddy the army's mission for decades to come, even as it enhanced the power of the central government. Wallace's idea of the "politics of the appetites," in which opponents seek to take over existing power structures with little change, was an apt description of the salvationist movement; and his "politics of identity" fitted those religiously motivated rebels in the Contestado, who sought a better life and rights for the "Brazilian Sons" at a time when everything seemed to be "for the peoples of *Oropa* [Europe]." However, the politics of appetite marshaled greater force and crushed the politics of identity.

CHAPTER 4

Patriotism and Modernization

[N]ascent societies have need of military elements to assist
their formation and development.
—*A Defesa Nacional,* Oct. 10, 1913

[M]ilitary defense is neither the principal, nor the first, nor
the most vigorous of our means of defense.
—Alberto Tôrres, *Presença de Alberto Tôrres*

With the end of the war in Europe conquerors and
conquered . . . will not hesitate to develop imperialist
policies, and South America, principally Brazil whose
riches had already stirred the greed of several [foreign]
syndicates, will be the objective of the conqueror's claws.
—General Antonio Ilha Moreira, "O Exército e a Nação"

While the Brazilian army had been preoccupied with the Contestado, the
First World War had broken out, and Brazilian officers watched in fascination
as the two model armies of Germany and France tested men, equipment,
organization, strategy, and tactics against each other. The European focus of
the national elites was starkly revealed in their nearly complete silence on the
fighting in the Contestado. Even though army operations there attracted
press coverage, the tone of commentary implied this was another backlands
affair that did not merit serious attention. It was fashionable for Rio de
Janeiro's society matrons to raise money for the suffering Belgians but not
for their displaced or wounded countrymen and -women in beleaguered
Santa Catarina. The war in Europe rather than that in the Contestado provided the backdrop against which the reform and reorganization plans that
had been developed during the previous years were put into practice.
Obligatory military service became a reality, and some officers hungered to
have their expanded army join the fighting in Europe. That desire was frustrated, but the physical expansion resulting from obligatory service further

extended the army's reach throughout Brazil and thereby increased the central government's ability to intervene in the states.

This chapter examines the officer corps' efforts to define the army, its mission, and its relationship to the society and political system. The resulting vision gave army leaders direction and energy, but it also sowed seeds that, as we shall see in later chapters, led some officers to revolutionary, violent solutions. We begin here with an analysis of ideological development.

Ideology of the Military's Role in Society

The First World War raised the consciousness of the Brazilian elites regarding their country's weakness, but they did not immediately agree on a proper course of action. Emotions for and against the warring sides ran high. Even antimilitarist Rui Barbosa argued that Brazil could not be neutral before the violation of international law. For him, by invading neutral Belgium, Germany had put itself beyond the pale. But Federal Deputy Dunshee de Abranches saw the war as a commercial conflict and opposed favoring the Allies because Britain's blockade of German trade and communications cost Brazil dearly in lost business. Caustically, he pointed to the irony of Britain rushing to save Belgium from "enslavement" while its own troops crushed "the liberty of Ireland." Retired diplomat Manuel de Oliveira Lima questioned whether the war might not allow the United States to enlarge the scope of the Monroe Doctrine to the detriment of Latin America. His articles in *O Estado de São Paulo* had such a pro-German tone that the British declared him persona non grata.[1] Intellectuals Olavo Bilac and Alberto Tôrres, who will be discussed below, urged strengthening Brazil to make it independent and autonomous, but, just as they differed on the war, they proposed different roles for the military. The ensuing debate over national defense centered on obligatory military service and shaped competing ideas of the army's role in Brazilian society. It brought to the surface three interpretations of the army's mission: that expounded by the military journal, *A Defesa Nacional;* that of poet and military booster, Olavo Bilac; and that of politician and writer Alberto Tôrres.[2]

The officers who founded and published *A Defesa Nacional* were a new phenomenon in the Brazilian army—they were educated, *and* they knew how to lead troops. Their task was to make themselves models for future generations, but in that effort they clashed with two older groups: the "doctors" and the *tarimbeiros.* The first had come out of the reform fever of 1890 that turned the military school into a center of positivist philosophy. "Everyone wanted to be a doctor: Dr. Lieutenant, Dr. Captain, Dr. General, or simply 'Sir Doctor' ['seu doutor'], . . . as many soldiers called certain officers." The *tarimbeiros* had come up through the ranks, with little formal education.

Many of them could barely read, seemingly believing that "illiteracy hard-ened the muscles." They must have been sorely irritated by the airs of the "Dr. Lieutenants," who discussed philosophy and quoted poetry. By late 1914 Second Lieutenant Francisco de Paula Cidade noted happily that ex-aggerated "doctorism" was on the decline and that there were few old-time *tarimbeiros* left on active duty. Even so, a significant number of officers pas-sively resisted modernization because they felt threatened by change or be-cause the innovations were being proposed and carried out by lower-rank-ing men.[3]

The *Defesa Nacional* group was made up of junior officers who had served in Germany and enthusiastic colleagues who wanted to learn from their expe-rience. Most of the latter officers were associated with the Escola de Guerra and the *Revista dos Militares* in Porto Alegre. Between 1905 and 1912 three contingents, totaling thirty-four officers, had spent two years in German regiments. The modern Brazilian army dates from their return home.[4] In addition to founding the important *A Defesa Nacional,* they and their associ-ates made up the so-called Indigenous Mission that instructed cadets at the Escola Militar between 1919 and 1923, thereby influencing officers who would lead the army into the second half of the century.

Significantly, these military reformers promptly embraced the nickname "Young Turks," after the Turkish officers who had reshaped the Ottoman Empire. Initially, their detractors had applied the name negatively, perhaps in part because *Turco* was then a pejorative term in Brazil for Middle Eastern immigrants, but the reformers adopted it enthusiastically. After all, the Ger-mans had also trained the Turkish officers; indeed, that training mission had been commanded by General (Baron) Friedrich Colmar von der Goltz, who in 1910 had been poised to assume direction of a similar mission in Brazil. It should be recalled that the professionalized Turkish officers seized power and reformed their country.[5]

Although it is true that members of the *Defesa Nacional* group saw the army's prime function as external defense, they did not think that the army should be aloof from society. To them being apolitical meant that officers should stay out of *party* politics, and all other extrainstitutional activities, in order to concentrate their energies on perfecting the army.[6]

They included military intervention in society among the army's roles. In their oft-cited first editorial the review's founders asserted that it was "an historic fact that nascent societies have need of military elements to assist their formation and development." Only when a society reached a high level of civilization could it be free of military tutelage, and only then could the military "limit itself to its true function." Although they did not want to in-ject unjustifiably "military elements into the country's internal affairs, the Army needs . . . to be prepared," they said, "for its stabilizing and conservator function" in a changing society. The army was "the first factor of politico-social transformation," and it had to "educate and organize the general mass of citizens." Their goal was to pass on to the society the virtues of a good army: hierarchical and social discipline; the abandoning of individual for collective interests; and a sense of duty and sacrifice for the Pátria. They observed that if military influence helped improve the old, cultured societies of Europe, how much more "in a country like Brazil," with its "retarded and unformed society," would it be "a powerful formative and transforming factor." Their goal was to construct an army that corresponded to the "legitimate aspirations of development and progress," convinced that "the social capacity of a people is measured and evaluated by its military organization." They could not cross their arms and trust to fate the defense of "one of the most opulent countries of Earth." These officers saw themselves as a "band of Cavaliers of the Idea," who would use reason instead of clubs to fight for their ideals. Convinced that "progress is the work of dissidents," their duty was to criticize in order to correct.[7]

By late 1914 they had an extensive reform program, which they recommended that the new minister of war, General José Caetano de Faria, put into practice. They stressed that he should begin at the bottom and work upward, first lowering the cost of maintaining the individual soldier so as to allow increasing the number of trainees to be inducted each year, in order to expand the reserves more rapidly. Their suggestions were substantive and aimed at improving efficiency. (1) They wanted the volunteers to report en masse to the barracks on a fixed date, rather than individually throughout the year, so that instruction could be organized effectively. (2) The health inspections of recruits should be more severe, and (3) only "morally" sound men should be inducted. (4) Obligatory military service should be put in operation to make the army "a part of the Nation," thereby replacing the "military class" with the "Nation in Arms." And because only the officer corps, as the military instructors of the citizenry, would be permanent, the cost of the nation's soldiery would be lowered. (5) The time of service for those already trained *(instruidos)* should be lessened to speed their entry into the reserves. (6) The number of units should be diminished to permit each an effective strength that (7) would allow proper troop instruction and prepare the officers for actual wartime command. (8) The army's peacetime organization should be the same as its wartime order of battle so that mobilized reserves could be easily incorporated. (9) The administrative services should be decentralized so that provisioning could be done at local levels to increase economy and to improve footwear and uniforms. (10) The latter should be national property so that stocks could be built up. (11) Instructional areas should be created in every garrison to train recruits under realistic combat field conditions. (12) The law establishing remount depots should be put in operation to supply the necessary horses and mules. (13) Finally, "political ambitions" should be kept out of the officer corps by a "serious and just promotion law."[8] In addition, *Defesa Nacional* officers argued for modern armament, ammunition for target practice, and, most especially, the contracting of a foreign military mission to help remodel and perfect the army.[9]

One of the Young Turks' first reforms was to train noncommissioned officers—corporals and sergeants—so that they in turn could train the recruits. This technical measure, in an army where it was not traditional and where corporals and sergeants were marginal figures, was revolutionary and probably contributed to later unrest among the subalterns.

The second conception of the army's role in society was that which poet Olavo Bilac, a self-styled "professor of enthusiasm," presented in his 1915–16 campaign in favor of obligatory military service. In his view the military's defense role was less important than its teaching function. Its principal mission was the civic education of the citizenry. By bringing all classes to the barracks, he argued, the army would act as a social leveler, teaching discipline, patriotism, and order. By making the army the people and the people the army, Bilac believed that the danger of a military caste was eliminated.

He depicted obligatory service as "a promise of salvation" for Brazil. Reflecting the prevalent middle-class view that Brazil was not a cohesive, unified nation, he saw the privileged elite classes wanting only self-pleasure and prosperity, the lower classes living "in the most extreme ignorance, displaying only inertia, apathy, superstition, [and] the absolute lack of conscience," while the foreign immigrants lived isolated by language and custom. The "militarization of all civilians" would give the society middle-class virtues, endowing it with the cohesion necessary to preserve itself. Military service would raise up the lower classes and level the upper classes.

To Bilac the urban middle classes were the true Brazilians. His views of the *povo,* the majority of the population, were laced with contradictions. "In the rude *sertões,* the men are not Brazilians, nor even true men: they are living things without a free and creative soul, like the beasts, like the insects, like the trees." The sertanejo looks "miserable and sad: thin body, colorless skin, bloodless arteries, blank look, enfeebled organism, lifeless soul, suppressed will, dim witted. He is the shadow of a man." "The cities," too, he said, "are full of lazy, barefoot, ragged enemies of the 'ABC's' and of bathing—brute animals, who have only the appearance and the wickedness of men." Yet, saying that the small educated minority had to perfect itself before trying to perfect the people *(Povo),* he enthused that "the people possess energies and virtues, stronger and purer than ours," that they only needed to be stimulated.[10]

Military service, Bilac asserted, would stimulate them, purify them, and return them to society as "conscientious, worthy Brazilians." The military would provide the discipline and order to reconstruct Brazil by uplifting the downcast millions. And blaming the rural oligarchies for the people's miserable condition, he argued that only the middle class possessed "complete intellectual and moral culture," "high-mindedness," and the capacity to place themselves above self, class, or partisan interests; therefore they were destined "to the sacred mission of governing and directing the multitude."[11]

The military, already possessing these high qualities, would help the middle class take power peacefully. The nation, that is, the remade people under middle-class leadership, would be the army; and the army, reformed, restructured, redirected, would be the nation. The officer corps, in Bilac's vision, was the army, its soul—"all the sensibility, all the intelligence, all the will of the corporation of soldiers." The officer was the priest of the cult of the Pátria and as such should flee from political ambition and involvement. The officer would be the regenerator and disciplinarian, the middle class would govern and direct.[12]

Bilac took this message to the core of modern Brazil—the south-central and southern states. Student, intellectual, and military audiences in São Paulo, Belo Horizonte, Rio de Janeiro, Curitiba, and Porto Alegre heard his rousing, patriotic speeches. Significantly, on October 9, 1915, he opened his crusade at the São Paulo Law School, which had eagerly embraced Rui Barbosa's antimilitarist campaign in 1910. Bilac's mission was to reconcile São Paulo, via its youth, with the military; indeed, it was to reconcile urbanites throughout Brazil with the military.[13]

The São Paulo speech was the rallying bugle of his campaign, in which he heralded the "militarization of all civilians" in the purifying "filter" of the barracks. Here he first annunciated the theme that ran through subsequent addresses: the image of Brazil lacking "faith and hope," of starving for an "ideal." He portrayed Brazil in crisis, in danger of dismemberment, as "an opulent land in which many people die of hunger, a Country without nationality, a Pátria in which patriotism is unknown," and in which the people were being "denationalized." His message was always the same: the exaltation of patriotism and the condemnation of doubt.[14]

Although he said constantly that he was not a militarist, that he did not want "a militarist regime, oppressing the Country," he did call on officers to be "fanatics" about their profession. His solution to the lack of national spirit, to extreme regionalism, to excessive foreign influence, was to blend the army and the people into a common democratic mentality. The officers were to be the saving teachers who would instruct the people. He envisioned the officers as political neutrals because "any partisanship diminished" their moral influence. He argued that they had to keep their distance from politics to preserve the trust, confidence, and respect of all.[15]

The task would, he assured his listeners, be "long, slow, difficult." They would not suddenly change the current generation; they had "to work for the future: only other happier generations, will enjoy the well being that we have created." The only remedies for the "national sickness are time, tenacity and devotion." He regarded the Contestado struggles as "ridiculous border conflicts" between states "poisoned by fanaticism."[16] One wonders what, if anything, he knew about what was then happening in the Contestado. The detachment from that conflict, evident in elite discourse, is striking.

Undoubtedly Bilac was sincere. In 1893 he had spoken out against what he regarded as the blossoming of militarism under Floriano, had been jailed briefly in Rio de Janeiro, and then had fled to Minas Gerais, where the state of siege did not apply, to get beyond the grasp of the police. But if he dreamed of a golden age in which wars would be forgotten and armies disbanded, he also believed that as long as there was danger of war, countries that did not prepare risked "humiliation" and "ruin." Reporting on General Hermes da Fonseca's 1905 maneuvers, Bilac had described them as "a *festa*, a radiant *festa*, because it is the beginning of a rebirth of military strength" that would give Brazil, in the unhappy event of war, "a disciplined and strong army."[17]

Writer and politician Alberto Tôrres offered a third vision of the military's role. Tôrres, a Flumenense who had served as state and federal legislator, minister of Justice and Internal Affairs, president of the state of Rio de Janeiro, and justice of the Supreme Tribunal Federal, had published two important and much-discussed books in 1914: *A Organização Nacional* and *O Problema Nacional Brasileiro*.[18] He agreed with Bilac that Brazil needed organization. He believed that the country had never been organized and that it was steadily losing what little organization it had.[19] But he could not accept Bilac's therapy. In his mind the barracks trained soldiers, not citizens; the transmitting of civic virtues was a different process than that which taught military skills. If a good soldier was virtuous, altruistic, and sympathetic, it was because he brought those virtues from home and from the public plaza. The barracks would not produce such qualities but rather would spawn "praetorians." He pointed to the kaiser's Germany as an example of how "military delirium" could cloud even the souls of the "children of Schiller and the descendants of Kant!" For him this "new idea of 'education by the barracks' [caserna] is one more page from the same book of . . . the old panacea of the authoritarian spirit" to use education to instill the virtues and qualities that those on the top of society think that those on the bottom should have. Within Bilac's "confused multitude of words, ideas, and sentiments" Tôrres saw an underlay of class and corporate differentiation in the idea of military primacy as a corrective for civilian degradation.[20]

In an article in *O Estado de São Paulo* (December 22, 1915), he doubted that "in a country without a 'society' and without a 'nation,' in a mixed people" without ties and solidarity, military training, even if under the command of a German general, could make Brazil into "a Turkey or a Bulgaria." Instead of a military solution, instead of the Turkish model, he proposed that they follow the examples of Japan, New Zealand, and Australia in building national unity and infrastructure. Because of Brazil's "anarchy of organization," he warned that obligatory military service would fail before it began.[21]

He opposed a permanent officer corps and army, which he regarded as a holdover from the old dynastic system. Such a corps necessarily, he argued, would become a privileged, disciplined, cohesive hierarchy, with a tendency to develop into an autocratic caste. It was an illusion to suppose that open recruitment that produced officers from the lower or middle class resolved the danger. The war in Europe, he asserted, demonstrated the need for a citizen army, a civilian militia similar to Switzerland's or to the United States National Guard. For proper training, he outlined a basic program of physical education, military maneuvers, and target practice.

In Tôrres's mind national defense was broader than military defense; "in truth," he said, "military defense is neither the principal, nor the first, nor the most vigorous of our means of defense." For him an ideal national defense was based on constitutional government, public education, an orderly legal system, a strong economy, caution with foreign credit, restriction of foreign investment and immigration, a cordial foreign policy, pacifist propaganda, and, finally, military strength.[22]

Somewhat contradictorily, considering his view of the dangers of a permanent officer corps, Tôrres would keep an officer corps to train troops that the states would be obligated to supply. Recruitment would be voluntary, with a draft being employed only to fill gaps.[23]

However, Bilac and Tôrres agreed on some points: the need for patriotism, for order, for a national ideal, for the elimination of apathy, and for national unity. Both argued that the military should stay out of politics, that a political army was a mere faction and no longer a true army. Politics would divide, separate, and pull the army apart. As Tôrres's biographer, Alexandre José Barbosa Lima Sobrinho commented, "a political army would be like a party that used, as a symbol, the national flag. The army can not be political, for the reason that it can not be and should not be a faction. . . . "[24]

In summary, the *Defesa Nacional* group wanted the army to modernize on the German model with the permanent officer corps training recruits called up by obligatory service and then discharged into an ever-growing reserve force. They viewed the army's mission as external *and* internal defense, with the latter requiring various forms of intervention in society for years to come. It would be their view that would set the future direction of the army's relations with the society and political system. Civilian thinkers Bilac and Tôrres both wanted to limit the military's role to specific functions, but Bilac's views were more palatable because he saw the army as a purifying instrument that could reform society via the educational role that he ascribed to obligatory service. This idea appealed to officers and meshed well with the interventionist viewpoint. Tôrres, however, doubted the compatibility of democracy with a standing army and favored a National Guard or civilian militia as an alternative—an attitude that officers rejected. Because death soon removed them both from the scene (Tôrres in March 1917; Bilac in December 1918), the military was able to adopt selected ideas from their writings and speeches without fear of embarrassing disclaimers. In later years, when the army was seeking closer ties with civilian society, it would proclaim Bilac its great civilian ally and friend. In 1939 President Getúlio Vargas decreed that Bilac's birthday, December 16, should be commemorated annually as "Reservist Day"; and in 1966 President (General) Humberto Castelo Branco raised the poet to the exalted status of "Patron" of Military Service. Not surprisingly, there are no commemorative plaques dedicated to Alberto Tôrres on the walls of Brazilian army installations.[25]

Army Reform of 1915

Of the three visions of the military's role discussed above, that of the *Defesa Nacional* officers had the greatest immediate and long-range impact on the army. Their influence inside the army was insured by the backing of General José Caetano de Faria, who served from 1910 to 1914 as chief of the general staff and from 1914 to 1918 as minister of war. Faria was sixty years old when he became minister in November 1914. He had been just shy of thirteen when he joined the army as a volunteer in January 1868. He participated in the occupation of Paraguay, entered the cavalry, and in 1875 was made an *alferes* (ensign), the beginning officer rank of the era. Although he did not have a bachelor's degree from the military school, he did complete the 1874 artillery course, and his promotions to lieutenant (1878) and captain (1884) were based on his "studies." His later career indicates that he believed an officer had to mix study with practical application. The early 1890s civil war netted him rapid promotions in 1894 from captain to major in April and to lieutenant colonel in July. He played an active role in suppressing the 1904 cadet revolt, which may have helped secure his general's stars. Army regulations specified that promotion to general was at government discretion. In 1905, although he was forty-sixth out of sixty-six colonels on the promotion list, he was raised to brigadier. In 1906 he prepared a training plan for cavalry brigades, much in the spirit, then in vogue, of getting the troops into the field.[26]

In the army of Hermes da Fonseca an officer such as Brigadier General Faria was clearly upwardly mobile. In 1909, as commander of the politically important Fourth Military District, which included Rio de Janeiro—an assignment indicating that he was well connected and was considered reliable—he organized the First Strategic Brigade, in a relatively short-lived and unpopular reformulation of the army's command structure, and became inspector general of the Ninth Military Region, which substituted the old military district in the table of organization. In 1910 he was president of the Promotions Commission, which gave him a voice in who would command the army in later years. His experience had taught him that the army needed to reform and to adopt the latest methods and arms in order to face potential adversaries (meaning Argentines), who were receiving direct German instruction. However, although he approved of sending officers abroad for training, he opposed hiring a foreign military mission on nationalist grounds. Rather, he believed that Brazilian officers themselves should filter, interpret, and adapt to the national army what they learned abroad.

It was to General Faria that the *Defesa Nacional* officers addressed the thirteen-point plan outlined above. They also worked on his 1915 reform; Young Turk Lieutenant Estevão Leitão de Carvalho, a *Defesa Nacional* founder, was one of Faria's immediate aides.[27] As chief of staff three years before, Faria had proposed remodeling the army using a divisional organization. He understood that an army made up of sundry units distributed in historical, political, or whimsical fashion over the national territory would have difficulty shifting to a war footing. He looked to the Russo-Japanese War (1904–5) for ideas. In his general staff reports he lauded the Japanese practice, based on Napoleonic norms, of maintaining expandable peacetime divisions that could reach combat readiness by adding individual reservists or recruits. In combat the Japanese replaced individuals rather than units; the men changed, but the unit remained. In contrast, the Russians created new units composed of poorly instructed reservists under the command of inexperienced officers. Russian divisions and corps were set up as they faced their enemy and were led by newly appointed commanders, advised by staffs whose members did not know each other or their troops. The outcome of the Russo-Japanese War left little doubt in Faria's mind which system was best. He cited the principle of German General Wilhelm Bronsart von Schellendorf, who in the 1890s had helped Emil Korner train the Chilean army, to the effect that "the first-line campaign army . . . would be the 'army of peace-time footing,' duly mobilized."[28]

In the officer corps the Contestado experience had been a graphic example that the Brazilian structure was more akin to the Russian than to the Japanese and German models. Faria knew all too well that to put units into the field, it had been necessary to borrow men, horses, and equipment from the widespread garrisons, which were left crippled in the process.[29] He also knew that little could be accomplished without funding, and for this he would need the backing of a Congress that had little interest in strengthening the central government. However, the First World War so alarmed the political elites that the Congress authorized a budget that permitted reorganization.

The 1915 plan was based on two fundamental considerations: that the army structure permit incorporation of reservists without destroying unit cohesion and that the peacetime army be able to shift to war footing, without creating new units. Faria's own strategic thinking centered on four ideas: (1) that the likely enemy would be landward, rather than seaward, that is, South American, rather than European or North American; (2) that the initial battles would be the task of the first-line troops; (3) that the Brazilian response would be offensive, carrying the war into the enemy's territory; and (4) that to safeguard the rear areas, they needed obligatory military service to produce a large and prepared reserve. Clearly influenced by European military writers, he repeatedly emphasized that modern war was between whole nations and that the mass of the population had to be ready to repel an invader. Obligatory military instruction was indispensable; citizens must, he wrote, "come to the barracks to learn to defend their homes, the honor and the sovereignty of the nation."[30]

The reform, or remodeling as Faria preferred it, had the long-range goal of implementing the *Defesa Nacional* program and the short-range goal of regrouping the army's units. The complicated and disliked structure of five strategic and one mixed provisional brigade was simplified to five divisions and seven military regions. Aside from the improved efficiency that this may have provided, it cut costs by reducing the number of general headquarters. It also increased the authorized size of a division from 14,249 to 16,876 and expanded its firepower from 42 to 56 cannon and 15 to 16 machine guns.[31] Officers debated whether these were enough, and Faria emphasized the harsh reality that the entire army was barely as large as mobilization plans specified for a single wartime division.

The minister complained in his 1915 *Relatório* that the budget only allowed a total force of eighteen thousand men, which, minus staffs, schools, and special assignments, left less than seventeen thousand for troop units. Many units, he observed, lacked enough men for proper training and functioning. Actually, the situation was worse than he portrayed it. On paper the Brazilian army was composed of ten brigades of infantry, four of cavalry, and five of artillery, yet only four infantry, three cavalry, and two artillery brigades existed in 1915, and their regiments and battalions were seriously understrength.[32]

Foreign observers were blunt in describing the army's weaknesses. In 1913 the British ambassador commented acidly that "as a fighting force against a really disciplined army, it may be looked upon as a *quantité négligeable,* but it is useful to the Government in the game of 'politics,' in which, indeed, it bears the chief part as the medium of enforcing the rule of the dominant clique." He compared it unfavorably with the Argentine army and then gave it a coup de grace: "I do not suppose for a moment that the Brazilian army, undisciplined, undrilled, of degenerate black blood, officered by commanders as conceited as they are ignorant, would have a ghost of a chance against any ordinary fighting force." It could not, he said, hold its "own even against the 7,000 military police of São Paulo," which a French mission had been training since 1906. As long as São Paulo had this force, state leaders could snap their fingers at any idea of Federal intervention; indeed, they could continue, the ambassador noted, to "dictate to the central Government."[33]

Clearly, Faria and other reformers had their work cut out for them. The minister admitted that Brazilians lacked the habit of military service. He wanted military instruction introduced into secondary schools and higher educational institutions, and he urged setting aside a number of government jobs for those completing military service, as well as giving applicants with reservist cards preference for official positions.

Partly to deal with the problem posed by the paulista and other state "police" forces, and partly to expand the trained reserves, he proposed a subtle incorporation by designating them the first-line reserve, arranging with the states exemptions from federal army service for state police officers and troops, and providing the state units with army instructors. He pointed to the 1893 revolts, the Canudos campaign, and the current Contestado situation as examples of emergencies in which it had been necessary to call on police units because they constituted the only available organized reserve. If it had a legal mechanism to regularize their reserve status, the federal army, he said, could make do with about thirty thousand men. He also proposed reorganizing the National Guard, under army control, to use it as the second-line reserve.[34]

Control of state military police and the National Guard was a constant in army thinking because their neutralization would enhance federal power thereby increasing the officer corps' sense of security. But before that objective would be attained much ink and blood would be spilled.

If the skeleton army was to be a true cadre force, expandable in a mobilization, it had to have reserves that could be called up, hence the interest in obtaining control over the state military police and the National Guard. But given the political considerations involved with these measures, the reformers saw revitalization of the *Tiro* units and emplacement of obligatory service as more likely of attainment.

After a burst of enthusiasm following the 1908 passage of the obligatory service law, the Tiros had declined in number and activity for two reasons: first, when the law did not take effect, many who had signed up as a way to escape active military duty saw no need to continue; second, local politicians had misused the societies as devices to collect votes. Faria was convinced that a functioning obligatory service law would revive the Tiros. He stressed their importance as a way of extending training beyond the small number of draftees the army would be able to absorb each year. One way to inject life into the Tiro movement would be to enforce the portion of the 1908 law (Article 17) that imposed a reserve obligation of light military training and once-a-month target practice on all those registered (alistado) but not drafted (sorteado). Apparently registration had taken place since 1908, although given the lack of enforcement, the poor communications throughout the country, and the absence of call-ups, the historian has to doubt that it was widespread or that it netted more than a small percentage of the draftable age group. At any rate, Faria thought that because no one had been drafted, all those registered could be called to fulfill their reserve obligation. This action would likely make the Tiro units more attractive.

He also intended to reward active marksmen who could pass appropriate examinations and were of good reputation by awarding reserve officer commissions in a rank structure that would progress from second lieutenant to captain. And to fit the Tiros into the army structure, he proposed linking each society with a battalion, making it, in a mobilization, the battalion's fourth company.[35] These steps would have created a true, active reserve force, but in the 1990s the Brazilian army still lacked such a reserve.

Obligatory Military Service

The restructuring and innovations that General Faria put into place rested on the notion that the army was to cease being the strong arm of "the dominant clique," to use the British ambassador's phrase, and become a cadre force. To do that successfully, the officer corps would have to distance itself from partisan politics, and it would need soldiers who could be trained and passed on to the reserve. To deal with the first and to signal that the era of *salvações,* of officers seeking to satisfy their ambitions by intervening in politics, was over, his aide, Young Turk Lieutenant Leitão de Carvalho, suggested that Faria use his New Year's address to the officers to urge them to concentrate on their military careers and to leave political struggles aside. The minister had the German-trained lieutenant write the proclamation, which he read to the surprised officers of the Rio garrison on January 2, 1915, as "an appeal of an old soldier." Bluntly, he told them that "we need to concentrate all of our energies on our professional work . . . [W]e can not strive for a greater degree of technical progress for the army, nor for greater troop efficiency, if we squander our energies by scattering them on activities foreign to the profession." They all must, he declared, abandon completely "political ambitions and collateral occupations and devote our activity, with decision and patriotism, to the work of the army."[36] Of course, a

New Year's proclamation could not immediately alter habits, but Faria set the tone, even if events of the next decade would show it to have been an overly idealistic tone. The speech provided a point of reference for those officers desiring an apolitical, professional career. For the ghostwriter, Leitão de Carvalho, it "defined my profession of legalist faith."[37]

The major problem facing the army of the mid-1910s was to get obligatory service finally into operation. After its passage in 1908, the law had lain dormant because the Congress had cut the army budget so drastically that the small authorized strength was filled by volunteers. The law reaffirmed the constitutional requirement that all Brazilians had a responsibility to defend the Pátria, but it said that the draft should be employed to fill those gaps not filled by volunteers. The existence of the draft provision was somehow to act as a goad for volunteerism. Those registered, but not drafted for a year of barracks life, were to receive simplified basic infantry training and to participate in marksmanship exercises and field maneuvers.[38]

Olavo Bilac's speeches were the main focus of the public relations effort, which included founding the National Defense League on September 7, 1916. The league sought to build an ideology of national defense on the ideas in Bilac's speeches, which it published and distributed. It had the active backing of the government, with President Braz and General Faria serving as honorary president and vice president. The willingness of national figures to associate their names with the league set an example that state leaders followed by sitting on regional directories. The league's conferences, patriotic demonstrations, its *Civic Catechism* and *Manual of Civic and Moral Education* contributed to an atmosphere of growing nationalism.[39]

This patriotic campaign did not occur accidentally. General Faria and chief of the general staff, General Bento Manuel Ribeiro Carneiro Monteiro, used the friendship of the latter's aide with Bilac to approach him about undertaking a national effort. Later, when criticism of the campaign arose, especially from Federal Deputy Maurício de Lacerda, who accused Bilac of receiving secret funds from the treasury, the government issued a notice in the *Diário Oficial,* saying that the Ministry of War had not given any funds "directly or indirectly, to help him in the campaign in favor of military service."[40]

Whether or not army funds were used, the idea for the campaign came from the high command and not from the poet. It is also clear that his first speech in the São Paulo Law School aroused passions on both sides of the question. Minister Faria and General Bento Ribeiro immediately sent congratulatory telegrams, Faria applauding Bilac's opinion that obligatory service would be the "source of resurrection of a strong Brazil." Army officers demonstrated their backing with a 250-place banquet in the Military Club on November 6, 1915. The menu cover carried the title "Tribute of the Army to Olavo Bilac, poet and apostle of National Defense."[41]

Some congressmen praised obligatory service as a way to reinforce national unity; others took exception, arguing that the army did not form character but that, on the contrary, its members' characters shaped the army. One
lawyer observed that in the barracks the Brazilian draftee would not find
"the teachings of Socrates, the philosophy of Plato, the eloquence of Cicero,
he will encounter the regulations of the Count of Lippe," noted for their
eighteenth-century harshness. A commentator in Rio's *Correio da Manhã*
noted that the draft had not yet been put into practice because "it is an ex-
otic plant in hostile soil." There was even a general, Gabino Besouro, who
was removed from his accumulated commands of the Fifth Military Region
(Rio de Janeiro) and of the Third Division because of his public opposition
to obligatory service on the grounds of illegality and the army's lack of
preparation to receive, what he assumed would be, an avalanche of draftees.
And, of course, there was the criticism of Alberto Tôrres discussed above.[42]

With the war raging in Europe and the Brazilian army licking its wounds
from the Contestado, thus did the elite debate the nature of Brazilian society, the role of the military, and the future of Brazil.

To turn the favorable mood of the moment into action, Leitão de Carvalho prepared telegrams for Faria's signature to "the presidents and governors of the states" asking that they set up the necessary local registration and
draft boards. The National Defense League actively sponsored speeches and
events that attracted press coverage and editorial discussion. The army command did not stand on the political sidelines but actively lobbied key members of Congress outside the chamber while its spokesmen defended its
funding and force-level requests on the floor. The majority leader of the
Chamber of Deputies, Carlos Peixoto de Melo Filho of Minas Gerais, met
with General Faria in the war ministry to discuss the military budget and
ended by arguing to his fellow legislators that "a Land Army, can not absolutely obey only budgetary criterion; the maintenance of a Land Army is
only done at the cost of the country's sacrifices" so as to have "the instrument of our sovereignty and the means of defending it, of guaranteeing it
in the present and in the future."[43]

From December 10 to 17, 1916, with due ceremony in the major urban
centers, the draft went into operation. On the tenth, at army headquarters
and in the presence of the president, Minister Faria, various army commanders, and political figures, with Tiro Battalion No. Seven presenting military
honors, the first drawing of names occurred. The assistant attorney general of
the republic extracted from the rotating urn the name of the first draftee, Alberto Garcia de Maltas of the município of Santa Rita. Some of the draftees
objected on procedural, constitutional, and religious grounds and asked relief from the courts. But by the end of January 1917 the Supreme Federal
Tribunal ruled unanimously that the law was constitutional. Forty-two years

after the first draft law (1874) and eight years after the second (1908) the army inducted its first draftees, thereby beginning its history as a cadre force.[44]

Sergeants' Revolt

The system did not function exactly the way Olavo Bilac had envisioned, however. There had been several conspiracies involving sergeants in the army, navy, Rio's Police Brigade, and Corps of Firemen that had social-economic roots and broad, long-range reformist goals. The army initially refused to consider the sergeants' demands for a new lower officer rank for which they could compete—they wanted something similar to the modern Warrant Officer rank in the U.S. Army. The sergeants objected to the favoritism inherent in the ministerial appointments to the administrative officer category. The high command argued that it was impossible to consider them for regular promotion since they lacked sufficient education even to assure legally their continuance as sergeants. Moreover, the nation could not "assume the responsibility of protecting the families of the battalion sergeants, because on the day that would be done there would not be an inferior [sergeant] who would not marry."[45]

The conspirators wanted to change the government from a presidential into a parliamentary republic, "to confiscate the goods of the politicians that have enriched themselves at the [country's] expense," to restructure the states' territories and political systems, to develop primary education, to allow free navigation for ships of all flags, *to adopt obligatory military service,* to regulate religious instruction, and to clarify the political rights of foreigners.[46]

General Abílio de Noronha, who conducted the official inquiry into the affair, asserted that civilian politicians had incited the rebels to mutiny with promises of high military posts once they had assassinated the officers. By his account the past governments of the republic were responsible for the lack of discipline that continually characterized the sergeants of the Rio garrison because they had not curbed the unscrupulous politicians who exploited the soldiers' frustrations. Little is known about the folklore of the enlisted ranks, but it is likely that the memory of the revolt that Sergeant Silvino Honorio de Macedo led at Fortress of Santa Cruz in January 1892 was still current in 1915. Like the present conspiracy, Sergeant Silvino's revolt involved civilian agitators.[47]

In 1915, when 256 sergeants were arrested, expelled from the service, and transported to points in the north, northeast, and Rio Grande do Sul, their exile won the "sympathy of the rank and file, of lower officers and of some higher ranking ones." Some historians see their demands as foreshadowing future movements; Edgard Carone has observed that "the *tenentista* ideology is, in great part, a continuation of that of the sergeants."[48]

Officially, Minister Faria and President Braz congratulated themselves that less than half of the six hundred or so soldiers wearing sergeant's stripes on their sleeves were involved, but they knew that the army was left seriously shorthanded.[49] The conspiracy certainly disrupted the chain of command; officers were disturbed to find that even sergeants that they had protected and considered *homens de confiança* were involved. Lieutenant Francisco de Paula Cidade expressed his dismay at discovering that a sergeant, whom he considered a trusted protégé, whose family he had helped during an illness, and whose sister frequently visited the Cidade household, was "a prominent figure in the conspiracy." Until the last arrests, officers did not know whom to trust or to what degree the sergeants commanded the loyalty of the troops.[50]

Once the conspirators were safely tucked away, Minister Faria sought to eliminate one source of dissatisfaction by substituting competitive examination for ministerial appointment in filling openings on the list of administrative officers. But in good paternalistic fashion, before changing the process, he promoted one of his former sergeants in the First Cavalry Regiment. The measure may not have been all that the sergeants desired, but Leitão de Carvalho claimed that thereby many became officers and started "on the road to a better future." He cited the case of Sergeant Joaquim Nunes de Carvalho, who used the administrative route to rise to colonel, retiring as a general.[51]

The Functioning of Obligatory Service

Not only were the upper enlisted ranks unhappy and rebellious, but in April 1915 the army concluded field operations in the Contestado, while throughout the year "the political situation . . . and enforcing court decisions" required "many troop movements" into Mato Grosso, Amazonas, Pará, and Piauí.[52] Such an army did not attract the sons of the urban middle class or the rural landowners. Indeed, it had difficulty attracting any suitable citizens. Of the 7,137 chosen in the draft lottery, only 3,709 reported for medical examination, and many of these were physically unfit.[53] But the high command put the best face on matters by emphasizing the legal way out of the year's service. Anyone holding a reservist card fulfilled his legal obligation, and membership in the Tiros, participation in army maneuvers as a volunteer, or attendance at a school offering military instruction qualified a man as a reservist. Not surprisingly, the Tiros found their ranks swelling, and new units formed continuously between 1916 and 1920. A side effect of this growth was the army's inability to provide the Tiro units with enough junior officers as instructors. As a result Faria approved creation of an instructors' training course, for sergeants and retired officers, that functioned in Vila Militar. It was the beginning of the army's sergeants' school and likely helped ease tension in those ranks.[54]

Primarily, the draft lottery was intended to create a reserve, and regardless of the propaganda about creating national cohesion and contributing to greater social equality, the "conscientious, worthy Brazilians" that the army took in were generally poor illiterates rather than middle- or upper-class sons. Although the lottery had important institutional and political effects, it did not, before World War II, radically change the social-economic composition of the rank and file, which continued to bare a striking resemblance to those of 1905. Two decades later Brazilians would continue to display, in General Eurico Dutra's phrase, a "visceral rebellion" against "the career of arms."[55]

Large numbers did not report either because they did not know they had been called or simply because they refused. Or as an American with experience in turn-of-the-century Brazil had put it: "Distances are so great that patriotism might leak away before the individuals reached any central barracks."[56] The lists of those eligible for the draft were based on municipal records, which in many parts of the country did not include all births and often failed to register deaths. At times hundreds of ghosts were being summoned to the colors. Local police forces and enlistment boards tended to look the other way when hometown boys decided that they could make better use of a year than playing soldier. The war ministry, as noted above, hoped to persuade the government to require a service certificate or a reservist card for all federal and state employment, but between 1916 and 1940 nothing reduced the considerable number who avoided their patriotic duty. The 1925 call-up of the First Military Region (Rio de Janeiro) can be taken as illustrative of the problem: of the 23,069 who were summoned, 19,122, or 82 percent, did not appear; and of the 3,947, or 17 percent, who did show up, 2,551 were either physically unfit or excluded for some reason, leaving only 1,396, or a bare 6 percent of those listed, to join the troops.[57] Throughout the years many were called, few came, and even fewer stayed.

Even though the system did not work well, it provided the mechanism and justification for the army's physical expansion and contributed to its increasing involvement in society and politics. Instead of opting for one or two national training camps, with subsequent distribution of trained troops to posts throughout Brazil, the army wished to keep the soldiers in their own regions. This would avoid the cost and administrative burden of transporting large contingents hither and yon, and it would give the army a local image. But to do this required at least one army unit in each state to receive and train the draftees and volunteers, and to do that would necessitate increasing the size of the army from an authorized eighteen thousand men to twenty-five thousand, which was the smallest number army leaders believed would allow the institution to deal with "questions of internal order" and also serve as a "nucleus of instruction." Such expansion, of course, would require more funding, an estimated 195 thousand contos, rather than the 1916 figure of 65 thousand contos.[58]

The army not only needed new facilities; it had to repair or rebuild existing ones, and it had to deal with the sharp price rises during the war. In 1917 some units, such as the Third Transportation Corps and the Fifty-eighth Battalion were in nonhygienic, disgraceful quarters. One unit in São Paulo was living in such a ruin that it was forced to rent a private building until new barracks could be built. Regional commanders all complained about troops' living in miserable conditions and about the lack of money to do anything about it.[59]

In October 1917, after German submarines had sunk several of its commercial ships over the previous months, Brazil entered World War I and rapidly raised the number of its soldiers to more than fifty-two thousand. The army had great difficulty merely housing, clothing, and feeding that number, not to mention training and arming them. Even though Brazil did not commit troops to the European battlefields, the war provided compelling justification for immediate expansion. By mid-1918 every state had at least one unit serving as a reception center for draftees. Moreover, General Faria opined that the war clearly demonstrated that it would be foolhardy to return "our army to the insignificant effectives that we had." With a national population of about twenty-five million, an army of twenty-five thousand meant that only one per one thousand were in uniform, which the minister observed was "very weak, in comparison with any other nation." And he argued that the cost was low when compared to Brazil's tremendous natural resource wealth, for which the army was protective insurance. Pointedly, he declared that military spending was helping the national economy because most of it was being spent in Brazil: food, forage, uniforms, leather for cavalry gear, all of the iron and some of the steel, military wagons, and all of the infantry's and part of the artillery's munitions were from private industry or army arsenals.[60]

The war gave the army its impetus for growth that continued over the next decades. According to General Dutra, the number of effectives rose from thirty thousand in 1920 to fifty thousand in 1930 and to ninety-three in 1940.[61] Although the proportion of soldiers to population would remain low in comparison to other countries, that is about 1.1 soldiers per 1000, the army's size increased at a faster rate than did the population. Between 1890 and 1930, whereas the population increased 162 percent, the army grew 220 percent.[62] And although there is evidence to support Alfred Stepan's comment that "political variables are frequently far more important for determining the role of the military in society than the absolute size of the armed forces,"[63] in the Brazilian case we have the army's numerical growth occurring simultaneously with its escalating political involvement. Growth by itself did not heighten its political function, but it is hard to imagine the army of 1905 providing the muscle for the Estado Novo dictatorship of 1937–45 or the 1964–85 military presidencies.

Whereas the draft lottery and the war provided justification for expansion in size and space, the army used its need for reserves to extend its influence over state police forces and the National Guard. Under a January 1917 law the war ministry made agreements with the state governments whereby state police and firemen would be considered auxiliary forces. Complete control would not be secured until the Estado Novo, but this was the first step. The National Guard became the army's second line, and under a 1918 decree it was to be remodeled; but, considered a rival force by many officers, it was eventually abolished. These measures allowed General Faria to note happily that for the "first time among us" the army controlled "all the forces which ought to constitute the military power of the nation."[64] A monopoly of fire-power always increases influence and power.

War Materiel and Industrial Development

More men meant that the army needed more arms. And just prior to the First World War the army had ordered a large stock of German weapons and equipment, which the British blockade prevented from reaching Brazil.[65] The shutoff of foreign arms convinced reformist officers that Brazil needed to produce its own armaments. *A Defesa Nacional,* echoing Florianista officers of the 1890s, argued for industrial development, hammering away at the protective tariffs that aided "fictitious parasitical industries" that imported raw materials or parts, a policy it described as "robbing the people to enrich a half dozen . . . " while "benefitting foreign production and ravishing the national economy." The editors favored industries that developed native resources.[66]

An adequate and secure supply of arms was necessary. In 1919 General Faria's successor as minister of war, General Alberto Cardoso de Aguiar, stated the matter plainly when he wrote that "obligatory service and the absolute independence from foreign materiel resources guarantee any country effective means of military defense."[67] All of the general staff's elaborate plans boiled down to obtaining sufficient men and guns, the two elements necessary for any army's existence. From the end of the Paraguayan War in 1870 down to the First World War, the army's policy was to import arms from abroad. At the end of the nineteenth century the army's arsenals were mainly repair facilities, which were often in shabby condition and lacked adequate storage space. Even so, in 1899 the minister of war had believed that "for our limited army, three arsenals . . . are more than sufficient."[68]

If prior to the First World War the army was not interested in weapons production, at least its officers were convinced they had to produce their own munitions. For them this was the "essential" element that if imported during wartime could be captured or lost at sea and would be subject to exorbitant prices and transportation costs.[69] In the first decade of the century war ministers repeatedly told the Congress that Brazil needed a properly equipped powder and shell works.

The constraints of underdevelopment cannot but impress the modern observer. When the cartridge and shell factory at Realengo that had blown up in 1898 was rebuilt a few years later, it continued to use imported German metal and powder in its shells.[70] Although the need was clear at the beginning of the century the Brazilian army continued to import munitions for years to come. To some extent this was because exchange rates and other fiscal constraints often favored imported items over nationally produced goods of similar quality. In 1909 the army set up a smokeless powder factory at Piquete in São Paulo using information from like facilities in the United States and Europe but found that although local pyrites could be used economically to produce sulfuric acids, both American cotton and alcohol were cheaper than the Brazilian products.[71] This kind of dependence would end slowly.

However, price was not the sole determinant; politics and graft entered the purchasing process, and not always favoring the foreigner. In 1915 an officer complained in *A Defesa Nacional* that locally made uniforms and tents cost considerably more than better ones imported from Germany. It was a mistake, he said, to underwrite Brazilian manufacturers, who enjoyed political influence, at the expense of the army because money was being wasted that could be better used for army expansion.[72]

The European-trained officers bristled with impatience at this situation. In a May 1914 editorial *A Defesa Nacional* remarked ironically that with "financial sacrifice" the cartridge-and-shell works at Realengo had expanded physically, acquired new machines, and imported an experienced European director only to find that it produced no more cartridges than previously. And worse, its artillery section had ceased to function at all. Moreover, despite having purchased expensive machinery to make shells, the staff contented itself with assembling cartridges from imported European casings. Blaming the workers, who, the editors charged, were accustomed to being paid for doing next to nothing, *A Defesa Nacional* called for a "radical cleaning out of the work force" as the only way to improve production. "National security demands the development of our factory to the point where we emancipate ourselves from abroad." The editors raised the La Plata menace, declaring that war in South America or in Europe could cut Brazil off from European supply and that the Argentine Republic was "more advanced than us" in this area.[73]

The 1910s also saw a discouraging beginning of military aviation. Although Brazilians look to Alberto Santos Dumont as a pioneer in world aviation development, he did his work in France and had little impact on the early days of Brazilian aviation.[74] The army's first air operation ended in disaster. A cavalry lieutenant, Ricardo Kirk, had learned to fly in France at his own expense and had the distinction of being the first Brazilian military aviator, but the army command was slow to use his skills. The high command also displayed that curious Brazilian attitude of depreciating local abilities when it set up a flying school under a contracted Italian. The Contestado campaign cut that effort short. Kirk and the Italian took their planes south and on his first reconnaissance flight Kirk crashed and died.[75] To instruct its pilots, the army turned to the civilian Aero-Club and the navy, which had moved ahead with hydroplane training. By 1918 the army had a half dozen aviators in the air and a few receiving training in France and Britain.[76] More important, two aviators assigned to the Realengo cartridge-and-shell works built an airplane, with the exception of the motor, from "national materials," declaring that Brazilians had the knowledge and materials to build any type of aircraft.[77] As in other areas, this beginning would be slow in bearing positive results.

Although foreign supply sources might be cheaper at times, the First World War made clear that such dependence was dangerous. The army had ordered and made some payments on thirty batteries of 75 mm cannon and a stock of machine guns in Germany only to lose them when hostilities prevented their shipment from Hamburg.[78] After Brazil joined the Allies in October 1917, Minister Faria observed that expanding the army from eighteen thousand to fifty thousand demanded triple the amount of quarters, uniforms, equipment, and arms; and he lamented that with imports nearly impossible, national producers were not able to turn out military necessities fast enough. To deal with the supply problem the army command took two steps: first, it established an Ordnance Directory *(Diretoria do Material Bélico)* to coordinate the army's arsenals and factories, which previously had functioned independently; second, it adopted as army policy the objective of liberation from dependence on foreign industry. Faria wrote that the war demonstrated "the necessity for each nation to be sufficiently strong to maintain its sovereignty and the inviolability of its territory." He warned that supposed "savings" in "national defense" would be repaid with "terrible interest" on the day an enemy invaded.[79]

The army's desire to liberate itself from dependence on foreign imports led it to seek Brazilian sources of iron and steel. It had an iron works at São

João de Ipanema, São Paulo, dating from 1808, that was all but abandoned after the government had tried unsuccessfully to sell it in 1895.[80] The army restored it, and by mid-1918 the Ipanema works was producing a rather low three to four tons of iron a day; but that was sufficient to encourage the war minister to send its director to the United States to study modern iron and steel production methods. What is interesting here is that the army's objective was to develop its own production capability rather than relying on private industry. Indeed, in a related effort it sought government monopoly of explosives to secure a market that would allow its factories to maintain a high level of production and a steady income.

However, it should be noted that there was debate within the officer corps over the proper role of private enterprise and reluctance to invest funds in projects that would not be immediately productive. Certainly officers were aware of the public discussion about developing Brazil's iron and steel capability that had been going on among civilians, and they must have agreed with sentiments such as those of Rio's *Jornal do Commércio,* which declared in 1912 that without a steel industry Brazil could not be "truly free and master of its own destiny." And they must have known that the number of metalworking foundries based on melted-down scrap was increasing apace with the wartime shortage of imported metals. Most of these foundries were in São Paulo, whose politicians subsequently opposed developing a steel industry based on smelting the rich iron ores of Minas Gerais.[81] Such narrow regionalist attitudes irritated nationally oriented officers, who debated the proper role of the federal government in industrial development. Some officers favored a military-run steel industry along the lines of the powder works, whereas others preferred that the government stimulate private initiative. There was agreement that the state must be involved and that steel, as much as gold, was "the nerve of war." But reform-minded *A Defesa Nacional* editors, expressing frustration that their repeated editorials on the need for a steel industry had been countered with the argument that such mills required "nonproductive expenditures," reprinted an article on American steel to show that the industry was productive in peace and war. They argued that even if Brazilian steel could not compete in the world market, at least it would cover "the necessities of the domestic market and of national defense."[82] Moreover, the nation could not successfully prepare for war without first creating a national steel industry. And the matter could not be left to the whims of the private sector. "We believe," said the editors, "that the Government of the Republic can not avoid the definite solution that the great question of the national steel industry demands. . . . It is necessary to found *the national steel industry*."[83] From then on the army stayed close to the steel question and would play a central role in the eventual creation of the major steel plant at Volta Redonda during the Second World War.

The artillery's inspector general stated the army's view of Brazil's situation when he wrote that "we need to be strong to be respected. . . . We have to prepare ourselves, if we want to continue to be an autonomous and independent nation." He especially urged immediate attention to a steel industry. "With the end of the war in Europe," he warned, "conquerors and conquered . . . will not hesitate to develop imperialist policies, and South America, principally Brazil whose riches had already stirred the greed of several [foreign] syndicates, will be the objective of the conqueror's claws."[84]

To improve Brazil's military stance, Minister Faria sent two study missions abroad during the war, one to France, to observe the conflict's effects on the "art of war," and the other to the United States, where it was to acquire technicians and material. The first mission, under General Napoleão Felipe Aché, was made up of twenty-eight upwardly mobile officers, several of whom would make general's rank in the 1920s and 1930s. They attended training courses, and some of them spent time with frontline units. The hero of the Contestado campaign, Major Tertuliano Potyguara, was wounded in action at St. Quentin in October 1918. One of the purposes of this group was to become familiar with the French army so that they could work with the French military mission that Brazil was getting ready to contract and that will be discussed in the next chapter. The army also sent medical personnel to set up a "Brazilian Hospital" near Paris. If the war had dragged on past 1918, it is possible that these contacts would have developed into Brazil's committing troops.[85]

In late 1917 the mission to the United States set itself up in New York City and immediately began meeting with manufacturers and visiting war plants and army arsenals. Faria had authorized the mission to hire an American metallurgical chemist and a superintendent from the Bethlehem Steel Company for the projectile section of the Rio de Janeiro arsenal and to purchase a wide range of arms, equipment, and machines. The American War Department exerted itself to assist the mission but made clear that because American factories were struggling to meet the demands of American and Allied forces, it would be able to do little to secure munitions or machinery for the Brazilians. The American ambassador in Rio de Janeiro had warned the secretary of state that most of whatever the Brazilians obtained would not go toward assisting the Allied war effort. The war would be over, he predicted, before the coast artillery, which the Brazilians wanted, could be installed and so would be used for "general defense and not against Germany." There was, the ambassador advised, a "strong popular prejudice" in Brazil against sending troops to Europe; moreover, General Faria did not believe that the army was sufficiently prepared. So despite pressures at home and abroad to the contrary, Brazil's major contribution would be supplying foodstuffs on a commercial basis.[86]

The Brazilian army's recent experience in suppressing the Contestado insurgency had revealed many organizational problems, and General Faria and the general staff used the world war as an excuse to correct the army's structural flaws and to increase its size. Its younger officers, especially the classes of 1917 and 1918, were spoiling to get into the fray, and their pent-up frustrations may have contributed to their revolutionary activities in the 1920s. As nominal allies the army leaders discovered that allied arms and munitions were beyond their reach during the conflict. The lesson of the First World War experience would influence the decision to take an active part on the battlefield in the next war.[87]

Military and National Reform

The reformists argued that aloofness from politics and loyalty to the federal government were marks of professionalism. They assumed that logical arguments would convince national leaders that defense was necessary. Apparently they did not consider that politics was neither neutral nor weighted in favor of the national good, nor did they realize that the elite urged them to be aloof from politics as a way of neutralizing their power. By the end of the First World War they came to understand, vaguely at first, that the political system was set against army reform because such reform would endanger that system; indeed, if the barracks really were turned into active centers of civic education, it could shake the exploitive social system. Although Marshals Deodoro da Fonseca (1889–91) and Floriano Peixoto (1891–94) had established and consolidated the republic, the political system took shape under Presidents Prudente José de Morais e Barros (1894–98) and Manoel Ferraz de Campos Sales (1898–1902), with the Partido Republicano Federal as the sole authorized party. It was an exclusive, rather than an inclusive, political system. The electoral process involved the local oligarchies, who chose the state governors, who in their turn, acting as the "grand electors," selected the president. In exchange for local autonomy the state governors had their congressional delegations support the president's programs. The system served to consolidate the state oligarchies, which, for the most part, were composed of families that had been members of the old monarchical parties. It also produced struggles for power in the states that led to the federal interventions that we saw in the previous chapter. The populous, powerful, and relatively rich states of Minas Gerais and São Paulo used their economic strength to dominate the system. The *política dos governadores,* as the system was often called, replaced the Florianista republic.[88]

This anti-Florianista republic and the state oligarchies strengthened the navy and the state police to create a counterbalance to the national army. Initially the army's reformers seem to have been so distracted with their work that they failed to see that their vision of a modern army was incompatible with both Brazilian society and the reigning political system. Eventually they would reach the conclusion that both society and the system would have to be changed.[89]

The reformers' intimate knowledge of the German army, the frustrations of the Contestado, and the attempt after 1916 to make effective use of obligatory service led them to examine their country more carefully. Their experience in Germany and the resistance to change that they encountered among fellow officers convinced them that their arguments would be more persuasive if they had a German military mission to back them. This is not to say that they had not had some success. They managed to have most of the combat arms regulations rewritten on the German model: often, in fact, these documents were mere translations into Portuguese. Critics charged that the translations were not well done and, worse, ill-suited for Brazilian troops and weaponry.[90] Be that as it may, partial success made them hunger for a more complete Germanization. Their enthusiasm was reflected in a lieutenant colonel's speech to a group of Pernambucan Tiros in which he crowed that "the new triumphant military spirit" would carry Brazilians, "in the near future, to the same role on the South American continent as the strong and powerful Germans play in Europe."[91]

They were confronted, however, with stubborn opposition, even before the outbreak of hostilities in Europe, from those who favored a French mission; the Francophiles argued, with some justice, that Brazilians felt more comfortable with the Latin French. Besides, it was not European experience per se that would be most applicable but European military techniques applied in a comparable setting, and the French were rich in military experience, with mixed populations and "native" troops in Africa and Asia. In addition, it seems that more officers knew French than German, if the movement of books in the army library is any indication (see Table 4.1): from 1910 to 1918 an annual average of 1,077 books in French were checked out compared to 18 in German.[92] Even Hermes da Fonseca, who admired the Prussian system and who sent the junior officers to Germany, conversed in French with German officials during his 1908 visit to Germany.[93]

In May 1914 *A Defesa Nacional* zealously campaigned in favor of inviting a German mission, editorializing that the French army did not have a general staff and that it was adopting German artillery tactics. Because "the French army is germanizing," the editors did not understand the hesitation in choosing "foreign officers to come to teach us the modern art of war" between "the original source of the greatest military advances and its timid and indecisive copy." They accused Brazilian financial and business interests of wanting to place "a formidable check" on German influences in the army in order to please "French high finance" and to secure the "fat commissions resulting

TABLE 4.1.

Army Library Usage, 1910–1918

Year	French	German	English	Guarani
1910	910	6	44	4
1911	1,076	4	56	1
1912	1,432	5	80	5
1913	—	—	—	—
1914	1,457	47	89	4
1915	1,305	22	55	1
1916	1,067	27	279	3
1917	1,045	30	128	0
1918	1,398	19	113	0
TOTALS	9,690	160	844	18

from future Brazilian government contracts with French equipment and arms manufacturers."[94] The Allied defeat of Germany put the matter to rest, although it did not curb admiration for the German model.

In 1915 the *Defesa Nacional* staff focused its critical analysis on the country and began to sound almost revolutionary. Major Raimundo Pinto Seidl, shocked at the ignorance of his troops, challenged other units to a contest to see which could eliminate illiteracy the fastest, and he persuaded the president to provide a bronze bust of the Duke of Caxias as first prize. The major declared that, with a national illiteracy rate of 80 percent, the best way to celebrate the coming centenary of independence in 1922 would be to eradicate illiteracy. His challenge went unaccepted.[95]

In 1916 the editors echoed Alberto Tôrres's assertion that Brazil was not a country, nation, or Pátria but "an exploitation." They listed as exploiters the politicians, judges, congressmen, public functionaries, and degree holders (bachareis), whose positions in society multiplied as their sons increased and who protested against "the *humiliation* of military service." The exploited were the farm laborers, the industrial workers, the commercial employees, "the people . . . who struggle, who work, who toil, who pay taxes of sweat and of blood. Only they have the right to give their lives for the PÁTRIA; the others reserve the right to sponge off it. In this sense there is no doubt— Brazil is an exploitation." Worse still, the editors lamented, "we are an improvised nation, without roots in the past, of indefinite ethnic formation, and, therefore easy to break up." For that reason, while preparing against a possible external enemy, they had to be aware of the more likely internal enemy: "the lack of national cohesion."[96]

In an editorial entitled "Above All We Should Be Brazilians," *A Defesa Nacional* called on its countrymen to wake up to reality; Europe was not falling over in amazement at the feats of Rui Barbosa or Santos Dumont. The self-congratulatory style of the Brazilian press was self-deluding. The people should not be fooled into dangerous complacency; rather, they should recognize their inferiority and work to reach the level of more advanced peoples. The editors asked why the elite did not turn their eyes toward Brazil and, instead of rushing to aid the wounded soldiers and the homeless children of Belgium and France, assist the victims of the Contestado? It was time to wake up, "to demonstrate by deeds that this land that witnessed our birth is ours, very much ours, and that our life is entirely hers, because she is the filter through which takes place the osmosis of life that came from our parents and passes to our children."[97]

Brazil was passing through a "delicate and decisive phase in its history," although it was closer than ever to "the road that could lead it to the definitive formation of an indestructible nationality." It also had never been so close to the "abyss of dissolution and ruin." And placing responsibility clearly on elite shoulders, the editors declared that "everything" depended "on the action of the *classes dirigentes* [ruling classes]." "Energetic and persistent activity, seeking general organization through military organization, could bring happiness to this *Pátria*," but "hesitant action, marked by fancy thrusts and acrobatic retreats, with an eye on popularity, will carry us fatally to defeat and dishonor." To guarantee that governmental action would not be in vain, the officers would have to become instructors and educators. The campaign for a national army first had to be won in the officer corps. Some officers still thought the idea impractical; others opposed it because of "philosophical *smartismo* [*sic*]" or thought it contrary to the "democratic character of the people."

A more revealing argument against an army based on generalized obligatory service was that Brazil's conditions were less akin to those of the European powers than to their colonies, where professional troops were the order of the day. Some officers feared drawing the lower classes into an active national role: universal obligatory service could weaken the oligarchy's power over the masses, and the draft did not apply to rural workers. *A Defesa Nacional*'s editors noted that the European powers maintained national armies at home to create cohesion; while in their colonies they relied on professional troops to avoid awakening sentiments of nationality in the natives. Happily, the editors stated, Brazil's leaders had embraced the idea of a national army as a vehicle to "secure a Pátria for Brazilians." "Thus, our duty is to march forward, always aiming at the happiness and greatness of the Brazilian nation. The path marked is the only one that can bring us a dignified and tranquil future. Whatever the obstacles that might arise, *to retreat would be cowardly.*"[98]

By the late 1910s the task the army reformers had set themselves was nothing less than the "formation of a people worthy of this marvelous Brazil." They wanted to see basic change in social behavior, particularly that of the elites. *A Defesa Nacional*'s editors, asserting that the long experience with slavery had weakened the Brazilian backbone, went on to attack "effeminate and hysterical *bacharelismo,*" which loved "declamatory speeches," "guitar serenades," and saw shame in any honest callus-producing work, whether with plow or sword.[99] An editorial lamented that this "immense and dazzling country" was a "*Pátria* so worthy of better sons." Instead of the "vacillating and defenseless nation" that it sheltered, Brazil "could nourish at her breast a virile and glorious nation."[100]

As the editors considered the "grandiose task" that lay ahead, they happily noted the flowering of a new generation that was beginning to cultivate the military spirit. Together the reformist officers and the young would make up for the "generations of moral collapse" by providing this "immense and lovely country" with sons worthy of its opulence. "Forward," the editors urged, "whatever the cost!"[101]

In a companion article Contestado veteran 2d Lt. Mário Travassos lamented the national bent toward pessimism, which he thought corrosive, depressing, and weakening. He asserted that optimism was "the only religion for Brazilians." Officers had divorced themselves from the positivist faith and taken shelter "in the sumptuous cathedral that our geographic frontiers form." The military schools were becoming more efficient. The graduating *aspirantes* actually knew how to ride, shoot, and conduct war games instead of merely being masters of abstract theories and having a taste for unsolvable questions. Brazil's war machine was being rebuilt. "The sleeping giant awakens." A small number of officers of all ranks had aroused the army. Travassos called on the majority to join them by putting aside their criminal "unpatriotic indifference" and their "pernicious inertia." It was no longer only the visionary "Young Turks" who spoke, he exalted, but the voice of the very nation.[102]

The ideas and sentiments expressed in these editorials encouraged officers to be critical of all aspects of Brazil and to begin the search for solutions to the problems that their analyses uncovered. But these were long-range issues and the reformers had more immediate goals.

Imposing the Young Turk Vision

The Young Turks and General Faria were in a race against time to impose their vision on the army before the Braz administration ended. As the war drew to a close, pressure to invite a French military mission to Brazil increased, stoked by paulista industrial and political interests tied to France. Even though the British and Americans wanted to sell armament to the army, they focused their efforts on competing with each other for the naval mission contract. Faria opened the door to acquisition of French artillery and aviation materiel but sought to preserve the adapted German doctrines that filled the pages of *A Defesa Nacional*.

The central educational institution of an army is its officer training school. It is the mold that forms the basic characteristics on which later schooling, training, and experience are built. The army had struggled since the closing of the school at Praia Vermelha in 1904 to strike a proper balance between professional military instruction and general education or, as it is called in Brazil, *cultural geral*. In 1913, 1918, and again in 1919 changes in the school regulations aimed at providing each in correct measure.

The 1913 regulation reiterated the prohibition, issued in 1905, against officers attending the military school. As observed in Chapter 2, the presence of officers, who had come up through the ranks, was a contributing factor to the school revolts of 1897 and 1904. The new regulations set an upward age limit of thirty and restricted access to men coming from one of the *Colegios Militares,* the army's version of a preparatory school, or to soldiers coming from an army unit. However, officers will be found in the student body as late as 1919 and will be factors in the revolts of the 1920s.

When officer preparation was moved from Porto Alegre to Realengo in 1911, it was conducted in two schools, the Escola Militar and the Escola Prática. They were separated by more than half a mile and initially had different commanders. Between 1915 and 1918 they were unified, and, supposedly, the practical was given precedence over the theoretical. Key to the development of the unified Escola Militar was its removal from the direct control of the minister of war and placement under the general staff.

During the period 1910–18 the general staff, which had been established in 1899, began for the first time to function as the army's core. The relationship between the general staff and the minister of war's staff was facilitated during Faria's years as minister by the fact that he had been chief of staff from 1910 to 1914. Prior to his chieftainship there had been seven chiefs, whose time in the post had ranged from one month to three years. Despite General Antônio Geraldo de Souza Aguiar's three-month interregnum between Faria and General Bento Ribeiro, these latter two officers gave the general staff whatever indigenous development it had prior to the coming of the French in 1919.

Under Faria the general staff planned the restructuring of the army that was put into effect in 1915. Led by Bento Ribeiro, it confronted the necessity for a Brazilian military doctrine that included war plans designating "theaters of operations and the type of warfare (offensive, defensive) and determining the means and general organization of the forces." From this plan would flow offensive and defensive plans, with emphasis, as a matter of national policy, on the latter. Bento Ribeiro recognized that the staff would be only as good as its officers, so he ended the haphazard selection process based on personal connections and favoritism and required that staff officers be graduates of the specialized course of their arm and of the general staff school.

He differed with Faria on how to reform the school system. Both agreed that "practical instruction" was weak and defective because there were not enough experienced instructors. Faria believed that the progressive spirit of the *Defesa Nacional* group could carry the day, but Bento Ribeiro thought that a foreign mission such as those that modernized the Argentine, Chilean, and Peruvian armies, as well as São Paulo's *Força Pública,* would be more effective. In 1917 the staff suggested inviting a mission, without expressing a national preference; but, of course, the possible choices, with the war then in progress, excluded the Germans and included the French, the British, the American, or the Japanese armies. Such an invitation would, because of the military necessity for doctrinal unity, require scrapping much of the German-inspired work of the Young Turks.[103]

To avoid this, the two generals compromised. Bento Ribeiro bowed to the minister's antipathy toward a foreign mission, perhaps thinking that ministers eventually leave whereas the general staff stays, and began revitalizing the military school with a select body of German-influenced officers.

In early 1918 *A Defesa Nacional* carried a number of editorials analyzing military education, arguing that an officer's preparation was a continuous process throughout his career and not something that began and ended in the three or four years of military school. That institution should have the restricted function of preparing combat arms officers to be troop instructors. Further training would be acquired in a series of schools to be attended throughout the officer's career. The editorials advised avoiding the French "vice" of overloading the training with "subjects without practical application, or of [only] remote necessity," and praised the "simplicity," short duration, and rationality of German military instruction. It would seem that the *Defesa Nacional* clique's admiration for German methods was not shaken by Brazil's declaration of war.[104]

Minister Faria did not say so publicly, but his actions indicate that he agreed with his young colleagues, with the caveat that the German methods should be introduced by Brazilians. And because by 1918 "our officers, with the exception of some old timers, all come from the military school," unity of origin would rapidly facilitate unity of doctrine.[105]

He focused on the Escola Militar, whose objective would be to produce graduates who, arriving at their first assignments, "could immediately commence to instruct their platoon or their section, without feeling ashamed amongst their company, squadron, or battery colleagues." In a fashion this was an ideal time to impose major changes on the Escola Militar because the financial crisis brought on by the war had required reducing the student body to two hundred, which was not sufficient to fill the 1918 deficit of 263 aspirantes in the units then being spread throughout Brazil. Everywhere unit commanders complained of a lack of officers, so for the 1918–19 school year the number of student openings was raised to 516, plus 31 lieutenants and 4 aspirantes held over from 1918; the enrollment was raised in 1919–20 to 811, which included 55 aspirantes taking advanced artillery and engineering courses and 756 *praças* (cadets). This expansion should have facilitated imposition of the new organizational structure and the revised curriculum.[106]

The general staff devised a competitive examination to select the new instructors. Prior to this time assignments to the school's faculty were based on favoritism. That a contemporary officer would later describe this decision as a "courageous service" gives some notion of the atmosphere in which it was made.[107]

To insure that the "practical instruction," as it was called, had the place of honor in the school curriculum, the general staff altered the grading system to give a coefficient of three for tactics, field duty, and military history; a two for armament, fortification, ballistics, and topography; and a modest one for analytic and descriptive geometry, calculus, and mechanic physics. Such an approach marked how far the army had come since the days when Benjamin Constant's and Colonel Dr. Roberto *Trompowsky* Leitão de Almeida's mathematics classes were the heart of the Praia Vermelha curriculum.[108] It is interesting that foreign language training was grouped under "practical instruction," with Spanish being given in years one and two, French in all three years, and English in the second and third years.[109]

The selected officers were assigned to the school in early December 1918, and soon the cadets nicknamed them the "Indigenous Mission." In the words of one of the officers, then 2d Lt. Odylio Denys, they condensed "the teachings of the ex-trainees of the German Army and adapting them to our environment were able to break the crust of backwardness and leisureliness that enveloped the traditional routine of the Army."[110] To take advantage of the new approach and to insure familiarity with the new methods, the aspirantes of the December 1918 *turma,* as classes were called, were kept at the school for another year to train with the new instructors. The unexpected result would be a combined 1919 turma that would contain the most technically professional rebels the army ever faced—the famous tenentes, who will be dealt with in the next chapters.[111]

The Faria Ministry Ends

With the various reforms in place, as the Braz administration was coming to an end in late 1918, Minister Faria could take some satisfaction in leaving behind an army on the road to modernization and different from that of a decade earlier. For once there would be continuity provided by General Bento Ribeiro's staying on as chief of staff. But the Brazilian army that had taken shape under Faria's leadership would face further change in the next years under French guidance and would be shaken by the revolutionary cycle that would begin in 1922.

However, those events lay in the future. In the second half of 1918 Faria acted to insure that his loyal subordinates were safe from the revenge of their enemies and detractors. For example, he packed *Defesa Nacional* founder Lieutenant Leitão de Carvalho off to Santiago as military attaché, telling him that he had been part of studies and reforms that upset a lot of important people and that if he returned to the troops just then, he would be like a "cockroach in a chicken-coop"; everyone would want to give him a peck. Leitão headed across the Andes, knowing that the job was not yet done and that the *Defesa Nacional's* junior officers had not been able to reform the army from the bottom up.[112] But there had been improvements, and now the army was about to receive a dose of French reform from the top down.

In this chapter we followed the discussions that generated the basic ideas of the army's developing ideology as it moved from being a professional army whose troops came from the dregs of society to a cadre or training army composed of a professional officer corps and draftees supposedly drawn from all social-economic levels. The pervasive influence of the German-trained Young Turks was most evident and lasting in their monthly review, *A Defesa Nacional*. Its editorials and articles were the arena in which the reformers proclaimed their doctrines that portrayed Brazil as a "Pátria so worthy of better sons" and then went on to outline how military training and social change would produce them. With their "Indigenous Mission" running the military school they put their ideas into practice and turned out the officers who would set the Old Republic on fire in the 1920s and bring it to an end in 1930.

CHAPTER 5

Professionalism and Rebellion

Brazil, a fertile and underpopulated country, is by its
well-known weakness, subject to great dangers in the
midst of the collision of these strong nations that clash
and will clash tenaciously to guarantee their existence
as autonomous peoples, economically powerful, and
financially sovereign.

—Brig. Gen. Alberto Cardoso de Aguiar

No one respects or seeks alliance with the weak.

—João Pandiá Calógeras

The streets of Rio de Janeiro were empty. A deadly fear hung over the Brazilian capital as the cadavers accumulated faster than they could be buried. The
Spanish influenza respected neither rank nor age. In October and November
1918, as the new government of ex-councilor of the empire and former
president of the republic (1902–6) Francisco de Paula Rodrigues Alves took
shape, its leader fought a losing battle against the illness in his Guarantinguetá
(São Paulo) residence.

The disease had arrived aboard the Royal Mail SS *Demerara,* which carried
two hundred cases contracted during a stop in Dakar. From its docking on
September 16 until an upper-class dance at the Club dos Diários on October
12, it spread slowly through the lower classes, but after many of the guests
took ill that night, a great leveling epidemic swept through rich and poor
households. Two weeks later an estimated five hundred thousand people—
half of Rio's population—were down sick, and a thousand bodies lay unburied in the Cajú cemetery. There were not enough hearses to carry the
bodies or enough grave diggers to bury them. Everything was paralyzed—
transport, schools, stores—as whole families were struck down. Food supplies,
especially milk and eggs, disappeared, causing some of the sick to die of starvation. The stench of death that had so marked Europe in the previous four
years spread through this tropical paradise with terrifying speed.

On October 25 the military took charge and set up four temporary hospitals. Fittingly, by All Saints Day the worst was over and the capital began to return to a degree of normalcy. The official death toll was 16,997, but other estimates reached 28,000. The army schools had suspended classes as officers and students took to their beds. The army's central hospital treated 1,442 persons with influenza, of whom 109 died. The experience set a serious tone as the postwar era began.[1]

With the president-elect too ill to function, his vice president, Delfim Moreira da Costa Ribeira, of Minas Gerais, took the oath as acting president on November 15, 1918. Although he himself was seriously ill with arteriosclerosis that caused sporadic memory loss, he struggled to run the country with the cabinet Rodrigues Alves had composed. For the army this meant a significant shift of direction.

The French Initiative

Minister of War Faria had opposed any foreign mission so as to avoid tying Brazil to a European power. When a contract for a German mission had been discussed during Hermes's government, he had opposed it "tenaciously" and was proud of having contributed to its failure. In a mood of self-congratulation he pointed to the difficulties that Argentina and Chile had during the war as a result of their officers having absorbed "the Germanic spirit." "The army," he asserted, "should be exclusively national in spirit, theories, doctrines, and even tactics." Although he thought it useful to send observers to Europe and to bring some foreign instructors to teach methods then in use on the western front, he doubted that the trench warfare employed there constituted a universal method or doctrine of war, especially for South America, whose great spaces and widespread populations kept the various national armies at some distance from one another. It was difficult to imagine trench warfare on the pampas of the Rio de La Plata or the rolling countryside of Rio Grande do Sul.

But General Faria had a deeper doubt: "I know our troops well, I know that our officers are very jealous of their rights and I do not believe that they will submit to the command of foreign officers." It would be better, he thought, to maintain the freedom to choose whatever they wanted from any source. He urged hiring foreign specialists in strategy, war gaming, mapmaking, aviation, and so forth. Indeed, he wrote the army's attaché in Paris about contracting French flying instructors, but he opposed an armywide foreign training mission.[2]

The idea of seeking military salvation abroad, of employing a large, army-wide foreign mission to teach the secrets of advanced military science, was old and had engendered considerable debate, as Faria's comments suggest. Such a mission had been aborted during the Hermes presidency mostly because German and French partisans checkmated each other. In 1917 and 1918, with Brazil at war with the German Empire, the idea of a mission rose to the foreground again. After Brazil's October 1917 recognition of a state of war, the rumor in Paris was that it would send troops to Europe, so Military Attaché Major Alfredo Malan d'Angrogne wrote Minister Faria, saying that his impression was that the French general staff would respond favorably to a request for a mission to train the mobilizing Brazilian forces. Malan lamented that, because of their country's military weakness, news of Brazil's entry into the war had been received in France with indifference, and he believed that a large mission to remodel the army, the military schools, the general staff, and the military administration would help the country garner respect abroad. He confessed to his friend General Augusto Tasso Fragoso that it was urgent to act because "Tomorrow could be too late."[3]

The Ministry of Alberto Cardoso de Aguiar

In 1918, with the government of mineiro Wenceslau Braz ending, the presidential power shifted to São Paulo in the person of ex-president Rodrigues Alves. The paulista elite's complex ties with France resulted, first, in the selection of a pro-French minister of war and, second, in the negotiation of a military mission contract with the French government.[4] The French had worked since 1906 to obtain such a contract. Paris had intended that the officers that São Paulo hired to train its *Força Pública* would be a demonstration of what its army could do. Having successfully blocked the Germans before the war—they even used the Faria's nationalist argument as a last resort—the French and their allies moved to insure a favorable outcome now.

Also in 1918 the French military attaché, Major (Viscount) Fanneau de la Horie, a former member of the mission to São Paulo, laid out the steps Paris should take: reestablish its mission in São Paulo as the *pivot de la manoeuvre;* arrange for Brazil to send an observation mission to France; furnish the artillery and aviation materiel that the Brazilians desired; finally, send a military leader who had the prestige, organizing ability, and temperament to "reorganize the Brazilian army."[5] Even though General Faria balked at hiring an armywide mission, he set the stage for doing so by sending the observation mission under General Napoleão Aché, by ordering French materiel, and by arranging for an aviation mission.

A curious and little-noticed aspect of the unfolding situation was the rise and appointment of Alberto Cardoso de Aguiar as Faria's successor. In army circles the likely candidates were experienced generals such as Augusto Tasso Fragoso, Luis Barbedo, and Setembrino de Carvalho. That Cardoso de Aguiar had been a brigadier general for only eleven months (January 12, 1918) before he became minister raised some eyebrows.[6]

An artillery officer with engineering training, Cardoso de Aguiar was fifty-four when he assumed the ministry. Among the eighteen colonels of artillery, he was one of four who were under the average age of fifty-nine. Having been sixty-ninth out of seventy-seven men on the combat colonels list in 1915, his sudden rise in the next two years must have set his competitors' teeth on edge. Promotion to general was never accidental; it had political ramifications and was made by the president, and appointment to minister was probably the single most important military-political decision a president made during the Old Republic. Cardoso de Aguiar had entered the army at sixteen (1880), was an *alferes-aluno* in the last year of the empire, went to second then first lieutenant in three days' time in January 1890, reached his captaincy in 1895, and stayed there for ten years before being made a major. He received his lieutenant colonelcy in 1911, a brevet colonelcy in October 1914, and his permanent colonelcy in January 1915. Three years later he had his two brigadier stars.[7]

He reportedly had wide knowledge of Brazil from his work on telegraph lines in Mato Grosso and the Palma strategic railway in Paraná, as well as having been acting chief of the commission mapping the country. He impressed the American attaché as "a man of good abilities, earnest and studious . . . [who had] good sense, capacity for work and organizing ability." He did not, according to this source, have a reputation for being allied with politicians. However, his election to the presidency of the Military Club indicated that he was popular with fellow officers and good at army politics. In the army he had a reputation as "simpático," intelligent, honest, hardworking, and reform minded.[8]

The secret to his rise was the combination of his competence and his connections. He had links to both Generals Faria and Bento Ribeiro, having served as head of the second section of the general staff under the former from 1911 to 1914 and as chief of the latter's cabinet from 1915 to 1918. These positions, especially the latter, normally were held by officers "of confidence." Moreover, he had political connections, as indicated by his service in 1914 as commandant of the Federal District's firemen's corps, while Bento Ribeiro was mayor of the district. He owed his ministerial appointment, if not his stars, to paulista politicians, especially Senator Álvaro de Carvalho, son-in-law of President-elect Rodrigues Alves. It is possible that he had promised to support contracting the French; however, that may not have been necessary, as he was known as a Francophile. Before his promotion, he had written to Malan in Paris saying, "France, valiant France, will be eternally our wise schoolmistress."[9]

The progressive officers received Cardoso de Aguiar's appointment with confidence in his abilities. Tasso Fragoso asserted that he "trusted him a lot, for his intelligence and honesty," although he hoped that he would free himself from "such futilities" as an excessive concern for "technical things and paper reforms." Leitão de Carvalho regarded him as "studious and capable" and a collaborator of General Faria's, and Pantaleão Pessôa thought him "a soldier of character and capability," who would be "a promise of justice" for the army. Certainly he would not be an ally of the "destroyers of good works."[10]

In the weeks after the new government took office on November 15, 1919, while the Congress debated authorization for a foreign mission, General Cardoso de Aguiar acted to hire the French. As early as November 29 he had told General Tasso Fragoso that he would contract French officers. Shortly thereafter, on December 4, he cabled Malan that the decision was made and that he wanted him to suggest a suitable general to head the mission. He wrote: "Not only do I want indisputable technical competence, I also want a young, healthy, far-seeing general with balanced judgment— qualities necessary [for the] delicate task to be intrusted." The selected general should visit Brazil to see firsthand what he faced and then should return to France to assemble his team.[11]

Clearly, the new minister must have been sure of his ground to have issued such orders prior to congressional approval. Between November 30, when it came out of committee, and January 3, 1919, when it passed, the bill was modified to remove mention of the mission's nationality, apparently to mollify the opposition, which had raised the possibility of an American mission in hopes of repeating the kind of stalemate that had prevented contracting a mission prior to the war. The Congress approved credits for "a Mission of foreign officers for the instruction of the Army. The Chief of said Mission to be attached to the General Staff as technical assistant." The Army and Navy Committee's interim report, however, had made quite obvious which "foreign officers" it had in mind:

The Government proposes to contract a Mission in France, the country closest to ours not only by race but in ideas and sentiments, almost identical in their general lines. It is natural that Brazil should seek teachers from the great military powers and especially from France whose army is giving most pronounced proofs of its valor and efficiency and has furnished the Commander-in-Chief for all the Allied forces. Furthermore, the Brazilian officers who entered the war sought France to learn and in France is a Mission under the direction of General Napoleão Aché. If these reasons are not sufficient it might also be stated that an Aviation Mission has already been contracted in France and that it would not be advisable to employ a Mission with different methods from another country for instruction in other branches of the service because confusion would result.[12]

The minister was determined to copy French organization and even uniforms.[13] Indeed, the latter, consisting of a dark blue tunic and red trousers with black stripes, were indistinguishable from those of French officers. It was almost as if he were applying the definition of a sacrament to the officer corps, an outward sign of inward grace. The French-style uniforms would turn the Brazilians into tropical Frenchmen.

The Young Turks had mixed reactions to Cardoso de Aguiar's French initiative. Some of the reformers reacted negatively, but Leitão de Carvalho wrote to his colleagues from Chile that their work had only begun and that by themselves they could not reform officer and troop instruction, eliminate "inveterate habits and customs," or acquire the experience of the recent war. He reminded them that not they but the government had chosen Germany as a prewar model, and with the defeat of that empire they had to turn elsewhere. As leaders of the progressive campaign, he declared that they should "give to the French mission the support that we would have given, before the war, to the German Mission, if it had been contracted." He was anxious to return to work with the mission "because we were not tied to the fortunes of Germany, but to the future of Brazil."[14] Other Young Turks either shared or soon adopted his attitude.

The *Defesa Nacional* group had its representative on the minister's staff, Captain Joaquim de Souza Reis Neto, and several of them held positions on the general staff (Captains Bertholdo Klinger, João Baptista Mascarenhas de Morais, Pantaleão da Silva Pessôa, Genserico de Vasconcellos, and Julião Freire Esteves).[15] These officers threw their weight behind the mission, several of them signing up for the new courses the mission established in order, one remembered, "to give the example of our submission." Leitão de Carvalho went so far as to move his family back from Santiago in hopes of gaining permission to end his assignment as military attaché a year early so as to study with the French. Chief of Staff Bento Ribeiro ordered him back to Chile but promised a slot in the 1921 General Staff review course.[16]

The Coming of the French

Malan's "delicate and thorny" task in Paris was to find a French general with the personal qualities that matched Cardoso de Aguiar's charge. The attaché worried that the names that came first to mind were generals who had commanded hundreds of thousands of men but whom he hesitated to invite to organize undermanned brigades or skeleton divisions. He knew that the chief of mission had to possess "tact, a certain diplomacy to deal with our touchy or ignorant and therefore arrogant Jacobins." "Among us," he reminded himself, "the chief doesn't demand: he asks, please." He and the Brazilian minister to France, Olyntho de Magalhães, to avoid making an open-ended request to the Ministry of War that they feared would net them someone's protégé, or an officer with political connections who would not satisfy their special requirements, sought the advice of Marshal Joseph Jacques Césaire Joffre, the hero of the Marne campaign. Joffre recommended Brigadier

General Maurice Gustave Gamelin, who had been his chief of staff, had held commands from battalion to division, and was young, in his mid-forties, tactful, and hardworking. Malan described him as being of medium build, black hair, blue eyes, and sporting a long blond mustache. He was not a poser and the Brazilian regarded him as "simpatico." He had found his man.[17]

It is noteworthy that Cardoso de Aguiar wanted Gamelin to make an inspection trip to Brazil immediately, before the two governments negotiated a contract. Undoubtedly he wanted to be sure of the selection, to give Gamelin the opportunity to see what he was in for, and to allow potential critics to see that he was less threatening in person than in their imaginations. As soon as the Congress voted in favor of a foreign contract, the minister requested that Malan make arrangements with the French government for Gamelin's visit. Malan and future war minister João Pandiá Calógeras, who was then in Paris for the peace conference, wrote to army friends and urged them to do what they could to give him a cordial welcome. Malan later wrote Tasso Fragoso that Gamelin was not a scholar but that he was a general. "Our backbiters, finding nothing to cut up, claim that we have found a man no one knows. We are not seeking a pure-blooded prizewinner; rather we need a fast-breaking colt who won't slacken on the course." He thought that the only thing they had to repent was taking so long to reach this point.[18]

In February 1919 Gamelin would arrive in Brazil for his precontract inspection. But before then the American army received passing notice. Officers repeatedly told the American attaché, Major Fenton McCreery, that his relations with Brazilian officers were "more intimate than those of any foreign attaches who have come to Brazil and that . . . [he had] been received more cordially." He reported that although Brazil would employ a French mission, the Brazilians expressed considerable "curiosity regarding our Army and especially regarding the rapid training, equipment and supply overseas of an enormous body of men." They were particularly interested in how civilians were trained to be officers. Several Brazilian officers stated that they hoped for an American mission. The army's surgeon general was inclined to model his service on that of the American army and hoped to go to the United States to study the medical corps.[19]

Minister Cardoso de Aguiar told the attaché that Brazilian officers should study in the United States to "acquire practical ideas and learn something more than theoretical tactics." Major McCreery assured his stateside superiors that he had not raised the matter and that he had "always confined my observations to remarking that we owed much to French officers in the training of our Army and that our officers had finally graduated and gone into the fight." Later on, the attaché presented the minister with forty-nine film reels with titles such as *Pershing's Crusaders, Field Service on the Western Front, Spirit of 1917,* and *The Remaking of a Nation* for showing on army posts.

Thanks to his efforts the American general staff suggested to the State Department that relations would be improved if Brazil were induced to send a military attaché to Washington because "Brazil . . . is ignorant of American military methods, and, if informed by one of her own representatives, would be favorably impressed and would be less prone to accept the anti-American falsehoods at present in current use there."[20] These glances toward the United States would not turn to serious flirtation until the 1930s, but they show that Brazilian officers were not narrowly pro-French or pro-German but were looking for the best methods.

The army that Gamelin encountered in early 1919 was considerably improved over that of 1900, but it must have made him realize that he had real work ahead. That year the army's authorized strength was 43,747, but the actual number under arms was about 37,000 with many units under recruited.[21] On paper it had five divisions, but in fact only two were organized and stationed so that they could function as such; the rest were more or less independent regiments and battalions spread over great distances. The two organized divisions were the Third, in the Federal District, and the Fifth, in Rio Grande do Sul. Whereas the Third Division's seven regiments and eight smaller units and the Fifth Division's sixteen regiments and twelve smaller units were within operational distances of each other, the First Division, like many others, had no fixed headquarters, and the battalions and regiments assigned to its two infantry and one artillery brigade were strung out from Manaus and Belém through Fortaleza and Recife to Corumbá and Cuiabá. The distribution of forces reflected the army's dual mission of external and internal defense: in the south they were placed to guard against possible invasions directly from Argentina or through Uruguay and to protect overland and sea communications with the south-central states; in the latter states and in the north, they were stationed to protect the ports and to maintain order in the large population centers and frontier areas. The British embassy's report for 1919 put it bluntly: "the distribution of the army more closely resembles that of a constabulary than of an efficient fighting force."[22]

The distribution pattern resulted naturally from the military's perception of the country's being constantly at risk of breaking up. According to Cardoso de Aguiar this was "incontestably the greatest danger that Brazil had to confront." And the army was the only instrument to hold the country together. Proper military organization would allow justice and tranquility to reign and economic and industrial development to proceed unimpeded while erecting "an unbending barrier to foreign ambitions, keeping Brazilian soil free of the foreign conquistador." Moreover, military strength would guarantee "our [external] commercial expansion."[23]

A problem uppermost in the minister's mind was the unequal burden that obligatory service was placing on some military regions whose populations were disproportionate to the number of troops that they had to supply. For example, the Fifth Region (the Federal District) had an official census tally of 975,918 and needed 8,292 troops, the Seventh Region's (Rio Grande do Sul) 1,682,736 people had to produce 11,814 soldiers, and the Fourth Region (Minas Gerais, State of Rio de Janeiro, and Espirito Santo) with 6,316,891 inhabitants required only 4,632 men for its units. As a result the Federal District and Rio Grande do Sul were overburdened, and because the former could not meet its quota, the other regions had to send conscripts there with the consequent expenses for sea and land travel. Acting president Delfim Moreira told the Congress that it was "against the interests of the conscripts to take them very far from their homes." The government proposed realigning the component states of the seven military regions to give them a base population more proportionate to their annual conscript levels. The actual numbers are less important than what the situation exemplified: first, the failure to think through major aspects of a program before putting it into operation; second, the resultant necessity to redo or reform the work of the preceding administration. Also, it is odd, that an army hierarchy so preoccupied with national unity insisted on a regional recruitment pattern rather than bringing conscripts to central training camps as a means of instilling national consciousness. Of course, by inserting a national institution into each region the army served to draw each closer to the central government. Moreover, the needs of the Rio garrison served as excuse for the practice of bringing recruits from Germanic colonies in Santa Catarina and Paraná to the federal capital. Tall, blond, blue-eyed soldiers, popularly called "Catarinas," made especially handsome guards in the eyes of a Europeanizing elite.[24]

The units in the Federal District—which an officer stationed in the north called the "bosom of Abraham"—were better quartered, fed, and supplied than elsewhere. It is indicative of an attitude that the *A Defesa Nacional* section containing news items contributed by officers from units outside Rio was entitled "Da Provencia" (From the provinces). This cast of mind labeled the whole country beyond the capital's limits as "the interior." As a consequence of this attitude and a desire for better access to influential contacts, officers did their best to spend much of their careers in the environs of Rio de Janeiro.

Three areas of the Federal District were traditionally military: Tijuca, where the Colegio Militar was located and where many officers resided; São Cristóvão, where the army's oldest regiment, the First Cavalry (1808), and a field artillery group, a battalion of light infantry, and a machine-gun company were quartered; and the Vila Militar/Deodoro area, which was home to the First Mounted Artillery Regiment, the First and Second Infantry Regiments, and two machine-gun companies. Illustrative of the army's facilities were those of the field artillery and machine-gun units. Their barracks at São Cristóvão were of brick and stone and built on three sides of a plaza. They were two-stories high, except in the sleeping quarters, where the ceilings were one and three-quarters stories over the floor. The rooms were spacious, airy, and full of light because of the high ceilings and the many tall, narrow windows. The soldiers' quarters consisted of two large rooms, one for conscripts and the other for sergeants, and a lavatory. The mess halls were separate and had tiled kitchens and modern ranges. The army's staple food was *feijoada,* the savory black-bean stew, served with boiled rice and *farinha* made from manioc flour. The troops also received meals of meat, potatoes, fruit, and coffee. There was an infirmary of ten beds, a dispensary, and a school building. The open-sided stables were brick floored and sported ironwork stalls and mangers. A foreign observer said that the horses were of fair size, a cross between native and European stocks, and in good condition but thin. They enjoyed a diet of corn, alfalfa, and a green fodder resembling marsh grass. There was a twelve-stall veterinary hospital and blacksmith and carpenter shops. To a practiced military eye, the wagons seemed too light for their purposes.

The men ranged in color, according to the American attaché, from black to white, displaying "almost without exception . . . evidence of African blood." He classed discipline and morale "a trifle below fair," which, showing his prejudice, he attributed to African emotions and mentality. They were armed with Mauser rifles, equipped with sword bayonets; the machine-gun company used eight Maxims and ammunition from Essen, Germany, and the field artillery had Krupp guns.

The central army hospital consisted of eight buildings modeled after the French hospitals of the era. The tiled floors and walls; the high-ceilinged, well-lit wards, with ample toilets and baths; the clean operating rooms, with their cabinets of French surgical instruments; and the Sisters of Charity bustling about in their great, white-winged wimples gave the place an air of salubrity. It probably had about three hundred patients in its wards at a time, and in 1919–20, 4,454 patients had been interned. The hospital's staff responded well during the epidemic of 1918, even taking on the added burden of one hundred sailors from the USS *Pittsburgh,* all of whom were treated and had recovered in a building renamed "President Wilson Pavilion." The army also had its own microscopic laboratory and chemical and pharmaceutical laboratory, which gave it independence in diagnosis and treatment. The latter laboratory had been improved during the war to make up for shortages of imported drugs and medicines.[25]

Vila Militar, the principal Brazilian military establishment, located about forty miles from downtown Rio de Janeiro, was, and is, reachable by train on the Central do Brasil from the terminal next to the army headquarters on Praça da República. The barracks, shops, and storehouses still string out along Avenida Duque de Caxias. Part of Hermes de Fonseca's 1907 construction program, they were similar to those in São Cristovão, but they benefitted from some modifications in later years. Across the street from the main group of buildings were comfortable houses for the officers and their families. The broad avenues served as drill areas for conscripts breaking in their new Brazilian-made black leather puttees and shoes, while learning the full-throated version of the unit's marching song. Each unit had an officers' dining room that also served as a place for social functions, where visitors such as General Gamelin and foreign attachés were entertained.

The Vila was home to the First and Second Infantry Regiments, the First Artillery Regiment, the Second Machine Gun Company, the First Engineers Battalion, the First Transport Corps, and the Infantry Course. The latter prepared sergeants in groups of about 150 at a time to serve as trainers of conscripts and of Tiro units.[26] Nearby to the east, in Deodoro, was the First Machine Gun Company; to the south behind the Vila was the Campo dos Afonsos, where the French Aviation Mission had been training would-be pilots since November 1918; to the west, in Realengo, was the Escola Militar, its cadets, and company of support troops; and further west, on the railroad at Santa Cruz, was the Second Artillery Regiment and the Ninth Machine Gun Company.[27] In that era, when the transportation units still lacked motor vehicles, the railroad was the principal link with the city. Because officers, cadets, and troops took the same trains, a careful etiquette was employed to maintain proper distance and poise. The annual training cycle created a rise and fall in the garrison's population, with the period between late December and February 1 being the low point.

The philosophy underpinning this military establishment had changed since the beginning of the century from a positivism that in its most orthodox form was atheistic and pacifistic to a form that stressed applying technology and method to any problem at hand. Because positivism as a way of thinking emphasized describing phenomena instead of understanding them, the resulting solutions to problems tended to be superficial. By the second decade of the republic, according to Francisco de Paula Cidade, positivism's hold on the military schools and on sectors of the high command had weakened and "disappeared from the bosom of the Army."

This decline of positivist influence was paralleled by the rise of a new Catholic spirit in the army. In 1917 the pastor of the parish in Realengo, Father Miguel de Santa Maria Muchon, encouraged a dozen or so cadets at the Escola Militar, including Juarez Távora, to form a Vincentian Conference to maintain their Catholic faith and to do good works among the poor of the town. The selfless dedication of these cadets during the influenza epidemic in bringing food to bedridden families made a profound impression on their indifferent, even hostile, colleagues. The mixing of St. Vincent de Paul's concern for the poor with August Comte's positivism and General Gamelin's professionalism would give some members of the coming military generation interesting, if confusing, intellectual roots.[28]

The French Arrive

This is the army that awaited Gamelin when he arrived in Rio de Janeiro in March 1919. Although some high-ranking officers looked forward expectantly to his arrival in hopes that he would clear the air of the "many asininities" floating about, others maintained a "deaf resistance," determined to end their careers, in General Tasso Fragoso's words, "without having done anything and without having learned anything."[29]

Gamelin did his best to reassure his hosts that he did not intend to turn everything upside down or strip the army of its Brazilian character. Most important, command would remain in Brazilian hands while the mission busied itself with training and instruction. The mission, he said, would endeavor to preserve the "national character of the troops and the national methods and systems." Contrary to the methods of "German Missions of instruction in foreign armies, whose principal object is to Germanize them and change their characteristic and traditional elements, the French Missions," according to Gamelin, undertook "to instruct the troops, conserving at the same time their national characteristics in the greatest possible degree."[30]

He made a five-week tour of army garrisons, being, he said, "especially interested in visiting those districts which present the problems of national defense now receiving the attention of the Government." Therefore, he considered it "absolutely necessary" to inspect boundary areas in Rio Grande do Sul, "without doubt the most interesting" in terms of Brazilian military traditions, so that he could have "a thorough and exact visual idea of the terrain and its accidents and its topography, in order to organize the localization of the forces and to determine the military elements adapted to the district." The terrain between Santa Maria and Cruz Alta and on to Porto Alegre reminded Gamelin of Champagne, although less wooded and more cut up by arroyos. A campaign in such an area would, he said, employ "every combat arm."[31]

A war on the "extended plains" of Rio Grande would be one of "movement and maneuvers," employing machine guns and long-range cannon to good effect. The "united front"–style of combat that characterized the western front would not occur there, but the war's lessons could still be applied. His impression of the southern garrisons was "much better than they told me it would be." He found "everything arranged for a good and efficient technical organization," and he greatly admired "the labor and devotion of the Brazilian officers." Diplomatically, he observed that with "rigorous instruction" and "a little more perseverance," and with "Cavalry from the south, Infantry from the north, the Brazilian Army will never lack men of the first class."[32]

Such reassuring, cooing words did not still criticism, however, especially among general staff officers. *O Jornal* of Rio de Janeiro responded to a critical article in the *Revista do Estado Maior* by praising the selection of Gamelin as "one who fought in the war and earned his promotions." The implication was, of course, that Brazilian generals had acquired their stars in different fashion.[33]

Inserting a foreign body, especially of expert advisers, into any organization is a delicate matter, so much more so in an elaborate, hierarchically structured, rank-conscious military institution. The decree (May 28, 1919) in which Acting-President Delfim Moreira authorized contracting a mission from France stipulated that "the Chief of the mission will be attached to the General Staff in the capacity of technical assistant and will have supervision of all activities assigned to officers of the mission." This provision recognized a separate chain of command for the mission, which, in effect, insulated its individual members from direct Brazilian control.[34] More bothersome was the contract, negotiated in Paris between May and September 1919, that created an awkward triangular relationship among the mission, the general staff, and the minister of war by making the first "answerable solely to the Minister of War of the Brazilian Republic through the Chief of Mission." By naming the head of mission the chief of staff's "technical assistant for instruction and organization" and requiring that he "must be consulted on all questions of instruction," a constant irritation was introduced into the Brazilian military system at a tense stage in its development. This made more difficult a solution to the continuous controversy over whether the chief of staff or the minister ran the army, an issue that took on special meaning with a civilian minister.

The four-year contract, which, considering the long-held French desire to secure it, should have given the Brazilians a strong bargaining position, was excessively favorable to the French. It forbade the army from contracting any "other foreign mission for military purposes other than technicians for the factories, arsenals and geographic services" and specified cancellation with a large indemnity in the event that any state hired non-French advisers for its police forces. It also limited acquisition of military hardware from other sources by giving French producers preference. The document provided extremely generous pay and periodic home leaves.[35] Why the Brazilian negotiators, who included Paris attaché Major Malan d'Angrogne and João Pandiá Calógeras, who in the midst of the negotiations was named the first and only civilian minister of war in the republican era, were not more hard-nosed and protective of Brazilian interests is not clear. However, the favoritism to the French is probably the reason that the terms were kept secret.[36]

By January 1920 some twenty members of the mission had established themselves in Rio de Janeiro. Although they wore their own uniforms, they were accorded the insignia and privileges of one rank beyond their French one. Their charge was to create the foundation of a modern army by establishing schools to train professional officers, improving the general staff's capability to direct the army, rewriting training and tactics regulations, devising a promotion system that would insure the rise of the most capable officers to the important leadership posts, and creating true tactical units.[37] They were assigned to the general staff school, where Colonel Eugène Durandin was made director of instruction, with the rank of brigadier general, a colonel was appointed director of studies, and four other officers were to be instructors. Lt. Col. Albert Barat, with the rank of colonel, and three assistants founded the Advanced Officers Course (Escola de Aperfeiçoamento de Oficiais, EsAO) at Vila Militar.[38]

The general staff school was already requisite for officers to serve on the army staff; therefore, it was the key institution from which to influence future planning and organization. Its student officers were drawn from majors and lieutenant colonels who would be the army's future commanders. To allow senior officers, who already had completed the staff course, to be exposed to French ideas, the mission set up a review course. EsAO prepared captains as company, squadron, and battery level commanders.

The graduates of these courses had the task of imposing unity of doctrine on the army. At that time, because the army regulations had changed so frequently in recent years, units were operating under different regulations. The EsAO graduates were particularly important in this process; they were assigned to units to act as instructors and official interpreters of the school's doctrines, with the idea that imposing "unity of doctrine" would intensify the speed with which the army would be transformed. Of course, in practice this meant a degree of tension between these bearers of the word and less-enlightened officers. The graduates of the general staff school's review and regular courses had the same mission but at a high level. The two schools marked, in the enthusiastic words of the minister of war, "the beginning of a new phase in the professional perfection of the Army."[39]

But to reach perfection, the Brazilian officers had to know French because their imported instructors did not speak Portuguese. A few Frenchmen made an effort to learn Portuguese, but they were the exception. Some Brazilian officers were put off by having to use a foreign language in their own country, and even more in their own schools, and by what they considered the "esoteric" phrasing of the French officers; "only the great initiates," one said, "were able to decipher the occult meaning of the lectures of the masters."[40] The Frenchmen were not experienced teachers so instruction had its shortcomings, as did the manuals that they prepared as texts. General Paula Cidade recalled that "they did not write their lessons with a literary preoccupation," nor did they provide references that would indicate the sources of the material that they borrowed liberally from published authors and French army manuals.[41] This latter practice set a bad example whose influence is still notable in army publications. On a lighter note, the language problems resulted at times in humorous misunderstandings and jokes that common soldiers, and likely officers, enjoyed at French expense.[42]

Despite the goodwill of the *Defesa Nacional* group, rumblings and uncertainties continued. It is not accurate to simply say that older officers opposed the French, whereas younger ones favored them; the matter was more complicated in that it flowed from the professional insecurities of some and the nationalism of others. And, despite all the talk of the common Latin soul, there was the barrier of cultural shock and clash that comes into play whenever people of different cultures work together. The mere fact of inviting a foreign training mission was an admission of Brazilian inferiority, so it would have been surprising indeed if there had been no tension between masters and pupils.

Some of the tension, however, between the general staff and the mission related to the former's lack of involvement in the decision-making process about the contracting and the use of foreign advisers. A May 1920 editorial in *A Defesa Nacional* noted that the general staff had been bypassed and was "a quiet victim, deaf to the disturbing rumors and secrecy of the [mission's] deliberations." There was danger that providing the new generation of officers with instruction that their seniors lacked would undermine the army's structure of authority. The professional gains would not compensate, the editors thought, for such an evil result.[43] Some of the very officers who had been in the forefront of the campaign to improve the army were antipathetic and distrustful. They had carried the reform process this far, and now it seemed that the foreigners would get the credit. They did not want their army to be a pale image of the French. They resented the idea of foreigners determining what was best for them.[44]

Gamelin used press interviews to reassure his hosts that the French had "not come to undo what has been done. We will try to preserve all the good things, expanding them where necessary. . . . [N]ot all the regulations of the Brazilian army are copies of the German Army and even if they were we would not reject them." Besides there were many similarities between French and German doctrine, and in any case both "had to be applied to the special case of Brazil." They would, he said reassuringly, "respect the military traditions of Brazil."[45]

The new general staff and EsAO courses opened with due ceremony on April 7 and 8, 1920, and at the same time a mixed Brazilian-French commission worked to revise army regulations. The objective of the commission was to form basic military doctrine for training and operations. This was a task in which the Brazilians tended to defer to French superiority; after all, that is why they had hired them. Although the Brazilians believed that they had chosen as their mentors the victorious masters of modern warfare, the next war would show that they had chosen badly. From their recent experiences in World War I the French had developed a military doctrine that, as it turned out in 1939–40, wrongly emphasized large-scale, static fortifications for defense and big infantry divisions as the basic elements of offensive maneuver. In the interwar period, despite Charles de Gaulle's efforts, they minimized the potential of the tank as an offensive weapon. Nor did they see the future importance of aircraft for support of infantry operations or for strategic bombing behind the enemy's lines. They ignored problems of battle control and the related need for efficient communications by radio and telephone. Their planners fought the Great War again, now on their sand tables trying to correct past mistakes instead of looking forward to a new type of warfare. And worse, right up to World War II, the French failed to "bring together the military and the nonmilitary branches of government for strategic planning in a systematic way, or even to coordinate the views of the rival services."[46]

The static type of warfare the French officers espoused turned out to be fantasy in 1939, and it should be recalled that General Gamelin, who would head the army in its disastrous defeat by the Germans, showed himself as commander-in-chief to be "defensive-minded, cautious, uninterested in tactical innovations."[47] This was the man that the Brazilian government entrusted with the future of its army.

There was little likelihood that the Brazilians would fight against foreign armies in a static, defensive war. Their country's huge territory, its poor communications, its small army, and lack of civilian interest in military matters counseled in favor of small, highly mobile tactical units trained for a war of movement. Although the French attempted to tailor their system to the Brazilian situation, perhaps calling on their colonial experience, much of their advice and teaching reflected doctrine derived from World War I, especially the emphasis on divisions as tactical units. Brazilian officers, dazzled by images of Napoleonic glory and the overwhelming industrial might involved in the recent European carnage, felt hesitant to criticize, so most accepted French ideas with little immediate protest. When that protest came, it would not be in classroom discussion but in insurrection. The discussion in Chapter 7 of the tenente rebellions and the Revolution of 1930 will show that battlefield success resulted from putting aside French methods in favor of traditional Brazilian techniques. So it is fair to say that "much of the [French] training prepared the Brazilians for the kind of war they would never fight."[48] As a critic wrote in 1928, "with all the teachings of the mission . . . our up-to-date generals" were not able to stop the Prestes column from marching back and forth across the map of Brazil.[49]

Military Industry

Although military and government leaders had adopted a foreign model to improve their personnel, they continued to dream of independence from foreign sources of arms and munitions. Increasingly their rhetoric linked autonomy and independence with national development of iron, steel, and coal industries. With the coming of peace the discussion of such development intensified. General Cardoso de Aguiar saw freedom from foreign sources of supply as a bulwark of defense. Without "organized industry" Brazil would always be dependent on foreign supply that could easily be shut off in a war situation. Maintenance of Brazilian independence depended, he argued, on the development of a metallurgical industry centered on steel production. He observed that if Japan, Switzerland, Italy, and Sweden could produce and export metal products when they were poor in coal and iron, then Brazil, which was rich in them, ought to be able to do likewise. The poor quality of Brazilian coal could be overcome by using electrically fired blast furnaces and charcoal; energy needs could be met from Brazil's tremendous forests, waterfalls, and rivers. The establishment of mills to produce steel

for our tools, our machines, our arms, our munitions, our ships, should be the principal objective of the government, because with iron will come the railroad that will open the backlands carrying progress to the isolated and deserted interior, allowing the rapid transport of merchandise; with iron we will also construct the great trans-Atlantic vessels that will carry our products in their holds in exchange for capital to enlarge our businesses and to give the country economic impetus.[50]

For General Cardoso de Aguiar defense was not only a question of arms; it involved the whole economy in industrial development, and he was aware of the links among international economic relationships, dependency, and national security. "Behind the label of peaceful economic competition," he reflected, "very often is hidden serious rivalries, whose consequences are truly bloody explosions."[51]

Of course, development of steel-based industry was long-range policy; however, for the short run the army had taken some action. The appropriately named *Usina Esperança* (Hope Mill) at the army's Ipanema ironworks had failed to produce a steel of the correct composition for artillery shells, so the minister of war had sent its director, Captain Antônio Mendes Teixeira, to the United States to study the problem with American specialists. And a foreign industrialist had produced a small amount of steel with Brazilian ores and had proposed to do so on a large scale if suitable concessions could be arranged.[52]

To "regularize" the production of the army's arsenal—which was responsible for fabrication of vehicles, parts for metal bridges, artillery projectiles, wagon breaks, stirrups and tools, besides repairing small arms and artillery pieces—as mentioned in Chapter 4, General Faria had sent, in late 1917, a seven-officer commission to the United States to purchase the latest machines.[53] By mid-1919 most of the machinery had been received and was being mounted, and Minister Cardoso de Aguiar thought that in another year they would be producing a sufficient number of artillery shells for training purposes and for building up modest stocks. To cover its short-run needs for weaponry, the army purchased arms in the United States and in France, where, it will be recalled, another commission had been observing the war and selecting aviation, artillery, and other equipment. But it is clear that the high command saw such foreign purchases as temporary expedients to cover current army needs until domestic production lines were in operation. As Acting President Delfim Moreira declared in his 1919 message to Congress, the difficulties of wartime had strengthened the conviction that the organization of military industry should be one of the government's "principal objectives," to be attained "whatever the sacrifices required" in order to "free ourselves gradually from foreign military industry."[54]

During the war period an Ordnance Directory (1915) had been inserted into the army's administrative structure to manage the arsenals, factories and depots, and everything else that pertained to arms production, acquisition, and distribution. Ministerial reports give the impression that initially the directory functioned merely as an umbrella for the subagencies without altering their outlook. In late 1918, with the appointment of Brigadier General Augusto Tasso Fragoso as ordnance director, things began to change. Although, at first, he saw the position only as a "good post for someone at the end of his life or with a horror of action," he threw himself into the work and was responsible in good measure for shaping army thinking regarding industrial development.[55]

Of special importance was Tasso Fragoso's emphasis on preparing a corps of technically trained officers, modeled on the artillery-engineers of Belgium, which would supervise Brazilian arms production. He urged employing foreign technicians as instructors for a program that would in the early 1930s grow into the army technical school, the forerunner of the present highly respected *Instituto Militar de Engenharia*. Later, as chief of staff (1922–29 and 1931–32), he would continue to influence industrial policy. His 1919 objective of seeking "complete military independence" would become the long-range goal of the Brazilian army.[56] But the gap between policy formation and implementation was often great in Brazil. The unrest of the 1920s and 1930s and the resulting institutional and national disorganization delayed turning plans into effective action. But for the historical record it is important to keep in mind that the impressive industrial development of the late 1930s and 1940s did not come out of the blue but had begun in these years. Let us now turn to the turmoil that was about to take hold of Brazil.

'Tenentismo'

The debate over the nature of the revolts of the 1920s, the so-called *tenentista* (literally lieutenantist) movement, has attracted scholars since Virginio Santa Rosa's *O Sentido do Tenentismo* appeared in 1932.[57] Whether the 1920s rebels represented the civilian middle classes or not will have to be resolved by others, but I will give the reader some idea about their representativeness among army officers.

First, a few things should be said about military contacts with civilian society. In the period in question about half of the officer corps was located in the Federal District. The military lived, not in isolation, but in proximity to civilians because of the location and physical arrangement of military garrisons. Barracks, as described above, were located on city streets, with the officers living in private housing throughout the city. Only a few of the newer posts, such as Vila Militar, provided some segregated officer housing. So officers' families used the same streetcar lines, the same stores, churches, and schools, and read the same newspapers as civilians. And given their relatively low pay they were as sensitive to economic fluctuations as anyone. Moreover, they had an institutional link with some civilians in the nationwide *Tiro* organization, which in 1921 had 266 companies "in all the principal cities of the country" comprising some thirty-five thousand men "of the better classes."[58] And the obligatory service system, however imperfectly it functioned, now brought officers into close contact with new recruits from civilian society.

In 1920 the bulk of the officer corps was in the lower ranks; fully 65.1 percent were second or first lieutenants, and 21.3 percent were captains.[59] They were rather old; many first lieutenants were in their late thirties, with fifteen to eighteen years of service. The older ones had studied at the Praia Vermelha academy, whereas those who had entered after it was closed in 1904 were either products of two short-lived institutions in Rio Grande do Sul (1905–11), the Escola de Guerra in Porto Alegre and the Escola de Aplicação de Infantaria e Cavalaria in Rio Prado, or the new Escola Militar at Realengo (1911).[60] The philosophical and practical changes that officer education went through in the first twenty years of the century were mirrored in these men. The lack of common educational backgrounds necessarily made it difficult to establish esprit de corps or provide the level of unity necessary for institutional cohesion. Indeed, I believe it was a factor that contributed to a willingness to break ranks and to rebel.

As for ideology, the Brazilian intellectual environment, populated with civilian writers such as Alberto Tôrres, who was discussed in Chapter 4, cried out for change. Tôrres's *O Problema Nacional Brasileiro* (1914) charged that the country suffered from self-ignorance, false optimism, regionalism, and lacked nationality and nationhood. Brazil needed organization and strong central government to direct national energies and to protect it from foreign exploitation. "Our nationalism," he wrote, "is not a sentimental aspiration, nor a doctrinaire program. . . . It is simply a movement of conservative and reorganizing restoration."[61]

A Defesa Nacional's editorials and articles contained ideas that paralleled Tôrres's, and he was often cited; but some themes, such as the population's undefined nature, the excessive regionalism, and the lack of organization, had been raised in earlier army writings, suggesting that some of these ideas originated with officers or were part of the contemporary intellectual milieu. Tôrres's ideas probably reached more officers in distilled form through the pages of the review than directly through his publications. Certainly *Defesa Nacional*'s biting analyses of institutional and national problems contributed to the ferment that beset the army in the 1920s. This does not mean that the editors and staff were prorevolution; they favored reform but within the system. They wanted to keep the governmental form; their criticism was aimed at making it work. The editorial board of 1920—Bertoldo Klinger, Pantaleão da Silva Pessôa, and Maciel da Costa—and contributors Manuel de Cerqueira Daltro Filho, Estevão Leitão de Carvalho, Newton de Andrade Cavalcanti, Francisco José Pinto, and Eurico Dutra were legalists, at least until the 1930s, who stood against military revolt. And even their commitment to legalism was conditioned by peer pressure, opportunity, loyalty to friends and commanders, and other personal considerations. As will be seen in Chapter 7, the question of who revolted and who stayed loyal is quite complex. But, without a doubt, the ideas expounded in *A Defesa Nacional* were an indictment of a corrupt system and could easily be read as a justification for revolt. As rebellion burst forth there would be a distinct toning down of its rhetoric.

By mid-1922 the officer corps had begun to divide into legalist and revolutionary currents. Both groups drew intellectual support from the editorials and articles of *A Defesa Nacional,* but they differed as to solutions. The legalists, or progressives as some officers referred to themselves, believed that by concentrating on improving the army, making it, in Bilac's poetic imagery, a school of civics, discipline, and organization, they would gradually create a national mentality conducive to defending the motherland. The revolutionaries also accepted the army's central educative role but saw intense regionalism and political corruption as impediments to carrying it out successfully. Once these were swept away, the saving grace of the nation-in-arms doctrine would be able to penetrate the remotest recesses of the country. Analysts have frequently commented that the tenentes had a weak program, in that they lacked postvictory plans. It may be that because as military men they agreed on what was wrong with Brazil, they focused, as they had been trained to do, on how to destroy the enemy instead of on how to rebuild. Their goal of an organized, self-aware, industrialized Brazilian nation required a strong central government, free compulsory primary education, obligatory military service, and government intervention in the economy to develop natural resources and to industrialize. They had the goals, but they were less certain about how to reach them.[62]

In diagnosing Brazil's ills and in envisioning what Brazil was to become there was little difference between the tenente rebels and the rest of the officer corps; where they differed was in their patience and choice of means. Indeed, who rebelled may well have been determined more by location and opportunity than agreement or disagreement over issues or goals.

It should be pointed out that army officers as a group were not the most intellectual Brazilians. Much of the analysis of *tenentismo,* indeed Brazilian civil-military relations in general, criticizes their ideas, programs, and actions as if they were intellectuals. In part this has occurred because of the necessity to deal with the written word; scholars are most familiar with officers who have left memoirs and other writings. However, a reading of ministerial reports over several decades reveals a considerable range of intellectual ability in the ministers of war and chiefs of staff, and a similar range can be noted in the pages of *A Defesa Nacional* or the *Revista Militar Brasileira.* If this were true among the formulators and leaders of Brazilian army thought, one can imagine that the range would be even greater in the rest of the officer corps. Officers were doers rather than thinkers. Of course, they had to have a certain writing ability to prepare the reports that were a constant in army life, which placed them several cuts above the mass of the population, but the kind of thinking that was required of an officer was mathematical in style; given this objective and these means, what solution would you propose? It was a limited thought process made even more so by the necessity of accepting command solutions as a matter of course.

Historians, too, have emphasized political events, such as the famous fake Bernardes letters insulting Hermes da Fonseca, neglecting events within the army that also contributed to revolutionary motivation. A review of those internal events will illustrate the increasing frustration and tension leading up to the outbreak of violence in 1922.

The Post–World War I Atmosphere and the Army

The First World War, as has been said, ended without Brazil's committing troops; instead of joyous homecoming parades, peace coincided with waves of strikes and the deadly Spanish influenza. In late 1918 the menace of Maximalism, as Bolshevism was then called, and anarchism threatened the army when, amid gunfire and bombs, a plot to seize the Rio de Janeiro military depot and the Catete Palace was foiled.[63] During 1919, while strikes and demonstrations, often accompanied by violence, disturbed Porto Alegre, São Paulo, Rio de Janeiro, and Recife, there were reports that the government suppressed the "Maximalist" newspaper *Spartacus* because it was "undermining the loyalty of the Army and the Navy." Although the American military attaché seemed disposed to accept the "general impression" that such rumors were "greatly exaggerated" and that there was "no wide-spread spirit of mutiny among the armed forces," hindsight suggests that studies of relations between labor and lower officer and enlisted ranks may well show the contrary to have been true.[64]

Of course, the strike violence encouraged the idea, commonly accepted by officers, that the Brazilian population was undisciplined. And if it was true that officers had an antilabor bias, their contacts with civilian businessmen in the National Defense League (founded 1916) may have stimulated it. José Murilo de Carvalho has pointed to these contacts as the beginning of an alliance between the military and economic groups looking to benefit from national-defense-oriented developmentalism.[65]

Perhaps as an indication of the lack of discipline, or at least of the level of distraction, in the army was the American attaché's observation that the army was "still far from being willing to get down to real work, for both officers and men, which is essential for successful training, and the European War appears to have had very little effect on this spirit."[66] Certainly there are many indications that the level of frustration in the officer corps was high, and frustration tends to divert attention from, rather than focus it on, "real work." The frustrations were related to the low esteem in which the public held the army and to dissatisfaction with pay, arms, equipment, and the army leadership.

Brazilian civilians simply did not like army service. Perhaps it was the memory of forced recruitment during the empire and early republic, or the more recent practice of local oligarchies and politicians having their enemies called up, or, as some officers suspected, a distaste for discipline, but whatever the cause Brazilians ran or hid rather than accept military training. It is probably indicative that the term used to describe such men was *insubmissos,* literally refusing to submit. By 1918–22 scenes such as occurred in the mineiro *município* of Sacramento in 1908, when two hundred women attacked the building where draft lists were compiled and destroyed them, were rare; the men simply fled or otherwise avoided reporting.[67]

Reviewing the period 1917 to 1923, General Tasso Fragoso lamented the increasing proportion of insubmissos as "dispiriting" and attributed their thousands to "intrinsic defects in the temperament and education of the people," but he added that Brazil's expansive geography, sparse population, and poor communications contributed to keeping many from even knowing that they had been called up. Moreover, the rigid policy of many commanders of locking up those that reported late added an unnecessary barrier. Table 5.1 illustrates the extent of the problem. Such a massive rejection of the army's cherished "Nation in Arms" *(Nação Armada)* must have produced deep frustration among the officers.

And there was tension inherent in the army, after years of reorganization along German lines, now being pressed into a French mold, under the watchful eyes of French officers. One foreign military observer commented that the French mission was "in effective control of the whole military organization."[68] Under French tutelage the army reverted to a sort of military adolescence, with everyone studying the new regulations, even superior officers returning to school for the "Review" course. With the French had come new weapons, some of which were war surplus and, even if the stories of bloodstained equipment were exaggerations, there was an uneasy suspicion that the army was being cheated. Artillery officers who reportedly still held "the German machine superior to the French," especially objected to the Frenchifying.[69] Artillery men regarded the Saint-Chamont cannon as "decidedly inferior" to the army's old Krupps. The Brazilian artillery was divided into field and coastal specializations. The field artillery argued that the number and weight of the complement the French wanted attached to each

TABLE 5.1.

Functioning of Obligatory Service, 1917–1923

Year	Called Up	Insubmissos	Exempted	Incorporated
1917	5,922	890	745	2,966
1918	41,564	14,500	7,625	17,615
1919	28,112	27,044	7,408	16,985
1920	24,088	22,663	4,783	14,382
1921	31,855	24,996	6,043	16,541
1922	41,516	30,185	6,541	15,471
1923	51,785	43,154	6,953	12,021

SOURCE: Gen. Div. Augusto Tasso Fragoso, *Relatório dos Trabalhos do Estado Maior Durante o Ano de 1923* (Apresentado ao Exmo. Sr. Marechal Fernando Setembrino de Carvalho), Rio de Janeiro, June 1924 (Rio de Janeiro: Imprensa Militar, 1924), 27. Data are drawn from graph between pages 28 and 29.

infantry division, although suitable for France with its network of highways and railroads, was too heavy and would be almost impossible to move rapidly over Brazil's rough dirt roads and trails. During the war the coastal artillery had sent some officers to train at the United States Coast Artillery School at Fortress Monroe, Virginia, and they were convinced of American superiority in this area. The cavalry denounced the French tanks as hopeless failures and thought that the English article was the best. The infantry was unhappy with the new automatic weapons, which officers regarded as less efficient than the German rapid-fire Mauser rifles. And officers derided the purchase of gas masks as ridiculous—the possibility of gas warfare in South America was too remote for consideration.[70] Some observers attributed the many accidents at the army's aviation school to old and defective French aircraft, although the civilian minister of war blamed the Brazilian pilots' rashness.[71]

The press attacked the mission and the minister of war for graft. Research did not reveal proof of such charges against the minister, but the evidence regarding shady activities by mission members seems strong. French officers controlled equipment purchases for the army in everything from felt hats and saddles to field kitchens and weapons. Reportedly, "certain high officers of the French Mission" extracted a personal fee of from "20% to 40% in excess of purchase price." The Brazilian army paid "this extra amount . . . without its official knowledge." It was "well known among business men in Rio" that the officers of the French mission were "grafting," and although it was not certain that the mission's ranking officers were getting a share, they certainly knew and "winked" at the practice.[72] Such profiteering must have irritated Brazilian officers, especially the lower ranked ones, who publicly accused some of their seniors with graft.[73]

The Calógeras Ministry and Chief of Staff Bento Ribeiro

The French mission was also involved in the growing frustration with national leadership. President Epitácio Pessôa, who had been chosen as a compromise candidate to replace Delfim Moreira, and who had concluded negotiations for the mission while still in France attending the Versailles conference before assuming office, had broken with republican tradition and named a civilian as minister of war. Even though José Pandiá Calógeras of Minas Gerais had a reputation as a federal deputy interested in national defense, some officers regarded his appointment as a diminution of military prestige.

During the empire it was common for civilians to serve as army ministers; however, in the collective memory of the officer corps that fact was associated with the emperor's lack of enthusiasm for the military. Perhaps the clearest measure of the corps' hostility to the idea is that Calógeras was the first and last civilian to hold the post. Curiously, it seems likely that he was a compromise selection calculated to avoid worse trouble with the officers. The two senators most frequently mentioned for the army ministry were especially anathema to the military.[74] So as a lesser evil, *O Estado de São Paulo* observed that "the selection of Calógeras narrowly averted real trouble with the military."[75] Calógeras and his navy colleague, also a civilian, Raul Soares, had the political virtue of being mineiros, thus securing the support of Minas Gerais for the Pessôa government.

Throughout his career Calógeras suffered the image of being a foreigner, a Greek, even though he was a native-born Brazilian, indeed a Carioca. His association with Minas Gerais came from his being a graduate of the School of Mines in Ouro Preto, his involvement in the province's abolitionist and republican movements, his being a charter member of the mineiro Republican Party, and his marriage into a prominent mineiro family. He represented the state in the Congress and served successively as Wenceslau Bras's minister of agriculture and of finance. He had a reputation for brusqueness and impatience with those who disagreed with his views, and he was not one to compromise. In Congress he was known for his expertise in economics, public finance, international affairs, and the armed forces. He was a strong supporter of Rio Branco's efforts to augment Brazil's international status and of Hermes' military modernization and professionalization programs.

In 1918 the ill-fated President-elect Rodriques Alves asked Calógeras to do a confidential study of government problems to guide the new administration. The frank and frequently critical study, published only after Calógeras's death, analyzed the difficulties facing each incoming minister, devoting great attention to the war ministry. He had recommended sending a sizeable expeditionary force to fight in World War I, financed with American or British loans, which, he argued, could be repaid with reparations from the defeated powers. The course of the war and the circumstances of Brazilian politics prevented the idea from being seriously considered.

He believed that under the empire the military had become a separate class and that the armed forces had to be reincorporated into national life. His solution was universal military service and professionalization of the officer corps, the latter to be carried out under the guidance of the French. Despite his reputation as a backer of military improvement, he was still a civilian and his appointment nearly led the military to prevent both he and Epitácio Pessôa from assuming office.[76]

With a civilian at the top of the structure, the leading general was the chief of staff, General Bento Ribeiro Carneiro Monteiro, who soon objected that the chief of the French mission was overstepping his bounds. The French viewed the general staff as functioning on the basis of "favoritism and private influence" and sought to make assignments and promotions depend solely on

merit. This attitude led them to interfere with appointments, details, and promotions, which General Bento Ribeiro regarded as beyond their advisory and
instructional functions. However, Calógeras sided with Gamelin.

Although there was certainly justice in the French suspicion of favoritism
in promotions and assignments, their intervention only irritated many officers' nationalist sensibilities. The so-called national element, who were also
pro-Germanization and were ill at ease with the French reorganization, saw
General Bento Ribeiro as their champion. Throughout 1920 and early 1921
Calógeras whittled away at Bento Ribeiro, detaching his loyal subordinates
one by one in a process calculated to isolate him. In February 1921 Bento
Ribeiro submitted his resignation, but the president refused to accept it.
Bento Ribeiro used his annual report to severely criticize the mission for
overstepping its limits, which led to the conflict's being aired in the press.[77]

Finally, an incident brought the matter to a head. Calógeras named a
French officer to give riding instruction to the instructors at the Escola Militar. Recall that in late 1918 the general staff had sent to Realengo as instructors a number of junior officers, who were members of, or influenced by,
the *Defesa Nacional* group, with the avowed purpose of inspiring the cadets
with their progressive ideas and military enthusiasm. This so-called Indigenous
Mission became legendary in the army. One member, Pantaleão Pessôa, a captain with eighteen years' service, who was close to General Bento Ribeiro,
asked to be relieved rather than humiliate himself by going through basic riding instruction from a Frenchman when he was an accomplished horseman.
Captain Pessôa saw this as part of the efforts of "zealous orthodox Francophiles" to root out German influence. Indirectly, Gamelin confirmed this
when he passed the word to the captain that the lessons were not his idea but
had originated with a member of the Calógeras staff. The president attempted
to smooth things over by offering to assign Captain Pessôa as General Bento
Ribeiro's aide. But rather than continue what he regarded as a losing struggle
with Calógeras that would upset army discipline, the general submitted his
resignation.

It was customary to transfer such positions with appropriate ceremony
and eulogistic speeches. But Minister Calógeras chose to ignore custom; he
ordered Bento Ribeiro's replacement, Major General Celestino Alves Bastos, to take over the very day he arrived from his former post in São Paulo.
General Bastos walked into Bento Ribeiro's office after 4 P.M. to tell him
Calógeras wanted the transfer made immediately. In less than two hours
Bento Ribeiro made his farewell to the staff, cleaned out his office, and was
on his way home in a private car, rather than the customary official one.

Bento Ribeiro was stunned; not only had he been ushered out without
due ceremony, but Calógeras had replaced him with an old friend, for whom
he had pulled political strings to secure his promotion to major general.[78]

Bento Ribeiro told the press that "in numerous cases" Calógeras had shown "his firm intention to injure me and [remove] me from the head of the General Staff. I could not continue to fill this post after the last events. An Army officer . . . is frequently obliged to smother his impulses in order to avoid conflict or crisis . . . but it cannot be demanded that an officer . . . shall consent to be injured in what a man must hold most sacred, his character and his self-respect."[79] The next day the commander of the Rio Military Region, General Luis Barbedo, a veteran of Canudos and a close friend of Floriano Peixoto, invited officers in the Federal District and vicinity to join him in visiting the ex–chief of staff's home to express their collective esteem for his professional merit and gratitude for his courtesies. Within hours regional commanders in São Paulo and Rio Grande do Sul served notice that any officers taking part in sympathy demonstrations would be guilty of an infraction of discipline, while in Rio de Janeiro, General Tasso Fragoso issued similar instructions to the Ordnance Department and Calógeras relieved General Barbedo.

General Bento Ribeiro gave a statement to the press, expressing his appreciation and saying that he could not receive the officers collectively but would be honored to do so individually. On April 23, astonishingly, more than a hundred officers, including General Barbedo and others of high rank, visited the deposed general. The United States military attaché was surprised. "This attitude of defiance," he wrote, "is a new departure in the Brazilian Army. There have been two serious revolts in the Navy during the Republic's life of 32 years, but the Army has always appeared stable and disciplined when judged by the South American standard."[80]

That the incident did not touch off the explosion that would come in the following year was probably because the general was more depressed than angry, and his habit of discipline was too strong to allow him to assume leadership of military dissidents. Besides, supporters like Captain Pessôa were immediately posted to barracks in Rio Grande do Sul and Mato Grosso.[81] And within four months Bento Ribeiro died after a short illness, removing, from what was about to become an extremely agitated scene, "the individual wielding the strongest personal influence in Army circles." A foreign observer thought that his death would "have a tranquilizing effect on the Army, as the devotion of a large section of the Army to General [Bento] Ribeiro's person and to his cause threatened to develop a feud within the Army."[82]

Even though successful in eliminating Bento Ribeiro, the Epitácio Pessôa–Calógeras administration was "too discredited" to do much about military discontent. Brazil's financial situation was not encouraging, the balance of payments was unfavorable, and creditors were protesting the government's slowness in paying its bills. Some army units were months behind in pay, and in some parts of the country the army had to cut troop rations.

Hardly the way to secure loyalty! And, strangely, the administration chose this fiscally difficult moment to sign a 120,000 conto contract with Roberto Simonsen's *Companhia Constructora de Santos* to build new military posts at thirty-six locations throughout Brazil. Admittedly, these facilities were sorely needed, but the contrast between the government's stinginess with pay and rations and its spendthriftiness with construction seemed suspicious to officers already aroused about graft.[83]

The slow promotion rate was also a nagging irritant. At the beginning of the 1920s it was common to encounter lieutenants with ten to fifteen or more years in rank waiting for captaincies to open. Certainly the promotion law under discussion in late 1921 did not contribute to easing frustration because it maintained the custom of promotion to first lieutenant and captain based on seniority.[84] Calógeras's solution to the recognition problem, apparently, was not promotion but decoration. He called for the reestablishment of "all our old civil and military orders," especially the Order of Aviz, which would be bestowed as a sign of "national gratitude" and "public veneration."[85]

Among some junior officers, particularly those who attended the military school during World War I, there was frustration at not having had a chance to fight in the war. The turmas of 1918 and 1919 apparently wanted to see combat. One such graduate, Delso Mendes da Fonseca, who directed Fort Copacabana's guns in the 1922 revolt, attributed the revolutionary current to those two turmas and explained their behavior by implying that they channeled their suppressed warlike urge into conspiracy. Certainly being an officer in an army whose government avoided combat when all the great nations were at war would not engender pride and satisfaction. In August 1918, explaining the official position to his friend Major Malan, Tasso Fragoso pointed to Minister Faria's notable role: "With Faria in the government not a single soldier of Brazil will go to France. No one knows the reason for this attitude in a man so intelligent and so pro-allied. I believe that it is fear of opposition on the part of the Francophiles here who dread seeing the Boches up close."[86] Of course, given Brazilian capabilities, it is difficult to see how sufficient mobilization, training, and transportation of troops could have been carried out. However, it would be the junior officer generation of this era, who as field grade and senior officers would lead the campaign for an active battlefield role in the next war.

It was in this atmosphere that the Military Club selected former minister of war and president of the republic Marshal of the Army Hermes da Fonseca as its president in May 1921. The *Correio da Manhã* (Rio) published the infamous falsified Bernardes letters insulting Hermes in October. Throughout the following eight months tensions rose as the press and the Military Club debated their authenticity. As in the 1880s a "military question" beset Brazil's political system at a time when multifaceted frustrations gripped the army officer corps. In both periods a progressive wave had raised the level of debate about professionalism. Slow promotions discouraged junior officers who found senior officers, who had accommodated themselves to the reigning system, blocking their upward mobility. And the existence of competitive foreign influences served to exacerbate a troublesome domestic situation.

The rebel tenentes rallied around Hermes da Fonseca and displayed their francophobia when they seized control of Fort Copacabana on the night of July 4–5, 1922, by throwing into the sea a new light 75 mm gun that St. Chamond had sent for testing.[87] On July 5, when they marched down Avenida Atlantica, they divided the officer corps and set Brazil on a revolutionary cycle that ultimately would bring down the republic.

CHAPTER 6

The Army of the 1920s

There is no possibility of [the government] abandoning
the regular Army, as it is the unit which holds the states
bound to the federal union.
—Major F. L. Whitley to Asst. Chief of Staff, July 31, 1923

[T]o instruct an army is a much greater task than merely
teaching it new methods of combat. . . . [I]t is necessary
to penetrate its core, in order to give it a mentality that
corresponds to the times.
—Gen. Francisco de Paula Cidade, *Síntese de Três Séculos
de Literatura Militar Brasileira*

The Army's air service remains paralyzed. . . . It is clear
that Mr. Bernardes has no confidence in a large element
in the Army and will take no chances on having bombs
dropped upon him.
—Capt. Hugh Barclay to Lt. Col. N. E. Margetts,
Aug. 31, 1926

Sailors and officers formed up on the deck of the battleship *Floriano* saluted
as Hermes da Fonseca came aboard on that gray, rainy, and cold morning of
July 5, 1922. He was tired and frustrated from the long night's vigil and from
racing about in automobiles seeking contact with what turned out to be nonexistent rebel units. The government had uncovered the conspiracy and had
struck first. Officers who had promised to raise the troops of Vila Militar
had been arrested before they could act. Now a prisoner, despite the courtesies due an army marshal and former president, his body reacted to the
pressure; he felt sweaty as the tightness in his chest turned into sharp pain.
The tension of the previous hours tore at his heart. General Alfredo Ribeiro
da Costa, commander of Vila Militar, had taken him into custody that morning at 6 A.M., at the home of his son, Mário Hermes (near the "Marechal

Hermes" railroad station), where he had waited in the garden for word from the conspirators. The rebellion had failed. The students at the Escola Militar in Realengo were confined to their barracks and being interrogated. Suspected officers were under guard and the troops of Colonel Sezefredo dos Passos had secured the streets leading to Fort Copacabana. There, Hermes' son, Captain Euclides, commanded the only rebel redoubt in Rio de Janeiro. And the next afternoon, the remnants of the Fort's garrison, the so-called volunteers of death would have their encounter with destiny on the sands of Copacabana.[1]

The internal struggle over the nature of the army and its relationship to the political and social systems burst into the open as partisans disputed their positions with guns in hand. The famous tenente revolts have come to be the focal point, if not the total history of the army in the 1920s. However, from 1922 to 1930 the tenentes were a minority in the officer corps, comprising about three hundred of the twenty-five hundred or so officers who were graduated from the Escola Militar do Realengo between 1913 and 1927. On the eve of the Revolution of 1930 their numbers probably did not exceed 600 out of an officer corps that then had 5,275 members, that is to say 11 percent of those on active duty. Indeed their movement did not yet have a name; they would not be called tenentes until after 1930.[2] Looked at from the perspective of the Revolution of 1930, the tenentes appeared to have won, and certainly many of them played important roles in subsequent Brazilian military and political life. But if the army's history in that decade is reduced to the story of the tenentes, then much that happened slips from view, and much that occurred subsequently is less understandable. The history of an army, because of the complexity of such an institution, needs to have a wide focus. Moreover, history should not deal only with the winners but should also give a sense of who lost and why. Despite the importance of the rebellions, there was more to the history of the army in the 1920s, as this chapter will show.

Brazil in the 1920s

The 1920s were important in Brazilian history because they were the crucible in which the old and new Brazil struggled to shape the future. The following sketch of Brazil in that decade will provide the reader with a backdrop against which to view the unfolding drama of the army. In the 1920s the changes that Brazil had been experiencing since 1889 were becoming clearer. On the eve of its centenary of independence its cities had the trappings of modernity, but its rural areas still had the aspect of the nineteenth century, if not the eighteenth. Its writers and artists could proclaim their vision of a new Brazil in São Paulo's famous Modern Art Week, but in the northeastern sertão, in the cacão groves of Bahia, in the sugarcane fields of Pernambuco, in the coffee plantations of São Paulo and Minas Gerais, indeed throughout the "interior," the *coroneis* controlled the lives of the poor. Organized labor was beginning to make its presence felt, but for years to come the political elite would consider its activities matters for the police.

In the thirty years since 1890 the Brazilian population had grown from 14,333,915 to 30,635,605. By 1920 the annual percent of increase was galloping along at 3.8 percent and would remain over 3 percent throughout the decade. The growth was at least partly a result of the arrival of immigrants after the World War. As the population grew, more of it was concentrated in the cities, until ten of them had more than one hundred thousand inhabitants each. Although the urban growth was notable, Brazil still had a rural ambience; its farms and grasslands held 69,703,000 head of cattle, horses, mules, hogs, sheep, and goats. There were few paved roads beyond city limits, and the railroads were concentrated in São Paulo's coffee and Pernambuco's sugar municípios. In wet weather the roads became nearly impassible, even for the versatile Ford Model T, which was much in evidence as the decade opened. Much of the country was underdeveloped except for a narrow coastal strip.[3]

To connect the developed centers of population strung along the 4,593-mile coastline, the country enjoyed at the end of 1926 the services of 582 steamers with a gross tonnage of 618,588 and 107 sailing vessels totaling 41,535 tons. The absence of all-weather roads and the local pattern of railways made sea travel a characteristic of interstate commerce and communications.[4]

People abroad had difficulty grasping the enormity of the country. In 1922, in response to a request from the British treasury to certify the entertainment expenses of the consul in Belém, the royal ambassador in Rio wrote to the Foreign Office that this was "tantamount to asking His Majesty's Ambassador at Paris to express approval of the cuisine of our representative at Mosul [in northern Iraq]." It was "difficult," he said, "for those who do not know Brazil to remember that the country is not one of normal size with normal means of communication, and that Brazil as a political entity is somewhat different from the Brazil of the map."[5]

The racial composition of the population continued to be a mixture of native Amerindian, African descendants, and European strains, with a small but growing number of Japanese. Foreign immigration was having more impact than in the past; in 1872 there had been 388,459 foreign-born in the country; between 1908 and 1920, 1,086,525 foreigners landed, bringing the total to 1,565,961. Publications prepared for Brazil's 1922 centenary of independence ignored racial proportion apparently because the educated elite was convinced (or, perhaps more accurately, hoped) that nonwhites were gradually and relentlessly being "bleached" out. The census bureau's mathematicians even created statistics that purported to prove that blacks were dying off at a higher rate (5.4 percent) than whites (2.8 percent), Amerindians (3.7 percent), or mulattos (2.8 percent). The British ambassador saw things differently: "Brazil, with the exception of its southern States, is not, and never can be a white man's country."[6]

The city of São Paulo alone had 100,000 Italians in a mostly white, total population of 548,000. As a result over the next decades the city's accent, favorite foods, and lifestyles would take on an Italian lilt. Located at twenty-five hundred feet above sea level, Europeans found its climate healthier than that of Rio de Janeiro or Santos. Its irregular street system, which covered several high ridges and intervening valleys, was paved as far as the outlying suburbs. Its electric streetcar network, the many motor cars and trucks, the clean, well-swept streets, and new public parks, businesses, and residential buildings gave it a modern appearance. Its population enjoyed ample fresh food from the numerous truck gardens that Portuguese, Italian, and Japanese immigrants had developed. The city's ten daily newspapers filled the corner news stands. Employment opportunities were to be found in the numerous industrial establishments engaged in the manufacture of machinery, sugar, chemical products, furniture, glass, earthenware, leather goods, paints, and cotton and woolen goods. The city was also the financial center for the state's coffee, cattle, and general agricultural interests. An American observer correctly predicted that it would one day surpass Rio de Janeiro.[7]

However, there were problems; the city was experiencing electric power shortages by middecade, especially when the dry season reduced water flows through the Light and Power Company's hydroelectric generating plants. The rapid growth of São Paulo's industries had produced such demand that periodic reductions in current were necessary. In the first half of 1925 street lighting was reduced, tram service cut down, and cinemas closed at ten P.M. Many industrial plants operated at half or three-quarters time, causing suffering among workers in need of full-time wages.[8]

Although São Paulo and immigration represented a new, perhaps more progressive, Brazil, other factors represented the drag of the past. Education in the 1920s was still something for the elites. "The governing class," a foreign observer noted, "does not favor much education for the masses." The physical labor that the elites wanted did not require education, which they believed only bred discontent, agitation, and strikes. They had "so far been free" of such irritations and wanted to keep it that way. Happily, other Brazilians realized that with at least 80 percent of the people illiterate, permanent development would be impossible.[9]

The scarcity of health care paralleled the lack of educational opportunities. Malaria, venereal diseases, trachoma, leprosy, Chagas disease, and hookworm were commonplace. Estimates of hookworm affliction (which was curable) among the rural population reached 90 percent, and three thousand stillbirths a year in Rio de Janeiro were attributed to syphilis. Poorly balanced diet contributed to general malnutrition in the countryside. Not without reason did Paulo Prado open his 1928 portrait of the country with the line: "In a radiant land lives a sad people." Indeed, the cartoonists of the day depicted Brazil as a character called *Zé Povo* (Joe People), a simple old guy who always got the worst of things.[10]

In the 1920s Brazil as a political entity was rife with internal dissension. There was a lack of cohesion and national consciousness; the gaúchos of Rio Grande do Sul, the paulistas of São Paulo, and the mineiros of Minas Gerais took more pride in their state identities than in being Brazilian. In January 1926 the federal capital's press reported on secessionist propaganda in Rio Grande do Sul in favor of forming a separate republic, either alone, or in company with Santa Catarina and Paraná. Meanwhile, paulistas often stated that if their state were independent, it could be the most prosperous republic on earth. After all, 50 percent of the federal government's revenue was reportedly collected in the state, and paulistas grumbled that most of it was spent on the poverty-stricken north.[11]

To sustain their relative independence from federal intervention the larger states maintained well-equipped police forces (see Table 6.1). In 1922 São Paulo's French-trained *Força Pública* contained 8,814 officers and troops,

TABLE 6.1.

State Forces in 1926

State	Authorized	Actual
Bahia	2,580	4,000
Ceará	1,000	1,000
Federal District	4,000	4,000
Minas Gerais	4,000	3,700
Pernambuco	2,381	2,381
Piauí	1,000	1,000
Rio de Janeiro	1,060	1,061
Rio Grande do Sul	3,182	8,597
São Paulo	14,254	14,254
SUBTOTAL	33,457	39,993
States under 1,000	6,059	5,828
TOTAL	39,516	45,821

SOURCE: Capt. Hugh Barclay, Rio, Mar. 18, 1926, no. 552: "Brazilian Organized Militia," 2006-70/6, Military Intelligence Division, General Staff, U.S. War Dept., RG 165, National Archives.

NOTE: Table shows authorized and actual effective strength as of January 1, 1926.

mostly garrisoned in the state capital; by 1926 its effective strength had reached 14,254. In 1891 it had been composed of eight infantry companies (2,267 men), and by 1927 it was truly a small army of seven infantry battalions, two cavalry regiments, one firemen's battalion, and an aviation squadron. Minas Gerais, Rio Grande do Sul, and Bahia kept fewer but still respectable numbers under arms.[12]

The above data have particular weight when one considers that the federal army's actual strength in mid-1925 was 3,045 officers and 36,000 troops and that these were distributed throughout the republic. If São Paulo, Minas Gerais, and Rio Grande do Sul had taken the field against the army, they would have had 26,554 troops among them. It is not surprising that they did not suffer federal intervention during the Old Republic nor that possession of these forces allowed them to stop a 1926 attempt to revise the Constitution in the direction of expanding the grounds for such intervention.[13]

From the perspective of Brazil's neighbors the state forces represented a threat and a blessing. The neighboring countries saw the state forces as army reserves, which gave Brazil a much larger army than it claimed in international conferences. This allowed Argentina to charge Brazilian diplomats with insincerity. However, diplomatic maneuvering aside, the neighboring republics understood that the state forces preserved the power of the states and thereby prevented the development of a strong, stable central government that could more effectively extend its influence beyond the borders.[14]

Troop Recruitment

The hard-won obligatory service system turned out rather differently than its proponents had hoped. From the beginning (see Chap. 4) the numbers of men who refused to answer their country's call were greater than the numbers of those who did. From 1917 through 1929, 619,753 names were drawn, of which 75,286 were exempted and of which 409,111 did not show up, leaving only 135,354 to enter the barracks. But even these figures are uncertain. Simple errors in addition marred the general staff reports throughout those years; moreover, for some regions the data were incomplete.[15]

The dream of obligatory service providing a cadre army that would generate a large, trained, mobilizable reserve was shaken by the realities of Brazil. As mentioned in Chapter 4, upper- and middle-class males escaped service, and the men who reported were too poor or too ignorant to have political influence or the means to seek a court order barring incorporation. For sons of what were then referred to as "good families" military service was "regarded as more or less of a calamity."[16] The situation grew so drastic in the midst of the July 1924 tenente uprising in São Paulo that military authorities in Rio de Janeiro gathered up vagabonds and loafers from the streets and docks of the capital in an old-fashioned *canoa* and subjected them to daily drills in the streets. The incident showed the divergence between legal methods and actual arbitrary practice. And even the legal procedures could have arbitrary results, as in 1928 when army medical examiners pronounced a one-legged man fit for service! Rio's *Correio da Manhã* asked in an editorial "what more is necessary to prove the demoralization of the military draft? All that is needed is a friendly word from a politician of even little influence, given at the moment of physical examination, and the favored one is pronounced unfit for service, in spite of an exuberant physique and robust health. But if the poor devil has no drag, then nothing can save him from a uniform—not even a wooden leg"!!

That case was certainly exceptional, but, as a foreign observer noted, there was no doubt that the law was "executed with the utmost partiality and favoritism." And "as a result," he declared, "there is little respect for the law and the youth of the country adopt every possible expedient for escaping military service."[17] Moreover, the draft became a weapon in the struggles between factions in the interior, where political bosses punished their adversaries by having their sons called up.

And because most of the recruits came from the lower end of the social and economic scale, they were darker and less educated than those who obtained exemptions. Mulattos and mestiços predominated in the ranks, except in the immigrant south. The army's health examination reports provide an image of the men from whom the recruits were selected. Although one has to approach the statistical data of that era with a cautious eye, a study that an officer of the army's medical corps, Colonel Dr. Arthur Lobo da Silva, compiled from the 1922 and 1923 records gives an idea of the recruits' racial composition, level of education, occupations, health, and even physical size. The records covered 38,675 men who reported for medical examines during those years. Of that total, 547 were caboclo, 3,707 black, 11,711 mestiço (which included mulattos), and 22,710 white. Curiously, the last were generally less healthy than the other three groups; 71 percent of whites were acceptable, compared to 77 percent of the mestiços, 80 percent of the blacks, and 81 percent of the caboclos. Whites also led in venereal diseases (489 out of 863); respiratory problems (475 out of 703); ear, nose, throat, and eye disorders (554 out of 733); and shortness (280 out of 575, the minimum acceptable height being 1.52 m).[18] In part, the greater number of health-related rejections for whites can be explained by the fact that most of the caboclos, mestiços, and blacks were from the north and northeast, where medical boards were not as rigorous as in the central and southern states. In the latter the whites examined were from the lower classes; those better off avoided the process as noted above. Table 6.2 shows the distribution of disqualifications among the four racial categories.

The majority of those examined were farm laborers (37.5 percent), workers (31.1 percent), and unskilled business clerks—"individuals without breeding, without education, and without certain means of livelihood." Among those examined, 30 percent were listed as illiterate (see Table 6.3). If accurate, this figure is notable because the national rate at that time was estimated at 70 percent.[19] However, one can suppose that a large number of those who never reported were probably illiterate. Certainly the level of literacy among soldiers was not high. In 1920 a foreign military observer declared, "Few [soldiers] that I have encountered could read or write." He also noted, "Soldiers seem to be recruited from the lowest and simplest of the peon class."[20] Whatever the exact percentage, it was high enough for the army to establish regimental schools to combat "the cancer of illiteracy." In 1926 Minister Setembrino asserted that the army had returned to civilian life "some hundreds of men who entered the ranks not knowing how to read and write, some of whom did not know whether or not they were

TABLE 6.2.
Rejections Based on Health Condition and Race

Condition	Caboclo	Black	Mestiço	White	Rejected
Venereal diseases	12	86	276	489	863
Digestive	1	—	28	29	58
Respiratory	13	47	168	475	703
Circulation	4	36	122	200	362
Genital, urinary	2	20	55	157	234
Nervous system	1	12	68	192	273
Eyes, ears, nose, throat	6	36	137	554	733
Malaria	4	6	70	78	158
Hernia	3	44	85	177	309
Verminosis[a]	—	5	60	76	141
Bones, joints	3	32	102	215	352
Weak physical condition	21	106	567	1,117	1,811
Physical defects	4	35	161	220	420
Too short (under 1.52m)	11	45	239	280	575
Tuberculosis	2	26	59	166	253
Other maladies[b]	16	134	348	539	1,037
TOTALS	103	670	2,545	4,964	8,282

SOURCE: Data from Arthur Lobo da Silva, "A Anthropologia no Exército Brasileiro," *Archivos do Museu Nacional* 30 (1928): 35.

[a]These figures are inaccurate. Col. Lobo da Silva wrote that the medical boards "did not make a systematic examination for [verminosis], because if they were to do so the rejections would rise to a fantastic percentage" because "the population of the interior of the country is subject to intestinal verminosis [parasites] in the proportion of 80 to 90 per 100" (40).

[b]Included are skin diseases, nonsyphilitic ulcers, anemia, obesity, traumatisms, maladies of the skin and cell tissues, infectious diseases, and miscellaneous illnesses.

TABLE 6.3.

Percentage of Illiteracy Among Draftees by Race

Race	Examined	Illiterate	Percent
Caboclo	547	231	42
Black	3,667	1,914	52
Mestiço	11,635	4,321	37
White	22,087	4,874	22
TOTAL	37,936	11,340	30

SOURCE: Data from Arthur Lobo da Silva, "A Anthropologia no Exército Brasileiro," *Archivos do Museu Nacional* 30 (1928): 35.

Brazilians."[21] However, that same year the American military attaché commented that the average soldier was "as a rule illiterate," and he was convinced that the teaching in the garrison schools was "not thorough or conscientious," although he recalled that "in every post which I have visited particular care has been taken to point out a score or more of desks and a blackboard."[22]

To what degree General Setembrino was committed to educating the troops was called into question by his frequent observation that an illiterate soldier with a "virgin memory" learned and remembered his duties more readily than one with some education. And what level of commitment to the education, to combating the "cancer of illiteracy," was involved in his abolition of the army library in 1925? He ordered the library, which dated from 1881, closed and its thousands of volumes scattered. A sadder, more senseless, more criminal act of anti-intellectualism is difficult to imagine; but, at least, he did not order the books burned.[23]

Discipline, an American attaché observed, did "not exist as is understood by an American officer." The troops, he went on to say, "do what they please, refuse details distasteful to them, etc." There was, in his view, "no recognition of constituted authority by the troops." The soldiers were "ignorant and illiterate" and were "easily persuaded to take part in uprisings, following their immediate commander without knowing why." Yet, despite being susceptible to "mob psychology," soldiers exhibited a strong fatalism that made them face "danger and death with a creditable degree of coolness and calmness." Surprisingly, considering the health problems and physical limitations, soldiers displayed impressive stamina. The endurance of both sides in making long marches with little rest and insufficient food during the tenente rebellions was favorably noted. Brazilian upper- and middle-class males, in general, regarded carrying parcels in public and doing physical labor as degrading; and, as far as they were permitted, enlisted soldiers mimicked such attitudes. The same pride involved in that behavior insured a high concern for a neat appearance in uniform. They loved to parade and endured drills, but when detailed to a work squad with a pick and shovel, they turned "sullen and rebellious."[24]

Although troop morale was not very good, the soldiers had a strong streak of passivity, and most were "quite satisfied as long as they [could] wear uniforms and parade in the city, and [could] have regular meals of rice and beans."[25]

The American attaché thought that the Brazilians lacked moral courage. "No Brazilian," he asserted, "can stand alone, no matter how thoroughly he may be convinced that he is right. In matters of opinion he must go with the crowd." The Brazilian would not defend, the attaché went on, an unpopular cause, and "ridicule would upset him completely." Lying and stealing were reportedly commonplace among the soldiers. Attaché Major Lester Baker declared that "truth among Brazilians is but a relative virtue" and that "they do not believe each other." When an American soldier accused another of lying, the major said, tension or perhaps a fight occurred, but among Brazilians it was just part of verbal exchange. The attitude toward stealing was also different. If a soldier took money from a comrade in the barracks, the thief would not be so much criticized as "the careless owner of the money who put temptation in the way of a poor fellow who could not be expected to resist." Those who allowed temptation to appear were to blame, not the one who succumbed.[26]

The same attaché declared that Brazilians were poor sports, that they loved to gamble and to compete but although they exalted in victory, they were sullen in defeat. Football games often ended in fights. He thought that an interservice game such as West Point and Annapolis played would result in "a bloody field of carnage." Thus, sports among the enlisted personnel had made little headway by the late 1920s;[27] however, the army would make an effort to establish physical education and athletics in the next decade.

The failure of the obligatory service system made it impossible to insure that all recruits served near their homes or even in their own regions. Because the largest troop concentrations were in the Federal District and in Rio Grande do Sul, those areas would have been overburdened had they supplied the nearby garrisons' annual needs. So each recruiting district was called on to contribute a quota for those regions. Further, because the army could not function without a nucleus of experienced soldiers, reenlistments were encouraged to the point that by 1928 one-half of the troops were volunteers and the other half were draftees. So as the decade came to a close, the army had moved a notable distance from Olavo Bilac's ideal of universal obligatory service. The nation in arms *(nação armada)* and the people in uniform *(povo fardado)* were rhetorical phrases rather than descriptive of reality.[28]

Army Leadership and Organization in the 1920s

Despite all the talk about professionalism and the structural changes resulting from French influence—the leadership style of the top officials, the struggle between the minister and the chief of staff, and the recruitment and training problems continued. Power was concentrated in the minister, but even he lacked authority over comparatively unimportant details of administration that could only be put into effect with a presidential signature. The United States attaché observed that "the Brazilian Minister of War has less authority than the American Secretary of War."[29]

After the brief experiment with civilian minister Pandiá Calógeras during the Pessôa government, the political elite returned that office to the generals. The two men who held the post in the remaining years of the Old Republic had deep roots in the old army that had come out of the empire rather than in the reformist wing of the officer corps. They supported modernization, but their concept of the army was as an instrument of a government and society based on the politics of the governors. They were what Brazilians would call *situacionistas* [supporters of those in power]. Fernando Setembrino de Carvalho (1922–26) and Nestor Sezefredo dos Passos (1926–30) had proven their mettle in defending the established order. Setembrino made his mark in the 1914 intervention in Ceará and in the Contestado, whereas the intestinal fortitude of Sezefredo dos Passos set the latter on his upward path.

Setembrino's earlier years as an engineer officer building railroads in Rio Grande do Sul called him to the attention of Marshal Hermes, who brought him to the capital, where, as chief of the war minister's office, he became an able power broker. He gained the trust and confidence of his superiors. His success as interventor in Ceará and then commander in the Contestado earned him the directorship of the ministry's administration department, which controlled the army's day-to-day life. In 1916 his colleagues elected him president of the prestigious Military Club, and in 1918 he received his third star as general of division. After a stint as commander of the Second Division with headquarters in Niterói, he was entrusted with the organization of the new Fourth Military Region that embraced Minas Gerais and Goiás and was headquartered in Juiz de Fora (Minas Gerais). As the senior federal officer in Minas he developed ties with the state's president, Arthur Bernardes, and later backed his candidacy for national president. During the "false letters" crisis that divided the officer corps in late 1921 and on into 1922, he took Bernardes's side. As the crisis peaked, on July 1, President Pessôa named Setembrino chief of staff to succeed General Alves Bastos. Although he did not officially take over until July 7, he happened to be in Rio when the rebellion broke out on the fifth. In the confusion he took decisive action to organize the government forces that crushed the challenge to Bernardes's claim to the Catete Palace. Bernardes rewarded his loyalty by appointing him minister when he took office in November.[30]

Interestingly, Setembrino's successor as chief of staff had a somewhat similar career as a military prop of the Old Republic. General of Division Nestor Sezefredo dos Passos was fifty-four years old when Washington Luís named him minister in November 1926. He had been born in Desterro (later Florianópolis), Santa Catarina, in 1872. At sixteen he had entered the preparatory course for the Escola Militar. In 1890 the now republican army sent him to take the first-year course in the Escola Tática e de Tiro de Rio Prado in Rio Grande do Sul. The following year he was assigned to a cavalry regiment that in 1893 was drawn into the Federalist Revolt. With the suppression of the rebellion he was discharged from the army and for a couple of years gave classes and engaged in business in Porto Alegre. Amnestied in 1895, he returned to the army as an *alferes-aluno* (a holdover from the imperial army in which this was the beginning rank) and served in an infantry battalion in Florianópolis. In 1899, now a mature twenty-seven, he returned to the Escola Militar, where in 1902 he received his bachelor's degree in mathematics and physical sciences. A second lieutenant that year, he moved up to first lieutenant in 1903. He saw service in Mato Grosso, where he participated with federal troops in the violent struggles for control of the state government in 1906 and where, under the command of Cândido Mariano da Silva Rondon, he built telegraph lines. He made captain in 1907. By 1911 he was back laying telegraph lines, this time from Amazonia south to Mato Grosso. From 1912 to 1916 he was in the Contestado region, where in 1914 he was promoted to major and took part in the fighting at Taquaruçu, Caraguatá, and Santa Maria (Santa Catarina). Now clearly upwardly bound, from there he went to Rio de Janeiro to take command of a battalion in the Second Infantry Regiment. Highly visible in Rio and having proved his worth, in 1917 he rose to lieutenant colonel and joined Minister General Cardoso de Aguiar's cabinet staff. Two years later he was a colonel and in 1921 earned the important credential of the French-run General Staff review course.

The uprising in July 1922 found him in command of the First Infantry Regiment at Vila Militar. During the early hours of July 5, in a struggle, he succeeded in disarming a rebellious lieutenant whose troops had surrounded the regimental casino. Earlier, having been alerted that several officers were en route on the train to join conspirators at the Vila, he had sent his executive officer *(fiscal),* Lt. Col. Álvaro Guilherme Mariante, to intercept them at the station. Mariante would later command a column against the tenentes and would earn his own general's stars. Sezefredo dos Passos's role on the night of July 4–5, and again on July 6 commanding troops confronting the rebels in Copacabana, prompted President Pessôa to promote him to brigadier general in August 1922 and helped secure him a post on the general staff. In March 1925 he and General Rondon directed operations in western Paraná against the tenentes in a series of notably violent engagements. The following year the outgoing Pessôa government promoted him to general of division.[31]

A third officer, who made a more indelible mark on the army, Augusto Tasso Fragoso, served as chief of staff from 1922 to 1929 and again in 1931 and 1932. A northeasterner, born in São Luis, Maranhão, in 1869, he entered Praia Vermelha in 1885, where by early 1889 he was an *alferes-aluno* and under the influence of Lt. Col. Benjamin Constant. His participation in the overthrow of the empire was rewarded with promotion to lieutenant in January 1890. A partisan of Floriano Peixoto, he fought against the navy rebels and was seriously wounded in the fighting at Niterói in February 1894, for which he was promoted for bravery to captain. Among his special assignments were some months as head of the Federal District's Department of Works and Transportation (1892) and service with the commission that selected the site of the future capital city of Brasília on the Planalto (1892–93). He spent nearly a year with the military purchasing commission in Europe, where he also sought treatment for muscular problems related to his wounds. Back in Brazil in 1895, he worked on coastal defenses and married Josefa da Graça Aranha, sister of the writer.[32] The next years found him assigned to various general staff duties and to work with the Bolivian boundary commission and the national mapping survey. In 1903, while engaged with the latter, he made major. He accompanied Marshal Hermes to Germany in 1908, and the following year saw him as military attaché in Buenos Aires, where he was promoted to lieutenant colonel. His experience there and as commander of the Eighth Cavalry Regiment in Uruguaiana from 1911 to 1913 shaped his thinking regarding Argentina. In 1914 he attained colonel, and after some months on the general staff, President Wenceslau Brás named him chief of his Casa Militar, thus bringing him into the highest political and military circles, where he worked with the president and Minister of War Faria to reactivate the reforms of 1908, particularly by establishing obligatory military service. Promoted to brigadier general in January 1918, he organized the Fourth Cavalry Regiment in Rio de Janeiro before agreeing at the end of that year to become director of the Ordnance Department. In February 1922 he received his general of division stars, and in November Artur Bernardes named him chief of staff. His length of service in that post eventually totaled seven years and five months, which made him the longest serving chief of staff. He also was a historian who turned out lengthy, detailed studies of the war with the Argentines in the 1820s and the war of the Triple Alliance against Paraguay in 1865–70. These works and his time as chief gave him enormous influence over army thinking.[33]

The personal relations between the chief of staff and the two ministers profiled above are worthy of comment. First, it should be said that tension between the general staff chief and the minister had been the order of things since the general staff was established in 1899. Although the minister supposedly named the chief and oversaw his work, in reality the president appointed both, which allowed the chief to bypass the minister and go directly to the president. Also the question of who commanded the army in peace and in war was unresolved, which meant that the limits of authority were blurred. Moreover, aside from the Calógeras ministry, both posts were held by generals whose predilection was to command. The army was small, regardless of its widespread distribution, and there was little room for two commanders. Ideally, the minister, who was a member of the government, and hence a political figure, ought to have concentrated on relations with Congress, on securing funding, and on policy matters, whereas the chief of staff should have focused on planning, organization, training, and the day-to-day running of the army. In actuality the ministers saw their position as commanders of the army and tended to centralize decision making and, indeed, planning in their immediate staff. Although this may have been the unconscious reflex of a general longing to leave his mark, some ministers saw the general staff as a threat to their authority and so bypassed it, making it marginal to army administration. Whatever the causes, a feature of the Brazilian army's history has been tension, if not discord, between the two top officers.[34]

In Tasso Fragoso's case he experienced frustration in his dealings with both of the ministers under whom he served in the 1920s.[35] Apparently Calógeras had wanted to have Tasso as chief of staff on the retirement of Alves Bastos, but because of the revolt of July 1922, President-elect Artur Bernardes prevailed on Epitácio Pessôa to appoint Setembrino, whose task was to maintain the army's loyalty. And he willingly played that role. In a letter to Bernardes, Setembrino declared that Brazil needed stability to be prosperous and that would be possible "only through the cooperation of the armed forces." He blamed the "true chaos" in the military on the ever present political exploiters—as if officers could not reach their own conclusions without civilian help—and said that it was necessary "to separate out the good elements, using them, rewarding their noble attitudes." But prophetically, he warned Bernardes against being too hard on "those momentarily diverted from the path of duty among whom [there were] many of real merit."[36] Bernardes did not heed that advice and refused clemency to the rebels of 1922, including former President Hermes da Fonseca, thereby insuring further turmoil.

Raised to minister, in November 1922, when Bernardes took office, Setembrino, with the president's approval, invited General Tasso to be chief of staff. Tasso saw the moment as opportune because he was "certain that the precious teachings of the French comrades" made it possible for them to recoup rapidly "all the lost time of previous years." Unhappily, in 1924, when renewed rebellion occurred, he found his trained staff officers being ordered off to the campaigns against the tenente rebels leaving him with a hollow shell. Worse, his hopes that the staff would gain profitable experience from conducting operations against the rebellion were dashed, because

Setembrino gathered the planning and direction of operations into his own office, "transforming his personal staff into the General Staff of the Army." Although this frustrated Tasso to the point of frequently considering resignation, Setembrino's personal treatment of him was so cordial that he could not bring himself to leave.[37]

His experience with General Nestor Sezefredo dos Passos was even less happy. Tasso had selected the general to be an under chief of staff, even though he did not know him well, because he was available for assignment, had the proper background, and, especially, because of his quick thinking in holding his regiment in line during the 1922 uprising. As Tasso's subordinate on the general staff, his performance was limited by his irregular appearance at his office, due, he claimed, to a grave illness in his family. Tasso pitied him and thought justifiable the little work that he did. He should have known better, but perhaps wanting to play kingmaker, he recommended to incoming President Washington Luís Pereira de Sousa that he name General Sezefredo dos Passos minister. Tasso recalled that he "nourished great hopes for General Nestor's cooperation," because he was "an intelligent officer, calm, professionally knowledgeable and of modest mien." Also the two had discussed frequently the needs of the service and various reform measures. But, especially, they had discussed relations between the ministers and the general staff and had noted the fits of "lack of confidence or jealousy" that beset ministers. Tasso remembered that General Nestor's opinion "regarding this was radical and in all perfectly in accord with mine" and that in other areas there had never been "the least symptom of divergence." Moreover, before assuming the ministry, General Nestor had made a point of going to Tasso's house to invite him to stay on as chief. All this had led Tasso to believe that a new era was about to begin in which "the General Staff would attain the position that in fact it ought to have, and the ties of confidence and harmony between it and the minister would be tightened."[38]

His deception could not have been greater. Once in office, General Nestor put distance between himself and all subordinate generals, treating them as inferiors. At regular intervals he received them together in his office, all standing, Tasso recalled, like "a confraternity of mendicants, each awaiting the opportunity to be heard." Such repugnant treatment of generals by a minister was unprecedented. Not only did relations with the general staff not improve; they deteriorated. For example, when the French contract was renegotiated (1927–28), Tasso learned of its contents only *post facto* when the French showed it to him. He finally resigned when he heard from a congressman that General Nestor had prepared and submitted to the Congress a new military training law, without consulting him. He sent his resignation to Washington Luís on December 30, 1928. Characteristically, he did not publicly explain his reasons.[39]

The inability of the top officers to work together was a serious institutional weakness. However, it was one that served to delay the army's emergence as a relatively independent political force, so perhaps civilian politicians deliberately avoided resolving the problem. Although Tasso was not able to do as much as he desired, he did raise the intellectual level of the general staff, solidify the tradition of staff map maneuvers in the field, further the cause of army aviation, and keep the French out of Brazil's defense planning. He also made certain strategic views, especially regarding Argentina, part of army thinking. Those views will be discussed below. And he was instrumental in spreading French-influenced professional instruction beyond the Rio de Janeiro garrison. He had the general staff supervise and regularize the process of "osmosis," as he called it, that disseminated the French doctrines throughout the army. A key feature of the process was direct staff contact with the troops. That this could be regarded as innovative says much about the army of the 1920s.[40]

The quality of an army is determined largely by its leadership, so the question of who gets promoted is of great concern. In the 1920s the Brazilian army began to impose stricter educational requirements in determining merit for promotion. Appointment to the then beginning rank of second lieutenant was based on one's standing at graduation from the military school; thence to captain it was based on seniority; to major one-third of the promotions were by seniority and two-thirds by merit; to colonel it was half by seniority and half by merit; and to brigadier it was at the discretion of the president from among the colonels of the combat arms, who had served in troop commands for at least a year at the rank of lieutenant colonel or colonel. The president used his own criteria for selecting generals of division. To encourage officers to take the French mission's Review and General Staff courses, the ministry warned that by 1929, no colonel in a combat arm would be promoted to brigadier general without one of the courses. In addition, they would need three years service as a field officer, of which two had to be in command positions. It was a marvelous plan, but in reality it was difficult to impose the changes; promotion boards continued to give weight to seniority despite the entreaties of the ministers.[41]

The informal criteria that presidents employed in selecting their generals sometimes had unforeseen results. President Epitácio Pessôa's daughter and biographer, Laurita Pessôa Raja Gabaglia, told the story of Colonel Clodoaldo de Fonseca's promotion. Epitácio, cautious in distributing the rank of general, had put off the promotion of this lackluster officer but gave in at the insistence of his older brother and chief of the Federal District police, General José da Silva Pessôa, who reminded the president that the colonel was a nephew of their deceased friend and patron, Deodoro de Fonseca. At the time Clodoaldo expressed great gratitude and declared himself at Epitácio's disposal for anything, anywhere. Ironically, in the July 1922 rebellion he was the only general to declare for the rising. He told the governor of Mato Grosso:"I am at the front of this regenerating movement."The affair demonstrated the need to professionalize the promotion process, separating it from *parentesco* and political and friendship networks.[42]

Leadership problems continued to plague the army, as did the use of unprofessional criteria for selection, such as family, parentela, and friendship ties. As General Tasso discovered, advancing an officer because he was simpatico, a friend of the family, or seemed to agree with you was ultimately detrimental to the army. Now let us take a look at the army's troops in this era.

The Officers

The officer corps was drawn principally from the southeastern and northeastern sections of the country and certainly from the small educated portion of the male population. Data on regional and state origins of the officers are fragmentary and scattered, but data on origins of students at the *Escola Preparatória e de Tactica do Realengo* in 1901–2 give an indication of where the captains through lieutenant colonels of the 1920s may have been from (see Table 6.4). The predominance of the southeast (40.4 percent) and the northeast (38.4 percent) as regions of origin reflected the economic and political power structure of the Old Republic. The civilian elites were not well represented. Many officers came from families with a military tradition or from relatively impoverished civilian ones. José da Silva Pessôa, the brother of Epitácio, pursued a military education and career after he and his four siblings were orphaned by the sudden death of their parents. His fellow northeasterner, Pedro de Góes Monteiro, entered the military for lack of better prospects and tenente leaders Luís Carlos Prestes, Antônio de Siqueiro Campos, João Alberto Lins de Barros, and the Távora brothers all came from modest economic backgrounds. When Estevão Leitão de Carvalho decided to apply to the military school, his teacher asked if his family was having difficulty paying his private school tuition. So in the Old Republic a military education and career were seen as a means of upward mobility. Gilberto Freyre observed that "numerous Brazilians of modest background and often mixed racial stock, craving social advancement and political participation, used the military schools as virtually the only means of ascent."[43]

The size of the army and of the officer corps sometimes befuddled contemporary observers. There was always a difference between the numbers that the Congress authorized in the army appropriation bills and the actual number of troops in the units. Indeed, some authorized units were never formed and existed only on organization charts. In the 1920s this practice allowed Argentine propagandists to paint a portrait of a dangerously strong

Brazil. The discrepancies could be striking as, in 1923 and 1924, when there were 4,706 officers authorized but only 2,913 on active duty, whereas for the troops the authorized strengths ranged from 42,808 in 1920 to 54,081 in 1923, even though the real number was in the high thirties, amounting from 60 percent to 70 percent of the level legislated.[44]

One effect of the shortfall in officer strength was the shortage of junior officers in 1923. The dismissal of rebellious cadets in 1922 had lowered the number of second lieutenants and necessarily placed added burdens on other

TABLE 6.4.

Preparatory Students' Regions and States of Origin, 1901–1902

Region and state	Number	Percent	Totals	Regional Percent
Southeast			387	40.4
Minas Gerais	69	7.2		
Espirito Santo	5	.5		
Rio de Janeiro	97	10.2		
Federal District	175	18.3		
São Paulo	41	4.3		
South			83	8.6
Paraná	17	1.8		
Santa Catarina	17	1.8		
Rio Grande do Sul	49	5.1		
Central West			70	7.3
Goiás	29	3.0		
Mato Grosso	41	4.3		
North			46	4.8
Amazonas	16	1.7		
Pará	30	3.1		
Acre	—	—		
Northeast			368	38.4
Maranhão	41	4.3		
Piauí	14	1.5		
Ceará	66	6.9		
R. Grande do Norte	22	2.3		
Paraíba	36	3.8		
Pernambuco	55	5.8		
Sergipe	42	4.4		
Alagoas	34	3.6		
Bahia	58	6.1		
TOTALS	954	100.	954	100.

SOURCE: Ministerio da Guerra, *Relatório apresentado ao Presidente da República dos Estados Unidos do Brazil pelo Marechal J. N. de Medeiros Mallet Ministro de Estado da Guerra em Maio de 1901* (Rio de Janeiro: Imprensa Nacional, 1901), 55; *Relatório . . . J. N. de Medeiros Mallet . . . 1902* (Rio de Janeiro: Imprensa Nacional, 1902), 33.

officers. Table 6.5 shows the authorized and actual force level by rank. Considering that the real 1923 troop strength was 38,346, that would mean that for each of the 2,913 officers there were 13 soldiers. If we exclude officers on special assignments, the general staff, and those on medical, dental, and veterinary duty, we would have 2,102 line officers and an officer-soldier ratio of 1 per 18. Such a ratio suggests a top-heavy army. But given the training mission and the necessity for a mobilization capability, it would not be surprising to find units with high officer-soldier ratios. However, various memoirs recall shortages of officers in units, and even the president observed that the lack of junior officers was prejudicial to troop training and was "overloading," he said, "the few officers among whom such duties are shared" (see Table 6.6).[45]

The image one gets of the army from American military attaché reports is mostly accurate. Some of the attaché's comments reflect the racism and ethnocentric biases prevalent in the United States at the time, but, those aside, the detail and the necessity of explaining clearly Brazilian society and culture to intelligence officers in Washington make these reports valuable for historians. The Americans rated the Brazilian officers' professional proficiency as low, below that of the Argentine and Chilean officers, and with "absolutely no basis for comparison with the American standard."

Regarding race and color, Major Baker thought that the army was appreciably more democratic than the navy. "Negro officers," he said, were "plentiful in the Army, but almost never encountered in the Navy, although the 'moreno' or mixed-blood type is numerous in both services." The social affairs

TABLE 6.5.
Proposed and Actual Officer Strength, 1924

Rank	Inf Auth/Act	Cav Auth/Act	Art Auth/Act	Eng Auth/Act	Special & General Staff Auth/Act	Medical, Dental, Vet. Auth/Act
Col.	36/31	17/14	33/22	18/8	20/20	7/7
Lt. Col.	41/36	22/22	49/39	21/21	34/34	19/16
Major	86/78	37/33	94/53	33/33	46/46	52/39
Captain	340/271	139/126	301/175	87/83	96/96	172/143
1st Lt.	484/374	247/199	470/195	93/34	129/129	287/126
2d Lt.	506/133	163/37	236/57	38/12	24/24	236/70
TOTALS[a]	1493/919	624/431	1183/561	283/191	349/349	774/462
SHORTFALL	574	193	622	92	0	312

SOURCE: Maj. F. L. Whitley to Asst. Ch. of Staff, G2, "Brazilian Army for 1924," Rio, Aug. 22, 1923, 2006-73, GS, WD, RG 165, NA. The generals were excluded from his calculations because they were at full strength (8 gen. divs. and 22 brig. gens.). The authorized figures were proposed to the Congress, but the bill did not pass.
[a]The total authorized strength (4,706 officers) minus the total actual strength (2,913) left a total shortfall of 1,793 officers.

TABLE 6.6.
Strength of Subaltern Officers, 1924

Rank	Authorized	Actual	Shortfall
Captain	1,135	894	241
1st Lt.	1,710	1,057	653
2d Lt.	1,203	333	870
TOTALS	4,048	2,284	1,764

SOURCE: Maj. F. L. Whitley to Asst. Ch. of Staff, G2, "Brazilian Army for 1924," Rio, Aug. 22, 1923, 2006-73, GS, WD, RG 165, NA.

at the *Club Naval* were more sought after by the Rio elite than similar functions at the *Club Militar.*

The requirement that army officers be graduates of the military school and the educational prerequisites necessary for admittance to that school excluded the vast majority of dark-skinned Brazilians from the officer corps. Moreover, it took political influence to get an appointment to the school; perhaps, as one report asserted, it was "the overwhelming element in determining selection."[46]

Another problem was graft, which was reportedly considerable. Officers who influenced or decided on purchases were courted with presents and money. Foreign manufacturers wishing to sell to the Brazilian army had to "grease the palms of the authorities."[47] Although the American observer attributed the prevalence of graft to deficiencies in moral instruction, it can also be explained as part of the political system's elaborate co-optation of senior officers; the more they benefited personally from the system the less likely they would be to attack it. During the uncertain years of the 1920s it is possible that such graft increased apace with the government's need to preserve the army's loyalty.

Another form of co-optation was the practice of special pay allowances, called *gratificações,* ostensibly for certain duties but in reality often given to certain officers in favor with the minister. A fluctuating exchange rate and price inflation made officers' salaries insufficient to maintain their families.[48] Prior to World War I the paper milreis was worth about U.S.$.33 [cents]; during the war it hovered around U.S.$.25 [cents], but by 1923 it had fallen to U.S.$.09 [cents] before rising slowly between 1924 and 1926 to about U.S.$.15 [cents]. Foreign exchange rates were important because Brazil imported much of the foodstuffs and most of the manufactured products that the urban middle classes consumed. In early July 1924 prices of necessities had become so exorbitant, and so many people were in such desperate situations, that the president suspended customs duties for sixty days on imported food.[49] In such circumstances any extra money would be helpful, and officers dependent on supplements would likely remain loyal. Of course, officers not receiving supplements would feel resentment.

Because the minister controlled supplementary pay, duty in a visible post in Rio de Janeiro had special attraction. If the assignment were to Vila Militar, it also meant a house at a token rent, which even Minister João Calógeras recognized was a form of favoritism that all officers should enjoy.[50]

Because of their low pay, most officers lived simply, often in inexpensive hotels. Memoirs give the impression that officers below the rank of colonel lived on the outer margins of the middle class. Sometimes a group of them would rent a house and live in the style of a student "republic." In one case the town of Itajubá, in Minas Gerais, loaned a house to the local engineer battalion for the colonel and his lieutenants.[51]

Pay was a constant worry and source of irritation in Brazil's inflation-prone economy. And although all officers hungered for promotion, it came with a special tax, which either they could pay all at once or half in a lump sum and the rest in twelve monthly installments. Pensions were financed by a *montepio,* a monthly deduction of one day's pay; however, in 1925 the pensions were still based on 1906 pay rates, whereas the deductions were at 1925 pay levels![52] Perhaps as a way of softening the harshness of the pension plan, the law gave officers with thirty years of service the right to retire with a brevet *(graduado)* rank one level above their own and to receive the pay of the higher rank. Those with thirty-five years received a real promotion to the next level, and those with forty or more received a promotion and were breveted yet another rank. So a colonel with forty years service could look forward to retirement as a general of division. Such a system encouraged both loyalty and long service from senior officers. On the 1925 list of eighty-four combat colonels, there were twelve with forty or more years, sixty-two with thirty-five years or more, and ten with more than thirty years.[53] Such a retirement mechanism was an important means of maintaining the loyalty of the army's top commanders.

At the end of 1928 the Congress changed the retirement law, restricting the *graduado,* or brevetment, rule to only the senior officer in each grade, who would thereby retire after thirty years with the rank and pension of the grade above his own; or, if he had forty years, he would move up two grades. But all other retiring officers would receive only their current rank and its attendant pension. Understandably, the new law was unpopular with the officers, especially colonels with more than thirty years service, and there was a wave of retirement applications before it went into effect. As a result, by late April 1929 the army lacked enough colonels and lieutenant colonels, so majors were placed in posts usually confided to the higher grade officers. The army could not merely promote such men because regulations required specified time between promotions. One of the senior officers who requested retirement was Chief of Staff Tasso Fragoso.[54] This retirement law contributed to the weakening of the command structure just as the Old Republic, and its army, was approaching the revolutionary year of 1930.

A curious aspect of the law was that officers in an "unassigned" status *(aggregação),* even if "absent without leave," were assured that their families would receive their base pay; those serving a jail sentence got half their base pay! This was a strange way to encourage discipline but emphasized that the army took care of its own, even its rebels.[55]

Officer Education: Realengo

The key to officer discipline and performance was education. Throughout the 1920s the army continued to search for a formula to produce the ideal officer. The seedbed of the corps was, of course, the military school at Realengo, located about fifteen miles from Rio proper on the Santa Cruz branch of the Central Railroad. The first two years of the three-year course were a mixture of general education and theoretical and practical military training that aimed at preparing platoon leaders; the third year was devoted to specialized instruction in one of the combat arms. The students were graduated as *aspirantes,* in which grade they served for a year or until a space among the lieutenants came available. The purpose of the military school was to prepare junior officers to function until they reached the rank of captain, at which level they would go to the Officers Advanced Course (*Escola de Aperfeiçaomento de Oficiais*—EsAO).

The Escola Militar do Realengo was located a short walk from the railroad station, providing easy access to the capital. In 1924 there were eight one-story barracks arranged in a quadrangle, each designed to hold seventy-five students in large open rooms. Each student had a small, narrow bed, with a thin, hard mattress, and a wooden footlocker for personal effects. In the mess hall they took meals at rectangular tables of eight, seated on backless benches. Variations of *feijoada* were the principal ration. There was no space for quiet study, and the library was small. The buildings and the grounds looked more like "a vast barracks" than a school. There were no recreation facilities, so students "killed time" by taking walks through the streets of Realengo. General Tasso Fragoso urged that, when it could afford to do so, the army build a facility on the model of West Point, as the Republic of Argentina was then doing. The student service uniform was a poor quality khaki that varied in tone from green to brown and was worn with leather leggings.[56] There was no special student dress uniform. Student status was indicated by a brass insignia in the form of a castle worn on the high collar. The Realengo student walking along Rio's Avenida Rio Branco had, in the chief of staff's opinion, the melancholy appearance of someone dressed in an unbecoming, borrowed uniform. One of the changes that the Revolution of 1930 would bring would be new dress uniforms modeled on those worn by Brazilian troops in the 1851–52 war against the Rosas government in Argentina.[57] At middecade the school was overcrowded because its preparatory course was functioning in the same set of buildings. From 1920 to 1929 the student population hovered between seven and eight hundred.[58]

The curriculum and staffing arrangements were "reformed" in 1924 and 1929. In each case the regulations followed the custom, in force since 1913, of providing detailed directives regarding instruction in the hope of regulating both content and quality. Jehovah Motta, who was a Realengo student in 1925–27, commented that "neither the commanders of the School nor the teachers" could carry out the directives. Indeed, he did not think it an exaggeration to say that "they had not read the 'instruction directives,' or if they read them, did not understand them, or, if they understood them, deliberately disregarded them." The teaching, "with few exceptions," he said, "was bookish, verbalist, [and] detached from the specified objectives." Some professors gave their classes in an "ambience of fear, and even terror," threatening impossible examinations and resulting in poor grades. Physics and chemistry were useless, he recalled, and descriptive geometry and mechanics were lost in calculations and abstractions. Topography was a mockery, and the course in fortification had no practical value. Students could reasonably question the quality of teaching that resulted in 86 failures in physics in the 1924 class of 139. Chief of Staff Tasso Fragoso wrote of "the crisis of professors," noting that among those with tenure, he saw few "really competent ones who desired to work." He cited chemistry and physics as particularly weak.[59]

The purely military training was better. The days of the enthusiastic "Indigenous Mission" were past, but energetic, upwardly mobile captains and lieutenants appeared on the roster of instructors. In 1924 and 1925, for example, of the twenty combat arms unit commanders, at least eight would reach general's rank; one, Alvaro Fiuza de Castro, would be one of the longest-serving chiefs of staff, and Euclydes Zenóbio da Costa would play an important role in the World War II expeditionary force and would be minister of war in 1954.[60] These were serious officers, who had been exposed to the French mission at the Officers Advanced Course (EsAO) and who wanted an efficient and modern army. They had perhaps a greater impact on the students than their American counterparts had on West Point cadets because Realengo did not have the West Point–style cadet command structure; rather, the officer instructors commanded the student units. This system brought them into close, daily contact with their charges, but it also lessened the cadets opportunities to practice command. The army's attitude was that command came after one learned how to obey.

Tasso Fragoso believed that the students should be selected more rigorously; he thought that "undesirable types" had been admitted. Influence and sentiment played a prejudicial role in deciding who got into Realengo. Surprisingly, despite the decade's unrest, by 1928 the numbers seeking admission had risen so much that General Tasso argued that the army could be more selective. He suggested that they should investigate candidates' morals and family reputations. And to improve the image of the military students, none should be admitted without a complete set of uniforms, presumably obtained at their own expense. He did not express concern that the cost of such apparel might exclude poorer candidates. It is likely, however, that they were already being excluded. The American attaché, Major F. L. Whitley, observed that the intelligence of the students was "notably superior to the average Brazilian youth of corresponding age" and that "the pronounced Negro type is comparatively rare in the student body."[61]

The rebellion of 1922 scarred Realengo. The effort to reinstate the expelled students was a constant irritant and would be a major problem after the Revolution of 1930. The second July 5 revolt in 1924 in São Paulo and Rio Grande do Sul was linked to the matter of amnesty and reinstatement of the 1922 rebels. Beyond this, the human, material, and financial resources required to suppress the Prestes Column meant that correspondingly fewer resources were available for military education.

The presence of the French military mission probably saved the army's school system from complete demoralization. From the outset of the mission, the French controlled two of the three principal institutions: the Escola de Aperfeiçoamento de Oficiais (EsAO), or the Officers Advanced Course, and the general staff school. The military school remained beyond their immediate influence until after 1922, when the minister decided that a French presence would improve discipline there. During the decade the French widened their influence over that institution, until in 1929 one of their number was designated "director of military instruction."[62]

Officer Education: EsAO

To the present, the memory of the French founders of the EsAO is cultivated as part of that school's traditions. The EsAO's mission was to prepare senior lieutenants and captains for the next stages in their careers as they moved into the field-grade ranks. The courses, which emphasized the practicalities of conducting military operations at the small-unit level, were given by the French officers, assisted by selected Brazilians who had completed either EsAO or the general staff school.

Opened on April 8, 1920, EsAO was to create a body of junior officers, who, as instructors in units spread throughout Brazil, would disseminate the new doctrines based on the experience of World War I. The objective was to end the confusion caused by units using different regulations and methods.[63] Located in a fine new building at Vila Militar, the school used the nearby troops for demonstration and training exercises. The lieutenants and captains who passed through its portals solidified the friendships, and perhaps enmities, that they had begun in the military school and established new and deeper relations with others from previous and later classes.

The French wisely embraced the "Young Turks," having Captain Joaquim Sousa Reis Netto, who had trained with a German infantry regiment in Hanover in 1910–12 and who helped publish *A Defesa Nacional,* assist the commandant, Colonel Albert Barat, thereby providing him with an intermediary respected by the Brazilian officers. Also the arrangement demonstrated that the French were not out to replace everything and everyone associated with the Germans. According to then Captain João B. Mascarenhas de Moraes, Colonel Barat controlled the Brazilian student officers' "natural tendency to slip into the abstract, when [treating] objective and concrete problems." The colonel did not hesitate to criticize their test answers, telling them that they needed to give more thought to their "deployment orders," that they wrote too much, and that they got off the subject too easily. The Brazilian officers were not accustomed to such criticism, which perhaps explains why one, recalling the school's first session, said that "it wasn't without sacrifice that I returned to the status of *cadet.*" It also helps to explain why the officers complained about the French. The transfer of ideas, technology, and experience were not as simple as some had thought.

The top student officer in that first class was Captain João B. Mascarenhas de Moraes, who as a general in World War II would command the Brazilian expeditionary force in Italy. Interestingly, he attributed his success in EsAO to the lessons that he had learned from the Young Turks. By 1945 he would embody the three foreign influences on the army—German, French, and American. Certainly he was correct in his judgment that EsAO was "the most efficient instructional institution" of the French years.[64] And because the school brought together junior officers who were normally stationed throughout the country, it became a center of conspiracy as they moved toward rebellion. Considering that 65 of the 131 officers enrolled in 1922 did not conclude the course, it is likely that most of that number were involved in the plotting. The danger of providing a seedbed for conspiracy did not weigh as heavily on Tasso Fragoso's mind as did the need to increase the number of captains and lieutenants studying at the school. He worried that at the 1923 level of about one-sixth of the 2,269 junior officers entering each year it would take at least twenty-two years to get them all through the course![65]

Officer Education: General Staff School

The general staff school was intended to be the capstone of the army's education system. When the French arrived in 1919, they set up a one-year "review" course to ease senior officers into the new system or to eliminate them. Throughout the 1920s the review course was a feature of military education. For the first two years of its existence that course had a larger enrollment than the regular three-year one. Indeed, it was difficult to convince officers to apply for the school. In 1923 only four candidates presented themselves voluntarily for the entrance examinations. Tasso Fragoso noted that with such reduced numbers it would not be possible to sustain the school, which would be embarrassing after the costly sacrifices involved in hiring foreign faculty. As a remedy he allowed the top graduates of the EsAO to be admitted without examination, and he arranged with General Gamelin to establish a correspondence course to prepare officers for the examination, which Tasso thought should not be such a "terrifying requirement."[66]

It was not just the examination that frightened officers; the program of study was more than many could handle. From 1920 through 1929, 664 officers entered the general staff school's three courses, but only 243 passed.[67]

Probably the major innovation of the decade was the creation of the army's aviation units and having the general staff school study their deployment. However, the tenente revolts, especially in 1924, made the government so suspicious that it withdrew financial support and grounded the aircraft. Parts were not purchased after 1921; planes became unserviceable, and personnel scattered. In 1926 the American attaché reported that "the Army's air service remains paralyzed. . . . It is clear that Mr. Bernardes has no confidence in a large element in the Army and will take no chances on having bombs dropped on him." The argument that Argentina was ahead of Brazil in aviation did not lessen President Bernardes's aversion. Even so, once Bernardes left office, the situation improved, new equipment was obtained, and flight training revived. In July 1928 United States Army Lieutenant James Doolittle put on a flying demonstration at the Campos dos Afonsos next to Vila Militar that deeply impressed the Brazilian aviators, who were then seriously endeavoring to make up the lost time. In 1929 the chief of staff was able to report that student officers at the general staff school had spent ten weeks at the Military Aviation School receiving orientation in the functioning of this important arm.[68]

The French Mission

The attitude of the Brazilians toward their French mentors, as noted earlier, was a mixture of admiration and irritation. As early as 1924 Tasso Fragoso, while praising the mission's work, asserted that he disagreed with Gamelin's design for the Brazilian infantry division. Gamelin's infantry was too heavy for "a war of movement, such as we will have to engage in with any of our probable enemies." But, even though Tasso wanted a lighter division, he thought it best to let the French doctrine take hold before attempting a change, perhaps two or three years in the future. He also thought that in a few years it would be well to revise the general staff course, giving it a "frankly national point of view," taking into account "our necessities" and the special remedial preparation that officers would require to take the course. He was implying that the fit between the mission and the army was not quite right.

Clearly, he viewed the mission as a temporary dose of medicine and that eventually the Brazilians could produce their own remedies.[69] The French were there to set standards, to show the officers what an international-class army was like; they were not there to create permanent dependence. How things would have worked out if the tenente uprisings had not occurred is impossible to say.

By middecade a certain disaffection was evident. In late 1924 the paulista authorities dispensed with the independent French mission that had trained the state *Força Pública* since 1906. Paulista officers carried on as the state expanded its forces to 14,200, creating a "formidable army" for the "Brazilian Prussia," as some observers referred to it. If São Paulo had provided the army with the example of hiring the French in the first place, it now pointed the way toward a more national solution.[70] By 1925 the French mission had graduated 172 officers from the general staff course. Tasso Fragoso claimed that whenever one of these officers appeared in operations against the tenente rebels, there was notable progress. "All that they learned they put into practice with the necessary adaptations," he wrote. If the troops had been equal to their leadership, he lamented, and if they had been equipped properly, the outcome would have been different. But the fact of the matter was that troop training was "very deficient and irregular."[71] Although the graduates of the general staff school were well versed in tactical theory, they did not put it into practice or pass the information on to rank and file. The army had the French doctrine but appeared unable to apply it in actual operations.[72]

In the late 1920s the principal training given to Brazilian army recruits was close order drill so that they would look good on parade; moreover, the corporals who supervised initial training knew little else. For all the emphasis on marksmanship in ministerial reports over the previous twenty years, the recruits still did not receive thorough instruction on the firing range. Indeed, the limited practice that they did receive resulted in little more than a waste of ammunition. Likewise, artillery gunnery training was not well organized, and target practice was nonexistent. During the Bernardes years, aviation training had languished, and motors rusted at Campo dos Afonsos field because the government feared the pilots might attack the Catete Palace.[73]

Perhaps it was indicative of the nature of the Franco-Brazilian relationship that the principal language of instruction was French and that Brazilian officers' deficiency in the language had finally reached such a point in 1926 that Tasso Fragoso thought it urgent to create a course in conversational French.[74] Whether they understood each other or not, the Brazilians resisted some French ideas and objected to the French involving themselves in certain matters.

At the outset the French developed a plan for the army's reorganization based on a peacetime strength of 74,534 men. Although the plan was decreed at the end of 1922, it was never put into effect because the Congress refused to vote sufficient funds to maintain such a force level, and throughout the 1920s Brazilians by the thousands refused to submit to military service. The actual Brazilian army was a weak reflection of the paper army. And worse, the Brazilian generals had no intention of implementing a plan, even if circumstances permitted, which they regarded as insufficiently attuned to Brazil's climatic and geographic conditions. Specifically they objected to the unduly heavy complement of field artillery planned for the infantry division. In France, with its highways and railroads, field artillery moved with ease, but with Brazil's rough dirt roads and trails such units would offer but little support and cooperation in infantry operations. Because the French advisers pushed their ideas aggressively, the Brazilian officers stubbornly refused to consider the plan seriously.[75] And the French probably did not understand that the matter was closed because the Brazilian refusal was nonconfrontational, hidden behind a wall of smiles, deflections, delays, and excuses.

General Tasso Fragoso objected to the French attempting to involve themselves in Brazilian war and operations planning. In 1926 the French wanted to include in the general staff course an examination of Brazil's military situation with regard to "certain neighboring countries," hypothesizing their probable line of attack and Brazil's best response. Tasso Fragoso at first tried to persuade the chief of mission, General Frederic M. M. Coffec, that operations planning fell in the general staff's area of responsibility and that Brazil had not contracted the mission to design its defense plans. Since the Frenchman persisted, Tasso Fragoso cut him off, saying "categorically . . . that this was a decision of the government." Perhaps this incident was what led Tasso Fragoso to prepare his own detailed study of Brazil's strategic situation.[76] The general's irritation with the French, and his efforts to make the best of the situation, are evident in various sections of his *Relatório* for 1927, especially those dealing with problems related to the replacement of General Gamelin, course content at the general staff school, and difficulties in getting the French government to supply advisers with the exact qualifications specified in the contract. The French were not taking the same care in selecting mission staff as they had earlier.

The Brazilians considered Gamelin's successor, General Coffec, who had arrived in January 1925, an intelligent person but with a "*vulgarissima* professional competence" that soon was apparent to all. He did not get on well with his mission subordinates, reaching the point of not speaking to his deputy, General Albert Quirin, whose own behavior toward his fellow Frenchmen was aggressive and antipathetic. The French ambassador eventually had to intervene to end the squabbling and to get the two senior officers out of the country. In September 1927, barely before the ink was dry on Tasso Fragoso's negative comments, General Joseph Spire, who had served in French missions in Poland and Czechoslovakia, arrived to head the nearly forty-member advisory group.[77]

In April 1928 Tasso Fragoso reminded Minister Sezefredo dos Passos that when the government invited the French mission, the idea was that it would stay a certain number of years and then Brazilians would take over. To that end each French instructor had one or more Brazilian assistants, whom they were allowed to choose themselves. Over time it had become clear that some of the French officers had deliberately avoided selecting highly talented men because, as Tasso Fragoso commented, "the more these assistants failed, the greater the probabilities of continuing the Mission in our service." Moreover, most of those selected were young, thus more submissive and impressionable, whereas Tasso Fragoso believed that national interest called for older officers, who could later be placed in higher positions.

To speed the process of freeing themselves from the mission, he urged that talented officers be sent to French army schools. His argument was striking. "The coming of the Mission," he lamented, "isolated us a little from Europe, above all France." Everything they knew came via the mission, which apparently wanted to keep it that way. Initially, Gamelin had asked that they not send officers abroad for the sake of unity of doctrine. But, Tasso Fragoso asserted, now "our interest dictates precisely the opposite"; attendance at foreign schools would be the best means of knowing precisely how they were organized and how instruction was carried out. For example, only after Captain Francisco Gil Castelo Branco returned from the cavalry school of Saumar did the Brazilian general staff obtain a clear notion of how it functioned. And an officer returning with a "diploma obtained after rigorous tests and impartial examination" would have, Tasso thought, enough prestige to introduce what he had learned. A number of such officers would allow the army "to emancipate itself from the French instructors" and to dispense with the mission "with greater security."[78] Although he was undoubtedly correct in his goals, they would not be realized.

In the general staff report for 1929 the new chief of staff, General Alexandre Henriques Vieira Leal, reviewed the mission's history, and he, too, suggested that its days were numbered. After asserting that in the first years the courses at the general staff school had been taught "more methodically" than at present, he reviewed the qualitative decline in several—Strategy and Military History went from twenty-four class periods in 1920 to one in 1928; Infantry Tactics never had a governing logic because the course changed every year; Cartography disappeared after 1924; and Military Transport, Mobilization, and Aviation either had been dropped or had been treated in two or three sessions a year. The irregularities were such that he proposed creating an office of inspector of instruction.

On a lighter, but obviously irritating, note he objected to various officers overextending their biannual paid home leaves in France. In one recent case an officer had stayed six and a half months instead of the regulation four. General Leal said it was time to think about terminating the contract.[79] Thus as the 1920s ended, the general staff was in the mood for change.

Meanwhile, the Americans had been expanding their contact with the Brazilian army. Because the French dominated the school system and the combat arms, the Americans moved into the service areas. In 1925 the director of the army medical service, who was impressed with American hospital organization, with the medical service's efficiency during the war, and particularly with the control of venereal disease in the American army, approached the American military attaché about arranging a visit to United States army facilities. In recommending that Washington issue an invitation, Harry W. Brown, the civilian clerk who was the mainstay of the attaché's office, said that "it would be an opportunity to strengthen our influence and offer assistance to a friendly nation which never has failed to appreciate such courtesies."[80] Similar visits of other specialists occurred; for example, the following year the army sent two captains to study American methods of making powder. Although the trip had not been arranged through official channels, the Ordnance Department set up visits to arsenals and exhibits, and provided them with "specifications" for smokeless powder.[81]

In July 1928 Lieutenant James Doolittle staged a demonstration at Campo dos Afonsos that General Spire, chief of the French mission, pronounced "the most wonderful exhibition of flying skill" that he had ever seen. Doolittle convinced the Brazilian army pilots that the American army–trained aviator was par excellence and that the Curtis Hawk aircraft was the world's best designed and constructed pursuit plane. Thereafter the military attaché began to receive inquiries from officers about attending the United States army's flying schools. The war ministry had declined previous American invitations (the last in 1923) because it did not wish to introduce doctrines that would compete with the French ones, but now the attaché noted that the French mission's influence was not "so strong" and asked the War Department for instructions. It responded that it favored "the attachment of army officers of all Latin American countries to our schools and military organizations." However, because the Brazilians had refused the earlier invitation, a formal one would "not again be given," but "an application received from the Brazilian government for the attachment of such Brazilian army officers as they desire . . . [would] be well received" and favorably acted on. Further, the instructions said: "We agree with you fully that contact at this time with our schools and our student officers would be of great benefit to the Brazilian officers and to the relations between our respective governments."[82]

The Americans were sensitive to the importance of having foreign officers train in the United States. "In fact," said one, "I consider this one of the very best methods of propaganda." Before the World War the Brazilian officers who had been sent to Germany, France, and the United States returned ardent admirers of the country in which they trained.[83] And now that some Brazilian army aviators were dissatisfied with the French mission and wanted to obtain American instruction and material, the Americans moved to secure the opportunity. Military attaché Major Lester Baker engaged in some covert espionage and obtained a copy of the secret Franco-Brazilian contract to have exact information regarding the terms of renewal of the aviation section's subagreement, which was renegotiated every two years instead of the mission's four. He advised the War Department that the Brazilian government had bound itself not to contract any other foreign military missions other than technicians for army factories, arsenals, and geographic service.[84]

The impetus for closer links between the Brazilian and American armies appears to have come from those Brazilian officers interested in specialized training and those unhappy with French armament, and from American officers convinced of Brazil's importance to hemispheric defense and its potential as an American market. United States ambassador Edwin Morgan did not initially favor having the Americans replace the French. Both he and army officials understood that "France would bitterly resent American penetration of the Brazilian army." The mission was part of France's overall program of penetration of South America in the interwar period, and the United States was not yet ready to begin such activity in earnest.[85]

Despite the statements from official Brazilian reports noted above, in public Brazilian officers usually professed satisfaction with the quality of French military instruction. But unofficial critics complained constantly that the French were more zealous about unloading quantities of French-made material than they were about recommending equipment best suited to Brazilian needs. However, by mid-1930 some officers publicly expressed their unhappiness with the quality of instruction. One officer writing, in *O Jornal*

(Rio), as a "military observer," called the training methods at the Escola Militar do Realengo antiquated and not suited to produce efficient officers. The French designed the course of study and supervised the instructional program, so such criticism amounted to condemnation of the mission's work.[86]

A combination of fiscal, trade, and political considerations kept the French mission in Brazil until World War II forced its recall in 1939. The Brazilians got much that they wanted from the French—a feeling of being modern and an endorsement of their inclination to intervene in society to mold better sons for the motherland. The French inspired Brazilian officers to think politically. Officers had to be above partisan politics; they had to be priests of the Pátria. This was the message that the Young Turks had brought back from Germany, and the French had confirmed that this was the true path to national salvation. As Frederick Nunn observed, "stress on being part of the nation, not apart from it, pushed staff officers toward the application of military solutions to national problems." With their personal and institutional military mission experience in Peru, Poland, Czechoslovakia, Rumania, and Greece; their League of Nations mandate service in Syria; and their colonial operations in Asia and Africa, the French gave the Brazilians the conviction that military power and national development were intimately linked. Their ideas about the military's role in society as a civilizing, stabilizing force likely encouraged the tenente rebels in their quest, as they certainly inspired the leading army personality of the following decade, Pedro de Góes Monteiro. As we will see in the next chapter, the tenentes and Góes Monteiro would start out in the early 1920s on opposite sides, but ending the decade together they brought down the Old Republic.[87]

Strategic Planning and Mobilization Plans

The expense of the French mission, indeed the expense of the army, was justified by its defense of the country against foreign enemies and of the government, or, more vaguely, the nation against turmoil and disintegration. In earlier chapters we saw examples of the army's being used in internal situations. Between 1889 and 1930 Brazil did not commit troops abroad and, except for the Acre affair, did not fight its neighbors, but the army planned for possible international conflict so that it would be ready, at least on paper.

Brazilian strategic planning was based on the premise of war with Argentina. The long, colonial-era struggle of the Spanish and Portuguese over the Rio de La Plata, the factional battles in Uruguay, unease over the outcome of the war with Paraguay (1865–70), and the 1895 arbitration of the *Missiones* border set the stage for twentieth-century relations between the two countries.

The tension in those relations was less a matter of actual intentions than of the perceptions the two sides had of each other. The Brazilians thought that they had ample reason to be cautious. At the turn of the century the Brazilian army was led by veterans of the war (1865–70) with, and occupation (1870–79) of, Paraguay. These veterans had witnessed the deterioration of relations with Argentina from alliance to jittery suspicion. The formative years of the Brazilian general staff (after 1899) coincided with the era of escalating tension. Some of the events that marked the period were United States president Grover Cleveland's arbitration in favor of Brazil in the Misiones–Las Palmas boundary dispute (1895), bitter personal relations between Foreign Ministers Zeballos and Rio Branco that peaked in the scandal of the faked Telegram Number Nine in 1908, and Brazil's purchase of powerful British dreadnaughts in 1910. The atmosphere clouded to such a point that Brazil did not send a delegation to the commemoration of the centennial of Argentine independence in 1910, during which Argentine cities witnessed anti-Brazilian demonstrations.

It was this situation that molded subsequent Brazilian army thinking regarding Argentina and certainly influenced Tasso Fragoso, who had served as military attaché in Buenos Aires from July 1909 to April 1911. His many detailed, lengthy memoranda analyzing the La Plata republic's capabilities were echoed in general staff reports for years thereafter. While in Argentina he became convinced that Brazil was militarily inferior, and he carried this idea with him through the rest of his career. He worried about the possibility of war, even though he believed that Argentina would not attack unless provoked.[88]

If war came, Tasso believed that because of Brazil's immensity Argentina would limit itself to seeking to destroy the navy and to invading Rio Grande do Sul in order to draw the army into decisive battle. Unable to move by sea, the Brazilians would be forced to depend on the narrow-gauge railway that linked São Paulo and Curitiba with Porto Alegre and Santa Maria, a railroad that Tasso Fragoso likened to the Trans-Siberian Railroad in the Russo-Japanese War. This was the railroad whose construction was one of the causes of the fighting in the Contestado discussed in Chapter 3. The hypothetical Argentine attack would come through Corrientes and Missiones at Uruguaiana, Itaqui, and São Borja. The Brazilians would have to fall back to defend the railway until they had assembled sufficient forces to counterattack. These ideas became the core of numerous staff reports in later years. As chief, Tasso Fragoso brought to the general staff like-minded officers, at least two of whom had also served as attaché in Buenos Aires.[89]

Tasso transmitted these strategic perceptions and attitudes to younger staff officers who carried them throughout their careers and passed them on to later generations of officers. A number of these staff officers came to play important roles in the army and nation; for example, Eurico Dutra, who would be the longest-serving minister of war (1936–45) and then president (1946–51), and Humberto de Castelo Branco, who would become chief of staff (1963–64) and president (1964–67).

Of course, internal factors, such as the 1912–15 unrest in the Contestado, also helped keep the army facing south. That campaign had provided combat experience, and officers carefully analyzed it for lessons.[90]

In October 1921 the French military mission legitimized the southern focus when it organized field maneuvers in Rio Grande do Sul—"the classic zone of your principal historic struggles"—based on an imaginary invasion by an Argentine-led coalition. Chief of mission, General Maurice Gamelin, told the assembled officers that the objective was to "familiarize" them with the neighboring armies in a situation approximating reality on "terrain of your eventual conflicts." But seeking to apply the lessons of the European war was risky. Gamelin commented that the previous year's maneuvers in the Paraíba Valley between Rio and São Paulo had the national press accusing the mission of provoking conflict between the north and south of Brazil. He cautioned the officers to keep this year's exercises confidential to avoid raising the accusation that "we want to set South America afire." The maneuver, which combined map and field exercises, stressed staging orderly retreats and counteroffensives in open country. The scarcity of railroads and the low level of support services were two limitations that the student officers, who had been drawn from the general staff school, EsAO, and the review course, had to confront as they "maneuvered" their brigades and regiments across the map and face of Rio Grande. These were lessons that many of the participants soon would put to use, although not, as the French had supposed, against foreign neighbors but against each other.[91]

It was a measure of the disorders resulting from the tenente rebellions and of his desire to keep the French away from defense planning that Tasso Fragoso himself wrote the 1920s most important analysis of Brazil's military situation. In this 1927 document he contrasted Argentine preparedness with Brazilian disorder. National defense was, he warned the government, "precarious." He urged improving recruitment procedures, obtaining equipment for training, giving more attention to aviation, establishing better communications with the south, refurbishing the arsenals, preparing reserve officers, acquiring trucks and automobiles, imitating Argentine horse-raising methods, holding more training exercises, nationalizing stretches of the frontier, and rearming and reorganizing the army. The lack of response to his suggestions may have been a factor in his decision to retire, as well as his role in arresting President Washington Luís and in turning the capital over to Getúlio Vargas in 1930.[92]

Barracks' Construction Program

The last section of this chapter on the 1920s deals with the army's endeavor to house itself and to provide adequate training areas. The massive construction program begun under Minister Calógeras and concluded under Setembrino de Carvalho was the largest government-sponsored building program up to that time. Despite the suspicions mentioned in Chapter 5, this program improved the horrendous living conditions with which the troops suffered and gave the army the basic physical plant that it would use for decades to come. Calógeras had come to the ministry with the conviction that the republic should not call young men to military duty and then make them live in "precarious and even unbelievable conditions." He went so far as to call the barracks existing at the start of the 1920s *senzalas immundas* (filthy slave quarters).[93] Moreover, the army's entire structure was supposedly based on the idea that the annual levies of citizens that it turned into trained soldiers formed a reserve that could be mobilized in an emergency, but the truth was that if a mobilization occurred, the army would not be able to accommodate the thousands of additional troops. And there were no buildings in which to store mobilization equipment and supplies. This problem was not new; ministerial reports had complained for years about the sorry state of army barracks, hospitals, arsenals, and storage facilities; what was new was that Calógeras did something about it. *A Defesa Nacional* cheered his initiative with an editorial, noting that "we are without barracks!" Its editors agreed with the minister that especially in Rio Grande do Sul the situation was miserable, that hardly a unit there was adequately sheltered against the harsh winter weather.[94]

The Federal District's Vila Militar, constructed in Hermes da Fonseca's time, was to have been a model for army bases throughout the country; but, as was often the case, once "The [Imperial] Court", as *ADN* editors derisively termed the First Military Region, was taken care of, the rest was forgotten. With President Epitácio Pessôa's support, Calógeras ordered the army's director of engineering to prepare a master plan. But the minister doubted the military engineers' ability to carry out the vast project and arranged for civilian companies, principally Roberto Simonsen's *Companhia Constructora de Santos,* to do the construction. Not surprisingly, this led some officers under General Candido Rondon of the Directorate of Engineering to feel slighted, but in the end even they had to admit that Simonsen's results were good. Their feelings were further smoothed when, later on, some of the projects were turned over to them for completion. The engineers likely had been mostly upset by Calógeras's assigning the initial planning to his own aide, Major Egydio Moreira de Castro e Silva, who throughout the project acted as the minister's liaison with Simonsen.[95] The massive program, involving construction of more than one hundred separate projects throughout the length and breadth of Brazil at a cost of about U.S.$23 million was unprecedented in Brazilian history. It also marked a departure from the practice of hiring foreign firms to construct public works.

Sixty-one new barracks (including five general headquarters), five military hospitals and numerous infirmaries, five warehouses, an airfield, a stadium, and a lake for pontoon training were built, and forty-five existing barracks were repaired, reconstructed, or expanded.[96] To avoid asking Congress to increase the army's appropriation, the program was financed via federal bonds, which required only congressional approval of money to pay the bonds' annual interest. The method spread the cost over many years, but, unhappily, it also added to the government's indebtedness and to criticism of President Pessôa. Even so, it was a price he was willing to pay; the situation had gotten so desperate that in 1919 the army put its arsenal and Fort São Pedro in Salvador up for auction to get money to build a new infantry barracks on city-donated land. Of course, although it may have made some fiscal sense to thin out its colonial and early imperial-era facilities, the army could not merely sell off all its old buildings.[97]

The program also marked the definitive establishment of the army in Minas Gerais and São Paulo. At the outset of the republic each of those states had one federal army unit stationed on its territory; an infantry battalion in the former and a cavalry regiment in the latter. In 1910, Minas still hosted the battalion and two messenger platoons, with a single infantry company of eight officers and ninety soldiers posted in Belo Horizonte and the rest in São João del Rei. Similarly, São Paulo city had a single infantry company of like size, and an infantry battalion and an engineer platoon in Lorena in the Paraíba valley on the road to Rio.[98] Prior to 1919 Minas was part of the First Military Region, with headquarters in Niterói. The army reorganization of that year reshuffled the components of the military regions but changed only one regional headquarters. It devoted a new military region entirely to Minas; its headquarters and that of a division were located in Juiz de Fora, on the road from Rio de Janeiro to Belo Horizonte. In all, Minas was graced with fifteen new units ranging in size from companies to regiments. Although this may have represented Calógeras's desire to give his state some financial benefit from the building program, it also represented the army's concern to better position itself vis-à-vis one of the powerhouses of the Old Republic. The added federal garrisons totaled four thousand troops in 1921, prompting the mineiros to increase their Polícia Militar from three thousand to four thousand by late 1922. With typical mineiro caution, while the newcomers were certainly made welcome, they also required watching.

Similarly, São Paulo had been the center of a military region (in 1910 it was labeled the Tenth Inspection Region, and by 1920 it was being called the Second Military Region) that embraced São Paulo state and the entire state of Goiás, which then extended north into Amazonia, encompassing the modern state of Tocantins. As a result of the construction program, São Paulo received twelve new units scattered throughout the state. Like the mineiros, the paulistas, in response, increased the number of their own state troops. In 1918 the Força Pública had 8,875 men under arms; by early 1926 it had 14,254. Although some of this buildup was likely a result of the 1924 tenente uprising and the subsequent necessity to guard against incursions by the Prestes Column, the figures strongly suggest that both states were mindful of the army's presence and used their forces to offset its power within their territories.[99]

Calógeras had aimed at completing the entire program in time for the Centennial of Independence on September 7, 1922. Aside from the obvious patriotic symbolism, he wanted the new barracks ready to receive the reserve troops that he planned to mobilize as part of the celebrations. Moreover, and perhaps principally, given his practical cast of mind, he wanted the program completed before the new administration took office for fear that it would not continue the projects left undone. But by the time the contracts were actually signed, in March 1921, their clauses spoke of the "majority" being ready rather than all. The delays caused by selecting so many new sites, and shipping materials, most of which were imported, over oxcart trails were frustrating but should have been expected. And, of course, the turmoil that afflicted the army after the July 1922 rising further complicated matters. What is amazing is that 70 percent of the program was finished by the end of the Pessôa government. Most of the remaining building was done during the ministry of Setembrino de Carvalho. A few facilities were left undone or unfinished when Simonsen agreed to a halt in Rio Grande do Sul in late 1924 because of the tenente rebellion there. Finally in January 1925 President Bernardes ordered all federal construction stopped for fiscal reasons.[100]

The barracks construction required a high level of organization and planning because many of them were located in places of difficult access. The lack of rail lines into frontier zones of Rio Grande do Sul and Mato Grosso forced the company to haul materials from the nearest railhead to building sites on its new Ford trucks. And because it could not depend on unskilled local labor, the Simonsen people set up special training courses and then moved its workers from one location to another, as one job was finished and a new one begun. Site selection often proved to be a political, as well as a technical, matter. Municípios were quite anxious to have the army select their locality because it contributed to the local economy. In places such as Campo Grande, Mato Grosso, that lacked water systems, Simonsen extended to the town the ones the company built for the barracks. For all the new garrison towns it meant an infusion of federal money, if only through the soldiers' pay. The documentation suggests that towns were not given an opportunity to compete for selection; indeed, even within a town there was some effort to keep the project secret until a site was chosen to prevent a sudden rise in land prices. In most cases municípios donated the land, but there were some, such as in Quitauna, S.P., where a landowner, seeking to profit unduly, had his land taken by eminent domain and then sought relief in court.[101]

A more serious problem was that senior officers, including generals, often did not understand that the new army based on obligatory service differed in function and method from the old army. Its units, Major Castro e Silva wrote, should "no longer be confused with those of the police." Hence it needed larger, spacious buildings, located in areas with sufficient room for training.[102] Officers who did not understand or sympathize with the new concepts forced some inappropriate site selections. For example, instead of the Eleventh Infantry Regiment being moved away from the center of São João d'El Rey, to a spot where its bugle calls would not disturb its civilian neighbors and where it could safely fire its rifles and guns, the regional and regimental commanders insisted that it be kept where it was.[103]

The garrisons resulting from this program, so-called Calógeras Barracks, are still in use as of this writing. Although similar in appearance, no two are exactly alike, thanks to the artistry of the Simonsen architects, who designed each one for its particular location. Most are of brick and cement, with airy, well-lit interiors, thanks to their high windows and ceilings. They usually have open areas for training, drills, and parades and are normally on a rise on the edge of town near the railroad or highway. All have walls or fences, complete with guard posts, enclosing the area; and access is via a formal, main gate. Many still use the original fixtures, windows, doors, and decorative tiles.

The gaúcho civil war of 1923 halted construction at the twenty-six garrison towns in Rio Grande do Sul, where in many cases the contending forces fought to control the new facilities. In July 1924 the tenente uprising in São Paulo affected work there and in areas supplied by train from there, some sites going months without rail shipments. At the end of 1924, work was suspended in Rio Grande, and in January 1925, as noted above, Bernardes stopped all federal construction projects. In May 1925 the Simonsen company turned over to army engineers the remaining fifteen incomplete sites out of the contracted fifty-three projects, thereby bringing to a close the Old Republic's largest construction program. A number of these barracks in Rio Grande do Sul, such as the ones in Passo Fundo, would be occupied by provisional battalions during the tenente rebellions and would be left in bad condition, much to the unhappiness of federal troops when they eventually took possession.

In the 1920s the army had reorganized itself, had established a high standard of training based on the advice of the French mission, and it had improved its facilities and armament. The future should have been bright. The organizational and physical elements that the "Young Turks" had seen as missing were now in place. But instead of realizing the dreams of the previous decades, the Brazilian army suffered disintegration and implosion in the Revolution of 1930.

CHAPTER 7

The Revolution of 1930

In tenentista values, the *"povo"* was already represented by
the Brazilian Army. . . . The Prestes Column wished to be
the agent of a "revolution" by the military for the Brazilian
people; thus it was not the agent of a social revolution.
—José Augusto Drummond, *O Movimento Tenentista*

"Rio Grande, on your feet, for Brazil! You can't fail your
heroic destiny!"
—Getúlio Vargas, *A Nova Política do Brasil*

At 5:30 on the afternoon of October 3, 1930, the air crackled with shots
aimed at the regional army headquarters in Porto Alegre. In the city's center
stores were closed and schools had sent their pupils home early because of
the rumors that had swept the city earlier in the day. In forty-eight hours the
rebel forces directed by Lt. Col. Pedro Aurélio de Góes Monteiro and lawyer
Oswaldo Aranha successfully overcame the few resisting officers and troops
throughout Rio Grande do Sul. The rapidity of the victory was a clear measure of the disintegration of the army's command structure. The fact that the
revolution's military commander was a lieutenant colonel was an indication
that most of the generals, and many of the colonels, remained loyal to the
regime and so had lost control of the army. They would be retired or passed
over by new commanders who were their junior in rank and age.

The Revolution of 1930 was marked more by telegram "battles" than actual combat. It was the culmination of the rebellions and conspiracies of the
1920s that so undermined the army that its command structure had collapsed rather than continue to defend the Old Republic.

This chapter examines the tenente revolts of 1924, the subsequent march
of the Prestes Column (1924–27), the revolutionary plotting, and the disintegration and implosion of the army in October 1930. The Brazilian army
was, as seen in the previous chapter, seeking to modernize, to rearm, and to

rebuild; so it must strike the reader as strange that junior officers, who seemingly would benefit the most from all the improvements, chose this time to rebel. It is a good example of how a determined minority can work its will when the circumstances are right. And, as each year passed, the circumstances favoring violent upheaval increased because in the 1920s the Old Republic reached its capacity for absorbing the changes that Brazil had experienced since the overthrow of the empire in 1889. Officers were not solely responding to pressures from within the armed forces but also to those from within the broader society. Change was in the wind and deeply affected the Brazilian army.

The Tenente Revolts

Historically, subaltern frustration and dissatisfaction with the political order had been a hallmark of the last years of the empire and had disturbed the new republic until 1904. The drive to professionalize the army had deflected such restlessness away from civilian society, but a new military question, similar to that which had driven the military to withdraw its support from the empire, had erupted in 1921. The "False Letters" episode in which presidential candidate Artur Bernardes supposedly insulted the former war minister and president, and the 1921 president of the Military Club, Marshal Hermes da Fonseca, upset officers; most, however, accepted the explanations Bernardes offered, and only a handful of lieutenants and captains continued to insist that he had insulted the honor of the military.[1]

As with previous displays of discontent, few senior men allied themselves with the restive officers. The most notable exception was Marshal Hermes, whose motivations still beg explanation; it is possible that the publicity resulting from the faked letters incident, the punishment he received for challenging the president's authority to intervene in Pernambuco, and his continuing desire to recoup his reputation that had been damaged during his presidency persuaded him to abandon his legalist position and lend his name to the movement. It may be that his sons influenced him. And there may have been a degree of truth in the British ambassador's analysis that he was an old man with diminished mental capacity, who was "very vain and only too willing to be made the figure-head of any political movement." The ambassador also thought that Hermes, whose "clever and ambitious" second wife, many years his junior, was "behind any political action he takes." All of the above may have been working on his emotions, as well as his unhappiness at seeing Bernardes defeat his candidate, and that of many officers, former president Nilo Peçanha.[2]

The campaign for professionalism had, in fact, contributed to the intensity, and maybe even the timing, of the tenente protest. In 1918 Minister of

War José Caetano de Faria and Chief of Staff Bento Ribeiro had reorganized the military school based on the philosophy that officer preparation should not begin and end in a three- or four-year period but should be a continuous career-long process (see Chapter 5). The military school, emphasizing practical matters rather than abstract theory, was to concentrate on training cadets to be junior officers in the combat arms. *A Defeza Nacional* editorials had argued forcefully for such emphasis, and the two senior generals agreed. Despite Brazil's participation in the war against Germany, Brazilian officers believed in the superiority of German methods.

The young, energetic officers of the so-called Indigenous Mission taught the cadets Brazilianized German tactics and procedures in a deliberate effort to modernize and to stimulate change in traditional army ways. As 2d Lt. Odylio Denys put it, their aim was to shake off the "backwardness and leisureliness" of the old army.[3] The classes, or turmas, of 1918 and 1919 passed through this special training program. These were the classes that supplied the bulk of the rebellious tenentes. Delso Mendes da Fonseca, a member of the 1919 class and one of the leading participants in the rising at Fort Copacabana, asserted that "two *turmas* . . . were responsible for the revolution throughout Brazil: the *turmas* of '18 and '19 of the *Escola Militar.*" "Where you had people *(gente)* from those *turmas,* those people were revolutionary. It was new blood that infiltrated the [army] organism." Their experience at the Escola Militar was key in forming a highly distinctive military generation. Oswaldo Cordeiro de Farias, a member of the 1918 class, recalled that because of the extraordinary training "we were incredibly united, like true brothers, and among us there wasn't jealousy or secrets. There was an unbreakable union that linked us like members of a family."[4]

Trained to a European standard, these junior officers believed themselves better prepared than their superiors, who were grounded in the Brazilian military experience. Moreover, many senior officers had been co-opted into the political structure, and junior officers such as Delso Mendes da Fonseca criticized them for allowing the army to be a buttress of the government, which added a political dimension to the tenentes' natural insubordination. That insubordination was likely influenced as well by the social unrest, strikes, and police repression that marked their years at Realengo. In at least one strike episode in nearby Bangu the cadets replaced police patrols after the latter killed a number of workers. The 1918 and 1919 classes also witnessed the upsurge in Catholic influence among the cadets spearheaded by the members of the São Maurício Conference, who, following the model of St. Vincent De Paul [French, d. 1660] and the inspiration of the local parish priest, Father Miguel de Santa Maria Muchon, assisted the poor and sick in the towns along the railroad from Bangu to Bento Ribeiro. The 1918 Spanish influenza pandemic especially provided opportunities for charitable works that took cadets into the homes of ordinary working people and exposed them to their daily struggles.[5]

Another contributing factor to tenente disgruntlement was the French military mission. Enough officers had opposed importing foreign instructors to create an atmosphere of tension around the mission. Even so, as we saw in the previous chapter, the French officers taught the general staff course and founded the Escola de Aperfeiçoamento de Oficiais (EsAO). Those junior officers who passed through French hands at EsAO believed that they were better trained than the senior officers, doubly so, if previously they had been instructed by the Indigenous Mission. Such a belief was bad for discipline and contributed to the tenente sense of superiority.[6]

It is paradoxical that the desire for reform that led to sending officers to Germany, to creating the Indigenous Mission at the military school, and to inviting the French also drew officers into political action. Frederick Nunn has emphasized that the German and French officer corps were highly political, with clear ideas about the importance of a strong army for the state's political health. Brazilians, and other Latin Americans, paid attention to the military's role in those countries while seemingly ignoring the checks and restraints on military intervention. In Europe, according to Samuel Huntington, military professionalism eliminated militarism, but, as we can see, in Brazil it contributed to it.[7]

The thrust of French instruction impelled certain officers to become political actors in order to reach the objectives that they had learned were essential if they were to have a modern army. The French mission had sought to reorganize the army by making officer training more systematic and by stressing that the general staff should be its organizational and command pinnacle. However, politicians hesitated to give the general staff much independence for fear of losing the army as a political instrument.[8]

As important as military reform was to them, the tenentes also wanted to change Brazilian society. Indeed, in their minds reform of both was mixed together. Although the specifics were vague, they preferred a less liberal and more authoritarian state that would intervene in the economy to achieve a fairer distribution of wealth. The movement was more negative than positive, and in practical, operational terms it was more a struggle for control of the army than for societal reform. Its confusion and quick collapse, after briefly having power within its grasp in 1930, show how immature it was. Certainly the interpretations of the movement are varied.[9]

In July 1922 what came to be labeled the tenente movement made its appearance on the national scene when a handful of the adherents staged a quixotic rebellion, principally at Fort Copacabana in Rio de Janeiro. The catalyst was the punishment President Epitácio Pessôa meted out to Marshal Hermes da Fonseca: when the president ordered federal intervention in Pernambuco, Marshal Hermes, as president of the Military Club, telegraphed the federal garrisons in the state advising passive resistance to carrying out the order, saying "governments pass and the Army remains."[10] The *tenentes* were outraged at the brief imprisonment Hermes received; they viewed the army as the creator of the republic and the civilian politicians as its betrayers. The fact that President Epitácio Pessôa had recognized as his successor Artur Bernardes (he of the "False Letters"), whom many officers regarded as an enemy, was further "evidence" of the mortal danger civilian politicians posed for the army and the state.[11]

Many officers, not just *tenentes*, voiced their anger within the confines of the Clube Militar. The debate was so ill-disciplined and vociferous that President Pessôa closed the club on July 1; four days later the revolt erupted. Although club leaders hastily disavowed the uprising, the then Captain Estevão Leitão de Carvalho surmised later that they must have played a clandestine role in its planning. Scattered units around Rio de Janeiro revolted: the Escola Militar, some elements of the First Infantry Regiment and of the Battalion of Engineers, and the garrisons of Forts Copacabana and Vigia. However, the remainder of the First Army Division stayed loyal and, with General Setembrino de Carvalho supervising the operations, easily crushed the revolt.[12]

The rebellion was full of ironies, not the least of which was that the rebels were a mix of members of the Indigenous Mission at Realengo, new graduates of that school, junior officers who recently had completed the French mission's course at EsAO, and at least one veteran of the 1897 Canudos campaign, Colonel João Maria Xavier de Brito, who commanded the military school. The majority were the products of the reform efforts of the previous decades, who used their costly training against the very system that had made it possible. It was ironic that Fort Copacabana fired the gun signaling the revolt because it was the army's most modern fortification, the apple of the eye of Minister Calógeras. He had treated the officers there with special attention, particularly Delso Mendes da Fonseca and Antônio de Siqueira Campos. The former fired the signal gun and by some accounts lobbed the shells into the patio of the war ministry, and the latter led the famous "18 of the Fort" down Avenida Atlantica to confront the army loyalists. Their roles must have pained the minister.[13] Other ironies are in the later careers of men on both sides whose paths would cross repeatedly over the next decades. One example was Captain João Baptista Mascarenhas de Moraes, who, commanding the Second Battery of the First Mounted Artillery Regiment, directed the cannon fire that helped convince the rebellious military students that Vila Militar was not going to join them. Some of the men he fired on subsequently served under him in the Italian campaign in World War II.

The course of events in his regiment show something of how the processes of conspiracy, rebellion, and response functioned. The regiment's barracks were located next to the EsAO, its batteries serving as demonstration units for the school, which permitted frequent contact between the regiment's officers and the student officers. At the end of June 1922, among the former were Second Lieutenants Filinto Müller and João Alberto Lins de Barros, who had graduated in January from Realengo as aspirantes and immediately assigned to the First Mounted Artillery. João Alberto joined Captain Mascarenhas's battery, which was beginning the training of new draftees. After a field demonstration for EsAO, João Alberto struck up a seemingly casual conversation with Mascarenhas in which he asked if he were satisfied with the "bad government of Epitácio Pessôa." Knowing that this was a subtle sounding of his position, the captain replied that since putting on the uniform he had served some bad governments but that he was consoled to see them later praised by the very newspapers that had heaped abuse on them. He made clear his "absolute respect for the decision of the ballot-box." After that conversation the regiment's captains watched the lieutenants more carefully. With Hermes's seventeen-hour punishment and the closing of the Military Club the unit went on alert. On the afternoon of July 4 the state of alert was first relaxed then reimposed as the senior officers sensed trouble. In the early hours of July 5, as the revolt began, the Second Battery's sergeants informed Captain Mascarenhas that Lieutenant João Alberto had urged them to join it. The regimental commander, Colonel João José de Lima, gathered all the officers in the Casino to question them on their attitudes toward the situation. João Alberto spoke first, criticizing the government for closing the Military Club and was followed in similar terms by all but two of the lieutenants. They were all marched off as prisoners, leaving the captains and the sergeants to take to the field against the Realengo students.[14] This sort of drama was played out in units throughout the army and shows that the "conspiracy" was long on conversation among the committed and short on insuring that at H-Hour the necessary personnel, equipment, and units were secure.

It is well to emphasize that the Hermes punishment and the closing of the club were pretexts rather than causes. The various memoirs and oral history testimonies, such as that of Delso Mendes da Fonseca, show a deep dissatisfaction with the society and the army's role in it. Such officers had come to believe that strictly "professional preparation was not enough . . . to fulfill completely their responsibility before the future of the country. It was no longer possible to serve governments . . . without analyzing the repercussions of any act on the future of the nationality." The situation had reached the point, according to this line of thinking, where the army could not simply follow orders without the risk of becoming an "automaton." Conversation and plotting had been going on for months before the outbreak. Delso recalled that it had taken him "nearly six months" to prepare

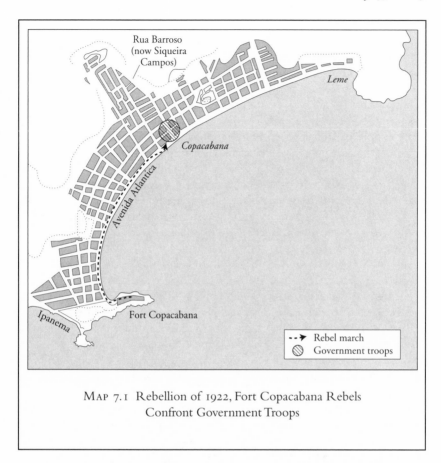

MAP 7.1 Rebellion of 1922, Fort Copacabana Rebels
Confront Government Troops

SOURCE: From *The Army in Brazilian History*, edited by Luiz Paulo Macedo Cavalho. Rio de Janeiro & Salvador, Ba.: Biblioteca do Exército & Odebrecht, 1998. 4 vols. Redrawn by Bill Nelson. Used with permission of Biblioteca do Exército, Rio de Janeiro.

the artillery control tables so as to be able to fire the great guns of Fort Copacabana on targets in the city. Indeed, the advance conversations had seemingly convinced so many officers to rebel that when representatives of the units in the Rio area gathered on July 4 at Fort Copacabana to discuss their plans, some of them, at least, believed that it would not come to a fight. Lieutenant Delso recalled that he left the meeting thinking: "Good, there won't be war. There aren't any opposing combatants; everyone is with us." He was wrong. Subsequent events showed that many who spoke loudly for action disappeared when the shooting started.[15]

What did not disappear was belief that change was necessary. Moreover, the punishments the rebels received hardened, rather than eliminated, the lines of conflict. The government's refusal to extend amnesty to the rebel officers was the single most important factor in the continuation of the movement. Participants in the civil war of the 1890s and in the military school rebellions of 1897 and 1904 had received amnesties after a period of punishment. Indeed, army regulations allowed an officer to be imprisoned for up to two years and still return to the corps, so punishments short of two years were considered tolerable. Although amnesty can be looked at as an example of Brazilian *jeito,* it clearly subverted discipline. The problem was that in attempting to change tradition at that juncture, the government contributed decisively to renewed rebellion.

On December 26, 1923, instead of the hoped-for amnesty the courts approved an indictment under Penal Code Article 107, meaning that the rebels were to be tried for attempting the violent overthrow of the Constitution and form of government. If found guilty, the leaders would be liable for ten to twenty years of imprisonment and the rank and file for five to ten years. Juarez Távora protested in his book *A Guisa de Depoimento sobre a Revolução Brasileira* (1927) that they were only seeking "violent vengeance" against President Pessôa; they did not nourish "any desire to change the form of government of the country or to alter, violently, the political constitution."[16]

In late 1923 they had been quietly sounding out potential adherents for a wider movement and had talked vaguely about taking advantage of the civil strife in Rio Grande do Sul to organize an uprising in the south. One rejected plan called for the seizing of Setembrino de Carvalho, who had gone south to negotiate a settlement, as he traveled back to Rio by train.

The indictments—symbolic of the government's stubbornness and oppression—forced those affected to make a choice. Of the fifty indicted, twenty-two were already imprisoned, and seventeen more soon surrendered, leaving eleven determined souls to carry on as legal "deserters." The solidarity of this group had been born in the Military School, had been deepened by their rebellion, and was now steeled by their common "desertion" and the clandestine existence that it imposed.[17] For this group the only route now open was that of "armed struggle," no longer seeking rebellion but revolution. Even those in prison argued for revolution. To save themselves, they had to bring down the government and the army's leaders. They had their fill of improvised "glory" in the 1922 insurrection; now they needed discipline and planning. First Lt. Granville Belerofonte Lima wrote to Captain Newton Estillac Leal, regarding the failed uprisings, that "the majority intend to live eternally conspiring instead of aspiring" thereby strengthening "the government that oppresses us."[18]

Perhaps he was frustrated by the two tendencies then observable among the discontented in the officer corps: one group wanted a carefully planned national movement with a definite schedule; the second thought that scattered barracks uprisings would be sufficient to provoke wider support. Although the first gradually won out, it was clearly the path of most resistance and doubt. What was needed "for a general transaction," Eduardo Gomes suggested, was something that would raise passions anew. And, he warned, they needed to have "a certain security in the sense of knowing on whom they could count."[19]

They also needed a leader. He had to be an officer who was free to move about, so it could not be someone involved in 1922. He had to be well-known and respected in order to command these unruly personalities, and he had to have enough political savvy and tact to garner civilian backing. To preserve hierarchy, he had to be a senior officer, and because they could not find such a man among those on active duty, they turned to the retired ranks to Colonel Isidoro Dias Lopes, who had been made a brigadier on retirement. He was a gaúcho from Dom Pedrito, Rio Grande do Sul. He was of the old army, having entered the ranks as a common soldier in 1883. In January 1889 he finished the Escola Militar in Porto Alegre and, as an ardent Republican propagandist, supported the new republic as that year closed. When the Federalist Revolt broke out in Rio Grande do Sul in 1893, he left the army and became the chief of staff of caudilho Gumercindo Saraiva, fighting against the state government of Júlio de Castilhos and the federal government of Floriano Peixoto. In 1895, when his side was defeated he went into exile in France. Amnestied in 1896, he rejoined the army the next year and became a student officer at the Escola Militar da Praia Vermelha in Rio. From 1900, when he became a captain, to 1917, when he reached lieutenant colonel, he held posts in various schools and barracks and, more important, commanded units in Corumbá, Rio de Janeiro, Bagé, Uruguaiana, and Cruz Alta. The tenentes regarded him as having proven his mettle as a rebel in 1893–95 and as one who understood the importance of amnesty. Moreover, he had already shown some disposition to conspire; after Artur Bernardes took office in December 1922, Isidoro had discussed some ideas for rebellion with former president Nilo Peçanha.[20]

The tenente desire to have a senior officer as leader went beyond respect for hierarchy; there was, as José Drummond has pointed out, "important realistic, practical and operational reasoning involved." A respected leader would, "by subordination, comradeship, or mere example," attract other officers to the cause. More profoundly, the tenentes yearned to diminish "effectively and/or symbolically" their isolation "within the army, and eventually to characterize their intervention as collective and institutional." It would be this desire for "*institutional* army cover" that would lead the tenentes to attempt unsuccessfully to attract Second Military Region commander General Abílio de Noronha to their cause in 1924 and to accept in 1930 the leadership of until then legalist Lt. Col. Pedro Aurélio de Góes Monteiro.[21]

In 1924, when the tenente leaders approached Isidoro about taking command, he hesitated until he had visited various barracks in São Paulo, Paraná, and Rio Grande do Sul to verify for himself the willingness of officers to rebel. At the same time the Távora brothers made their way incognito through units in those same states, plus Santa Catarina, Minas Gerais, and Rio. Joaquim Távora met with civilian leaders in the Contestado, perhaps remembering the talent that people in that region had shown as warriors. Others visited units in Mato Grosso and smuggled messages in and out of the prisons of Rio. Completing their survey, they met in São Paulo and drew up four lists of forces: (1) those units with officers who were friendly, (2) those who would assist, (3) those who would be of easy adhesion, and (4) those who were enemies. Their objective at that point was to organize simultaneous rebellions throughout the country to lessen the government's ability to snuff out the movement quickly as it had in 1922.[22]

How individual officers decided to join the rebellion reveals that politics was probably less important than pressure from friends and a belief in the movement's likely success. A paulista *Força Pública* major, improbably named Indio do Brasil, testified later that although he had no ill will against the leaders of the state or the police force, he followed Major Miguel Costa because he "lacked courage to deny him any aid in any area due to his friendship and the favors that he received." Belief that the movement did not have sufficient war material and personnel to succeed kept the best known midrange officer, Major Bertoldo Klinger, from adhering. His regiment, the Fourth Artillery in Itu (S.P.), was one of the centers of conspiracy. Given his prestige as a founder and longtime editor of *A Defesa Nacional,* he was highly respected. He had served in the office of Chief of Staff Bento Ribeiro and had been sent to Peru as military attaché from February 1921 to June 1922 because of his outspoken criticism of the French mission. Even though his Itu unit did not rebel in 1922, his image as a critic of the government's military policies led to constant tenente overtures throughout the next year and a half. He affected a seeming willingness to talk, which kept the conspirators hopeful that they could win him over. Indeed, at one point he agreed to take a leadership role in organizing the rebel staff.

They used festivities, such as Soldiers' Day in May 1924, as cover for their discussions. The Itu barracks was host that day to all the units of the Second Military Region for ceremonies and sports competitions. Even fugitives such as Juarez Távora blended into the crowd and conversed with Klinger. He, in turn, gathered the officers of his command to discuss the rebels' plans, and argued persuasively that they lacked sufficient ordnance for such a large-scale movement. The plotters finally conceded that the Itu regiment was out, but, even so, they believed that once the uprising occurred, it would join them.[23]

The tenente objective was to seize power, which meant that they had to win control of Rio de Janeiro. But the increasingly frequent labor strikes, public meetings, and street demonstrations focused so much police attention on the capital city that plotting there became more dangerous. As it grew clear to the tenente leaders that they would not be able to raise enough barracks to take over the army, they turned to São Paulo as a useful objective. Many of them were already there, using the cosmopolitan crowded streets as cover. In a sea of foreigners and migrants from throughout Brazil they could pass unnoticed. Moreover, they believed that the 1922 rebellion in Rio had failed because rich São Paulo had lent its strong arm to the federal government. This time their idea was to cut off that arm at the first blow, thereby securing a solid position from which to consolidate the revolutionary movement. If they held São Paulo, and if all the promised units arose, they could dominate the approaches to Rio via the Paraíba valley and isolate the federal capital. But for such a plan to work they had to control Barra do Piraí on the way to Rio, and this they would never do.[24]

As might be expected, they had some difficulty setting a definite date for the uprising and getting absolute commitments as to who would act first. From February to June 1924 the leadership met with conspiring officers at Jundiaí (SP) and in São Paulo, and repeatedly set dates—March 28, May 13, May 28, June 26—that came and went without rebellion because one or another unit, such as the Fourth Infantry Regiment in Quitaúna (SP) or Klinger's Fourth Artillery in Itu (SP), was not secure. The death, on April 1, of their important civilian ally, former president Nilo Peçanha saddened them, and Klinger's definitive withdrawal from the movement discouraged participation by officers in Paraná, Rio Grande do Sul, and part of São Paulo. Regional Commanding General Noronha heard the rumors and repeatedly sought assurances from his commanders that their units were loyal and, as late as June 26, asked Minister of War Setembrino to remove Lieutenant Colonels Olinto de Mesquita Vasconcelos and Bernardo de Araújo Padilha from the Second Artillery Group and the Fifth Cavalry Battalion because of evidence of their involvement. Whether his words of warning to federal and state officials had as little impact as he believed is unclear, but certainly the police in Rio and São Paulo tightened their surveillance.[25] In desperation, at the end of June, they selected July 5, so full of the symbolism of the Fort Copacabana uprising two years before. They had to act while they still could.

Seizure of São Paulo

In the early hours of July 5, 1924, five tenentes, including Captains Joaquim and Juarez Távora and Newton Estillac Leal, took over the barracks of the Fourth Cavalry Battalion in São Paulo city, armed eighty soldiers, and joined

Major Miguel Costa and his Força Pública troops in turning the police headquarters into General Isidoro Dias Lopes's revolutionary command post. The rebels tried unsuccessfully to take the Palace of Campos Elíseos, the center of the state's government. In the city itself the two sides were more or less evenly matched, each with about one thousand men, as they struggled for control. The rebels seized the telegraph building, several police stations, and, most important, the railroad stations. But to win they had to gain rapid control of the entire city, convince fence-sitting units and many opposing troops to join them, and to move east through the Paraíba valley to Rio. The government forces merely had to hold together and keep the rebels bottled up in the city. On July 8 this realization led Isidoro to order withdrawal before they were trapped. Miguel Costa and various tenentes initially refused to obey, but on reflection Costa wrote a letter to the governor, offering surrender in return for amnesty and reinstatement in the Força Pública. But, fortunate for them, the other side was even more nervous. Before dawn on July 9 the governor and his forces abandoned the city, so Costa's letter went undelivered and Isidoro's order to retreat was rescinded.

The tenentes soon found that planning to deal with a captured city of 647,000 was rather different from actually doing so. They seem to have thought that everything would continue to function while they went about their military business. Now they found that they had to deal with food and water supply, electrical power, transportation, and public order. Anarchist labor leaders tried to reach accommodation with the rebels, who made foodstuffs available to those in need. Indeed, a rebel officer, João Cabanas, broke into the municipal market and ordered its contents distributed free to poor families. The unemployed, which now included workers whose factories were either closed or damaged, and ordinary people sacked stores and warehouses, some of the latter the property of industrialists such as Francisco Matarazzo. Tolerating sacking, and even helping to carry it out in some instances, secured some popularity for the rebels and relieved some of the social tension produced by the fighting. The city's Commercial Association protested to General Isidoro, who responded with the formation of a civil police force and attempts to reestablish order. By the end of the occupation some 103 commercial and industrial establishments had suffered losses resulting from "fire, sacking, bombardment, robbery and rebel requisitions."[26]

Meanwhile, the federal forces had deployed in such fashion that the war of movement that the rebels had envisioned was no longer possible. Minister of War Setembrino, at the first word of the rising in São Paulo, had ordered General Eduardo Socrates, commander of the First Military Region, whom the reader met in the Contestado campaign (Chapter 3), to block the approaches to Rio. But he was able to do much more than that. By July 7 he had set up his command post in Barra do Piraí, which had been one of the key objectives that the rebels never reached, and quickly moved on through Caçapava to Mogi das Cruzes on the outskirts of São Paulo. In so doing, his forces blocked rebel passage to eastern São Paulo, Minas Gerais, and Rio. In the meantime the dreadnaught *Minas Gerais* closed the port of Santos. And General Socrates had Col. Tertuliano de A. Potyguara, who also had honed his repressive skills in the Contestado, seize the São Paulo railway thereby cutting off access to Campinas. The rebels were being surrounded. Civilian "patriotic battalions" under the leadership of planters and merchants, who included the next president, Washington Luís, and future presidential candidate Julio Prestes, blocked the way to Paraná and the possible adhesion of southern garrisons to the revolt. But even with all this government activity the rebel forces increased their number with desertions from federal units and the enlistment in their cause of paulista workers, most of whom were foreigners with combat experience in World War I. About three hundred Germans, Hungarians, and Italians formed national units. All together the rebels numbered about thirty-five hundred by July 11.[27]

The next day General Socrates ordered his artillery to begin the bombardment of São Paulo. The repressive techniques that had worked in the Contestado were now applied to a major city. Under the pounding of the big guns the civilian population, suffering hundreds of casualties, began to flee the city. The archbishop of São Paulo and civic leaders appealed to President Bernardes to halt the bombardment and relayed Isidoro's offer not to use his artillery if the government forces would abstain from firing theirs. Bernardes had Setembrino reply that the federal forces could not wage war without artillery because it would only prolong the resistance, which was doing greater moral damage than the "easily repaired" physical damage caused by the shells. The minister suggested that instead of appealing to the government to stop the bombardment, they should appeal to the "enemy's" bravery not to "sacrifice the population and to evacuate the city to accept combat in open country." Although some paulistas were irritated that Setembrino termed the rebels "enemies" and their insurrection "war," when the year before, during the rebellion in Rio Grande do Sul, he had called the combatants "brothers," civil leaders, such as José Carlos de Macedo Soares, president of the Commercial Association, tried to arrange negotiations using General Abílio de Noronha, the captured commander of the Second Military Region, as intermediary. Their efforts proved fruitless.[28]

On July 22 federal aircraft added their bombs to the shells castigating the city. The barrages continued day and night, but curiously the rebel-held barracks were the least hit. It was the civilian neighborhoods that suffered the most damage and loss of life. Paulista reporter Paulo Duarte charged that the army fired freely on the city without setting proper targets, with the result that "the Santa Casa [hospital] filled with women and children; the cemeteries shamefully overflowed with cadavers and the revolutionary ranks lost not a single man." Certainly he exaggerated. The tenentes lost Joaquim Távora, "the head and heart of the Tenente movement, who was chiefly responsible for launching the São Paulo uprising." But civilian deaths did reach five hundred.[29]

While all this had been going on, unbeknownst to the tenentes, whose telegraph and telephone lines had been cut since the beginning, revolts had occurred in Bela Vista, Mato Grosso, and in Aracaju, Sergipe on the twelfth, and in Manaus on the twenty-third. Faced with government determination and numerous civilian "patriotic battalions" led by local "colonels," the revolts had little chance of success. Lieutenant Augusto Maynard Gomes, one of the leaders in Sergipe, later explained that he hoped to attract federal forces away from São Paulo, the "principal theater of struggle." The Bela Vista conspirators, Lts. Pedro Martins da Rocha and Riograndino Kruel, were subdued promptly by their regiment's sergeants and sent to Rio as prisoners. In both Aracaju and Manaus, the rebels had to form governments for the cities after the governors fled. In the first they tried to convince retired general José Calazans to take charge, but failing, they set up a junta composed of four tenentes; while in Manaus, they assembled a commune that included civilians. The commune sent a vessel downriver to secure the fort at Óbidos and took various socioeconomic measures that included levying taxes on the rich to benefit the poor, breaking food-supply monopolies, seizing the English-owned slaughterhouse and market, and forcing its managers to pay the company's long-owed taxes. Minor officials in Sergipe and Amazonas responded positively, some perhaps even opportunistically, to tenente telegrams informing them of the new governments, but the precariousness of their situation was, perhaps, best captured by their desperate refurbishing in Aracaju's railroad shops of three cannon from the 1820s for the city's seaward defenses. However, in Sergipe the repression came by land, ending tenente control after twenty-one days. At Manaus, they held on for thirty days before abandoning the city to an expedition led by General João de Deus Mena Barreto. The Aracaju jails and public buildings were soon overflowing with real and imagined rebels and sympathizers. The numbers of the accused reached 606 before the courts lowered them to 252. The manhunt for Lieutenant Maynard finally caught him in São Paulo, whence he was shipped back to Aracaju in February 1925. In both Manaus and Aracaju, with their small populations and tight societies, the trials were great spectacles that served to heighten public discussion of national and local problems.[30]

Meanwhile in São Paulo, on July 26, army airplanes dropped leaflets warning the population to abandon the city so that legalist forces would be able to act freely against the rebels. Panic ensued as thousands filled the highways seeking refuge. In the previous twenty days, by rail, auto, truck, and foot, some two hundred thousand had left, but what of the remaining four hundred thousand and more civilians? It was simply impossible for so many to evacuate the city. Did Setembrino and Socrates think that São Paulo could be leveled the way Canudos and the Contestado towns had been? After all the French training, was the Brazilian army reverting to its old methods? It certainly appeared so. This might explain why army commanders spread confused explanations among their troops that they were suppressing a general strike, an Italian uprising, or a revolt by the Força Pública seeking higher pay.[31]

Isidoro's various attempts at securing an accord with the government that would at least give the rebels amnesty were rebuffed. The leaders understood that they would be wiped out, along with a good part of the city, if they stayed. On the night of July 27 they staged a careful withdrawal of three thousand troops on thirteen trains, via the Northwest Railroad, toward Mato Grosso, where they hoped to hook up with sympathetic units. This withdrawal was executed so smoothly—complete with two field guns still firing as the last train pulled out—that, in Neill Macaulay's apt phrasing, "the artillery-obsessed government command knew nothing of the evacuation until the next morning." Finding the route blocked to Mato Grosso, and after losing the bloody and decisive battle for Três Lagoas, whose possession would have given them control of the railroad on the western side of the Rio Paraná, they moved downriver to Foz do Iguaçu and resolved to hold on in that corner of Brazil fronted by Argentina and Paraguay.[32]

The subsequent story of how these forces, joined by more from Rio Grande do Sul, formed the so-called Prestes Column and marched hither and yon for fifteen thousand five hundred miles through thirteen states until February and March 1927 is well known, so here I will give only a summary. The news blackout that the Bernardes administration imposed on the rest of the country did not work in Rio Grande do Sul, where Argentine and Uruguayan newspapers and radio broadcasts, which were daily fare, spread word of the rebel forces. And the government's practice of arresting suspected officers, or constantly transferring them from one command to another, served to call attention to the rebellion and spread disgruntlement.

The Rio Grande garrisons in Santo Angelo, São Luís, São Borja, and Uruguaiana rose at the end of October 1924 and joined with the gaúcho forces of "General" Honório Lemes who were unhappy with the settlement of the state's 1923 civil war. They proved to be very colorful with their regional garb and antiquated weapons but of little effective use in defeating the federal, state, and provisional forces arrayed against them. By early January 1925 the two thousand men under Captain Luis Carlos Prestes marching to

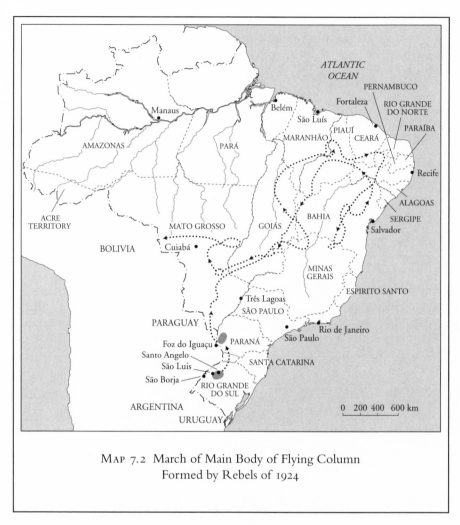

MAP 7.2 March of Main Body of Flying Column
Formed by Rebels of 1924

SOURCE: From *The Army in Brazilian History*, edited by Luiz Paulo Macedo Cavalho. Rio de Janeiro & Salvador, Ba.: Biblioteca do Exército & Odebrecht, 1998. 4 vols. Redrawn by Bill Nelson. Used with permission of Biblioteca do Exército, Rio de Janeiro.

hook up with Isidoro's rebels had dwindled by about half from desertions, while federal forces led by General Candido Rondon awaited them in Paraná and Santa Catarina with about twelve thousand men. With considerable effort Prestes managed to reach Foz with about eight hundred men and some fifty women. There he found that Isidoro had enough, as had many of the other rebel officers and troops, many of whom crossed into Argentina and exile. Miguel Costa and Prestes became the dominant personalities of the remaining rebel force that surprised Rondon by crossing the river into Paraguay and on into Mato Grosso.

After some initial disagreements about strategy, the rebels adopted one that amounted to less a war of movement than a moving "armed protest demonstration" that would serve as a constant call to action against the hated Bernardes. The idea was not to defeat the forces sent against them, much less the old objective of seizing power in Rio de Janeiro; the objective now was to stay alive, to keep the column moving and seemingly invincible. In that, they succeeded as they moved through state after state from Mato Grosso to Maranhão and back, before seeking refuge in Bolivia in 1927. The army, despite the thousands of men it put into the field, increasingly showed little disposition to fight opponents who were some of its best officers. As General Eurico Dutra would later recall, the attitude of most officers was "let him pass." They simply did not have the will to fight because many officers, especially the lieutenants, captains, and majors, agreed with the rebels.[33]

Even so, the fighting widened the generational split that had been developing in the officer corps since the founding of *A Defesa Nacional* in 1913. One of the founders, Major Joaquim de Souza Reis, whom many officers considered the best mind on the general staff, shot himself to death because he felt humiliated for being relieved of his post when he could not suppress the rebellion.[34] The Brazilian army was slowly crumbling as an institution and as a fighting force. It would take much of the 1930s to reconstruct it. The roster of combatants on both sides includes many of the major actors in Brazilian military and civilian politics of the next decades. The fighting would produce the political-military elite that shaped Brazil between the Revolution of 1930 and the military takeover of 1964.

Throughout the country rebels, sympathizers, suspects, and relatives were arrested, some beaten and tortured. One account placed the number of detained in São Paulo at about ten thousand. Some prisoners disappeared; others were killed openly. Neither advanced age nor female sex nor military status were protection against arrest. One old German of nearly eighty years was detained in an interior town for having shouted "vivas" for Isidoro when the retreating revolutionaries passed by. The prisoners in São Paulo had to buy their own mattresses to soften the hard floors on which they slept, and they paid the guards to bring them food and newspapers. Many also bought their freedom. According to Lourenço Moreira Lima, who witnessed these things from his cell, "the Paulista police made the Revolution a good business. The prisoners, especially well-off persons from the interior, became a splendid source of revenue." And as might be expected, lawyers, such as the brother of Governor Carlos Campos, used their connections to free those with money. Even officers who fought against the rebels faced arrest for criticizing government actions.[35]

The revolt convinced many Brazilians that military service was not for them, and they questioned maintaining a rebellious army. Chief of Staff Tasso Fragoso lamented that "no one wanted to join the ranks of the Army for fear of the disorders." Many obtained court orders freeing them from the draft, but most simply refused to answer the call. In 1925, of the 73,250 drafted throughout Brazil, fully 59,638 did not show up. The army was "almost without soldiers; . . . the results could not be sadder," observed Tasso. The prestige that the federal forces were rapidly losing was seemingly flowing in the direction of the civilian patriotic battalions and state police. The government, much to the disgust of knowledgeable officers, was now paying for two armies: the federal and the state/civil forces. The declining civilian support was demonstrated by the continuing refusal to serve; in 1927, of the 49,084 called up, 25,412 refused to appear. The Brazilian people *(povo)* were resisting passively but effectively. The tenente revolts undermined the army and the moral authority of the central government.[36]

In 1925 Tasso Fragoso put the best face on it by asserting that "to the glory of the Brazilian army, the late uprising thinned its ranks, but did not annihilate it." And even though some critics were saying that "the excessive instruction" given officers had contributed to the rebellion, the chief of staff argued that professionalism was the only means to prevent further troubles. For an officer corps in which "no one wants to leave Rio" for distant garrisons, he saw the field experience gained in suppressing the rebellion as good preparation for a foreign war. From this point of view, he said,

we should congratulate ourselves for the events which yanked us out of the monotony of the barracks. At last we carried out important maneuvers with troops, in conditions extraordinarily close to a real war. The officers that moved through Paraná, through Rio Grande do Sul and through Mato Grosso, will never forget this unexpected training that allowed them to feel the urgent necessity of guarding our frontiers. The soldiers returned to their homes with a solid experience of life in the field and of the exceptional effort that the defense of Brazil could one day require of its sons.

Noting that the French military mission had by then trained 172 general staff officers, who he said had made an excellent showing in the operations, he asserted that if the troops had been equal to the stature of those officers and if they had proper equipment, they could have suppressed the revolts more rapidly. If nothing else, he believed that they now understood better the problems that they would have to face in a war with neighboring countries.[37]

The Rise of Góes Monteiro

Tasso Fragoso's exercise in positive thinking aside, the unsuccessful pursuit of the Prestes Column revealed all the weaknesses of the Brazilian army and of its relationship with the political system. Some officers who fought against the column would shortly join with the tenentes and disgruntled civilians to unleash the Revolution of 1930; the most important among such officers was Pedro Aurélio de Góes Monteiro. He had risen quickly, having gone from lieutenant at the end of 1923 to lieutenant colonel in late 1928; he would be chief of staff of the revolutionaries in 1930 and minister of war in 1934. More than anyone else he would reconstruct the army in the late 1930s and set it on the increasingly interventionist course it would follow in subsequent decades.

Góes, as he was known, was from Alagoas but spent so much time in Rio Grande do Sul that he identified with the gaúcho state. Born in December 1889, he entered the army preparatory school at Realengo in 1903 in search of free education. The school commandant, Hermes da Fonseca, prevented it from joining the 1904 revolt of the military school at Praia Vermelha, so 1906 found Góes at the new Escola de Guerra in Porto Alegre. Curiously, there he crossed paths with several men who would later play crucial roles in his own and Brazil's national life. During the heated Rio Grandense state elections of 1906 he joined a group of law students, led by Getúlio Vargas, and wrote on military themes for their newspaper. Although he and Vargas apparently had little or no direct contact until 1930, they did know people in common, and thereafter their lives were intertwined, with Góes leading the revolutionary forces in 1930, playing a major role in establishing the Estado Novo dictatorship in 1937, in deposing Vargas in 1945, and in heading the Armed Forces General Staff in the reelected Vargas government of the early 1950s.

After being declared an *aspirante* in 1910, Góes was assigned to a railroad battalion commanded by Setembrino de Carvalho. Promoted to second lieutenant in 1914, he served in Rio Grande cavalry units until 1916. After his marriage that year to Conceição Saint Pastous, of a traditional family of Alegrete, he took an engineering course in Rio and absorbed the ideas of the Young Turks of *A Defesa Nacional*. In 1918 he returned south to command a squadron of the cavalry regiment in Quaraí on the frontier with Uruguay and was made a first lieutenant the following year. Through his wife's family he got to know an up-and-coming young lawyer, Oswaldo Aranha, who had an office in Alegrete and who was a business associate and friend of Getúlio Vargas, who also serviced clients in that part of the state from his office in nearby São Borja. Aranha would be the civilian coordinator of the Revolution of 1930 and would serve in subsequent governments as finance minister, ambassador to the United States, and as foreign minister. In 1921 Góes was summoned back to Rio to take the new French course at EsAO and continued on to the general staff school in which he was a student when the July 1922 revolt broke out. Although as a student officer he stayed on the sidelines, he supported the government in the crisis. The French instructors were pleased with him, and during the 1923 civil strife in Rio Grande do Sul, the army assigned him to develop a plan to defend the state government. Made a captain the following year, he was sent to Santos to help organize federal forces after the tenente seizure of São Paulo. He made no secret of his disagreement with the indiscriminate bombardment of the city. Once the tenentes withdrew, he returned to double duty—teaching at the general staff school and serving in the operations section of the general staff.

At the start of 1925, while on a vacation trip to Rio Grande do Sul, Góes received orders to become chief of staff of Colonel Álvaro Guilherme Mariante's detachment, which was to be part of the forces assembling in Paraná under General Cândido Rondon. He participated in the operations that pushed the now combined Prestes-Miguel Costa column up against the Paraguayan frontier. After the rebels crossed into Paraguay on April 27–29, 1925, Góes and Mariante spent a short time in Mato Grosso on the staff of General Malan d'Angrogne, then were called back to Rio. For two months Góes was at the general staff school before being sent to Uberaba in the Mineiro Triangle, where federal forces unsuccessfully attempted to block the rebel advance into Goiás.

In January 1926 the now General Mariante took him to Bahia, again as his chief of staff, where he hoped to trap the rebel column. Góes organized "hunting groups" made up of gunslingers *(jagunços)* in the pay of local landowners. But although the Mariante-Góes team moved from Bahia to Minas Gerais to Sergipe to Goiás, and finally to Mato Grosso, they were unable to stop, let alone defeat, the rebels. With the latter safely interned in Bolivia in March 1927, Góes, a major since October 1926, returned to his teaching duties in Rio.[38]

Later that year Mariante, the appointed director of army aviation, made Góes head of his staff (similar to an executive officer) and in October 1928 saw him promoted to lieutenant colonel. With this second swift promotion in the space of two years, Góes had entered that tier of the officer corps where exercising true influence and power began to be a real possibility. His studies with the French military mission had strengthened his native self-confidence, provided a body of military doctrine, and inspired him to think, to write, and, even more, to talk about the army and its difficulties. To his mind the army was at the core of most national problems and their solutions. Its condition reflected the political health of Brazil.[39] He was highly critical of army life, which irritated many officers, especially highly placed ones. However, he was even more critical of the federal government's attitude toward the army, which he believed kept it inefficient.[40]

Knowledgeable foreign observers also thought that the army was undisciplined and shot through with political intrigue. The various state military police forces were showing themselves to be better in battle than the federal army, which some thought did not want to destroy the Prestes Column because victory would mean the end of double field pay. The political elites doubted the army's capacity to defend the Old Republic's political system. Not surprisingly, leaders of the larger, richer states strengthened their police forces to ensure the survival of their own portion of the system.[41]

Góes was particularly shaken by the deplorable performance of the army. While pursuing the column, his coordination of mixed forces of hired gunslingers, assorted hangers-on of various landlords, and state police from Bahia, Pernambuco, Alagoas, and Minas Gerais had made a deep impression on him.[42] Elsewhere civilian "patriotic battalions" provided the muscle that the army lacked. It was difficult to make such forces work together and especially galling that civilian and police units often were more effective than the regular army. The experience unsettled Góes. It was, he thought, the lack of military preparedness that permitted the column to survive. According to the Constitution, the armed forces were to insure internal order and to defend national integrity and honor, but he was now convinced that they were not able to fulfill those missions.

What if Brazil were invaded? he wondered. The army needed plans to confront its most likely enemy, Argentina, and such plans had to embrace agriculture, industry, transportation, and finances, as well as intelligence, supply, and massing of forces. But after this experience he doubted that the current system could provide what was required. "In war," he wrote in an analysis of the campaign, "it is not the army that mobilizes, it is the whole Nation, that fully mobilizing its vital forces, goes to fight." Criticizing the army's response to the tenente uprisings, Góes asserted that modern armies could not wait until danger appeared to improvise a reaction, especially in an underdeveloped country. The Brazilian people had to see the army as part of the whole rather than as something apart; the army's "greatness or decadence is a function of the greatness or decadence of this *Whole*." It would take decades to build an adequate defense system because it was not a matter of rebuilding but of constructing an entirely new army. If action were not taken, he feared that Brazil would fall apart. He warned that the experience with the rebellion foreshadowed what would happen if the country were invaded.

In his report on the Mariante detachment from which these comments came, he also disparaged his fellow officers, saying that most of them were uninterested in learning military doctrine and stubbornly resisted the French mission's efforts to teach them. The average officer, in Góes's view, did little to improve himself after reaching captain; rather he strove to stay in Rio, far from the hardships of interior garrisons and close to those who influenced promotions. "He no longer studies. Doesn't produce. And to mask his ignorance, he doesn't hesitate to use all manner of tricks." Góes argued for a new promotion system that would stimulate officers to improve themselves continually. In his mind he was "a voice crying in the desert" with the message that Brazil's armed forces had "little of military value."[43]

Subconsciously perhaps, Góes was slowly reaching the point of decision. Although the chaos of the 1920s had contributed to his rise, his desire to improve the army, and undoubtedly his own ambition, brought him eventually to the conclusion that only a massive change in the national leadership would create the proper environment for military reform. Seemingly, other officers were going through a similar process. From 1927 to 1930 there were no open rebellions, but there was plenty of criticism of the government and ample warnings of revolution. Góes himself, while on the aviation staff, warned in reports that it was either "national reconstruction" or revolution. His superiors ignored him, and he blamed *caudilhismo* [regional strongmen] for closing the ears of civilian leaders to his admonitions.[44] But the civilian and military leaders could not overlook the repeated warnings in the press.

Revolution in the Wind

Some newspapers, such as Rio de Janeiro's *Diário Carioca,* branding the government *entreguista* (traitorously giving in to foreigners), charged that its readiness to assume foreign debts had delivered Brazil into the hands of imperialists. It was not the United States or Europe that was to blame; "they are doing exactly what we would have done in their place. Our principal enemy is among us. . . . It is the bad governments . . . who sold and delivered us to foreign powers. . . . [O]ur major enemy is the president of the republic." *A Manhã* (Rio) mused that if after ten years the French military mission's success could not be demonstrated on the battlefield, either the officers could not understand French (the language of instruction) or the French officers could not teach. Collectively, editorials and stories in such vein pointed to revolution as the solution. The *Diário Carioca* captured the growing mood when it declared that "a radical transformation even more complete than the one which took place on November 15, 1889 is needed." São Paulo's *Diário Nacional* put it bluntly: "Brazil is moving quickly toward a revolution."[45]

In July 1929 discontented politicians began considering that course. President Washington Luís's selection of fellow paulista Júlio Prestes as the official candidate for the 1930 election infuriated mineiro leaders because under the rules of the "politics of the governors" the next president should come from Minas Gerais. In early 1929 the Liberal Alliance was born when mineiro politicians and their confreres from Rio Grande do Sul consulted about challenging the paulista choice. To attract the gaúchos, the mineiros proposed the candidacy of their state president, Getúlio Vargas. Almost immediately the Alliance leaders raised the possibility of rebellion in the likely event that they lost the election. They understood that victory at the ballot box was remote because the government counted the votes.[46]

Although most army officers were not happy with the current president—they resented that he kept his predecessors' policy of refusing to give the tenente rebels amnesty—only a few active-duty officers threw themselves into the plotting at the outset.[47] Subsequent events would show that few officers cared enough about the government to defend it with their lives.[48]

The tenentes were initially reluctant—if not hostile—to the idea of associating with the civilian plotters. These civilians were the type of men, indeed in some cases, the very same men, they had fought to depose. Eventually, they succumbed to Oswaldo Aranha's persuasion and agreed to cooperate rather than continue their isolation. Even though a "second generation" of tenentes had responded to the new call of rebellion, they were still a minority of the junior officers. Curiously, the government, by scattering them to garrisons throughout the country, inadvertently helped spread the conspiracy. The plotters eventually would win over or neutralize enough officers—chiefly in the northeast and Rio Grande do Sul—to make the movement irresistible.[49]

When gaúcho Getúlio Vargas declared his candidacy, many officers, especially in Rio de Janeiro and Rio Grande, expressed their disenchantment with the reigning system by working openly for him. The federal government sought to keep such activity under control, but tensions rose steadily. As in earlier rebellions it is likely that some officers did not make a conscious decision for one side or the other but were swept along by majority opinion in their units and/or by the strength of their friendships on one side or the other.

Góes Monteiro's case is illustrative. The army command suspected that if rebellion broke out, it would occur in Rio Grande do Sul, so it began to place trusted officers in garrisons there. But when Minister of War Nestor Sezefredo dos Passos ordered Góes Monteiro to take command of the Third Independent Cavalry Regiment at São Luís das Missões, he felt persecuted because he considered this "the worst garrison" in Rio Grande and because his superiors there, including the regional commander, General Gil Antônio Dias de Almeida, were his enemies. The minister may have been testing his loyalty and getting him out of Rio at the same time. He was, after all, on the aviation staff and many of the air officers reportedly favored Vargas. Moreover, in July 1929 he had allowed himself to be photographed with opposition politicians on the very day that Vargas announced his break with President Washington Luís. The encounter was accidental and social, but the newspapers gave no reason for his presence, so it is possible that the scene may have raised some doubts at army headquarters.

It is more likely, however, that General Nestor saw Góes as an officer who had proven his skill and loyalty against the Prestes Column, who knew Rio Grande well, and who could be depended on to hold the area around Vargas's hometown of São Borja. The Washington Luís government feared that after the March 1930 elections, the defeated Vargas forces would revolt employing the firepower of Rio Grande's *Brigada Militar* and the civilian provisional units under rural political chieftains. Rather than being flattered, Góes was angered by the assignment, telling a friend "It doesn't matter to me. But they will pay dearly!"[50]

At this point the influence of family and *parentela* made itself felt. In January 1930, en route to his post in São Luis, Góes paused in the port city of Rio Grande, where his favorite brother Cícero Augusto, an infantry captain involved in the plotting and stationed in nearby Pelotas, sketched the agitated local situation for him. And, from the moment his ship docked in Porto Alegre, Oswaldo Aranha orchestrated a pressure campaign by relatives—Góes's brother-in-law Antonio Saint-Pastous, and his second cousin on his mother's side, tenente João Alberto—and various other conspirators. He had him meet with Vargas, who reminded him of their student days. Aranha sounded him out, saying that "the elections will be fraudulent and we are going to make a revolutionary movement to end this oligarchic system that dominates and oppresses Brazil." Góes shrugged off the appeals, telling Aranha: "I am a legalist officer, I come to command a unit in Rio Grande do Sul and I have no reasons to change my mind."[51] Of course, he did have his own reasons and would eventually come around. But it must have been a difficult decision; either he could stay loyal to a regime he was sworn to uphold, but that he thought was bad for Brazil and for the army, or he could gamble his life and career.[52]

How the revolt's military command was created is a complicated question. Clearly, Góes became the commander. But to some extent it was by default. Virgilio de Mello Franco said that Colonel Estevão Leitão de Carvalho, commanding the barracks at Passo Fundo, and Colonel Euclydes de Figueiredo in Alegrete were worked on, the former being told that if he joined, Góes and Figueiredo would accept his leadership.[53] It must have been difficult for the tenentes to think of serving under an officer who had fought against them. But they had already compromised their principles by joining the Liberal Alliance, which included politicians that they had rebelled against—Epitácio Pessôa and Artur Bernardes! Indeed, vice presidential candidate João Pessôa, throughout the 1920s, had been a justice of the Supreme Military Tribunal that had tried and sentenced tenente rebels.[54] On the brighter side, the alliance also included their old civilian allies: the gaúcho "liberators," paulista democrats, and Federal District opposition politicians. Disagreeable as the arrangement might be, it was their only path to victory.

Tenente Oswaldo Cordeiro de Farias observed years later in an interview that "if we staged an exclusively military uprising, without the popular cover that the political element could give us, it would be a repetition of '22 or '24."[55] "Effectively isolated in the Army," as José Augusto Drummond pointed out, the tenentes "were not in condition to be fussy in selecting their civilian allies."[56] And in the past they had consistently sought the support of higher ranking officers; if they could not get a general or two to join them, they would have to settle for an up-and-coming lieutenant colonel. For its part the Liberal Alliance absorbed tenente demands (such as the secret vote, better election laws, treatment of social problems, and, especially, amnesty for them) into its platform. However, it was the tenentes who became one of the strong arms of the dissident oligarchies of Rio Grande do Sul, Minas Gerais, São Paulo, and Paraíba, rather than the reverse.[57]

What the civilian conspirators wanted was to absorb the tenente mystique, and to that end they had approached Luís Carlos Prestes, then in exile in Buenos Aires. In late 1929 and early 1930 Prestes met secretly in Porto Alegre with Vargas and Aranha and took money from them to buy arms abroad, but he had already moved too far to the left. He no longer shared the goals of the veterans of the column. He thought that Vargas wanted his endorsement more to win votes than to launch the revolution Brazil needed. In May 1930 he shocked his former comrades by denouncing the Liberal Alliance as "bourgeois." His rejection set the tenentes adrift because now they were more interested in a successful revolt that could give them an amnesty and allow them to repair their disrupted lives and careers than they were in revolutionary idealism or doctrinaire ideology.[58] Prestes's refusal pushed the rebellion toward the political center, making it easier for the politicians to control.

The ups and downs of the next months are well known: after the government pronounced Julio Prestes the victor in the "elections," revolutionary ardor dissipated to such an extent that the project seemed dead; however, the assassination in Recife and the dramatic funeral in Rio de Janeiro of conspirator João Pessôa, Vargas's vice-presidential running mate and state of Paraíba president, revived it.[59] During the interlude before the murder, Góes told Aranha that even if it took "one, two, ten, twenty years to secure victory I now carry in my mind the fixed idea of a regenerated Brazil." If

Aranha was no longer disposed to go forward with their plans, he would organize a secret society within the army for national regeneration.[60]

Góes's São Luis barracks was not the best place from which to maintain contact with the conspirators in Porto Alegre. The region's commanding general, Gil Antonio Dias de Almeida, suspected that Góes was plotting, which meant that he had to cover his movements carefully. Because of *mineiro* leader Antonio Carlos's vacillation and refusal to accept responsibility, the revolt could not begin until after September 7, when Olegário Maciel would be sworn in as head of government in Minas Gerais and could bring that state's forces to bear. Góes stayed in the interior after his last meeting with Aranha in June until early September. Then he arranged a clever excuse to travel to Porto Alegre without arousing the general's suspicion. From mid-August, his brother-in-law Dr. António Saint-Pastous, a physician, and his brother, Cícero, used, with appropriate acting on his wife Conceição's part, her feigned illness as a telegram code. For example, on September 1, Cícero telegraphed: "Possible come soon, P.Alegre, attend operation?" and on the seventh, "you are not understanding gravity illness Conceição, ought to depart urgently to see her."[61] The government intercepted many of the plotters' telegrams and letters but could not, or did not, expend the energy to decipher the codes, which were changed weekly, while the rebels listened in on all the radio traffic among the Rio Grande units, and between them and Rio; and they received copies of general staff messages from "friendly functionaries" in the telegraph and post office.[62]

Góes's journey across Rio Grande to Porto Alegre was carefully stage managed. He met with military and civilian plotters at the various railroad stations—Santo Angelo, Cruz Alta, Juí, Tupanciretã, Santa Maria, and Cachoeira do Sul. Some would board the train at one town and ride to the next to avoid arousing suspicion. Preserving his legalist facade gave an ironic cast to a number of his conversations. For example, in Cruz Alta, where his friend Major Eduardo Guedes Alcoforado, who was not involved in the plot, had assembled the garrison's officers for a surprise luncheon at the train station, Góes asked the post commander, Lt. Col. João Baptista Mascarenhas de Moraes, if he had any messages for the regional commander. Mascarenhas, who would lead the 1944–45 expeditionary force to Italy, naively told Góes to say that he had his troops in hand and that he was keeping conspiracies out of his units. Góes observed that he, too, considered his own regiment invulnerable. But Góes must have been thinking "If you only knew what 1st Lt. Nelson Gonçalves Etchgoyen is organizing among your officers and sergeants!" When the revolt broke out, many of the officers would either not report to the barracks or would not resist because they had pledged to remain neutral. Guedes Alcoforado, finding his battalion without officers, would turn the unit over to the rebels, and the regiment's sergeants would disarm and arrest Mascarenhas.[63]

In Porto Alegre Góes went over the military operations plan with the plotters,[64] probably pleased that he had succeeded in keeping secret his role in the projected insurrection. In fact, he was such a model commander that an inspector commended him for the degree to which he had improved the morale and discipline of the São Luiz troops.[65]

The legalists were not completely in the dark; the signs were everywhere that rebellion was afoot. There were mysterious movements of the *Brigada Militar,* municipal guard units and provisional battalions being assembled throughout the Rio Grande countryside, arms and munitions disappearing inexplicably from army storehouses, rumors flying about at an alarming rate—all serving to keep the state's army garrisons in a constant state of alert. At the end of August, General Gil, the regional commander, asked permission of the minister of war to concentrate his troops in the interior of the state to make them less vulnerable to being picked off separately and to prevent the plotters from having access to sympathetic officers and sergeants. General Nestor did not see the need (even though conspirators cut the army telegraph lines in the midst of the generals' exchange), saying that peace reigned throughout Brazil; "the danger of the revolution had passed." A few days later the rumors reached such pitch that General Gil felt compelled to call in three units to Porto Alegre just to show that they would respond to his command.[66]

In the process nerves were wearing thin, and soldiers were increasingly willing to heed appeals such as in this manifesto addressed to "the Riograndense Soldier" and circulated in Passo Fundo on September 23:

In the thrilling moment when Rio Grande, united . . . takes to the field to avenge the stained national honor, trampled under the boot heels of the bastards of the Republic, what will you do [que farás tu], Riograndense Soldier? Will you raise, perhaps, a weapon to fire against your brothers?

Remind yourself, Gaúcho soldier, that there, in those columns that you are going to face, are your civilian brothers, your childhood friends, those with whom you ate from the same *churrasco* and drank from the same *chimarrão*.

Will you commit . . . the crime of fratricide? No! You can't fire on us, soldier of Rio Grande, beloved brother, who so many times we clasped in our arms in fraternal embrace. Come with us, come beloved brother, share the same ideal, for the redemption of the *Pátria* and the salvation of the Republic!"[67]

In Rio de Janeiro General Nestor had gathered so many of the general staff's functions into his own office that he had cut himself off from the broad flow of information that the staff would normally process. Worse, he had alienated respected generals with large followings in the officer corps,

Tasso Fragoso, João de Deus Mena Barreto, Francisco Andrade Neves, Malan d'Angrogne—the very men to whom the conspirators appealed. On September 12 former federal deputy from Rio Grande Lindolfo Collor arrived in Rio to seek the generals' support. But tact was necessary. Rather than invite Tasso Fragoso to join the revolution, he told him that he had come to him as one known to esteem Rio Grande do Sul, to inform him of their plans, to alert him. To this display of confidence Tasso responded that he opposed rebellions against "constituted authority," but if this were really to be a countrywide revolution he assured Collor that he would not remain neutral but act patriotically when the time came.[68]

The Federal District's police, under Coriolano de Araújo Góes Filho, were strikingly unsuccessful in preventing such meetings because of the prominence of the people involved. They could use strong-arm methods with the *povo* but not with the elite.[69] Undoubtedly, they were also restrained by two other factors; first, President Washington Luís simply did not believe that revolution was possible and discouraged aides and others from bringing him rumors and reports of plotting; second, the power of the presidency, in matters of political policing, simply did not run beyond the borders of the Federal District. So with a handicapped police force, an isolated and egocentric minister of war, a divided officer corps, and a stubborn president, the odds tipped steadily in favor of the revolutionaries.

Officers who joined the revolution, such as Góes Monteiro, agreed with the tenente critique that a paulista clique controlled the political system to its own benefit. Some worried that the economic crisis was making communism attractive to the ignorant masses. The military situation depressed many officers; as Góes asserted, there were no leaders, no troops, no materiel. The army's fragile disciplinary structure would crack at the first blow. Revolution would be the vehicle of national regeneration. Mussolini's Italian fascism provided a compelling example of what could be done; and, of course, the army would have an important role. The problem would be to keep the army from being ensnared in partisan politics. Such ideas motivated officers to adopt one of three courses of action: join the revolution; remain neutral; or offer a token defense. The officer corps was not about to fight to the death for the Washington Luís government.

By the end of August Góes had written plans for political reform aimed at creating an authoritarian state to "regenerate" Brazil. Rather than accept the fragmentation and collapse of Brazil, he argued for unification by force.[70] Of course, neither the tenentes nor the Alliance politicians wanted him to write political plans. They were getting more than they bargained for in this lieutenant colonel, who before the decade was out would reshape the army and its political doctrine. Interestingly, earlier in 1930 Góes had done a report on preparedness for one of the army staffs that gave him the chance to think through connections between politics and military readiness. It contained familiar statements about the army providing a common, unifying national vision, about Brazilianizing immigrants, and about achieving progress by using the government to solve national problems. Most of the report stressed the army's institutional needs, such as a new promotion system, staff and command reorganization, creation of regional logistical services, and a more reasonable division of authority. He depicted the situation in the units as desperate: morale was poor, materiel deficient, and discipline undermined by political agitation. Rapid, honest action was necessary.[71] Perhaps Góes was trying to warn the ministry to act while there was time, or maybe he hoped to convince his readers that revolution was the only way to save the army and the country so as to justify his actions.

Góes's genius lay in expressing ideas that were acceptable to, or latent in the minds of, many officers who wanted to see Brazil changed but who opposed popular uprisings and who doubted the elite's ability to make a revolution. His own goal was a military revolution that left the social situation as unchanged as possible. The *povo* were to be passive observers, not active participants. Góes wondered uneasily if Brazil was capable of a "useful revolution." What would happen when mobs took to the streets? "Revolutions," he cautioned thoughtfully, "always lead to the unknown. Things rarely happen the way you want them to."[72]

But Góes worked hard to see that things went exactly the way he wanted. He managed to keep his role as revolutionary chief of staff hidden from his superiors and unsympathetic fellow officers. Arriving in Porto Alegre in mid-September, supposedly for his wife's surgery, he set up a covert headquarters that operated in the small hours of the night. Oswaldo Aranha's network of agents obtained copies of the regional command's messages that greatly facilitated revolutionary planning.[73]

The rising itself, on October 3, 1930, was to occur simultaneously throughout the country. The earlier postponements taught the conspirators something about the precariousness of their communications system, and it probably was no surprise when the confused messages to the northeast delayed action there until the wee hours of October 4. In any event the key was the successful rising in Rio Grande do Sul.

The plan was clever, as it had to be because the rebels could not move beyond Rio Grande until the state's fourteen thousand federal troops were neutralized or enticed to join their side. The attack was set for 1730 hours on Friday, October 3. At that hour, at the end of the week, most officers would have gone home, and soldiers not on leave would be having supper. For days before the third, police from the Civil Guard unit near the Regional Military Headquarters in Porto Alegre had relieved their men in the downtown area by marching a column of twos through the streets, dropping off the replacements and collecting those going off duty. By accustoming the federal troops to their comings and goings, they eliminated suspicion and made themselves an ideal surprise-attack force. On the afternoon of October 3, as they marched past at 1730, they suddenly wheeled and rushed the entrance to the headquarters. Trenches, supposedly waterline repair ditches, had been dug in the streets. Surrounding buildings—the tower of Our Lady of Sorrows church, the St. Raphael convent, the *Brigada Militar* barracks, and the Hotel Majestic—that provided clear fields of fire from their windows had been occupied. Gunfire burst from all directions. About three hundred men made up the attacking force. The plotters had expected shops and stores to be closing and the streets clogged with people heading home from work. But word had spread through the city early in the afternoon. Schools let their pupils out early, and by late afternoon stores downtown had sent their clerks home and lowered their metal grates. In fact many curious bystanders were on the streets waiting for something to happen. The revolt was a secret only to the unobservant.

Ironically, General Gil had gone that morning to have his eyes examined; it seems that he should have had his ears checked as well. On returning to the headquarters about 1300, he was told that Oswaldo Aranha would read a revolutionary manifesto at a rally that day, and he received reports of anonymous telephone warnings of imminent revolt. Then from Passo Fundo, Colonel Leitão de Carvalho radioed that armed men had taken over the post office and the regiment's civilian provisioner had been ordered by the local intendant not to provide some requested supplies. From Bagé, Colonel José Meira de Vasconcellos informed him that he had learned the revolt would start that very day in Porto Alegre, and from Alegrete came word of groups rustling horses from the army's pastures in the middle of the night. At 1500 General Gil sent word to the capital's units to stand ready. But many of them had already dismissed their troops, and in other units compromised officers hid the order. The general was slow to believe that Vargas could be involved. The messenger that he sent to inform Vargas of reports from around the state returned about 1630 with the reply: "Tell the general that precautions will be taken." Some of the "precautions" included army conspirators removing firing pins from machine guns and locking doors to ammunition rooms in the regional headquarters itself! By the time the attack was underway, Oswaldo Aranha had several of the crucial firing pins safely tucked into his shirt pocket.[74]

Armed civilians and police arrested officers and soldiers who had been given leave as they walked along the streets. At one barracks the officers, summoned by the dinner call, were set on by rebels. The eight men on the three floors of the regional headquarters were no match for the three hundred firing on the building. General Gil and a medical officer, Major João

Cavalcanti Ferreira de Mello, took refuge in the general's quarters, where the doctor was wounded. One of the general's daughters grabbed the downed man's revolver and with her father held off the attackers from one of the pantries. With his quarry immobilized, Oswaldo Aranha bid him surrender, which he agreed to do only after receiving a letter from Getúlio stressing the uselessness of further resistance and giving him guarantees in accord with his rank and "the esteem that he merits in Rio Grande do Sul."[75]

Of the fifty in the force that actually assaulted the regional headquarters, eleven were killed and fourteen wounded. An old soldier, known only as Vicente, sweeping the floors was shot dead; as was the head of Porto Alegre's Reserve Officer Training Corps (CPOR), Major Otávio Cardoso. Curiously, the memoirs, from which much of this detail is drawn, do not provide over-all figures on wounded and killed. Likely this is because the record keeping collapsed along with the army's command structure.[76]

Elsewhere, the rebels surprised loyal units in their barracks, the soldiers were weary not only from the day's routine but also from the weeks of alerts and false alarms that had kept them at the ready; resistance was weak and un-certain and overcome at most places in only a matter of hours, if not min-utes. A few held out longer, but in three days the state was secure.[77] At São Angelo the infantry regiment and artillery battery surrendered after being threatened with having their families' throats slit in front of the barracks. In Vargas's town of São Borja, the Second Light Infantry Regiment, despite having one of the leader's relatives among its officers and having soldiers from the locality, held out for several days before crossing the Uruguay River into Argentina. The Vargas relative and another officer later adhered to the revolutionary movement. Góes apparently did not risk conspiring in his own Third Regiment because under the command of a captain, who after declar-ing for legality waited until October 7 for orders that never came. The unit did nothing; most of its officers eventually sought refuge in Argentina. Colonel Leitão de Cavalho had been promised that his Eighth Regiment would not be attacked if it did not take offensive action, but local rebel chiefs lost control of some trigger-happy types from outside the area, who began shooting at the barracks. In the ensuing firefight two soldiers were mortally wounded. Leitão dissolved the regiment before surrendering the buildings and grounds. He and a number of his officers eventually were sent to the prison ship in Porto Alegre harbor. Significantly, they were not relieved of their side arms and swords until reaching the vessel. The rising found Colonel Euclides Figueiredo absent from Alegrete, attending field exercises in Livramento, where, being assaulted by civilians outside of his hotel, he was knocked unconscious and his aide and orderly wounded. The state *Brigada Militar* took the Livramento cavalry and infantry barracks by surprise.[78]

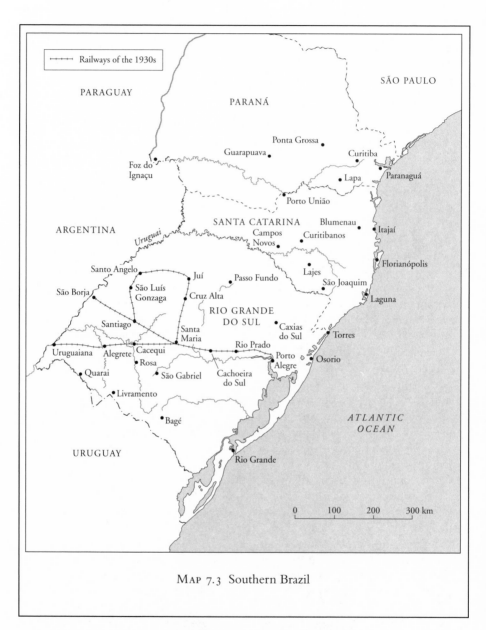

MAP 7.3 Southern Brazil

SOURCE: From *The Army in Brazilian History*, edited by Luiz Paulo Macedo Cavalho. Rio de Janeiro & Salvador, Ba.: Biblioteca do Exército & Odebrecht, 1998. 4 vols. Redrawn by Bill Nelson. Used with permission of Biblioteca do Exército, Rio de Janeiro.

What had appeared to make strategic sense back in the Calógeras ministry (1919–22), when the modern Rio Grande barracks were built, namely scattering them in regimental-sized units in defensive array across the map of the state, proved disastrous as a defense against domestic conspiracy and piecemeal attack. The fourteen thousand federal troops were dispersed in twenty-one garrisons, ranging in effective strength from two hundred to one thousand men. Although they outnumbered the state's forces in each locale, except in Porto Alegre, and were better trained and armed, spread apart as they were, with compromised and/or cut communications, with officers and sergeants committed to the revolution, and with troops drawn from the region uneasy about firing on friends and relatives, the army in Rio Grande do Sul collapsed. Its officers either surrendered, went into exile, or tied red scarves around their necks and joined the revolution.

Captains and below tended to embrace the revolution, whereas majors and above were stronger in support of legality. Junior officers, who stayed with their superiors and resisted the rebels, if only for a brief time, did so out of a sense of loyalty to their particular commanders rather than to the system or the federal president. They maintained resistance until their commander released them from their obligation to him. Since it is doubtful that many senior officers felt personally loyal to Washington Luís—his refusal to grant amnesty to the rebels of 1922 and 1924 was too sore a point for that—one can surmise that those who fought against the 1930 movement did so because they were legalists, believing that the army did not have the right to rebel against constituted authority; or perhaps they believed that their personal commitments bound them to act this way or that they had more to gain by staying with the government. Leitão de Carvalho is usually cited as the premier legalist, partly because in his book he constantly asserted that he was, but it is noteworthy that he had been promoted to colonel in the midst of the crisis in September 1930.[79]

But even legalists had a peculiar self-definition because they did not arrest those who whispered conspiracy, nor, apparently, did they reveal to higher commanders that they had been approached. It should be noted that Brazilian officers did not take an oath to uphold the Constitution but to obey superiors, so personal ties played an important role maintaining discipline. It was a very paternal system in which personal ties and friendships were influencing factors. Even Góes advised General Gil's aide, 1st Lt. Afonso Henrique de Miranda Correia, who wanted to join the movement on the morning of October 3, that he should stay with his general because he trusted and depended on him.[80] Enjoying a superior's confidence, being his *homen de confiança,* involved the reciprocal duty of loyalty in the unwritten code of the officer corps.

That relatively few officers opposed or refused to join the revolutionaries can be seen by comparing the authorized strength in each rank in Rio Grande do Sul units with those that General Gil listed as being held prisoner in Porto Alegre harbor or as having fled the country. Bearing in mind that all units were not up to authorized strength and that General Gil was not able to list all officers who resisted, Table 7.1 shows an overwhelming trend either toward passivity or acceptance of the revolution.

The table can only be suggestive of the numbers of officers who chose to rebel and of those who resisted, but until better figures are developed, it

TABLE 7.1.

Revolution of 1930 in Rio Grande do Sul. Officer-Authorized Strength Compared to Officers Who Stayed Loyal and Those Who Rebelled

Ranks	Branch of Service					Posted in RGS			Percent
	Inf	Cav	Art	Eng	unknown	Total	Loyal	Rebel	
Colonels	3	1	4	1		9			89
Loyal	3	3	1	0	1		8		
Rebel		1						1	
Lt Cols	6	12	11	2		31			54.8
Loyal	9	0	1	0	4		14		
Rebel					17			17	
Majors	19	12	21	2		62			59.6
Loyal	10	4	2	1	8		25		
Rebel	9	8	19	1				37	
Captains	67	65	60	12		210			87
Loyal	15	3	3	0	6		27		
Rebel	52	62	57	12				183	
Lts	85	130	108	17		343			88.6
Loyal	9	21	3	3	3		39		
Rebel	76	109	105	14				304	
2d Lts	110	104	56	12		285			82.5
Loyal	28	12	4	3	3		50		
Rebel	82	92	52	9				235	
Totals						937			
Loyal							163		17
Rebel								777	82.9

NOTE: For Authorized Strength see the *Almanak do Ministerio da Guerra para o Anno de 1931* (Rio de Janeiro: Imprensa Militar, 1931), 17–19, 187–89, 267–69, 367–69. These authorization levels had been in effect throughout most of the 1920s. They may not be completely accurate for the number actually present in the state on Oct. 3. General Gil de Almeida, *Homens e Factos de uma Revolução* (Rio de Janeiro: Ed. Calvino Filho, n.d.), 327–32, noted that his list did not include some officers from garrisons in São Borja, Itaqui, Uruguaiana, and Alegrete. But he did include the majority of those who stayed loyal and were imprisoned or who crossed borders out of Brazil. José Murilo de Carvalho said that "more than 300 officers presented themselves as prisoners to the rebel command," but he did not give a source (see José Murilo de Carvalho, "Armed Forces and Politics in Brazil, 1930–1945," *Hispanic American Historical Review* 62, no. 2 ([May 1982]: 194 fn. 2.) It is possible that the figure of three hundred was that high in the first day or two after October 3, but I suspect that many who initially stayed with their senior officers out of personal loyalty soon were released from that commitment and joined the rebels.

shows that the vast majority or 758 of the 920 officers below full colonel billeted in Rio Grande joined the revolution.

The rebellion succeeded because the army's command structure had been thoroughly undermined. The conspirators had convinced 82 percent of the officers, and an unknown but large number of sergeants in many units, that their future, the army's, and the country's would be better under a new set of leaders. The attacks on the various units succeeded largely because of compatriots on the inside and the overall lack of disposition to fight. The revolutionaries' objective throughout was to minimize losses on both sides.

Interestingly, even in rebellion certain military courtesies and customs were observed. After the Seventh Light Infantry Battalion in Porto Alegre stubbornly held out for hours against heavy fire from small arms and artillery, its commander and Góes negotiated a formal surrender document saying that the unit had fulfilled its military duty. Then, instead of just arresting the defeated officer, he was allowed the usual ceremony complete with speeches transferring the battalion to its new rebel commander. Moreover, all of the battalion's soldiers opted to join the rebels with whom they had just been fighting.[81]

The Road to Rio

Now employing the railroads, the revolutionary forces moved north across Santa Catarina to Porto União and on to Ponta Grossa in Paraná, while cavalry rode up the coastal route. Federal units in Paraná joined the revolution and deposed the state government.

Minas Gerais was cause for worry. Tenente veteran Oswaldo Cordeiro de Farias coordinated the rebel activity in that state, but since he was only a first lieutenant, command was exercised by the brother of the fallen João Pessôa, Lt. Col. Aristarcho Pessôa Cavalcanti de Albuquerque. They were unable to turn any of the federal garrisons to their side. The revolutionary forces consisted of the state's Força Pública and armed civilians led by local political leaders. The rebels dismantled the federal forces command system by seizing General José Joaquim de Andrade ten minutes before the attack on the various barracks. In Belo Horizonte the Twelfth Infantry Regiment held out for five days in a futile struggle against a state police battalion, and units in Juiz de Fora and Tres Corações were immobilized in their barracks. Soldiers of the Tenth Light Infantry Battalion of Ouro Preto at their first encounter with the rebels either ran for the hills or adhered to the revolution. The Eleventh Infantry Regiment in São João d'El-Rei capitulated after a brief exchange of fire. Mineiro forces soon were poised on the Minas borders with São Paulo and Rio de Janeiro.[82]

In the northeast the resistance was overcome similarly in three days. There, in addition to federal garrisons, *Tiro* units, such as the 333d of Recife, joined the revolt. Only in Paraíba did things not go smoothly; there the key conspirators were aides of the governor and the commander of the military region, neither of whom were involved. When the attack came, at 0100 hours on October 4, nearly twelve hours after the rising began in the south, it took the life of General Lavanère Wanderley, the regional commander, and five of his staff. Likewise the Twenty-third Infantry Battalion's commander, Colonel Pedro Àngelo Correia, died resisting his own men. By October 12, in the south, revolutionary forces were at the Paraná–São Paulo border, approaching Itararé, a town inside São Paulo at the crossing of the São Paulo–Rio Grande railroad with the *Nordeste* line, the capture of which would clear the way to São Paulo and, eventually, Rio de Janeiro.[83]

There was no battle at Itararé but rather a stalemate. Torrential rains pounded the region from October 5 to 24, making military operations difficult when not impossible. Loyalist federal army units and the paulista Força Pública set up defensive positions at the town, tested rebel lines with small unit probes, and exchanged artillery rounds. But neither side showed much interest in a big battle while they waited for the weather to improve and the political climate to reveal itself. Góes, his regular army colleagues among the revolutionaries, and the tenentes were not interested in physically destroying the federal army but in gaining control over it. They would need the army to maintain order and to prevent the masses from making their own revolution. Given the revolutionary fervor that was growing across the country, time was on the side of revolution. Meanwhile, rebel forces from Minas Gerais and the northeast continued to press toward Rio de Janeiro.[84]

The capital was alive with rumor and plotting. In the barracks of Vila Militar and in the corridors of the Ministry of War on the *Praça da República* the generals and colonels reexamined their loyalty to President Washington Luís. Each day from October 10 onward the number of legalists declined. The lack of response to the call-up of reservists in the First Military Region demonstrated that the government did not have popular support. Stories of nepotism began to appear; the sons and son-in-law of the president reported for duty but soon were assigned to the president's military staff. People pointed to the president as the principal person responsible for provoking the revolution. General Tasso Fragoso saw him as "authoritarian and without the slightest political vision." As legalist enthusiasm fell, plotting became the order of the day.[85]

The generals had to act before the army was totally defeated, subverted, or before it melted away, if they wanted to have a say in its future. The more optimistic among them may have hoped to gain control of the situation and somehow keep Vargas from reaching power. But there was not a chance of that. General Malan d'Angrogne wrote in his diary that the "general mood is frankly favorable to the triumph of the revolution" but that it should "end, as quickly as possible" to save the country and "our beloved Rio Grande" from prolonged bloodshed.[86] Tasso Fragoso had come to believe that if the generals led a "pacification" movement, it would "be easier to preserve the troops' discipline, maintain social order, limit abuses, and avoid personal vendettas." Passions had reached such a point that intervention at the top was necessary. As early as October 19, Col. Bertoldo Klinger and Lt. Col. José Antonio Coelho Neto went around to various generals in the name of Gen. João de Deus Mena Barreto seeking signatures for an "operations order" calling on the president to step down.[87]

Tasso Fragoso's decision "to rebel" is especially interesting because at age twenty he had participated in the coup against the empire, and subsequent experience had given him second thoughts about revolutions. He said that he had rebelled in 1889 because he believed that the monarchy was a transitory governmental form that shortly would disappear. The laws of human evolution, he thought, demanded a republic; his love for Brazil had compelled him to help the inevitable process along. Although not repenting of his decision, he came to believe that "partial risings" that turned the government over to the military diverted the army from its true mission. But by October 1930 he recognized that the country was in the midst of a "true national revolution such as had never been seen." It was no longer fitting for the military to defend a government that the nation did not support. "The armed forces are the servant of the nation and not of a government." To his mind the difficulty was to be able to recognize the decisive moment when one should refuse to serve as an "instrument of oppression."[88]

On the morning of October 23 General Mena Barreto and his son went to Tasso's house to say that all was ready and to ask him to join them. They discussed the text of a manifesto appealing to the president to resign out of patriotism, and Tasso agreed to approach other generals. That afternoon, Tasso went to the ministry, where his friend Chief of Staff Alexandre Henriques Vieira Leal made clear that he stood with the government and that Tasso should not tell him any secrets. He would stay with the president because he had given his word, not because he agreed with him. The other generals with whom Tasso talked thought that rebellion was justified and either committed themselves outright or excused themselves saying that they could not abandon their posts out of loyalty to their immediate superiors.[89] That night, on orders from Minister of War Sezefredo dos Passos, agents unsuccessfully tried to arrest Colonel Klinger at his home. Very deliberately he had taken to sleeping in his office, where he could trust the sentries. The minister sent General Leal with several officers and *secretas* [plainclothes agents] to bring in General Mena Barreto. However, finding that he was not at home

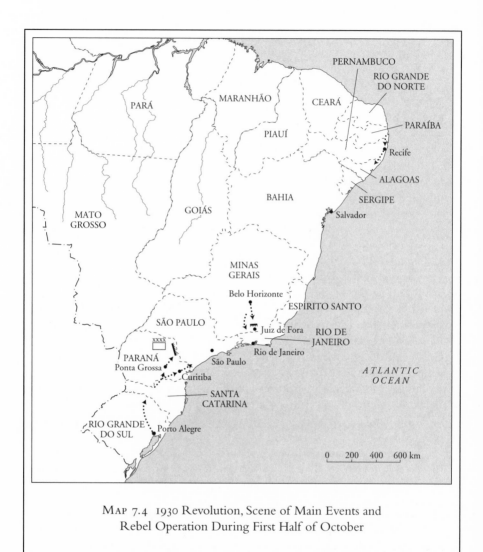

MAP 7.4 1930 Revolution, Scene of Main Events and
Rebel Operation During First Half of October

SOURCE: From *The Army in Brazilian History*, edited by Luiz Paulo Macedo Cavalho. Rio de Janeiro & Salvador, Ba.: Biblioteca do Exército & Odebrecht, 1998. 4 vols. Redrawn by Bill Nelson. Used with permission of Biblioteca do Exército, Rio de Janeiro.

and being told that he was at Fort Copacabana, General Leal deliberately led his party in the opposite direction, probably wishing to avoid a fight. In any case the rebellious generals now had no choice but to act. Mena sent a car to bring Tasso to the fort late in the evening. The scene of the first tenente revolt of 1922, the fort now was the stage for a generals' revolt.[90]

Across the city at the *Praça de República,* between 0100 and 0300 of October 24, Minister Sezefredo and General Leal summoned various generals to the ministry for an emergency meeting. They discussed the Mena Barreto operations order. General Malan affirmed that he had not signed it because he did not command troops, and without soldiers to back him up it would have been a useless, "platonic" act. He asserted, however, that his "simple military obligation" was now superceded because his "duty as a Brazilian required stopping the bloodshed and impeding the ruin of the country." He thought that they should demand that the president resign.[91] General Nestor asserted that the problems in the country were being caused by political parties struggling for control and not by the government. Various officers blamed the minister and the chief of staff for hiding the gravity of the situation from the president. After a couple of hours General Nestor declared that he had heard enough and left for the Guanabara Palace to confer with Washington Luís.[92]

At 0600 Generals Tasso and Mena began working the telephones. Tasso urged Generals João Gomes Ribeiro, commander at Vila Militar, and João Alvares de Azevedo Costa, commander of the Fourth Military Region, to join them. Shortly thereafter, the minister of war called Mena:

> [minister] João de Deus, this is Nestor. I have your papers. How is it that you are involved in this? You, who all your life, always, were on the side of legality? Come over to our side!
>
> [General Mena] It is not possible. The orders are given and being executed. This is precisely about restoring legality. It is you who should join your comrades, to free yourself of your political commitments.
>
> [minister] You all are going to deliver BRAZIL to communism.
>
> [General Mena] This won't happen while I live.

Colonel Klinger called his friend General Azevedo Costa in Juiz de Fora and brought him over to the "pacification movement." And General Mena advised the commanders of the Federal District's *Polícia Militar* and Firemen's Corps *(Bombeiros)* to stay out of the fray. About 0830 General Malan's son-in-law brought word that the general had decided to join them, and immediately they placed him in command of the Third Infantry Regiment at Praia Vermelha and the Fortress of São João in Urca. Generals José Fernandes Leite de Castro, Firmino Antonio Borba, Alvaro Mariante, and Pantaleão Telles Ferreira cast their lot with them as well. A steady stream of officers of various ranks had been arriving at Copacabana, and crowds filled the streets of Rio. In some parts of the city looters took advantage of the distraction of the authorities to sack stores, and the government-leaning newspaper *O Paiz* was burned, giving the city a chaotic air.[93]

In the Botafogo district the assembly of the Third Infantry and the civilians it had armed and their march down Rua Farani and Rua Pinheiro Machado to Guanabara Palace had aspects of a comic opera. Generals Tasso, Mena, and Malan joined regimental commander Colonel José Pessôa Cavalcanti de Albuquerque, nephew of President Epitácio Pessôa, at the head of the motley column as they pushed their way down the streets through the crowds of bystanders and on into the palace gardens. Instead of a fight the palace guard received them with *vivas* and palm branches. In the distance the crowds could hear the cannons at Forts Copacabana, Vigia, and São João booming a fifteen-gun salute, one round for each state then in revolutionary hands.

Curiously, even at this stage, perhaps out of lifetime habit, the rebellious generals respected the position and authority of the president. Deferential in the extreme, considering the circumstances, Tasso, Mena, and Malan waited somewhat nervously for Washington Luís to receive them, but finally, tiring of the game, they walked in on him. After saluting, Tasso noted their regret at being obliged to act as they were and expressed his concern for the president's life, to which the latter replied that was "the only thing that is not worrying me." The generals were taken aback by the president's refusal to accept the coup; apparently he hoped that he still might face them down. Their problem was to get him to concede to being deposed and to leave the palace peacefully. They feared that if they used force, they might incite the mobs in the garden and the streets to uncontrollable violence. The story of their negotiations and the involvement of Rio's archbishop, Sebastião Leme da Silveira Cintra, who had returned from Rome in the midst of the crisis with the Red Hat of a cardinal, is well known. Simply, late in the day Washington Luís gave in and agreed to leave the palace in the company of Cardinal Leme and General Tasso, who drove him to Fort Copacabana, from whence he would eventually leave Brazil for exile.[94] If the rebellious generals recognized the symbolism and irony of using Fort Copacabana to launch their revolt and to imprison the president, they did not say so in their memoirs. But it was a fitting end to the process set in motion in 1922.

If the Rio officers and their "pacification movement" thought they could fend off the victorious October 3 forces, they were mistaken. Their action in deposing Washington Luís gave them some negotiating power, and it stopped the bloodshed, which could well have descended ever deeper into civil war. On the very day of the coup in Rio, Góes Monteiro was about to issue orders for attack at Itararé. Because the revolutionaries were committed to carrying on the fight, the generals had little choice other than to surrender power to Vargas on November 3. If they had any doubts, his triumphal passage from the south to Rio de Janeiro and his tumultuous reception in the capital demonstrated where popular sentiment lay.[95]

General Tasso Fragoso, although the highly respected senior officer of the army, did not suffer from an acute desire for political power. His whole career suggests the truth of his testimony that he was relieved to pass the burdens of authority over to Vargas. It should be noted that although Tasso may have embodied much of the soul of the army of 1930, his rebellion and that of his colleagues did not constitute the same sort of institutional coup that Brazil would experience in 1937, 1945, or 1964. The coup of October 24 was a coup first and foremost of senior officers against the army's own command structure, against the president, the minister, and the chief of staff. It was indicative of the disintegration of the Brazilian army.

The officer corps and sergeants had split into six groupings. First, there were the tenentes, including the veterans of 1922, 1924, and the Prestes Column and the so-called second generation, who joined as they came out of the military school late in the decade. Second, there were the moderates clustered around Góes Monteiro, formerly legalists with ties to the gaúcho, mineiro, or Paraibano oligarchies. At the top of this group there were a couple of dozen field-grade officers like Góes, but its bulk was made up of lieutenants and captains who followed their seniors in October 1930 without sympathy for the tenentes; indeed, they would later form the lower-ranked core of opposition to tenente influence in the army. Third, there were the opportunists who, during an attack or after being taken prisoner, had adhered to the movement. Fourth were those who resisted. Some, as we have seen, fled the country; about ten, including the regional commanding general in Paraíba, were killed. Fifth were the "pacifiers" who overthrew Washington Luís and, failing to negotiate a new government acceptable to the revolutionaries, passed power to Vargas. Sixth were the pacifists who did not define their position and awaited the struggle's outcome. The sergeants are difficult to categorize because of the lack of studies of their role. In all likelihood they were spread across the above groups. Both rebels and government forces handed out lieutenant's commissions to sergeants to fill gaps in the chain of command. That the above listing is possible indicates the extent of the collapse of discipline and organization. It is also important to emphasize that the various groups above were not the only armed forces involved in the revolution. There were the military police forces of the Liberal Alliance states and the large number of armed civilians led by state politicians, military police officers, or local *coroneis*.[96]

The revolution spotlighted the army's fall from grace. The revolutionaries of 1930 did not see the army as the *nação armada,* or "the people in arms," but as the principal military enemy that had to be eliminated or neutralized to insure victory. As Leitão de Carvalho observed, "the Brazilian army was the principal victim of the revolution."[97] The army was the bulwark of the old regime, not the agent of a New Brazil. Throughout the country the regional headquarters and commanders were the revolutionaries' initial targets. Their objective was to uncouple the chain of command, to neutralize the army's functional capacity so that it could not defend the government. And in that effort they succeeded so well that it would take much of the coming decade to put the army back together.

In 1889 army officers had lent their sabers to the creation of the republic; the brief period of rule by generals in the 1890s gave way to oligarchic rule and to the positioning of the army as the principal instrument for extending the authority of the national government across the map of Brazil. As the basis of the Old Republic was eroded by the social-economic changes of the early twentieth century, so too did the contradictions between the army officer corps' modernizing objectives and the strong-arm role it played in maintaining the established order undermine its self-confidence and self-esteem until it was incapable of resisting revolution.

CHAPTER 8

The Army and Revolutionary Politics

[E]verything has to do with the army.
—Oswaldo Aranha

The Revolution and the Army

The Revolution of 1930 ushered in a period of profound and turbulent change. And as unstable as the army was, it was the only national institution that the central government had at its disposal, so mastery of it was key to everything. At the end of the decade Oswaldo Aranha would comment to a foreign diplomat that "everything has to do with the army"[1] And Aranha's friend and colleague Lieutenant Colonel Pedro de Góes Monteiro would be one of the principal actors within the army in bringing about this predominance. In assessing the revolution and the political role of the army, Góes wrote his famous dictum: "Because the army is an essentially political instrument, its collective consciousness should be shaped so as to bring about the politics of the army and not politics in the army."[2] It should be said that army regulations supposedly limited political involvement. Article 73, for example, forbade "initiating, taking part in or tolerating religious or partisan political discussion inside a barracks or military establishment"; and Article 74 banned "public manifestation regarding partisan political topics." Along with the regulations specifying the rules of discipline (particularly those listed under Article 338) they would be repeatedly violated and ignored.[3]

After the revolution the army was in crisis, if not in chaos. From the outside a superficial glance would see its barracks, schools, communications systems, and personnel seemingly continuing as before, but closer examination would note that the command structure had many gaps and new faces but, most especially, that it now had a parallel, revolutionary chain of command under Góes Monteiro. Its members may have been clear to insiders at the time, but because the parallel structure issued no almanacs listing positions, historians are left with memoirs, newspaper references, and correspondence to figure out who was who.

In the next years there was a struggle for control of the army that eventually would blend the revolutionary army with the old army. This internal conflict had philosophical, traditional, practical, economic, political, and geopolitical aspects that were reflected in the various debates, reforms, foreign influences, revolts, and personal enmities and friendships discussed in earlier chapters. The influence of the rebels of the 1920s, called tenentes after 1930, would lessen with time, even while their moral and symbolic importance increased and eventually became a staple of Brazilian historiography and of army hagiography. The officer corps would be reconstituted with great pain and the army restructured slowly so that by November 1937 it was able to support Brazil's first long-term dictatorship, the Estado Novo (1937–45). But the process of reconstruction would be affected by frequent conspiracies and minor unit rebellions during 1931 and 1932, the São Paulo civil war of 1932, unrest and plotting at various levels in 1933 and 1934, by unruly sergeants stimulated by the example of Sergeant Fulgencia Batista taking power in Cuba, by adjustments to the new Constitution adopted in 1934, by the communist revolt of 1935, by the fierce repression of 1936, and by the slide toward dictatorship in 1937. It is to be marveled that the army accomplished anything against the backdrop of those events. In retrospect it is clear that in the 1930s the army was pushed, pulled, and self-propelled into the center of Brazilian politics to a degree that surpassed its experience at any time since the 1890s.[4] But what makes this period different from the past is that for the first time in the republic the military had an effective civilian moderator in Getúlio Dornelles Vargas.

In applying social science analysis to the post-1930 army, Edmundo Campos Coelho saw it developing from an organization into an institution. Its institutional status involved strengthening or creating specific agencies to form leaders who were consciously socialized and indoctrinated; isolating leaders from their followers so as to minimize pressures from below; and perfecting mechanisms to insulate the army from harmful outside influences, at the same time deepening and improving internal communications.[5]

On November 3, 1930, after forty-one years as a republic, Brazil once again entered a protracted period of regime change that would extend over several years. And as with the earlier period ushered in by the toppling of the empire, the violence and the real revolution came afterward. It was clear that the Liberal Alliance led by Getúlio Vargas had won, but what did that mean for the army? The Rio generals' last-minute deposition of Washington Luís had made unnecessary a war for São Paulo and Rio de Janeiro, thereby muddling who had won militarily. Were the old generals, such as Tasso Fragoso and

Mena Barreto, or the revolutionary officers, such as Góes Monteiro, Juarez Távora, and Oswaldo Cordeiro de Farias to reshape and reconstruct the army?

Revolutionary experience in other countries counseled that the new regime should not trust what remained of the old military command structure. Perhaps Vargas did not know the story of President Francisco Madero of Mexico, who had placed his trust in the federal army after driving out Porfirio Diaz in 1910, only to be rewarded with arrest and murder by his generals; but Vargas's instincts, sharpened in the often violent politics of Rio Grande's frontier, made him keenly aware of his dependence on armed strength.[6] Over the next years he would maneuver skillfully until both revolutionary and federal forces were dependent on him and once again there was one national army.

Vargas closed the Congress, state legislatures, and municipal assemblies and abrogated the Constitution of 1891 and those of the states. He replaced the governors of the states with his appointed interventors, seven of whom initially were military officers. Alone among the states, Minas Gerais kept its elected governor, Olegário Maciel. With a flurry of decrees Vargas swept the Old Republic into the archives.

Gradually Vargas assembled his cabinet, insisting on making his own choices. He believed that the "mentality created by the Revolution no longer permitted use of the old processes, applying purely political criteria" balancing the desires of state leaders.[7]

The driving force of the revolution, Oswaldo Aranha, became minister of justice, from which post he directed a tribunal that investigated the corruption of the deposed regime. Other ministries went to those with revolutionary credentials: Joaquim Francisco Assis Brasil, longtime gaúcho opposition leader, who the tenentes in 1924–27 had regarded as the civilian head of their movement, took over the Agriculture Ministry, although he spent most of his time on other political affairs; José Maria Whitaker, a paulista banker, former president of the Bank of Brasil (1920–22), assumed the Ministry of Treasury, providing foreign bankers reassurance of financial stability; José Américo de Almeida, native of Paraíba and security secretary of the "martyred" Governor João Pessôa, had been the civilian leader of the revolution in the northeast, took over the Ministry of Transportation and Public Works, which included the postal, telegraph and antidrought services; the Ministry of Foreign Affairs went to *mineiro* Afrânio de Melo Franco, whose son Virgílio had played a leading part in the conspiracy and whose own long experience in diplomacy made him an attractive and internationally recognized spokesman for the new regime; Lindolfo Leopoldo Boekel Collor, early collaborator and agent for Vargas, assumed the new Ministry of Labor, Industry, and Commerce; and finally, the new portfolio of Education and

Health went to Francisco Campos of Minas Gerais. Vargas may have had "revolutionary" motives for each selection, but he also managed to cover some of the traditional regional interests: Rio Grande do Sul had Agriculture and Labor; São Paulo had the Treasury; a northeasterner had Public Works, with its locally lucrative antidrought programs; and Minas had Foreign Affairs and Education and Health.

In the military posts he kept the officers that the old system had produced: Brigadier General José Fernandes Leite de Castro as minister of war, Brigadier General Alfredo Malan d'Angrogne as chief of the general staff, and Brigadier General Francisco Ramos de Andrade as head of the so-called *Casa Militar,* the president's personal military staff. All three had been approached by Vargas agent Lindolfo Collor before the outbreak and had supported removal of Washington Luís. Leite de Castro and Andrade Neves were natives of Rio Grande, and Malan had spent many years in the state; all three favored modernization and had extensive experience in Europe.[8] Curiously Leite de Castro, in the excitement of deposing Washington Luís, had not wanted to step aside for Vargas. According to General Malan he had asserted, "We made the revolution and the people want us to take charge of the country."[9]

Making him minister of war was an example of Vargas's habit of keeping potential power grabbers close and so intimately involved that they would be neutralized and co-opted. The general soon became an ardent backer of the revolution and of the tenentes. His personal staff of eleven officers included seven tenentes, among whom were Major Eduardo Gomes, a survivor of the Fort Copacabana rising of 1922; Newton Estillac Leal, a future minister of war and son of a colonel that the reader met in the Contestado; Captain Oswaldo Cordeiro de Faria, a Prestes Column veteran; Captain Dulcido Espirito Santo Cardoso, who was in the 1924 rising in São Paulo and imprisoned thereafter for fourteen months; and First Lieutenant Filinto Müller, who had been an artillery commander in São Paulo in 1924 and who would become infamous as chief of the Federal District police.[10]

Even with such well-placed allies, Colonel Góes Monteiro did not trust the Rio garrison's officers and continued bringing revolutionary forces from the interior and maintaining a parallel command structure. At this stage Vargas confided to his diary that his own dictatorial powers should be limited so as not to violate the ideals of the revolution by continuing the restrictive methods of the old regime.[11] However, he did not act on the thought. He must have come to think that limiting his power as provisional dictator would threaten the new regime.

Vargas was at the center of an unruly coalition, whose components had goals that clashed with each other. After all the talk of revolution, he and his colleagues were to find that ideas were one thing and implementing them another. He tolerated, even encouraged, rivalries among ministers and other intraregime competitors until one side was exhausted politically or until a consensus emerged. He was very patient and had trained himself to listen to and to study those around him, including his enemies, until he understood how to deal with them. He feared failure more than his adversaries ever suspected. At several points from 1930 onward he regarded suicide as the way to deal with disgrace. Affable and attentive, he left cabinet ministers, advisers, and his numerous correspondents with the impression that he took them and their ideas, wants, and worries seriously. What he really thought on an issue he often entrusted only to his diary, whose very existence was unknown to other than a few family members until 1995! Hollywood studios never would have cast him in a film as a dictator; he simply did not look the part. Short, increasingly pudgy and balding with the years, he was not the man on horseback that the 1930 revolutionary posters portrayed; rather he proved to be an affable cigar-smoking golfer, whose best hole was the nineteenth.

The tenentes wanted more than they could accomplish. Vargas gave them his ear but kept them so busy with immediate political tasks that they were never able to build their own base of power and became steadily, although gradually, more dependent on him. He had tenentes assigned to the federal district's military police, to various ministries, and to the states, either as interventors or assistants. Counting officers of all ranks, there were seventy-four men with such assignments in 1931. Into the next year the tenentes were riding high. Indeed, Vargas played them against the regular army and vice versa. The tenentes, urged on by Góes Monteiro and Aranha, formed the 3rd of October Club, with branches throughout the country to provide a forum for discussing revolutionary doctrine and an extragovernmental vehicle for spreading it.[12] The very existence of the club and its branches became a bone of contention with some general officers who objected to the extrainstitutional organization as a threat to discipline.

The stalwarts of the "Old Republic," including the former president, former minister of war, former mayor of Rio, and former senators such as Antônio Azeredo had been sent off into exile. Most important, by the end of November 1930 Vargas began a purge of the officer corps, starting with senior officers "whose attitude was incompatible with the Revolution." This cleanup extended over the next year. Of the nine generals of division (equal to a U.S. major general), the then top rank, only two were spared, Tasso Fragoso and João de Deus Menna Barreto. Of the twenty-four brigadier generals, seven survived the initial retirements.[13] The cuts into the list of combat colonels went even deeper; some forty colonels were pensioned off. And considering that the list then legally had ninety-nine spaces (although in 1931 it only had 83 names), these retirements severely limited those officers available for future promotion to general. By the end of the decade Getúlio had a hand in shaping the top ranks of the army to a degree as no civilian since Pedro II.

In this atmosphere promotions were an especially delicate matter. The commanders of the reconstituted army had to understand and have the ability to reach reformist goals. Arguments over promotions caused personal and institutional tensions, pressures, and afflictions. In addition to the question of how to balance the services of those who opposed the old regime with those who defended it, Brig. Gen. Firmino Antonio Borba, whose presidency of the promotions commission was set aside by the appointment of commission member Brig. Gen. Malan d'Angrogne as chief of the general staff. Borba publicly refused to attend further meetings because he believed that date of rank, which gave him seniority, should take precedence over position, even that of chief of staff. The dispute distressed Malan so deeply that on January 6, 1931, at the end of the workday, his aide found him slumped in a chair in his dressing room, bathed in sweat and unable to speak. He was taken home in an ambulance, but the medical doctors could not reverse the effects of the stroke. He lingered for a year, but the army lost one of its best officers to the emotional trauma that continued to hamper its reconstruction. Not long afterward, however, the minister and president revised army regulations to say that the chief of staff was to chair the commission.[14]

The debate over promotion standards united Góes Monteiro and Bertoldo Klinger in objecting to the criteria and the way Vargas carried out the March 1931 promotions because the "selection was infected with personal considerations of the moment." Góes protested to Minister Leite de Castro that he had not expected his new colonelcy, nor did he feel that he merited it.[15] Góes, Klinger, and other such professionally oriented officers saw a politically based promotions system as a major obstacle to improving the army's professional standards. Political criteria, they argued, as had the fallen Malan, could not take priority over performance in training and in command. In mid-February, in order to reassure the revolutionary-minded, Vargas signed a decree authorizing administrative retirement of officers not sufficiently prorevolution. These included eight of the twenty-three colonels then serving in the artillery, including Young Turk Colonel Olyntho de Mesquita Vasconcelos after he had the nerve to write to Vargas protesting his being passed over in the promotions to general. He objected that the promotion processes of the "new Republic . . . are the same as the old and the [type of] men are the very same." He accused Getúlio of relegating to a secondary level those men who had struggled for a decade against the governments that the revolution had replaced and of rewarding those who had been committed to, and favored by, those very governments, especially that of Washington Luís. "The current promotions," he fumed, "were a great injustice by Your Excellency" against those "who had placed above their own interests, the principles and the well-being of their Pátria." Curiously, among those promoted to brigadier general were three of his Young Turk colleagues: Col. José Maria Franco Ferreira of the cavalry and Cols. Cesar Augusto Parga Rodrigues and Bertoldo Klinger of the artillery.[16]

In that same month, giving shape to his dreams of reforming the army, Góes Monteiro compiled a list of proposals with fellow revolutionary officers Captain Alcides Gonçalves Etchegoyen and First Lieutenant Jurandir da Bizarria Mamede. Nineteen other officers joined them in signing what they called a "secret pact" to work toward desired reforms. While the revolutionary government was reorganizing the country, the document declared that, the armed forces must guarantee the regime's survival. Until a constitution could be written (no deadline specified), Vargas needed and deserved the military's unequivocal support. The signers identified three regional military spokesmen—Góes Monteiro for the south, Leite de Castro for the central states, and Juarez Távora for the north. They would gather revolutionary officers' views and convey them to Vargas. The document called for commanders at every level favorable to the revolution, and asserted that those who had not pledged themselves to the revolution should be purged or at least assigned to locations where they could do no harm. Revolutionaries should control the crucial promotions commission. Such an attitude contradicted Góes's professional emphasis noted above. But then, throughout his career Góes Monteiro often assumed contradictory positions. Critics pointed out that the three delegates to be charged with revolutionizing the army were the very ones who, until then, had been unable to restore order and discipline in the army. As Captain Heitor da Fontoura Rangel pointedly declared: "Until now the army hasn't known how to govern itself, how can it aspire to govern States or the Republic?!" Officers of like mind refused to sign, unwilling to support what they regarded as an emerging "republic of soldiers and workers, of sergeants and illiterate lieutenants" commissioned from the ranks; in short they feared that the revolution would produce a Soviet-style regime. But their deepest concern seems to have been the subversion of military hierarchy.

How could captains or colonels command generals? It would be an inversion of hierarchy. Setting aside the traditional chain of command, they argued, would destroy what discipline remained and would force out capable, honest officers:

Six months [have] already passed and disorder, anarchy and indiscipline still prevail in the army! What have the revolutionary military chiefs done up to now . . . to benefit the army or Brazil? . . . The revolution was meant to restore the broken, ruined, and disorganized Brazil. We are to take care of the Army and the civilians to look after the politics and administration of the country. They are the majority, we the minority. This duty is their's [*sic*], that is our's [*sic*]. . . . We must all unite around

President Getúlio Vargas, delegate of the people and our commander-in-chief, leaving him free to think and to act. . . . [W]e must remain firmly united at his side, aiding him as he needs, with unselfishness, sincerity, and loyalty.[17]

What they needed to do was to fulfill the promises of the Liberal Alliance, the promises of the revolution. But how could they do that with officers who were not convinced revolutionaries? Of course, part of the problem was that 1930 was a reformist movement rather than a truly revolutionary one. It did not intend to eliminate poverty or even redistribute national wealth or income; it did not propose to cut up the huge fazendas that dominated agriculture and restructure landholding more equitably; it did not set out to eliminate illiteracy. The revolutionaries wanted an honest government that would promote modernization that included industrialization and economic development but with little restitching of the social fabric.

A developmentalist revolution had no models at that time (the Soviet one being unacceptable), so the rhetoric on all sides tended to be that of some version of liberal democracy. In some ways what was taking shape could be compared to the various goals and programs of Franklin Roosevelt's New Deal, without its redistributive aspects. But that example in the United States was still a few years in the future, so at this point the Brazilians were on their own. In this context the military goals of men such as Góes Monteiro looked more like the reformist ideas of the "Young Turks" of 1913. It was agreement of officers on those reform goals that allowed the various factions of the 1920s and of 1930 eventually to work together for the good of the service. They could agree that Brazil was a Pátria "worthy of better sons"[18] and that it needed a modern army to defend its untold riches from narrow-minded regionalist politicians and envious, greedy foreigners. The country had to be changed enough so that it could be adequately defended. The problem was that the rhetoric available was that of the eighteenth-century American, French, and Spanish-American Revolutions against foreign oppressors and/or monarchial institutions. The revolutionaries of 1930 liked the jargon of those revolutions but not their realities. The revolution that they had in mind was to be from the top, not from the bottom.

And at its top the army was in a crisis of leadership. With Malan gone, the general staff not only had no head but lacked its two subchiefs as well. The next ranking officer was Col. Arnaldo de Souza Paes de Andrade, who had commanded the government troops that had blocked the revolutionary forces in the south of São Paulo. He invited his friend, Colonel Leitão de Carvalho, one of the leading reformist Young Turks of the 1910s, who had turned away an offer to be military commander of the 1930 forces and who was still under a cloud of suspicion that kept him without assignment, to become interim deputy chief. To revolutionary officers it looked as if the reactionaries of the "old army" were regaining control. They would have even more reason to regard the general staff dubiously in the paulista crisis of 1932.

At least some of the government's practices had a familiarity about them. As governments had done during the Old Republic, the Vargas regime was careful to see that the retired officers, including the ones it had forced from active service, had reasonably comfortable pensions. It also followed the old practice of cutting enlisted personnel and using the savings to cover pay increases for the officers. In early 1931 the retired list included 15 marshals (a wartime rank), 80 major generals, 324 brigadier generals, 102 colonels, 126 lieutenant colonels, 363 majors, 323 captains, 191 first lieutenants, and 581 second lieutenants. By comparison the active officer ranks consisted of 11 major generals, 26 brigadier generals, 109 colonels, 164 lieutenant colonels, 301 majors, 717 captains, 875 first lieutenants, 239 second lieutenants, and 504 second lieutenants *commissionados.* Both active and retired ranks received moderate pay increases in early 1932.[19]

Clearly, the competition among captains and first lieutenants had to have been fierce. If all the majors were replaced simultaneously, *which would not occur,* only 42 percent of the captains could hope for promotion. Upward movement necessarily meant that many would be forced out, or they could expect to stay in rank for long years. A frustrated officer corps did not make an efficient vehicle of reform. And the already crisis-ridden lower-officer ranks acquired an additional frustration in late May 1932. The revolutionary movements of the 1920s complicated officer corps membership and relative position within each rank. Probably the most controversial issue regarding army personnel was the status of the academy students expelled in 1922. In the fabled uprising of July 5, 1922, aimed at preventing the inauguration of President-elect Arthur Bernardes, the officers of the academy at Realengo had led an attempt to take control of neighboring Vila Militar. Immobilized by artillery and armored cars, they had surrendered in failure and were summarily dismissed from the army.

One of the tenente aims in the Revolution of 1930 had been a general amnesty and reinstatement of all those officers and academy students ejected during the 1920s, and they successfully lobbied with Vargas and Leite de Castro for its enactment. As a result 508 discharged students, after a decade of civilian life, were reinstated and put through a year's course and then declared first lieutenants—the rank they would have held if they had not been expelled. This action stirred a hornet's nest of discontent because they were placed and numbered on the army list ahead of first lieutenants who had entered the army after 1922, including those who had fought against the Old Republic. Overnight these latter lieutenants, with six or seven years of postacademy service and advanced training, found themselves pushed back by 508 positions on the army list by men who were less prepared. In response 163 first lieutenants sent a collective protest telegram to Minister of War Leite de Castro.

Matters were made more awkward by the fact that many of the 1922 group had remained aloof from the later revolutionary activity, whereas those they were squeezing had been the backbone of the Revolution of 1930. Each group acquired a distinctive label. Those of 1922 were called *picolés* (popsicles) because they had been cool to subsequent conspiracies, or, as some said, they came ready-made as junior officers; and the lieutenants of 1930 were tagged *rabanetes* (radishes), as being red radicals outside and white conservatives inside. There was deep sentiment across the ranks that the picolés were undeserving. Back in 1925 Tasso Fragoso, as chief of staff, had warned against such reinstatement, arguing that "it was an error to give into impulses of the heart allowing backsliders and laggards to achieve by toleration what they could not obtain by intelligence or work."[20]

The minister retaliated by ordering the protesters confined for thirty days in punishment for their "offense against discipline." Word of his action provoked a storm of telegrams, from officers all over the country, expressing solidarity with the 163 offenders, thereby inviting similar punishment. If he continued arresting those who signed telegrams, he would shortly have to imprison the majority of the officer corps. Vargas called on First Lieutenant Juracy Magalhães, federal interventor of Bahia, to "mediate" between the harassed minister and his unruly officers. Humiliated by the situation, Leite de Castro struggled to control the army. Only the tenentes supported his efforts to reintegrate the rebels of 1922; most officers saw an injustice being done to those young officers dislodged from their earned places on the official list. The compromise solution was to create parallel rolls of first lieutenants, those of 1922 and those commissioned later, who would rank with, but not before or after, each other. Those who felt prejudiced by future promotions could seek redress in the military courts.

The Civil War of 1932

The realities of Brazilian politics intruded into these internal army debates and further split the already fractured officer corps as 1931 slipped by. The major political problem was how to impose rule of the central government on the state of São Paulo. Given that the Liberal Alliance had turned to violence to strip São Paulo of its control of the presidency and thereby its domination of the "politics of the governors" system, it is understandable that the more radical tenentes wanted to keep the state's power in check. The appointed interventor, João Alberto Lins de Barros, native of Pernambuco, became the focal point of paulista complaints and found it nearly impossible to govern the state. It was not just that he was a northeasterner, in effect a foreigner to paulistas; it was that he superseded the Partido Democratico (PD), which had been in opposition within the state's politics since 1924 and which had been a member of the Liberal Alliance and which saw itself as a partner in the revolution. The party had contributed to the ouster of Washington Luís, and its leaders believed that one of their number should be interventor in their own state. This was not simply a question of ego, or even state pride, but also a practical matter of who controlled the vast patronage system that the revolution made available, because the interventor appointed the heads of the state's municípios, cities, and various agencies. João Alberto gradually placed army officers in those positions, excluding the state's politicians affiliated with either the allied PD or the Partido Republicana Paulista (PRP) of Washington Luís. The paulistas complained that the state was suffering military occupation and that they were being treated differently from other states with military interventors.

The PD was particularly embittered. During Vargas's passage through the state en route to take office in Rio, people had lined the railway tracks waving and cheering, and in towns, including the capital, he had been received in a climate of triumph and euphoria. The president of the PD, Francisco Morato, who had been named governor by the short-lived *junta pacificador* when it imprisoned the president in Rio, had expected Vargas to confirm his appointment. The dynamics within the "revolutionary group" produced a different scenario. Gaúcho leaders Antonio Flores da Cunha and João Neves da Fontoura favored Miguel Costa, the paulista Força Pública officer who had played a key role in the 1924 rising in São Paulo and the subsequent "Miguel Costa-Prestes Column." He was one of the troop commanders in October 1930, and after the death of Siqueira Campos, he had been touted as the great "paulista revolutionary hero." In the triumphal crossing through the state his name was often bracketed with Vargas in the cheers at railway stations. Apparently he refused to accept the position and opposed the appointment of Morato. When the latter met with Vargas on the "Victory Train," Getúlio told him that João Alberto would be the "Military Delegate of the Revolution" to the state but that it was a provisional appointment and the state government or secretariat would be composed of "notable civilian personalities."[21]

Also, the paulista workers had embraced Vargas as their hero. He had promised social justice and a government that would speak for the workers. João Alberto was representing the new regime, not merely his own point of view. The workers had celebrated the defeat of their state's politicians in October 1930 by burning down the hated prison, locally called the Bastille of Cambuci, where labor leaders had been imprisoned, tortured, and murdered. As Joel Wolf commented, Cambuci was symbolic of "the false promises of working-class life in the São Paulo of the 1920s." Getúlio's pledges of "improved conditions, a minimum wage, mandatory vacations, consumer cooperatives, and the regulation of women's and children's labor" were what brought throngs into the streets to cheer his name. The worldwide Depression had made itself felt in reducing market demand at home and abroad, causing the city's factories to cut production to a few days a week and throwing some one hundred thousand men and women out of work. Nervous industrialists stockpiled arms and made special arrangements with the police for protection. Vargas maneuvered to harness the workers' enthusiasm without provoking a social revolution.[22]

From October 1930 until February 1931 the PD had "shared" government with João Alberto, naming its members to key posts, such as mayor of the state capital, chief of police, and secretary of treasury. The PD accepted this division of power as unavoidable during this revolutionary period. However, as interventor, João Alberto suggested by his actions that his idea of revolution differed from that of the PD. Without consulting the chief of police, he allowed the Partido Communista Brasileira (PCB) to reorganize and to hold a major rally that ended with the police knocking heads. Even more disturbing was his decree ordering the State Bank to divide up certain *fazendas*. Then there was the threat of a military-sponsored Revolutionary Legion of São Paulo. In November 1930 aircraft had leafleted the state capital with a call for a popular movement in support of the revolution and against politicians. The leaflets were signed by the military revolutionaries João Alberto, Miguel Costa, and Colonel Mendonça Lima. At that stage the Revolutionary Legion was part of Oswaldo Aranha and Góes Monteiro's unsuccessful effort to form a national revolutionary party.

All of this put João Alberto in suspicious light. Not only was he an officer foreign to São Paulo, but, worse, he evinced communist tendencies! PD leaders pressured Vargas to replace him and they urged that the Rio government take charge of "social questions." João Alberto defended himself, arguing that he had no ties to communists, who were so few that they could be tolerated as inconsequential. Instead of removing him, Vargas, pressed by Aranha and Juarez Távora, confirmed him as head of the state. As if to soften this move, the state government issued a communiqué, in defense of "public order" and "private property," prohibiting communist and anarchist "agitation." At the same time, to assuage the problems of the working class, the interventor formed a committee to study the "labor question." Like Henry Ford in the United States, the paulista industrialists did not want the national government telling them how to deal with their workers. If there were to be unions and negotiated hours and wages, they wanted the state government, not Rio de Janeiro, to control the process. João Alberto's insistence that they negotiate with their workers provoked owners to close their factories in mid-1931.

Strikes, lockouts, and street violence formed the social backdrop against which the political and military events were played out.

Paulista elite calls for João Alberto's replacement with a civilian from the state and their clamor for a constitutional convention perhaps had more to do with their desire to protect their own interests than with distress about the interventor's origins or their commitment to constitutional government, much less democracy. Repeatedly they referred to their desire to restore the state's autonomy. They opposed national intervention in economic and social policies so much that they were willing to start a civil war to regain control of the state. On January 17, 1931, the PD issued a manifesto breaking with Vargas. And on the twenty-fifth a public rally commemorating the founding of the city deteriorated into an attack on the gaúcho center and tearing down of the Rio Grande do Sul flag. With this hostility symbolically aimed at the Vargas government, the Liberator Party of Rio Grande sent telegrams of solidarity to the PD, and in mid-February the PD solidified a United Paulista Front with its old enemy the Partido Republicana Paulista. Miguel Costa and his followers in the Partido Popular Progressista stood with the federal regime. Vargas's signing, on February 24, of an electoral law setting the date for voting for a constituent assembly to draft the new Constitution was not enough to appease the irritated spirits.[23]

Lack of discipline up and down the chain of command characterized the army in 1931 and on into 1932. In January 1931 soldiers and sergeants of the Fifth Infantry Regiment in Lorena (SP) demanded the replacement of the regimental commander, and sergeants of the Third Infantry in Rio de Janeiro tried to appeal directly to Vargas to remove their commander. In March Minister Leite de Castro reportedly asked a group of officers meeting in Niterói for their support against opponents in the government. In the next month a "Proclamation to the Army" circulated in posts in Rio Grande appealing to "old" and "new" revolutionary officers to unite in installing a military dictatorship that would eliminate the cancerous regionalism that sought to splinter the armed forces. In moments of great change such as the present the document proclaimed that the army should tutor and direct Brazil. In October officers opposed to the "revolutionary" activities of their colleagues issued a pamphlet entitled "Union of the Military Class," calling for reestablishment of discipline and complete dedication to the profession. Generals Mena Barreto, Pantaleão Teles Ferreira, and Bertoldo Klinger publicly expressed their support for renewed discipline. On October 29–31, 1931, a revolt of the Twenty-first Light Infantry in Recife spread to the dock and streetcar workers, requiring units from Paraíba, Rio Grande do Norte, and Ceará to end the uprising. A twenty-three-year-old first lieutenant of artillery, Ernesto Geisel (who would be president of Brazil from 1974 to 1978), persuaded the holdouts to surrender.

In its early planning this revolt may have been part of a broader conspiracy involving the commander of the Seventh Military Region, Brigadier General José Sotero de Menezes Jr., who was transferred shortly thereafter and subsequently implicated in a plot to overturn the government for which he was exiled to Portugal. The Twenty-first Infantry's commander and executive officer were killed in the fighting. The unit distributed twelve hundred rifles to civilians, which likely explains why 1,024 civilians were arrested in the aftermath along with 15 officers, 60 sergeants, and 300 soldiers. The revolt in Recife pointed up a question that interlaced discipline and promotion policies, namely what to do with the hundreds of "Commissioned Lieutenants." The rebelling battalion had a half dozen such men, all of whom were reported to have been promoted from enlisted ranks during the Revolution of 1930. Supposedly, many "commissioned lieutenants" had so little education and were so lacking in military aptitude that they could not obtain permanent commissions, but although they held officer status, they supposedly were often a disruptive influence in their units. The sudden rise from enlisted man to officer allegedly had gone to their heads. However, this interpretation does not appear to be supported by the career information in the army list for 1931; out of 504 such *Commissionados* in the combat arms, only 111 could have been commissioned in late 1930. Officers wanting to keep their own ranks closed to sergeants may have used the revolt to spread negative propaganda.[24]

In May 1932 there was another rebellion of sergeants in the Eighteenth Battalion of Light Infantry in Mato Grosso, followed by a discovered conspiracy of "communist" sergeants and junior officers in Rio de Janeiro that resulted in hundreds of arrests, followed in June by contradictory movements in the Federal District and Rio Grande do Sul for and against Minister Leite de Castro. Each of these conspiracies appeared to have had links with civilian politicians.[25] The total of all these revolts and conspiracies indicated the incredibly low level of discipline and effective command in the army. Harry W. Brown, the quartermaster corps clerk, who was the backbone of the military attaché's office in the United States Embassy, concluded a report on some of the foregoing by commenting that "after thirteen years of interested observation of the Brazilian Army and its undertakings, [I am] forced to the conclusion that the organization has reached its low ebb of morale, discipline and efficiency."[26]

Enforcement of military discipline reflected a traditional saying in Brazilian politics: "for our friends, everything; for our enemies, the law." Acts of indiscipline were punished according to the malefactors' connections, rather than army regulations. For example, on February 24, 1932, a civil-military group, "the 24th of February Club," which wanted an immediate return to the 1891 Constitution, had scheduled a demonstration to celebrate the provisional regime's new electoral code. Minister of Justice Maurício Cardoso and Rio chief of police João Batista Lusardo (effectively head of national police services) gave permission for the commemoration but later were forced to cancel the affair because of threats of violence from the "3rd of October Club." A street fight that would have involved officers on both sides was thus avoided. Not content with suppressing free assembly, the 3rd of October Club organized three truckloads of soldiers to assault the offices and employees of the antiregime *Diário Carioca* (Rio), which had been editorializing for return to constitutional government and had just published an article critical of the tenentes. The justice minister and police chief, both gaúchos, demanded that Vargas order arrests, but Army Minister Leite de Castro asserted that "the 'boys'[the tenentes] had done to the *Diário Carioca* what he would have done if he were twenty years younger." Vargas, according to Lasardo, answered their protests: "But what do you want me to do? If the boys did this because the *Diário Carioca* was attacking me? I can't be against them!" No one was punished. The principal newspapers of Brazil protested the attack with an unprecedented 24-hour suspension of publication.[27]

The two gaúchos resigned, and Interventor Flores da Cunha, who was in Rio and had observed these events, wavered in his loyalty. The politicians of Rio Grande do Sul, who had so fervently supported the revolution, were on the verge of a complete break with Getúlio because of his alliance with the "boys."

The provisional president saw himself as trying to maintain military backing. His diary shows that he knew that soldiers from the First Cavalry Regiment were involved and, somewhat different from Lusardo's report, noted that Leite de Castro told him that he could not restrain the officers who were disposed to attack any other newspapers that criticized the government and the military, and he feared that contrary disciplinary action would provoke a greater military crisis. To himself Getúlio wrote: "I have to choose between the military forces that support the government and a subversive journalism, backed and instigated by politicians against the government. I am at a cross-road that demands a decision."[28]

Leite de Castro's unwillingness to punish those officers and soldiers who assaulted the *Diário Carioca* frustrated their immediate superior officer, General João Gomes Ribeiro, commander of the First Military Region, which included Rio de Janeiro. Unable to move the minister to act, he issued an order of the day condemning disorder and calling on the region's troops to avoid politics and to hold fast to their military duties. Minister Leite de Castro responded by transferring Gomes's subordinates without consulting him, and subordinate officers slighted him by going over his head to the minister to settle matters within Gomes's authority. His fall from grace was noted in the newspapers, and the minister let the reports stand. Vargas decided to replace

Gomes with Góes Monteiro. In late May the commander of the Third Military Region in Rio Grande do Sul, General Andrade Neves, asked for replacement because he too was frustrated by ministerial meddling in his command, most especially the transfer of his aide Major Rangel, quoted above, from Porto Alegre to Uruguaiana. Rangel regarded his transfer as retaliation for his open comments favoring return to constitutional government and his refusal to join the 3rd of October Club branch recently opened in Porto Alegre. He publicly said that he was the victim of the tenente clique in control of the minister's office. Andrade Neves's great popularity in the state led to protests at the prospect of his departure. The situation was potentially volatile because gaúcho politicians had formally withdrawn their support of the Vargas government. Paulista political leaders and opinion makers, such as Júlio de Mesquita Filho of the newspaper O Estado de São Paulo, worked to build a united front with the gaúchos believing that they needed Rio Grande do Sul for an armed showdown with the provisional government.[29] They envisioned an alliance with Rio Grande and Minas Gerais that would by their simple unity topple Vargas and make a fight unnecessary.

To make matters worse, while Góes Monteiro was head of the Second Military Region (São Paulo, Mato Grosso, and Goiás), he went from ally to opponent of native son Miguel Costa, who commanded the state's Força Pública, and controlled the Revolutionary Legion. This latter organization had been founded in November 1930 to "guarantee" tenente reforms, which broadly sought a strong, central government capable of intervening in Brazil's economic and social life; of checking the power of private latifundios, trusts, and monopolies; and of protecting the national patrimony from absorption by foreign syndicates. It called for rejection of foreign models in favor of Brazilian solutions to Brazilian problems. In April 1931, in disagreement with Costa's active politicking and Interventor João Alberto's backing of it, General Isidoro Dias Lopes tried to resign as commander of the Second Military Region, but Vargas put him off. A rebellion on April 28, 1931, of Força Pública officers and PD politicos against Costa and João Alberto was snuffed out with the arrest of some two hundred police and the subsequent transfers or replacement of army officers, including General Isidoro. This affair was likely connected to strikes and layoffs in paulistano industries and to João Alberto's forcing factory owners to negotiate with workers.[30]

Góes Monteiro was supposed to bring peace to this hotbed of discontent; instead, the state's ambience grew more poisonous. Góes's fondness for giving newspaper interviews resulted in hundreds of confusing and contradictory remarks. João Alberto felt isolated and resigned in July 1931.

To calm the agitation, Vargas accepted the idea of appointing a civilian paulista as the state's interventor. The first name that seemed to gain approval was the longtime editor of the Estado de São Paulo, Plínio Barreto, who for a few days during the Revolution of 1930 had been provisional governor. But Miguel Costa raised objections that included an article Barreto had written in 1922 criticizing the rebels of July 5. The choice then fell on a state judge, Laudo Ferreira de Camargo, whose ties to the PD provided a base of support, but also contributed to the rising hostility of Miguel Costa and his labor allies. Once installed as interventor, Camargo insisted that Costa give up one of his two positions, either remaining as secretary of state security or as commander of the Força Pública. He then compelled a decision by creating a new secretariat of justice that included security, thereby demoting the position and its occupant. As a result, tension in the state rose higher. Camargo managed to make matters even worse by granting amnesty to various officials of the pre-1930 government and reappointing several judges who had been deposed by the revolutionaries, which raised federal objections that he had overstepped his authority and led to his resignation in November 1931.[31] Vargas then turned back to the army for what he hoped would be a safe interventor, Colonel Manuel Rabelo.

In the midst of all this confusion the Bank of England sent Otto Niemeyer to Brazil to review the financial and debt situation with an eye to preserving Brazil's ability to maintain the value and exchangeability of its currency. At the end of July, while worrying about conspiracies, revolts, and endless rumors, Vargas was reading the Niemeyer report that recommended budgetary balance and exchange stabilization, as well as creation of a privately held central bank on the model of the Bank of England. In late September the country's English finances collapsed, halting pound/*milreis* convertibility, and in response the government suspended Brazil's foreign debt payments. The sudden inability to obtain foreign exchange and letters of credit pushed down the price of coffee, which, of course, hurt São Paulo, the center of King Coffee's realm.[32]

The Revolutionary Legions in São Paulo and Minas Gerais had grown in numbers and noisiness, and although they probably were not real military threats, they appeared to reinforce the already formidable state forces of the country's two richest states. On September 30 Vargas was sufficiently worried to summon a night meeting of his kitchen cabinet, which he referred to as "the revolutionary soviet," made up of Oswaldo Aranha, General Leite de Castro, Rear Admiral José Isaías de Noronha (navy minister), General Góes Monteiro, Major Juarez Távora, and the new interventor of the Federal District, Dr. Pedro Ernesto. They discussed the two legions, the attitudes of Miguel Costa and of the mineiro government. Vargas argued that it was necessary to secure the predominance of federal military forces over the police of the two states, "so as to be able to act later." He ordered Leite de Castro to take the appropriate steps.

Góes Monteiro and Interventor Rabelo both requested that more federal troops be sent to reinforce the garrisons in São Paulo. But Vargas decided to avoid the alarm that such sudden troop movements would cause by calling Miguel Costa to Rio for a chat. He convinced him that it would be best to give up command of the paulista Força Pública.[33] It is not known what he said, but Getúlio was obviously persuasive.

Góes Monteiro's extremely rapid rise to brigadier general was an exception to the peacetime promotion rules. His career embraced most of the years of this study. He had entered the preparatory school of Realengo in 1903, and he and his schoolmates had been kept out of the 1904 so-called Vaccination Revolt by its commandant, Col. Hermes da Fonseca. And because the government closed the Escola Militar da Praia Vermelha for its role in the revolt, Góes and his fellow graduates of the preparatory had to go to Porto Alegre to continue their studies at the Escola da Guerra. This bit of fate set him on a path that linked this son of Alagoas to Rio Grande do Sul in intimate ways. As a military student he was drawn into the political agitation that still afflicted the state from the violent conflicts of the early 1890s. He joined the group of law students who were publishing a partisan newspaper, *O Debate,* under the editorial orientation of student Getúlio Dornelles Vargas, for whom the young Góes wrote on military topics. Graduated as an aspirante in 1910, he was assigned to the Railroad Battalion in Cruz Alta, then under the command of Gen. Fernando Setembrino de Carvalho. Promoted to second lieutenant in 1914, he was assistant to the commander of the Second Cavalry Brigade in Uruguaiana. Before reassignment to Rio for an engineering course in 1916, he fell in love and married Conceição Saint Pastous, of a leading family of Alegrete. It would be his brother-in-law who in 1930 would bring him into face-to-face contact with Oswaldo Aranha, then constructing the revolutionary conspiracy. It was the depth of Góes's involvement with the Rio Grande-Uruguay-Argentine frontier region that contributed to his credibility with both the federal army authorities and the revolutionaries in 1930. While in Rio de Janeiro in 1916–18, he was attracted to the teachings of the Young Turks and their Indigenous Mission at the military school. In 1918 he returned to the Rio Grande frontier to command a squadron of the Sixth Independent Cavalry Regiment in which post he was made a first lieutenant. In 1921 he was back in Rio studying with the French military mission; and when the flag of rebellion rose in 1922, he was in the general staff school. The French gave him high marks and praise that, together with his familiarity with Rio Grande, led to a request from the minister's staff that he prepare a plan of defense for the state government against its opponents in the state civil war of 1923–24. In it he outlined the use of provisional forces to be raised among the gaúchos of the frontier zone. Two of the outstanding leaders of such units in that conflict were Flores da Cunha and Oswaldo Aranha, both of whom later led provisional corps against tenente rebels Prestes, Cordeiro de Farias, and brothers Nelson and Alcides

Etchegoyen. In January 1924 Góes was promoted to captain and named instructor of strategy at the general staff school. The tenente seizure of São Paulo in July 1924, led to his being sent to Santos, where a chance meeting with the admiral commanding the port's occupation resulted in his preparing a plan of attack that became the basis of legalist plans to defeat the rebels. At several points, after the rebels retreated from the paulista capital and evolved into the Prestes Column, Góes was frequently the legalist operations officer that organized forces in the field against them. He played that role in the fighting in Paraná, western Minas Gerais, and in Bahia, usually under his mentor General Mariante. In October 1926 Góes rose to major. The next year the Prestes Column sought exile in Bolivia, and when Mariante became commander of army aviation, which had just been recognized as a new combat arm, Góes went with him as his chief of staff. In October 1928 Góes was promoted to lieutenant colonel, which is the rank he held when he went to Rio Grande in January 1930 to assume command of the Third Independent Regiment of Cavalry in São Luís das Missões.

According to the 1929 rules, promotion to colonel required two years in a command position. From colonel to brigadier general was a presidential choice from a recommended list. Góes made colonel in March 1931, and in May Vargas named him a general. It is possible that he was not on the list submitted to the president, which may be why he initially said he did not want promotion. Certainly two months between colonel and general was highly unusual. But as the above career sketch indicates, he had no reason to be embarrassed about the quality of his performance to that point.[34]

Generals Gomes Ribeiro's and Andrade Neves's disaffection from Minister Leite de Castro and the constant complaints and rumors that questioned his loyalty led Vargas to begin the difficult search for an acceptable successor. In late May 1932 General Gomes's request to be relieved from the First Military Region in Rio gave Vargas a graceful way to get Góes Monteiro out of São Paulo by putting him in that post. In addition to deepening tension in that state and rumors of plots at every hand, the "popsicle" and "radish" controversy discussed above was in full flavor! Gomes had been approached by Col. Euclides Figueiredo about raising the garrison in Rio on the side of a revolt in São Paulo, and his vague response made the colonel believe that he was with them. He had replied that if it were truly a national movement, with Minas, São Paulo, and Mato Grosso joining together, "I believe that the garrison here will cooperate." Things did not work out that way, and police carefully watched General Gomes. His son José, a lieutenant, did join the paulista cause as an aviator, and died in an attack on a ship at Santos in September 1932.[35]

The paulistas showed more verve and energy in organizing their propaganda than in conducting an effective military campaign. Unhappily for them,

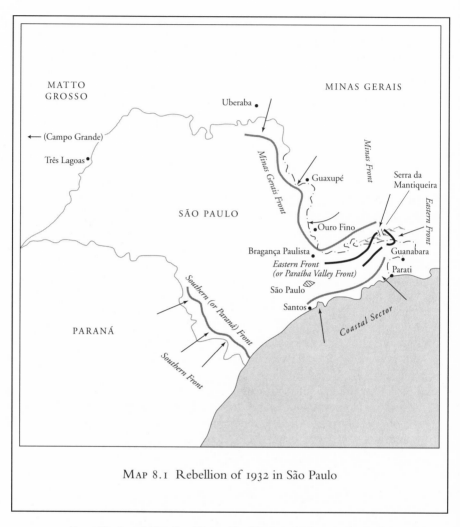

MAP 8.1 Rebellion of 1932 in São Paulo

SOURCE: From *The Army in Brazilian History*, edited by Luiz Paulo Macedo Cavalho. Rio de Janeiro & Salvador, Ba.: Biblioteca do Exército & Odebrecht, 1998. 4 vols. Redrawn by Bill Nelson. Used with permission of Biblioteca do Exército, Rio de Janeiro.

their planners showed more wishful thinking than cold analysis of capabilities. It is ironic that they attracted Bertoldo Klinger, who made brigadier general in 1931 and who was chief of the Mato Grosso Military District, to be commander of the rebellion's forces. The reader will recall that Klinger had declined to accept the command or to participate in 1930 because he believed that the revolutionaries lacked sufficient strength. Yet here, he signed on to a poorly organized and under-supplied operation, with little chance of success. Perhaps now he regretted his decision in 1930 to the point of clouding his judgment?

Certainly he had gained a reputation for eccentricity; some observers even regarded him as "erratic." In April 1932 he may have revealed his attitude toward common Brazilians when he led troops from units in Campo Grande and Bela Vista to restrain and arrest peasants *(camponeses)* around Ponta Porã who were resisting the takeover of their lands by the Company *Mate Laranjeiras*.[36] Clearly he was willing to do more than express disagreement with the tenente 3rd of October Club's social reform ideas. Klinger relieved the tedium of his assignment in Cuiabá by sending telegrams to newspapers, friends, and dignitaries on all sorts of matters. Not long after roughing up the peasants in the border area, he launched a vague telegram to the effect that if he had to return to Rio, it would be at the head of his troops. He followed that with a "coded" message to Colonel Rabelo, commander of the Second Military Region (SP), advising that he should not permit himself to be used by "scheming politicians"(apparently meaning Vargas) to turn out another São Paulo government.

Rabelo may have stifled his irritation, but tenente Captain Asdrúbal Gwyer de Azevedo, who was then in charge of public works in the state of Rio de Janeiro, attacked General Klinger in brutal terms, linking him to the impending paulista rebellion and, perhaps, making a veiled reference to the Mate Laranjeiras affair mentioned above:

Not content with betraying revolutionists in 1924 through cowardice and betraying General Sezefredo in 1930 through the instinct of self-preservation, you insist[ed] upon being traitor to revolutionary principles, seeking to disturb order with your idiotic telegrams. . . . you should remove the uniform that you cover with slime. . . . To provoke renewed shedding of generous Brazilian blood is appropriate merely for highwaymen whose only ideal consists in extorting . . . public money. Revolutionists who repel your unworthy ambition understand how to maintain the noble attitude demanded by the ideal to which they are dedicated and which you cannot comprehend. The government's excessive indulgence, which made you a general, is to be blamed for your behavior. The traitors to the country should not deceive themselves, because the revolutionists, in spite of all their errors of generosity, will continue to the very end in their firm purpose of defending the collective public against the insatiable vultures to which you have united yourself.[37]

As the public statement by a captain addressed to a general the foregoing is a startling example of the indiscipline reigning in the army but also an indication of the confidence of revolutionary officers such as Captain Gwyer. There is no way of knowing how many officers might have agreed with Gwyer's assessment, but Klinger, for all his Young Turk reformist efforts of earlier decades, had by the 1930s become a controversial figure. After the paulista conspirators gave him the command of their forces, he generated even more controversy.

Klinger had promised the paulistas that he would arrive from Mato Grosso at the head of five thousand troops. Paulista planners highlighted his importance by agreeing that any federal attempt to remove Klinger from his post would trigger their revolt before their planned July 14 date. It is revealing to compare Góes Monteiro's deliberately low profile, just before the Revolution of 1930, with Klinger calling national attention to himself.

In June 1932 Vargas was faced with intensifying tension over São Paulo and growing complaints from officers about Leite de Castro, who, Oswaldo Aranha had warned Vargas a year earlier, was trying to promote to general's rank officers who were "reactionaries and personal friends."[38] The tenente factions, those who had participated in the 1920s revolts and those, like Góes Monteiro, who came out of 1930, wanted a deepening of the revolution to eliminate remaining men, ideas, and practices associated with the Old Republic. Perhaps Leite de Castro's greatest failing was his inability to reestablish order in the army; he had even asked Vargas to declare a state of siege to allow him to impose his will. Such an act would have been too reminiscent of the old regime and would likely have provoked a national uproar. At first Vargas thought to bring in General Andrade Neves but then decided that he needed him alongside Flores da Cunha in Rio Grande do Sul. João Alberto and Góes Monteiro suggested a retired officer who had left the army in 1923. Augusto Inácio do Espírito Santo Cardoso had been a legalist then, but his brother General Joaquim Inácio Batista Cardoso, and his two sons Lts. Ciro and Dulcídio Espírito Santo Cardoso, had been active conspirators, which had been enough for the authorities to suspect him and for the promotions board to pass him over.[39] His promotion to brigadier general had been of the honorary type that came with retirement. The new minister was sixty-five years of age—hardly the paragon of professionalism that middle aged Young Turk Klinger wanted in the army leadership! And he let it be known. He sent one of his staff with a letter to the new minister that said that his appointment was "absurd." Leite de Castro had been removed because he "sanctioned assaults on discipline" and had acted on the advice of a handful of extremists led by "your son Captain Dulcidio, a late-coming red extremist." Klinger doubted that the minister could pass a physical-fitness examination and declared that he lacked the moral qualities for leadership, that he had not taken the general staff course, and that he did not have the reasoning ability required to connect the army's problems with other national issues. He wondered how the government had reached the surprising conclusion that it had no active-duty general who would be appropriate, after it had retired so many and "fabricated others en mass."[40] The government could only conclude that Klinger had gone too far and had to be retired.

It is indicative of the respect that Klinger's early career as a Young Turk had won for him that Lt. Col. Pantaleão Pessôa, chief of staff of the First Military Region, had intercepted the emissary and held the message while his boss Góes Monteiro attempted unsuccessfully to dissuade Klinger by telegraph and by telephone. Trying to reassure Klinger of the regime's good intentions, Góes asked how he thought the situation could be resolved? In response Klinger accused the government of hypocrisy in its appointing a minister, "who physically, morally, and professionally could only be a figurehead." "Finally," Klinger asked Góes, "who better than we soldiers, who know that war is not an end but a means, to reestablish peace. If this can be resolved peacefully, so much the better. It's in the hands of the government."[41] Góes had gone as far as to send Klinger copies of telegrams from regional political and military leaders to show him that the paulistas were deluding themselves into thinking that they had the support of Minas Gerais or Rio Grande do Sul. Góes, who admired Klinger's background and respected his abilities, pleaded with him that he should use again the courage it took to "state the true situation of the country" and "the need for union and tight collaboration among all of us in the army," to come to Rio so that they could defend him and give "sincere explanations of *our attitude* and of how *we think we can contribute* to the well-being of the Brazilian people" (emphasis added). If he did that, Góes argued, his retirement could be set aside, and "we will not lose your precious collaboration and the Army will not lose your services in this hour of extreme difficulties. I appeal to your noble virtues to listen to me and to come here to end the worries resulting from the latest incident in which you were involved."[42]

The exchange also tells something of standards of discipline in the army; talking, writing, even plotting were tolerated until some action took place. If Klinger had taken back the message, it would have been seen as an intemperate outburst, which calmer thought had shown to be improper. As if he wanted to cut off chance of his own retreat, Klinger sent copies to other officers and the letter's contents were soon an open secret. The document, sent on July 1, finally reached Minister Espírito Santo Cardoso on the sixth, and two days later he telegraphed Klinger that Vargas had ordered his retirement, that he should step down from his command and report to Rio.[43] Col. Euclides Figueiredo, who had his doubts about the quality of paulista planning and had tried to convince Klinger to back down so that he would not lose control of the Mato Grosso troops, was shocked at the general's lack of concern for the "revolution" he had committed himself to lead. Figueiredo knew Klinger well, going back to their training in Germany, their founding and editing of *A Defesa Nacional,* and their joint efforts to professionalize the army. In his view after their defeat, Klinger had betrayed their ideals and their dreams.

Klinger appeared unconcerned that his intemperate action had mortally wounded the paulista cause before a shot was fired. General Bertholdo Klinger "was one of those men," Figueiredo wrote, "whose will can not be bent, even by arguments of the purest reasoning; once having made a decision as leader, he shut his eyes and ears, regarding the matter closed. The order was to be executed. He judged himself incapable of error and depreciated the observations of those around him." Instead of attracting support, his action isolated him. The paulistas, and federal officers attracted to their struggle, did not want the high national interests that they asserted they were defending— legal order, military hierarchy, sincerity of political proposals, respect for state autonomy—mixed in the public mind with "the insubordination of a general." Now, the man who was to command them, "in an armed uprising in the name of Law, was bearing as credential the stigma of military indiscipline." Perhaps worse, in Figueiredo's view, was that Klinger had obeyed the very government he had promised to rebel against, and in his last order-of-the-day, which he had written for the transfer of command, urged his troops to remain calm, maintaining "order in true discipline." In exasperation Figueiredo bemoaned that Klinger had not uttered a single word to incite the Mato Grosso units to follow him; in effect, he had "abandoned" the paulista cause.[44] The man whom many in the army considered its best prepared officer showed himself to be inflexible and a poor leader.

The articulation of conspiracies, as noted in discussing earlier revolts, often moved along networks of friends. Behavior in such matters had unwritten rules that took precedence over army regulations and the prescribed norms of discipline. A striking example is the case of Colonel Figueiredo. A star during the high tide of the Young Turks, his career took a wrong turn with the events of 1930. In the paulista crisis he was sought out by both sides, and his decisions would result in his spending most of the remaining Vargas years in exile in Argentina. He sired future generals, one of whom, João Batista, would be the last president (1978–85) of the military cycle (1964–85). The new minister, Espírito Santo Cardoso, was his "old friend and chief . . . [who] in all of my life as a soldier had never failed to show his respect and with whom in that delicate moment, it was important to display the maximum loyalty." He felt embarrassed when the minister called him to meet with him about the rumors he was hearing. They talked frankly, "brother to brother, as patriots and as friends, each strong in his point of view, but respecting that of the other." The colonel made clear that he had a "commitment of honor" to the paulista cause and that he could no longer obey the government. The minister, "as a man of honor," could only lament the wrong path his friend was taking; he appealed to him as they took their leave, "knowing it was in vain, but it was his duty as chief to try." If he had thought to order Figueiredo's arrest, his "gentlemanliness" and "sentiments of friendship" held him back. Understandably, the colonel hurried from the minister's office to the elevator and out of the building. And from then on, he did not appear in public and did not sleep at home.[45]

Another case was that of Col. Eurico Gaspar Dutra, who was sounded out on July 4, 1932, at his hotel in Tres Corações (Minas Gerais), where he was commanding the Fourth Cavalry Regiment, by Capt. Benjamim C. Ribeiro da Costa. The captain presented himself as emissary of Colonel Figueiredo, bearing an invitation to join their side in the coming uprising. Dutra replied that he could not accept because he was a legalist by principle. Moreover, he was grateful to Minister Espírito Santo Cardoso, who, at the suggestion of his son Capt. Dulcídio Cardoso, had taken him out of Mato Grosso and had given him this regiment. Dutra had stood against the Revolution of 1930 and had been sent to the Eleventh Cavalry Regiment in Ponta Porã on the border with Paraguay in November 1930. He was a well-regarded officer who stood out on the general staff under Tasso Fragoso in the late 1920s, when he also became known throughout the army as one of the editors of *A Defesa Nacional*. In 1931, on Klinger's staff, the general praised him highly, saying that "with him on staff no mission is difficult for a commander." In his diary Dutra noted his gratitude to the minister and his son and concluded that "I desired to be loyal to both." It is interesting that one of Dutra's officers was the unsuccessful emissary's brother, Capt. Thales Ribeiro da Costa, who later distinguished himself in the fighting for the railroad tunnel through the Mantiqueira mountains.[46]

Thanks to Klinger's grandstanding, and the paulistas' believing that "maybe" and "might" were commitments, the conspirators moved their pronouncement of revolt from the fourteenth to the ninth of July. How many officers had told them, as Col. Basílio Taborda, recruiting for the cause among general staff officers, had told Figueiredo when he departed for São Paulo on the eighth: "You can go tranquilly, in 48 hours we will respond from Vila Militar to the liberating call of São Paulo!"[47] Colonel Taborda would join his friend alone; the troops of the Vila stayed with the provisional government.

On July 9 the paulista Força Pública and all the army garrisons in the state declared themselves in rebellion against the national government and assumed blocking positions on the approaches to the Paraíba River valley to the east, along the railroad through the Mantigueira mountains to Minas Gerais, and in the west on the roads into Paraná. Their only chance for victory would have been a rapid attack along the Rio de Janeiro–São Paulo road to carry the war to the capital before the federal forces got organized. Instead, they went on the defensive because they were convinced that they really would not have to fight, that once Minas, Rio Grande, and Klinger's Mato Grosso troops joined them, Rio's units would depose Vargas. But the governor of Minas and the interventor of Rio Grande stayed loyal to Vargas, so their state forces would be invading São Paulo, not joining it; and, of course, Klinger lost his command and arrived in São Paulo alone.

An attempt by the new commander of the Fourth Military Region (Minas Gerais), Brig. Gen. Firmino Antônio Borba, to bring the region's units to the paulista side was foiled by Juarez Távora, who rushed from Rio to Juiz de Fora, where he arrested General Borba and replaced him with Col. Jorge Pinheiro, who was immediately promoted to brigadier general. A federal officer, Col. Cristóvão Barcelos, traveled on the train with Távora to Belo Horizonte, where he assumed the post of chief of staff of the Polícia Militar of Minas.[48]

The navy blockaded the port of Santos preventing munitions being shipped into São Paulo from abroad. The paulistas had to make do with the arms and shells in possession of the revolting garrisons. Local industry did its best to produce what it could and kept workers happy with overtime pay and free medical and dental clinics.[49] Law students enthusiastically enrolled in provisional units but made poor soldiers when combat became real.

Figueiredo, with Klinger still en route from Mato Grosso, assumed command of operations almost as soon as he arrived from Rio by car on the morning of July 9. At the outset he had the twelve thousand troops in the federal garrisons and nine thousand in the *Força Pública* units. He placed the largest contingents athwart the railway and road along the Paraíba to a few miles inside the state of Rio de Janeiro line. From the outset the posture was to defend the state's borders from invasion. In military theory this positioned the paulistas on interior lines and the federal forces on exterior lines, with the former regarded as superior for supply and communications. However, the advantages of interior lines can be lost if the supplies of men and materiel are inadequate for the war's objectives. Moreover, as Napoleon in his *Maxims of War* observed, "the transition from the defensive to the offensive is one of the most delicate operations in war."[50] If this were so for the great captains of history, how much more so for a makeshift army, with its many units of green volunteers and a shortage of experienced officers?

But neither side was capable of waging an energetic offensive campaign. As can be inferred from the foregoing pages, the federal army did not inspire confidence in its loyalty, and when some officers abandoned their posts and slipped into São Paulo, fears rose in government circles that it would crumble as in 1930. Vargas noted in his diary that there were "deficiencies of all sorts, felonies, betrayals, inertia." For his field commanders the provisional president turned to men he trusted. He named Góes to command what he significantly called the "expeditionary troops" of what later would be labeled the Army of the East. He placed his wife's uncle, retired Brig. Gen. Waldomiro Castilho de Lima, in charge of the government forces advancing into São Paulo from Paraná. The general staff, again headed by its longtime chief Tasso Fragoso, who had been called back to duty, was slow to prepare operations plans; and in the first hours of the crisis some of its officers tried to prevent the embarkation of troops. Tasso's return to active service would be short-lived. To prevent pro-paulista agents from communicating with units in Rio, Góes ordered several units out on a pointless night march and had the rest board Central do Brasil trains, buses, and trucks borrowed from the electric power company and a brewery. These units took up positions near the São Paulo boundary at Barra do Piraí, and at a place called Volta Redonda, which in the 1940s would become the center of Brazil's steel industry. With no plans forthcoming from the general staff, Góes himself took over the task of writing up the operations orders to crush the rebellion. His basic idea was to wage a war of attrition. São Paulo simply did not have the resources to win. He likened its situation to a miniature of that of the Central Powers in World War I; "isolated and invaded from various directions, its economy and resources will breakdown. . . . Its advantage of being able to maneuver on interior lines, using its excellent railway network and roads, will disappear or be neutralized with the passage of time." All that was needed was to squeeze it ever tighter and prevent supplies from reaching it.[51] He also hoped to avoid great loss of life and materiel so that the scars of this messy conflict would not be beyond healing.

Neither side was notably strong in the air at the beginning of the fighting. The federal forces had a mixed collection that included several French single-engine biwinged Potez TOE for observation and bombardment; six American-made Waco CSOs (single engine, biwinged with mounted machine gun); one Amiot bomber; a few British De Havilland Moths, the only craft equipped with radio and so could be used as artillery spotters; and a single Nieuport Delage fighter. The Potez and the Wacos carried out 90 percent of the thirteen hundred missions and the twenty-five hundred hours of flight. One of the Wacos was delivered to the paulistas on July 21, when its pilot used his training flight from Campo dos Afonsos to join their cause. Because the paulistas obtained their first aircraft from rebelling units stationed in their territory, the makes were the same as the federal craft, except they were fewer and lacked synchronization between their machine guns and propellers, and so were at a disadvantage in aerial combat. In August, Constitutionalist (the name the paulistas favored) agents bought nine Curtis Falcons from the American Curtis Wright Corporation's assembly plant in Chile.

American and Chilean pilots flew these planes to Paraguay and southern Mato Grosso, where they passed them to the paulistas. Two were lost in the ferrying operation, one in a crash in Argentina, and the other was seized by Paraguayan authorities; a third had its propeller damaged in a failed attempt to synchronize its machine gun. With a top speed of about 140 miles per hour, capability of vertical dive bombing, a maximum elevation of forty-six hundred meters, and a flight range of 620 miles the Curtis Falcons were the most advanced aircraft used during the conflict. But the federal side had an important resource that the Constitutionalists lacked: the 103 officer and 34 sergeant aviators it had trained between 1928 and 1932. The government immediately ordered 150 new Wacos, 10 of which were readied in time to see action.[52]

The paulistas concentrated their aircraft in the south, against General Waldomiro's forces, because at the outset he did not have planes. It would be late August before the federal side established parity in the air on that front. The federal army did not achieve complete control of the air over São Paulo, but with the increasing number of planes and with trained pilots to fly them the advantage was tipping in their direction.

Flores da Cunha sent Brigada Militar units to the Paraná front and to Rio, as did the interventors of Bahia and Pernambuco. Vargas threw himself into getting his generals the troops and arms that they needed. He noted that his minister of war, Espirito Santo Cardoso, proved to be "an energetic and serenely calm man." However, complaints continued about the slowness, and even "sabotage," of the general staff. Not content to sit in his office attending telephones and correspondence, on July 14–17, Getúlio took his military and civil advisers and General Espirito Santo Cardoso to visit Góes Monteiro's headquarters in Barra Mansa and to see units within less than two miles from the paulista lines. Such excursions displayed the deliberate calm that he believed he had to maintain to reassure the public and those around him.[53]

From behind the palace walls Vargas was fighting against the Old Republic's leaders, Borges de Medeiros in his home state of Rio Grande, and ex-president Artur Bernardes in Minas Gerais. Both used their considerable influence to undermine the national government in the name of state autonomy. Their agents worked on contacts in the respective state military police units to convince them to give up the struggle. Their activities constantly worried Vargas, but his intelligence service kept him informed and he was able to counter their moves. He also ordered the retirements of officers who had joined the paulistas, as well as those who had refused to fight. And instead of holding hostage those paulistas employed in the capital's civil service, he had the navy transport all those who wished to go to São Paulo.[54]

He deliberately projected an image of calm determination and strength, edged with compassion.

By the end of July Góes's Army of the East was fighting along a twenty-five-mile-wide front in the Paraíba valley. The Rio de Janeiro–São Paulo road that, along with the railroad, was the focus of his operations was an all weather, two-way gravel-over-red-clay road that measured twenty feet wide. Feeder roads outside the two cities were gravel on clay but were one way and ten feet wide. "Heavy traffic could pass over them only in dry weather." The paulistas destroyed all the bridges on the main routes and dug five-foot-deep trenches across the roadways.[55]

On August 9 Vargas could confide to his diary that "the rebels were falling back on all sides." About the same time he was meeting with paulista emissaries and sending the rebels the message that "I intend, after extinguishing the revolt, to adopt a provisional constitution until the Constituent Assembly can vote a definitive one." He even asked for their suggestions for the provisional Constitution. On August 10 he saw his "tribe" again, when the Fourteenth Auxiliary Corps of the Brigada Militar of Rio Grande do Sul, from his hometown of São Borja, passed through Rio de Janeiro under the command of his brother Benjamin Vargas. His son Lutero and two nephews were soldiers in the corps. This unit and its personnel would play a role in the rise of a major figure in subsequent army and national history. They were assigned to Col. Eurico Dutra's command, fighting to take the Mantiqueira railroad tunnel on the Minas border with São Paulo. Afterward Benjamin Vargas praised Dutra so convincingly that Getúlio promoted him to general and eventually made him his minister of war, which post he would hold longer than anyone in Brazil's history, 1936–45, and then he would follow Vargas as president, 1946–51. It is difficult not to see a stroke of fate in Dutra's relationship with Benjamin Vargas and the gaúchos from São Borja.

In mid-August Góes described the situation to Getúlio and offered some advice. There had been few changes in the situation, but although "we advance little, we always advance." Given their "deficiency of means" it would be best not to expect victory soon but to "temper the spirit for a persistent and drawn out war against the pride and near fanaticism that the Paulista plutocracy cultivated to its own benefit with absolute disdain for the rest of Brazil . . . the nineteen states that support your government." São Paulo was militarily inferior, "but it had summoned its political will, its industry, [and] its economy entirely in the service of victory." Klinger, he wrote, had at his command the "will and organization of seven million men, who day-by-day become more convinced that we want to destroy and ruin their state." On the federal government side he saw much dispersion of effort. He advised

Vargas to concentrate "in his hands all the vital strength of the country and to channel it towards victory." For himself, he only wanted to be part of that victory; "having been unable to prevent the catastrophe that threatens us, I want to contribute sincerely to reduce its affects and to serve Brazil defending your government."[56]

As was typical of August weather, the rains and cold winds blew up from the south, depressing spirits and turning the roads and trenches into muddy messes. The paulistas added to the gloom by using their 105 mm howitzers to shell heavily the federal positions in the Paraíba. Meanwhile, the government struggled to get armaments that it had purchased in France liberated and shipped. The French, whose army had trained the paulista police since 1906 and the federal army since 1920, alleged humanitarian concerns, but Vargas believed that they resented purchases made in the United States and elsewhere.

Klinger initiated negotiation with the government via the navy, whose officers were not enthusiastic about the war. The general seems to have disagreed with the paulista civilian leaders over how to end the fighting. They likely agreed that Vargas should be replaced, but Klinger wanted to go farther and have the military take over the national government. The men of 1930 saw this idea as counterrevolutionary and unacceptable. But it coincided with Borges de Medeiros's argument in Rio Grande do Sul, and his influence was then weakening support for the provisional government among the state's Brigada Militar units on the Paraná front. An army pilot on that front flew his plane over the lines and joined the paulistas, and one of General Góes's staff went over as well. To make things worse, in the far north the Fort of Óbidos, which guarded the narrows of the great Amazon River, rebelled. August appeared to be keeping its reputation as the month of political disasters. Suspicion was in the air; Vargas and Góes could not get the army's arsenals to produce fast enough; the mineiro government suspected the general of plotting with his old [and supposedly secret] patron, ex-president Bernardes; Góes distrusted the mineiro leaders who he thought were arming their troops but holding back their attack to see how things worked out; others whispered to Vargas that Góes was conspiring with Klinger to impose a military dictatorship. Meanwhile, bombs went off in downtown Rio de Janeiro, and the gathered crowds shouted Vivas for São Paulo.[57]

Near the end of August the gloom lifted as the mineiros went on a forceful offensive. By late September both Borges de Medeiros and ex-president Bernardes were taken prisoner in their respective states and placed under navy guard on a coastal island. Vargas promoted seven new generals in front-line commands. In the wee hours of September 29 Klinger telegraphed Vargas proposing a suspension of hostilities. Getúlio told him to send an emissary to General Góes. There was confusion in paulista ranks for a few days as various delegates tried to get better terms than unconditional surrender. The officers of the state's Força Pública refused to obey either Klinger or the rebel government and deposed the latter, assuming control of the state until federal authorities arrived.[58]

A myth came out of this civil war that it was responsible for pushing Vargas into reconstitionalizing the country; but as noted above he had already scheduled elections for the constituent assembly, and from his diary it is clear that his private sentiments supported his public statements. Far from contributing to constitutional government the paulista rebellion added unnecessary death, expense, confusion, betrayal, and indiscipline to a situation that already had too much of all that; indeed, it probably contributed more to smoothing the road to dictatorship five years later.[59] The argument that the revolt forced Vargas to fulfill his pledge to hold a constitutional convention was based on the view that he was deeply insincere and would have avoided convening such a convention but for the paulista pressure. How could his sincerity or lack thereof be proven? In the absence of proof the paulistas were able to claim that their sacrifice had not been in vain. But the 1995 publication of Getúlio's secret *Diary* undermined that argument because now we know what he was telling himself at the time. In 1931 he believed that "at least three years of dictatorship, administering free of clientage politics and of the parties" were necessary to reach budgetary equilibrium, and that this had been sabotaged by the United Front of Rio Grande, led by "two lunatics," Borges de Medeiros and Raul Pilla, who also prodded the paulistas to revolt. The hurried return of the country to constitutional rule was already underway, with May 3, 1933, proclaimed as election day, when the fighting started. The paulista demands for state autonomy had been satisfied, even the transfer of the commander of the military region. Vargas noted that they had been so satisfied with the state government that he had put in office that it was kept throughout the revolt. He believed that the state government had not desired revolt but had to accept the decision of the military conspirators or face deposition. In a 1937 meeting with Vargas, Valdemar Ferreira, who had been São Paulo's secretary of justice during the conflict, placed the blame for the revolt on General Klinger and his fellow military conspirators. At the very least it is time for historians to reexamine the paulista revolt of 1932.[60]

The paulista war did have important results. It eliminated tenentismo as an influential force in national politics and within the army. The tenentes and their 3rd of October Club were opposed to constitutionalization, so their demise had made it easier for Vargas to negotiate. It brought the army closer than at any previous time to enjoying a monopoly of force within Brazil. Gen. Waldomiro Lima, who became military governor of São Paulo on October 10, 1932, immediately set out to eliminate some sectors of the

Força Pública. By the time he left the state the following July, the Força Pública, although still in existence, was a police force rather than a small army, a reduction in status that would be confirmed in law two years later. The officer corps was more aware of the damage that had been done to the army and more officers were determined to repair it. The war also showed how poorly prepared the army was for combat. A new wave of reorganization and rearmament marked the next years, as did the conviction that dependence on foreign sources of arms and munitions had to end. Brazil needed its own arms industry, and the efforts to create it would lead to a tighter alliance between Vargas and the military and would affect the directions Brazilian foreign relations took up to the outbreak of World War II.[61] The paulista war also brought forward officers who would lead the army through the world war and beyond into the 1960s and 1970s.

Paulista industry had learned that it could get more efficient production out of its workers by extending benefits than by threats and violence. The state's industrialists became advocates of mixing comprehensive welfare with capitalism. They gained, in Joel Wolfe's analysis, "a new appreciation of the government's power to guarantee social peace, and therefore high levels of production. . . . [T]hey began to accept key components of Vargas's program of state-sponsored corporatist unionism."[62] But whatever the lessons learned, the paulistas were not able to manufacture enough weapons and munitions to outclass the government's superiority in both. However, they took advantage of what they had. The Piquete powder factory had been in their hands and had turned out "a cheap and very efficient explosive." The Matarazzo factory in São Caetano had turned out 250,000 cartridges a day for rifles and machine guns and had produced four hundred 75 mm artillery shells a day; and the paulistas had manufactured 160 trench mortars of 90 mm, with extreme range of fifteen hundred meters, from the axles of railway cars. And at peak production, the shops were making three thousand hand and rifle grenades a day. The seventy thousand men the paulistas put into the field were not unarmed.

But they were not enough to resist or overcome the eighty thousand that the federal forces deployed against them. Indeed, the government could afford to keep "at least one battalion of 75 mm artillery guns and a considerable number of Infantry in Rio throughout the campaign." The federal aircraft, with their guns synchronized to fire through their propellers, were "vastly superior in quantity and quality" to the paulista equipment which required firing automatic rifles from the sides of the planes. Both armies made extensive use of air bombing against troop concentrations. Federal air raids shook paulista morale, dropping bombs on Campinas daily and then on the return flight strafing paulista trenches. But it was not numbers of troops or quality of equipment that brought on the paulista defeat; it was principally the "lack of good officer material at the front." In the fighting outside Campinas the state Força Pública "repeatedly withdrew, leaving the volunteer units in a precarious position." Worse, lower-ranked officers were "very negligent, often deserting the men for days. Such conditions led to repeated retreats, and the result was a gradual loss of morale among the volunteers." In the aftermath of the war rioting occurred in São Paulo city on September 28, 30, and October 13 because the population believed that "they had been sold out by the military leaders in the field."[63]

The casualty reports on the 1932 civil war were vague and at variance with one another. The U.S. Army attaché estimated that the federal forces had suffered 1,050 killed and about 3,800 wounded. Among the 50 officers killed in the Paraíba valley was Góes Monteiro's favorite brother, Ciro. After touring the battle areas U.S. Army attaché Sackville concluded that "hard fighting did not take place in this rebellion. The federal forces seemed content to gradually surround the rebel armed forces and proceed to starve them out. Although the Paulista people remained staunch to the end, the pressure was too great and Paulista morale at the front broke under the strain." He correctly observed that the manner in which the Vargas government handled São Paulo now would determine the future; harsh treatment would deepen the resentment that led to the war. "Kindness would probably win them over in time." He thought that Vargas was likely tacking in that direction because he did not send federal "troops into the Paulista capital until the Paulista state troops had restored order in the city."[64]

One major weapon that was missing from the war's battlefields was the tank. In March 1932 the army had abolished its only tank company. Among the secondhand French equipment purchased after the arrival of the military mission were a dozen tanks. The tanks were virtually obsolete when they arrived, and "the Brazilians never acquired any notable proficiency in handling the tanks." In the dozen years that followed they "deteriorated to a point where all [were] out of commission." U.S. attaché clerk Harry Brown thought that "dissolving of the single Tank Company [would] result in no substantial loss so far as the Army's efficiency is concerned." But of course, he wrote that comment before the outbreak of hostilities with São Paulo.[65]

In Góes Monteiro's mind the lack of tanks was only a tiny part of the problems that needed to be corrected. While field operations were still underway he analyzed what needed to be done. He wrote Vargas that the paulistas had in their hands all the elements necessary for victory but that they did not know how to take advantage of them. If they had mobilized properly and had used their road and rail net effectively, they could have surprised Rio with a powerful offensive. The government had been saved by paulista ineptitude, not by its own military prowess. Politically Brazil's nationalism and the federal ties had been weakened because the national structure was "fragile, confused, and susceptible of breaking apart." What was needed to strengthen unity, Góes declared, was "a greater political [and] nationalist centralization." The paulista affair was a reactionary attempt to return to the past under the false banner of "reconstitutionalism." What Vargas needed to do, his commanding general urged, was "to complete the Revolution, to decree a Constitution for the country that would satisfy the necessities and possibilities of the whole, without uncertainties, imitations and fantasies that are inadequate for the Brazilian people, who must be understood as they really are." Similarly Góes turned a cold, hard eye on the Pátria's military:

The Federal Army and the auxiliary troops of the states are not more than a conglomeration of units weak in personnel and material, poorly equipped for war and suffering the effects of an already advanced dissolution caused by defective organization, by lack of relationship to the military needs of the country, and by a decade of intestinal struggles, in which [they have] been actively involved, and by which [they have] been steadily enfeebled, morally and materially, especially the officer corps, which has felt most intensely the influence of political factionalism and consequently has not applied itself to the profession as it should.

The High Command . . . leaves everything to be desired and will be, in posterity, chiefly responsible for the state of collapse and anarchy of the armed forces, compromising the future of the Nation . . . sacrificing the national interests in favor of particular, regional, and personal interests.

The Revolution of October should have changed or begun to transform this order of things and the mentality that it has produced. But, the raw material, the substratum of certain elements who call themselves *revolutionaries,* are not very different from the so-called "*reactionaries*" or "*decadent ones.*"

It is necessary, that all Brazilians of good will combat in all its forms this profound evil—in the mentality, habits, customs, passions and exaggerated individualism—that casts a threatening shadow over the sick Nation.

Góes pleaded for reinvigorated, "disciplined, strong, homogeneous, well equipped and well commanded military forces" as the next step. "Cost whatever sacrifice it costs, only this will allow us to face the future without great worries and nervousness." He wanted to increase the army to one hundred thousand men and to give it exclusive control over all questions of arms and military mobilization.[66]

The immediate post–civil war task was to reorganize the army again and to insure that officers kept on active duty were securely supportive of the government. The "touchstone" for the army, Góes reminded Vargas, was the question of promotions. Although according to regulations the president was supposed to be involved only in selecting the top ranks, he involved himself in discussions of all ranks down to captains, lieutenants, and even sergeants. In fact, he reviewed and "organized" the promotions list the army board proposed and then gave it to the head of his own military staff, Col.

Pantaleão Pessôa, and to General Góes for comment. Minister of War Espirito Santo Cardoso and his predecessor, General Leite de Castro, suggested names meriting advancement. At least one colonel, José Gay, asked Getúlio in a private audience to promote him. The president declined, noting in his diary, "I will not promote to general a mere wearer of rank." Góes warned that if the few hundred officers who justly merited promotion by virtue of their service in the Revolution of October and in the recent campaign were not attended, the situation would get worse. A new promotion law was badly needed "to avoid arbitrary and political promotions that would cause new problems for the government." Above all else it was "now necessary to re-establish the most rigorous discipline in the ranks and to prepare them for any emergency." He had approved, with a few deletions and additions, the captains' list that Vargas had sent to him. As for lieutenants, Góes thought that following the order of date of rank was the safest procedure, but there were some who should be promoted for merit because of their service in the civil war. "It would be difficult for a lieutenant who spent 3 months in the trenches to accept that someone more junior, who did not take part directly in the military operations should be promoted before him." The same could be said for those junior officers who had played a part in the Revolution of 1930 but whose assignment during the late conflict was not at the battle line. The problems of sergeants and of the *commissionados* were also serious. The former should be paid better, and the latter should get greater benefits than run-of-the-mill "dead weights." It was "extremely necessary," Góes argued, to improve the officer corps, "especially in the higher ranks, including the generals . . . by purging the incapable elements." Also the enlisted ranks should be increased, "particularly in São Paulo and other sensitive spots." The regime's vigilance should not stop. It was "preferable to spend more on the army and prepare it well, than to risk having to spend 100 times more facing greater threats to public security." The army had to be put into excellent condition morally, professionally, and materially. "Discipline, the most rigorous that can be obtained, will be a question of life or of death. And in the [military] regions outside of Rio, the officers and the sergeants should be carefully selected and be entirely trustworthy, so as not to be contaminated."[67]

Careful control of retirements and promotions gradually removed senior officers promoted before 1930. By 1937 the list of combat colonels, from which future generals were chosen, contained only five officers promoted prior to the revolution out of a total of 104 colonels.[68]

Góes Monteiro believed that with the paulistas defeated, the army was free to turn its attention to the dangers that confronted the Pátria. As noted above, the civil war provided an excuse to cleanse the officer corps of the inept, the lazy, and the agitators. As the victorious general, Góes was rapidly increasing his influence. He had knocked Klinger from his almost mythical position as Young Turk reformer, and Góes, not the German-trained officers, would be credited with shaping the new Brazilian army. His immediate reward was promotion, on October 6, 1932, to the top active duty rank of General of Division. He was forty-two years old, but already he was not keeping in the physical condition that his position demanded. Over the next decade his health would frequently restrain his ambition. Although he worked hard at seizing his opportunities, he was also careful not to overdo the limelight. For example, in October 1932, when he was about to return to Rio from his headquarters in Resende, politicians from Rio visited him to learn his arrival time in the capital so that they could stage a flashy welcome. He consulted his chief of staff, Col. Pantaleão Pessôa, who observed that a public acclamation might be inconvenient for the government, so they set the general's return for between 2 and 3 A.M. It was a deliberate demonstration of his determination to support the government, or at least Getúlio.[69]

The paulista rebellion had a profound effect on Góes, more than his comments in the oft-cited Coutinho interviews would suggest. Among his papers there is an unfinished manuscript analyzing operations that he led himself, in which he cast the Vargas government as gullibly guiltless and the paulista leadership as dastardly scoundrels, out to plunder their state and nation. They were *conquistadores,* "monopolistic, selfish industrialists" with no concern for their countrymen. In a defense of his role in the civil war Góes smoldered about "the blindness of the Brazilian oligarchs," whose insanity made them want to destroy the army. Their aim in splitting the officer corps was to control Brazil. In his noticeably truculent farewell speech at the demobilization of his "Army of the East" he warned the soldiers to be vigilant because the Pátria would always need them. They should stay watchful and keep their bayonets close by. They should act, he said, "nipponically" (a sly reference to the Japanese attacks in China) whenever "the internal enemy" raised its head, even in the army itself. Attached to the text there is a handwritten page entitled "Enemies," in which Góes grumbled about the "occult forces" that were seeking to destroy Brazil. There are no names, or even clear hints, as to whom he was referring to, but there was no mistaking his anger and conviction. When he was particularly stressed and frustrated, this line of thought erupted but usually in private. At that moment he must have been feeling great pressure, perhaps related to his grief at the death in combat of Cícero (or Ciro), his favorite brother.[70]

Góes also warned Vargas that a complete restructuring of the army was urgently needed. Argentina could rapidly mobilize better-armed troops than could Brazil, and Argentina presumably was Brazil's most likely opponent in any future foreign war. Góes was particularly concerned about equipment; modern equipment was desperately needed, as the paulista rebellion had shown—São Paulo's equipment and the substantial contribution the state's industry had made to its war effort favorably impressed Góes and his staff officers. He did not immediately connect the need for arms and equipment with industrialization; his first worry was to obtain arms, as quickly as possible, which meant that he focused on importation as the immediate solution. Although he favored improved production and standards in army arsenals and civilian plants, he let others make the arguments for grander, longer-range industrialization.

Constituent Assembly and the Constitution of 1934

At the end of the civil war Vargas revived his promise to call a constituent assembly. And Góes Monteiro's public image as Brazil's newly victorious and youngest general thrust him into active participation. Góes joined the committee, under the leadership of Foreign Minister Afrânio de Melo Franco, that wrote the proposed text for the elected assembly's consideration. Between mid-November 1933 and mid-July 1934 the assembly debated the suggested clauses, accepting most of the recommended text but rejecting a unicameral legislature in favor of the two-house variety and adding the novelty of employer and laboring class representatives in an unsuccessful attempt to weaken the clout of big state delegations. Executive power was vested in the president and cabinet, with no vice president. The vote was extended to both sexes over eighteen and was mandatory for all males and for female public servants. Women were excluded from obligatory military service, which now became a constitutional rather than a legislated requirement. Góes Monteiro had wanted to extend military service to females, excluding them only from combat roles, but he could not make his view prevail.

As in 1891 the civilian delegates wanted to keep the military involved in politics. Indeed, the new legislature, thanks to amnesty laws, would have exiles of 1930 and 1932 elected to its chambers, giving the regime's enemies a status and a platform from which to protect their interests and from which to attack the government. Like its predecessor, the 1934 Constitution declared the armed forces to be "permanent national institutions and within the law, essentially obedient to their hierarchical superiors." Their purpose was "to defend the Pátria and guarantee the Constitutional powers." As Alfred Stepan noted, "this in effect authorized the military to give only discretionary obedience to the president, since obedience was dependent upon their decision regarding the legality of the presidential order." Oddly, this provision had been opposed by Deodoro da Fonseca in 1891 as being bad for military discipline. That it survived into the 1934 document indicated that the politicians wanted to impose constitutionally an interventionist or moderating role on the military that they could use to call soldiers to their

side in disputes between the executive and the Congress.[71] To the extent
that the Constitution sought to preserve the practices of the Old Republic,
it was a blow against the centralizing tendency of the Revolution of 1930
and against hopes to insulate the military from politics.

What this exercise in democracy did was to draw the army more intimately into politics. The military was at the margins of the succession crisis
caused by the death of the "president" of Minas Gerais (the only state governor allowed to keep the old title in tribute of his role in 1930). On December 12, 1933, Getúlio's decision *not* to appoint either Virgílio de Melo
Franco or Gustavo Capanema led to the resignations of minister of finance
Oswaldo Aranha and, Virgílio's father, the minister of foreign affairs, Afrânio
de Melo Franco. Flores da Cunha, backing Capanema, threatened to resign
as interventor in Rio Grande do Sul. Reports and rumors of conspiracies
swirled about the government. Vargas convinced Aranha and Flores to stay,
but Melo Franco's family pride was too wounded for him to withdraw his
resignation. The affair nearly destabilized the regime and caused Minas and
Rio Grande to build up their state forces to seven thousand and thirty-five
hundred respectively, which in turn upset the officer corps.[72]

Shortly before the crisis over Minas Gerais, a column appeared in the
Gazeta do Rio by "Coronel Y." that criticized the politicians' misuse and
abuse of the army. It and its companion pieces show that military matters
were discussed in the public press, that officers were much preoccupied
with the effects of politics on the institution, and that they were concerned
to educate the public. The columns have more pointed importance because
they were written by Captain Humberto de Alencar Castelo Branco, then
assistant to the director of studies at the military school in Realengo. The
army, he wrote, was neither an apparatus to control the rulers of the nation
nor a partisan militia. He criticized political officers who gave themselves
over to such roles, distorting the armed forces' true mission of national defense. "Our politicians," he charged, "do not study, as a rule, the vital questions of a permanent army." They saw the army as they did their local state
police, as a force to impose the will of the party in power. He called on the
constituent assembly to study military issues and to think of national defense as part of the "sacred interests of Brasil."[73]

While the above had been going on, Paraguay and Bolivia went to war
over the Chaco; Peru and Colombia came to blows over Leiticia; Generals
Góes Monteiro and Tasso Fragoso engaged in a bitter exchange in the newspapers over their actions in the paulista civil war; and Generals Waldomiro
Castilho de Lima, interventor in São Paulo, and Manuel de Cerqueira Daltro
Filho, commander of the Second Military Region (São Paulo), fell to arguing publicly over their roles in the state's politics. In mid-October 1933,

a few days after Argentine president General Agustín P. Justo visited Brazil, Getúlio's brother Benjamin led a troop of soldiers, relatives, and friends from São Borja across the Uruguay River into Santo Tomé, Argentina, to settle a local cross-border dispute. They were met with gunfire, and several of the Brazilians were killed, including two Vargas nephews. Getúlio, calling it a "sad night," was embarrassed by his brother's intemperate behavior, but the incident tells much about the roughness of the southern borders. Some of the Argentine government's irritation was soothed in late December 1933, when Brazilian authorities in Uruguaiana arrested Argentine colonel Gregorio Pomar and his followers, who were preparing to invade their homeland.[74]

In December the "phantasma of military dictatorship" hovered over the political scene, never quite assuming definite shape but usually fluttering around Góes Monteiro's name. General Espirito Santo's decision to step down as minister of war gave Getúlio the opportunity to draw the increasingly ambitious young general closer to his side by offering him the ministry. This post would give Góes the position in which he could realize his dream of army reforms. Instead of instantly grabbing his opportunity, Góes worried Vargas by asking for time to consult with other generals and then keeping his distance from the president. From the latter's *Diary* it appears that they did not see or talk to each other between December 20 and January 10, which for them, and considering the crisis in progress, was a long time.[75] Oswaldo Aranha, whose continued support also troubled Vargas at that time, spoke against naming Góes as minister of war, telling the president that General Andrade Neves had told him that Góes did not have the influence in the army that the president supposed. Moreover, Aranha said that Góes had offered him one hundred thousand contos to unite with him against Flores da Cunha, as their "common enemy."[76] Whatever the truth of this odd offer, Góes Monteiro's antipathy toward Flores continued to grow until his removal from Porto Alegre would be preparatory to declaring the Estado Novo dictatorship in 1937. On the night of January 18, attempting to squeeze further commitments from the president before accepting the ministry, Góes showed Vargas a letter he had written on the army's needs. Vargas told him that they were beyond such maneuvering and that he would provide what he could, but Góes should stop raising difficulties and assume his new post.[77]

In what was likely an attempt to weaken Vargas by splitting his military support, Bernardes delegates from Minas Gerais raised Góes Monteiro's name for president long enough for him to get bitten, as the Brazilians say, by the "blue fly" of presidential ambition but not long enough for an unstoppable groundswell of support to develop. His short flirtation with the blue fly was, perhaps, encouraged by whispering among officers and politicians of coup plots to impose him as dictator, in the event that his candidacy failed. The tenente 3rd of October Club issued a manifesto of support. How much truth there was in any of the reports and rumors is an open question. Certainly the number of letters and telegrams in the Vargas papers shows that there were a lot of reports, but the center of plotting was always somewhere other than where the person writing was located. For example, Flores da Cunha in Rio Grande telegraphed Vargas that an officer from a unit in São Paulo alerted him that telephone calls from the minister of war's office to officers in that state had said that General Góes would resign as minister and if not elected president would stage a coup d'état. What seems most likely is that either the rumor mill was simply running freely with no direction or that an unknown group was deliberately spreading false rumors in hopes of provoking a crisis. In any case the theme that runs through the Vargas responses was caution, vigilance, and avoiding displays of police power. He suggested to Flores that he telegraph Góes to tell him that he had *not* met with the commanders of the state's Brigada Militar, that he had not mobilized provisional units or blockaded army posts, or done anything hostile toward the army. Vargas responded to comments by Bahia's interventor, Captain Juracy Magalhães, about rumored plotting, that he should act only when certain that the rumors were true. Vargas urged "energetic measures, excluding the *Força Pública*, the preference being retirement for suspected officers, [and] inviting the principal, responsible civilians to leave the State."[78] It is ironic that Góes Monteiro, who publicly and privately attacked regionalism as the gravest danger to the Pátria, should get drawn into a web spun by regional politicians.

From time to time during these months Vargas asked himself if he should resign and leave all the headaches to others.[79] Flores da Cunha was hearing so many rumors of a coup to implant a military dictator that he proposed sending to Rio a gaúcho police detachment to act as Getúlio's personal guard. The president thought that such a step would be "useless, if not irritating." Oddly some of the men (for example: General Rabelo and Oswaldo Aranha) who later would be most identified as antidictatorship entertained the idea in this interval. Generals Manuel Rabelo and Góes Monteiro agreed that the "storm that was brewing, would degenerate into a civil war of tragic consequences for the Pátria and could be prevented only if the army and navy imposed a constitution that wouldn't be another fantasy . . . but a reality, whose efficacy and utility are assured." Rabelo reminded Góes that he had once concurred that the positivist Constitution of Rio Grande do Sul was the "only means to end the uneasiness that walks the land." Under his scheme Vargas would stay as president and would be sworn in before the two armed services, which "embody national aspirations and the will of the free people of Brazil." Having done this, Rabelo assured his colleague, they would "save Brazil from the anarchy that threatens it . . . the chaotic situation in which we are living . . . , and enter a clear and defined phase of strength and responsibility. . . . Either Brazil saves itself this time, or we will no longer be able to foresee its future." Rabelo told Vargas of the generals' conversation, gave him a copy of a proposed proclamation, and urged Getúlio "to stage this coup to avoid the revolution." Vargas promised to study the matter but said that he preferred to try to have the *constituente* improve the Constitution via debate. Separately, General Daltro Filho, interventor in São Paulo, criticized the assembly, saying that he favored a "dictatorial republic." On April 9 and 10 secret meetings of generals in Rio de Janeiro urged Góes to tell Vargas that if he insisted on standing for election as president, blood would flow. Góes refused to carry the message. But with his name in contention, his frequent exhortations in the press that the army should stay out of politics rang hollow. Vargas noted that the general's candidacy brought "politics into the heart of the army," dividing it into supporting and hostile groups.[80] In April General João Guedes da Fontoura, commandant of Vila Militar, gathered 170 of the officers of the vila's units and obtained their consent to a declaration affirming their support of the government and respect for the constituent assembly and expressing solidarity with General José Maria Franco Ferreira, regional commander in Rio Grande do Sul, who likewise had expressed his loyalty to the government.[81]

In early April José Carlos de Macedo Soares, an influential paulista who would become foreign minister under the constitutional government, worried over the split opinion in the country regarding liberal democracy. He observed that the "fiction of election of the President of the Republic was no longer enough to give him the power to exercise his office." The revolution had undermined the prestige of authority in Brazil, and informed opinion, he said, was influenced by contemporary great thinkers who were writing that democracy had failed, as the strengthening of presidential powers in the United States, Belgium, and France seemed to verify. He told Vargas that he had sounded out a number of army officers and was impressed at the uniformity of opinion; "almost all are against liberal democracy." The officers saw Brazil on the road to corporatism. Curiously, the Constituent Assembly, in revising the draft Constitution, had shown its preference for the very same liberal democracy that the officers opposed. Góes's candidacy was supported, Macedo Soares said, by the old-time republicans, so there were basic contradictions in the general's candidacy.

According to Macedo Soares, Góes would not be willing to play a Nestor Passos or Marshal Hermes, but he might accept backing from outside the liberal democratic tradition, perhaps rising to power "on the crest of a clearly popular movement." Surprisingly, on May 27 Vargas wrote in his *Diary* that Aranha had suggested that they launch a fresh revolution that would dissolve the Constituent Assembly and declare a new Constitution for the country. The truth of this cannot be verified by other sources, which are silent on it.[82] However, other conspirators apparently continued to whisper and to meet secretly. On June 4 the chief of the federal district police briefed Vargas about a "politico-military" plot to launch a surprise coup on the night of the assembly's election of the president, taking him prisoner and giving the government to General Góes. The only plotter identified clearly was Lt. Col. Gustavo Cordeiro de Farias of Góes's ministerial staff. One of the most fascinating aspects of all this was that aside from the months of the paulista revolt, Getúlio did not resort to martial law, states of siege, or press censorship to govern as dictator.[83] Under the coming constitutional regime such measures would become nearly constant.

Finally, Vargas stood as candidate for constitutional president, along with General Góes and Antônio Augusto Borges de Medeiros, the Rio Grandense political boss. On July 16, 1934, Vargas won with 175 votes, against 59 for Borges and 4 for Góes. Several days before the election Góes offered his resignation, asserting his steady loyalty but admitting that he had been led astray by "false friends" in a sordid intrigue against the army. He had not wanted to be candidate in opposition to "Your Excellency's honored name." His candidacy was "the dark point in the long and transparently frank association that I have had with Your Excellency." He blamed "enemies of the army," "certain cynical men." He wanted to reestablish the atmosphere of trust between them and thought that he should leave the ministry and return to the army ranks to give Getúlio freedom to implement the army reorganization that they had agreed on. Aside from the financial difficulties and the "complications accumulated during the first republic and the revolutionary period," he saw only one grave obstacle to "institutional order, that had not been possible to correct, and that was that it had not been possible to divert "the active army from the attractions, competitions and struggles of party politics." He reaffirmed his belief in Getúlio's "patriotism and capacity to find the means to overcome the difficulties and to restore our position on the Continent." Vargas reciprocated these statements of loyalty by keeping him as minister; indeed, his diary entries make clear that he considered fellow gaúcho Borges de Medeiros the opposition candidate rather than Góes.[84]

Thus did Brazil return to constitutional rule but, unhappily, under a national charter that lacked precise terminology in its attempts to check presidential powers by listing them and making them less discretionary. Contemporary observer Karl Loewenstein commented that "Janus-headed as the constitution appears it was probably the predestined link between the liberal past and the more social-minded if not collectivistic future."[85] The states drew up new constitutions and held elections, and the local 1930 factions struggled with the old oligarchies, who saw their chance for a comeback. The national assembly became the legislative battleground between the state autonomists and the Vargas centralists. The president had immediate doubts, believing that it would be difficult to "direct the country" under the new Constitution, and he began to think about drawing up another "project."[86]

The period of elective government did not calm the continual turbulence that afflicted Brazil, and the army would often be a major actor in the series of crises that marked the era. Góes Monteiro's oft-stated goal of keeping partisan politics out of the army and of developing a unified institutional political stance proved to be impossible without dictatorship.

CHAPTER 9

Security of the Pátria

[W]e lack almost everything.
—Getúlio Vargas, Dec. 24, 1934

There is a small percentage in all echelons who are good
soldiers and would be good in any Army, but unfortunately
their efficiency is all but lost in the general medium of
questioned loyalty and lack of discipline.
—Maj. William Sackville, April 18, 1935

To construct an army with a high standard of professionalism, Brazil needed to reform its military education system and provide its regiments and battalions with modern arms and equipment. And to be sure that its assigned missions were adequate to the threats it faced, the army had to develop intelligence gathering and analysis. Because Brazil's great distances were traversed by few railroads and by fewer paved roads, the airplane was a godsend that allowed observation and communication with many points of the national map that had been rarely seen by outsiders and maintenance of physical contact with places that were weeks or months away from Rio de Janeiro by overland or water transport. And to halt national dependence on imported manufactures, there was consensus among Brazil's elites that industrialization had to take place. In the turbulent 1930s it would have been wildly optimistic to think that any of this could occur without struggle, discord, and iron determination. Wars between Brazil's neighbors helped focus its officer corps attention on the essentials of soldiers, arms, and training. Awareness of the realities of the threats they faced also heightened corporate awareness and a sense that their lives were being sold too cheaply. The struggle over adequate pay seemed petty to some observers, but many officers believed that they could not survive on their salaries. The pay crisis of 1935 permits an unusual perspective on the inner workings of the officer corps, its fragile discipline, and its self image as a military organization.

Military Academy Reform and the New Academy
of Agulhas Negras

An informed outsider's view of the army at this juncture can be obtained from the reports of the U.S. military attaché, Major William Sackville, who toured army posts for a firsthand look. His viewpoint and analysis were descriptive and comparative. After attending the graduation ceremonies at the military school at Realengo, Sackville noted that the cadets lived in large rooms with bunks for seventy-five, more akin to American enlisted barracks than the three or four cadets to a room at West Point. They ate at long tables in the mess hall. The atmosphere was more appropriate for a barracks than a school. The main building was two stories high with a central archway that gave entry into the inner courtyard, which was flanked by a continuous two-story building on all sides, with another archway leading into the second inner patio with a similar but one-story structure around it, and a third arch by which one entered the third patio, with its parallel bars and basketball court. On hot nights studious cadets, teasingly called *cranios* (skulls, i.e., brains) by the less motivated, would take their books and folding tables out under the exterior lights in the second and third patios until the wee hours. On finally turning in, they might encounter classmates returning from "over the wall leave" adventures in Realengo, Bangu, or other suburbs. If the officer of the day happened to make a bed check, the wall-climbing adventurer might find his cot dismantled and placed in the bathroom. It was in these large quarters that the cadets studied, sang or beat out sambas, or slept in slack moments. It was the constant contact of the quarters that unified and tightened the "comradeship that united us like brothers, in good and bad situations."[1]

The corps of cadets totaled 750 in the three-year course, which at that point consisted of a two-year basic curriculum, with the third year devoted to the cadet's combat arm. The graduating class of 1933 numbered 220. "Cranios" of 1930–33 such as Golbery do Couto e Silva, Mozart de Souza Andrade, Raymundo Ferreira de Souza, Fritz de Azevedo Manso (all infantry), José Campos de Aragão (artillery), and Dirceu Araujo Nogueira (engineer) would be the captains of the Estado Novo, the majors and lieutenant colonels of the second Vargas era of the early 1950s, the colonels of the coup of 1964, and the generals of the post-1964 army.[2]

The commanding officer, Brigadier General José Pessôa Cavalcanti de Albuquerque, was the brother of Vargas's assassinated vice presidential running mate, João Pessôa, whose violent death had sparked the Revolution of 1930. He was the nephew of President Epitácio Pessôa (1919–22) and brother of Aristarcho Pessôa Cavalcanti de Albuquerque, who had played a central role in the Revolution of 1930 in Minas Gerais. He was also an officer of

considerable distinction, who was a product of, and a participant in, the reform efforts of the previous decades. Born in 1884, at seventeen he entered
the army as a student at the Preparatory and Practical School of Realengo,
to ready himself for admittance to the military school of Praia Vermelha. It
was 1903, and in 1904, as seen in Chapter 2, the latter school got swept up in
the riotous events of that year that led to its closing and the transfer of students to Porto Alegre for completion of their studies. He observed Realengo
commandant Brig. Gen. Hermes da Fonseca's success in keeping the school
out of the 1904 uprising and Hermes' efforts to energize the discipline, training, and professionalization of his students. In 1909 his first troop assignment coincided with a high point in Hermes' reforms and the return of the
first group of officers sent to Germany for training. In 1912, as a lieutenant,
Pessôa participated in salvationist operations in his home state of Paraíba in
the movement discussed in Chapter 3. He was an instructor in the Tiro program in Bahia and São Paulo, and in the latter organized and trained a volunteer unit at the law school in support of Bilac's campaign for obligatory
military service. With Brazil's entry into World War I he was sent to Paris for
a course in the military school of Saint-Cyr and was assigned as a squadron
commander in a French army unit whose soldiers were Turks. He later attributed his French and Belgium Cross of War decorations for bravery to
his extremely aggressive Turkish soldiers, who at least once presented him
with a necklace of enemy ears. Downed by typhoid, in Hemingwayesque
fashion he fell in love with a beautiful English, Red Cross nurse, Blanche
Mary Edward, who became his wife. Returning to Brazil in 1920 as a captain, he organized the army's new tank unit, which two years later helped
close off Vila Militar from the rebellious advance of Realengo military students. Promoted to major, he served as second officer of the military school,
then interim commander of the First Cavalry Regiment; success in that assignment led to command of the Third Independent Cavalry Regiment in
São Luis, Rio Grande do Sul. One wonders what his wife, Mary, thought of
frontier life amidst the gaúchos? The Revolution of 1930 found him a colonel
in Rio de Janeiro, where he led the seizure of Guanabara Palace during the
deposition of Washington Luís. After a brief period as Federal District fire
chief, he took command of the military school of Realengo.[3]

The term *cadet,* which in the old Portuguese tradition was a title with airs
of nobility, had been abolished by the republican government in the radical
surge of 1898. In August 1931, in order to link the army's basic officer's school
with the traditions of the previous century, Vargas decreed the establishment
of the Corps of Cadets, complete with a new blue uniform and shako head-
gear modeled on the uniform of 1852 (used in the campaign against Juan
Manuel Rosas of Argentina). A smaller version of the campaign sword of
the duke of Caxias and a red-tasseled fourragère completed the distinctive

uniform known as the *azulão* (big blue) in army parlance. On August 25, the birthday of Caxias, Vargas handed the new blue flag of the cadet corps to the first-ranked cadet, Antonio Pereira Lima. The cadets were encouraged to see themselves as elite soldiers, future officers. A cadet of this era recalled that they were proud and honored to wear the school uniform. Even the harassed first-year boys (the *bichos*) felt they were worthy men *(gente)* in that uniform.[4]

Pessôa changed some of the academy's basic traditions with simple modifications, such as imposing health and physical examinations each year instead of just at the start of the three-year course. It had been traditional for the third-year class to coast on the laurels of the first two years, by, for example, not carrying packs and equipment on field exercises. Pessôa insisted that every cadet maintain the full program until the very end. No more gliding; laurels had to be constantly defended. He used his persuasion and social connections to secure invitations for his splendidly dressed cadets to parties at the leading clubs of the capital, such as the *Tijuca* Tennis Club and the *Fluminense,* successfully injecting the army's cadets into the higher reaches of society. With cadet status in mind he ended the practice of punishing rule infractions with imprisonment in army jails or units where his charges would be mixed with common soldiers. Instead, punishments were completed within the school. His stress on dignified public comportment and status led him to expel a few cadets who were provoked into street brawls in nearby Bangu, even though the cadets thought that they were defending the school's honor. Also contributing to the change of status were new recruitment policies that limited to 50 percent the number of graduates of the three Colégios Militares in Fortaleza, Porto Alegre, and Rio de Janeiro, selecting the remaining half by competitive examinations from civilian secondary schools. That the school was attractive to young men of civilian background was shown by the one thousand who sat for the 1932 examinations, of whom only eighty were accepted.

Among the latter was a seventeen year old from São Paulo city, Carlos de Meira Mattos, who had been a soldier in the paulista forces and whose parents had tried to dissuade him by saying that "they will not want a Paulista revolutionary in the Military School." He insisted and was admitted to the ranks of the "big blue." Meira Mattos's career would stretch through World War II service in the Italian campaign to be a major figure in the postwar army and commandant of Pessôa's dream school, the Academia Militar das Agulhas Negras in 1969–71. In retirement his many books on geopolitics would elevate and set a high standard for Brazilian strategic thinking.[5]

General Pessôa remodeled the old buildings, but in accepting the assignment to Realengo he had imposed two conditions: first, that he could move the school away from "the tumultuous atmosphere" of the capital; and second, that he would have a free hand in doing so. In 1931, after looking at possible sites in the states of Rio, São Paulo, and Minas Gerais, he selected one opposite the city of Resende, in the state of Rio de Janeiro, not far from the São Paulo line. This beautiful location was dominated by the majestic Itatiaia mountains, the highest in Brazil, with the distinctive Agulhas Negras (Black Needles) peak marking the horizon. There, far from the political intrigues of Rio and São Paulo, Pessôa believed that a new type of officer could be prepared. His dream school was one of the things delayed by the paulista civil war. By January 1933 an architectural firm had been selected. A wooden block model of the planned facility was on display at Realengo, and the army had estimated its cost at about U.S.$4,500,000. The problem was that the government did not have the money. Oswaldo Aranha, then minister of treasury, fearful of destabilizing market prices, objected to Pessôa's idea of funding it with extra coffee sales to the United States. Some officers criticized plans for such a "luxurious" academy because its graduates would find the army's regular units so rough and ragged that they surely would become disheartened. With determination and conviction, José Pessôa shut his ears to negative voices and pressed on, perhaps believing that the most secure way to overcome opposition was to build fast. He pushed the architectural plans to completion and scheduled a cornerstone laying ceremony to conclude a week of cadet corps field exercises in late October 1933.[6]

Those exercises were unusual in their scope and location in that they involved the full corps and that they took place in the area where Agulhas Negras now stands. They became famous in army lore because they marked the high tide of French influence and because certain of the officers who directed the cadets became the generals who led the army in the fateful 1960s.

The curriculum of the school aimed at balancing professional military training with university-level general education, under the guidance of the French military mission, in the person of Realengo's director of studies, Lt. Col. Paul Langlet, and his upwardly mobile assistant, Captain Humberto de Alencar Castelo Branco, a prized pupil of the mission, who would himself leave a profound mark on the army's history as chief of the general staff and as president of the republic. Among the school's officers were also found Major Mário Travassos, and Lts. Newton Fountoura de Oliveira Reis, Breno Borges Fortes, Paulo Enéas F. da Silva, and Amílcar Dutra de Menezes. In later years Travassos became a pioneer formulator of Brazilian geopolitics, Dutra de Menezes headed the government propaganda department during the Estado Novo, and Borges Fortes served as chief of the general staff.[7]

Pessôa's insistence on proper behavior and self-discipline was not always shared or understood by the cadets. In response to his punishment of a few cadets for disorderly conduct a mass "strike" occurred. His disagreement with then Minister of War Góes Monteiro over his handling of the affair led to his replacement. But even so, he continued to push construction of the new academy at Agulhas Negras.

In the remaining years of the decade the Vargas regime focused its efforts on raising the quality of military training and education, providing adequate arms and equipment, and shaping strategic doctrine so as to balance Brazil's national goals with its capabilities and potential. Of course, all of these goals were interrelated, and their pursuit would have profound affects on the Brazilian society, economy, politics, and, ultimately, international standing.

War in the Chaco and Amazonia

In order to improve training, the army had to keep existing units functional and to increase its force level to man and equip units that existed only on paper. The paulista war had required a sudden armed forces expansion, heavily based on the mobilization of short-term state provisional and police units, but the army also expanded its own numbers so that, at the end of hostilities, it had under arms 63,524 men, who were kept until the end of the year. In 1932, while the São Paulo crisis had preoccupied Brazilian leaders, a decades-long border dispute between Paraguay and Bolivia exploded into the Chaco War (1932–35); and in the western Amazon, from September 1932 until early 1933, Peru and Colombia engaged in small-scale combat for control of Leticia and surrounding territory. The proximity of these conflicts to the Brazilian frontier towns of Corumbá on the upper Paraguay River and Tabatinga and Benjamin Constant on the Solimões River worried the Vargas government enough to keep 60,000 soldiers on active duty, even though the budget for that year called for a reduction to 54,500. By March 1934 the general staff had submitted to Vargas a plan for a provisional reorganization of the army that envisioned a force of 74,000 soldiers.[8]

The high level of Getúlio's anxiety is best captured in secret correspondence in late 1934 with Oswaldo Aranha, who had left his cabinet post as minister of treasury to become ambassador to the United States in July 1934. The president wrote that he had not consulted any advisers, but he had returned from a trip in the south deeply troubled by the Paraguayan situation and its possible ramifications for Brazil's relations with Argentina. His worry coincided with the views of the general staff, which he said, was "very alarmed." The Chaco question had taken an obscure turn and seemed to be getting more complicated. Now "militarily strong, with a victorious army of 70,000 men," Paraguay "won't know what to do with these people after the war"; it would not have jobs for them, so, Vargas correctly predicted, a victorious general returning at the head of "a discontented army" might well topple the civilian government. He feared that Paraguay might "create problems on our frontier in Mato Grosso, provoking an incident that would bring Argentina into the conflict." Buenos Aires, he declared, had been "openly supporting Paraguay, providing all manner of supplies, concentrating troops on the border of Bolivia, even occupying some border posts of that country and advocating the reabsorption of Bolivia, [which had been] part of the [colonial] viceroyalty of the Prata." One of the loudest voices calling for such action was the Argentine minister of war, General Manuel A. Rodríguez. The Argentine government provided loans to keep Paraguay fighting. The two countries treated Brazilian attachés with "visible suspicion" and would not let them visit the war zone. "Our policy," Getúlio noted, "has been cordial friendship with Argentina and abstention of interference in the Chaco question." While keeping that policy, "we must take military precautions," which alone might avoid future problems. However, "we lack almost everything." What, he wanted to know from Aranha, was American thinking about all this, "and to what point will they accompany us?" We do not have money, and "two things we need at the moment: some units for coastal defense; one or two cruisers, submarines and one or two gunboats on the Paraguay river."

Aranha responded that Roosevelt had asked that they do nothing regarding the Brazilian fleet without consulting him because the American president had "decided to do everything he could so that everything could be built [in the United States] on the best and cheapest terms." Aranha warned that they had keep this to themselves, that the slightest leak could compromise their efforts to secure American arms. "The truth . . . Getúlio, is that these people are convinced that in case of war we will be with them." However, they were "alarmed with our lack of interest in this post since the time of Domicio da Gama" (1911–18), and the Americans did not understand how Brazil could twice renew the French military mission's contract and not keep the American naval mission. It was "because of this that "THEY BEGAN TO CONQUER THE SYMPATHY OF THE OTHERS, especially Argentina, to which they have already conceded a naval mission." "I tell you," Aranha wrote, "that everything is possible to obtain, but it will all have to be done with discretion, with secrecy." Not a word could get out, he cautioned.[9]

The general staff had kept an eye on the two sides for years as they had maintained an uneasy peace, thanks to Chile warning Bolivia to stay calm and to Argentina, under President Hipólito Yrigoyen (1916–22, 1928–30), keeping a brake on Paraguay. But in 1930 Yrigoyen's toppling by the military had eliminated that restraint. Indeed, throughout the 1930s the Brazilian military worried a good deal about their Argentine counterparts. During the paulista civil war the Brazilian military attaché in Buenos Aires, Captain Riograndense Kruel, reported that "the Argentine ambience, popular, as well as official is, in general, sympathetic to the Paulistas." Kruel said that rebel agents were able to smuggle supplies and aircraft from Argentina into Brazil. This alone would have made Brazilian intelligence officers nervous, but in their analysis of the Chaco situation they saw Argentine interests at work. As of 1929, the great majority of the private properties in the Chaco were owned by Argentine citizens or enterprises, fully 10,500,000 hectares of the total 22,000,000 hectares in dispute were in Argentine hands; of the 30,000 Paraguayans resident in the region, 18,000 worked for Argentine businesses, which held half of the million head of cattle being raised there; 198 miles of the Chaco's 260 miles of railroad were Argentine. In total Argentine investments in the conflicted zone, according to the Brazilian analysts, far exceeded the 1929 figure of 40,000,000 pesos. They also believed that reports of oil in the Chaco played a role in Argentine backing of Paraguay. They asserted that Argentina considered Paraguay "an extension of its commercial markets and [that] its territory constitutes indirectly a tributary geographical element of its own political economy." Moreover, they believed that Brazilian diplomacy was being outmaneuvered in the neighboring republics by the astute Argentine foreign minister, Carlos Saavedra Lamas.

The war restrained Brazil's plans for ties with Bolivia. In 1928 the two countries had signed a protocol whereby Brazil would help with the construction of railroads linking Santa Cruz de la Sierra to ports in the Amazon basin, and to those on the Paraguay River, thereby giving Bolivia access to Manaos in the north (and to the world via the great river) and to Corumbá in the east. Via the latter it would have a rail link with São Paulo, "whose industries would find a good market in Bolivia." This Brazilian plan clashed with Argentina's project of building a railroad north into Bolivia; it also competed with Chilean and Peruvian efforts to orient Bolivia in the direction of the Pacific.

In addition to Brazil's competition with Argentina over their neighbors, the army analysts pointed to an Argentine-Paraguayan threat in the border region of Mato Grosso. In 1870 the area had changed hands as a result of the Brazilian defeat of Paraguay, however the numerous Paraguayan inhabitants still objected. A number of the great latifundios were Paraguayan owned, and the army had reports that many of the cowboys were being signed up for the Paraguayan army in violation of Brazilian neutrality. Especially, the Brazilian officers pointed to the Argentine-owned company "Mate Larangeira [which] constitutes a danger for the interests of National Defense . . . in case of war with that country." To emphasize Mate Larangeira's untrustworthiness, the analysts noted that "in all the internal struggles from 1922 to 1932, this company always aided the rebels against the government, whether by providing money, or by raising troops, in great part Paraguayans, as happened particularly in the 1932 revolution of São Paulo." Clearly, the Brazilian officers did not trust either the Argentines, with whom in the mid-1930s Brazil was maintaining very cordial relations and active trade, or the Paraguayans, "given the perfidious and contemptuous character that the Paraguayans always showed in diplomacy and concerning the rights of other countries, when it involved satisfying their interests and ambitions." The officers worried that to attack Puerto Suarez (in Bolivia, opposite Corumbá, on the Mato Grosso border) the Paraguayans would have to cross Brazilian territory, violating not only neutrality but national sovereignty.

In the great conflicts around the world in the 1930s the Chaco War may have been a small affair, but for Brazil it was an immediate problem that affected its relations in the Rio de La Plata region for decades to come. One interesting sidelight was that army intelligence, frustrated by the difficulty of securing accurate information, apparently attempted to make up for its lack of military attachés in Asuncion and La Paz at the outset of the war by having First Lieutenant of Cavalry Nemo Canabarro Lucas serve on the Paraguayan side. On his return to Brazilian service he helped produce the study of the war on which the foregoing is based.[10]

The Army's View of Brazil's Strategic Position in the 1930s

The general staff's study of the Chaco War was part of the process of organizing the country's first modern military intelligence service. Brazil sent military attachés to various "interesting countries." An early result of this effort was a detailed study of Brazil's "military situation" that would provide a basis for the military and foreign policies in the years prior to World War II. A summary of this 1934 document will give the reader some insight into the strategic thinking of the Brazilian leadership. The analysis suggests that for all the apparent internal divisions among the elites, Brazilian policy ultimately was based on a coherent and realistic appraisal of the country's relative strength and position in South America and in the world.

The analysts observed that the great powers were shaken by internal economic and social crises that had unsettled the world order and had produced a "*reciprocal and permanent distrust*" that made any durable agreement impossible." As a result "Brazil as an ally could be pulled into another world war, or it could be the cause or theater of a war." The analysts saw "serious threats" looming over "South America in general and over Brazil in particular" from "*various expansionist currents,*" among which were the following:

– the Japanese—the most dangerous, because it is the most systematic and methodical, the most absorbent and best directed;

– the Germanic—which threat existed before the European conflagration [WWI] and which broke out again with the wave of intensive *racist spirit* and scientific-military philosophy;

– the North American—that is above all economic, not threatening directly our political independence, but tending to make us vassals. American expansion, that is accomplished principally by *means of the exportation of capital and via commerce in gen-*

eral, tends to clash here with the Japanese, that is carried out by the export of labor, whose effect is more radical and dangerous. The collision of these two currents could result in an attack against our independence or, at least, against our integrity;

– the Italian—that by its origins and nature is less dangerous, has concentrated, however, too much in certain regions of the country, tending indirectly to threaten a break in the national unity of the people, and to exercise strong influence on part of public opinion in event of a European war.

The German immigrants could similarly endanger national unity and resolve.

In case of an *"extra continental"* war, Brazil could only defend itself with a preventative policy. Internally, it would have to control the immigrant population, spreading it throughout the country to avoid concentrations of those with the same origins, neutralizing direct assistance from foreign governments, forbidding foreign colonization companies, insisting on obligatory teaching and use of Portuguese, and imposing an *"intense nationalization"* of those born in Brazil to cut their ties to the countries of origin. Externally, Brazil would have to make alliances. No one South American country, the general staff analysts noted, in the next two or three decades, would have sufficient military strength to fend off a great power aggressor. If the bigger South American countries allied, they would have enough military power to make "difficult, expensive, and dubious, attempts at *conquest by any method.*" This idealized South American alliance would involve development of military industries and a continental system of communications. Alas, the analysts lamented, the history of South American disputes and rivalries made such an alliance unlikely.

The authors reminded their superiors that Brazil, as the only Portuguese-speaking country in the hemisphere, was isolated and so could only count on itself. Although the United States was similarly alone vis-à-vis the Spanish-speaking countries and although this Brazilian-American commonality as outsiders had led to a "more or less intimate cooperation" in the past, expanded United States influence would not be "without grave inconveniences." "Economically we are their dependents, because they buy our principal product [coffee] in much greater quantities than all other countries, while we buy relatively little from them." Furthermore, coffee was not a necessity, and in wartime it could be obtained elsewhere. The United States, the report warned, "could itself constitute a threat for us . . . depending on the evolution of its post-war international policy."

All this meant, the army analysts opined, that Brazil had to organize its military power, which would "liberate it from *North American dependence,* without prejudicing an even greater closeness with the great confederation of the north, thereby satisfying, in broader fashion, the necessities of national defense." The analysts warned that, in case of war, "without the aid of the United States or of another strong industrial power, the situation of any South

American nation is precarious, because none of them possesses sufficient military industries." In the meantime, as Brazil developed its industrial capabilities, its defense against extracontinental aggression, lay in "*preventative* measures", principally diplomacy.

If a new war followed the pattern of the great war of 1914–18, "our position is naturally on the side of the *Entente,* especially if Argentina and the United States line up on that side." However, the report cautioned that Brazil "should not assume an attitude diametrically opposed to that of Argentina, which could cause a war with that nation, for which we are not prepared."[11]

This threat analysis shows that as early as 1934 Brazilian authorities were measuring the dangers that were accumulating on the world scene and were considering how best to protect the country. In summary, the Brazilian army leaders believed that they had to depend on their own wits and resources and that they should use the crises that lay ahead to obtain the greatest advantage for Brazil. However, when considering a possible world war and the problem of equipping and preparing its armed forces, the Brazilian military and presidential papers repeatedly point to the United States as the logical source.[12] Later in the decade Brazilian espionage in Argentina turned up a 1933 document, with revisions made in 1934 and 1935, that outlined *"Plano Maximo"* for possible war with Brazil. The plan assumed United States support of Brazil; indeed, the Argentines saw themselves as the principal barrier to American imperialism on the South American continent and thought it possible that Washington might prod Brazil into a conflict with Buenos Aires to eliminate their opposition.[13]

There were also domestic reasons for wanting to build up federal military power. The Revolution of 1930 had pushed aside the oligarchic, state-based coalitions, but the danger of an uprising of remnants of the old system was always latent. Indeed, as noted above, some officers and some civilian politicians saw the 1934 constitutional government as a return of the state coalitions that the 1930 revolution had thrown out. As noted earlier, the period of the constituent assembly in late 1933 until July 1934 was full of windy conspiracies and wispy specters of dictatorship. In army thinking the internal and external threats could best be checked by organizing for a war against strong foreign enemies, which preparation ought to give them sufficient resources to maintain "internal order." Chief of Staff Francisco de Andrade Neves stated candidly that keeping internal peace and order was as influential in the distribution of troops throughout the national territory as were recruitment, mobilization, or strategic reasons. They had to be ready for "rapid intervention" of a "preventive character." The experience in the country's "intestinal wars," notably the recent one with São Paulo, had shown their infantry division to be too heavy, so they had to develop "a lighter and more mobile combat unit." Army policy, or, better, mission, was that "the interests of internal politics committed to the Army the role of guard of peace and defender of order in the Republic."[14]

The foregoing analysis should be sufficient to indicate that the Brazilian leadership prior to the Second World War had linked national development and security with international trade and finance, and that they were worried about moves that might endanger the country, but that internationally they saw themselves naturally on the side of the liberal powers, particularly the United States. Further, there was agreement among the key leaders that the dangers that afflicted the world also offered opportunities. Factions developed as the world crisis deepened, and opinions differed as to which side offered the most with the least danger. For some foreign observers the internal debates took on ideological coloring that muddied their analyses.

The Army and Industrialization

The links among Brazilian external and internal security concerns, army reorganization and rearmament, foreign policy, and industrialization grew tighter as the 1930s progressed. Back in 1919 and 1920 the army minister's reports and the presidential messages to Congress had emphasized that ending dependence on foreign arms imports and "the organization of our military industry will be the greatest patriotic achievement of the generation that brings it about" because it would "secure the country's economic emancipation and independence." President Epitácio Pessôa had connected arms production to the development of a national iron and steel industry. He and his predecessors had recognized that establishment of such an industry was tied to broad economic development, and within the army it was understood that such development was ultimately a means of national defense. Vargas and his administration implemented a set of policy objectives that had been argued and imagined for decades. Being the implementers, rather than the creators of the objective of industrialization takes nothing away from Vargas or his advisers. The circumstances of the 1930s, nationally and internationally, provided opportunities that previously had been foreclosed. The slowness of the process of turning goals into realities can be best understood by recalling that Brazil of the 1920s was not just underdeveloped; it was undeveloped. The majority of Brazilians were illiterate, and the tiny educated elite did not have the problem-solving or organizational mentality required to take the country into the modern age. Higher education under the empire had been limited to medical, law, and engineering faculties; the first university, that of Rio de Janeiro, dated from 1920. By 1937 and the Estado Novo there would be only a total of four universities. Those institutions were not engaged in preparing a modernizing cadre, but, as education reformer Anísio S. Teixeira observed, they "were removed from most pressures that might have made them responsive to the broader needs of society," existing in "a closed world of remote and distant studies."[15] The universities, their faculties, and students were disengaged from the ideas, goals, and regimentation of the military, and neither seemed to understand the other, with dangerous future results. So instead of the universities leading Brazil into the modern age, that role was left to the politicians and the military.

There was so much to be done that it was nearly overwhelming. How could sophisticated development occur in a country where the bull cart and mule train were still common means of transport—the army remained preoccupied with horse and mule raising until the eve of World War II—and wood was the major source of energy? The goal of steel and arms production involved a leap of centuries, from animals and wood to the gasoline-powered internal-combustion engine and hydroelectric power.[16]

Indeed, the army's experience with its own arsenals showed just how difficult the road ahead would be. In the 1920s it became clear that the purchase of the latest machines, dies, and tools was not enough. Leadership was a basic problem. Customarily, officers detailed to the arsenals were selected haphazardly, without regard to their technical knowledge or managerial abilities. And the workers they directed had no incentives to produce because nobody, according to the then minister of war, was prepared "to appreciate and reward real merit." He complained that "a job in an arsenal is considered an opportunity to loaf." Without proper technical supervision workers did almost nothing. The army brought in some French technicians to remodel "this ramshackle ruin," which Brazilians, the war minister lamented, had deceived themselves into thinking was "a first-class department for the manufacture of military material," when in reality, it was "nothing more than a heap of junk." The litany of problems went on for paragraphs.[17]

The rebellions of the 1920s, the Revolution of 1930, and the paulista civil war of 1932 more or less froze this situation into the late-1930s. Those events, particularly the last, demonstrated the army's material weakness. Weapons and equipment research all but ceased as the army struggled to hold itself together. In the paulista conflict the government forces fired an average of 265,000 rifle cartridges a day, while its Realengo arsenal produced only 65,000 per day. In 1932 the army's total expenditure was more than twenty million rounds, whereas Realengo had managed to arm 17,442,535 cartridges, of which only 1,335,189 used shell casings produced locally. And it took a special budgetary allowance to make that possible. The army had to buy munitions in the United States, France, Holland, and Austria to overcome rebellious forces that relied solely on captured army and state police stocks and improvised production. The situation was similar in artillery-shell production and in the refurbishing of rifle and machine-gun barrels. The army's arsenals and factories could produce about one-third of its needs. The ordinance director blamed this on the semiabandonment of those institutions. By comparison, in the mid-1930s Argentina had a reserve stock of 380 million cartridges as against Brazil's 46 million. The worries of Vargas and his generals about the Chaco War were based on a realistic assessment of Brazilian capabilities.[18]

Clearly, Brazil needed the ability to produce its own arms, and to do that it had to industrialize. Between 1934 and 1938 the ordnance chief argued for a variety of measures that reflected evolving army policies on industrialization. Instead of merely exporting its massive ore deposits and importing finished goods, Brazil should create industries to make iron, steel, copper, lead, zinc, aluminum, and other metal products. Ordnance reports called on the government to attract private investors with fiscal incentives, with the easing of customs restrictions on the necessary foreign-made machinery, and with guaranteeing a basic, beginning market by specifying that government factories would buy a certain portion of the resulting production. The army had been studying the metallurgical problem since 1931, and its officers had concluded that during the turbulent 1920s the institution had not seriously faced the question. They pointed out that although the ordnance department dated from 1915 and that the various technical courses in construction, armament, chemicals, and electricity had begun in 1918, still little progress could be noted. The army's senior officers and promotion policy did not encourage the technical and specialized training required. Without officer specialists the army was dependent on civilian experts, whom the Brazilian universities were simply not producing. The immediate solution was the old one of contracting foreign specialists and buying whole production lines and processes in Europe or North America. In 1937 the ordnance chief observed that his department was "a technical section without technicians." Only then, he commented hopefully, were the army's schools beginning to graduate the desired technicians, and he regretted that their effect would not be felt for several years. Among other reasons, the new officer technicians would have to train a specialized workforce. The fruits of these endeavors would be evident after World War II, when the wartime construction of the Volta Redonda steel complex and growth of the automobile industry in the 1950s secured Brazil's industrial rise.

Army Aviation Extended the Reach of the State

The 1930s also witnessed the invigoration of the army's air service and the growth of aviation in general. The São Paulo civil war demonstrated the value of military aviation and led to the physical expansion of the air arm, now well equipped with the 150 aircraft purchased in the United States during the conflict. This was "the largest purchase of War Equipment ever made by a Brasilian [*sic*] Government outside of the two dreadnaughts they bought from England" in 1910. The conflict also had increased army attention to antiaircraft artillery. Overall the fighting had helped turn Brazil into an aviation-conscious society. In Vargas it already had a leader fascinated by flight and convinced that aviation would be the most rapid and effective means to tie the farthest reaches of Brazil's roadless expanse to the nation-state. To Vargas "aviation will be the historic destiny of Brazilians."[19]

Prior to the 1932 conflict the training regimen of pilots at the flight school at Rio de Janeiro's Campo dos Afonsos held them within six miles of the field. To break free of the distance limitation and to gain practical experience of flying conditions, a group of pilots including Major Eduardo Gomes and First Lieutenants Antonio de Lemos Cunha and Casimiro Montenegro Filho suggested to the minister of war that they form a military airmail service (*Correio Aéreo Militar,* CAM). This idea provided the army and navy with a civilian justification for the costly imported aircraft, to gain valuable flight experience, and a way to extend the military and the central government into the still shadowy interior. It allowed sharing equipment and infrastructure costs with the Ministry of Transportation and Public Works. And it was a productive manner to "channel" the energy and enthusiasm of the pilots and ground crews into a useful and welcome service to society. Beginning with triweekly flights between Rio de Janeiro and São Paulo, they gradually extended the service to Goiás, Mato Grosso, and through Minas Gerais up the São Francisco River to Juazeiro and Quixadá in Ceará by late 1932. CAM pilots were very comfortable in the air by the time hostilities began. Some pilots, such as Captain José Candido da Silva Muricy, literally landed from airmail runs and took to the air again on combat missions. He commented that it was painful to find friends on the paulista side in his gun sight, but he had been determined to do his duty.[20]

This activity had coincided with the entry into Brazilian air space of nascent foreign commercial airlines, whose Brazilian subsidiaries—Pan American's Panair do Brasil (1930), France's Aeropostale, and Lufthansa's Condor—and the growing state-based air companies of Varig (RGS) and Vasp (SP) needed pilots familiar with conditions and routes. Indeed, in 1936 the government decreed that the foreign subsidiaries and state lines must have completely Brazilian crews, most of whom would be recruited of necessity from the military.[21] In 1934 Pan American's *Brazilian Clipper* inaugurated service from Miami to Rio de Janeiro via the coastal route. Perhaps I should remind contemporary readers that back then there was not yet long-distance night flying, so "flying down to Rio" was a five-day trip. It took the *Brazilian Clipper* three days to fly the 2,645 miles from Belém, at the outlet of the Amazon, to Rio de Janeiro. In August 1934 it was a significant event when two army pilots flew their Waco Cabin-64 from Fortaleza to Rio de Janeiro during the same day, in sixteen hours. Vargas and his family loved to fly, and he used flight to shorten travel time whenever he could. During his long period in office Brazil stepped over the rail era and soared into the air age.[22]

The purchase of American aircraft led to the sending of pilots to the United States for advanced training. However, differing ways of doing such things nearly led to very negative results. The Brazilian authorities did not ask the United States ambassador or the military attaché to make arrangements for visits to American army flying fields or aircraft factories, yet the officers expected to take courses and to learn American ground, squadron, and group organization and to see the latest types of military air equipment. Apparently the Brazilian embassy in Washington was to make arrangements. Despite the breach of protocol, the American military attaché in Rio advised his superiors in the War Department that the Brazilians were willing to pay more for high quality aircraft and that "a policy on the part of the Army Air Service of encouraging these Brazilian officers to inspect equipment and learn our methods of instruction will bring future dividends to the country." The Brazilians especially wanted to make extensive visits to manufacturing plants to gain technical knowledge about the proper use and maintenance of their new aircraft and armament. A representative of the Du Pont Company, who was anxious to sell powder for the .50 caliber ammunition being used in the aircraft machine guns, observed that the visit was "a fine opportunity for us [North Americans] to gain their good will in such a manner that America will continue to furnish them with equipment in the future." In his view the War Department "could materially aid in pushing American Air Force Equipment" and that "a thousand and one things [could be] done officially or semi-officially to so impress the Brasilians [*sic*] so that no orders will be diverted to Europe in the future." The officers en route to the United States were "the best flyers in the Brasilian Army and exercise the most influence" in it. Clearly, American business saw its interests at stake in competition with European companies. The perceptive Du Pont agent commented:

I know what would be done by the British Air Force or the French or the Italians had these men gone to those countries. Certainly our Army should do no less. There are no other people in the world with whom courtesy and friendly treatment go so far as with the Brasilians. We've got the stuff to give them, so let's do a good job while we have the chance. . . . I shall be most interested to know what was done by our Army Air Force by way of "Sales Aid" to American Manufacturers. It's high time we stop pussyfooting; we ought to strike back at Europe the way she strikes at us. Righto![23]

The U. S. Army Air Corps authorities gave approval for visits to Mitchel, Wright, Selfridge, Randolph, and Kelly Fields, but they expressed concern that there would be little to see because the tactical school at Maxwell had ended its current session, and that elsewhere there were few officers present, because many of them were then on duty with the Civilian Conservation Corps. Unhappily, the War Department initially refused permission for the Brazilian flyers to visit the Martin Company's factory in Baltimore, where a new bomber was under construction. The company asked for a reconsideration because the plane had already been delivered to the Air Corps in Dayton, Ohio, and it wanted to show off its manufacturing facility and the new flying boats it was making for Pan American Airways. When the Brazilians realized that their visits to Martin, Curtis, and United Aircraft facilities were restricted to one- to three-day visits rather than the more lengthy training stays that they had envisioned, they complained to their superiors in Rio, and there was sufficient talk in the war ministry of recalling them that representatives of the American firms involved peppered the Rio embassy, the War and State Departments with letters and cables protesting such short-sighted treatment. Colt Fire Arms (which made machine guns for aircraft) and United Aircraft agents in Rio reported that "the officers spoken to at the Ministry of War here, were deeply disappointed." The agents warned that "it would be inimical, not alone to American trade interests, but also to the spirit of good will which prevails between the two countries, to allow this matter to remain as it is. Brazil went to quite some expense and trouble to send the mission to our country, and, under the circumstances, it is left with the alternative of suddenly recalling it."

As a propaganda or publicity venture the aviators' tour of the United States had mixed results. Some of the officers returned to Brazil "more or less embittered" and spoke "in favor of European material." They asserted that "they were not permitted to learn much of anything, that protracted visits to the plants that really interested them were not facilitated." One, who intended to study armaments, was allowed only three days at the Colt factory. From the documents it seems that most of the officers did not speak English, and it is not clear if interpreters were provided. The armaments specialist was later sent to Italy and France, whose governments were seriously seeking to sell arms, while the United States moved to tighten its arms exports because of its increasing fears for world peace. On the positive side two influential officers, Captains José Candido da Silva Muricy and Nelson Freire Lavanère-Wanderley, requested permission to attend the Advanced Flying School at Kelly Field, San Antonio, Texas. It is an indication of how new training foreign officers was for the United States that the decision was handled at the level of the secretary of state and Chief of Staff Douglas MacArthur, who approved "in view of the importance with which it is regarded by your Department."[24]

Foreign Arms Purchases as Interim Solution

The decision to buy arms abroad continued the old pattern, but this time it was intended as a stopgap until industrialization could be carried out. The efforts were to go forward simultaneously. In 1933 Vargas appointed two commissions to "create and develop military industries" and to buy arms in Europe, the latter commission was headed by former war minister Leite de Castro.[25] That commission's officers negotiated with the Swedish Bofors company for artillery, but the attempt failed because of Brazil's inability to pay in gold or hard currencies. Because they affected Brazil's ability to pay for arms, the army joined the debates over trade and debt policies. The choices were not easy. If Brazil paid its debts, it would have to sacrifice national defense. The British and the Americans preferred that debts to their citizens holding mature Brazilian bonds be settled before seriously discussing arms sales. That attitude and the menacing clouds of war made London and Washington less open to Brazilian concerns about arms. Moreover, in the first half of the decade the Washington Naval Treaty of 1922, limiting naval tonnage, was still in force (it expired in 1936), which made it illegal for Britain or the United States to sell warships to the Brazilians. Washington did not want to see funds that could pay bondholders diverted to other purposes. As a result continental European manufacturers appeared more attractive than they otherwise might have. The informal compensation trade agreement with Germany in June 1935 had army support because arms could be purchased with raw materials, such as cotton. That year, too, Krupp was again available as a source of arms. Considering that old Krupp cannons were still in use or on display in army posts, there was a certain continuity in the Brazilian army again looking to Germany for its equipment and arms. The purchases would take place in 1937 and 1938, and the onset of war would interfere with delivery.[26]

President Roosevelt, as mentioned earlier, had said that he wanted to have the desired Brazilian warships built in shipyards in the United States, but ultimately, after making commitments and raising the Vargas government's hopes, strenuous Argentine protests caused Washington to reverse itself. Prior to the world war the United States was not able to provide the army with arms or equipment. One of the reasons the Brazilians decided to send troops to Europe was to get arms. But its inability to supply armament did not prevent Washington from pressuring the Vargas government to manage its trade policies in favor of American interests. The Brazilian general staff paid close attention to those same policies because they affected the country's ability to buy abroad. As debates went on inside the army regarding such policies, the officer corps appeared to group into pro-American (later Allied) and pro-German (later Axis) camps. The European crisis produced deeply conflicted and complicated responses in the Brazilian officer corps. Certainly, there was admiration for Germany's reconstruction of its armed forces and its military industries and spreading acceptance of the idea that in facing the uncertainties ahead, Brazilian national security demanded a strong, efficient, centralized government committed to defense. It was easy for contemporary foreign observers to see nefarious Axis influences in the statements and attitudes of Generals Dutra and Góes Monteiro, but historians must look more deeply. The secret reports of the general staff provide a view behind the public facade. At the end of 1936, Brazilian army intelligence specified the "ambitions and demands of Germany, Italy and Japan . . . [for] a new division of lands" as a "latent danger for Brazil." Moreover, in recommending that a military attaché be assigned to the Washington embassy, the general staff's intelligence section asserted that "our foreign policy counsels us, by all its principles, a greater closeness with the United States of America, our principal support in case of war." The reciprocal interests of the two countries linked them together as the inter-American conference in Buenos Aires that year had shown. The army would benefit from tighter relations with the American military as demonstrated in the "very dedicated and loyal" work of the American coastal artillery mission.[27]

In his report for 1936 the chief of the general staff noted that the army as the "institution responsible for defending the Pátria" had to be "interested in stimulating . . . industrial mobilization." The view of the general staff was that "our economic emancipation" would be the only way that Brazil would have "efficient armed forces." That goal would be reached when Brazil solved its "*great national problems (steel mill, combustibles, etc.)*" (italics added). In this moment of grave international tension, when the European powers were arming themselves, the chief declared that "Brazil could not be an exception." The officer corps, he lamented, was working hard, but the material deficiencies undermined everything. "Practically, we are disarmed. Even our very rifles are in a sad state."[28]

With this lack of preparedness the senior officers particularly were extremely sensitive to the national political situation. During 1934 the formation of political parties, state elections, and adoption of state constitutions heated political activity to the boiling point. The parties were organized at the state level to defend or oppose various local interest groups. They did not unite into national parties and generally tried to use the national government to enhance their power in their respective states. The state police forces, which they had created in the 1890s, defended the state power holders and their municipal allies. State governments were not impartial but the creatures of private interests. It was this situation that the Revolution of 1930 was to reform. The 1934 restoration of elective politics tossed the states into internal political struggles. In São Paulo the importance of the state police can be seen in the repeated bickering over control of that organization. For example, in February the interventor Armando de Sales Oliveira protested to Vargas that General Daltro, commander of the Second Military Region, was attempting to control the state police in favor of the Partido Republicano Paulista.[29] By late April rumors of a possible coup against Vargas stirred the political stews in the states. Flores da Cunha in Rio Grande began mobilizing the provisional battalions of the state brigade. Senior officers, such as Dutra and Góes Monteiro, saw Flores's actions as a challenge to the national army. By August there were local political feuds, some with gunplay, going on in Maranhão, Rio Grande do Norte, Ceará, Piauí, and Mato Grosso. In Natal (Rio Grande do Norte), perhaps mimicking what they thought was happening in Rio de Janeiro, officers of the Twenty-fifth Light Infantry encouraged the interventor to resign, noting a fall in his public support. This latter unit would be involved in the communist revolt in Natal in November 1935.[30]

Military Tempest: Pay and Discipline

The officer corps was upset that the security legislation had come in the midst of heated public discussion about boosting military salaries. General João Guedes da Fontoura, commander of the First Infantry Brigade at Vila Militar, had headed a committee of army and navy officers that drew up the initial pay proposal submitted to the Congress.[31] It would have doubled the pay of the whole army and navy. When congressional hearings went against the proposal, General Guedes Fontoura lost his sense of proportion and threatened to parade his troops in front of the Congress to help its members see reason. The situation was complicated and dangerous. Back in early July 1934, when Vargas had been signing decrees legalizing decisions of his "provisional government" prior to the promulgation of the new Constitution, the army had proposed that he raise salaries, but then he and the minister of the treasury were implacably cutting budgets; indeed, reductions in the Ministries of Justice, Foreign Affairs, Education, Agriculture, Transportation, and Navy had shaved off over 140,000 contos. The story floated that he had promised raises to get army backing in the election for president, but this is not supported in documentation or in his own diary. On September 12, 1934, he had agreed with the navy minister and the chief of staff of the fleet that the navy would get new ships if it could find builders who would take payment in export goods. Later that month pressure had mounted for an economy-wide improvement in pay scales. In military circles petitions were circulating that requested readjustments vis-à-vis civil servants or an elevation in military pay. Vargas had reached agreement with his war and treasury ministers that one hundred thousand contos would be set aside for rearmament and nineteen thousand contos for salary adjustment.[32] General Pessôa, head of Vargas's military staff, thought Guedes Fontoura and others demanding salary increases were working against the government. How could generals seek raises, he asked, when the army was economizing by keeping units understrength and under-armed?[33] The constitutional government was operating on a deficit budget whose origin went back to the costs of the civil war in 1932 and was looking to reduce expenses, not increase them. The ministers of finance, Oswaldo Aranha (until July 24, 1934) and Artur de Souza Costa (1934–45), refused to sanction increases without new taxes. Sensing opportunity, the civil servants demanded parallel raises. The press wavered between favoring better pay for public servants, civilian and military, and expressing fear for the stability of the republic's finances. Army discipline was teetering. General Guedes da Fontoura reportedly told officers that if the pay raises were not approved, he would bring down the government. On the last day of 1934 Vargas noted in his diary that the military had issued a document demanding salary increases, and the supreme court justices solicited raises as well. Getúlio lamented: "And there isn't money, exports are declining, the exchange rates are falling, we can't pay the foreign debts." A few days later, in the new year, he noted that the two most important and urgent issues were payment of the foreign debt and military pay raises.[34] Vargas wanted the generals in command of troops to be trustworthy and loyal to him, but there is no evidence that he attempted to buy their fidelity.

Curiously, for a centralizing, antiregionalist regime, the 1930 to 1945 era is the only one in which the *Almanaque do Exército,* the army's official list of active-duty officers and the principal publication for keeping track of promotions and assignments, gave the officers' states of birth. During those fifteen years the greatest number of generals from a single state came from Rio Grande do Sul (twenty-seven), which had the largest concentration of army posts. The Federal District and the state of Rio de Janeiro contributed sixteen officers who rose to general, and the northeast collectively had twenty-six. I have not found any document that explains how origin affected promotions. It is noteworthy that São Paulo did not have a single son reach general's rank, and Minas Gerais had only one.[35]

Vargas had tried, however, to placate officers who had fought with São Paulo in 1932 by promoting a good number of them. General Eurico Dutra noticed this and commented in his own diary that Vargas was seeking "the peace so necessary for order and national development." But other senior officers had different ideas; they did not like the new Constitution or the federal system that they believed threatened national unity, and, somewhat contradictorily, they did not like the national security law being debated in the Congress, so they were whispering about a coup to install a military dictatorship.[36] In the first months of 1935 rumors and reports of military conspiracies continued to reach the president and his aides. The amnestied rebels of 1932 joined the plotters, with General Klinger secretly linking arms with General Guedes da Fontoura. It is very possible that among those whispering in the shadows, the agitation over salaries, rather than being a true issue, was really a vehicle to rile officers against the government. It is unlikely that there was widespread inclination in the army to resort to arms to force pay concessions. But it should be noted that real income had fallen 30 to 40 percent since 1929, and even middle-class bank employees, who had been resistant to associating themselves with striking factory workers, were becoming more radical in 1934–35. So officers must have been feeling real financial pressures.[37] On April 9, 1935, Minister of War Góes Monteiro sent a coded message to all generals regarding the pay situation. And on April 15, at the urging of Chief of Staff Olímpio da Silveira that the army's leadership take a decisive attitude, Góes convened a meeting of the Rio area generals in his office and said he would resign if the raises were not approved, and the attending generals agreed that they would refuse to be appointed his successor. If this did not amount to a high-command mutiny, it was uncomfortably close; Vargas called the idea "a white revolution." It was a precarious argument that, because the minister's post was political, it fell outside the normal obedience rules. The generals apparently did not consider that legally Getúlio could appoint a civilian. However much the single civilian minister of war during the republic, João Pandiá Calógeras (1919–22), had been lavishly praised at his funeral in April 1934, there was no inclination to repeat the experience of a civilian minister. Oddly, military autonomy was supposed to insure institutional distance from political intrigue, but clearly that was not happening. As bits and pieces dribbled out into the press, public apprehension increased. In an apparent attempt to calm the atmosphere, chief of staff General Benedicto Olympio Silveira told reporters that he insisted on order and discipline and that the army's "just aspirations" would be obtained legally and constitutionally. General João Gomes, commander of the First Military Region, went further, saying that it was "unthinkable that the army ever could turn its guns against the public or could assume the role of oppressor of the civilian population." And General José Pessôa, commander of the military school, wrote to Góes that he disagreed with his fellow generals' "mode of action." He feared that their attitude could have "funereal consequences." General Pantaleão Pessôa, who had not been invited to the meeting, wrote years later that the generals' position was "grave, undisciplined, and even ungrateful, because the President was the one most favorable to the increase and only asked that it be done in regular fashion." The crisis was fast going from bad to worse.[38]

The pay crisis then generated a disciplinary imbroglio with political and regional ramifications. Officers in Second Pontoon Battalion (Engineers) in Cachoeira do Sul (RGS) telegraphed Minister Góes, rebuking him for his statements and for not punishing the blustering General Guedes da Fontoura. They insisted that Góes state emphatically that the army recognized that its pay was a congressional decision and that, whatever the outcome, the army would be the "bulwark and defender of public order." What was fascinating about this event was that the officer who wrote the telegram and organized the protest, Captain Ciro Carvalho de Abreu, had been a member of Góes's immediate staff until shortly before; in fact, he had written the text before flying from Rio to take up his new post. Revealing even more how discipline functioned in the army, before heading south, he went to see his brother-in-law, General Pantaleão, at his home, showed him the text, and told him that he could not use the country's arms to get a pay raise, that he felt humiliated by the situation. He counted on his friends in the south to join him in dignified protest and said that after raising the Cachoeira unit he would wait there for his punishment! The general pointed out that what he proposed was "a revolution and that the army suffered from such acts of indiscipline." But he noted in his memoir that he did not say more to dissuade him because "inside I was wishing to be a Lieutenant to accompany him." Pantaleão then telegraphed Governor Flores da Cunha that Captain Ciro was en route and asked Flores to intercept him, to read the text, and to advise him; "we need to avoid new difficulties."[39]

Góes sent this offensive document to Gen. Div. César Augusto Parga Rodrigues, commander of the Third Military Region in Porto Alegre to impose the usual punishment for insubordination, thirty-days confinement to barracks. Quickly, similar telegrams arrived from other Rio Grande garrisons backing Cachoeira's position and inviting like confinement. One of the protesting officers was the president's uncle, Artillery Colonel Argemiro Dornelles, who could not be punished because he had immunity as a member of the state assembly.[40]

Flores sent Colonel Dornelles scurrying back and forth to Cachoeira trying to calm down the garrison's officers, who now threatened to rebel if the punishments were carried out. Dornelles reported to Flores and to Vargas that the Cachoeira officers believed that the "army was not for sale" and that they were defending its honor. Vargas appealed to Flores "with the affection of a friend, and by virtue of the function that I exercise, that you muzzle our friends there. . . . I have to solve this, and I will. I appeal to your Brazilian sentiment to avoid taking the moral responsibility on yourself of a civil war. . . . Everything is moving toward an entirely satisfactory solution." The plotters buzzing around Gen. Guedes da Fontoura included such regime opponents as Klinger and Figueiredo, but Vargas found it reassuring that the officers of the Vila Militar units were split, some agreeing with their general, others not. This was not the moment he counseled Flores to criticize Góes, who was doing his duty. "We need to be ready and united."[41]

The American military attaché, Major William Sackville, filed a report saying that "discipline in the Brazilian army is poor, compared to American standards." Morale had been undermined by the "frequent revolutionary movements. The troops will revolt on slight provocation. . . . [T]he loyalty of any particular unit must always be questioned." Some of this he blamed on shaky personal relations among officers, who had fought against each other in the 1932 civil war or earlier rebellions. Petty personal jealousies and feuds affected army administration. "Business is not carried on between Departments," Sackville observed, "so much by regulations as by barter." It was generally understood that "the quickest way in which to obtain a desired result is to offer inducements in one form or another. . . . There is a small percentage in all echelons who are good soldiers and would be good in any Army, but unfortunately their efficiency is all but lost in the general medium of questioned loyalty and lack of discipline."[42]

In early March Vargas noted, in his gaúcho lingo, that "I am becoming convinced [that] to give greater firmness and efficiency to discipline in the army and navy, it is necessary to change the lead oxen."[43]

In this ambience it is not surprising that the officer corps' faith in the constitutional regime's liberal democracy was evaporating.[44] Dedicated, self-sacrificing patriotism seemed to be fading as well. Vargas received continuous police and army reports of military-politico conspiracies involving opposition figures who were using the pay crisis and the Security Law as pretexts to stir opposition to the government. The crisis reached a peak behind the superficial calm of Holy Week. To avoid involvement, some generals took leave for the spa-towns of Minas Gerais. The president spent the holy days in Petrópolis, where, seeing the image of the suffering Christ in a Good Friday procession, he reminded himself that it "should encourage resistance rather than despair." That night at police headquarters in Rio de Janeiro, Police Chief Filinto Müller, First Military Region commander General João Gomes, and Minister of Justice Vicente Rao met for a long time about who to replace with whom and what needed to be done to tighten army discipline. The next day Gomes carried their recommendations to Vargas. His only modification was to move Eurico Dutra from head of aviation to replace Guedes Fontoura at Vila Militar. In the preceding days Dutra had done his own shuffling of the command at the aviation school, especially replacing Colonel Newton Braga, who had said he would not fight any troops that rebelled, with Lt. Col. Eduardo Gomes. On the morning of April 20 many officers, including General Klinger, came and went at General Guedes da Fontoura's Vila Militar residence. Dutra set infantry at the ready to defend the aviation school and early the next morning, Sunday, went to take command of Vila Militar. In a tense scene in front of Guedes's house as he was leaving for Mass, the outmaneuvered general angrily told Dutra that he would not pass the command, that "he was disgusted with the army and fed up with traitors." Dutra took over the headquarters without the usual transfer ceremony. In the May promotions Vargas made Dutra a general of division and moved him again to head the First Military Region, vacated by General João Gomes, who became minister of war, replacing Góes Monteiro, who remained temporarily without assignment.[45]

With the threat of a coup and threatened military dictatorship headed off, Vargas then resolved the pay crisis that was still nearly crippling the administration. The army and navy ministers tried to no avail to convince their subordinates to recognize the country's perilous financial situation; even with the currency's falling in value army officer corps sentiment refused to give up a pay increase. Vargas commented that even with the shifts in command "the army is infected with an impressive lack of discipline." The Congress that was ending its term on April 27 proposed creation of a special commission to make a detailed study of federal taxation and expenditures as part of a broader effort to reconstruct the republic's economic and financial system. As a stopgap measure the outgoing deputies passed a monthly bonus to be added to the pay of all federal employees until the new Congress (starting May 3) designed a permanent solution. If paid for twelve months the bonus would push the treasury's deficit from 1.5 million contos to more than five million. The value of Brazil's currency, the milreis, had been falling in the previous weeks. It then stood at roughly seventeen milreis to the U.S. dollar.[46]

Getúlio reacted by vetoing the civilian portion of the bill, using the constitutional provision that fiscal measures were to originate with the president, not the Congress. Because he had submitted the military pay scales but not the civilian, he felt justified in vetoing the Congress's largess. Opponents charged bad faith, but there was no prospect of getting a new bill passed over the partial veto. Some officers, such as General Manuel Rabelo, commander of the Seventh Military Region in the northeast, argued that the bonus would "burn the hands" of officers accepting it. But in the poorly paid armed forces, faced with the declining milreis and raising prices, there was little enthusiasm for further debate.[47]

To deal with the deficit resulting from the bonus, the army simply stopped taking recruits into the ranks. The 1,700 sergeants who had been made lieutenants *commissionados* for their service in the Revolution of 1930 were denied further promotion and were being gradually weeded out by retirement so that by late 1935 there were 1,125 on active duty. Because of the peace policy of accepting former rebels back into the ranks, the officer corps was blotted; instead of the 5,485 officers authorized in the budget there were 6,173 on the active list (this did not include those out of ranks filling political positions). The return of the 1932 rebels took place in 1934. The magnitude of the cost can be seen in this hypothetical example: *if* the extra 688 officers had all been captains (they were not), their basic monthly pay would have amounted to 1,444:800$000, which over a year would mean an addition to the army expenses of 17,337:600$000.[48] Table 9.1 shows that the total army budget for 1936 was 39,600,113:000$000. Giving amnesty to rebels and returning them to the ranks may have had clear political and cultural justifications; however, the scale of such restorations in the 1930s produced costs that weakened the government's solvency.

Over the decades that this book covers, government figures on military budgets were questionable and of little analytical value because in many years total expenditures were not the same as announced annual budgets. Additional allotments, public and secret, were the norm. That is why there is little budgetary analysis in this book. But in 1935 the amounts designated for the armed forces were better documented, closer to reality, and the relationship between increased pay for officers and cuts in numbers of enlisted personnel was so clear that discussion could not be avoided; in fact, it allows me to point out a major factor that would otherwise be hidden in the revolts of November 1935.

TABLE 9.1.

Brazilian National Defense Budgets, 1919–1936 (in U.S. $)

Year	National Budget	Army Budget	Army Percent of Total	Navy Budget	Navy Percent of Total	Defense Percent of Total
1919	159,345,212	21,662,500	13.58	12,900,000	8.07	21.65
1920	93,040,401	13,917,574	14.96	6,418,236	6.89	21.85
1921	121,706,883	19,205,711	15.77	9,266,565	7.61	23.38
1922	153,903,808	16,167,088	11.00	12,056,844	7.80	18.80
1923	155,815,981	17,159,344	11.40	9,748,800	6.50	17.90
1924	145,274,106	20,730,455	11.00	11,241,301	6.40	17.40
1925	184,806,705	21,719,989	11.75	12,156,424	6.58	18.33
1926	205,936,281	25,754,742	12.50	14,348,566	6.96	19.46
1927	214,371,516	23,374,537	10.90	14,464,539	6.75	17.65
1928	250,567,920	30,665,760	12.23	17,370,360	6.93	19.16
1929	254,084,040	33,136,800	13.04	18,677,040	7.35	20.39
1930	211,937,880	32,443,432	15.31	18,561,679	8.76	24.07
1931	156,317,258	23,733,881	15.18	14,741,948	9.43	24.61
1932	160,159,084	16,612,500	10.37	9,286,674	5.79	16.16
1933	207,916,354	24,817,526	11.93	12,467.694	5.99	17.92
1934	195,463,010	32,562,600	16.66	19,185,300	9.82	26.48
1935	223,409,772	36,810,067	16.47	19,215,498	8.60	25.07
1936	241,142,099	39,600,113	16.43	20,621,823	8.55	24.98

SOURCE: "Funds Used for National Defense, Brazil, Period of 1919 to 1936," MID Chart, 2006-147, MID, GS, WD, RG 165, NA. Researchers preferring amounts in milreis will find them in this document.

In a broad sense it may help the reader form an idea of Brazil's military spending to provide a summary that was prepared by United States army intelligence in 1936. Table 9.1 shows the percentage of the national budget assigned officially to the army and navy; it is not likely that the figures include secret or even additional moneys given to the military after the initial announcement of the annual budget.[49]

Achieving evenhanded discipline proved to be very difficult. Although the conventional view is that the government tolerated the integralists and persecuted the ANL (National Liberating Alliance), at least in 1935 the government applied the Security Law against army and naval officers who participated in either ANL or integralist demonstrations. But it was one thing to change commanders, and it was another for them to exercise complete control over their subordinates. On May 16 the Military Club showed its defiance by electing Gen. Guedes da Fontoura president, but support for an institutional move against the government had faded. The national crisis appeared to have shifted to the political arena. But the government could not resolve its financial problems and still maintain the armed forces. Vargas had committed himself to rearming, reequipping, and generally modernizing the military. The Reorganization Plan of 1934 would cost funds now increasingly in short supply, if not nonexistent. As American attaché Major Sackville, observed "the situation of the federal treasury has grown more and more difficult, and the prospect of balancing the federal budget more and more hopeless. The increased burden occasioned by the raise in pay to the armed forces presented a problem for which there was but one solution—reduction of the effectives." In fact, cutting the number of the army's soldiers had begun as early as July 1, 1935. This was done by simply not replacing those who completed their training. Debates in the Congress portended a "drastic cut in the Army for 1936." In late October some army officers anonymously called for a session of the Military Club to protest troop reductions and to plan actions to prevent them. Minister of War João Gomes, whom the U.S. military attaché described as "the firmest disciplinarian the Brazilian Army has had in many years," called on Federal District police chief Müller to investigate the identity of the agitators and to act rigorously against those holding unauthorized meetings. Minister Gomes called the reported reductions "nothing more than wild rumor" and asserted that "no modification will be made in the efficiency of our land forces." Further, he insisted that the problems that he and the chief of staff faced were "not subject to public discussion, because they are intimately related to National Security."[50] The officers who had called clandestinely for protests faded deeper into the shadows, but a few weeks later the army was shaken by barracks uprisings.

Presumably the general staff would be important to fulfilling Vargas's desire for readiness and unity. The foregoing events resulted in repeated shuffling of regional and high command generals. General Daltro's public appearance, with government-opponent retired Colonel Figueiredo, had caused his replacement in the second regional headquarters by Benedito Olímpio da Silveira. This newly promoted general of division stayed in São Paulo only from May to August 1934, when he was called back to Rio to head the general staff. General Olímpio da Silveira was one of the few generals to have survived the purge after the Revolution of 1930. He had opposed revolutionary movements since his student days in the 1890s. Highly regarded by fellow officers, he served on the general staff under Tasso Fragoso from 1923 until, as a colonel in 1926, Minister Sezefredo dos Passos made him head of his office staff, where he stayed until 1929. He was promoted to brigadier general in October 1929, and when Tasso Fragoso resigned in August 1932, in the midst of the paulista civil war, Olímpio da Silveira acted as chief of staff until General Andrade Neves took over in early September. Two years later this seasoned staff officer succeeded as chief of staff and threw himself into managing the reorganization of the army that he had helped prepare since the end of the civil war. His health broke under the strain. He fell ill and died on May 15, 1935, having been chief for nine months.[51]

Vargas took the opportunity to place his closest military adviser, General Pantaleão da Silva Pessôa, as chief of the general staff. He was a practiced staff officer, having served as head of Góes Monteiro's staff during the paulista civil war, and since October 1932 he had worked in daily contact with the president as chief of his personal military staff (called the Casa Militar); under the constitutional government of 1934 he also had acted as secretary general of the National Security Council. In early 1935 he had worked in favor of the national security law that so upset officer opinion and aggravated the emotions generated by the campaign for higher salaries led by General Guedes da Fontoura. He was also a friend of Flores da Cunha, which friendship disturbed his now delicate and tense relations with his former boss, Góes Monteiro. Vargas promoted Pessôa ahead of more senior officers to general of division on June 27 and made him chief of staff on July 4. In this perilous time of rising indiscipline in the army, he had chosen Pessôa because "of the dedication with which he had served my government." Vargas thought that his appointment would provoke "much jealousy, but I am certain," he told his diary, "that he is the best one for the post."[52]

He would have occasion to regret that decision. As things turned out, the men he depended on to discipline the army succumbed to temptations themselves. Instead of proving to be a durable, dependable team, these men showed the president during the next year that his ability to judge men was not perfect.

CHAPTER 10

The Army and Ideological Politics

Integralism['s] . . . propaganda is useful in the sense of
disciplining [public] opinion. However, I don't have much
confidence in its leaders.
—Getúlio Vargas, *Diário*

In November 1930 *Careta,* a Rio de Janeiro magazine, carried a cartoon that
showed a 1930 revolutionary marching between the outstretched arms of fascism and communism, with the cartoonist's warning below: "Careful . . . !
You have to pass untouched between the two." The loss of Prestes to communism assured that the left would capture the loyalties of some army personnel. The right could turn to fascism or Nazism, but all three "isms" were
foreign ideologies that had limited appeal to nationalistic Brazilians. Contemporary, on-the-scene observer Karl Loewenstein noted that Brazil was not
fertile soil for Bolshevism. In the 1930s its level of industrialization was low,
and in much of the country labor relations were more akin to feudal paternalism than to those existing in modern industrial societies. Communism,
he wrote, "never was a real danger to the bourgeois order." Integralism, a
Brazilian version of fascism, had the distinct advantage of being native. It
adopted the motto on the Brazilian flag—Order and Progress—as its own,
along with "God, Country, Family"—ideas dear to all Brazilians. Amherst
College political scientist Loewenstein was not impressed with integralism's
"hodgepodge of conflicting ideas" and was at a loss to label its program as
"more infantile than imbecile, or vice versa."[1]

Debut of Right-Wing Political Ideology:
The Integralista Movement

In the midst of the uneasy atmosphere of mid-1935, political ideologies
made their dramatic debut on the Brazilian political stage. In July 1935 Vargas
had met nearly daily with government officials and congressional leaders

about multiplying communist activities, which were stimulating responses from the political right. General Pessôa was an asset as a bridge in that direction. The general was in sympathy with the independent, right-wing political movement that paulista novelist Plínio Salgado had launched in October 1932. Ação Integralista Brasileira (AIB), as described in Salgado's founding manifesto, aimed to protect Brazil under the motto "God, Pátria, and Family" against the threats of the failure of politics, national disunity, class struggle, materialist Communism, capitalist greed, and European models of social and economic organization. The basic objective of the movement was the creation of an "integral state," which would differ from the "liberal state" with its fraudulent system of representation based on sham political parties and supposed universal suffrage. As early as 1927 Salgado had denounced what he saw as the phony character of Brazil's democracy and the chasm between liberal ideology and the country's reality. To his mind history had produced two Brazils, that of the interior, which since colonial days, when it was far from the reach of Portugal, had been "the Brazil that was really Brazilian, really nationalist . . . [with its] spontaneous, barbarous, and wild life." The second he saw resulting from independence and greater contact with Atlantic trade and the influences of Europe, which facilitated the "domination and oppression of the coastal cosmopolitan elite over the sertanejo populations of the interior. Integralism supposedly would reconcile the two Brazils by spiritual and moral action rather than by violence.[2]

Facilitated by the contemporary revival of Catholicism, symbolized powerfully by the erection (1931) of the huge statue of Christ the Redeemer on Corcovado Mountain overlooking Rio de Janeiro, integralism was part of the intellectual ferment of the 1930s. That ferment was stimulated by the rapid expansion of the book publishing industry. For example, between 1931 and 1937 *Companhia Editora Nacional* increased its printings from 350,000 to 2,000,000. Editor and publisher José Olímpio recognized that the Revolution of 1930 and the rise of the new middle class had changed the intellectual climate and had created a new market for Brazilian authors.[3] Ideas entered the political debate to a degree unmatched in the nation's past. Salgado's analysis and solution to Brazil's problems appealed to the multiplying thousands of white-collar office employees and professionals and likely those former civil servants cut from government payrolls by the collapse of the Old Republic's patronage system. It is significant that those who donned the movement's green shirts, with Sigma armbands, and shouted a Tupi word *(anauê)* with their straight-armed salute, were more literate than most of their fellow citizens. About 40 percent were secondary-school graduates, and 25 percent held university degrees. In 1934 the AIB claimed that it had 180,000 members, which, with some exaggeration, it asserted rose to nearly a million in 1937. In the frequent integralist parades upper-class women marched with laborers, poets, lawyers, priests, and small businessmen. Wealthy Brazilians supported the movement, and it received advice and financial aid from the Italian embassy. Its militia disrupted communist and National Liberating Alliance (ANL) rallies. In a startlingly short time integralism became "the largest mass political movement in the history of Brazil to that time." Contemporary observer Karl Loewenstein noted that "for the first time in Brazilian history a political party had begun to obtain a real mass basis."[4]

When the Congress passed the Security Law in late March 1935, Vargas commented in his *Diary* that "Integralism is an organic form of government and [its] propaganda is useful in the sense of disciplining [public] opinion. However, I don't have much confidence in its leaders, and the way they have tried to approach the government does not inspire confidence."[5] What came to worry Vargas, and ultimately the military chiefs, was that this growing movement intended to govern Brazil and was creating a shadow structure in anticipation. Salgado headed a hierarchy of leaders and supervisory bodies at municipal, state, regional, and national levels. The movement had disciplinary courts, health clinics, milk dispensaries, schools, and reading rooms. It published newspapers (e.g., *A Ofensiva & O Povo*) and a review in Rio de Janeiro *(Anauê),* and it had the support of newspapers in several states. It even marketed its own brand of cigarettes. It also built up extensive files on members and enemies. Its importance increased steadily after the communist revolt of 1935, and by late 1937 it could not be ignored. The suddenness of shifts in political views was illustrated by the rapid change of attitude by Vice Admiral Henrique Aristides Guilhem, the minister of navy. The minister had lobbied to include the green shirts among banned organizations under the security law, but after some communist slogans appeared on the walls of his residence, overnight he became an integralist enthusiast. The ministers of war and of justice enjoyed teasing him about his sudden conversion.[6]

Many commentaries categorized integralism as Brazilian fascism, but spokesmen for the movement anxiously drew distinctions between it and European fascism and German Nazism. They argued that integralism was compatible with Papal encyclicals on social organization, *Rerum Novarum* and *Quadragesima Anno* and that Catholic philosopher Jacques Maritain's condemnation of fascism and Nazism should not be applied to integralism because it was "not the same thing as those two regimes; it is considerably different." They declared that "Integralism affirmed the existence of God and the immortality of the soul. It conceived of the family and of [state] authority according to Christian teachings. . . . It opposed class hatreds and struggles . . . and regarded the nation as a society of families . . . [and] the moral elements of Nationality as being Religion and Family." The movement's concept of property was the same as that of Leo XIII and Pius XI. The integralist state would be corporative, in harmony with the Church's orientation.[7]

General Pessôa wrote articles for the integralist weekly *A Ofensiva,* but he asserted in his memoirs that he "was never an Integralist," that while he was in military service he thought it improper to belong to any political party. However, he admired the AIB's "splendid civic campaign," which he believed had done some good for the country.[8]

His friendship with Flores da Cunha, his support of integralism, and a speech that he gave in São Paulo in which he attested to the army's devotion to the Pátria and asserted that democracy was the "natural tendency of Brazilians" contributed to his downfall. In the January 19, 1936, speech he declared that the "army aspired to see the solidarity of all Brazilians placed above political incidents." He denied that the army desired to "dominate internal politics" or to install "militarism," and most especially it did not consider a change of regime necessary. Afterward a friend told him that he liked the speech but doubted that it would be interpreted correctly, and that for General Pantaleão it would "divide the waters." His days as chief of staff were definitely numbered.[9]

Moscow-Sponsored Revolts in Brazil

One of the strangest events of the 1930s was also one of the most miscalculated. In distant Moscow the Comintern decided to mount its next major upheaval in Brazil. Soviet agents in Buenos Aires had successfully attracted famed tenente Luis Carlos Prestes to the cause of world revolution. Curiously, the Brazilian Communist Party rejected his request for membership because its leaders considered him a bourgeois intellectual, without working-class background. He went to Russia for several years (1931–34), where he supported his mother and sisters by working as an engineer. The Russian Communist Party also refused him membership. However, in October 1934, the Seventh International Communist Congress, basing itself on exaggerated reports about the Brazilian situation, decided in favor of armed revolution in Brazil under the leadership of Prestes. At the end of December 1934, using false passports, he left Moscow for Brazil via the United States, in the company of Olga Benário, who was to look after his security and who eventually became his lover. As early as July 1934 the Comintern officials were assembling its team of revolutionary coordinators and moved them like pieces in a far-flung chess game across the globe. Alone or as married couples they moved through Europe to the United States or from China to Argentina to converge in Rio de Janeiro: Arthur Ernst Ewert (and his wife Elise Saborowski) and Johann de Graaf were German; Rodolfo Ghioldi, Argentine; Pavel Stuchevski, Ukrainian; and Victor A. Baron, American. These agents arrived with a set of plans for an insurrection that was to begin in the northeast and spread south. They kept a studied distance from the Brazilian communists and maintained an active and revealing telegraphic correspondence with Moscow. Graaf and Stuchevski separately studied Portuguese with the same Berlitz instructor. Incredibly, these elite revolutionaries gathered openly in bars in Leblon and enjoyed the beaches of that district and Ipanema.[10]

Meanwhile, the ANL was organizing itself into a broad front of socialists, communists, Catholics, and democrats opposed to fascism, imperialism, latifundia, and the government's repressive laws and decrees. The timing of its formation resulted from intensifying political activity throughout the country as the states held constitutional conventions to shape their governments to the new national regime. In most states, the Vargas interventors were elected governors, allowing for a legalization of the existing situation. For those in opposition locally or nationally this was their brief moment of opportunity. The ANL was officially founded in March and opened its mouthpiece newspaper *A Manhã* (Rio) in late April. In the same month Prestes arrived in the capital but stayed in hiding so effectively that the police thought he was in Russia in August when the Seventh International elected him to the Comintern. By all reports the Comintern's other members had no idea of conditions in Brazil, and they readily accepted the exaggerated reports of revolutionary readiness that the Brazilian Communist Party presented. However, Prestes should have known better; likely he was swept along by the headiness of being suddenly grouped with the elite of world revolution—Stalin, Mauilski, Dimitrov, Thorez, Togliatti, Mao Tsé-Tung, Dolores Ibarruri, and Bela Kun. From the outset Graff, a double agent working for British Intelligence, kept London abreast of their plans. The British ambassador alerted Vargas without revealing his source. As can be seen from the general staff's 1934 study of potential threats to Brazil, the Soviet Union and communism had not made the list. So the sudden emergence of the Soviet plot was startling. This is not to say that the army or the government was not aware of the potential dangers of communism, but they tended to think in terms of the local Brazilian Communist Party rather than Soviet actions. The army was watching communist activity in its own ranks, particularly among the sergeants who continued to be unhappy with their status.[11] In the public debate about conducting commerce with the USSR, the *Correio da Manhã* asserted it would "only be harmful to our internal security," the *Jornal do Brasil* (Rio) noted that communists were spreading throughout the country, and the *Estado de São Paulo* warned, "If we do not protect ourselves against that danger, we will be lost." It was the hour, the *Diário Carioca* (Rio) advised, for the government to "grow some claws." Army commanders were reporting on suspicious characters and publications in their localities. And the political police, the *DOPS*, in São Paulo and Rio de Janeiro were keeping an eye on ANL leaders and raiding meetings.[12]

The events of November 1935 are part of army history for several reasons: Prestes was a military school graduate, still carried on army rosters as a captain of engineers, who had deserted; the instruments of insurrection were army units; among the results of the affair was that the army closed itself off even more from society; it made the army deeply anticommunist and suspicious of social-economic reformers; finally, Prestes was touched by, or was a participant in, many of the events and trends discussed in earlier chapters.

The early life of Luís Carlos Prestes was so exemplary and so linked to the major reform trends in the army that looking at his early career suggests that he likely would have reached general's rank had he not become a revolutionary. He was born in Porto Alegre in 1898, the son of an officer of engineers and a primary-school teacher. His father's death in 1908 at the rank of captain left the family (wife, four daughters, and Luís) with a skimpy army pension. In 1910, with the help of General Bento Ribeiro, a friend of his father, Prestes was admitted into the Colégio Militar in Rio. In due course in 1916 he entered the military school of Realengo, where, influenced by teachers from the Colégio and the Catholic revival at Realengo, he accepted baptism into the Church. It was the era of the Young Turk–inspired Indigenous Mission (see Chap. 4). His friends and classmates included such later tenentes as Juarez and Fernando Távora, Antônio de Siqueira Campos, Carlos da Costa Leite, Eduardo Gomes, Oswaldo Cordeiro de Farias, and Newton Prado. Completing the basic course in 1917, he then spent two years studying engineering, during which he reached *aspirante-a-oficial*. Because of the Spanish flu epidemic, exams were postponed, and it would be January 1920 before his class was awarded the Bachelor of Physical Sciences and Mathematics degrees. They were the last class to receive the bachelors, which was dropped in the French-influenced reforms. His first assignment was to the First Railroad Company in nearby Deodoro, spending a stint as part-time instructor at Realengo in 1921. He attended the debates at the Military Club regarding the authenticity of the Bernardes letters; in the famous vote he opposed a formal inquiry because he did not believe the army could intervene. He spent six months on sick leave. In the situation that led to Hermes de Fonseca's arrest Prestes attended the planning meeting mentioned above (see Chap. 5) but missed the revolt because he was bedridden with typhoid fever. In September 1922 he was assigned, with Fernando Távora, to the commission that was supervising barracks construction in the south (see Chap. 6), but in February 1923 he asked to be relieved because the commission did not have the ability to oversee costs or to stop the obvious corruption that he witnessed. In October he was made captain, having been praised by the regional commander for his efforts to pacify competing sides in the Rio Grande civil war of 1923.

He was then assigned as chief of construction of the First Railroad Battalion in Santo Angelo (RGS), where he came face-to-face with administrative graft, reinforcing his desire for political reform. And working with several hundred illiterate soldiers strengthened his views on the need for social change. During this time he was in communication with his classmates who were planning the revolt of 1924. To avoid breaking his oath of loyalty he went on extended sick leave before its outbreak, but, not being notified, he missed the uprising. Finally, in September 1924 he resigned from the army and worked as a civil engineer in the Santo Angelo area, keeping in touch with his colleagues as they withdrew to Foz de Iguaçu. On October 29 he led the kidnapping of the commander of his former battalion and presented a fake telegram to the officer of the day, supposedly from the regional general, ordering Prestes to take charge. Later, the battalion commander felt so humiliated that he committed suicide with a shot to his head.

Meanwhile, his classmate Lt. Siqueira Campos raised a cavalry unit in São Borja, Lts. João Lins de Barros and Renato da Cunha Melo did likewise with a horse artillery unit in Alegrete, and Capt. Fernando Távora took over the engineer battalion in Cachoeira do Sul. After joining gaúcho provisional forces under local caudillos led by Honório Lemes, they fought their way through government troops to join eventually with the rebels from São Paulo. This movement was highlighted by such maneuvers as withdrawing from between two government units so quietly that the government troops attacked each other and by cutting a trail through roadless country to reach Iguaçu.[13]

But in 1935 Prestes was leading a very different form of revolution, and the Brazilian Communist Party was long on bombast and short on cold analysis of its influence and its capabilities. It reported strengths that it did not have, and then its leaders seemed to believe their own exaggerations. The British double agent was the Comintern's military adviser to the Brazilian communists, which likely meant that he also acted as a provocateur. With frequent missteps the affair declined from a grandiose revolution to a tragedy. From the perspective of nearly seven decades there seems little chance that the communists could have succeeded. But fear of communism inclined army leaders to ascribe to the Reds a popular appeal and an organizational ability that they did not have. In a way the attention of international communism highlighted Brazil's importance, and its leaders could not minimize that status. Moreover, the annual draft to fill the army's ranks constantly reminded officers of the sharp inequities in their society, and the fear of social revolution ran deep in the nation's history and in the elites' psychology.

Because of its rhetoric about the working classes, the army's senior officers saw communism as more dangerous than fascism, Nazism, or Brazilian integralism. These would keep the existing social order, whereas communism aimed to turn it upside down. But the Prestes-led communists' revolutionary methods were not innovative. Although they made gestures toward organizing the laboring classes, their main effort followed the well-worn path of subverting the army to gain power. The officer corps tolerated and, as this book has shown repeatedly, worked within certain norms when engaging in rebellion. It was "acceptable," despite regulations to the contrary, not to betray friends who revealed their involvement in plotting for political ends. But ideological insurrection was an unfamiliar, foreign import that was unwelcome. If "bad Brazilians" were condemnable, those who betrayed the motherland to a foreign power—*entriguistas*—were beyond forgiveness, and foreigners who threatened the Pátria summoned fury from deep in the undercurrents of xenophobia that flowed beneath Brazil's placid cordiality.

In Brazil the communists mixed their two strategies of united front political action and armed rebellion. In the political ferment stimulated by the adoption of the 1934 Constitution and the subsequent formation of state governments the Brazilian left, desiring antifascist, nationalist rather than regionalist politics, clustered in the ANL, founded at the end of March 1935. This organization was infiltrated by communists and naively named Prestes its honorary president, which implicated it in the November communist revolt. However, Hélio Silva was likely correct when he commented that it was not Prestes the communist leader but the popular hero, the knight of hope, who was acclaimed enthusiastically by the crowd.[14]

On April 4, 1935, Vargas signed national security law no. 38, which extended the government's repressive authority. Among the actions declared crimes against the political order were attempts to use violence to change the Constitution or form of government; to instigate collective disobedience to the law; to incite the military or the police to disobey the law, to break discipline, rebel or desert; to provoke animosity between the armed forces and civilian institutions; to encourage hate among the social classes; to promote, organize, or direct any activity aimed at subverting or modifying the political or social order by means not permitted in law; further, it prohibited any parties, centers, associations, or boards, of any type, that sought to subvert, by threat or violence, the political and social order. Military officers who practiced any of the above or belonged to any such groups, would be removed from their positions, and implicated foreign-born residents would have their naturalizations canceled. All these crimes would be processed in federal courts. And only the "public power" could create militias of any type, excluding only the boy scouts, *tiros,* and others legally authorized. It would be wrong to assume that Law no. 38 was aimed principally at the ANL, because at that moment the government saw a variety of additional dangers: increased restiveness in the states where new constitutions were being drawn and elections held; the pay crisis that was causing unrest in the military; fall in currency values and an accompanying rise in living costs; and the bleak international situation. Many army officers objected angrily to the law because it singled them out for special attention, which they argued was insulting and unnecessary. Actually the military's connection to the new security law may have been subsequently overshadowed by the dramatic events of late 1935. For Vargas it was a measure that would allow more rigorous control of the army.[15]

Meanwhile, the left ineptly provided more reason to end the constitutional regime. Prestes sought to associate the ANL, and a projected November rising, with the tenente movement of the 1920s by issuing a proclamation on the anniversary of the 1922 Fort Copacabana uprising on July 5. In it he provocatively called on the masses to organize for war against the "hateful Vargas government" and for a "popular national revolutionary regime." "All power," he declared, "to the ANL." Flexing its muscles, six days later, the government invoked the national security law to close the ANL. By that point Prestes and his small band had convinced themselves that they had enough adherents in the military to make armed revolt possible; they saw the unrest over pay and reduction of the army's size as their opportunity to attract supporters. Moreover, as the army began to discharge sergeants and corporals, Prestes worried that he would lose key men. It became a matter of acting soon or losing existing supporters.

As in all past revolts, coordination was a problem, especially so because many of the so-called commitments were not firm or did not exist. Coordination failed. In late November, instead of exploding together, a firecracker string of bursts occurred in Natal, Recife, and Rio de Janeiro. Indeed, the incidents in the northeast had more to do with affairs inside the army than with communism, Moscow's hopes, or Prestes' plans. In the region, particularly Recife and its environs, the lower classes had fervently backed the Revolution of 1930—five years later the burned-out shells of mansions of the rich were mute reminders of the crowds' fury—but because little had changed, the people's impatience was growing. Internal army factors influenced the course of events. After the revolution the provisional government recognized the role played by the noncommissioned ranks by setting aside the rule that sergeants and corporals must leave the service after eight years of active duty. But the Constitution of 1934 restored the limitation. As a result men in those ranks exhibited frustration, bitterness, and discontent.

Prior to November happenstance linked labor and military unrest. There were strikes at the Great-Western railroad shops on Recife's outskirts. Along the rail bed workers, shielded by their wives and children carrying a Brazilian flag, repeatedly blocked trains near where the tracks passed the barracks of the Twenty-ninth Light Infantry Battalion. The Twenty-ninth was charged with clearing the tracks and its gentleness indicated sympathy for the strikers' plight. A shot from an unknown assailant killed a supervising lieutenant. Later investigation showed that sergeants, involved in the seizure of the battalion barracks on November 24, had not moved their families into recently constructed quarters nearby, ostensibly to keep them away from the fighting. As fate would have it, there was a momentary absence of leadership in Pernambuco. Governor Carlos Lima Cavalcanti had gone to Germany as guest of the Zeppelin company, whose transatlantic base was in Recife. The commander of the Seventh Military Region headquartered there, General Manuel Rabelo, had gone to Rio de Janeiro to discuss the construction of new barracks. The state's military police commander, army Captain Jurandir Bizarria Mamade, was in Rio Grande do Sul, representing Pernambuco in centennial commemorations of the Farroupilha civil war (1835–45); in his stead another army captain, Afonso Augusto de Albuquerque Lima, was the senior police officer. Both men would have notable roles in Brazil's subsequent regime changes, particularly that of 1964 and its aftermath.[16] Moreover, a large part of the state's police force was then in the interior, pursuing the famous bandit gang of *Lampião*. After the revolt's failure they would pick up rebels fleeing into the hinterland.[17]

The first uprising in Natal involved relatively few sergeants and soldiers (about 110 men, or 25 percent) of the Twenty-first Light Infantry Battalion, whose choice of Saturday, November 23, during a school graduation ceremony attended by the governor and many Rio Grande do Norte officials, meant that defense in the city was minimal. Recall that the Twenty-first Battalion was the same unit that had rebelled in Recife in 1931. It had been transferred to Natal as a control measure, but the problems persisted; because its soldiers had been involved in recent street fights, the government had sent a trusted colonel to discipline it. Several soldiers had been slated for expulsion but for some reason were still in the barracks. It is indicative of the style of discipline that jailed soldiers who were behaving were allowed to spend nights at home. As customary on Saturdays, the officers left the barracks at noon, leaving the single officer of the day in charge. He was seized by the revolting sergeants and corporals. As Hélio Silva observed, for those men communism was something that would solve Brazilian problems; "the majority knew nothing of communism." They were aided by unemployed ex-civilian police whom the current governor had dismissed when he took office. The governor escaped to a French ship in the harbor, and the rebels, more or less, held Natal until Wednesday morning November 27, when they fled at the first sign of army units arriving from neighboring states.[18]

The next day, on the outskirts of Recife, rebels seized a building at the Twenty-ninth Light Infantry Battalion. After hours of defense they were forced to surrender. Other points of rebellion were contained and suppressed. Meanwhile, in the city center, the planned attack on the Seventh Regional headquarters fizzled when supposedly committed insurgents failed to show up, and commanders emptied the building by sending everyone home for lunch. One of the actual communists involved in these events, Sergeant Gregório Bezerra, finding no one to arm at headquarters, rushed to the Reserve Officers Training Center, where he fired at several officers, killing one and pinning the others down. Although bleeding badly from a wound, he raced into the street trying to persuade passers-by to join him; in what has to be the most extreme example of Brazilian improvisation, he convinced and armed two sympathetic newsstand attendants. Later, having been taken to a hospital by an army doctor committed to the revolt, he was arrested while on the operating table.[19]

These events had put the authorities in Rio de Janeiro on alert. The president requested and the Congress voted the first state of war since 1930. Even so, the explosions in Rio de Janeiro were more serious. Oddly, Minister of War João Gomes professed disbelief at the warnings of Chief of the General Staff Pantaleão Pessôa. Gomes went so far as to suggest that Pessôa's service as head of Vargas's Casa Militar had addicted him to "rumors and revolutions." Even when Pessôa gave him two revolvers, with special copper bullets used only by the municipal police, that were being distributed to conspirators, Gomes objected that he "did not believe in revolution" and that his police contacts told him it was not anything dangerous. General Pessôa was so unnerved by the minister's attitude that he gathered his most trusted staff officers and set up an impromptu command center in his own house. At about midnight Pessôa went by the Ministry of War and found the building closed! He then went on to Dutra's First Regional Headquarters and then to the Catete Palace to reinforce the guards at the president's residence and offices. He ordered that the lights be turned out and that Vargas not be disturbed.[20]

During the early hours of November 27 revolts erupted in the Third Infantry Regiment barracks in the old military school building at Praia Vermelha and at the aviation school at Campo dos Afonsos, next to Vila Militar. From a tactical point of view, if rebels could have gotten the aviation school's aircraft aloft, they could have caused serious trouble, at least until they ran out of gas; however, they were too few to hold the airfield against the troops of Vila Militar. Attempting to stage a rebellion from the Third Infantry Regiment barracks at Praia Vermelha was suicidal. The barracks was hemmed in on the narrow neck of land between the massive sheer stone faces of Mounts Babilônia and Úrubu on the side toward Copacabana and by Urca and famed Sugar Loaf on the bay side. There was neither a way to retreat nor to stage a sortie. The planners had hoped to take over the regiment rapidly and move its troops speedily to seize Guanabara Palace and its presidential resident. But hope had not been backed up with careful preparations. It was insane to choose Praia Vermelha as a key point of revolt in 1935, just as it had been in 1904. Perhaps it was even crazier because at the end of November 1935, two-thirds of the soldiers of the regiment were recent recruits who did not yet know how to shoot; others had not yet been issued uniforms! Aside from rescuing the captured officers and soldiers, it is not clear why loyal forces had to use violence against the trapped mutineers. Hunger and thirst would eventually have driven them to surrender.[21]

That afternoon, November 26, a potentially more serious attempt had been short-circuited at army headquarters. There was a report in American intelligence files that telephone calls had summoned several generals to a meeting at the war ministry. Dutra, now the commander of the First Military Region, was suspicious of the call he received and raised the alarm. Supposedly, rebels were to seize the ministry and murder the assembled generals. If this was true, it is odd that it does not appear in contemporary accounts. However, it is certain that a company of the 2nd Infantry Regiment had arrived to help protect the ministry. Its commander, 1st Lt. Augusto Paes Barreto, tried to convince the commander of another unit to join him in seizing the building. Instead of agreeing, that officer informed General Dutra, who had the subversive lieutenant arrested. Dutra told the other lieutenants in the company that at the first sign of rebellion they were "summarily to shoot" mutinous soldiers.[22] The uncertainty as to when or where the explosions might occur caused tension to mount. About 1 A.M. Dutra ordered all units to maintain vigilance under arms. At 2:50 A.M. officers at the Third Infantry Regiment telephoned that there was shooting in the barracks. The rebels fired across the patio at the two machine-gun companies that resisted. When his company captain was wounded early in the exchange, 2d Lt. Fritz Azevedo Manso took command and played a notable role in the resistance.[23] Troops rushed from army headquarters, Vila Militar, and the military police barracks in the city's center, and backup battalions came down from Petrópolis and crossed on the ferry from Niterói.[24]

As dawn was breaking, Vargas approached Praia Vermelha but because of the intense firing could not reach the command post; instead, he drove back across the city to the army headquarters, where he got the latest news from Generals Gomes and Pessôa over a cup of coffee. At 7 A.M., accompanied by his two military aides, he headed to Campo dos Afonsos to check on the aviation school. En route he passed a heavy artillery group hurrying to Praia Vermelha. Ignoring warnings from officers encountered along the way, his car passed through groups of mutinous soldiers who had thrown down their weapons and were fleeing the scene. The president talked with wounded Lt. Col. Eduardo Gomes, with school commander, Lt. Col. Ivo Borges, as well as with cheering soldiers against a backdrop of burning buildings and hangers. None of the expensive aircraft had been lost.[25]

One bright spot on this dismal day was the military school in Realengo. With its history of rebellion—1897, 1904, 1922, and the strike in 1934—it would have been reasonable to expect its cadets to be involved. After the protest strike had forced General José Pessôa's transfer, in less than a year two other generals had failed to bring discipline to the school. In July 1935, Col. João Batista Mascarenhas de Moraes arrived, determined to change the atmosphere with constant inspections and by making his presence felt constantly. In the early hours of November 27 officers from the nearby aviation school alerted him to the revolt. He had reveille sounded and formed the nearly thousand cadets in the patio, armed them, and, with dawn breaking, had them marching down the Rio–São Paulo road toward Campo dos Afonsos. They captured some of the fleeing rebels. Although the school's active role was minor in these events, it was important for what did not happen; its cadets "for the first time in Brazil left [their] barracks in the defense of order and [national] institutions."[26]

Meanwhile, Minister Gomes had taken the precaution at 11 P.M. of telephoning Lt. Col. Oswaldo Cordeiro de Farias, who was then taking the course at the general staff school, and ordering him to bring as many trusted student officers as possible to the ministry. From there Gomes sent Cordeiro and his friends to Praia Vermelha to join with troops from nearby Fort São João to prevent anyone from leaving the Third Regiment.[27] The Guards Battalion, under Brig. Gen. Francisco José da Silva Jr., took up blocking positions just before 4 A.M. and opened a steady fire.[28] Some troops on Mounts Babilônia and Urca were able to fire into the central patio and to throw back sorties from the building's side galleries. General Dutra took a direct role in the placement of machine guns and, along with Minister Gomes, exposed himself to rebel fire. When the two generals moved forward for a closer look, Dutra's aide fell at their feet with a fatal wound. Civil police officers fired tear gas grenades into the building. About 8 A.M. a battery of four howitzers, placed in the street and in the Yacht Club property, blocking the exit from Praia Vermelha down Avenida Pasteur, pounded the building with shrapnel at the point-blank range of 150 meters, which caused it to burst into flames. Simultaneously two aircraft machine-gunned the barracks. Observing the former military school building in flames, General Gomes commented to Lieutenant Colonel Cordeiro that "your father was fortunate because he did not live to see the destruction of our school. Praia Vermelha is the Army. . . . And I am the one destroying it!"[29] Dutra may have had similar thoughts; he was there as a student during the 1904 uprising. After about an hour of bombardment a bugler sounded the short notes of "cease fire," and Dutra sent in a messenger calling on the rebels to surrender.

Note his formal language: "*Senhor comandante revolucionário* of the 3rd RI. The general commander of the 1st Military Region—your commander—

counsels you immediately to put down your arms and to surrender; your situation is unsustainable and it is advisable to avoid useless sacrifices." Mutineer Captain Agildo Barata responded with a message to his comrades of the Guards Battalion, pleading with them to switch sides. In his message to Dutra he hoped that the general would "accept their point of view and free our Pátria from Getúlio's claws. The movement is not communist, but national, popular, revolutionary, with the worthiest of our colleagues at its head: Luís Carlos Prestes." Shortly after 11 A.M. aircraft returned to dive-bomb the barracks, convincing Captain Barata that they were indeed "entirely alone." His men talked about their impossible situation and had their bugler sound "cease fire." At 1 P.M. a white flag appeared. Barata wrote in his memoirs that he had hoped, as a condition of surrender, to get immunity for his sergeants and soldiers but that Dutra's troops had "abused" the cease fire by "infiltrating" the left, or Babilônia, side of the barracks. Barata's spokesmen were met with gunfire, surrounded, and disarmed. General Dutra immediately hurried into the barracks patio, where, refusing to speak with Captain Barata, he ordered the rebels into formation. Dutra, determined to control his men, stopped a captain, who was waving a pistol and shouting, "Which one is the son of a whore Agildo Barata," growling at him through clinched teeth: "Shut your mouth!" At that point the president walked through the smoking rubble into the patio. The building was burning, smoke and sparks blowing about, and a light rain was falling. The rebel prisoners lining up, the wounded being treated, the weary faces, the destruction under the gray sky was, for Vargas, "a desolate spectacle."[30] There was a report that Minister Gomes angrily had ordered the rebels shot as they were captured but was countermanded by Vargas. However, Dutra years later contested the truth of this, even though in a somewhat different context; he said that Gomes had told him: "Let's bomb everything. . . . I don't want any of that rabble to come out of there alive."[31]

Surprisingly, amidst all this shooting and destruction there were only two deaths: Major Misael Mendonça, on the government side, and Lt. Tomás Meireles, one of the mutineers. Tragically, Lieutenant Meireles died in a confrontation with his close friend Lt. Armando Pereira, who afterward suffered anguish from killing his friend.[32]

None of the testimony of those on the scene speaks of soldiers being killed in their beds, but this soon became the tag line of references to the rebellion. It is true that some troops on ready alert were on their beds, fully dressed and armed. But this was a control measure to keep them from subversive contacts. They were even escorted to the lavatories. No account says they were sleeping. Others were in formation under arms in the patio. General Pessôa recalled that he repeatedly urged the various school commanders and his friends among unit commanders to be alert and cautious. The rebellion, including Natal, Recife, and Rio, resulted in 22 dead and 159 wounded on both sides.[33]

In the wee hours of 1936, in his New Year's Eve radio address to the Brazilian people, President Vargas warned against the forces of evil and of hate that threatened the nation. He referred to "our communists imitating the apostles of Russian Bolshevism" in the "shameful outbreak" of November 27, during which there were scenes of "disgusting betrayals, even cold and calculating murder of trusting and *sleeping* colleagues" (my italics).[34]

The sleeping reference was repeated at the burial ceremony on November 28 and thereafter at annual commemorations. For example, in Natal at a commemoration of the thirtieth anniversary of the "Communist Conspiracy of 1935," General Antonio Carlos da Silva Muricy asserted that at Campos dos Afonsos the conspirators "assassinated their colleagues, some of whom were sleeping." Ever after communists and the treacherous 1935 rebellion were linked in the army's collective memory.[35]

News reports of the outbreak in Natal had prompted the Congress to approve a state of siege that imposed press censorship, and in December it agreed to expand the government's exceptional powers by a ninety-day state of war, which would be continually renewed. Effectively, this allowed a brutal wave of repression that swept ANL officials and members, communists, mere sympathizers, and the innocent into the overflowing jails. Ships in the Rio harbor became floating prisons. In March 1936 even congressional immunities were lifted to permit the arrest of a senator and four deputies. Dr. Pedro Ernesto Batista, revolutionary of 1930, civilian tenente, and honorary army colonel, the Vargas family's private doctor, member of Getúlio's "black cabinet," and the first elected mayor of the federal district, was arrested for conspiracy.[36] The tension was inescapable, especially in parts of Rio where police agents staged house-to-house searches for Prestes and his Comintern colleagues. Their arrest, and the murder of American Victor A. Baron, the plotters' radio operator, who was tortured into revealing Prestes' hideout and who, mysteriously, fell to his death from a window in police headquarters and the brutal treatment of Harry Burger became international causes, provoking demonstrations and negative editorials in the United States and Europe. The enduring symbols of the repression would be novelist Graciliano Ramos, whose book on the experience, *Memórias do cárcere* shaped the image of the Vargas era for many literate Brazilians, and Olga Benario, Prestes' pregnant companion and Comintern appointed bodyguard, who was deported into the hands of the Gestapo and death years later in a gas chamber. Assis Chateaubriand, owner of the newspaper syndicate, *Diários Associados,* captured the reality of the moment: "The recipient of all that Luís Carlos Prestes has lost is Getúlio Vargas."[37]

An interesting question is how much of the repression should be seen as the responsibility of the army? It was carried out by the civilian federal district police, but under the command of army Captain Filinto Müller. He was on detached duty and outside the regular chain of command. But he was a commissioned officer (*aspirante,* Jan. 1922), who would return to uniformed duty in July 1942 as a member of the minister of war's staff. Was the army responsible for his behavior during his time as chief of police? The post had been filled before, and would be afterwards, by army officers, and the promotions board regarded such duty as service toward the next rank. But does that mean approval of behavior? At meetings of the generals of the Rio de Janeiro area during 1935 to 1937, the consensus was that sterner measures had to be taken and that legal appeals for more humane treatment for Harry Berger should be rejected as softheaded. So it is logical to think that Müller must have believed that the army's senior officers supported his brutality.[38]

Communist ideology and foreign involvement set these events apart from the many other rebellions in the 1930s. Discipline in the Brazilian army involved continuous subordination. Obedience was an absolute value, the core principle of the army. As Vanda Maria Ribeiro Costa observed "the rhetoric of subordination takes its fundamental inspiration in the analogy of the army with the family." It sought to induce "total submission with the promise of paternal affection that equalized all the sons." To obtain absolute confidence and willing, voluntary submission, "the chief had to be more than chief, he had to be a friend." For the recruits to internalize obedience, they had to see their officers the way they did their fathers. True discipline, advised Captain Gerardo Lemos do Amaral, required instructors to make their soldiers love them. He pictured "the army as a family living in the shadow of the flag. . . . Each one seeing their companions as brothers in the military family." However, this rosy imagery was undermined by a structure that eliminated the professionalization of sergeants. The sergeants instructed the recruits, handled routine administration, and made the units function. Yet they could not hope to better their lot. Soldiers in this model would never grow up to be adults; such status was only for the officers. "While the rhetoric included everyone, in practice the kingdom of the military family was reserved for the officers." The language of equality clashed with the reality of subordination. The army may have been a *grande familia,* but it was one in which its different hierarchical levels could not be familiar with each other. The closure of the Sergeant's School in 1931 had cut off a ray of hope, which may have been stimulated by the admission of sergeants in the School of Arms, but this too proved a short-lived experiment. In 1937 all sergeants with more than ten years service were discharged. All of this shaped the manner in which rebellions were plotted and carried out. Revolts tended to be short, marked by truces for negotiation, considerable conversation back and forth in a continuous search of accommodation. Absolute ruptures were to be avoided.[39] But when the best-loved son betrays the father's affection, the response must cut the bonds that bind them. The Third Infantry Regiment and the aviation school were "elite units" to which the army had given the ample resources needed to complete their missions. "For this very reason," General Gomes stated, "the methods of repression, that were used, involved maximum violence. . . . The resulting damages were considerable, not only here but in Natal and Recife; but, the principal of authority was salvaged."[40]

"Difficult people these military . . . "

Moscow's clumsy attempt at generating revolution in Brazil failed to attract the masses, but it gave added justification to those officers and politicians who saw the constitutional regime of 1934 as a backward step to replace the fiasco with a centralizing government that they believed could save Brazil from its ills. In the days after the suppression of the November 1935 rebellions Vargas noted in his *Diary* that there were civilian and military demands for "exemplary punishments." The Constitution did not permit the death penalty and limited the length of imprisonment. Tougher laws were needed so that the government could control the army and fight communism.[41]

Catholic church leaders demonstrated their solidarity with the government, and Alceu Amoroso Lima, lay commentator and confidant of Archbishop Sebastião Cardinal Leme, used his column in *O Jornal* (Rio) to state views favoring a strengthened state, corporative organization of the economy, and elimination of regionalist politics. He applauded Vargas as "the man Brazil needs to save it from chaos and Soviet imperialism." The press, which had been slow to agree with the government's suspicion of the ANL before the rebellion, was now united in calling for strong measures. On November 30 *O Jornal* demanded that Congress give the government new powers that matched the threat to Brazil. "The weapons to preserve us from communism have to be forged from the same steel as those used to attack us."[42]

It was embarrassing that it was the army, which should have been secure from communist infiltration, that served as the vehicle for it. The Communist Party "had no real ties to the factory [workers] commissions" and, as historian Joel Wolfe commented, "the plotters did not even attempt to organize working-class support in São Paulo." Labor was unimpressed and kept its distance from the events of November, but it was to suffer from repression none the less. The affair provided a convenient excuse to crackdown on independent labor organizing and protesting activities, and to force workers into the government's industrial relations system.[43] A mirage was concocted to convince the country that the threat was indeed real and serious. But how could a threat so easily defeated be truly dangerous? General Gomes, after all, disbelieved until the last moment. The use of artillery and air bombardment against immobilized men armed with rifles and machine guns may well have been related to Gomes wanting to cover his earlier inaction, but it was also in line with the excessive force the army had employed at Canudos in 1897, the Contestado in 1915, and São Paulo in 1924. It is also possible that collectively the generals were truly shocked, frightened, and angered that the Soviet Union would try to launch a revolution in Brazil.

On December 3 Minister Gomes summoned all the generals in the Rio area to his office. He proposed that they endorse the immediate expulsion from the army of those involved in the revolt and that they seek harsher measures against future subversion. Góes Monteiro, who had been on the sidelines with little to say publicly about these events, was the only one to come with a written position paper. He was concerned, as usual, to have the army present a united front before the country. Expulsion from the service was a matter that directly affected the status of officers before civil and military law, and, in some way, the rules governing it in the past had touched everyone in the room. There was debate over how to interpret the revolts; some generals attributed them to the reduction of troop levels, opposition to reenlistment of sergeants, to poor living conditions, or to overall lack of discipline. Góes Monteiro blamed the liberality of the 1934 Constitution (of which he was one of the authors), which in giving soldiers the right to vote had opened the barrack's doors to contact with politicians and with "foreign" ideas.

For years he had been preaching that Brazil's politicians schemed against the army to preserve their personal and regional influence and power. Such men, in his view, "lacked rational education and had facilitated the very evils about which we complained." "Our patriotism," he had declared back in May 1935, "can not allow such a situation to endure." For the "greatness of Brazil to rest on a solid footing . . . the efforts of all good Brazilians . . . [were needed] to immunize the army against the seductions of partisanship."[44] The other generals were intimidated by Góes and coming with a prepared memorandum allowed him to direct the discussion and its outcome. He advised that they should stand with Gomes because any more such events could cause "national disintegration and complete social subversion." Calling the revolts "the most terrible crisis through which the Brazilian nation had yet passed," he asserted that the nation's existence was menaced because the army, the nation's backbone, was in fatal condition. They had to act decisively as one, not merely to punish the rebels but to solve the nation's institutional problems. Brazil was sick, and its illness had infected the army; Góes argued the Pátria and its army could be saved only by heroic and dangerous treatments. He outlined three possible courses of action: (1) keep the Constitution and have anarchy and chaos; (2) pursue constitutional reform as a temporary solution; (3) stage a coup d'etat, abolish the Constitution, and impose rule by a junta until a new national charter could be written. This last course, he admitted, risked splitting the armed forces.[45] Góes believed that the army had to be united intellectually to face the country's ideological divisions. Constitutional amendments, he asserted, should be rushed through the Congress, which should dissolve itself after forming a constituent assembly to draft a new Constitution and give power over to the president. Góes ended by observing that everything that involved the "rights or interests of the armed classes should be resolved internally, without any outside interference." "Turning them into police will be preferable to dissolution."[46]

Perhaps to signal that unit rebellions were no longer to be tolerated as part of Brazilian military lore, that same day Getúlio and Gomes signed a decree dissolving the Twenty-first and Twenty-ninth Light Infantry Battalions and the Third Infantry Regiment, creating in their place the Thirtieth and Thirty-first Battalions and Fourteenth Regiment. This action coupled with the expulsion of rebel officers from the service, with loss of all patents and benefits, went far beyond the symbolic to eliminate the tolerance that had made past rebellions survivable.[47]

The Congress began considering the amendments on December 6. The prevailing attitude in the legislature was to consider "intestinal commotion," to use Vargas's phrase, "as equivalent to a state of war." When Gomes told the president that he intended to speak to congressional and state leaders, Vargas told him not to, that he, himself, would coordinate congressional approval of changes in the Security Law and the constitutional amendments. Vargas told other visitors that the government was decided on a "severe repression" of communism and that those who agreed should follow him and those who didn't should get out of the way.

General Gomes carried the generals' demand for constitutional reform to a cabinet meeting on December 7. He declared that they were crossing a pit filled with ashes that could burst into flames at any moment, and criticizing the liberalism of existing laws, he requested exemplary punishment of military and civilian conspirators. Minister Gomes declared that the rebel officers had committed the "crime of high treason against their *pátria.*" In addition to breaking their "sacred oaths," and using the nation's weapons against it, the Third Infantry officers had affronted Brazilian society with their sneering laughter as they were being escorted to jail! Beyond supporting Gomes, the ministers decided to create a strong system of censorship and a National Security Tribunal.[48] A week after the cabinet meeting the presidents and the majority leaders of the two chambers of the Congress met with Vargas to discuss the proposed amendments and to witness his signing the bill strengthening the Security Law. A few days later, on the seventeenth, the Chamber of Deputies approved the amendments by wide margins, and on the twenty-first the Congress extended the state of siege for another ninety days and authorized the president to consider it equivalent to a state of war. On December 31 Vargas signed a law nullifying the commissions of the rebel officers. That law made it a crime for officers or sergeants to belong to subversive parties or to those that preached violence against government or society. The law specified that breaches of discipline were punishable by retirement; and an assault on a "superior, inferior, or comrade" while committing any of the crimes listed, would merit a sentence of ten to twenty years at labor; if the aggression resulted in death, the sentence could be extended to twenty to thirty years at labor. Foreigners implicated in security crimes were subject to immediate expulsion, and the law reduced the time allowed for trials to be held and completed.[49]

Whether these laws could be applied to crimes committed prior to their passage was left a bit vague. In any case the officers who were stripped of rank and emoluments consisted of three majors, nine captains (including Prestes, who was still on the deserter list nearly ten years after leaving his barracks in Rio Grande do Sul), eight first lieutenants, four veterinary lieutenants, and four second lieutenants. For failing to resist sufficiently the subversion of the Third Infantry Regiment, two majors and ten captains were retired by a presidential decree. Col. Afonso Ferreira, the regimental commander, who in spite of being alerted to the danger of a revolt had given officers of dubious loyalty command of troops, was absolved of blame, but he never held another command. He was promoted to brigadier general in May 1937 and retired from the service.[50]

A storm of anticommunism shook the government, stirred the press into screaming headlines, and shifted Brazil even further to the right. In the Congress the red scare was coordinated by Deputy Adalberto Correia, of the Partido Republicano Liberal of Rio Grande do Sul. He had participated in rebellions in the state as far back as 1923 and had been a leader in seizing the federal arsenal in Porto Alegre in 1930. He was newly elected and likely saw red-baiting as a means of rapid political ascent. It is curious that he was the brother of Octávio Correia, the civilian who went to his death when he joined the tenentes in their deadly march down Avenida Atlantica in July 1922. It is not clear why or how he was appointed chairman of the new National Commission for the Repression of Communism. The deputy was out of his depth on the national scene, but played a notable, if minor, role in the events that connected the communist plot of November 1935 to the dictatorship of November 1937. In May 1936 he joined mineiro Deputy Pedro Aleixo in leading the attack on the minority opposed to suspending the congressional immunities of four deputies and a senator accused of involvement in the November 1935 plot. One military observer of the era called him "half crazy." It could even be that his stubborn persecution of Rio's mayor, Pedro Ernesto, may have gone beyond Getúlio's own desire to rein in his populist family doctor. Given the configuration of power in the federal capital in 1936 one has to wonder about Deputy Correia's sanity in giving interviews attacking the minister of justice and Federal Police Chief Müller. In fact, the press censors cut at least one interview, which he stubbornly had mimeographed and distributed; clearly he was obsessed and likely had a tenuous hold on reality. Whether he was being manipulated or was out of control will have to be left to other historians.[51]

The anticommunist commission served to keep public opinion stirred up. Its investigative and prosecuting authority extended nationwide, although it is doubtful that it could force state authorities to do its will. Supposedly it could dismiss government employees, arrest them, and counteract communist propaganda, and it was charged with developing a national plan for repressing communism. Because it accepted anonymous accusations, many of those denounced were victims of personal enemies or labeled communist because they were different from local norms. One woman was processed by the Security Tribunal because her name appeared in the address book of a supposed communist and because she belonged to the *União Feminina do Brasil.* The image of the communist was mixed up with that of a foreigner, so suspicion of immigrants became the order of the day. The law requiring that foreign-owned businesses have a workforce that was two-thirds national was added justification for numerous dismissals. The commission regarded injustices suffered by the few as acceptable to protect Brazil from communism. The commission was behind the arrests of Federal District mayor Pedro Ernesto, former district secretary of education Anísio Teixeira, and army Colonel Filipe Moreira Lima, among others. Pedro Ernesto's arrest was the most important, and his odyssey generated enormous sympathy. Indeed, he was one of the most popular men in the country. Who was responsible for the decision to arrest the populist leader? In his diary Vargas wrote that he would approve an arrest order only if sufficient proof existed. When it took place he noted: "I confess that I did it with sadness. I have a crisis of conscience. I have doubts that this man is corrupt or a traitor, is misunderstood or a deceiver. Perhaps the future will tell."[52]

General Góes Monteiro, who without assignment had sat out the months after giving over the ministry to General Gomes, saw in the developing political crisis the opportunity to centralize power in the federal government while increasing the army's autonomy from politics. But it did not work that way. True, the Congress scrambled to increase the president's power; however, in doing so it also gave him more authority over the military by specifically vesting the president with authority over promotions, assignments, and punishments of officers. In effect the constitutional amendments took from the armed forces the legal supervision over internal discipline. Years later Góes objected that having done its duty, the military was punished with loss of autonomy.[53]

In early 1936 gathering storms were darkening the political-military atmosphere. Generals were arguing over their authority, politicians were secretly forming alliances and buying arms for their state police forces, and Vargas was attempting to hold off open contention among possible successors in the scheduled 1938 elections. In several states there were silent struggles over who would administer the "State of War" decree and associated investigations. In Pernambuco, for example, regional commander General Rabelo was miffed at not being appointed and so asked to be relieved. Vargas attributed the Recife and Natal revolts to Rabelo's habit of giving press interviews that raised social issues in disturbing fashion. His positivism could be interpreted, according to the president, as having a kinship with communism. Rabelo had gone so far as to say that "the communist movement had its roots in the misery of the masses."[54] Governor Flores da Cunha of Rio Grande do Sul was working to create a tripartite pact with Governors Valladares of Minas Gerais and Armando Sales Oliveira of São Paulo to insure the latter's election as president. Both Rio Grande and São Paulo were importing arms and looked to be readying for a fight if necessary. Flores was having a serious problem holding the loyalty of political factions in his state. The gaúcho provisional units that Flores controlled worried federal army commanders, particularly those at a distance in Rio de Janeiro. Góes Monteiro and Flores were completely at odds; Góes was a confirmed centralist, whereas Flores was an equally strong proponent of state autonomy. But his idea of autonomy did not exclude his own political meddling in neighboring Santa Catarina and in the State of Rio de Janeiro. At times he appeared to fancy himself a latter-day Senator Pinheiro Machado, the kingmaker of the early republic. Left to fester, the rival Góes-Flores visions of Brazil would eventually require Vargas to side with one or the other, and such a decision would set Brazil's course on either preserving old-style regionalism or establishing centralized government.

What is evident is that the Revolution of 1930 had not eliminated the way the Brazilian leadership at the national or state levels thought about politics. The revolution had interrupted the political game, sidelined some players, but the actual mentality and traditions had not been changed. The politics of the governors still functioned in the sense that the governors spoke for their states, and even if Minas and São Paulo no longer had final say, they still tried to influence outcomes. Vargas himself was playing the old game even as he manipulated the rules to fit shifting political realities.

The explanation of why the Estado Novo dictatorship was established is left vague in the general histories and in monographs on the 1930s, including this author's earlier writings, but it is not sufficient to say that Getúlio liked power or that his supporting generals were antiliberal. The Estado Novo constructed much that we associate with modern Brazil. It did not just happen; it was the deliberate creation of the men who have appeared in these pages, and their actions demand explanation. For the army this was a major turning point in its history, so events cannot be left simply in easy myths or misty generalizations.

Politics or factionalism within the army were very much alive in April and May 1936. Góes Monteiro was usually at the center of disputes over key policy matters, such as Amendment 2 to the Constitution, which allowed the annulment of officer commissions. Góes did not want to accept this provision and actively stirred up sentiment in the officer corps against it. He sketched out alternative texts and even circulated in the army a bulletin objecting to the government's action. This seems to have provoked more ill will between Góes and Gomes than it did between him and Vargas.[55] Góes also was irritated with the promotions of general officers because he believed that several on the list did not measure up to the professional standards he had sought to impose during his time as minister.[56]

To put it mildly, Góes and his successor as minister did not get along. Gomes was typical of many ministers of war in that he had little regard for the plans and ideas that he inherited and either let them slowly die from inaction or made his own substitutions. He was from the "old army," a student at Praia Vermelha when the empire was overthrown; as a lieutenant he fought on Floriano's side in the civil war of 1893–95, during which he had distinguished himself in commanding the seizure of the cruiser *Aquidabã*. Clearly the various Old Republican governments considered him safe, so he wore lieutenant colonel's rank by mid-1920. His colonelcy came in 1923 "for merit," and he made brigadier general in December 1924. He led troops in Piauí and Ceará against the Prestes Column, which must have been a factor in his attitudes in 1935. His popular standing in the officer corps was indicated by his election to the presidency of the Military Club in 1928. Despite his opposition to the Revolution of 1930 he survived the retirement purge. As mentioned earlier he had promised to join the paulista side in 1932 but kept at his post in Rio de Janeiro instead. One of his sons, flying for São Paulo, was killed in combat. In the next years he distinguished himself as regional commander in Curitiba (Fifth R.M.) and Porto Alegre (Third R.M.) and was back in Rio de Janeiro to command the First R.M. in 1935, just as the national security law took effect and the salary question was agitating the army. He and Góes Monteiro, then minister of war, had a rather public dispute over the army's position in the salary crisis. The reader will recall that the outcome of the crisis removed General Guedes da Fontoura from command of Vila Militar and involved criticism of Góes by his ex-ministerial staff aide Captain Ciro de Abreu and other officers in Cacheira, RGS. The emotions stirred up got very complicated. Flores da Cunha's relations with Góes deteriorated and the latter's relationship with Panteleão Pessôa (who was Captain Ciro's brother-in-law and a good friend of Flores da Cunha) reached the breaking point. Góes held him responsible for the captain's action. Although there is no evidence linking Gomes to pressure on Góes to step down, indeed Góes laid the blame on Flores; later the deposed minister included Gomes among his enemies because he made negative comments to the press about Góes's effectiveness.[57]

In May 1936 a new round occurred in the Góes Monteiro–Gomes feud, caused by comments regarding Gomes that Góes supposedly made to some officers. The custom in such situations was for the offended officer to request written comment on the alleged remarks. Gomes took Góes's request seriously enough to send telegrams to the regional commanders alerting them that unnamed "ambitious characters who were trying to regain important political positions" were seeking to divide the army so that it could not oppose their plans. The timing suggests that this "alert" was aimed at Góes, but it would be interesting to know if the regional generals had a special secret codebook to interpret such messages?

Góes immediately denied making any remarks to anyone save Gomes himself. In the background was the mutual disdain the two generals had for one another. Their disagreement over the second amendment to the Constitution was certainly not the cause of their ill will. The tension became public indirectly when the *Correio da Manhã* (Rio) reported that there was a movement in the armed forces against the amendment, and that many officers had signed a petition sent to Vargas. The minister's staff issued an emphatic denial that such a petition existed. General Dutra, commander of the First Military Region, assured a reporter that the story was not true. Dutra circulated the clipping to his officers with a warning to do their duty and to maintain their loyalty.[58]

A review of 1936 and 1937 shows that the coup d'etat of November 10, 1937, was not a foregone conclusion and that it did not flow solely from the decisions of Getúlio Vargas.

The trend toward dictatorship was bolstered by the determination of certain paulista leaders to regain the presidency; by the survival of pre-1930 political ideas, imagery, and goals; by politicians who could not accept the candidates that came out of the political jockeying that was leading up to the presidential elections of 1938; and by generals convinced that "liberal" democracy, and specifically the regime of 1934, would not supply the arms, equipment, and men necessary to build a modern army. There was a consensus forming in the political leadership that drastic action was necessary to avoid greater calamities. For the army to support such a move changes had to be made in the individuals holding the various commands. In retrospect some of this appears to have been manipulated by Vargas, but appearances are often deceiving. Many of the changes in commands were more accidental than planned. If we could go back to 1931 and ask knowledgeable officers to guess who would be the three or four top officers in late 1937, I doubt that they would have been correct. Look at the list of generals who became gravely ill and/or died during those six years: three chiefs of the army general staff, Alfredo Malan D'Angrogne (1932), Benedicto Olímpio da Silveira (1935), and Arnaldo de Sousa Pais de Andrade (1937); Generals José Victoriano Aranha da Silva (1931), João de Deus Mena Barreto (1933), Ptolomeu de Brasil (1935), and Manoel de Cerqueira Daltro Filho (1938); and those who self-destructed, such as Brigadier Generals José Sotero de Meneses Jr. (1931), João Meira de Vasconcelos (1932), Generals of Division Augusto Tasso Fragoso (1932), Pantaleão da Silva Pessôa (1936), and João Gomes Ribeiro Filho (1936).[59] Although it is common to pair Eurico Dutra and Góes Monteiro as the minds behind army support for the Estado Novo, it took a lot of happenstance to bring the two men together as minister of war and chief of the general staff in late 1937. This is not to take away any of the luster from Getúlio's reputation for political orchestration but rather to emphasize the accidental aspects of the scenario with which he had to work.

João Gomes Ribeiro Filho's fall from Getúlio's grace had interlaced political and military aspects. In September 1936 he reportedly sent word to paulista governor Armando de Sales Oliveira that he was sympathetic to his candidacy and that he considered himself a minister of São Paulo. This occurred amid constant reports and rumors of military preparations in São Paulo and Rio Grande do Sul. Vargas received firsthand accounts from members of his family in Rio Grande of Flores's mobilization of provisional corps. Allegedly, some twenty thousand provisionals were organized, and arms were arriving in the state. Flores was supposedly making arrangements with like-minded allies in Paraná. At the same time Flores appeared to be maneuvering to become a substitute candidate for the presidency. Oddly, the governor lost control of, and certainly the loyalty of, the state's congressional delegation *(bancada),* many of whose members met regularly with Getúlio on Tuesday evenings at Guanabara Palace. General Góes Monteiro had been assigned as inspector general of the garrisons in the south so that he could coordinate the government's counter moves. He found the situation so explosive that he threatened to resign unless Minister Gomes acted quickly to reinforce the army in Paraná and Rio Grande. Gomes hesitated because he feared that federal reinforcement would make the situation worse.

To checkmate Flores da Cunha it was necessary to have trusted officers in charge at each level, starting with the First (Rio), Second (São Paulo), Third (Porto Alegre), and Fifth (Curitiba) Military Regions. Within those regions the various brigade commanders would be crucial. The military police of the several states, especially the Brigada Militar of Rio Grande and the similar forces in São Paulo and Minas Gerais, would have to be allied or neutralized, and the famed gaúcho provisionals would have to be disarmed and disbanded.

Because slightly less than a third of army units historically had been stationed in Rio Grande do Sul, many of the officers had been born and raised in the state. And because many officers had their early assignments in the state, if they had not found a wife among their military school–era sweethearts, they married Rio Grandense women. Even northeasterners such as Góes Monteiro, whose wife was from Alegrete, RGS, adopted gaúcho speech and mannerisms. Further, the local recruitment pattern of the Brazilian army meant that nearly all of the troops in the units scattered around the state were gaúchos. Divided loyalties did not make a strong army. A showdown might produce a repeat of the 1930 collapse. In this situation bluff, bluster, and diplomacy proved to be the weapons of choice.

In August 1936 General of Division Dutra commanded the First Military Region, providing security to the national capital; Brigadier General Almério Moura headed the Second Military Region; Brigadier General Emílio Lúcio Esteves was chief of the Third Military Region; and Brigadier General João Guedes da Fontoura headed the Fifth Military Region (in Curitiba). The previous two years had seen considerable movement in those positions; in that time the current commanders had two predecessors in the First, three in the Second, two in the Third, and five in the Fifth. Generals Esteves and Guedes were gaúchos, whereas Dutra was from Mato Grosso and Moura from Maranhão. At least one army observer attributed the fact that Guedes had survived the fiasco over salaries to an old friendship with Vargas from school days.[60] The truth of that analysis is uncertain. Guedes da Fontoura's career would suffer fatally in the coming crisis with Flores da Cunha. It is notable that, except for Góes Monteiro, the general officers involved in this crucial moment were not former tenentes or 1930 revolutionaries but the so-called

TABLE 10.1.

Brazilian Army Units, 1934–1936

Branch	Units Total	In RGS
Infantry	14 regiments	4
	30 light battalions	3
Cavalry	14 regiments	12
	5 divisional regiments 1	
Artillery	9 mounted regiments	3
	5 mule-back (dorso)	1
	6 coastal groups	0
	3 howitzer groups	1
	6 mounted batteries	6
	8 coastal batteries	0
Engineers	2 pontoon battalions	1
	4 sapper battalions 1	
	3 independent communications companies	1
	1 mounted communications battalion	1
Aviation	3 regiments	1[a]
	3 regiments (being formed)	0
TOTAL	116	36

SOURCE: MG, *Relatório . . . João Gomes Ribeiro Filho . . . Maio de 1936* (Rio de Janeiro: Imprensa do Estado-Maior do Exercito, 1936), 154[-]57.
NOTE: The total number of units of various sizes and missions was 116 (36 posted in Rio Grande do Sul).
[a]One of the three was in Curitiba.

legalists. Perhaps useful as a symbol of that group of officers would be Brig. Gen. José Joaquim de Andrade, who was then commanding the First Infantry Brigade and Rio's Vila Militar, and who had shown his mettle in the suppression of the November rebellion, but who as a colonel had commanded the Twelfth Infantry in Belo Horizonte during its famous resistance to the Revolution of 1930. He was assigned to the Fifth Infantry Brigade in Santa Maria, the principal garrison in the south. As can be seen in Table 10.1, the concentration of army forces in Rio Grande was truly impressive.

During the slowly evolving struggle for control of Rio Grande, two regional commanders would be shifted elsewhere because of their tolerance of Flores da Cunha's attempts to stay in office, but significantly Gen. Div. César Augusto Parga Rodrigues and Brig. Gen. Emílio Lúcio Esteves were not retired. Indeed, 1937 would find them heading respectively the Second Military Region, in São Paulo, and the Fourth Military Region, in Juiz de Fora.[61]

Minister Gomes Sabotaged Government
Policies and Undermined Morale

Gomes had suffered a decline in popularity during 1936. Partly this was due to whispers of scandal and partly because his administration left much undone. And he irritated Vargas unnecessarily. For example, as part of the commemoration of "Soldiers Day," on August 25, the army was to award the medals of the Order of Military Merit. As president and grand master of the order, Vargas had to authorize each one. Noting that the list was somewhat loaded with officers who had rebelled in 1932, he wrote the selection committee that it would be well to include some other names and suggested his uncle General Waldomiro. The committee responded by adding some names but remarked that it could not include the general because he had "a bad name in the army." So Vargas refused to approve any medals. Although the minister was not openly involved, little of that nature would occur without his knowledge.[62]

For 1936 the Congress had authorized seventy-four thousand troops, but actual strength was not much over sixty thousand. At the same time the officer corps was at its authorized forty-eight hundred regulars and eleven hundred temporary appointments. What was happening to the money not being spent on the missing fourteen thousand soldiers? This question is especially interesting because the congressional appropriation for 1936 was somewhat larger than for 1935. Yet in October the "Grand Maneuvers of the General Staff" scheduled to be held in the Paraíba valley near Taubaté (SP) were reduced in scale because of a lack of funds. Perhaps to save face, the School of Arms at Vila Militar transported its student officers, sergeants, and school troops to the Taubaté area for modest field exercises. Even this scaled-back event was regarded as important enough to warrant the presence of the minister, the chief of staff, the commander of the second military region, various brigade commanders, ranking officers of the paulista Força Pública, French and Brazilian officers of the School of Arms, and the Argentine and American military attachés. And to be sure that the guests ended the day pleasantly, according to the American observer, "the Grand Maneuvers of the Brazilian Army for 1936 [were] modified into a barbecue."[63]

And Minister Gomes's reputation was hurt by his lack of enthusiasm for putting Góes Monteiro's 1934 reorganization plan into effect. That plan had envisioned dividing the ministry into four departments: the general staff, personnel, general administration, and technical war material. The first two had existed, and the major innovation would be gathering numerous separate agencies into a general administration department. Failure to bring this new department into being was "glaring proof that the 1934 plan was far from realization." Inquiries at all levels brought "uncertain and even evasive" responses. In September 1936 Congress formally recognized the situation by stating that the 1934 plan was still in force but that now the military authorities had until the end of 1939 to complete it.[64] Even more serious was the arms and material situation. At its October 1935 meeting, Gomes had explained frankly to the National Security Council that the army's weaponry and material were in a "chaotic state." In March 1936 a special credit of 1.5 trillion milreis had been opened to begin a ten-year program of procurement. But when the new minister took office in December, the same deficiencies existed. Worse still was Gomes's approval, back in October 1936, of São Paulo's purchase abroad of arms and munitions for its Força Pública. Because the orders included 7,000 Mauser 7 mm rifles and carbines, 372 Madsen 7 mm machine guns, 10 million 7 mm cartridges, and 8 antiaerial 20 mm machine guns, it would appear that they were not intended for normal maintenance of public order. When the existence of these orders was discovered in late January 1937, the army seized the shipment in the port of Santos and transported the materiel to Rio de Janeiro.[65]

In September and October Vargas received constant reports of Flores da Cunha's military preparations, and he met repeatedly with Góes Monteiro, who was anxious to act but growing more and more frustrated with the vacillations and sabotage of General Gomes. On November 30 the Góes-Gomes crisis reached its inevitable crossroads when the minister's orders to Góes were clearly inadequate for his mission. Dispirited, Góes asked to be relieved. Moreover, Gomes censured General Esteves for going over his head to Vargas to complain that he was not receiving the arms and munitions he had requested. Exasperated, the president wrote in his diary: "Difficult people these military."[66] One has to admire Getúlio's legendary calm because this drama was playing behind the scenes while Vargas was hosting Franklin D. Roosevelt, and he was mourning his mother, who died at the end of October. Finally Vargas had General Francisco José Pinto, who had succeeded General Pessôa in July 1935 as chief of the president's military staff, tell Gomes to support his policy or to resign. On December 3, in their usual meeting on military matters, Vargas noted that Gomes made "a last attempt not to follow instructions" and, because the president insisted, later in the day Gomes sent the president his letter of resignation.[67]

It is noteworthy that Vargas allowed Gomes to leave with his public reputation intact. In July there had been a police report to the effect that there was growing hostility among army officers toward the minister. On November 25 Police Chief Müller had given the president a report on the minister's scandalous behavior with a group of young, pretty officers' wives. In return for sexual favors he was supposedly taking care of their husbands' career needs.

Talk about subverting military discipline! He went into "reserve" status on March 12, 1937, and was retired as a general of division in January 1940.[68]

Minister João Gomes's December 1936 removal from power illustrated the complexities of the political-military situation. The role and power of the minister of war in the Old Republic had not been clearly defined; most presidents had allowed their ministers to manage the army, but Vargas saw himself as the commander in chief of the armed forces and was determined to exercise direct control where he saw fit. Gomes could not make a case for strengthening discipline by channeling the president's orders through him to the chain of command because he had been subverting presidential instructions. Historically, the army worried about the power of the states' military police forces. After 1930 the army had gained more control over the states' military police, but its control was often more symbolic than real. Army officers were detached from regular duty to take command and staff positions in several states, usually at the request of the interventor or the governor, but many, if not all, such officers were natives of the state involved, with personal ties to the governor, so their loyalty to the national government had to be verified before it could be trusted. As 1936 turned into 1937, paulista governor Armando Sales resigned his post so that he would be eligible to run for president in the January 1938 elections. Significantly, he entered his candidacy against the advice of General Góes Monteiro, who told him that he would not have army support. Also within the state he faced opposition. Perhaps he was blinded by the opportunity to be the agent of São Paulo's regaining control of the national government? Oswaldo Aranha had another explanation for Armando's determination; namely that he saw the presidency as the only way to resolve the financial difficulties that his governorship had caused.[69] But Flores da Cunha's backing of his candidacy doomed it, and the reassertion of regionalism gave politics an increasingly sharp edge, the well-honed edge of the bayonet blade.

Vargas maneuvered among the would-be candidates to succeed him by encouraging some but refusing to name his own choice. There was an Old Republic feeling to national politics as the various factions and parties tried to get the president to sort out their internal disputes. The major threat to what was left of the Revolution of 1930 was a potential alliance among Flores da Cunha of Rio Grande, Armando Sales of São Paulo, and Valladares of Minas Gerais. The reality of such an alliance and the threat it posed to centralization is uncertain, because it did not occur, but that does not mean that the effort had no results. It crashed on the rocky crags of mineiro politics as Valladares struggled with Antonio Carlos Ribeiro de Andrada for dominance of the state.[70] Ever a realist, Valladares decided it was better to be at Getúlio's side, so he stayed loyal to his political creator, leaving his would-be allies in militarily exposed positions. Minas Gerais and its state troops were the balance wheel of the national political moment.[71]

Immediately upon receiving General Gomes's resignation the president invited General Eurico Dutra to assume the ministry. Since the suppression of the November revolt Dutra's star had risen rapidly. As commander of the First Military Region he had been visible to the Rio newspapers and to Vargas. He was then fifty-three years of age, trim and looking every bit a general, especially in his gleaming cavalry boots. He would be the longest serving minister of war in the history of Brazil, holding the post until 1945. Ironically, considering his role in repressing the 1935 rebellion, he had participated in the 1904 rising of the military school of Praia Vermelha. Dismissed with the other mutinous students, his career dreams had turned nightmarish. Humiliated, he had waited in Cuiabá for the amnesty that came in November 1905. It was the first and last time that he took part in rebellious adventures. In 1906 he entered the School of War in Porto Alegre, where he was a contemporary of Pedro de Góes Monteiro and where they both were active, with law student Getúlio Vargas, in a civilian-military student organization, Bloco Acadêmico Castilhista and its newspaper *O Debate*. Although they do not seem to have been close friends, they certainly knew each other.

In 1908 Dutra was declared an *aspirante* and assigned briefly to the Seventeenth Cavalry Regiment in Ponta Porã on the frontier with Paraguay in his native Mato Grosso. After courses in the artillery and engineering school, where he specialized in mechanics, ballistics, and metallurgy, he served in the Thirteenth Cavalry Regiment in the federal capital, where he was promoted to second lieutenant in 1910. Between 1912 and 1915 he was a cavalry instructor in several of the army's schools in the Rio area, including Realengo. In the latter year he joined the prestigious First Cavalry Regiment, also in the capital. In 1916 he published a book, *Duas Táticas em Confronto*, comparing the use of cavalry by the German and French armies. He also served on the editorial board of *A Defeza Nacional*, placing himself firmly among the reformist modernizers of the officer corps led by the Young Turks. He personalized that connection by marrying Carmela Leite, the widow of José Pinheiro de Ulhôa Cintra, an engineer officer in the third group sent to Germany (1910–12). He took the general staff course (1920–22) under the French military mission during which he was promoted to captain. In January 1922 he was one of the 529 officers who signed the Military Club motion condemning President-elect Bernardes for supposedly insulting the military. But he was on the government side in the spasm of rebellion in July of that year, and, concluding the staff course as the top student with the rare *très bien*, he found himself the next year in the operations section (third) of the general staff under General Tasso Fragoso. During the tenente rebellion in São Paulo in 1924 he acted as general staff liaison with army forces in the field. After serving as operations officer for General Mena Barreto's Detachment of the North, which put down the tenente rebellion in Amazonas and Pará, Captain Dutra returned south to the staff of General Otávio de Azevedo Coutinho, then in operations (Feb. 1925) against the units that had fled São Paulo and had dug in between Foz de Iguaçu and Catanduvas, Paraná. The chief of staff of one of the neighboring government detachments, that of General Mirante, was Captain Góes Monteiro. Before Captain Prestes' troops arrived in the area from Rio Grande, Dutra was called to the staff of the First Military Region, in Rio, where he advanced to major in May 1927. Between then and May 1929, when he was made a lieutenant colonel, he spent a year with the Ninth R.C.I. [Independent Cavalry Regiment] in São Gabriel (RGS), followed by a period heading a military court in Rio and several more months on the general staff. As the 1930 plotting intensified, he spurned invitations to join, instead staying firmly in the double command of the Fifteenth RCI and the cavalry school, both in Rio. On October 21–24, 1930, he was leading the Fifteenth toward Minas Gerais. The cessation of hostilities on the twenty-fourth made his projected invasion unnecessary. A new day had dawned in Brazil, and he must have appeared sufficiently aloof from politics to have escaped the postrevolution retirement purge. His punishment for not supporting the revolution was command of the Eleventh R.C.I. in Ponta Porã, where he had his first assignment as an aspirante. Shortly thereafter, Brigadier General Klinger took command of the Mato Grosso military district and requested Dutra as his chief of staff. They knew each other from *A Defesa Nacional* and worked well together, and Klinger had high praise for his staff chief. In December 1931 Dutra made full colonel and was ordered to command the Fourth R.C.D. [Regiment of Division Cavalry] in Tres Corações (MG), where the civil war of 1932 found him. His gratitude to Vargas for giving him the colonelcy and the Fourth Regiment kept him loyal to the government and brought him into contact with Benjamin Vargas, on whose recommendation, together with that of Oswaldo Aranha, who observed his leadership in the Mantiqueira mountains, the president made him a brigadier general on October 4, 1932. From the depths two years before, his career was now firmly on an upward trajectory. His status in the officer corps was signaled by his election as president of the Military Club for 1933–34. The circumstances of his career that carried him in the salary crisis of 1935 to substitute General Guedes da Fontoura as chief of the First Infantry Brigade at Vila Militar were described earlier.[72]

The configuration of personalities that historians associate with the Estado Novo reached their positions of power through the internal politics of the army and of the regime. The accidents of sickness, sexual desire, regional loyalties, and personal ambition played minor roles in shaping the roster of the high command of the Brazilian army in late 1936. Perhaps a different minister of war or chief of staff would have produced different outcomes in the crucial events of 1937. The threat to Brazilian unity from regional politics, represented by Flores da Cunha, had more substance than historians have thought. And the red menace may have been more nightmarish than real; however, fear is not always realistic or controllable. For good or ill Brazil was about to embark on a path to dictatorial modernization.

CHAPTER 11

The Generals and the Estado Novo

We want nothing. We only wish to work for the Army and
for the salvation of the *Pátria*.
—Minutes of meeting of generals, Sep. 27, 1937

[T]he *Pátria* and the regime will be under our guard. . . in
defense of internal order, of political integrity, of national
sovereignty. This is our mission.
—Marechal Eurico Gaspar Dutra, Nov. 10, 1937

Dawn lit the sky beyond the mountains across the bay, and rain puddles
dotted the streets of Rio de Janeiro as the state's military police rode up to
the Monroe and Tiradentes Palaces to guard the closed congressional chambers. The city center slowly came alive as the electric streetcars disgorged
their passengers. The newsstands posted the morning papers, which head-
lined the appointment of Francisco Campos as minister of justice but said
nothing about Armando Sales's manifesto read the day before in the Congress. The placid appearance of the capital city belied the fact that a revolution was occurring. Before noon on November 10, 1937, Brazil would have
a new Constitution and would begin eight years of dictatorship. It was to
be a salvationist dictatorship that would, Getúlio Vargas told the radio audience, "restore the nation . . . allowing it to construct freely its own history
and destiny." The complicated course of events, maneuverings, conspiracies,
and politics that produced that momentous day involved the Brazilian army
to an unprecedented degree. Central to the relationship between Vargas and
the generals was a pledge, or *compromisso,* that he had made to equip and
arm the army and navy in return for social and political peace in which his
government would develop Brazil's economy and infrastructure. The Pátria
was to be made safe. Generals Pedro de Góes Monteiro and Eurico Dutra
believed that they were saving Brazil from catastrophe and insuring its future security.[1]

Politics of the Generals

When Dutra took over the ministry from João Gomes in December 1936, he had no intellectual or emotional links with tenentismo or with the Revolution of 1930; rather his military thinking was rooted in the institutional reformism of the Young Turks and *A Defesa Nacional*. He felt gratitude to Getúlio Vargas for his promotions to colonel and to brigadier general. His long ministry and his partnership with Góes Monteiro would fortify the centralization of the national government, modernize the army, take it to war against Germany, eliminate political regionalism as a threat to the Pátria's integrity, and make the armed forces the moderator of the political system for the next half century. At this crucial juncture of Brazilian history he was an actor of considerable importance.

His personality contrasted with the typical army officer who often exhibited native or adopted gaúcho mannerisms, especially energetic, emphatic, loud speech marked by rolling *r*s. Dutra had "a gentle manner, small hands and a soft handshake, listened carefully, spoke little, low, sibilant, whispering the words."[2]

It is important to observe that Góes Monteiro was not Getúlio's initial choice for chief of the general staff and that he would be appointed at Dutra's insistence. Rather the uncle of the president's wife was the first pick. General Waldomiro Castilho de Lima would have been a logical choice at that critical point because of the family ties; indeed, he had soldiered under Getúlio's father, Col. Manuel do Nascimento Vargas, in the civil war in 1894. Likely Vargas thought General Waldomiro's Rio Grandense roots might be useful in the coming showdown with Flores da Cunha. He had a typically upward career until the outbreak of tenentismo in the 1920s. He stood with the government in 1922 because he believed in discipline. In October of that year he was made commander of the Third Infantry Regiment at Praia Vermelha. His growing sympathy for the tenentes attracted the suspicions of the Artur Bernardes government, which retired and imprisoned him on the desolate Island of Trinidade, in the mid-Atlantic. Freed by the Supremo Tribunal Federal in 1925, he kept away from politics until the crisis of 1929–30. He was involved in the attack on the Third Military Region headquarters in Porto Alegre on October 3, 1930, and played notable roles in later military operations. During the 1932 civil war he commanded the federal forces confronting São Paulo in the west. After the paulista collapse he was military governor and then interventor of the state. As such he showed interest in improving the lot of workers and in defending the state's interests. In October 1933 he returned to the army as inspector general of the First Group of Military Regions (the south). From June to August 1935 he took the general staff school's intelligence course for senior officers and topped the class. The practice at the time was to give the first-placed students in the army schools a period of study or practical experience in Europe. In France, where he was attached to the general staff, General Gamelin pinned a medal on him and arranged a tour of the supposedly impregnable Maginot Line. Mussolini, not to be outdone, invited him to fly over the battlefields of Ethiopia and gave him a medal to commemorate his daring. He returned to Brazil at the end of October 1936. On the same day that Vargas called Dutra to the ministry, he persuaded General Waldomiro to assume command of the First Military Region, preparatory to elevating him to chief of the general staff.[3]

Dutra wanted tighter control over the officer corps. One of his first steps as minister was to call back officers serving outside the ranks. On January 21, 1937, he sent to the Congress a report on officers who were serving on detached duty with federal ministries and at the disposition of state governors. In all there were sixty officers assigned outside the army, some of whom had been away for years. In December Dutra had ordered nine officers back to active service and had a sharp exchange of telegrams with Flores da Cunha, who protested that the recall discriminated against Rio Grande do Sul. On the first list of those receiving recall orders were three of the seven officers who were at the disposal of Governor Flores. Their cases showed blatant abuse of detached assignments: Lt. Col. Agnelo de Souza, with nearly thirty-three years in the army, had never served with troops, had been outside the army since 1932, and at the service of the Rio Grandense governor since 1934. But "everyone knew that he remained almost continuously in the Federal Capital." And then there was Major Leopoldo de Barros Bittencourt, also with thirty-three years of service, who had only "one year, eleven months and eight days" with troops, and that was when he had been a second lieutenant. He had served at the disposition of Rio Grande do Sul since 1924, twelve years! The third case was Major Armando Nestor Cavalcante, who had been promoted to his current rank for merit but had not yet done troop duty as a major. He was attached to the Porto Alegre government in 1932. Dutra's December recall left Flores with only the commander of the Brigada Militar.[4] Under the guise of responsible administration Dutra struck a largely unseen blow that weakened Flores.

Getúlio intended to place his wife's uncle at the head of the general staff, but it did not work out that way. In May 1937 as plans moved forward to isolate Rio Grande with federal troops, on May 4 it seemed to Vargas that the trend of events was toward "peace and conciliation of interests," but ten days later it appeared that "Flores [was] preparing an armed movement." Toward the end of the month Vargas invited his wife's uncle, General Waldomiro Lima, to become chief of staff. But then the army's internal politics spilled over into public view.

Several generals, alarmed that civil war could result from the pressure on Flores, met at the home of General José Pessôa, where they drafted a condemnation of the maneuvers in the south. These "pacifying generals," who included Waldomiro Lima, afterward, apparently met individually with Dutra, who on May 19 had issued a proclamation to the army insisting that the troop movements had nothing to do with the presidential succession but were aimed at safeguarding "national order, institutions, and integrity." All of the measures he had taken as minister, he declared, were to put the army in position "to fulfill its mission of maintaining internal order and of carrying out the decisions of the legally constituted government." But it also was a public admission that federal military preparations had been made "to forestall any resistance by Rio Grande do Sul." Regarding presidential succession, Dutra wrote that the army should be "a vigilant and dispassionate spectator, willing and able to give its cooperation so that the succession could be carried out by legal means, within constitutional norms and according to electoral law." He charged his "Comrades" to remember that "now and forever, the honor and integrity of the *Pátria,* the prosperity of the Nation and the tranquility of the Brazilian Family," rested on "our unity of vision, on our firm cohesion and on our conscious and unyielding discipline." Despite the high-sounding language, the proclamation was the "first indication that any fears . . . [were] felt for the morale of the army."[5]

Immediately, in response to the generals' protest, Góes Monteiro sent a letter to all the generals in the Rio area, demanding to know who had attended the meeting at General Pessôa's house. Góes was fuming because the generals' protest had deflated his invasion plans, and he feared that some of the senior officers were seeking to undermine him. This was an odd situation. Góes had no legal authority to query his fellow generals, but their respect or fear made them answer. Some replied that no meeting had occurred, and some said that only a few generals had attended a discussion of current affairs at Pessôa's house. They assured Góes that they had not talked about him. The few who admitted protesting to Dutra said that they did so to avoid civil strife. One bravely asserted that his conversation with Dutra was privileged. Two raised doubts about Góes's actions in the south; to these he replied dryly that he would divulge, on request, documents supporting his plans. Last, to one general, who had expressed his patriotic desire to avoid civil war, Góes sent a self-conscious lengthy apologia, oozing fervent affirmations of military honor. In all of his replies he stressed that his mission was of paramount importance to the nation.[6]

The incident epitomized the immense influence Góes enjoyed in the army: fifteen general officers replied swiftly and thoroughly to his eccentric demand; a few were brief, but most responded carefully. However, the incident also showed that Góes and Vargas did not have absolute power; several generals had warned the most powerful men in the country that their support had limits. It also showed that a perhaps sizable portion of the army could have been provoked to mutiny over what would have been, until less than a decade earlier, fairly common practice, that is federal intervention in a state. The incident emphasized, as well, the special regard officers had for Rio Grande do Sul. Rio de Janeiro and Mato Grosso were intervened without much ado. Last, it offers evidence of the anxiety Góes was suffering; to have sent the original letter to the generals was startling enough, but his troubled replies showed that the undoing of his plans had affected him deeply.

The public facade of army unity began to crumble as the press got wind of the generals' meeting. "Poor guys!" Vargas wrote in his *Diary*. "It seems that Flores is more a general than they are. It would be preferable, instead of sabers, to give them pillows to embroider." General Waldomiro denied that the generals were conspiring, but Góes Monteiro told Vargas that his wife's uncle had been carrying on secret communications with Flores da Cunha. Getúlio turned to Dutra, who had come with Góes to see him, saying that the government had to take vigorous measures to prevent the political scene from "dissolving into military anarchy."

In the midst of this backstage crisis, what the public saw was the minister of justice releasing three hundred and some political prisoners. But even this was playacting. The "political" prisoners were in reality, Vargas admitted, pickpockets and street toughs arrested during the state of war. Dutra added to the peaceful facade by telling the press that the army had no objections to ending the oft-renewed state of war. So, censorship ended, constitutional rights returned. But beyond public view the drama continued. Vargas met with General Waldomiro on June 11 to tell him that the government knew what he was up to and that he could no longer be considered for chief of staff; in fact, Góes Monteiro would assume that position. The general denied involvement in political maneuvers and said he would resign as commander of the First Military Region if Góes became chief. Indeed, Dutra had already made clear that Góes's appointment was required for him to stay on as minister. The Góes-Waldomiro confrontation became public when General Waldomiro had his lawyer give the press his letter charging General Góes with character defamation. Minister Dutra considered this a breach of discipline and ordered him imprisoned for four days at Vila Militar. Waldomiro, in his turn, labeled this action an abuse of authority and appealed to Vargas. Dutra removed him from command of the First Military Region and attached him to the president's military staff. There outside his jurisdiction he would be the president's problem.

General José Pessôa weighed in with an "energetic" letter to Vargas defending himself against the conspiracy charge and lamenting that "certain elements" (meaning Góes) had reached "high posts of responsibility, where they may more easily gratify their morbid thirst for fostering contention and disorder." He bound himself to resign from the army immediately if the charges proved true and asked that his accuser "proceed with like dignity" if the reverse be the case. In response, the president ordered him imprisoned for six days.

General of Division Firmino Borba, now head of the First Military Region, opened a military inquiry into the two generals' charges against Góes Monteiro. The American military attaché recalled the 1932 argument between Góes and Tasso Fragoso and noted that then Góes had not been disciplined for his verbal excesses, in marked contrast with Pessôa and Waldomiro's punishments. The attaché worried that the quarrel could split the army "into factions openly arrayed against each other. Rancor and ill-feeling of long standing may come out into the open."[7]

Rather than splitting the army between the two victors of the São Paulo civil war, it solidified the general officers. The Góes-Waldomiro struggle came to an end with charges and countercharges before the Supreme Military Tribunal and the arrests and brief imprisonments of Generals Waldomiro and Pessôa. General Borba's inquiry report "attempted to place all of the officers involved in as favorable a light as possible." However, the sidelining of these two prominent officers served as an object lesson to other senior officers who might think of opposing the unfolding course of events. Waldomiro was given some minor military judicial inquiries to conduct and died of a stroke in February 1938. Pessôa was left without assignment until March 1938, when he was sent to command the Ninth Military Region in Mato Grosso, the army's traditional banishment posting, where his troops hunted bandits.[8] The "politics of the generals," as Vargas called the episode, ended with the army under the command of the Dutra-Góes duo. They would be the longest serving minister and chief of staff in Brazilian history.

While these events claimed the officer corps' attention, the politicians had come up with two candidates for the January 1938 elections. Armando de Sales Oliveira formally launched his candidacy in São Paulo. Vargas's man, Governor Benedito Valladares, dramatically announced in a radio address that "Minas Gerais will not lend itself to any movement of coercion or violence" to resolve the presidential succession. Some commentators wondered if the address meant that Valladares had broken with Vargas? A convention of politicos from around the country, which Valladares organized in Belo Horizonte, raised as their candidate José Américo de Almeida of Paraíba. Fascinating though it is, the ill-fated electoral campaign is the backdrop for the main drama and need not take our attention away from the march to dictatorship.[9]

With the army secure the government moved against Flores da Cunha. For Vargas, Flores represented the keystone of potential state-level political opposition to centralization; politicians in other states were not likely to move without his leadership. Góes Monteiro had pushed military preparations close to completion in the first three months of 1937. Indeed there were so many reports of paulista and gaúcho arms purchases abroad that Vargas noted in his *Diary* that it seemed as if the two states were arming "for a war to conquer Brazil."[10]

With public attention focused so intently on political figures, it is not surprising that some "normal" military events escaped scrutiny. The annual cycle of training in the army of that time began in May and ended in the following March. Individual recruits and draftees moved from the manual of arms through small-unit tactics to ever-larger configurations until they could function in combined divisional operations. Such large training operations depended on funds being available to regional headquarters. In March 1937 the Third Military Region received the necessary funds and staged maneuvers in the Santa Maria area and at Portão, about thirty miles north of Porto Alegre, near Novo Hamburgo. The plans of the two maneuvers seemingly aimed at defending against forces attacking along the rail line from Uruguaiana and from Santa Catarina, but because Brazilian units played both offensive and defensive roles, the training had immediate application in case of confrontation with the state's Brigada Militar and provisionals. The two weeks of maneuvers involved about ten thousand infantry, cavalry, and artillery troops, and included use of observer aircraft. The American attaché noted that "the real purpose of the exercises was to train the organization in troop movements and supply."[11] Surely Flores was well aware of this training and what it portended.

Oswaldo Aranha, passing through Brazil for the Pan American meeting in Buenos Aires, had tried to reconcile Flores and Getúlio. For the president the solution was simple. Flores should keep quiet, not stir things up, and he would not be hostile to him. Effectively that would mean that Flores would stop his newspapers from attacking the federal government, or sending circular telegrams to other state governors, or negotiating resistance agreements with them. He had even tried to get Uruguay to pledge neutrality in the event of conflict between Rio Grande and Rio de Janeiro. Oswaldo convinced the two former friends, now protagonists, to meet. On April 2 Flores and Getúlio talked alone about the presidential succession. They agreed that neither of them was committed to a particular candidate; in fact, Flores said he was willing to try to convince Armando Sales to withdraw his name. In what would be their last meeting, both were cordial and conciliatory. Flores said he would remain for fifteen days in Rio at Vargas's disposition, but five days later, unexpectedly, he telegraphed that he had to return south immediately. The power balance in the gaúcho state assembly was by a precarious one-vote margin that had shifted against him. Getúlio's brother Benjamin led the opposition state deputies against Flores. The Vargas brothers crafted a strategy that they hoped would provoke Flores to some hostile response that would justify federal military intervention. On April 25 the opposition deputies requested that for peace and security in the state the administration of the special state of war powers be transferred from Flores to General Emílio Lúcio Esteves, the Third Military Region commander. To the surprise of all, the normally explosive Flores restrained himself. General Esteves, or his staff, had convinced Flores to accept the slap peacefully. Even so, Dutra canceled the leaves of all officers and urged Esteves to concentrate army units in Porto Alegre. The general replied that such troop movements could provoke an unnecessary confrontation. In effect Esteves, a gaúcho from Taquara, in the serra region of eastern Rio Grande do Sul and for several years chief instructor of the state Brigada Militar who made no secret of opposing federal intervention, acted as a buffer between Flores and authorities in Rio de Janeiro. In any case the national state of war expired on June 18 and so was no longer a tool to irritate Flores.[12]

However the struggle against Flores was not over. Góes sent his assistants Col. Gustavo Cordeiro de Farias and Major Arthur Hescket Hall to Rio Grande to be his eyes and ears. They radioed assessments of the political and military situations, as did General Esteves, who stayed until July to oversee the continuing disarming of provisional units. On June 29 Esteves telegraphed that the provisionals had been disarmed and disbanded completely. And as of mid-July regiments and battalions sent south in preceding months were still there awaiting further orders.[13]

On that same day the war ministry circulated a warning to all commanders that in adjusting to the return to constitutional status they should be alert to inflamed political passions arising from the presidential election campaign. Some civil authorities, it noted, would likely "confuse liberty with licence and justice with tolerance. The army must be calm, exact and vigilant so as not to be taken by surprise. As the army's responsibilities expanded, so too did the forces which might rise against it." The most dangerous enemy continued to be communism because it is "organized and persistent subverting the results of centuries of civilization and endangering our sacred homes." Góes Monteiro, who most likely wrote this inflated prose, concluded by recalling the tragic events of November 1935 and the vandalism that they must never forget![14]

On July 2, after his seriously ill friend, General Pais de Andrade, had resigned as chief of staff, Góes succeeded him.[15] While Góes shuffled regional commanders, Dutra flew to inspect units in Rio Grande do Sul. On July 5 he and Vargas had discussed the trip, and for the first time the two spoke openly of federal intervention. Dutra said that he wanted to impress on the Rio Grande garrisons the need to be "aggressive" if new groups of state irregulars turned up nearby. Vargas was concerned that, if intervention came, the troops must carry out "any order of the government." Dutra conferred with officers in Curitiba, Paraná, and further south with those of some reinforcement units in Tuberão on the narrow coastal plain of Santa Catarina. In Porto Alegre, Flores da Cunha, whom Dutra addressed as "general" because of his 1930 honorary title, staged a "grandiose" reception at the airport and had his official car carry the minister to the headquarters of the Third Military Region to meet General Esteves. The latter was saddened at the news that he was to be moved to another military region. Dutra met with "General" Flores, who took the opportunity to stress the peaceful intentions of his government but noted that if necessary "he would know how to defend the dignity of the state." He asserted that he had dissolved the provisionals, except for about eighteen hundred, who were engaged in essential services. Flores provided a special train to carry Generals Dutra and Esteves to the key military center of Santa Maria. In conversations with Brigadier General José Joaquim de Andrade and the officers of the Fifth Infantry Brigade, Dutra perceived that they wanted to stay out of local politics and placed some restrictions or limitations on federal intervention.[16] Andrade and Esteves were agreed that they should avoid armed conflict. Officers in Cruz Alta expressed similar restrictions regarding intervention.

Dutra and Esteves made the circuit of Uruguaiana, Alegrete, São Gabriel, and Bagé. At each Dutra emphasized the need for "unconditional obedience." On July 14 at the Ninth Independent Cavalry Regiment in São Gabriel, where he had served as a major in 1927–28, Dutra gave a brief speech in which he reminded the officers, "Obedience makes the army an impersonal force, entirely subordinated to the powers of the Nation." Moreover, he declared that "it was not up to us to debate [the government's] decisions, but only to carry them out, with loyalty and with the impartiality that ought to characterize us."[17]

Meanwhile, back in Rio de Janeiro, Góes Monteiro had been rearranging the top commanders. General Guedes da Fontoura, who had been such a headache in mid-1935 and had been posted to command the Fifth Military Region in Curitiba was, like his brother-in-law General Esteves, cool to the maneuvers against Flores and was moved to a supposedly higher post as inspector general of the First Group of Military Regions (south). As had been shown during Góes Monteiro's tenure, the inspector general was only as powerful as the president, the minister of war, and now the chief of staff wanted him to be. For Guedes da Fontoura, who was made a general of division, it was an empty post. He would be retired in November. Góes had placed the Fifth Military Region in the capable hands of one of his trusted men, and fellow northeasterner, baiano General of Division Manoel de Cerqueira Daltro Filho. He had been commanding the invasion forces that were poised to strike

Rio Grande had Flores resisted. Now he awaited new orders. Esteves would be transferred to the Fourth Military Region in Minas Gerais, whose state troops would insure that he did not give into any sudden impulses to aid Flores.

In early August Góes and Dutra reshuffled the commands once more to gain even tighter control. This time Daltro Filho went to the Third Military Region, Esteves stayed in Minas, and Brigadier General José Meira de Vasconcellos went to the Fifth Military Region. Colonel Mascarenhas de Moraes took over the Ninth Military Region in Mato Grosso, and, more curious, Gen. Div. José Maria Franco Ferreira became inspector general of the Third Regional Group, which apparently did not yet exist. Major Mitchell, the U.S. military attaché, commented that this latter assignment was "one of the mysteries, or at least surprises, with which Brazil's military administration abounds." As the generals moved, their lower-ranked trusted officers also shifted.[18]

At the same time Dutra tightened the screws on Flores by demanding that Rio Grande return all of the weapons that the army had loaned the state as far back as 1930! No consideration was to be given for worn-out material nor for normal losses and disappearances. The state could either return the arms or pay for them. Flores made a conciliatory reply and requested that the army and his state seek an impartial judge to reach a settlement. But Dutra asserted that was not acceptable because the question was an army matter and only the army and the national government had authority to resolve it.[19]

August, that darkest of Brazilian months frequently marred by political crises and problems, lived up to its reputation in 1937. At the end of July "official" candidate José Américo gave a fiery address to a political rally in Rio's Esplanada do Castelo, laying out his priorities if elected: cleaning up public finances; restructuring public administration; improving public transportation and housing; breaking up the great rural properties; stimulating exploitation of mineral resources and of war industries for national defense; careful separation of executive, judicial, and legislative powers; and guarantees for political and individual rights. On July 31 Minister Dutra issued a stern circular to the military regions, cautioning that the presidential campaign could turn violent because "we are not accustomed to political clashes of such vast proportions." Left to themselves, "the masses could easily slide into aggressive violence and disorder, with nothing to keep them within reasonable limits. . . . It is then that the national Armed Forces exercises its most legitimate and elevated mission . . . as guardian of internal order." The army, he emphasized, must "stay aloof from the political struggle . . . to be respected, to be able to impose authority wherever it is called, it must be impartial." Therefore the officers must keep their eyes on national interests that must supersede "political aspirations, regional ambitions, [and] ideological concerns."[20]

On the night of August 3, at the request of the military ministers, Vargas met with them, the minister of justice, and Chief of Police Müller, who presented an alarming report on the danger of communist propaganda. The minister of justice, to whom Müller was supposedly subordinate, was upset because he had said nothing to him in advance. They decided that the chief should make a written report and request authority for specific countermeasures. The next day, Plinio Salgado, Integralista candidate for the presidency, gave a radio address warning of a communist coup plot. That same day José Américo told Getúlio that he and Edmundo Bittencourt, founder of *Correio da Manhã* (Rio), were trying to persuade Flores to resign. He also cautioned the president that there was danger of a coup; Góes Monteiro had told him that if the politicians did not reach an understanding, the army would act. During August there were almost daily rumors of either a communist uprising, an Integralista *putsch,* or a military coup d'état, which, according to the U.S. Embassy, was causing uneasiness in the government and in business circles. On August 7 a political rally in São Paulo against Armando Sales was broken up with gunfire. Rumors of conspiracies and warlike preparations in Rio Grande continued to run hot. The death on August 8 of recently resigned chief of staff General Pais de Andrade added to the somber mood. On the fifteenth, in Campos, state of Rio de Janeiro, an Integralista rally ended in a riot that left thirteen dead and several injured. On the eighteenth General Dutra instructed regional commanders to be set for public disturbances; every major unit was to have a subunit on ready alert. He also ordered the Central do Brasil railroad to be prepared on short notice to transport troops. And the next day General Daltro Filho, who had assumed command of the Third Military Region on the seventeenth, telegraphed Vargas that officers in the region were saying that they would oppose any assault on Rio Grande's autonomy and that Flores was determined to resist intervention. Daltro discovered that his own headquarters staff included a number of officers allied with Flores, so gradually he arranged orders for the dubious ones to be sent elsewhere. To underscore the precariousness of the situation, General Daltro sent by courier a report with photographs of sixteen groups of road workers, who were really provisionals paid by the state Brigada Militar. Daltro also reported that discipline in the Paraná garrisons was shaky. Moreover, Governor Flores was communicating with São Paulo regarding a broad movement against the national government. And Flores, Daltro reported, intended to place Getúlio's wife's uncle General Waldomiro in command. Once again the specter of civil war hung over Brazil.[21]

The gaúcho provisionals were "great fighters," partly because they were on their home ground and knew each other, and partly because they all had either had a year of army training or were former members of the Brigada Militar. They were well armed, and, enjoying local prestige, they exhibited considerable pride. A nagging question that remains to be answered more fully than is possible here is how were they paid? Did the Brigada's budget include money for provisional battalions? Juracy Magalhães commented that "the provisionals were paid by the central government, under the table." This was, he said, "a sore point with many officers" and a reason why Góes Monteiro's operation against Rio Grande had a good reception among them. If Juracy was correct, why did Vargas not simply pull the financial support from under the provisionals?[22]

It should be no surprise that, with all these complicated matters, Vargas did not feel very well and grew even more anxious when Argentina, England, and Germany opposed the agreement that he had worked out with Roosevelt to lease six old American destroyers for naval training purposes. The Brazilians especially resented the Argentine attitude. Brazilian newspapers, regardless of their sentiments toward the federal government, rose to defend the acquisition of the vessels as a matter of national honor and expressed disappointment and exasperation with Argentina, which was then building seven destroyers.[23]

In the midst of this national and international turmoil Vargas was experiencing an even more personal turmoil. He was involved in the only known extramarital affair of his life. He complained of irritability and mood swings and noted in his diary that his wife, Darcy, was having explosions of jealousy. On August 19 his personal and presidential frustrations caused him to wonder if "perhaps they'll push me to get out of this with a brusk and unexpected decision." Was he having thoughts of resigning, or of suicide?[24]

Did Vargas's dark mood reflect that of the country, or was he projecting his own perceptions? Indeed, what was he thinking? His diary entries grew more cryptic. Certainly José Américo's speeches were making politicians nervous and were rapidly undermining his candidacy. However, Vargas, in a diary entry on the twenty-third, seemed to minimize the dangers that the electoral campaign was stirring up, writing that "the communist, Integralista, and . . . Rio Grande phenomena did not have the significance" that "the champions of democracy" wanted to give them. He thought that José Américo's extreme positions were mainly a "candidate's pose" and that he did not have the same "misgivings" as alarmed political leaders.[25]

On August 25 the corps of cadets paraded in front of the Caxias monument, then located in the Largo do Machado, to commemorate Soldier's Day, the birthday of the army's patron and "spiritual guide" Luiz Alves de Lima, the duke of Caxias. A brief digression will give the reader a clearer idea about the significance of this event.

Luiz Alves de Lima, the Duke of Caxias

Twelve years before, the army did not have a tradition of patrons. The army practice of adopting symbolic patrons for its branches and academy classes came into being and flourished between 1923 and 1938. It had begun when a member of the Instituto Histórico e Geográfico Brasileiro suggested in 1923 that the army officially commemorate the 120th anniversary of Caxias's birth and the 100th of his entry into the army. Minister Setembrino de Carvalho ordered that henceforth appropriate army formations would mark the day. In January 1925 the Realengo Military School graduating class, or turma, charmed by the French army use of symbolic patrons, had selected the empire's only duke and greatest general as their class patron. During their Thanksgiving Mass the students passed out "holy cards" on which was the duke's picture and a listing of his victories. Caxias's rise was advanced by the Realengo students' decision to take him as class patron. Later, Minister Setembrino, who had attended the Mass, ordered that Caxias's birthday be commemorated as Soldier's Day. From then onward Caxias was to be regarded as the exemplar soldier of the Pátria. Recalling his life was to be, as Celso Castro suggested, a symbolic "antidote against lack of military discipline." However, it would not be enough merely to give speeches about Caxias as "prototype of Brazilian military virtues"; it was necessary for soldiers to internalize, according to Castro, "his moral character and to renew annually the promise to follow his example." After 1930 there was an important shift of emphasis away from legality and discipline to a "fusion of the army and the nation," with Caxias as the central figure in the struggle for the "*Pátria's* unity and integrity." As the political closing of 1937 reached its high point in the Estado Novo, the emphasis was on Caxias's military leadership in the service of a strong State. José Murilo de Carvalho observed that in the closing of ranks behind the dictatorship, Caxias was even more the symbol of military and national unity. Articles in professional military journals on Caxias increased notably in the 1930s.[26]

Vargas, unlike his predecessors, made a point of participating in Soldier's Day commemorations. Another new feature was that the ceremonies involved the military school students. Col. José Pessôa, as mentioned earlier, consciously created new "traditions" in his reorganization of the military school of Realengo. The two most notable were the adoption of the "big blue" uniform used in the Caxias-led 1852 war against Rosas of Argentina and the addition of a scaled-down version of the duke's saber as part of the cadet's dress uniform. To emphasize the unity and continuity of the officer corps, Pessôa and his colleagues developed what became an evocative feature of military school ceremonial. Pessôa regarded the Caxias saber as "a talisman guiding [the cadets] to a life of great success, of love of the army and of fidelity to their *pátria*." The short sabers did not become the property of the individual cadets but were passed down to successive classes for use during their school years. Beginning in 1933, and continuing to the present, the class about to be graduated passed its sabers to the first-year men, who accepted them with an oath that includes the statement, "I receive the saber of Caxias as the true symbol of military honor." The ceremony was first held in Rio de Janeiro in front of the statue of Caxias.[27] Much has been made of the fact that the resurrection of Caxias as an ideal role model took on more intensity with the Estado Novo, but we should not lose sight of its being a process of several years and the work of a variety of officers. In 1899 his memory was honored with an equestrian statue erected in the then fashionable Largo do Machado, which space bore the duke's name until the statue was moved to its present location. The nature of the army, of the officer corps, and of its relationship to the country was on the minds of senior officers. One of the historic philosophical problems was the role that positivism had played in military education in the nineteenth century. The belief of its adherents that war would disappear and that humanity's positive aspects would predominate had led to minimizing military studies. By the 1930s professionalization had the upper hand, but some of the old positivist symbols were still very much in evidence. The army *Almanac,* as it still does, carried Benjamin Constant Botelho de Magalhães as number seven in the list of brigadier generals, by virtue of an 1891 congressional resolution permanently retiring that position in his honor. In 1926 his image as a historic figure was enhanced by a splendid monument located on the edge of the Praça da República facing the war ministry. As the emblematic figure of military positivism, Benjamin Constant had been the role model for generations of officers. The fact that Benjamin Constant's monument was moved in the 1940s from its prominent position to a less-conspicuous location in the vast plaza could easily be misinterpreted as the result of a clash of military philosophies that replaced the positivist with the duke. The reality was more prosaic. Rio de Janeiro's urban renewal, beginning in 1943, included broadening of the street that became Avenida Presidente Vargas. That urban development included constructing the mausoleum in front of the then war ministry, in which the duke and his wife's remains were reentombed on Soldier's Day, August 25, 1949. The mausoleum was graced by the equestrian statue mentioned above.[28]

Caxias was a symbol of Brazilian unity, military dedication, and international respect. In the special August 1935 issue of the *Revista Militar Brasileira* in honor of the duke's memory, then Minister of War General João Gomes had suggested to soldiers that when they began to doubt the future of their Pátria, they should recall Caxias, "who was always full of faith, patriotic love . . . [and] lively hope in the destinies of Brazil."[29]

The Cohen Plan

Soldiers certainly needed a lot of faith in the future of the Pátria at this juncture in Brazilian history. All the ink that has been spilled over the Cohen Plan episode has not clarified why a fake document was used to justify the reimposition of a state of war. It is well known that the document was written by Captain Olímpio Mourão Filho, an Integralista since 1932, organizer of the party's paramilitary militia, member of its council of four hundred, and, in 1937, chief of its secret service. He was also serving in the intelligence section of the army's general staff! He wrote the document that became the Cohen Plan, as an Integralista defensive exercise against a supposed communist coup d'etat. Plinio Salgado rejected it for party use as too fantastic. But Chief of Staff Góes Monteiro used a portion of the document as justification for a government request to the Congress to reimpose the state of war.

The episode raises questions for which the current state of research does not provide answers. The fact that Captain Mourão was not charged under national security law no. 38 of April 1935 for organizing an unapproved militia is likely the most glaring evidence that the law was applied selectively. If the government needed communist documents, why didn't it use some of those captured with Prestes and the other Moscow agents? Who knew it was fake? General Mariante, Góes Monteiro's mentor in the 1920s and in 1937 president of the Supreme Military Tribunal, obtained a copy from Mourão, who explained exactly what the document was; General Góes, who seems to have gotten a copy from Mariante, also knew; Major (later General) Aguinaldo Caiado de Castro, who encountered Mourão typing the document in a general staff office, certainly knew as well. Mourão asserted that when he heard that such a document was about to be made public, he hurried to Góes's office to protest, but the chief of staff curtly told him to shut up. Did Góes tell Vargas or Dutra that the Cohen Plan was false? The former's memoir and the latter two's diaries provide no answer. Does it matter?

What is certain is that once again significant army involvement in politics was stimulated, at least partly, by lies. In 1889 it was the lie that the imperial government was going to dissolve the army and arrest Deodoro and Benjamin Constant; in 1922 it was the forged letter in which President Bernardes supposedly insulted the army; and now in 1937 it was the allegedly communist Cohen Plan. If there was no communist plot that demanded a salvationist military response to safeguard Brazil, why did the generals support the coup of November 10, 1937?

Vargas–Góes Monteiro–Dutra Alliance
to Strengthen Brazil Militarily

A constant theme that has run through this book has been the army's worry about the poor state of its arms and equipment, the difficulties of mobilizing and training sufficient soldiers to have adequate armed forces to defend the country against internal and external enemies. In 1903 Sergeant Getúlio Vargas had seen firsthand the precariousness of mobilization on the frontier; the Revolution of 1930, the paulista rebellion of 1932, and the communist barracks revolt of 1935 each revealed weaknesses in Brazil's army and navy. With the world stumbling toward some terrible, yet still unknown, crisis, Vargas linked the solution to Brazil's political predicament, with national defense. Governments in France and the United States, not to speak of Germany, Italy, Poland, and Portugal, were solidifying their control over national policy formation and execution. Why should Brazil not do so too?

Vargas and Dutra's worries about the army's possibly negative response to orders to intervene in Rio Grande do Sul, let alone to a change of regime, were behind the new code of military discipline imposed by executive order. The extremely detailed code cited "everything a soldier or officer has been known to do, everything it might occur to him to do, and quite a number of acts it probably never would enter his mind to do." Officers were not to appear in public in their greenish gray cotton service uniform but rather in their neater, dressier, woolen garb. Only enlisted men could wear their uniforms in places considered *not respectable!* Various provisions aimed at keeping a social distance between officers and troops. Officers were to treat soldiers with "urbanity" and recruits with "benevolence." However, subordinates were to comply "instantly with every order received from a superior." The new rules would be subject to severe testing in the next few months.[30]

For most of the 1930s Góes Monteiro had been impressing on Vargas the military's desperate need for basic reforms. As ministers of war and chiefs of staff had noted for years, Brazil was all but disarmed; its fleet and its army had human talent and a full array of schools but scarcely any arms or munitions. This was not news, but the world panorama in 1937 was exceptionally frightening. The Spanish Civil War indicated that Brazil had been lucky in 1932 not to have attracted foreign intervention, but it likely would not have such good luck twice. The Soviet Union's involvement in the 1935 fiasco raised fears that it would try again if the chance presented itself, and Nazi Germany had already been much too attentive to the status of German communities in southern Brazil. Argentina had just shown in the Destroyers' Affair that it was a "false friend." Old fears of losing rich, untapped, and, often, undiscovered natural resources gave Brazilian officers and knowledgeable politicians nightmares.

Back in March 1935 Ambassador Oswaldo Aranha had written from Washington to Góes Monteiro that he had fallen in love with democracy:

But my friend, it is necessary not to confuse this ideal form of government with its deformed examples. Our problem, my dear friend, consists, only in giving military organization to the military to safeguard authority, maintain the unity and to defend the integrity of the country and, more, to improve the race and the land, to educate the people and to give liberty to Brazil. . . . Russia, Germany, Italy are in perpetual economic convulsions, stuck in unstable situations that will toss those peoples into war or anarchy. We should not drag Brazil down such mistaken paths. *I confess that it seems that a regime of force would be useful to us. . . . The military organization of Brazil is an internal and external necessity.* . . . The world is getting mixed up and our continent is growing nervous.[31]

Brazil could afford to arm, and it must do so. "Brazil can and should equip itself, if it does not, it will pay more than we can calculate."[32] In June 1937 Aranha wrote Vargas, "My opinion is that we must arm ourselves, making purchases abroad, *whatever it costs. If we don't do so quickly and immediately, it will cost much more*, materially and morally." He suggested a way to create a special defense fund as a pacific measure to avoid even greater sacrifices in the future.[33]

Vargas, Dutra, Góes, and, as just seen, Aranha agreed that Brazil had to modernize its armed forces. A modern army would hold the country together against the centrifugal forces of regionalism and defend it against foreign enemies. It would also set an example of educated modernity for the Brazilian people. By September 1937 the first three were more or less in agreement as to the course they were following. In a sense Vargas had become a captive; he would have to carry out their plans or risk being deposed. The two generals could back down, but Vargas could not.

Góes and Dutra wanted a modern army with all its attendant arms and equipment. The arrangement was straightforward. They were to give Vargas internal peace and security, and he would get them the arms and the modern industries that would support continued military development. Góes wanted to make the 1934 reorganization plans a reality. On September 1, 1937, Vargas presided over a meeting of the National Security Council, which included the cabinet ministers and the chiefs of staff of the army and navy. This was only the third time it had met since its formation in 1934, so it is not an exaggeration to say that it was an unusual event.[34] They discussed the equipping of the armed forces and the need to create a new source of revenue to pay for it.

As Stanley Hilton has shown, during 1934–36 the army had been negotiating with the German Krupp Corporation and with the Swedish Bofors company for modern artillery to be paid for with natural resources.[35] The navy engaged in similar activity with the Italian government for submarines and with the American government for destroyers. In January 1937 the then chief of staff Paes de Andrade had warned, "we are practically disarmed." And in his annual report to the president in May 1937 Minister Dutra had written:

[I]t would be to lie to the Nation to say that we are armed, in condition to guard it and to defend its enormous patrimony. The truth . . . is that Brazil is a disarmed State. . . . We have a proud, patriotic, and brave people. We know the energy stored in almost fifty million inhabitants. . . . It is sad but true to confess that we do not possess sufficient material resources to deal with even our internal requirements. . . . We can not stand still while the rest of the world advances.[36]

National policy was to become a mix of seeking immediate arms purchases abroad and a longer-term goal of developing heavy industry.

Vargas committed himself to arming and equipping the military and building a national steel complex in return for military backing of extending his presidency with dictatorial powers that would eliminate politics and regionalism. The public implementation of this arrangement proceeded in the hesitant, indirect way in which Getúlio usually maneuvered.

The signals that he flashed were certainly mixed. It is most common for historians to see his contradictory moves as deliberate diversions intended to confuse. It is more likely, however, recalling his behavior in 1930, that such moves really indicated his indecision and caution. In his September 7 address to the nation he asserted that it would be the last time he would commemorate "independence day" as chief of state. Was he serious or trying to lull opponents? Over the next few days politicians, including Governor Valladares of Minas, who had been supporting José Américo, became dismayed by the candidate's speeches and attitudes and wanted to drop him in favor of a third or conciliatory candidate.[37]

Then on September 13 the political scene exploded. Former mayor of Rio, Dr. Pedro Ernesto, acquitted by the Supreme Military Tribunal, was released from jail. Rio de Janeiro erupted into an impromptu, out-of-season Carnaval. The city government declared a holiday, and the crowds swelled with city workers. Praça Onze, the traditional gathering spot for samba groups, was so full of people that his car could not enter. To reach the Castelo Esplanade in the city center, where he was to speak, his car was pushed along by the cheering throngs. They passed directly in front of the Ministry of War, from whose windows officers, soldiers, and civilian employees watched the spontaneous outpouring of affection and loyalty. The doctor had stayed neutral in the presidential race, so both José Américo and Armando Sales backers had organized demonstrators. In his talk in the Esplanade he stressed that he had not been involved in the 1935 revolts, that "I am not, was never, and will never be a communist." But he remained silent on which candidate he supported. Days later, on September 29, he announced his backing for Armando Sales. Michael Conniff noted that the public outpouring for Pedro Ernesto "inadvertently precipitated" action by the coup planners.[38]

During the next few days Vargas met with Valladares and Dutra. They agreed that a substitute third candidate was impossible to arrange. Extending Vargas's mandate legally was also not possible, so "they decided upon the revolutionary solution." To this point it is likely that Vargas and his collaborators had been moving toward a congressionally approved extension of his term, but from here onward they pursued an extralegal solution. Such an interpretation would explain why Dutra could say that their discussion on September 18 was the first time Vargas had spoken openly with him about reacting "against the situation that was developing, by staging a revolution from the top down, that is, unleashed by the government itself." The president complained that the Congress had done nothing useful and opposed the executive's initiatives; at that moment he was particularly concerned about the fate of his proposal to create a central bank. The only solution was to change the regime and reform the Constitution. But the general said Vargas commented that "he would make the revolution" only if Dutra collaborated with him; Dutra was silent for a few moments and then replied that "he could count on him, but he could guarantee nothing regarding the army." They would begin by eliminating Flores in Rio Grande. Feelers went out to Plinio Salgado that gave him the idea that by collaborating with a change of regime, he could be sure that Integralism would have a major place in the new Brazil.[39]

Curiously, even as Vargas was moving to break the back of regionalism, he was willing to use, and thereby strengthen, a proponent of regionalism in the person of Governor Benedito Valladares of Minas Gerais. Because the conspirators assumed that there would be some resistance in São Paulo and Rio Grande do Sul, they had to have mineiro state troops on their side. Valladares demanded two conditions in return for his support: that the army accept the revolution and that the Força Pública of Minas, except for two battalions, not be federalized but remain under his command.[40]

On September 19 Valladares called on Dutra, saying that Vargas had asked Plinio Salgado to join the movement, that he wanted something in return, and that he would get a ministry. The governor suggested that they limit the participation of Salgado and Góes Monteiro to keep them from dominating the scene. In another conversation the following day, Valladares lamented the impossibility of finding a third candidate and affirmed strongly that their only path was "revolution," headed by Getúlio. He gave Dutra rough drafts of a suggested presidential manifesto and of the Constitution that Francisco Campos was preparing. He pointed out that the latter would extend Vargas's term for another six years.[41]

In what has often been described as a cold and calculated series of events, there was actually considerable emotion. The most striking example was the official response to the popular celebration of Pedro Ernesto's acquittal. On September 22 the government declared a holiday, complete with the closing of commerce, and held a commemoration for the dead soldiers of November 1935. Vargas and the generals gathered at the grave site in Rio's São João Batista cemetery for prayers and speeches. For the president the ceremony was a "reaction to the unrest in the political ambience." The event was odd in its timing and likely would have been forgotten except for what happened next. The Chamber of Deputies entered a prolonged debate over entering the graveside speeches into the official record of the chamber, which led General Newton Cavalcanti, commander of the First Infantry Brigade at Vila Militar, and key enthusiast in the army for Integralism, to charge that there was "a communist current or grouping within the National Congress itself."[42] The debate expanded to examine the crisis in Brazilian democracy and rumors that General Góes Monteiro was plotting a coup. He issued a formal denial that he had ever thought of such a thing and asserted that in serving the Pátria his greatest desire was to put the army in condition to face any danger to national integrity.[43]

In the following days Vargas showed his solidarity with the army by attending field exercises at the Jericinó maneuver grounds; he also strengthened his ties with the army's aviators by delaying Pan American Airways permission to open a new route from São Paulo and Curitiba to Asunción, Paraguay. The military airmail service carried mail over that route and was reluctant to give it over to a foreign company. He understood the importance of keeping the aviators and bombardiers content.[44]

On the morning of September 27 Dutra convoked a crucial meeting in his office. Those invited were Góes Monteiro (chief of general staff), Almério de Moura (First Military Region), José Antonio Coelho Neto (director of aviation), Newton Cavalcanti, and, the most powerful and feared captain in Brazil, Filinto Müller (police chief of Federal District). They had received copies of the report on the Cohen Plan from Góes, which Dutra assured them was "not a government fantasy." The Ministry of Justice's actions were "fomenting" rather than repressing "the energies that are ready to explode." The laws, Minister Dutra asserted, were not working. "The armed forces, particularly the army, constitutes the sole element capable of saving Brazil from the catastrophe ready to erupt." "It is necessary," he concluded, "to act and to act immediately." Newton Cavalcanti, referring to the Cohen Plan document, declared that the communist intention was "to liquidate the army itself." The undermining of the Congress was shown by its refusal to include in its record the speeches of a few days before. The looming of a new communist threat, he asserted, "required immediate action in defense of the army, of democratic institutions, of society, of the very family threatened with death. . . . *[I]t is necessary to act, even outside the law,* but in defense of the corrupted law and institutions." General Coelho Neto, the newest of that rank, observed that they had to involve the navy and Vargas himself. Several generals stated that the Chamber of Deputies must be purged of its reactionary, weak, and incapable members. Dutra and several of the others insisted that "the constituted authorities should be maintained. The movement will carry with it the President of the Republic, whose authority will be strengthened."[45]

In an aside Góes Monteiro charged that José Américo was bankrolling the fellow traveler newspaper *O Popular* (Rio) and Coelho Neto recalled that the candidate had not attended the graveside ceremony on the twenty-second. He noted the communist plans required "a military movement that amounted to a coup d'etat." Absolute secrecy was necessary, he added; their plans should be "a generals' secret." They should sign an agreement that "they did not want a military dictatorship." Captain Müller spoke up: "It is necessary that the Armed Forces, conducting this movement, stay outside the government, to guarantee the operation and the constituted government." He also suggested that arrests be summary with no right of defense and that forced labor camps be established. Cavalcanti declared that the two service ministers should direct the operation, at the side of the president, to secure for him, with force, the exceptional powers required. Success, he went on, "demanded an immediate return to a state of war without any restrictions, as well as declaring of Martial Law in all of its fullness." Dutra chimed in that it should apply to the whole country for "the salvation of Brazil." They should, he said involve the entire army, and especially the air arm. General Almério de Moura, who had kept his own counsel thus far, referring to the accusations made against Góes Monteiro, said that they had to be careful not to let the movement be confused with military dictatorship. Cavalcanti defended himself against the charge of being an Integralista. "I am not," he said; he opposed political influence, even Integralism, in the army. "Only use them, if needed, as enlisted troops, but never as [Integralista] militia." Góes and Cavalcanti seemingly summed up the group's feelings: "We want nothing. We only wish to work for the Army and for the salvation of the *Pátria*." The next day they all signed the minutes, pledging themselves to the "exclusive purpose of saving Brazil and its political and social institutions from the disaster that was about to occur . . . excluding from their intentions any personal gain or any idea of military dictatorship." It is ironic that on that day the Chamber of Deputies approved entering the celebrated speeches into the record of its debates.[46]

The next day General Dutra and Vice Admiral Henrique Aristides Guilhem (naval minister) went to Guanabara Palace to speak with Vargas about the need to resume the state of war. The two ministers agreed to provide an explanation that the president could send to the Congress. Later, at his office, Dutra told his colleague generals that this would be the "most viable way" for them to have some legal basis to attack communism and to arrest congressmen and other such acts. On the twenty-ninth Vargas sent the ministers' petition to the Congress. It is noteworthy that in his *Diary* Getúlio's references to the request for the state of war distanced him from it. He usually added a comment such as "in accord with the request of the military ministers."[47]

The ministers' document was addressed to Vargas and was so lacking in detail that it is difficult today to see it as a serious request for extraconstitutional powers. It is worth quoting at length to remind the reader what Brazil of 1937 was like. The ministers evoked the ghosts of 1935 by declaring "just as in 1935 the threats are evident . . . [and] many people do not believe, attributing the ostensive preparations to maneuvers of biased politics, fantasies of salaried authorities." To counter the communist threat, the ministers claimed that they had already done what they could. But despite their efforts the "crime against the *pátria* committed in November of 1935, is about to be repeated with greater energy and more certainty of success." The situation

is not a fantasy of the authorities. . . . Documents of communist origin, from abroad or edited in our own territory, are copious and precise. The aggressive attitudes of the elements recently freed are public and evident. The public manifestations, in which naive people were led to honor false idols, organized by devotees of the red creed, did not show the least embarrassment in their offensive exhibitions. The declarations of certain red newspapers, some signed by Federal Deputies, do not leave the slightest doubt. The repressive laws and measures requested by responsible authorities were criminally delayed. The minister of Justice has not taken promised measures of defense against the dangers that threaten the very existence of the nation. [They then referred to the Cohen Plan, without naming it.] . . . [T]he nation already knows the communist plan of attack uncovered by the General Staff of the Army. It is a carefully designed document that treated the psychological preparation of the masses and the unleashing of pitiless terrorism. There are even more evident proofs. There is a communist grouping within the very Congress, protected by parliamentary immunities. Their names are known. They are preparing the ruin of the *Pátria,* when they ought to be the first to unite it. The laws that we have are not sufficient. We have secure intelligence that the explosion will occur before the general election of January 3rd of the coming year, which communism wants to prevent. The existing laws impede the police from acting to prevent all of this. Our laws are ineffective and useless. They have only served to put at liberty those who the Police caught in the act. The armed forces can not be silent. For them not to act is a crime against [national] institutions, against society, against religion, against the family, against the *Pátria,* against Humanity itself. The Armed Forces are the only element capable of saving Brazil from the catastrophe ready to explode. . . . The struggle will be violent without quarter. . . . We have the example of Spain. . . . Thus it is necessary to act, and to do so immediately, without stopping for any considerations. Above everything is the salvation of the *Pátria*. . . . [S]peaking for the generals and admirals of the armed forces of Brazil . . . speaking for all of Brazil . . . [we] ask for an immediate return to the state of war.[48]

On September 30, the day the foregoing document went to the Congress, the government radio program *Hora do Brasil* featured an announcement about the general staff's "discovery" of the Cohen Plan, and the next day's headlines took the story, and the government's appeal to restore the state of war, to the streets and byways. During the previous days General Daltro Filho had reported shipments of arms from abroad into Porto Alegre, information on the location of secret arms caches, and Flores da Cunha's expanding the numbers of Brigada Militar troops. As Vargas had commented in his *Diary* on September 27: "things were becoming clearer."[49]

On October 1 the debates in the Congress centered on the legitimacy of the supposed dangers. Some deputies and senators naturally wanted to see the documents mentioned but not submitted. Others said that to ask for the documents would be to question the honesty of the armed forces chiefs, who would be held responsible by their colleagues in uniform and by history. The Chamber approved the measure 138 to 52 and the Senate 21 to 3. And that night Vargas signed the decree reimposing a state of war on Brazil. Unlike the earlier states of war, this time it was to be supervised nationally by a commission, named on October 7, made up of Minister of Justice Macedo Soares, General Newton Cavalcanti, and Admiral Dário Pais Leme de Castro; in the states the governors were in charge, except in São Paulo, Rio Grande do Sul, and the Federal District, where the authority rested with Generals of Division César Augusto Pargas Rodrigues (Second Military Region), Daltro Filho (Third Military Region), and Captain Filinto Müller (police chief). The attitudes of the national commissioners were extreme. Admiral Pais Leme de Castro told reporters that "anyone not against communism is a communist," and General Cavalcanti concurred, saying that "the enemies of the Pátria" were "the communists and the indifferent." The commission's plan called for summary judgments, the detention "of all communist sympathizers," and the creation of a "Federal Police" empowered to suppress communism. Even Masonic Lodges and spiritist centers were to be closed.[50]

The decision not to have the governors in the two suspect states implement the state of war required that the Força Pública in São Paulo and the Brigada Militar in Rio Grande do Sul be placed under the commands of the two military regions. In the previous weeks considerable negotiation and maneuvering had placed army sympathizers in key positions. Dramas large and small took place as police officers weighed their options, loyalties, and futures. Neither police force was in the mood for civil war. But even so, from day to day and week to week, tensions mounted and uncertainty hung in the air. São Paulo showed no resistance, encouraged, perhaps, by the state troops that Minas Gerais placed along its side of their joint border.

What would Flores do? Gaúchos were born and bred loyal to Rio Grande. Could the governor marshal those sentiments? The archbishop of Porto Alegre, Dom João Becker, discussed the impasse with Flores, seeking an honorable way out short of violence. Flores recognized that the Brigada had gone over to the army and that the provisionals were listening to their Brigada officers. He was alone. In a symbolic gesture of gallantry, he donned his general's uniform on Sunday morning, October 16, and made the rounds of the Brigada barracks in Porto Alegre to make his farewells. Then, in defiance and pride, he refused to sign a decree giving the Brigada over to the army. Instead, the next day he resigned and took the waiting Varig aircraft to the Uruguayan frontier. There would be no more gaúcho caudilhos like him. On the nineteenth Vargas decreed federal intervention in his home state and named General Daltro Filho as interventor. For a short time, until the general fell into a fatal illness in December, Rio Grande had an outsider, a Bahian, at its head. Worry that the paulistas might react against the intervention in Rio Grande led Dutra to order his old Fourth Cavalry Regiment in Tres Corações (MG) to a position closer to the São Paulo line and to request Valladares to concentrate mineiro police in similar fashion. The paulistas kept quiet. But in Rio Grande do Sul there were sufficient problems with arms that Flores had ordered abroad and suspicious behavior by some Brigada officers that it would be the end of October before Daltro Filho could turn his attention to his civil responsibilities. Indeed, his chief of staff, Col. Oswaldo Cordeiro de Farias, commented that it took thirty days to get the situation under control.[51]

Back in Rio de Janeiro Generals Góes Monteiro and Newton Cavalcanti were showing Vargas documents accusing the governors of Bahia and Pernambuco of having plotted with São Paulo and Rio Grande do Sul against the federal government. Cavalcanti also complained that Minister of Justice Macedo Soares was not cooperating in running the state of war commission with Admiral Pais Leme de Castro and him. One can imagine Vargas groaning to himself as he wrote in his diary: "A crisis is created, or rather a new crisis." The president was convinced that Flores's departure was for the best. Such regionalist leadership had been running "against the centralizing and coercive tendency" of the national government. If Flores had been able to hold out long enough, Vargas speculated, he would eventually have been "supported by military elements diverted from their mission."[52]

From October 20 onward Dutra met or spoke with Vargas on a daily basis. Curiously, Vargas did not note all of these conversations, but Dutra, who was now using the fateful term "coup d'etat," kept a record. On the twenty-first they talked about replacing Minister of Justice Macedo Soares with Francisco Campos, and on the twenty-third they disagreed about intervening in São Paulo; Dutra fearful that intervention could cause a widespread reaction, even in the army. He preferred leaving São Paulo alone and intervening instead in Pernambuco and Bahia. In the end all three were intervened. In these days, too, in addition to the federalization of two battalions of Minas Gerais troops, the military police forces of the other states were taken over by federal authority.[53]

The next major step was to delude Salgado and his green shirts into thinking that they would have an important function in the new regime. Francisco Campos, who was writing the new Constitution on the model of the Polish and Portuguese documents, had developed a friendly relationship with the ostensible Brazilian führer and went so far as to get his comments on the draft document. On Sunday, October 24, in his Guanabara Palace residence Vargas met with the core conspirators—Minister of Justice Macedo Soares, Minister of Labor Agamenon Magalhães, Governor Valladares, and Generals Dutra, Góes Monteiro, and Newton Cavalcanti—to discuss how to carry out the "constitutional reform." They talked about military measures to control Pernambuco, Bahia, and São Paulo, the likely "nonconformist states." They did not reach consensus regarding how to legalize the new Constitution. General Cavalcanti contended that the Congress should approve it. Others preferred that the government declare it effective and subsequently submit it to a plebiscite. Dutra noted in his diary (perhaps referring to a separate conversation) that he and Vargas had agreed to present the draft Constitution to the National Security Council, followed by a presidential manifesto to the nation and the coup d'etat. Two days later Vargas met with Plinio Salgado in the home of a mutual friend. They got on well, Vargas regarding him as "shrewd and [an] intelligent hick." The president gave Salgado to understand that in the reorganized government the Education Ministry would be his.[54]

Emissaries from Valladares and Vargas winged their way to get agreement of the state governors for the change of regime. Pernambuco and Bahia were skipped and marked for deposition. Valladares later thought "it interesting to point out that when 'a revolution' was staged by the government, which was above suspicion, it was possible to carry it out openly, without the people suspecting."[55]

That is not to say, however, that success was guaranteed. Some unidentified generals were "conspiring" to mount a counteraction. Such plotting, which unfortunately for historians has left few traces, may have motivated Minister Dutra to take the precaution of face-to-face meetings with certain generals and to do some shifting of regional commanders. On October 26 he visited artillery units getting ready to proceed to Pinheiros (S.P.); then he went to Vila Militar to be assured that General Cavalcanti was convinced of the necessity of their moves and would cooperate fully. On Sunday the thirty-first he was in Juiz da Fora talking with Fourth Military Region commander, General Lúcio Esteves, whom he found securely committed to the government. While in Minas Gerais Dutra stopped by some army units and two state police units. The tension he felt exploded when General Waldomiro flagged down his car on the highway back to Rio. Vargas and uncle Waldomiro had been at a barbecue at a *fazenda* near Petrópolis, and the general had made some suggestions of measures he might take as inspector general of the group of regions that included São Paulo. Vargas told him to submit the ideas to Dutra. Instead, in their beside-the-road conversation Waldomiro presented them as if they were the president's orders. The minister got so upset that he wanted to resign then and there. Getúlio, who had hoped for a bit of rest in the mountains, had to return to Rio the next day to "put things back in place." One can imagine that he and Dutra must have had an interesting exchange about Uncle General Waldomiro![56]

The incident raises a question about one of the most famous events leading up to the Estado Novo: did Getúlio plan to "review" the Integralista parade of November 1, or was his presence inadvertent, as the foregoing seems to suggest? Certainly it was a dramatic event that marked the high tide of Integralism. Hundreds of trucks had carried green shirts to the Praça Mauá from where they marched down Avenida Rio Branco, along the Avenida Beira-Mar, past the Hotel Gloria, where "Führer" Plinio Salgado saluted them, then on by Guanabara Palace, from whose window Vargas and General Cavalcanti observed their show of strength. That evening Salgado gave a radio address in which he withdrew his candidacy for president in favor of Vargas's continuing in office. He said that he and his followers were in "solidarity with the President of the Republic and the armed forces in the fight against communism and anarchical democracy. . . . [Further, they favored] a new regime without which it will not be possible to save the institutions and traditions of Brazil." Rather than becoming president, he wanted "simply to be the adviser of my country."[57]

The next day, All Soul's Day, was a public holiday, but even so, it was busy at Guanabara Palace. Vargas met with gaúcho allies, federal Deputies João Neves da Fontoura and João Baptista Lusardo, bringing them up to date. Lusardo then left for Rio Grande, where he told political colleagues that the coup was set for November 15 and that Vargas wanted them to behave as if nothing was about to happen. Finance Minister Souza Costa, who was the architect of the government's finances, was arguing for an end to the artificial support of coffee prices via government purchase and burning or dumping into the sea of millions of tons. Months before, in May, he had negotiated an agreement with the Roosevelt administration that allowed Brazil to separate United States and European foreign-debt negotiations, thereby facilitating a repayment plan, and he had obtained guarantees of U.S.$60 million to finance a Brazilian central bank. Because an important part of the plan for regime change involved suspending foreign-debt payments to allow arms purchases, Souza Costa's views carried considerable weight with the conspirators. Police Chief Müller and Francisco Campos put in appearances; with the latter the president went over some changes in the language of the Constitution and of the accompanying manifesto. Generals Dutra, Cavalcanti, Deschamps, and Daltro Filho made their reports and heard the latest on the "coming political and constitutional reform."[58]

On November 5 the *Correio da Manhã* (Rio) broke the news that serious intrigues involving the government and the armed forces were afoot. Vargas wondered "how the censor let [the story] be published?" He wired Valladares, who had sent Deputy Negrão de Lima to inform the northeastern governors of the impending coup, to put out the story that Negrão's mission had been to search out possible "legal political solutions." After trying to calm worried congressmen, he received a letter from Minister of Justice Macedo Soares wanting to resign his post. The generals had long been impatient with his efforts to maintain a liberal attitude toward human rights and the regime's facade of the rule of law. The day before, General Cavalcanti had complained to Vargas that he could no longer work with the minister, whom he accused of "sabotaging" the State of War Commission. And later Macedo Soares came by the palace to say that he was worn out and suggested that either the general be removed or new commissioners named. Thinking on it for a night he had decided to quit. Significantly, on the afternoon of the fifth Vargas met with the two service ministers, General Góes, and Police Chief Müller, with whom he discussed the events of the day. "After hearing them, I resolved to accept the resignation of the minister of justice," telling them that Francisco Campos would replace him. That night Campos accepted the post, and Vargas and his new minister talked about "the constitutional reform."[59]

On the afternoon of November 8 opposition leaders met at the home of candidate Armando de Sales Oliveira, who told them that he was sending a letter to the military chiefs "denouncing the sinister conspiracy that was being hatched in official circles against [national] institutions." "If some powerful force," he warned, "does not intervene in time . . . a terrible blow suddenly will shake the nation to its deepest foundations. . . . A long prepared plan is about to be executed by a small group of men, so small that they can be counted on one hand, intending to enslave Brazil. . . . The nation turns to its military leaders: in suspense, awaiting the killing blow or the saving word." Apparently, José Américo had declined to sign the manifesto on the advice of friends, who thought it would likely hurt him more than do any good in stopping the coup. Ironically, at about the same time, Generals Dutra and Góes and Admiral Guilhem were at the home of Francisco Campos going over the text of the new Constitution.[60]

The next day, in the Chamber of Deputies, João Carlos Machado (an ally of Flores da Cunha) read to the deputies Armando Sales's appeal to the military to resist the coup. In the Senate Paulo de Morais Barros, the nephew of President Prudente de Morais (1894–98), did the same. João Baptista Lusardo, who had returned quickly from Porto Alegre, was on hand to witness the scene in the chamber. The "atmosphere was," he thought, "revolutionary." He hurried to the Catete Palace to inform Getúlio. He warned that "tomorrow the Nation will know everything. . . . Either you stage the coup today, gaining the upper hand, or their revolution will be in the streets. Call Dutra and Góes. It has to be today." In the meantime the Armando Sales manifesto was reaching the barracks and the lower-officer ranks. As Dutra left his home in Leme, he told his family: "Either Dr. Getúlio unleashes the coup today, or he won't be able to." In trying to stop the plot Armando Sales succeeded in precipitating it.[61]

In the course of the planning Dutra and Góes strove to lower the profile of army involvement, perhaps because of what Getúlio called "the intrigue and division of the military." It was to that division and because D-Day was known to be the eleventh that it was "necessary to precipitate the coup, taking advantage of surprise." With Müller, Campos, and Dutra, Vargas arranged the final steps. Dutra ordered the First, Second, and Third Military Regions to stand ready and alerted the other regions that highly important political events were about to occur and that they should be ready to act if need be. However, it would not be federal troops stationed outside the closed houses of Congress but the Federal District's military police. At 6 A.M. Müller informed the acting president of the Senate that the Congress was dissolved, but Pedro Aleixo (Minas Gerais), president of the Chamber of Deputies, suffered the embarrassment of being turned away by the police. Also in the early hours Dutra went to the São Cristóvão district to check on the readiness of the First Cavalry Regiment and the guard battalion. Vargas had João Batista Lusardo inform José Américo of the coup. Awakened very early by the head of his campaign committee, the candidate accepted the inevitable and went back to sleep, as he said, "in obscurity," satisfied that he had done what he could. "It wasn't I who failed; it was Brazil itself that was deaf."[62]

On that overcast November 10 at ten in the morning, the cabinet, save for the dissenting minister of agriculture, signed the new Constitution. During the day eighty members of Congress sent congratulatory messages. Those associated with Armando Sales were under house arrest. In the afternoon the foreign minister called in the American ambassador to assure him that there would be no changes in foreign policy and that the government would be very liberal toward "foreign capital and foreigners who have legitimate interests in Brazil." That night, at eight, Vargas addressed the nation by radio. The political parties, infected by regionalism, he claimed, were subverting order, threatening national unity, and endangering Brazil's existence with their polarizing rivalries and encouragement of civil disorder. To avoid Brazil's disintegration he had decided to restore the national government's authority. He reviewed the country's economic and military needs: suspension of foreign-debt payments, construction of railroads and highways into the vast interior, and reequipping of the armed forces. All of these he linked directly to "the important problem of national defense." He emphasized that it was "urgently necessary to provide the armed forces with efficient equipment, that will make them capable of assuring the country's integrity and independence." For those reasons there had been no other alternative than to "installing a strong regime of peace, justice and labor."[63]

Dutra's Proclamation to the Army

The afternoon newspapers of November 10 gave front-page space to General Dutra's statement, which was also circulating in the barracks. In the peculiar military language that characterized such declarations he sought to clarify the army's mission:

It was up to the army, to the armed forces not to permit that the people's aspirations be frustrated by the eternal enemies of the *Pátria* and of the regime. The army had to be free from contamination by partisan political passions, ideological conflicts, personal, group, or regional interests. Seductive temptations would arise that had to be resisted. It would not be proper for the army to influence the political destinies that the politicians chose to follow. That was not its mission. It was much simpler, but that did not make it less noble. Carrying it out, in this moment of uncertainties, safeguarding the interests of the *Pátria,* while being faithful to the principles of obedience, discipline, work, instruction, serenity, discretion, unselfishness, self-denial, in short patriotism. The politicians could not find acceptable solutions and so turned to exceptional measures. The army did not shape the internal political scenario, it did not foment the discord among the competing factions. What it did do, and would continue to do, was to contain explosions, to constitute a barrier to partisan ambitions, expelling from its ranks undesirable elements, snuffing out immediately the smallest outbursts of disorder. . . .

As everyone knows, today a new Federal Constitution was proclaimed, one that those competent in such matters believe will better attend the demands of the present moment. Perceiving the lacunas and defects in the statute of 1934 . . . new directions were set for our democratic regime, better suited to its federative continuity.

. . . Any disturbance of order will be a breech through which might rush the enemies of the *Pátria,* the adversaries of democratic rule. We must avoid this, carrying out with calmness and with firmness our mission.

If we proceed thus, Brazilian society will continue to be confident in us. . . . [T]he *Pátria* and the regime will be under our guard . . . in defense of internal order, of political integrity, of national sovereignty. This is our mission.[64]

And it was a mission sanctioned by the army's patron, the duke of Caxias. In 1939 at the commemoration of August 25 in the Third Military Region, General Estevão Leitão de Carvalho said that current events had made Caxias an even more immediate historical figure. "Truly," he said, "the opponent of caudilhos, tireless defender of national unity, bulwark of Order and of Authority, *Caxias is the precursor, the symbol of this victorious reaction incorporated in the Estado Novo* and which is being carried out . . . with the fiber and patriotism of the soldiers of Brazil." He went on to emphasize that "we are on the road to realizing the ideal of our Patron: consolidating national unity morally and politically, under a regime of authority, with a numerous Army, well provided for and disciplined, assuring internal peace and making the country respected abroad."[65]

What did Vargas get from this army support? Clearly the presidency until October 1945, more work, and personal sacrifice. He may have loved power, but surely his motivations were more complex than enjoying being president. He drove himself to work long hours, often alone with huge reports; he carried on correspondence with an enormous number of people; and after a long day of audiences and conferences, he often had other meetings and conversations until late at night. Unlike other such leaders in Latin America he was not much for speeches from palace balconies but used the radio to reach his citizenry. It was an effective device but not as emotionally satisfying as speaking from a balcony to cheering crowds. His thirst for power had other elements driving it. He and the generals shared a dream, perhaps not with the same details, but they dreamed of a great, prosperous nation spread over a gloriously beautiful portion of the earth, living and producing in security and happiness. Vargas was dedicated to the improvement of Brazil and was confident in his ability to make the right decisions for his country. However, he was careful to seek advice and not to get too far ahead of elite opinion. He did not rob the treasury, and after his demise his family was not notably wealthy. Even his hometown, São Borja, did not benefit greatly from his years in power; the road to it was not paved until 1972, and rains on the pampa turned the road to his own *estancia* into a ribbon of mud as late as 1973! This is not an apology for him but rather a statement of known facts.

The evidence available does not make clear whether the dictatorship was Getúlio's idea or that of the generals. Getúlio once joked with a high-ranking officer, who was also a friend: "In 1930 I made the revolution with the Tenentes, in 1937 with the Generals." His daughter said that he acted to prevent a military dictatorship, but the minutes of the generals' meeting of

September 27 stated that they did not want one.[66] Does it matter who first expressed the idea? Perhaps not, but it does matter why the army supported dictatorship. On a personal level the coup insured that Dutra and Góes Monteiro would remain in charge of the army, allowing them to shape its continuing professionalization according to their lights.

The army, represented by its top generals, wanted to safeguard the country. They believed that the army could not do so under the regime of 1934, so they toppled the constitutional government in the name of the higher good of the security of the Pátria. Vargas made a pledge, or *compromisso,* that he would equip and arm the armed forces so that they could carry out their assigned duty; in return they would provide the muscle for a regime of force and national development. On November 17 Vargas wrote Aranha to explain why he had changed the Constitution and to say that he needed him in Washington to obtain American capital for a great reform and development program centering on "large acquisitions of material for our military and railroads."[67] In a series of speeches in early 1938 he repeated the quid pro quo in various ways. In his New Year's radio address he said that Brazil had "a mission in America and in the world" of mobilizing the riches of half a continent, which "we can not leave undefended. We are stubbornly working on the equipping and preparation of the armed forces, which bring together thousands of Brazilians disposed to sacrifice everything for the integrity of the *Pátria.*" In Porto Alegre, a week later, he told an elite audience that he was happy to be back in his native Rio Grande, now safe from the dangers of civil war, and once again able to work in safety and confidence. They would have to be, he concluded, "soldiers and workers in the great project that is beginning." Even more pointedly, in his address at the banquet offered to him by the Second Independent Cavalry Regiment in his hometown of São Borja, he declared that he had "tried always to enhance the prestige of the army, because the greatness of the country is founded on the army. . . . I have counted on the army, principally, to put down the 'political bosses,' who were attempting to set up a regional hegemony to supercede the authority of the central power, weakening Brazil. Today, all this is assured. The Constitution of the 10th of November re-established definitely, the predominance of the central power." This mission of the armed forces was to guarantee order so that there would be public confidence. He then stated the *compromisso* succinctly: "Give me order and tranquility and I will restore the finances, develop the economy, construct all that which our raw materials could give us; . . . the iron necessary for our industries and for our progress, from locomotives to aero-planes. . . . For this . . . I need order. But I trust in you who are the Nation."[68]

The clearest statement of this *compromisso* was that of Góes Monteiro in his general staff report for 1937. Góes opened the forty-one page document with the charge that the 1934 law specifying that army reorganization was to be completed within three years had not been fulfilled. Simply put, the army was "useless for the field of battle." He did not mention former minister Gomes, but he clearly had him in mind. The images that he sketched were extremely discouraging. The army was, he said, "fragile, more fictitious than real," its big units were "dismantled . . . incapable of being mobilized in reasonable time and employed in any situation." The general staff's worries about Brazil's military weaknesses, he wrote, had intensified with the news that Chile was renewing its army's equipment and that Argentina was improving its armament, expanding its weapons industry, and generally developing its military capabilities. In the United States President Roosevelt was calling for the "prompt and intensive equipping of its armed forces." The nations of the globe were preparing for war. "The violence in Abyssinia, China, and Spain were," the general asserted, "true practice wars to test the means of destruction and protection" in rehearsal for a great and decisive struggle. Neither pacifist illusions nor Brazil's turn-of-the-century Krupp artillery would be able to protect it. On Brazil's very borders the "ex-belligerents of the Chaco, despite the interminable peace conference in Buenos Aires, had returned to the path of complete rearmament, in expectation of another appeal to arms." Góes warned that "the moment, in which we are living, imposes a radical transformation of [our] military organism . . . [because] we remain paralyzed, about a decade behind." They had the responsibility to restore Brazil's armed forces in order to "redeem us from the previous inertia and to free us from the depressing situation in which we are entombed." These circumstances motivated Góes and Dutra "to solicit insistently from the President of the Republic all the measures required for the reform of our [army's] structure."

He ended the report with a review of the "internal situation" in which he cast the struggle with Flores da Cunha as the "extermination of *caudilhismo.*" He said that he had battled "with all of his soldier's soul for inviolable national unity and for the prestige of authority." In November 1935 "subversive elements . . . following instructions from Moscow," he declared, had threatened that prestige. And finally, "the secret document captured last year" (the Cohen Plan) had led "all the country's classes, through their legitimate representatives, to agree that exceptional powers, in such emergency, should be given to the Sr. President of the Republic." The need for the declaration of a state of war amounted, in his mind, to a condemnation of the 1934 regime as incapable of "promoting the happiness of the *pátria.*"

The country's peaceful atmosphere after November 10, he warned,

should not delude us. Brazil, today more than ever, needs to be a militarily strong power, able to neutralize, on any field, the aggressions of our internal and external enemies. The army, in whose soul resonates, in a special way, the yearnings of the purest sentiments of *Brazilianess, places its hopes in the promises of the Government, that, without doubt, will not stop championing its complete restoration,* in the very favorable situation that we are traversing. If this rare opportunity is not taken, it would be reason for the army to give up believing that it would ever be possible to carry out its high purpose. I already said, and I repeat, that the military problem can not allow incomplete, unilateral solutions. . . . All Brazilians must contribute to, and be responsible for, the common task of National Defense.[69]

Góes had the "firm conviction that the action of November 10 responded to an inevitable national necessity and, at least, [was] a barrier against the political-military decomposition that had progressed to a well advanced degree. The regime, that ceased to exist, would not have permitted a defined and consistent position before the whirlwind that upsets the world." The Constitution of 1934 was proof, Góes lamented, that Brazilian statesmen had turned their backs on the "politics of reality." They had evoked the ideas of other countries without paying attention to how those countries actually solved their problems. The 1934 regime had the trappings of constitutional rule without the mechanisms, mentality, and traditions that made such a government work. The army would do its part, and "the government will do the rest, fulfilling the *compromisso* (pledge) it assumed to equip the Armed Forces so that they can carry out the roles reserved to them."[70]

In May 1938 Dutra stated the *compromisso* more succinctly, writing that the government "only wished peace and tranquility to develop the country economically and financially. In order to carry out its program of national renewal the government depends on the army." In his annual report to the president he affirmed that "the army no longer is interested in questions of party politics." And, clarifying somewhat, he assured Vargas that if any rare intervention occurred, it would be "under the command of authorized chiefs to assure liberty, maintain law and order." As a mere spectator of the political scene, following unfolding events from outside, "the army, every day more," the minister assured the president, "constitutes the support on which the Government can count, anytime that noxious elements try to subvert order or attack the integrity of the *Pátria*."[71]

It has been the view among scholars that after the overthrow of the emperor in 1889 the army, as Ronald M. Schneider put it, "assumed the function of the moderating power."[72] The previous chapters do not support this view; rather, it is from 1937 onward that the army, in the persons of its senior officers, asserted the institution's right to be national moderator. Vargas's "compromisso" opened the gate, and the generals marched in.

The politico-military agreement that underpinned the Estado Novo called for short-term rearmament and reorganization of the armed forces and long-term industrialization centering on a steel mill. Vargas had pledged both, and the generals wanted both. Throughout the 1930s the general staff had pointed repeatedly to the United States as the best source of arms and of investments in industry. But just as Brazil was taking the turn toward more centralized and authoritarian rule, Germany was becoming an important market for Brazilian goods, particularly cotton and food stuffs, and an enthusiastic arms supplier. The famous pre–World War II American-German competition for Brazil had its origins not in ideology but in the need of the Brazilian armed forces to arm themselves.

In June 1935 the Vargas government had arranged an informal compensation trade arrangement with Germany that through elaborate exchange mechanisms allowed Brazil to use its natural or agricultural products to obtain German manufactures. The United States objected strenuously to this closed system, which removed Brazilian-German trade from the broader international system based on gold and convertible currencies. As a result of the close linkage between obtaining arms and Brazil's international trade, the military was more than an interested observer of foreign commerce; it was a direct participant in the debates that shaped the government's policies.

The Brazilian government's attitude toward the United States prior to the turn of events above was to see the northern republic as a natural ally. After their cordial meeting in late 1936, Vargas proposed to Roosevelt that their representatives discuss full military and naval cooperation, including building of a naval base in Brazil for American use in the event of a war of aggression against the United States.[73] But Washington did not act, and Brazilian leaders turned to their own needs and solutions. The high American prices and unfavorable payment conditions led the Brazilians to turn to Europe, ordering artillery in Germany, light infantry arms in Czechoslovakia, and warships in England and Italy. In the United States they ordered aircraft and material to build some destroyers.[74]

The Brazilian generals were painfully aware that their coastal artillery guarding entrances to the country's ports could not stop an Argentine, let alone a German, naval attack. Rio de Janeiro had only two 305 mm guns, and their range was shorter than the guns on Argentina's *Rivadavia* and *Moreno.* And, according to Chief of Staff Góes Monteiro, it would take five years to make their defense plans operational. An American military adviser reported that "the capital of Brazil is at the mercy of any determined, well informed and efficient naval attack."[75] It was to remedy the vulnerability of the ports and land frontiers that the army placed an order in Germany for [U.S.]$55 million in artillery and accessories in March 1938. The weapons were to be paid for mostly in compensation marks earned in the trade arrangement outlined above. From at least June 1936 Vargas had been worried about how to pay for the armaments. On June 15, 1936, he had noted in his diary that the only way to make the necessary purchases would be "a great reduction in payment of the foreign debt" and that could not be done under "the political regime that we are following."[76] Thus, in order to buy arms to safeguard the Pátria, it was necessary to cut foreign-debt payments, which required eliminating the Congress and creating a new regime. Ultimately, defense policy drove the Vargas–Dutra–Góes Monteiro alliance that resulted in the Estado Novo.

Epilogue

With the imposition of the Estado Novo the army was securely the central government's principal instrument of control. The idea of the army as a politically neutral institution, as a vehicle of social reform, as the "vanguard of the people" was replaced with the idea of "the army as an essential part of the state and an instrument of its policies." It became "the vanguard of the state" rather than of the people.

José Murilo de Carvalho's insightful analysis of the contending currents in the post-1930 army showed that the tenentes, whom he labeled "reformist interventionists," formed an alliance with the professionally oriented officers who were concerned to reestablish discipline and hierarchy in order to achieve the army of their dreams. The resulting "conservative interventionism" had its fullest expression in the Estado Novo. Professional officers who boasted of their stubborn legalism praised the dictatorship as "a regime of political peace and of real concern for the armed forces." The professionals accepted the army's political intervention because, Murilo explained, it was "beneficial to the specific interests of the military establishment."[1] The 1930s also saw the army increasing some of its linkages with society by strengthening punishments for draft evasion and requiring a certificate of military service for public jobs and for voting, by increasing the number of military-run shooting clubs (Tiros de Guerra), and by imposing reserve officer training on male university students. A decree-law of May 19, 1938, specified that no one could leave army ranks "without knowing how to read, write, count, and possess an elementary knowledge of Brazil and its geography and constitution." However, to control the flow of ideas and divisive political attitudes from society into the army, there was a coinciding effort to isolate officers from political factionalism. The elimination of competitive politics with the establishment of the Estado Novo and the regime's constitutional disenfranchisement of military personnel symbolized the conservative interventionists' desire to protect the army from harmful outside influences. The army also restricted access to the military school to those who had acceptable racial, familial, religious, educational, and political characteristics. Ideological indoctrination became the norm in training at all levels. Officers were even forbidden to attend civilian institutions of higher learning because the army schools were sufficient.[2]

These repressive measures, the suspension of political activities, and the government's support of rearmament and modernization gave the army a coherence and unity it had not had since before 1922. Its numerical growth from a 1930 level of 47,997 to a 1940 level of 93,000 and its acquisition of modern weapons gave it muscle and the means to employ it. World War II and the military alliance with the United States gave the military more equipment, enhanced its organizational and individual skills, increased its prestige, and, ultimately, gave it what it had lacked since 1870: combat seasoning against a foreign enemy. The experience of the Força Expedicionária Brasileira in the Italian campaign, also gave the army a popular status somewhat separate from the Estado Novo, which allowed the Febianos to return as heroes and permitted the high command, again under General Góes Monteiro, to step into the successionist crisis of October 1945 to depose Getúlio Vargas and to cut short the political mobilization of the masses that the generals believed would upset the social order. Not to have acted would have violated the implicit agreement with the elites when the latter surrendered their independent state military forces to federal control.[3]

We correctly speak of the age of Vargas in Brazilian history, but it is difficult to imagine what directions the 1930s and 1940s would have taken without Góes Monteiro and Eurico Dutra. Even though, since 1930, Getúlio had given every general officer his stars, their primary loyalties were to the army institution and its hierarchy, not to the president and his regime. The army under Dutra and Góes Monteiro became, as Aspásia Camargo noted, "an autonomous and interventionist army, capable of acting with its own legitimacy."[4]

The elected government over which Dutra presided from 1946 to 1951 was supported by the conservative interventionist army and not a suddenly democratic entity. Indeed, as president Dutra made the point that he still belonged to the "classe militar," that he would not neglect its needs, and that he would guide the army politically. Pointing out that "united and disciplined, our Armed Forces—guarantors of the constitutional powers—are vigilant in the defense of the Country, Law, and Order," Dutra drew a significant parallel: "Thus it was on November 15, 1889 and on October 29, 1945." In his mind the overthrow of Pedro II and of Getúlio Vargas were analogous and for the same purpose—"For the greatness of Brazil."[5]

The army now sought to remake Brazil by indoctrinating the elites with an industrial vision of the country's future. Just as the dreams of the 1910s were based on reforming society via obligatory military training, the post–World War II dreams would be given life by educating the elites. General staff officers preserved the propaganda that obligatory service was a great social leveler of classes, races, and regions; a nationalizer of immigrants; and "a great and complete school of democracy" but admitted that the modern, mechanized, technical army required educated recruits and that "there was no longer room, these days, for illiterates and those without skills in the barracks." Indeed, by the mid-1950s, either because of lack of education and skills or in order not to interfere with agriculture and the rural social structure, the army recruited in only five hundred of the two thousand municípios in Brazil.[6] Instead of reform flowing from the bottom up, it continued to flow from the top down.

The Escola Superior de Guerra (ESG), founded in 1949, was intended to integrate and militarize the civilian elites by inviting selected persons to study at the school and by organizing special courses for local elites throughout Brazil. In the 1950s, expanding on the doctrines of the French military mission (1919–39) and of the Joint Brazil–United States Defense Commission (1942–52–77), which emphasized the need for officers to study the elements of the economy and the society that contributed to national mobilization, the ESG's military-civilian student body examined inflation, banking reform, land-tenure reform, voting systems, transportation, and education, as well as guerrilla and conventional warfare. As Alfred Stepan noted, "fundamental aspects of Brazilian social and economic organization were depicted as needing change if Brazil were to maintain its internal security."[7] And because of staff interlocking between the ESG and the Escola de Comando e Estado Maior do Exercito (ECEME), the former's doctrines were mirrored in the latter's and so had been extended to the whole officer corps.

From the early 1950s onward the conservative interventionist mode attempted to dominate army behavior, as the high command reigned in Getúlio Vargas's attempts to base his now elected government (1951–54) firmly on populism. But at the same time the liberalized atmosphere of what Thomas Skidmore called the "experiment in democracy," allowed the reappearance of political factionalism in army ranks, "thereby crippling a second time," as José Murilo de Carvalho noted, "its capacity for political control."[8] The internal army struggles over possible participation in the Korean War and regarding the creation of the federal oil and electric monopolies, Petrobrás and Electrobrás; the firming of the Vargas legacy after his August 24, 1954, suicide; the dissension in the ranks produced by Marshal Henrique Lott's preventative coup of November 1955, which permitted Juscelino Kubitschek and João Goulart to take office as president and vice president; and the military's disunity in the 1961 crisis provoked by the resignation of Janio Quadros and the succession of Goulart were all symptomatic of the military's malady and dissension. Some would argue that the nationalist faction that stood against sending troops to Korea and favored government intervention in the economy, as in the case of Petrobrás, formed a leftist wing of the military, but that assumes a level of behavioral and ideological consistency that seems to me unproven.[9]

The army was willing to intervene in 1964 because enough of its officers believed that it was in the institution's interest and therefore to Brazil's benefit. In the early 1960s the army was being increasingly called on to provide troops to maintain order during elections and to police the borders against smuggling and contraband, which caused wear and tear on equipment and deterred proper training for war. As these extramilitary duties began to be almost routine, army leaders complained that the negative effects were increasing because of a lack of funds to maintain their limited stocks of equipment. In 1962 the army was devoting 93.8 percent of its funds to personnel, leaving only 6.2 percent for materiel. Army Minister Amaury Kruel complained that the army had been subjected to a "survival" budget since 1958 and that most of its armament and equipment was either obsolete, required replacement, or was too far gone to fix. In 1962 every regional army headquarters reported that it was not in condition to schedule regular exercises, and there was such a generalized "disbelief and lack of incentive" that many officers concluded that their efforts were useless. General Kruel prophetically alerted President Goulart that the deficiency of funding to carry out its missions was creating a "calamitous situation" in which the army was being "economically and financially asphyxiated." As a result, "the Brazilian army," Kruel warned, "is experiencing an anguishing and progressively accelerating process of devitalization that, inexorably, will deviate it from its basic purpose."[10]

Clearly the coup d'état of 1964 was motivated by more than budgetary limitations, but it is also true that General Kruel's prediction was correct. As in 1937 Brazil had reached another crossroads that presented conflicting visions of the future. The noisy, even chaotic, social reforms favored by Goulart and his party looked like communist revolution to generals who had been captains in 1935–37. Unable to accept the messiness of electoral democracy, they reached for what they knew best. Kruel had warned President Goulart that "the army will not accept your policies and sooner or later you will be alone with your friends and I will not be able to stay with you."[11]

The limits of tolerance were pushed to their maximum as officers viewed events such as the sergeants' revolt of September 1963 and the Sailors' Association demonstrations of March 1964 with a sense of déjà vu. The political mobilization inside and outside the armed forces and the challenges to the chain of command reminded them of the 1930s and of October 1945.

And steadily the logic of 1937 and 1945 grew more attractive. In the months prior to March 1964 the staff and student officers of the ECEME played a key role, convincing officers via meetings and newsletters that they should support a movement against the government. They believed that rational economic development and internal security (and, one might add, the army's well-being) would occur only if the economic and political structure were altered and that the civilian leaders were unwilling or unable to make the necessary changes.[12] Edmundo Campos Coelho saw the postwar military as suffering from a severe identity crisis, which he said had its origin in the identity crisis of the Brazilian state, which lacked a focal institution that everyone accepted as the "incorporation of national authority." He thought that in 1964 the army leadership intended to make the army that core institution, shaping the rest of the national state around it.[13]

The problem with that idea was that although there was widespread acceptance in the officer corps of the necessity to act against the Goulart government (admittedly some officers resisted and were later purged), there was less consensus for maintaining military control once the mess had been cleaned up. Even though the hard-liners successfully imposed authoritarian rule, this produced an underlying sense of malaise because the military's organizational structure, field training, and weapons systems were geared for use against conventional forces or, to less extent, guerrillas. So as the military institutions adapted themselves to their assignments after 1964 (and especially after 1968), many officers were ill at ease with their internal security roles. These smacked of police work, and officers reacted angrily when words such as *milicia* (militia) or *milico* (militiaman) were applied to them.

In late 1965 and early 1966 those officers who favored defining their mission primarily as internal security won a victory over the Humberto de Castelo Branco faction, which favored returning the purged government to civilian politicians. The hard-line officers, clustered around Minister of the Army (and ex-tenente) Artur Costa e Silva, then imposed authoritarian rule.[14] The result was two competing conceptions of military professionalism: one that Alfred Stepan called the "new professionalism" of internal security, and another that defined the profession in terms of conventional warfare primarily against foreign opponents. Officers adhering to the latter view regarded troop commands and normal staff assignments as more "military" than internal security duty. The tension between these two visions of professionalism frequently appeared over the years in my conversations with officers who resented the internal security activities of their colleagues, even when they may have half-heartedly justified the necessity for them.[15]

The Estado Novo accelerated Brazilian industrialization, centralized governmental power, created the bureaucracy that implemented that power, extended the state into the far interior, and projected the country onto the world stage. It is difficult to imagine how Brazil could have reached the good and the ill of its present condition without its peculiar dictatorship. Certainly the modern army and its companion armed services were affected by those years. The men who made the decision for dictatorship in November 1937 were responding to domestic concerns embodied in their desire to assure the security of the Pátria.

They feared that war would catch them ill prepared, but they certainly could not have envisioned the scope of the conflict that was unleashed in 1939. They were unprepared for the rapidity of world events in the next five years. Vargas's consensus style of decision making was not fast enough to keep Brazil apace of the war's demands and of its opportunities. Often, even though the eventual decisions were correct, they came after the most opportune moment had passed, so the benefits from them were not as great as they might have been or as had been hoped. For example, if the Brazilian army had a trained corps of infantry ready in 1943, it could have fought in the invasion of North Africa, thereby gaining greater prestige from its war effort. As it was, it could not field a corps a year later and therefore gained less stature internationally. The reduction of the army's links to society in the early Estado Novo prevented the officer corps from understanding the social and economic changes that the war provoked in Brazil. The fateful decision to end Vargas's rule in October 1945 by coup d'etat, rather than by legal process, projected the army into politics in the double role of moderator and of participant and contributed substantially to the crises that culminated in the series of military presidencies from 1964 to 1985. During those twenty-one years Brazil lived under an odd regime. A purged Congress functioned most of the time, as did adjusted state and local governments. It was a tutelary democracy with successive generals overseeing the process. There were no caudillos, in the Spanish-American sense, and succession to the presidency was by officer consensus. Yet direct participation in politics was limited to senior generals; the rest of the officer corps was expected to continue normal professional activities. This required heavy emphasis on institutional unity, acceptance of command decisions, and denying outsiders information about internal divisions. General Góes Monteiro's desire to keep politics outside the barracks and to present a unified political position was the ideal. But it proved much more difficult to achieve than Góes could have imagined. The army itself suffered a decline in capability during the military presidencies. By the time the Constitution of 1988 was enacted, it was clear that the idea of a national security state had been rejected by voters.[16] From now on it would be up to the whole society to provide soldiers worthy of the Pátria.

REFERENCE MATTER

Notes

ABBREVIATIONS

ACS	Army Chief of Staff
ACB	Arquivo Castelo Branco
ADN	*A Defesa Nacional*
AE	Arquivo do Exército
AFSC	Arquivo Fernando Setembrino de Carvalho
AGV	Arquivo Getúlio Vargas
AHE	Arquivo Historico do Exército
AOA	Arquivo Oswaldo Aranha
BAO	Brazilian Army Officers Project (based on army's annual officer list or *Almanac*)
Batt.	Battalion
BiblioEx	Biblioteca do Exército
CDOC-EX	Centro de Documentação do Exército, Brasília
CPDOC	Centro de Pesquisa e Documentação de História Contemporânea do Brasil, Fundação Getúlio Vargas, Rio de Janeiro
DGFP	Documents on German Foreign Policy
DHBB	Dicionário Histórico-Biográfico Brasileiro
EsAO	Escola de Aperfeiçaomento de Oficiais
FDRL	Franklin D. Roosevelt Library, Hyde Park, N.Y.
FEB (BEF)	Força Expedicionária Brasileira
FSC	Fernando Setembrino de Carvalho
GMP	Góes Monteiro Papers
GS	General Staff
GV	Getúlio Vargas documents (archived at AGV)
Inf. Reg.	Infantry Regiment
MID	Military Intelligence Division
MG	Ministerio da Guerra

MMB	Modern Military Branch
NA	National Archives, Washington, D.C.
RG	Record Group
UFMG	Universidade Federal do Minas Gerais
WD	War Department (U.S.)

PREFACE

1. Vanda Maria Ribeiro Costa, "Com Rancor e Com Afeto: Rebeliões Militares na Década de 30," *Política e Estratégia* 4, no. 2 (Apr.–June 1986): 193. "Para mim o senhor é um coronel do Exército . . . apenas momentaneamente estamos em campos opostos."

2. Alain Rouquié, *The Military and the State in Latin America* (Berkeley: University of California Press, 1987), 330.

3. Alfred Stepan, *The Military in Politics: Changing Patterns in Brazil* (Princeton, N.J.: Princeton University Press, 1971); and Alfred Stepan, ed. *Authoritarian Brazil: Origins, Policies, and Future* (New Haven, Conn.: Yale University Press, 1973). See also Frank D. McCann, "Origins of the 'New Professionalism' of the Brazilian Military," *Journal of Interamerican Studies and World Affairs* 21, no. 4 (Nov. 1979): 505–22.

4. See Frank D. McCann, *The Brazilian-American Alliance, 1937–1945* (Princeton, N.J.: Princeton University Press, 1973), 444.

5. José Murilo de Carvalho, "As Forças Armadas na Primeira República: O Poder Destabilizador," *Cadernos do Departamento de Ciência Política [UFMG]*, no. 1 (Mar. 1974): 113–88; idem, "As Forças Armadas na Primeira República: O Poder Desestablizador," in *História Geral da Civilização Brasileira*, vol. 9, bk. 3, *O Brasil Republicano*, ed. Boris Fausto (Rio de Janeiro: DIFEL/Difusão, 1977), 183–234; idem, "Forças Armadas e Política, 1930–1945," in CPDOC, *A Revolução de 30: Seminário Internacional* (Brasília: Editora Universidade de Brasília, 1982), 109–187; idem, "Armed Forces and Politics in Brazil, 1930–45," *Hispanic American Historical Review* 62, no. 2 (May 1982): 193–223. José Murilo de Carvalho also had important influence on my thinking about the nature of the republic thanks to his books: *Os Bestializados: O Rio de Janeiro e a República que não foi* (São Paulo: Companhia das Letras, 1991); and *A Formação das Almas: O Imaginário da República no Brasil* (São Paulo: Companhia das Letras, 1990).

6. Edmundo Campos Coelho, *Em Busca de Identidade: O Exército e a Política na Sociedade Brasileira* (Rio de Janeiro: Forense-Universitária, 1976), 19, 27.

7. My thanks to André Moysés Gaio for calling Goffman to my attention. Gaio wrote a very interesting discussion of the literature on the military in his thesis: "Em Busca da Remissão: Os Militares contra o Regime: Uma Análise das Eleições do Clube Militar em 1984" (master's thesis, Universidade Federal de Minas Gerais, 1992). See also Erving Goffman, *Asylums: Essays on the Social Situations of Mental Patients and Other Inmates* (Chicago, Ill.: Aldine, 1962), 4–9.

8. Anthony F. C. Wallace, "Identity and the Nature of Revolution," in *Latin America: The Dynamics of Social Change*, ed. Stefan A. Halper and John R. Sterling (New York: St. Martin's, 1972), 178–80.

9. Roderick J. Barman, *Brazil: The Forging of a Nation, 1789–1852* (Stanford, Calif.: Stanford University Press, 1988), 225. On the functioning of parentelas as units of regional power see Billy Jaynes Chandler, *The Feitosas and the Sertão dos Inhamuns: The History of a Family and a Community in Northeast Brazil, 1700–1930* (Gainesville: University Press of Florida, 1972); and Linda Lewin, *Politics and Parentela in Paraíba: A Case Study of Family-Based Oligarchy in Brazil* (Princeton, N.J.: Princeton University Press, 1987).

10. Rouquié, *Military and the State,* 104.

CHAPTER 1

1. The historiography of these events is ample and growing. See, e.g., Ernesto Senna, *Deodoro: Subsidios para a historia—Notas de um reporter* (Rio de Janeiro: Imprensa Nacional, 1913); George C. A. Boehrer, *Da Monarquia à República: História do Partido Republicano do Brasil (1870–89)* (Rio de Janeiro: Ministério de Educação e Cultura, 1954), 275–91; Raimundo Magalhães Jr., *Deodoro: A Espada contra o Império,* vol. 2, *O Galo na Tôrre* (São Paulo: Companhia Editora Nacional, 1957), 31–82; Heitor Lyra, *História da Queda do Império,* 2 vols.(São Paulo: Companhia Ed. Nacional, 1964), esp. 2:272–88; José Maria Bello, *A History of Modern Brazil, 1889–1964* (Stanford, Calif.: Stanford University Press, 1966), 50–57; June E. Hahner, *Civilian-Military Relations in Brazil, 1889–1898* (Columbia, S.C.: University of South Carolina Press, 1969), 24–33; John Schulz, "O Exército e o Império," in *História Geral da Civilização Brasileira,* vol. 6, ed. Sérgio Buarque de Holanda and Pedro Moacyr Campos (São Paulo: Difusão do Livro, 1971), 235–58; William S. Dudley, "Reform and Radicalism in the Brazilian Army, 1870–1889" (Ph.D. diss., Columbia University, 1972); Emilia Viotti da Costa, *The Brazilian Empire: Myths and Histories* (Chicago, Ill.: University of Chicago Press, 1985),202–33; Murilo de Carvalho, *Formação das Almas,* 35–54; Renato Lemos, *Benjamin Constant: Vida e História* (Rio de Janeiro: Topbooks, 1999), 368–411. The painting of Deodoro was done from life by Henrique Bernadelli; there is a full-page reproduction in *Agulhas Negras: Tradição e Atualidade do Ensino Militar no Brasil* (Rio de Janeiro: AC & M Editora, 1993), 163.

2. Schulz, "O Exército e o Império," 235–58; esp. 239; on army as a penal institution see Peter M. Beattie's excellent "Transforming Enlisted Army Service in Brazil, 1864–1940: Penal Servitude Versus Conscription and Changing Conceptions of Honor, Race, and Nation" (Ph.D. diss., University of Miami, 1994), esp. chaps. 6 and 7.

3. Senna, *Deodoro,* 245. He names two captains, one alferes, and a cadet as the ones who gave the information. For a clear account of the Vintém [penny] crisis see Thomas H. Holloway, *Policing Rio de Janeiro: Repression and Resistance in a Nineteenth-Century City* (Stanford, Calif.: Stanford University Press, 1993), 260–62.

4. Holloway, *Policing Rio de Janeiro,* 263–64. The lower classes, to whom Castro was a defender and hero, took to the streets to stone police and attempted to set fire to the ministry of justice, causing the imperial cabinet to end a meeting and to flee out the rear doors. See Nelson Werneck Sodré, *História Militar do Brasil* (Rio de Janeiro: Editora Civilização Brasileira, 1965),145.

5. Raimundo Magalhães Jr., *Deodoro: A Espada contra o Império*, vol. 1, *O Aprendiz de Feiticeiro* (São Paulo: Companhia Editora Nacional, 1957), 303–16; quote on 314.

6. The marques da Gavea was Manoel Antonio da Fonseca Costa (1803–90), who, amazingly, spent seventy-six years in the army! He was adjutant general from 1880 to 1888. Alfredo Pretextato Maciel da Silva, *Os Generais do Exército Brasileiro de 1822 a 1889 (Traços Biográficos)* (Rio de Janeiro: Biblioteca Militar, 1940), 2:356–60.

7. Schulz, "O Exército e o Império," 235–58 (Schulz's discussion of the "military question" is the best in the literature—clear, concise, and well-documented). Robert Conrad, *The Destruction of Brazilian Slavery, 1850–1888* (Berkeley: University of California Press, 1972), 187, 193, 201–2, 218–19.

8. Sergio Buarque de Holanda, *O Brasil Monárquico: Do Império à Rúpúbica*, vol. 7, *História Geral da Civilização Brasileira* (São Paulo: Difusão Européia do Livro, 1972), 314–16; Jeanne Berrance de Castro, "A Guarda Nacional," in *História Geral da Civilização Brasileira*, vol. 6, ed. Sérgio Buarque de Holanda & Pedro Moacyr Campos (São Paulo: Difusão do Livro, 1971), 274–98; Holloway, *Policing Rio de Janeiro*, 66–75. Apparently regular officers were assigned guard duties periodically.

9. *Relatório aprensentado á Assembléa Geral Legislativa na Quarta Sessão da Vigesima Legislatura pela Ministro e Secretario de Estado dos Negocios da Guerra Thomaz José Coelho d'Almeida* (Rio de Janeiro: Imprensa Nacional, 1889), 7–8. In 1888 the army's authorized strength for enlisted men *(praças)* was 13,500, and in 1889 it was 16,616. A reorganization was in progress, and the minister noted that "não podem actualmente todas os corpos ter o pessoal completo da nova organização" (8).

10. Francisco de Paula Cidade, "O Exército em 1889: Resumo Histórico," in Biblioteca Militar, *A República Brasileira* (Rio de Janeiro: Almanak Laemmert, 1939), 231–304. Cidade, a colonel, was one of the best historians of the army for intriguing details.

11. João Camillo de Oliveira Tôrres, *A Democracia Coroada: Teoria Política do Império do Brasil*, 2d ed. (Petrópolis: Editora Vozes, 1964), 455–57.

12. Emilio Fernandes de Souza Docca, "A Questão Militar," in Biblioteca Militar, *A República Brasileira* (Rio de Janeiro: Almanak Laemmert, 1939), 50–56.

13. Lyra, *História da Queda do Império*, 2:35–36.

14. This insight is from Eiko Ikegami, *The Taming of the Samurai: Honorific Individualism and the Making of Modern Japan* (Cambridge, Mass.: Harvard University Press, 1995), 42–43.

15. John Bushnell, "The Tsarist Officer Corps, 1881–1914: Customs, Duties, Inefficiency," *American Historical Review* 86, no. 4 (Oct. 1981): 759; see also Edward M. Coffman, *The Old Army: A Portrait of the American Army in Peacetime, 1784–1898* (New York: Oxford University Press, 1986), 63–66, 69–70.

16. Roberto Kant de Lima, "Bureaucratic Rationality in Brazil and in the United States," in *The Brazilian Puzzle: Culture Borderlands of the Western World*, ed. David J. Hess and Roberto A. Damatta (New York: Columbia University Press, 1995), 260–61.

17. It is instructive to note that classic studies of the military by Huntington, Lieuwen, and Johnson do not even have the terms *discipline* or *obedience* in their indices. See Samuel P. Huntington, *The Soldier and the State: The Theory and Politics of Civil-Military Relations* (Cambridge, Mass.: Harvard University Press, 1957); Edwin

Lieuwen, *Arms and Politics in Latin America* (New York: Praeger, 1960); John J. Johnson, ed., *The Role of the Military in Under-developed Countries* (Princeton, N.J.: Princeton University Press, 1962).

18. Senna, *Deodoro,* 10.

19. Cláudio Moreira Bento, *O Exército na Proclamação da República* (Rio de Janeiro: SENAI, 1989), 90–91. Col. Francisco de Paula Cidade noted the gap between the army's disciplinary code and the way officers applied it without formal boards or councils, decreeing punishments, including whippings and executions, on their own authority in the interest of not wasting "paper, ink, or time." Arbitrariness tended to make commanding officers rules unto themselves. See Cidade, "O Exército em 1889," 272–76.

20. Lyra, *História da Queda do Império,* 2:354–56, 365–69; Charles Simmons, *Marshal Deodoro and the Fall of Dom Pedro II* (Durham, N.C.: Duke University Press, 1966); Henry H. Keith, *Soldados Salvadores: As Revoltas Militares Brasileiras de 1922 e 1924 Em Perspectiva Histórica* (Rio de Janeiro: Biblioteca do Exército, 1989), 41–43. On the motivations of the coup participants see William S. Dudley, "Institutional Sources of Officer Discontent in the Brazilian Army, 1870–1889," *Hispanic American Historical Review* 55, no. 1 (Feb. 1974): 44–65; and William S. Dudley, "Professionalism and Politicization as Motivational Factors in the Brazilian Army Coup of 15 November 1889," *Journal of Latin American Studies* 8, no. 1 (May 1976): 101–24.

21. *Almanak ... 1889,* 73–75; it gives location, date of creation, name of director. For a study see David L. Wood, "Abortive Panacea: Brazilian Military Settlements: 1850 to 1913" (Ph.D. diss., University of Utah, 1972).

22. Benjamin Constant, for his role in the creation of the republic, was promoted to brigadier general "by acclamation" in January 1890, and, on his death in 1891, the provisional government honored him by decreeing that he be carried in perpetuity as number seven on the brigadiers' list in the Army Almanac. I thank Peter M. Beattie for sharing his article, "National Identity and the Brazilian Folk: The *Sertanejo* in Taunay's *A retired da Laguna.*" Beattie notes that army-educated authors were more prominent in shaping the symbols and issues of national identity than was the case in Spanish-American countries.

23. Bento, *O Exército na Proclamação da República,* 64.

24. Francisco Ruas Santos, *Coleção Bibliográfica Militar* (Rio de Janeiro: Ed. Biblioteca do Exército, 1960), 9–125. Alain Rouquié made the point that the army's control of officer education contributed to the growing autonomy of the military from the civilian sphere; see Rouquié, *Military and the State,* 61–66.

25. Cidade, "O Exército em 1889," 232–304; Bento, *O Exército na Proclamação da República,* 80–85.

26. Ildefonse Favé, *Curso de Arte Militar,* trans. Joaquim Alves da Costa Mattos (Rio de Janeiro: Tipografia Militar de Costa & Santos, 1882); summary and comments in Gen. Francisco de Paula Cidade, *Síntese de Três Séculos de Literatura Militar Brasileira* (Rio de Janeiro: Estabelecimento Gustavo Cordeiro de Faria, 1959), 259–60. Cidade noted that the faculty of the military school did not think a translation of this book was necessary "because all the students knew French," so over their opposition

the book was translated for use by the *tarimbeiro* officers who neither knew French nor had the opportunity for formal study.

27. On the shooting see Francisco de Assis Barbosa, *A Vida de Lima Barreto* (Rio de Janeiro: José Olympio Editora, 1975), 25; Murilo de Carvalho, *Formação das Almas,* 75–128.

28. For a discussion of the broader scene leading up to the coup see Emilia Viotti da Costa, *The Brazilian Empire: Myths and Histories* (Chicago, Ill.: University of Chicago Press, 1985), 202–33; Sérgio Buarque de Holanda, "Do Império à República," *Historia Geral da Civilização Brasileira,* Tomo 2, Vol. 5 (São Paulo: Difel/Difusão Editoral, 1972), 224; João Quartim de Morães, *A Esquerda Militar no Brasil: Da Conspiração Republicana à Guerrilha dos Tenentes* (São Paulo: Edições Siciliano, 1991), 39–49; Renato Lessa, *A Invenção Republicana; Campos Sales, as Bases e a Decadência do Primeira República Brasileira* (São Paulo: Edições Vértice, 1988), 23–46.

Machado de Assis's novel *Jacob and Esau* (Berkeley: University of California Press, 1965) captured the ambivalent response of the public to the change of regime in the situation of the pastry-shop owner who had just put up a new sign proclaiming the "Imperial Pastryshop" and was afraid he would lose monarchist clients if he took it down or republican ones if he left it up, and the reverse if he changed it to "Republican Pastryshop," so in the end he opted to use his name, "Custódio's Pastryshop."

29. Barbosa, *A Vida de Lima Barreto,* 26–30.

30. Magalhães, *O Galo na Tôrre,* 134–37.

31. Ibid., 207–26. Benjamin Constant was the great loser in these internal struggles.

32. Ibid., 238–57; Edgard Carone, *A República Velha,* vol. 2, *Evolução Política* (Sao Paulo: Difusão Européia do Livro, 1972), 71.

33. A Mexican source reported that Blaine provided Deodoro with money with which to buy congressional votes; see Daniel Cosío Villegas, *Historia moderna de México* (México, D.F.: Editorial Hermes, 1954–74), 6:700.

34. Alfred Stepan, *Military in Politics,* 75–77.

35. Carone, *A República Velha,* 2:54–78.

36. See June E. Hahner, *Civilian-Military Relations in Brazil,* 56–72; for a novel that accurately captures the feel of the fighting in Rio Grande see Erico Verissimo, *Time and the Wind* (New York: Macmillan, 195l); the best scholarly treatment is Joseph L. Love, *Rio Grande do Sul and Brazilian Regionalism, 1882–1930* (Stanford, Calif.: Stanford University Press, 1971), 57–75; and Bello, *History of Modern Brazil,* 131–38. The massacres perpetrated by army Col. Antonio Moreira Cesar in Santa Catarina show that mistreatment of prisoners was carried out not only by unlettered gaúchos.

37. Hélio Silva, *1889: A República não Esperou o Amanhecer* (Rio de Janeiro: Civilização Brasileira, 1972), 170, 196; Carlos Eugênio de Andrada Guimarães, *Arthur Oscar, Soldado do Império e da República* (Rio de Janeiro: Biblioteca do Exército, 1965), 102–15.

38. Many of these men would be active for a long while. Prudente de Morais brought those expelled from the army back to active duty. Both sides contributed to the army's subsequent leadership. Mallet and Setembrino de Carvalho became ministers of war. Arthur Oscar suppressed Canudos, and Piragibe opposed the 1904 military school uprising.

39. The twenty-six-day siege ended with the death of Lapa's commander, Col. Antônio Ernesto Gomes Carneiro. The resistance was credited with discouraging the Federalists from advancing on São Paulo, an event of such importance to Florianists that a bronze panel on Floriano's monument in Rio was devoted to Gomes Carneiro. José Feliciano Lobo Vianna, ed., *Guia Militar para o Anno de 1898* (Rio de Janeiro: Imprensa Nacional, 1897), 289. The eulogy likened the Lapa resistance to a sea wall that broke up the waves of that "storm of crimes." "Que vergonha, senhores inimigos da Republica!!" (Arthur Vieira Peixoto, *Floriano, Biografia do Marechal Floriano Peixoto* [Rio de Janeiro: Ministerio da Educação, 1939], 405–9). Both sides used Uruguayan gaúchos often from Brazilian-owned estancias across the border.

40. Bello, *History of Modern Brazil,* 110, 135–36, 145; Hélio Silva, *1889,* 232–33, 243–45; for analysis of the executions on the island of Anhatomirim see Carlos Humberto Corrêa, *Militares e Civis num Governo sem Rumo: O Governo Provisório Revolucionário no sul do Brasil, 1893–1894* (Florianópolis: Ed. UFSC & Ed. Lunardelli, 1990), 141–48. Corrêa concluded that it is not clear who ordered the executions and that the number killed is uncertain but was small. Some of the violence in Rio Grande was personal vengeance. Reportedly, Adão de Latorre, who slit the throats of republicans captured just before the assault on Bagé, was avenging the brutal rape of his wife and daughters by these same men; John C. Chasteen, *Heroes on Horseback: A Life and Times of the Last Gaucho Caudillos* (Albuquerque: University of New Mexico Press, 1995), 108–9; Love, *Rio Grande do Sul,* 60–71.

41. Bello, *History of Modern Brazil,* 136.

42. Steven C. Topik, *Trade and Gunboats: The United States and Brazil in the Age of Empire* (Stanford, Calif.: Stanford University Press, 1996), 102–3; José Afonso Mendonça Azevedo, *Vida e Obra de Salvador de Mendonça* (Rio de Janeiro: Ministério das Relações Exteriores, 1971), esp. 380–81.

43. Topik, *Trade and Gunboats,* 126–27. The U.S. Naval Institute also compared Brazil's vessels to those of the U.S. Navy in 1893; see idem, note 22.

44. Ibid., 126.

45. Ibid., 124–27.

46. Ibid., 128–30; June E. Hahner, "Jacobinos versus Galegos: Urban Radicals versus Portuguese Immigrants in Rio de Janeiro in the 1890s," *Journal of Interamerican Studies and World Affairs* 18, no. 2 (May 1976): 129–30.

47. Teresa A. Meade opens her book with a description of the street violence of Sept. 11–12, 1893, but ignores that it took place after the Naval Revolt began on Sept. 6. See Teresa A. Meade, *"Civilizing" Rio: Reform and Resistance in a Brazilian City, 1889–1930* (University Park: Pennsylvania State University Press, 1997), 1–2, 51–54.

48. On civilian dress see Carone, *A República Velha,* 76; *Jornal do Brasil* (Rio), June 30, 1895, reprinted in Arthur Vieira Peixoto, *Floriano,* 315–17.

49. Quoted in Topik, *Trade and Gunboats,* 156.

50. Ibid., 163.

51. Quoted in ibid., 147.

52. For a full account of the events outlined in the last three paragraphs see ibid., 135–77.

53. Bello, *History of Modern Brazil,* 138.

54. Edgard Carone, *A República Velha,* vol. 1, *Instituições e Classes Sociais* (São Paulo: Difusão Européia do Livro, 1972), 358.

55. Jehovah Motta, *Formação do Oficial do Exército: Currículos e regimes na Academia Militar, 1810–1944* (Rio de Janeiro: Ed. Companhia Brasileira de Artes Gráficas, 1976), 249–50.

56. Ibid.

57. Floriano Peixoto, message to Congress, Rio de Janeiro, May 2, 1894, in Câmara dos Deputados, *Mensagens Presidenciais, 1890–1910* (Brasília: Câmara dos Deputados, 1978), 101 (my translation).

58. Motta, *Formação do Oficial,* 251.

59. Ministerio da Guerra, *Relatório apresentado ao Presidente da República dos Estados Unidos do Brasil pelo General de Divisão Bernardo Vasques, Ministro de Estado dos Negocios da Guerra em Maio de 1895* (Rio de Janeiro: Imprensa Nacional, 1895), 19–23. Hereafter the form for all ministerial relatórios will be MG, *Relatório . . . Vasques . . . 1895* (minister's name and date substituted as appropriate); MG, *Relatório . . . Vasques . . . 1896,* 17–18. Prudente J. de Morais Barros, Rio de Janeiro, May 3, 1895, message to Congress, in Câmara dos Deputados, *Mensagens Presidenciais, 1890–1910,* 116–18. Career data on Gen. Mendes Ourique Jacques from *Almanaque do Exército, 1895.* On Floriano's funeral see Arthur Vieira Peixoto, *Floriano,* esp. 223. For the effects the school's insubordination had on national politics see Hahner, *Civilian-Military Relations in Brazil,* 160–62.

I have used the term *military students* rather than *cadets* because the title of cadet was associated with the monarchy and had been proscribed; moreover, the Escola Militar of the era was not merely an officer candidate school but an institution offering a preparatory program, a general studies program, and programs in infantry, cavalry, and artillery. Both officers looking to further their education and soldiers *(praças de pret)* seeking officers' commissions attended. Even field-grade officers might be found among the students. In 1896 Major Tristão de Alencar Araripe and Lieutenant Colonel Alberto Ferreira de Abreu received their bachelor's degrees along with seven other officers. See MG, *Relatório . . . Vasques . . . 1896,* 18. The practice of senior officers returning to study seems to have been customary; Floriano Peixoto received his degree in 1871, when he was a lieutenant colonel with fourteen years of service.

60. Gen. Medeiros Mallet, who Floriano had expelled, would be named to an important commission in October 1896 to draw up regulations for the new general staff and then would be promoted to major general (General de Divisão) in November 1897, whereas ardent Florianista, and conqueror of Canudos, Arthur Oscar would find himself frozen in grade.

61. MG, *Relatório . . . Vasques . . . 1896,* 3–4.

62. MG, *Relatório . . . Argollo . . . 1897,* 3.

63. The army was split over a number of internal and external issues. June Hahner, in *Civilian-Military Relations in Brazil, 1889–1898,* takes the position that Prudente selected his ministers of war on the basis of their commitment to civilian rule to help depoliticize the army (152). Increased professionalism would lead to depoliticization. In this view the army had entered politics because the imperial government had ignored it.

64. MG, *Relatório . . . Vasques . . . 1895,* 4–5.

65. Ibid., 4–16; *Relatório . . . Vasques . . . 1896,* 4–5. The commission to draw up the general staff and quartermaster regulations was composed of Brig. Gen. João Nepomuceno de Medeiros Mallet (who had returned to the army in October 1895), Major Pedro Ivo da Silva Henriques, and Major Francisco de Paula Borges Fortes. It was named in October 1896 and submitted its recommendations by May 1897 (*Relatório. . . . Argollo . . . 1897,* 4).

The United States army was also debating its future in the 1890s; see James L. Abrahamson, *America Arms for a New Century: The Making of a Great Military Power* (New York: Free Press, 1981), 19–62.

66. Scholars have been fascinated with the community's leader, Antonio Conselheiro, ever since. Although the usual veterans' campaign memoirs appeared, the military side of the affair has been superseded by the sociological, religious, and political. Maria Isaura Pereira de Queiroz, *O Messianismo no Brasil e no Mundo* (São Paulo: Dominus Editora, 1965), 200–219; Duglas Teixeira Monteiro, "Um Confronto entre Juazeiro, Canudos e Contestado," in *História Geral da Civilização Brasileira,* ed. Boris Fausto (Rio de Janeiro: DIFEL/ Difusão, 1977), 9:58–71; Ralph della Cava, "Brazilian Messianism and National Institutions: A Reappraisal of Canudos and Joaseiro," *Hispanic American Historical Review* 48, no. 3 (Aug. 1968): 402–20; Hahner, *Civilian-Military Relations in Brazil,* 171–79. Edmundo Moniz, in *A Guerra Social de Canudos* (Rio de Janeiro: Civilização Brasileira, 1978), gives attention to the political-military aspects, but unfortunately his book is not annotated. The best summary of current interpretations is Robert M. Levine, "'Mud-Hut Jerusalem': Canudos Revisited," *Hispanic American Historical Review* 68, no. 3 (Aug. 1988): 525–72; and Robert M. Levine, *Vale of Tears: Revisiting the Canudos Massacre in Northeastern Brazil, 1893–1897* (Berkeley: University of California Press, 1992).

67. Levine, *Vale of Tears,* 4, 8; Levine, "'Mud-Hut Jerusalem,'" 545–46; Lt. Pires Ferreira's after-action report ("Parte") is quoted at length in Tristão de Alencar Araripe, *Expedições Militares Contra Canudos: Seu Aspecto Marcial,* 2d ed. (Rio de Janeiro: Biblioteca do Exército, 1985), 9–21; and Luiz Viana to Minister of War Dionísio Cerqueira (Dec. 14, 1896) is also quoted in Araripe, *Expedições Militares Contra Canudos,* 35; Euclides da Cunha, *Rebellion in the Backlands* (Chicago, Ill.: University of Chicago Press, 1944), 183–88. About 150 sertanejos died. Araripe's book includes excerpts from officers' after-action reports and is more accurate on many military details than is da Cunha's famous work.

68. See da Cunha, *Rebellion.*

69. Della Cava, "Brazilian Messianism," 411.

70. Ibid., 407; da Cunha, *Rebellion,* 137–39.

71. Teixeira Monteiro, "Um Confronto," 68. The Conselheiro's Trinitarian theology followed the classic sequence of creation, elevation, sin, punishment, promise, remission, and reconciliation. His surviving manuscript is in Ataliba Nogueira, *Antonio Conselheiro e Canudos: Revisão História* (São Paulo: Companhia Editora Nacional, 1974).

72. See Moniz, *A Guerra Social de Canudos:* "Na *Utopia,* de Thomas More, estava a origem histórica e ideológica de Canudos" (253).

73. Della Cava, "Brazilian Messianism," 411. A *fazendeiro* is a large agricultural landowner, equivalent to *haciendado* in Spanish.

74. Ibid., 412–14. Rui Facó was correct in assigning the fazendeiros a keen interest in the destruction of Canudos, but the situation was more complex than rebelling sertanejos on one side and fazendeiros on the other. However, the army's action ultimately helped preserve the existing social-economic system of the region. See Rui Facó, *Cangaçeiros e Fanáticos, Gênese e Lutos* (Rio de Janeiro: Editora Civilização Brasileira, 1976), 90: " . . . os grandes fazendeiros. . . . Eram os principais interessados no assalto a Canudos, no esmagamento dos 'revoltosos' que tão mau exemplo transmitiam aos demais explorados do campo." For the complexities of Bahian politics see Consuelo Novais Sampaio, "Repensando Canudos: O jugo das oligarquias," *Luso-Brazilian Review* 30, no. 2 (winter 1993): 97–113. On the role of the rural colonels see Victor Nunes Leal, *Coronelismo, Enxada e Voto, O Município e O Regime Representativo no Brasil* (São Paulo: Rd. Alfa-Omega, 1976); and Maria Isaura Pereira de Queiroz, *O Mandonismo local na Vida Política Brasileira e Outros Ensaios* (São Paulo: Ed. Alfa-Omega, 1976), 163–216.

75. Araripe, *Expedições Militares Contra Canudos,* 9–11. Sólon cited the principle of Brazilian law that said "what the law does not specify, no one has the right to specify."

76. Pires Ferreira's after-action report *(Parte)* is quoted at length in Araripe, *Expedições Militares Contra Canudos,* 14–18.

77. Araripe, *Expedições Militares Contra Canudos,* 25–38. At one point in the Vianna-Sólon dispute, the governor detached the state police from the force and ordered them to move forward to Monte Santo (32). Febrônio de Brito to Col. Saturnino Riberiro da Costa Jr. (Commandant 3d Military Dist.) Monte Santo, Jan. 24, 1897, in Henrique Duque-Estrada de Macedo Soares, *A Guerra de Canudos* (1903; reprint, Rio de Janeiro: Biblioteca do Exército, 1959), 9–13. Consuelo Novais Sampaio placed General Sólon and Major Febrônio and their behavior in the context of Bahian state politics; see "Repensando Canudos," 108–9.

78. da Cunha, *Rebellion,* 33–38.

79. Ibid., 207.

80. Ibid., 211.

81. Ibid., 212–15; and Febrônio de Brito to Col. Saturnino Riberiro da Costa Jr. (Commandant 3d Military Dist.), Monte Santo, Jan. 24, 1897, in Macedo Soares, *Guerra de Canudos,* 9–13.

82. da Cunha, *Rebellion,* 310; Marcos Evangelista da Costa Villela Jr., *Canudos: Memórias de um Combatente* (São Paulo: Ed. Marco Zero, 1988), 21.

83. Manuel Benicio, Canudos, July 24, 1897, *Jornal do Comércio* (Rio) Aug. 7, 1897, in Walnice Nogueira Galvão, *No Calor da Hora: A guerra de Canudos nos jornais, 4a expedição* (São Paulo: Ed. Ática, 1974), 263.

84. Macedo Soares, *Guerra de Canudos,* 11.

85. da Cunha, *Rebellion,* 223.

86. Moniz, *A Guerra Social de Canudos,* 133–134. This force was patched together with his Seventh Infantry Battalion, the reconstituted Ninth Infantry, the understrength Sixteenth Infantry from São João del Rei, Minas Gerais, some of the

Thirty-third Infantry, a battery of the Second Artillery Regiment, and a squadron from the Ninth Cavalry.

87. Umberto Peregrino, *"Os Sertões" Como História Militar* (Rio de Janeiro: Biblioteca do Exército, 1956), 70–71.

88. Moniz, *A Guerra Social de Canudos,* 134. Vianna had opposed José Joaquim Seabra's candidacy, which was pushed by Vice President Manoel Vitoriano; see João Dunshee de Abranches, *Como se Faziam Presidentes: Homens e Fatos do Início da República* (Rio de Janeiro: José Olympio Editora, 1973), 12–13.

89. His words were "Ve? Não há doentes. Siga" (Moniz, *A Guerra Social de Canudos,* 139). See also Macedo Soares, *Guerra de Canudos,* 22.

90. Moniz, *A Guerra Social de Canudos,* 140–41. Dr. Ferreira Nunes said, "Os ataques hão de repetir-se cada vez mais amiúde e se ele tem o imcômode em momentos de combate, pode nos ser fatal." Moreira César: "Não tenho medo de morrer e não hei de morrer sem ir a Canudos."

91. da Cunha, *Rebellion,* 246; the artillery unit especially had a difficult time because it had to smooth the way for the four Krupp L-24 cannon and push them when their mules could not, or would not, pull them up hillsides; see Villela, *Canudos: Memórias de um Combatente,* 16–19.

92. da Cunha, *Rebellion,* 265; Villela, *Canudos: Memórias de um Combatente,* 20–21. The latter notes that from time to time during this march sertanejos fired at the troops.

93. Araripe, *Expedições Militares Contra Canudos,* 58–62, 68–69; Villela, *Canudos: Memórias de um Combatente,* 21–23. The various participant accounts give different times for the colonel's wounding.

94. Araripe, *Expedições Militares Contra Canudos,* 62–69; Macedo Soares, *Guerra de Canudos,* 19–27 (Macedo Soares wrote that the "archive" of the expedition survived, but he did not say where it was, and I found no other reference to it; see 27); Villela, *Canudos: Memórias de um Combatente,* 23–32.

95. "É tempo de murici, Cada um cuide de si . . . " (quoted in da Cunha, *Rebellion,* 267).

96. Later, rumor and government propaganda would say that monarchists were supplying the sertanejos with modern arms, but their modern weapons clearly came from their attackers. See reporter Favila Nunes account in *Gazeta de Notícias* (Bahia), Oct. 17, 1897, in Galvão, *No Calor da Hora,* 203. Initially Euclides da Cunha had difficulty believing this was the source of arms. See his *Canudos, Diário de uma Expedição* (Rio de Janeiro: José Olympio Editora, 1939), 98–101. See also Araripe, *Expedições Militares Contra Canudos,* 60–75. A survivor of this disaster, who was a gunnery sergeant in the artillery battery and who returned with the final expedition, told of officers leaving soldiers on the road to get along as best they could; it took him fifteen days to reach Queimadas; Villela, *Canudos: Memórias de um Combatente,* 23–51.

97. Thomas Thompson (U.S. Minister), Petrópolis, Mar. 12, 1897, Despatch #550: "Opposition to the Government by religious fanatics in Bahia," Department of State Records, Microfilm Vol. 60, Sep. 18, 1896–Aug. 31, 1897, Roll 62, NA. Thompson observed: "There is no doubt that this band are antagonistic to the Republic, but I cannot see that they are in any position to materially aid the efforts of the Monarchist

party in their aim to restore the Empire." He noted that reports of monarchist aid to Canudos were "greatly exaggerated." Hahner says in *Civilian-Military Relations in Brazil* that the assassins were officers (172). For a list of their names and for the quotations from the *O Estado de S. Paulo* see Maria de Lourdes Mônaco Janotti, *Os Subversivos da República* (São Paulo: Ed. Brasiliense, 1986), 139–45 and n. 90.

98. Moniz, *A Guerra Social de Canudos*, 153–58; Janotti, *Os Subversivos da República*, 138–39, discusses the three republican currents that both combined and clashed at that time. The Castilhistas of Rio Grande do Sul defended federalism as a way to insure centralization of power in the state; the militarist Florianista current supported an authoritarian presidency, perhaps to the extreme of a dictatorship; and the paulista "Burguesia," with its coffee interests and its links to international capital, favored oligarchic, conservative rule with civilian control of the military.

99. Moniz, *A Guerra Social de Canudos*, 158–59.

100. Prudente de Moraes, message to Congress, Rio, May 3, 1897, in Câmara dos Deputados, *Mensagens Presidenciais, 1890–1910* (Brasília: Câmara dos Deputados, 1978), 152. "Canudos vai ser atacado em condições de não ser possivel novo insucesso: dentro em pouco a divisão do Exército, ao mando do general Arthur Oscar, destroçará os que alli estão envergonhando a nossa civilisação."

101. Hélio Silva, *1889*, 272–73; Dunshee de Abranches, *Como se Faziam Presidentes*, 34–35; Raymundo Faoro, *Os Donos do Poder, Formação do Patronato Político Brasileiro* (Porto Alegre & São Paulo: Ed. Globo & Ed. de Universidade de São Paulo, 1975), 2:558; Vianna, *Guia Militar para o Anno de 1898*, 315, 318, 320; and Table 1.2 is based on MG, *Relatórios, 1895, 1896, 1897, 1898*.

102. MG, *Relatório . . . Mallet . . . 1899*, 66. The shipment left Hamburg on May 5. For arms at Canudos see Macedo Soares, *Guerra de Canudos*, 45.

103. Dunshee de Abranches, *Como Se Faziam Presidentes*, 34–35; MG, *Relatório . . . Cantuaria . . . 1898*, 4–5, 16–17. The military students asked that their punishments be reconsidered because "they represented the Republic," to which the minister responded that the "Republic was all of its citizens" (Janotti, *Os Subversivos da Republica*, 148–49).

104. MG, *Relatório . . . Cantuaria . . . 1898*, 18.

105. *Folha da Tarde*, Rio, July 17, 1897, in Galvão, *No Calor da Hora*, 35.

106. Vianna, *Guia Militar para o Anno de 1898*, 396. For the ways army recruitment was laid on the poor in previous decades see Joan E. Meznar, "The Ranks of the Poor: Military Service and Social Differentiation in Northeast Brazil, 1830–1875," *Hispanic American Historical Review* 72, no. 3 (Aug. 1992): 335–51.

107. MG, *Relatório . . . Argollo . . . 1897*, 9. For example, the Battalion Tiradentes, which was related to the archrepublican Club Tiradentes, had been dismissed on Mar. 24, 1897.

108. MG, *Relatório . . . Cantuaria . . . 1898*. See chart in Anexo C, "Repartição de Ajudante General, Mappa da força do Exército, segundo a lei de fixação vigente no anno de 1897, de accordo com os ultmos mappas parciaes." Dated Dec. 31, 1897, it shows unit strengths and locations. In 1897 there were 80 second lieutenants, 1096 *alferes*, and 9 *alferes alumnos* who were carried on the extraordinary list.

109. Beattie, "Transforming Enlisted Army Service," 301–31.

110. *Folha da Tarde* (Rio), July 17, 1897, in Galvão, *No Calor da Hora,* 34.

Eu ando desconfiado,
Olhar baixo, lábios mudos,
Com medo de ser pegado
Para o açougue de Canudos!

111. *A Bahia* (Salvador), Sep. 12, 1897, in Galvão, *No Calor da Hora,* 43.

Nos somos de pega-pega
Os rebotalhos, os miúdos:
Que aos grandes não se *bodega*
Para mandar pra Canudos!
Voltaremos da refrega
Tortos, zarolhos, ossudos,
Se não levarmos *fubega*
Inda outra vez em Canudos!

112. Galvão, *No Calor da Hora,* 36. Joseph Love noted that many of the Uruguayan gaúchos who followed their Brazilian Federalist landlords in raids into Rio Grande in 1893 were from a department of Uruguay peopled by Spaniards from Maragatoría. Hence, Maragatos. See Love, *Rio Grande do Sul,* 62. For a discussion of *jagunço* see Maria Isaura Pereira de Queiroz, *O Mandonismo,* 219–28.

113. The battalions sent to Salvador were the Fourteenth Battalion, from Pernambuco; the Fifth Battalion, from Maranhão; the Twenty-seventh Battalion, from Paraíba; the Twenty-fifth and Thirtieth Battalions, from Rio Grande do Sul; and the Ninth and Sixteenth Battalions from Bahia. Those shipped to Sergipe were the Twelfth Infantry and a battery of the Fifth Artillery, from Rio, and the Thirty-first and Thirty-second battalions, from Rio Grande do Sul; they were added to the Twenty-sixth Infantry of Sergipe, the Thirty-third of Alagoas, the Thirty-fourth of Rio Grande do Norte, and the Thirty-fifth of Piauí. *Relatório . . . Cantuaria . . . 1898:* Anexo A, "Forças em Operações na Bahia." This document contains after-action reports and unit lists, as well as listings of those killed and wounded.

114. MG, *Relatório . . . Argollo . . . 1897,* 9; and *Relatório . . . Cantuaria . . . 1898:* Anexo A, "Forças em Operações na Bahia," 8, 12, 19.

115. BG Claudio do Amaral Savaget, Salvador, Aug. 6, 1897, "Relatório," in MG, *Relatório . . . Cantuaria . . . 1898:* Anexo A, "Forças em Operações na Bahia," 13.

116. BG Claudio do Amaral Savaget, Salvador, Aug. 6, 1897, "Relatório," in MG, *Relatório . . . Cantuaria . . . 1898:* Anexo A, "Forças em Operações na Bahia," 14. Savaget was forced to pause at a place called Simão Dias for seven days at the end of June so that his supplier could organize his transport and because of the "muitos casos de estropeamento de praças, devido não só aos pessimos caminhos, pedregosos e lamacentos, como tambem e principalmente, pela falta de habito dos nossos soldados ás marchas prolongadas, á pé descalço" (emphasis added).

117. Cidade, "O Exército em 1889," 247. "Quando as tropas marchavam para guerra, a mulher e os filhos acompanhavam o soldado." For numbers see Macedo Soares, *Guerra de Canudos,* 88. Whether the women were legally soldiers' wives or more casual *vivandeiras* makes little difference here.

118. BG Claudio do Amaral Savaget, Salvador, Aug. 6, 1897, "Relatório," in MG, *Relatório . . . Cantuaria . . . 1898:* Anexo A, "Forças em Operações na Bahia," 15.

119. Ibid., 16.

120. Ibid., 17.

121. Manuel Benicio, *Jornal do Comércio* (Rio), Aug. 9, 1897, in Galvão, *No Calor da Hora,* 297.

122. Lelis Piedade, *Jornal de Notícias* (Bahia), Sep. 7, 1897, in Galvão, *No Calor da Hora,* 345. This woman was the wife of a soldier in the Fourth Bahia police battalion. I have translated *companheira* as wife because it was often used that way in popular speech and because the legal nature of the relationship is unimportant here.

123. Savaget, Salvador, Aug. 6, 1897, "Relatório," in MG, *Relatório . . . Cantuaria . . . 1898,* Annexo A, "Forças em Operações na Bahia," 18.

124. Benício, *Jornal do Comércio* (Rio), Aug. 9, 1897, in Galvão, *No Calor da Hora,* 297.

125. Savaget, Salvador, Aug. 6, 1897, "Relatório," in MG, *Relatório . . . Cantuaria . . . 1898,* Annexo A, "Forças em Operações na Bahia," 19.

126. Benício, *Jornal do Comércio* (Rio), Aug. 3, 1897, in Galvão, *No Calor da Hora,* 240–41.

127. Capt. Alberto Gavião Pereira Pinto to Lt. Col. Emygdio Dantas Barreto (C.O. 3d Brigade), Favella, June 30, 1897, in MG, *Relatório . . . Cantuaria . . . 1898,* Annexo A, "Forças em Operações na Bahia," 85–87; Brig. Gen. João da Silva Barbosa, Favella, July 17, 1897, "Relatório," in ibid., 69–72; da Cunha, *Rebellion,* 313. The Seventh's losses took place during fighting on June 28 as the army attempted to attack. The second major to be shot was Carlos Frederico de Mesquita, who later as a general would command early operations in the Contestado (see Chap. 3).

128. The artillery incident involved a display of raw courage and determination. Early on the twenty-eighth gunnery sergeant Marcos Evangelista da Costa Villela Jr. was taken to the hospital in a rear trench where, pinned against the earthen wall, the doctors removed a slug from his arm without anesthesia and doused the wound with an acid to stop the bleeding. After recovering from the searing pain and with his arm immobilized against his body by bandages, he returned to the battle. Gathering up an inexperienced gun crew from among a Bahian police detachment, he made the now lone cannon do its deadly work. He would be responsible for destroying one of the day's major sertanejo assaults. He mentioned the colonel's orders regarding shooting cowards. See Villela, *Canudos: Memórias de um combatente,* 64–68.

129. Savaget, Salvador, Aug. 6, 1897, "Relatório," in MG, *Relatório . . . Cantuaria . . . 1898,* Annexo A, "Forças em Operações na Bahia," 20.

130. Manuel Benício, *Jornal do Comércio* (Rio), Aug. 3, 1897, in Galvão, *No Calor da Hora,* 245.

131. Ibid., Aug. 8, 1897, in Galvão, *No Calor da Hora,* 290.

132. da Cunha, *Rebellion,* 343.

133. Manuel Benício suggested as much in *Jornal do Comércio* (Rio), Aug. 3, 1897, in Galvão, *No Calor da Hora,* 244.

134. John Reed, *Insurgent Mexico* (New York: D. Appleton, 1914). There is no study for Brazil comparable to Elizabeth Salas, *Soldaderas in the Mexican Military: Myth and History* (Austin: University of Texas Press, 1990).

135. Benício, *Jornal do Comércio* (Rio), Aug. 8, 1897, and Aug. 9, 1897, in Galvão, *No Calor da Hora*, 290–91, 299–300; Macedo Soares, *Guerra de Canudos*, 183–84, 187–89; da Cunha, *Rebellion*, 337–40; Villela, *Canudos: Memórias de um combatente*, 69–73. This last source said that he existed for fourteen days on grease from the cannon, limes, and bits of meat and that once he shamefully stole another's food while it cooked.

136. Benício, *Jornal do Comércio* (Rio), Aug. 10, 1897, in Galvão, *No Calor da Hora*, 305, 312.

137. da Cunha, *Rebellion*, 348.

138. Macedo Soares, *Guerra de Canudos*, 35–36, 39. Da Cunha mentioned Pajeú several times in *Rebellion*. The expedition's sertanejo guide, "Captain" Jesuíno, held him responsible for the deaths of his family and offered his services to get revenge; Villela, *Canudos: Memórias de um combatente*, 83–84.

139. Manuel Benício, *Jornal do Comércio* (Rio), Aug. 3, 4, 8, 1897, in Galvão, *No Calor da Hora*, 247, 252, 294.

140. Brig. Gen. João da Silva Barbosa to Brig. Gen. Arthur Oscar de Andrade Guimarães, Canudos, Aug. 7, 1897, in MG, *Relatório . . . Cantuaria . . . 1898*, Annexo A, "Forças em operações na Bahia," 60–64. Benício, *Jornal do Comércio* (Rio), Aug. 6, 1897, in Galvão, *No Calor da Hora*, 257–60.

141. Macedo Soares, *Guerra de Canudos*, 233–37.

142. Ibid., 246.

143. Benício, *Jornal do Comércio* (Rio), Aug. 6, 1897, as in Galvão, *No Calor da Hora*, 262; Moniz, *A Guerra Social de Canudos*, 219.

144. Benício, *Jornal do Comércio* (Rio), Oct. 23, 1897, in Galvão, *No Calor da Hora*, 336–38.

145. *Diario de Notícias*, Bahia, Aug. 24, 1897 (datelined Canudos, Aug. 13, 1897), in Galvão, *No Calor da Hora*, 122–23.

146. Macedo Soares, *Guerra de Canudos*, 275–76.

147. Since most went under their own power with an allotment of three days' rations that would barely satisfy a man for one day, let alone the five it took to reach Monte Santo, *evacuated* hardly seems the proper word to describe the frightful withdrawal of the halt and the lame.

148. Macedo Soares, *Guerra de Canudos*, 177–79, 249–54; da Cunha, *Canudos, Diário*, 119–20; and da Cunha, *Rebellion*, 466–68; Galvão, *No Calor da Hora*, 281, 292, 332–33. Some wounded stayed awake nights on the trail guarding their burros from other soldiers, and some rented animals from civilians; Villela, *Canudos: Memórias de um Combatente*, 84–87.

149. Benício, *Jornal do Comércio* (Rio), Aug. 9, Oct. 6, 1897, in Galvão, *No Calor da Hora*, 298, 333; see also discussion on 113–14 of Galvão.

150. See Jonas Correia, introdução to Macedo Soares, *Guerra de Canudos* (1959 ed.), xxi–xxii.

151. Benício, *Jornal do Comércio* (Rio), Aug. 4, 1897, in Galvão, *No Calor da Hora*, 253.

152. Moniz, *A Guerra Social de Canudos*, 195–99.

153. These typical phrases are from Col. Pedro Antonio Nery (Thirty-fourth Inf. Batt.) to Citizen Col. Julião Augusto da Serra Martins (C.O. 5 Brigade), Canudos, June 29, 1897, in MG, *Relatório . . . Cantuaria . . . 1898*, Annexo A, "Forças em

Operações na Bahia," 37; and Lt. Col. Emygdio Dantas Barreto (C.O. 1st Brigade) to Brig. Gen. João da Silva Barbosa, Canudos, Aug. 4, 1897, in ibid., 65–69. The republican term *citizen* appeared frequently in army correspondence in the 1890s.

154. Moniz, *A Guerra Social de Canudos*, 201.

155. Macedo Soares, *Guerra de Canudos*, 224.

156. Col. Antonio Olympio da Silveira (C.O. Arty. Brigade) to Brig. Gen. João da Silva Barbosa, Fort Sete de Setembro (Canudos), Oct. 5, 1897, in MG, *Relatório . . . Cantuaria . . . 1898,* Annexo A, "Forças em Operações na Bahia," 138–40; da Cunha, *Rebellion,* 439–44, quote from 444; see also da Cunha, *Canudos, Diario,* 69, 80, 92–93; Lelis Piedade, *Jornal de Notícias* (Bahia), Sep. 18, 1897, in Galvão, *No Calor da Hora,* 378 (describes a throat slitting); Macedo Soares, *Guerra de Canudos,* 312–13, 334–35, 387–88, 391–95.

157. Macedo Soares, *Guerra de Canudos,* 394.

158. da Cunha, *Rebellion,* 439.

159. Macedo Soares, *Guerra de Canudos,* 262.

160. Correia, introdução, xiv–xvi.

161. The newly summoned battalions were the Twenty-eighth Infantry from Minas Gerais, the Thirty-ninth of Paraná, the Thirty-seventh of Santa Catarina, and the Fourth and Twenty-ninth of Rio Grande do Sul.

162. Edmundo Moniz maintained that Bittencourt approached other generals but that none would accept the brigade, so he was forced to confide it to Arthur Oscar's brother. Moniz also said that "Like Girard, the more enlightened generals, knowing what was going on, did not want to participate in a fratricidal and unpatriotic war that compromised the honor of the army instead of safeguarding it. Only discipline kept them silent and from going public to unmask the small minority responsible for that irrational adventure." Unhappily, his book offers no citations to allow verification; however, it has the ring of truth. Moniz, *A Guerra Social de Canudos,* 207–8. Although I am persuaded by Moniz's argument, it should be noted that another possible reason for hesitancy to accept such a command was the condition and strength of these units. Their arms, and even their uniforms, were old, and they were seriously under strength in the "volunteer" ranks. By regulation, each infantry battalion was to have 425 men, but these had 240 (Twenty-ninth), 250 (Thirty-ninth), 322 (Thirty-seventh), 250 (Twenty-eighth), and 219 (Fourth)—for a total of 1,281 instead of the regulation 2,125. Curiously, all but one were over strength in officers; they had 27 (Twenty-ninth), 40 (Thirty-ninth), 51 (Thirty-seventh), 47 (Twenty-eighth), and 11 (Fourth). The last, from São Gabriel, Rio Grande do Sul, was composed entirely of *alferes* or sublieutenants. Euclides da Cunha provided the figures; see *Rebellion,* 393. For regulation strengths for 1897 see MG, *Relatório . . . Cantuaria . . . 1898:* Anexo C, "Mappa da força effectiva do Exército."

163. da Cunha, *Rebellion,* 397–98.

164. Macedo Soares, *Guerra de Canudos,* 311.

165. Ibid., 333–37.   166. Ibid., 341.

167. Ibid., 350–53.   168. Ibid., 358.

169. Ibid., 364.

170. Favila Nunes, *Gazeta de Notícias,* Oct. 28, 1897, in Galvão, *No Calor da Hora,* 210.

171. *O Comércio de São Paulo,* São Paulo, Dec. 27, 23, 24, 1897, in Galvão, *No Calor da Hora,* 498–99, 504, 507–8.

172. MG, *Relatório . . . Cantuaria . . . 1898,* 33; Macedo Soares, *Guerra de Canudos,* 406.

173. Suely Robles Reis de Queiroz, *Os Radicais da República—Jacobinismo: Idelogia e Ação, 1893–1897* (São Paulo: Ed. Brasiliense, 1986), 61–80; Hélio Silva, *1889,* 286–90.

174. The assassin was from Alagoas, Floriano's home state, and had attempted unsuccessfully in previous months to position himself to strike at Prudente. That he was tortured in prison was indicated by the condition of his feet and that he was found dead in jail on Jan. 24, 1898, with weights tied to his feet. The official report said that he hung himself. Suely Robles Reis de Queiroz, *Os Radicais da República,* 61–80; Hahner, *Civilian-Military Relations in Brazil,* 179. The officers are listed in Hélio Silva, *1889,* 291–92. For a social science analysis of the political effects of these events see Renato Lessa, *A Invenção Republicana: Campos Sales, as Bases e a Decadência da Primeira República Brasileira* (São Paulo: Edições Vêtice & Instituto Universitário de Pesquisas do Rio de Janeiro, 1988), 73–94.

175. His brother, General Carlos Eugênio de Andrada Guimarães, complained bitterly about it in his *Arthur Oscar,* 125–31.

CHAPTER 2

1. The *Panther* incident occurred in late November 1905, when crew members from the German cruiser visiting the port of Itajaí, Santa Catarina, went ashore and seized a deserter. This led Rio Branco to protest vigorously to the kaiser's government and to receive an apology. Although it did not involve any army response, the Brazilian navy did detail two of its larger ships to keep an eye on the *Panther.* See José Joffily, *O Caso Panther* (Rio de Janeiro: Paz e Terra, 1988). Later another deserter turned up in the Contestado among the rebel forces.

2. For the economy of the Old Republic see Steven C. Topik, *The Political Economy of the Brazilian State, 1889–1930* (Austin: University of Texas Press, 1987); and Steven C. Topik, "The Old Republic," in *Modern Brazil: Elites and Masses in Historical Perspective,* ed. Michael L. Conniff and Frank D. McCann (Lincoln: University of Nebraska Press, 1989), 83–102.

3. MG, *Relatório . . . Mallet . . . 1900,* 4–5.

4. MG, *Relatório . . . Mallet . . . 1901,* 35.

5. Ibid., 6.

6. MG, *Relatório . . . Mallet . . . 1900,* 9.

7. MG, *Relatório . . . Mallet . . . 1901,* 72.

8. Ibid., 72–73.

9. Francisco de Paula Cidade, "Marechal Hermes Rodrigues da Fonseca," *Revista Militar Brasileira,* July–Dec. 1955, 235.

10. MG, *Relatório . . . Mallet . . . 1901,* 74–81.

11. Ibid., 94.   12. Ibid., 109.

13. Ibid., 31.   14. Ibid., 32.

15. MG, *Relatório . . . Mallet . . . 1900,* 12.

16. MG, *Relatório . . . Mallet . . . 1901,* 105.

17. Ibid., 22.

18. Carone, *A República Velha,* 1:355–56; Oliveira Tôrres, *Democracia Coroada,* 224–25.

19. Dermeval Peixoto, *Memórias de um velho soldado (Nomes, coisas e fatos militares de meio seculo atrás)* (Rio de Janeiro: Biblioteca do Exército, 1960), 108.

20. Cidade, "O Exército em 1889," 275–77. The expression *metia o pau* was still heard among army officers in the 1990s, although it then meant cracking down in less violent fashion.

21. Peixoto, *Memórias de um velho soldado,* 108–12. These were called, in order, *surras* (lashing), *marche-marche* (double-time marching), *solitária* (solitary), *palmatória* (switch), and *estaqueamento* (staking).

22. Ibid., 132–33. A mutiny occurred at Fort Santa Cruz on Nov. 8, 1905, in which two officers were killed before the neighboring Fort São João cannonaded the rebels into surrender. Edgard Carone, *A República Velha,* 2:214; MG, *Relatório . . . Francisco de Paula Argollo . . . 1906,* 12–13.

23. Ademar de Brito, *O 52º batalhão de caçadores e a 3a companhia de metralhadoras pesadas* (Rio de Janeiro: Biblioteca do Exército, 1944), 47.

24. Capt. LeVert Coleman, Rio, Aug. 31, 1912, War College, Division 4392, Record Card, RG165, Old Army and Navy Branch, NA; *O Estado de São Paulo,* Feb. 9, 12, 1913, cited in Carone, *A República Velha,* 1:357–58.

25. MG, *Relatório . . . Mallet . . . 1900,* Annex 1. Actual outlays for 1900.

26. Augusto Sá, *Exércitos Regionaes ou O Problema de uma organisação para o nosso exército* (Porto Alegre: n.p., 1905), 12–14; Armando Duval, *Reorganisação do Exército* (Rio de Janeiro: Imprensa Nacional, 1901), 53. Duval said that authorized strength was 30,100 officers and soldiers but that actual strength was 17,917.

27. MG, *Relatório . . . Mallet . . . 1902,* 21. The salary total is based on the 1897 figures because those for 1902 are not at hand, so the number should be read as suggestive rather than actual.

28. MG, *Relatório . . . Mallet . . . 1900,* Annexo B, "Leis e Decretos." These figures are based on Decreto 3573 of Jan. 23, 1900, which set the wages for the *Fabrica de Cartuchos e Artificios de Guerra.* The first-class workers were paid 8$000 a day, the fifth-class $500. I arrived at the annual figure by assuming a six-day workweek for fifty-two weeks, so the actual figures might be less because of unpaid absences.

29. Robert M. Levine, *Pernambuco in the Brazilian Federation* (Stanford, Calif.: Stanford University Press, 1978), 25.

30. J. C. Oakenfull, *Brazil (1913)* (Frome, U.K.: Butler and Tanner, 1914), 564–65. For a price index see Levine, *Pernambuco,* 189. He used 1912 as base year. From 1914 to 1937 prices climbed: with 1912 as 100, 1915 was 132; 1920, 289; 1925, 341; 1930, 243; 1935, 265; 1937, 327.

31. Oakenfull, *Brasil (1913),* 569–70. The *Jornal do Comercio* (Rio) estimated in 1913 that between 1887 and 1912 food costs had risen 671 percent; clothes, 537 percent; household goods, 611 percent; and medicines, 1,940 percent!

32. Cidade, *Síntese de Três Séculos de Literatura Militar Brasileira,* 341.

33. Cidade, "O Exército em 1889," 246.

34. On public education during the Old Republic see Jorge Nagle, *Educação e sociedade na primeira república* (São Paulo: Editora da Universidade de São Paulo, 1974).

35. MG, *Relatório . . . Mallet . . . 1900,* 105; *Relatório . . . Mallet . . . 1901,* 213.

36. MG, *Relatório . . . Mallet . . . 1901, 209–11.*

37. *Relatório . . . Mallet . . . 1900, 101–3.*

38. Nancy Stepan, *Beginnings of Brazilian Science, Oswaldo Cruz, Medical Research, and Policy, 1890–1920* (New York: Science History Publications, 1976), 55.

39. Quoted in Barbosa, *A Vida de Lima Barreto,* 135.

40. Gilberto Freyre, *Order and Progress: Brazil from Monarchy to Republic* (New York: Knopf, 1970), 179–80. In common with the noble titles of the empire these military titles were based on personal "merit." See discussion in Lilia Moritz Schwarcz, *As Barbas do Imperador: D. Pedro II, um Monarca nos Trópicos* (São Paulo: Companhia das Letras, 1998), 191–95.

41. MG, *Relatório . . . Mallet . . . 1901,* 52–62; Umberto Peregrino, *História e Projeção das Instituições Culturais do Exército* (Rio de Janeiro: Biblioteca do Exército, 1967), 58–59.

42. MG, *Relatório . . . Mallet . . . 1901, 55; Relatório . . . Mallet . . . 1902, 33;* Estevão Leitão de Carvalho, *Memórias de um soldado legalista* (Rio de Janeiro: SMG Imprensa do Exército, 1961), 1:23. Leitão said that his class, or *turma,* at Realengo, which entered Praia Vermelha in 1901, contained these 1897 veterans who wore martial-looking goatees and mustaches, as well as sergeant's stripes.

43. For a study of the affair from the perspective of Bolivia see J. Valerie Fifer, *Bolivia: Land, Location, and Politics Since 1825* (Cambridge, U.K.: Cambridge University Press, 1972), 92–134.

44. The most complete study of the Acre Crisis is Charles E. Stokes, "The Acre Revolutions, 1899–1903: A Study in Brazilian Expansion" (Ph.D. diss., Tulane University, 1974).

45. Ibid., 184–92.

46. *Folha do Norte* (Belém), Sep. 23, 1900, as quoted in Stokes, "Acre Revolutions," 197.

47. Ibid., 197–98, 242–43.

48. Consul K. K. Kenneday, quoted in ibid., 202.

49. Ibid., 317.

50. Bolivia would have benefited directly from the taxes on rubber, and it would have received 60 percent of the syndicate's profits. Bolivian leaders thought that these revenues would more than cover the country's annual budget (ibid., 322).

51. Ibid., 249.

52. Luiz Viana Filho, *A Vida do Barão do Rio Branco* (Rio de Janeiro: José Olympio Editora, 1959), 307.

53. Rio Branco to José Verissimo, Petrópolis, Feb. 16, 1903, Arquivo da Academia Brasileira de Letras, as quoted in Viana Filho, *Vida do Barão,* 332.

54. See above for a discussion of troop strength; MG, *Relatório . . . Mallet . . . 1901,* 127.

55. MG, *Relatório . . . Argollo . . . 1904,* 6–7. In 1904 two officers were members of Congress, thirty-five were state deputies or senators, and eight were municipal officials.

56. Alzira Vargas do Amaral Peixoto, *Getúlio Vargas, meu Pai* (Porto Alegre: Editora Globo, 1960), 3–5; "Getúlio Vargas," *Dicionário Histórico-Biográfico Brasileiro* (hereafter *DHBB*), 4:3437.

57. MG, *Relatório . . . Argollo . . . 1904,* 6.

58. It is noteworthy that when Paraguay threatened Mato Grosso in the 1860s, the imperial government conducted surveys to link it with the Atlantic; but after the war and the passing of danger the road project "fell into profound oblivion" (MG, *Relatório . . . Mallet . . . 1901,* 171).

59. Luiz Viana Filho, *Vida do Barão,* 344–45; Charles A. Gauld, *The Last Titan: Percival Farquhar, American Entrepreneur in Latin America* (Stanford, Calif.: Institute of Hispanic American and Luso-Brazilian Studies, 1964), 126–59. Gauld noted that Farquhar shipped some twenty thousand laborers to build the "mad Mary," as the American engineers called the railroad.

60. L. E. Elliott, *Brazil Today and Tomorrow* (New York: Macmillan, 1917), 112–13. The films also were intended to show how attractive the far interior was. Elliott agreed: "The tale of the magnificent work in the interior done by the Rondon Commission is an epic of the Brazilian interior, and one of its great merits has been the proof that this unknown country is no terrible jungle, but an open, honest country awaiting the plough" (129). There is a rich collection of the photos from these expeditions in the Rondon collection in the Biblioteca do Exército's Fort Copacabana facility. Studies of Rondon and his work would enrich the history of the Old Republic; there are several dissertations slumbering in these files.

61. The first official report on the telegraph projects is in MG, *Relatório . . . Fonseca . . . 1908,* 60–61. A list of officers who served on the telegraph commission (the Fifth Engineer Battalion) is in the *Almanak do Ministerio da Guerra para o anno de 1912* (Rio de Janeiro: Imprensa Militar, 1912), 86–87; "Cândido Rondon," *DHBB,* 4:3012–14. David H. Stauffer, "The Origin and Establishment of Brazil's Indian Service: 1889–1910" (Ph.D. diss., University of Texas, Austin, 1955); Eulália Parolini et al. "A Contribuição de Rondon para a Antropologia Brasileira," *Revista do Exército Brasileiro* 119, no. 2 (Apr.–June 1982): 7–19.

62. Oakenfull, *Brazil (1913),* 189–93. Here there is a list of stations, along with their kilowatt power and range. In 1913 Rio had 173.6 miles of telephone line, and service was about to connect it to São Paulo. But then telephone service was limited to local in-town connections in Porto Alegre, Belo Horizonte, Bahia, Manaus, Belém, and Recife. In J. C. Oakenfull, *Brazil in 1911* (Frome, U.K.: Butler and Tanner, 1912), 142–43, there is a list of the thirty-seven principal rail lines and the combined track of twenty-seven smaller ones, totaling 13,221,810 miles in operation, with another 2,329,863 then in construction. In general, these were narrow-gauge, point-to-point lines that were not networked for long-distance travel.

63. Theodore Roosevelt, *Through the Brazilian Wilderness* (New York: Charles Scribner's Sons, 1919), 333; so many spiders spun webs on the lines in the rainy season that they short-circuited it (239). Claude Lévi-Strauss, *Tristes Tropiques* (New York: Atheneum, 1968), 250–51.

64. MG, *Relatório . . . Argollo . . . 1904,* 3.

65. Ibid., 3–5.

66. E. Bradford Burns, *A Documentary History of Brazil* (New York: Knopf, 1966), 283–84.

67. In a decree reforming military education dated Apr. 14, 1890; text in Edgard Carone, *A primeira república (1889–1930) texto e contexto* (São Paulo: Difusão Européia do Livro, 1969), 249–50.

68. France and the United States experienced similar movements to establish universal military training and to reform military institutions. See Richard D. Challenger, *The French Theory of the Nation in Arms, 1866–1939* (New York: Columbia University Press, 1952); and John G. Clifford, *The Citizen Soldiers: The Plattsburg Training Camp Movement, 1913–1920* (Lexington: University Press of Kentucky, 1972). Much of the terminology used in France was taken over into the Brazilian debates.

69. Carone, *A República Velha*, 1:162.

70. MG, *Relatório . . . Argollo . . . 1905*, 4.

71. Ibid., 5.

72. Luis Mendes de Morais, *Reforma do Ensino* (Rio de Janeiro: Villas Boas, 1904), i–v. His proposed regulations for an Escola Prática do Exército were dated Mar. 7, 1904, and his introduction to his full set of proposed reforms was dated Oct. [n.d.] 1904. Mendes de Morais was minister for three weeks in 1909 under Nilo Peçanha.

Goltz's writings popularized the idea of the nation in arms among Brazilian military thinkers. For him military strength reflected a nation's cultural level, the citizen and soldier were synonymous, and the army bound citizenry and state together. For a discussion of his writings and influence on South American armies see Frederick M. Nunn, *Yesterday's Soldiers: European Military Professionalism in South America, 1890–1940* (Lincoln: University of Nebraska Press, 1983), 82–85.

73. Mendes de Morais, *Reforma do Ensino*, vii.

74. MG, *Relatório . . . Argollo . . . 1905*, 5.

75. Ibid., 6.

76. Ibid., 4.

77. Capt. Dr. Liberato Bittencourt, "Pelo soldado Brazileiro," *Revista Academia Militar* 1, no. 9 (Jan. 27, 1904): 455–61. Copy in Centro de Documentação do Exército (hereafter CDOC-EX), Brasília.

78. Motta, *Formação do Oficial*, 230–40; 258 n. 33; 263 n. 72; Leitão de Carvalho, *Memórias*, 1:25–27.

79. Carone, *A República Velha*, 2:198–207. For analysis of the cultural changes of the era see Jeffrey D. Needell, *A Tropical Belle Epoque: Elite Culture and Society in Turn-of-the-Century Rio de Janeiro* (Cambridge, U.K.: Cambridge University Press, 1987).

80. Leitão de Carvalho, *Memórias*, 1:23–30; Carone, *A República Velha*, 2:208–9. In 1903 Gen. of Division Olympio da Silveira had commanded the First Military District (Amazonas and Pará) during the Acre crisis and oversaw the occupation of the territory, and Brig. Gen. Silva Travassos headed the Third in Bahia. MG, *Relatório . . . Argollo . . . 1903*, 12. On the positivist role see Robert G. Nachman, "Positivism and Revolution in Brazil's First Republic: The 1904 Revolt," *The Americas* 34, no. 1 (July 1977): 20–39.

81. Hermes held this post only briefly, from Sep. 12 to Dec. 24, 1904. His action in support of the government was rewarded by promotion to major general in July 1905. He had just turned fifty in May. Hermes da Fonseca Filho, *Marechal Hermes: Dados para uma biografia* (Rio de Janeiro: n.p., 1961), 56–57.

82. Carone, *A República Velha*, 2:208–10; Glauco Carneiro, *Historia da Revoluções Brasileiras* (Rio de Janeiro: Edições O Cruzeiro, 1965), 1:136–50; Leitão de Carvalho, *Memórias*, 1:41–48.

83. Innocêncio Serzedello Corrêa, *A revisão constitucional* (Rio: Litho-Typographia, 1904), 3, 16, as quoted in Nachman, "Positivism and Revolution," 35.

84. Nachman, "Positivism and Revolution," 36. José Murilio de Carvalho emphasizes the social-economic aspects of the uprising in the streets in *Os Bestializados: O Rio de Janeiro e a República que não foi* (São Paulo: Companhia das Letras, 1987), 91–139.

85. The 1904 revolt's cast of supporting actors included officers who would play major roles in coming years. Several would become minister of war. On the legalist side there were Hermes da Fonseca (1906–8), José Caetano de Faria (1914–18), José Fernandes Leite de Castro (1930–32), and João Gomes Ribeiro Filho (1935–36). Among the rebel students was nineteen-year-old Eurico Gaspar Dutra (1936–45), who was wounded and who, after the longest term as minister in army history, joined Hermes as the second general to be elected president (1946–50). Estevão Leitão de Carvalho had the distinction of being one of three alferes and nine student officers who refused to rebel, whereas his future colleague in the reform movement of the next decade, Bertoldo Klinger, joined the rebels. Indeed, the list of military students nearly corresponds to the list of generals, colonels, and lieutenant colonels who led the army in the 1930s.

86. MG, *Relatório . . . Argollo . . . 1906*, 14–16.

87. Motta, *Formação do Oficial*, 288–97. For a helpful discussion of bachurelism see Emilia Viotti da Costa, *The Brazilian Empire: Myths and Histories* (Chicago, Ill.: University of Chicago Press, 1985), 196–98. Viotti da Costa observed that "the armed forces seemed to be the only group capable of 'modernizing' the country without popular mobilization" (198).

88. MG, *Relatório . . . Argollo . . . 1905*, 17. This first group included: Capt. Emilo Sarmento, Lt. Constantino Deschamps Cavalcante (both infantry); Lt. Cassiano da Silveira Mello Mattos, 2d Lt. Bento Marinho Alves, 2d Lt. Manoel Bourgard de Castro e Silva (both artillery); and Lt. Estellita Augusto Werner (cavalry).

89. Motta, *Formação de Oficial*, 296.

90. See Cidade, *Síntese de Três Séculos de Literature Militar Brasileira*, 338.

91. The Fourth District comprised, in addition to the capital district, the states of Rio de Janeiro, Espirito Santo, Minas Gerais, and Goiás.

92. On Hermes see Cidade, "Marechal Hermes Rodrigues da Fonseca," 229–42; Umberto Peregrino, "Significação do Marechal Hermes," in Peregrino, *Euclides da Cunha e Outros Estudos* (Rio de Janeiro: Récord Editora, 1968), 111–48; Fonseca Filho, *Marechal Hermes*, 371–80.

93. General de Divisão Hermes Rodrigues da Fonseca (Commander Fourth Military District) to General Francisco Antônio Rodrigues Sales (Chief of General Staff), n.p., Feb. 16, 1906, no. 3, 418: "Relatório das manobras de 1905 nos Campos de Santa Cruz," in *Primórdios da organização da defesa nacional*, ed. Mario Hermes da Fonseca and Ildefonso Escobar (Rio de Janeiro: Tipografia Glória, Pinho, & Manes, 1943), 43–45. General Hermes ended his report by saying that he had described "much that we still need, to have in this district an army corps ready to be mobilized from one moment to the next."

94. See Frank D. McCann, "The Nation in Arms: Obligatory Military Service During the Old Republic," in *Essays Concerning the Socioeconomic History of Brazil and*

Portuguese India, ed. Dauril Alden and Warren Dean (Gainesville: University Press of Florida, 1977), 211–43.

95. Alfonso Celso, *Porque me Ufano do Meu Paiz* (Rio de Janeiro: Livaria Garnier, 1900), 197–98. For a discussion of the role of intellectuals in this developing nationalism see E. Bradford Burns, *Nationalism in Brazil; a Historical Survey* (New York: Praeger, 1968), 51–71; see also E. Bradford Burns, *A History of Brazil* (New York: Columbia University Press, 1970), 267–71; for a summary account of the period see Pedro Calmon, *História do Brasil* (Rio de Janeiro: José Olympio Editora, 1959), 6:2092–2112.

96. Euclides da Cunha, *Rebellion,* 481. For an excellent discussion of da Cunha's thought see Thomas E. Skidmore, *Black into White: Race and Nationality in Brazilian Thought* (New York: Oxford University Press, 1974), 103–9.

97. "Ao mesmo tempo em que o Barão afastava as possibilidades de conflito armado com as demais potências, eliminando . . . as questões de fronteiras, espalhava-se no Brasil um espirito não propriamente de belicosidade, mas de sobranceria" (Afonso Arinos de Melo Franco, *Um estadista da república, Afranio de Melo Franco e seu tempo,* vol. 2, *Fase nacional* [Rio de Janeiro: José Olympio Editora, 1955], 625–26). See also E. Bradford Burns, *The Unwritten Alliance: Rio-Branco and Brazilian-American Relations* (New York: Columbia University Press, 1966).

98. MG, *Relatório . . . Cantuaria . . . 1898,* 20; *Relatório . . . Mallet . . . 1900,* 8; *Relatório . . . Argollo . . . 1904,* 27.

99. Hermes and Escobar, *Primórdios,* 17–19, photographs between 176 and 177; Calmon, *Historia,* 6:2157. Calmon noted that "no tiro 7, do Rio, se alistaram personalidades ilustres, que o povo, admirado, via desfilar, fuzil ao ombro, na canícula, enèrgicamente." The cost of Tiro activities indicated that its members were not poor or working class. At Sunday shoots they spent about 4$500 on shells, which, added to their monthly dues of 5$000, meant that Tiro cost them 23$000 a month, 276$000 a year, plus the expense of their uniforms, 19$800. Figures are from Hermes and Escobar, *Primórdias,* 18; and MG, *Relatório . . . Caetano de Faria . . . 1917,* Annex B, 43.

100. The shifting nature of civil-military relations can be seen here. The early congressional supporters of obligatory service lottery were James Darcy of Rio Grande do Sul and Carlos Peixoto Filho of Minas Gerais, leaders of the so-called kindergarten faction that was challenging Senator José Gomes Pinheiro Machado's dominance of the government. The nature of Brazilian politics was such that by mid-1909 these men would be opposing Hermes da Fonseca's candidacy for the presidency on grounds of Caesarism, whereas Pinheiro Machado would be supporting it. See Bello, *History of Modern Brazil,* 202–7; Carone, *A República Velha,* 2:229–36; Love, *Rio Grande do Sul,* 136–64.

101. Hermes and Escobar, *Primórdios,* 71–76.

102. Afonso Pena to Mar. Hermes da Fonseca, Petrópolis, Feb. 24, 1908, in Hermes and Escobar, *Primórdios,* 54.

103. Carone, *A República Velha,* 2:228.

104. MG, *Relatório . . . Fonseca . . . 1907,* 3–6.

105. Ibid., 7.

106. Ibid., 11–12.

107. MG, *Relatório . . . Fonseca . . . 1908,* 26–27; Capt. Francisco Ruas Santos, "Resumo Histórico, Periodo de Outubro de 1896 a Dezembro de 1950," Estado-Maior do Exército, Rio de Janeiro, Nov. 5, 1951, 4–5, CDOC-EX, Brasília.

108. The Brazilians were not alone in having difficulty grafting a general staff onto their army; in the same period the U.S. Army was experiencing a similar problem. Major Marc B. Powe (U.S.A.), "A Great Debate, The American General Staff (1903–16)," *Military Review* 55, no. 4 (Apr. 1976): 71–89. James L. Abrahamson analyzed the struggle to impose the American staff onto that army's bureau structure in *American Arms for a New Century: The Making of a Great Military Power* (New York: Free Press, 1981), 66–67, 123–24, 167–68.

109. MG, *Relatório . . . José Bernardino Bormann . . . 1910,* 23–41.

110. MG, *Relatório . . . Bormann . . . 1910,* 79.

111. Fonseca Filho, *Marechal Hermes,* 75–79; Leitão de Carvalho, *Memórias,* 1:102, 143; Manuel Domingos Neto, "L'Influence Etrangere dans La Modernization de L'Armee Bresilienne (1889–1930)" (Paris: Thése presentée a' l'Institut des Hautes Etudes de l'Amérique Latine, Université de Paris III, pour l'obtention du Doctorat IIIe'me Cycles, 1979), 208.

The German mission was to be composed of twenty to thirty officers under General (Baron) Friedrich Colmar von der Goltz, a well-known military writer *(La Nation Armée)* and reorganizer of the Turkish army. See Fonseca Filho, *Marechal Hermes,* 122. On German experience in Turkey see Ulrich Trumpener, *Germany and the Ottoman Empire, 1914–1918* (Princeton, N.J.: Princeton University Press, 1968). On the export of European military ideas and practices see Nunn, *Yesterday's Soldiers.*

112. Leitão de Carvalho, *Memórias,* 1:102.

113. Joseph L. Love, *São Paulo in the Brazilian Federation, 1889–1937* (Stanford, Calif.: Stanford University Press, 1980), 168–71.

114. The U.S. Army military attaché files for Brazil were destroyed in 1925 and 1926 to make space at the War College, but the index cards for 1903 to 1916 with document summaries survived. See Index Cards, "Coastal Defenses—Brazil," no. 5978, War College Division, Old Navy and Army Branch, NA. See entries for May 17, 1912; Dec. 31, 1912; and Jan. 4, 1913. For a discussion see Frank D. McCann, "Influencia Estrangeira no Exército Brasileiro," *A Defesa Nacional* (hereafter *ADN*), Jan.-Feb. 1985, 86–87.

115. Domingos Neto, "L'Influence Etrangere" 212.

116. Ibid. Fleury de Barros apparently had political connections. In 1900, while a lieutenant in the old general staff corps, he found time to serve as a deputy in the Rio de Janeiro state legislature. *Almanac do Exército, 1900,* 21. Fonseca Filho, *Marechal Hermes,* 126, commented that Brazilian journalist Agenor de Carvoliva accompanied Hermes. His articles appeared in the *Jornal do Brasil* (Rio).

117. His reports cited in Domingo Neto, "L'Influence Etrangere." Fleury de Barros was later made military attaché in Paris.

118. Ibid., 213.

119. Fonseca Filho, *Marechal Hermes,* 124. Hermes' son was sensitive to the implication that the marshal had been won over in questionable fashion. In his account he quoted from French newspapers to the effect that by accepting German instructors and excluding the French ones from São Paulo, the Brazilian govern-

ment was insulting France. He asserted that the compliments came "after" Hermes had declared his position (see 124–25).

120. Nilo Peçanha, Rio de Janeiro, May 3, 1910, in Câmara dos Deputados, *Mensagens Presidenciais, 1890–1910,* 700.

121. For the French-German competition see Christopher Leuchars, "Brazilian Foreign Policy and the Great Powers, 1912–1930" (D. Phil. diss., St. Antony's College, Oxford University, 1983).

122. Domingos Neto, "L'Influence Etrangere," 214–15.

123. Le capitaine d'artillerie Brevete Demars a M. le Ministre de la Guerre (Etat-Major de l'Armée 2è Bureau), Paris, Oct. 19, 1911, "Compte-Rendu de la Visite du Senateur Antônio Azeredo a Paris en 1911," in ibid., Appendix, i–vii.

124. Love, *São Paulo,* 195, 202.

125. See Domingo Neto, "L'Influence Etrangere." See note 123, Appendix, iv–v.

126. P. C. Knox (Acting Secretary of State) to Secretary of War, Washington, Oct. 14, 1911, 832.20/1; and Edwin Morgan (U.S. Ambassador), Rio, Nov. 13, 1917, #1052, 832.20/16, both NA Microfilm "Brazil 1910–29," Roll 17; Capt. LeVert Coleman, Rio, Dec. 31, 1912, summary 31 and Jan. 4, 1913, summary 29, in Index of War College materials, War College Division, Old Navy and Army Branch, NA.

127. Cidade, *Síntese de Três Séculos de Literatura Militar Brasileira,* 341 (emphasis added). Cidade, then a young aspirante, had suggested publishing the *Revista* and would later work with the German-trained group in getting out *A Defesa Nacional.*

CHAPTER 3

1. Bello, *A History of Modern Brazil,* 204–15; Raymundo Faoro, *Os Donos do Poder, Formação do Patronato Político Brasileiro,* 2d ed.(São Paulo: Ed. Globo/Ed. Univ. de São Paulo, 1975), 593–602; Luiz Viana Filho, *A Vida de Rui Barbosa,* 7th ed. (São Paulo: Livraria Martins Editora, 1965), 329–39; Love, *São Paulo,* 112–15.Sertório de Castro, *A República que a Revolução Destruiu* (1932; reprint, Brasília: Editora Universidade de Brasília, 1982),157–75; Murilo de Carvalho, "As Forças Armadas na Primeira República: O Poder Desestablizador," 218–20.

2. See Wallace, "Identity and the Nature of Revolution," 172–86.

3. Vespasiano D'Albuquerque to Fernando Setembrino de Carvalho, Rio, Mar. 5, 1914 (teleg), Arquivo de F. Setembrino de Carvalho 14.03.05/10, CPDOC-Rio.

4. Melo Franco, *Um estadista da república,* 2:702. The career data was drawn from *Almanak . . . 1912* (Rio de Janeiro: Imprensa Militar, 1912), 7–16, 21–24, 57–60,187–95, 321; Combat Colonels list, 17–18; *Almanak do Ministerio da Guerra para o anno de 1914* (Rio de Janeiro: Imprensa Militar, 1914), 9–17, 27–29, 65, 140, 205–9; Combat Colonels list, 21–22. In 1912 the states with officers as governors were Sergipe, Pernambuco, and Goiás; in 1914 they were Sergipe, Pernambuco, Alagoas, and Ceará. In 1912 officers were senators from Amazonas, Piauí, Ceará, Paraíba, Santa Catarina, and Federal District; but in 1914, the list was reduced to Amazonas and Santa Catarina. In 1912 officers served as federal deputies from Rio Grande do Sul, Minas Gerais, Federal District, Goiás, and two from Ceará; in 1914 the list had shrunk to Rio Grande do Sul, Goiás, and two other states that I was unable to identify.

5. The question here centers on what is old and new about the military's role in Brazil prior to 1964. Alfred Stepan's "new professionalism" could easily be applied to the officer corps of this era; see his *Authoritarian Brazil: Origins, Policies, and Future* (New Haven, Conn.:Yale University Press, 1973). See also Frank D. McCann,"Origins of the 'New Professionalism' of the Brazilian Military," *Journal of Interamerican Studies and World Affairs* 21, no. 4 (Nov. 1979), 505–22.

6. Edmar Morel, *A Revolta da Chibata,* 3d ed. (Rio de Janeiro: Ed. Graal, 1979), 63–74.

7. Comment on the sailors' revolt is based on Fonseca Filho, *Marechal Hermes,* 141–48; for the events in Portugal see Douglas L. Wheeler, *Republican Portugal: A Political History, 1910–1926* (Madison: University of Wisconsin Press, 1978), 32–61.

8. Fonseca Filho, *Marechal Hermes,* 141.

9. Brazilian Army Officers project (hereafter cited as BAO) no. 120. The BAO consists of biographical career data, compiled by the author, on 554 general officers. Data are drawn largely from the army's annual *Almanac.*

10. Fonseca Filho, *Marechal Hermes,* 153. Edmar Morel quoted João Candido, who led the sailors' revolt on the *Minas Gerais,* as saying that Gregorio do Nascimento became a police agent *(tira);* see Morel, *Revolta da Chibata,* 201.

11. MG, *Relatório . . . Emygdio Dantas Barreto . . . 1911,* 5; strength figures are from MG, *Almanak do Ministerio da Guerra para o anno de 1915* (Rio de Janeiro: Imprensa Militar, 1915), 658; Alfredo Souto Malan, *Uma Escolha, Um Destino: Vida do Gen. Malan d'Angrogne* (Rio de Janeiro: Biblioteca do Exército, 1977), 129.

12. Carone, *A República Velha,* 2:272.

13. Ibid., 271; Fonseca Filho, *Marechal Hermes,* 161–63.

14. *Correio da Manhã* (Rio), Dec. 30, 1911, quoted in Carone, *A República Velha,* 2:284.

15. List of retired officers in MG, *Almanak . . . 1914,* 465–75.

16. The foregoing is based on a comparison of MG, *Almanak . . . 1912,* 8–16, 21–24, 57–61, 121–27, 187–98, with MG, *Almanak . . . 1914,* 465–75. Table 3.1 is not all inclusive but provides enough examples to illustrate the point.

17. Carone, *A República Velha,* 2:284.

18. BAO 89.

19. Herculano Teixeira d'Assumpção,"Atividades Militares em Belo Horizonte" (typescript), Dec. 12, 1947, prepared for Estado-Maior do Exército, CDOC-EX, Brasília, 24.

20. The situation in Ceará that led to federal intervention has been examined from a local perspective by Ralph Della Cava, *Miracle at Joaseiro* (New York: Columbia University Press, 1970); for a national viewpoint see Carone, *A República Velha,* 2:277–93.

21. Della Cava, *Miracle,* 132.

22. Carone, *A República Velha,* 2:291.

23. MG, *Almanak . . . 1914,* 10–17. And because Hermes expanded the Promotions Board with his men in 1912–13, he extended his reach down to the lower officer ranks; see MG, *Almanak . . . 1914,* 590.

24. On combining the regions see MG, *Relatório . . . Vespasiano Gonçalves d'Albuquerque e Silva . . . 1914,* 76.

25. His instructions were in the following telegrams:Vespasiano Gonçalves d'Albuquerque e Silva to F. Setembrino de Carvalho, Rio, Feb. 16, 1914, 14.02.16; Feb. 18, 1914, 14.02.18/2; Feb. 19, 1914, 14.02.19/2, all Arquivo Fernando Setembrino de Carvalho (hereafter AFSC), Centro de Pesquisa e Documentação de História Contemporânea do Brasil, Fundação Getúlio Vargas, Rio de Janeiro (hereafter CPDOC-Rio).

26. Della Cava, *Miracle,* 153.

27. F. Setembrino de Carvalho, "Antes, Durante, Depois" (typescript), n.p., n.d., 14.00.00/1, AFSC, CPDOC-Rio. He condemned Rabelista atrocities while ignoring similar ones by their opponents. Della Cava noted that Padre Cícero bitterly denounced "brutalities inflicted by *cangaceiros* in Floro's pay (frequently against *cangaceiros* employed by the *rabelistas*)." See Della Cava, *Miracle, Juazeiro* 155.

28. Rabelo denounced a conspiracy in a telegram to Hermes, Fortaleza, Feb. 20, 1914, 14.01.20/4: he objected to interventions in state affairs in telegrams to Setembrino, Fortaleza, Feb. 24, 1914, 14.10.24/14 and Feb. 26, 1914, 14.02.26/3, all AFSC, CPDOC.

29. Sebastiao do Rego Barros to F[ernando] S[etembrino de] C[arvalho], Rio, Feb. 25, 1914, 14.02.25/11, AFSC, CPDOC-Rio.

30. Vespasiano Gonçalves d'Albuquerque e Silva to FSC, Rio, Feb. 28, 1914, 14.02.28/7; Feb. 28, 1914, 14.02.28/8; Mar. 3, 1914, 14.03.01/3; [name missing] to FSC, Rio, Mar. 3, 1914, 14.03.02/6, AFSC, CPDOC-Rio.

31. *O Estado de São Paulo,* Mar. 1, 1914, quoted in Carone, *A República Velha,* 2:290.

32. Ibid., 290–92;Vespasiano d'Albuquerque to FSC, Rio, Mar. 5, 1914, 14.03.05/10, AFSC, CPDOC-Rio; Robert A. Hayes, "The Military Club and National Politics in Brazil," in *Perspectives on Armed Politics in Brazil,* ed. Henry A. Keith and Robert A. Hayes (Tempe: Arizona State University Press, 1976), 150.

33. Deputy Agapio Santos to Manuel Satiro, Rio, Mar. 6, 1914, 14.03.05/9; Vespasiano d'Albuquerque to FSC, Mar. 5, 1914, 14.03.05/10; Pamplona [rest of name missing] to FSC, Rio, Mar. 3, 1914, 14.03.07/5, AFSC, CPDOC-Rio. Two active-list generals and a full colonel were among the arrested officers—Maj. Gen. Gregorio Thaumaturgo de Azevedo, who had been assistant chief of the general staff from Nov. 29, 1911, to Mar. 21, 1912, and was without assignment during 1914; Brevet Maj. Gen. Feliciano Mendes de Morais, who from Nov. 29, 1911, was listed as commander of the Fifth Strategic Brigade, headquartered at Aquidauana, Mato Grosso; and Col. Coriolano de Carvalho e Silva, listed as officer of Fourth Engineers Battalion, Margem do Taquary, Rio Grande do Sul. All had taken part in the agitation of previous days in Rio. The latter two were obviously not with their units. MG, *Almanak . . . 1914,* 11–12, 19, 612, 615.

34. Fonseca Filho, *Marechal Hermes,* 219. Hermes' own view was that "[t]he Government had been so cautious in the use of the measures which the state of siege authorized that, since the day of its declaration until today (May 3, 1914), the normal life of the city was not interrupted. . . . Were it not for the knowledge of the decree's existence . . . the population of this great Capital would not have perceived that the constitutional guarantees were suspended" (Hermes R. Fonseca's 1914 report to Congress, Câmara dos Deputados, *Mensagens Presidenciais, 1910–1914* [1921; reprint, Brasilia: Câmara dos Deputados, 1978], 313).

35. Hermes R. da Fonseca to FSC, Rio, Mar. 6, 1914, 14.03.06/7, two telegrams, AFSC, CPDOC-Rio.

36. Herculano de Freitas (Minister of Interior) to FSC, Rio, Mar. 9, 1914, 14.03.09/3; Marcos Franco Rabelo to FSC, Rio, Mar. 16, 1914, 14.03.16/2, AFSC, CPDOC-Rio. The last contains his instructions as interventor.

37. Pinheiro Machado to FSC, Rio, Apr. 12, 1914, 14.04.12/2, AFSC, CPDOC-Rio.

38. FSC, Decreto (incomplete), June (2?), 1914, 14.06.02?/1; Padre Cicero to FSC, Juazeiro, Mar. 2, 1914, 14.05.02, AFSC, CPDOC-Rio.

39. See Maurício Vinhas de Queiroz, *Messianismo e Conflicto Social: A Guerra Sertaneja do Contestado, 1912–1916)* (São Paulo: Editora Atica, 1977); Duglas Teixeira Monteiro, *Os Errantes do Novo Seculo, Um estudo sobre o surto Milenarista do Contestado* (São Paulo: Livraria Duas Cidades, 1974); Queiroz, *Messianismo no Brasil;* Todd A. Diacon, *Millenarian Vision, Capitalist Reality: Brazil's Contestado Rebellion, 1912–1916* (Durham, N.C.: Duke University Press, 1991).

40. F. Setembrino de Carvalho, *Relatório apresentado ao General de Divisão José Caetano de Faria, Ministro de Guerra pelo . . . Commandante das Forças em operações de guerra no Contestado, 1915* (Rio de Janeiro: Imprensa Militar, 1916), 3. Copy in Arquivo do Exército, Rio de Janeiro. Hereafter cited as FSC, *Relatório . . . Contestado.*

41. Herculano Teixeira d'Assumpção, *A Campanha do Contestado,* 2 vols. (Belo Horizonte: Imprensa Oficial do Estado de Minas Gerais, 1917), 1:72–73. The results of the 1938 nationalization can be seen clearly in cemeteries in southern Brazil; for example, in the cemetery in Gramado, RGS, the graves to the left of the main path are pre-1938 and have inscriptions in German, and those to the right are post-1938 and are in Portuguese, even though the family names are German.

42. Nilson Thomé, *Trem de Ferro, A Ferrovia no Contestado,* 1st ed.(Caçador, Santa Catarina: Impresora Universal, 1980), 100. Duglas Teixeira Monteiro speculated that the introduction of so many workers from port cities that had been experiencing labor disputes may have further stirred the agitated scene; he called attention to the violent repression of railroad workers, who rebelled against nonpayment of wages. See Teixeira Monteiro, *Os Errantes do Novo Seculo,* 44.

43. Farquhar's activities and point of view are presented in Gauld, *The Last Titan,* 160–79. Gauld says Farquhar built the railroad straight for speed efficiency, but then he throws an extremely benign light on the "titan." There are photos of the railway, the lumber mills, and the "security force" and army personalities in Fundação Roberto Marinho, *Contestado* (Rio de Janeiro: Ed. Index, 1987).

44. Vinhas de Queiroz, *Messianismo e Conflicto Social,* 73.

45. Teixeira Monteiro, *Os Errantes do Novo Seculo,* 31.

46. Wallace, "Identity and the Nature of Revolution," 172–86.

47. The idea of monarchy in the Contestado is interesting. From Duglas Monteiro's analysis and the theory of Wallace on renovation movements it is clear that monarchy here did not mean restoration of the Braganças but renewal of life and salvation from the oppression of the corrupt republic. The core fact in the idea of a monarchial movement in the Contestado was the fanciful crowning of a "king of the feast," which was traditional in rural Brazilian festivals. Although more common during the *Folia do Divino* (feast of the Holy Spirit), it was not unknown as part of

Bom-Jesus. Usually a priest crowned the "king" in church. The "king" was in fact a sponsor of the event, whose duty was to see that it was held properly. At Taquaruçu, José Maria took the priest's role and crowned a local fazendeiro and supplier of cattle to the "monk's" followers, Manuel Alves de Assunção Rocha. On Aug. 5, 1914, at the redoubt of Taquaruçu, this "emperor" of the constitutional monarchy of the Brazilian-South signed a "Letter to the Nation," pledging himself to a thirty–item program of such sophistication that it is doubtful that he composed it. Because the "crowning" associated with the *Folia do Divino* was widely known, perhaps the "letter" was an attempt to give credibility to the monarchial idea? For the thirty items see Luís da Câmara Cascudo, *Dicionário do Folclore Brasileiro* (Rio de Janeiro: Instituto Nacional do Livro, 1962), 486–87. This aspect of the affair could use further clarification. See Vinhas de Queiroz, *Messianismo e Conflicto Social,* 88. Moreover, in the rustic Catholicism of the rural south, *monarquia* was suggestive of the coming of the millennium, of Christ's kingdom on earth. Their struggle took on the aspect of fighting the forces of evil, of the anti-Christ, so that they could secure salvation among the blessed hosts. See Marco Antônio da Silva Mello and Arno Vogel, "Monarquia Contra República: A ideologia da terra e o paradigma do milênio na 'guerra santa' do Contestado," *Estudos Históricos* 2, no. 4 (1989): 190–213.

48. Col. (Inf.) Alcibíades Miranda, *Contestado* (Curitiba: Lítero-Técnica, 1987), 31–38. Col. Miranda served in the campaign in the Tenth Batt. of the Fourth Inf. Reg. and later in the mopping up phase under Colonel Pyrrho. His manuscript, which is clear and exact on military operations, was completed in 1939, but publication was delayed until 1987, so studies before that date did not have the benefit of it.

49. Apparently he deserted from one of the two, maybe even from both. Vinhas de Queiroz in one place says it was the army and in another the state police (see *Messianismo e Conflicto Social,* 79, 103). Of course, he could have been a double deserter, as the state police often attracted former army men with higher pay and better uniforms.

50. Ibid., 109–110. 51. Ibid., 117.

52. Ibid., 119. 53. Ibid., 122.

54. FSC, *Relatório . . . Contestado,* 12. 55. BAO no. 99.

56. BAO no. 147. "Sezefredo dos Passos," *DHBB,* 3:2624–25; there is a photo of him. He would become minister of war in the 1920s (see Chap. 6).

57. Lt. Col. Duarte de Alleluia Pires to Brig. Gen. Alberto Ferreira de Abreu, Espinilho, Feb. 10, 1914 (teleg.) in FSC, *Relatóro . . . Contestado,* 12–13; Vinhas de Queiroz, *Messianismo e Conflicto Social,* 129–31.

58. Dermeval Peixoto, *Campanha do Contestado—Episódios e Impressões* (Rio de Janeiro: 2° Milheiro, 1916), 160.

59. For Alleluia Pires see MG, *Almanak . . . 1915,* 213, 495; for Sezefredo dos Passos see note 56 above. On his wound see FSC, *Relatório . . . Contestado,* Annexo 23, 255.

60. MG, *Almanak . . . 1914,* 14, 611; BAO no. 102. At Canudos the then Major Mesquita commanded the Ninth Infantry Battalion from Bahia. He was mentioned frequently in the after-action reports in MG, *Relatório . . . Cantuaria . . . 1898,* Annexo A. In the South Mesquita replaced Abreu as commander of the Second Strategic Brigade, headquartered in Curitiba, which post the latter had accumulated with that of inspector general (commander) of the Eleventh Military Region.

61. Abreu thought that because the sertanejos' basic tactic was to close and use their machetes, if police had known how to use bayonets, they would have carried the day.

62. The foregoing is based on Abreu's 1914 report, quoted at length in FSC, *Relatório . . . Contestado,* 30–37.

63. *O Estado de São Paulo,* São Paulo, Jan. 4, 1915, 1. He was interviewed in Rio Grande do Sul returning from the Contestado. He believed that the affair was the result of the political maneuvering of local politicians.

64. This event involving Matos Costa occurred at Santo Antonio do Madeira (modern Porto Velho, Rondonia); see Morel, *Revolta da Chibata,* 172–75.

65. Vinhas de Queiroz, *Messianismo e Conflicto Social,* 160–62. It is possible that if the government had accepted responsibility for Taquaruçu, paid indemnity to those who had lost relatives, and provided land to the dispossessed, it might have avoided further bloodshed.

66. FSC, *Relatório . . . Contestado,* 22. Matos Costa's behavior here is all the more interesting considering that he was not above using violence. At Canudos, where he served with the Twenty-ninth Infantry, he was cited for being "untiring" in killing the *jagunços* and endangering his own life by throwing dynamite bombs; Col. João Cesar Sampaio (CO Sixth Brigade) to Brig. Gen. Carlos Eugenio de Andrade Guimarães (CO Second Column), Canudos Camp, Oct. 5, 1897, MG, *Relatório . . . Cantuaria . . . 1898,* Annexo A, "Forças em Operações na Bahia," 145. In Acre in 1910, while delivering prisoners from the sailors' rebellion, he reportedly shot several to maintain discipline over the others; see Morel, *Revolta da Chibata,* 175.

67. Vinhas de Queiroz, *Messianismo e Conflicto Social,* 164.

68. The full text of the sign sheds some light on the deep frustration the rebels felt at having the government seemingly desert them in favor of foreigners: "We were in Taquaruçu attending to our devotion and not killing nor robbing, Hermes cowardly sent his forces to bombard us wherein they killed women and children therefore the cause of all this is the bandido Hermes and therefore we want the law of God which is the monarchy. The government of the Republic drives out the Brazilian Sons from the lands that belong to the nation and sells [them] to the foreigner, we now are disposed to make our rights prevail." [Translation attempts to capture the tone of the rebels' expression.] d'Assumpção, *Campanha do Contestado,* 1:245. See also Dermeval Peixoto, *Campanha do Contestado,* 74.

69. d'Assumpção, *Campanha do Contestado,* 1:245. The Portuguese read: "Nois não tem direito de terras tudo é para as gentes da Oropa." This corruption of Europa was common in Rio Grande do Sul in that era, see Editôra Globo, *Vocabulário Sul-Rio-Grandense* (Porto Alegre: Editôra Globo, 1964), 327.

70. Vinhas de Queiroz, *Messianismo e Conflicto Social,* 168–73.

71. Ibid., 177–78.

72. FSC, *Relatório . . . Contestado,* 28–30.

73. Vespasiano de Albuquerque to Setembrino de Carvalho, Rio, Oct. 26, 1914, AFSC, CPDOC.

74. David L. Wood, "Abortive Panacea: Brazilian Military Settlements, 1850 to 1913" (Ph.D. diss., University of Utah, 1972).

75. Initially, too, he referred to the settlements as *aldeias,* a term for village (usually a rustic, poor one, often of native people and/or mestiços) that in Setembrino's *Riograndense* parlance could also mean the houses of soldiers' families located around a barracks. He dropped this relatively nonthreatening term for the more warlike redoubt *(reduto).* Ironically, *reduto* can also mean a place of refuge. The labels, of course, have importance because the army used terminology that aided soldiers to think of their fellow countrymen as fierce, treacherous enemies, whereas the sertanejos employed terms that helped them to resist.

76. FSC to Vespasiano de Carvalho, n.p., Nov. 20, 1914, in *Relatório . . . Contestado,* 78.

77. Ibid., 39–40; Vespasiano de Albuquerque to FSC, Rio, Sep. 23, 27, 1914, AFSC, CPDOC.

78. Dr. Hermogeneo Pereira de Queiroz e Silva, Curitiba, May 18, 1915, in appendix to FSC, *Relatório . . . Contestado,* 329.

79. Ibid., 48–49; career data in *Almanaque do Exército, 1914,* 174; Editorial, *ADN,* Apr. 10, 1915, 197–98.

80. Gen. Setembrino de Carvalho, "General Headquarters of the Operations Forces," Sep. 26, 1914, as in his *Relatório.*

81. Ibid., 50–51. The Tenth Infantry Regiment was from Porto Alegre; the Fifty-sixth Light Infantry Battalion's home barracks was in the old military school at Praia Vermelha in Rio; the Fifty-eighth Light Infantry was from Niterói; the combined elements of the Fourth, Fifth, and Sixth Cavalry Regiments were from the Missões region towns of São Nicolão, São Luiz, and São Borja, in Rio Grande do Sul. See listing of unit stations *(paradas)* in MG, *Almanak . . . 1914,* 617–18. For an interesting discussion of Bley Netto's economic and *compadrío* relations in the region see Diacon, *Millenarian Vision,* 17, 38. There are pay lists of the civilian scouts in "Relação dos civis empregados com declarações dos vencimentos, Forças em Operação no Contestado (F.O.C.), Caixa 12a, Arquivo do Exército—Rio.

82. Staff Article, "Uma mobilisação," *ADN,* Aug. 10, 1914, 370.

83. Editorial, *ADN,* Oct. 10, 1914, 1–2. The most up-to-date analysis of the causes of the insurgency is Diacon, *Millenarian Vision.*

84. Francisco de Paula Cidade, "Os Fanáticos, Liame Historico," *ADN,* Oct. 10, 1914, 13.

85. A Second Sergeant (of the Forty-third Battalion of the Fifteenth Infantry Regiment, who was with Capt. Potyguara's column, maintained in a letter to his daughter (June 17, 1915) that the "fanáticos" dug up army and civilian scout cadavers to cut their throats in the belief that doing so would prevent their resurrection on the Last Day; see Themistocles Cavalcanti de Queiroz, "A Luta no Contestado," *Revista do Clube Militar* 31, no. 152 (1957): 49–57.

86. Cidade, "Os Fanáticos," 13–14.

87. FSC, *Relatório . . . Contestado,* 60–67. In 1914 Colonel Socrates was a federal deputy from Goiás; MG, *Almanak . . . 1914,* 209. At least two of the officers involved in this round of fighting became generals. Aspirante Henrique Teixeira Lott (BAO no. 262; *DHBB,* 3:1937–43) led a platoon of the Twelfth, and Major Fernando de Medeiros (BAO no. 175) commanded the Fifty-sixth Light Infantry. The latter

arrived well armed; see Vespasiano de Albuquerque to FSC, Rio, Sep. 12, 1914, AFSC, CPDOC.

88. FSC to Col. Felipe Schmidt, n.p., Nov. n.d., 1914, Annex 32 to FSC, *Relatório . . . Contestado,* 334–36.

89. MG, *Almanak . . . 1914,* 21–22. Schmidt was listed as no. 10 and Setembrino as no. 41.

90. FSC to Vespasiano de Albuquerque, n.p., Nov. 20, 1914, quoted in *Relatório . . . Contestado,* 79–80. On the problem of officers see Francisco de Paula Cidade, "Recrutamento de Oficiaes," *ADN,* Nov. 10, 1914, 50.

91. FSC, *Relatório . . . Contestado,* 85–86, 90; d'Assumpção, *Campanha do Contestado,* 2:60–63; Vinhas de Queiroz, *Messianismo e Conflicto Social,* 213–14.

92. Diacon, *Millenarian Vision,* 127. In these views Tavares was closely associated with another dislodged official from Canoinhas, Bonifácio Papudo (Bonifácio José dos Santos).

93. Antonio Tavares Jr. to Maj. Atalibio Taurino de Rezende, Itajahy, Dec. 18, 23, 1914; Jan. 2, 4, 1915; and Maj. Taurino de Rezende to Tavares, Moema, Dec. 20, 1914, Jan. 4, 1915, Annexes 16–20, FSC, *Relatório . . . Contestado,* 229–33.

94. d'Assumpção, *Campanha do Contestado,* 65–72; Vinhas de Queiroz, *Messianismo e Conflicto Social,* 214–17. Antonio Tavares, like Bonifácio Papudo, had lost his Canoinhas municipal post in 1914 and had joined the rebellion to settle scores; see Diacon, *Millenarian Vision,* 127.

95. FSC, *Relatório . . . Contestado,* 82–84. Potyguara eventually made general (BAO no. 153) and fought against the tenentes (see Chap. 7).

96. Most of those surrendering had Brazilian/Portuguese style names, but a minority had names such as Becker, Kosky, Leffel, Baffz, and Schinowski. A typical list had 275 males and 800 women and children. "Relação Nominal dos Fanaticos e Suas Familias Apresentadas," [n.d., n.p.] Linha Leste, Cel. Julio Cezar G. da Silva, Doc. 19, Forças em Operações no Contestado, Caixa 12, Arquivo do Exército (Rio).

97. Details on early surrenders are in Diacon, *Millenarian Vision,* 126–27. FSC, *Relatório . . . Contestado,* 89–90; *O Estado,* Florianópolis, May 18, 1915, as quoted in Vinhas de Queiroz, *Messianismo e Conflicto Social,* 218. Pedro Ruivo brought 42 men with him into scout *(vagueano)* service; he received 10$000 (milreis), and they received 5$000 each per day. There were several such groups of civilians. The army records list them by name, with days of service and pay. Relação dos civis empregados com declarações dos vencimentos, Forças em Operações no Contestado, Caixa 12, Arquivo do Exército (Rio).

98. FSC to Col. Felipe Schmidt, Pôrto União, Feb. 18, 1915; and F. Schmidt to FSC, Florianópolis, Feb. 19, 1915, in FSC, *Relatório . . . Contestado . . . 1915,* 240–41; Vinhas de Queiroz, *Messianismo e Conflicto Social,* 220.

99. José Caetano de Faria to FSC, Rio, Jan. 29, 1915, AFSC, CPDOC. He said that the Italian government had protested mistreatment of its nationals and that he was delivering to Foreign Minister Lauro Muller FSC's report on the matter. Faria to FSC, Rio, May 19, 1915, AFSC, CPDOC. In this handwritten letter Faria said: "O caso das relamações estrangeiras sobre individuos mortos por forças civis já esta dando que faser e parece que custará caro. Os inqueritos provaram infelismente que

houve degollamentos por parte dos taes civis; a propósito, permitta que recommende todo o cuidado no seo [*sic*] relatório se tiver de referir-se a esses fatos." On the murder by Potyguara's troops see d'Assumpção, *Campanha do Contestado,* 2:393–96.

100. Ricardo Kirk and Ernesto Darioli to Col. Eduardo Socrates, Pôrto União, Jan. 19, 1915, in FSC, *Relatório . . . Contestado,* Annexo 13. General Faria is BAO no. 80; for his career and ministry see Chap. 4.

101. José Caetano de Faria to FSC, Rio, Jan. 29, 1915, AFSC, CPDOC. Estillac Leal and Leovigildo Paiva were promoted for "merit" on Jan. 20 and 27 respectively; see *Almanak . . . 1915,* 32, 175. On pay and taxes see R. Bonjean (Revenue Office) to FSC, Curitiba, Feb. 10, 1915; Col. Frederico Rossani to FSC, Rio, Mar. 1, 1915; and R. Bonjean to FSC, Curitiba, Mar. 12, 1915, AFSC, CPDOC.

102. Col. Francisco Raul d'Estillac Leal was an imposing-looking officer, complete with a stylish handlebar mustache. Thanks to several articles on the campaign that he published in *A Defesa Nacional* and the two volumes that one of his officers wrote, his name came to be associated with the affair. He seems to have been an effective officer in everything except leading his troops to victory. His articles entitled "Do Contestado, Observações colhidos nas operações da columna sul," appeared in *ADN,* Aug. 10, 1915, 357–61; and *ADN,* Oct. 10, 1915, 27–30. The junior officer author was Herculano Teixeira d'Assumpção. See d'Assumpção, *Campanha da Contestado.* The quality of his leadership did not prevent him from retiring as a marshal. As a later war minister, João Pandiá Calógeras, would observe, "as promoções ao generalato raramente foram felizes. Obedeceram a considerações políticas e pessoais, a relações de amizade, muito mais do que às conveniências do serviço. . . . [O] que mais pesou no critério da eleição foram a simpatia, serviços políticos, parentes influentes e empenhos, e não, como deveria ser, o crisol do valor profissional, de dedicação à tropa, do esfôrço militar" (João Pandiá Calógeras, *Problemas de Administração,* 2d ed. [São Paulo: Companhia Editôra Nacional, 1938], 96). Two of his sons, Newton [*DHBB,* 2:1751–58] and Zeno Estallac Leal [*DHBB,* 2:1760–61], as junior officers would be on opposing sides in the disturbances of the 1920s—the former a tenente and the latter with the government—and would serve respectively as minister of war (1951–52) and chief of staff (1956–58).

103. Vinhas de Queiroz, *Messianismo e Conflicto Social,* 218. See photograph in FSC, *Relatório . . . Contestado,* photo no. 12, after 261. Diacon, *Millenarian Vision,* 127.

104. Heitor Mendes Gonçalves was declared an *aspirante a official* in January 1911 on completion of officer training in Rio Grande do Sul (at the Escola de Guerra in Porto Alegre 1907–9 and at the Escola de Aplicação de Infantaria e Cavalaria in Rio Pardo, 1909–11). He was born Oct. 1, 1889, and entered the army on Mar. 21, 1907; MG, *Almanak . . . 1912,* 393. His would be the last class of those prepared in Rio Grande between the closure of Praia Vermelha in 1904 and the opening of Realengo in 1911. For a memoir of the Rio Grande schools see Francisco de Paula Cidade, "Revivendo o Passado—Meio século mais tarde: a Escola de Guerra," *Revista do Clube Militar* 31, no. 152 (1958?): 105–14. According to Cidade a good number of the schools' graduates saw action in the Contestado (112). The graduates of the Rio Grande schools would be the captains and majors of the 1920s, and like Pedro A. de Góes Monteiro, class of 1910 (the chief of staff of the revolution of 1930), the lieutenant colonels of 1930 and the generals of 1930s and 1940s. The Contestado

would be that officer generation's introduction to warfare, and, save for World War II, their later experiences would be one form or another of civil war.

105. BAO no. 246. João Pereira de Oliveira was declared an *aspirante* in Jan. 1911 after completing training in the Rio Grande do Sul schools. He was born in 1884 and entered the army Apr. 7, 1903.

106. BAO no. 147; Nestor Sezefredo dos Passos was in the Contestado from 1912 to 1916; he had recently been promoted to major. He was born in 1872 and participated in the civil war of 1893; at twenty-seven years of age he was a member of the class of 1902, of the Escola Militar at Praia Vermelha. He would rise to general and become minister of war in 1926. For a full career sketch see Chap. 4.

107. Vinhas de Queiroz, *Messianismo e Conflicto Social,* 223–24.

108. Based on FSC, *Relatório . . . Contestado,* 105–13.

109. Alcibiades Miranda, *Contestado,* 91–93. He noted that the cemetery next to his tent in the camp had only five graves by Mar. 2; the rest lay in the forest until after Apr. 5. Then the dead were buried where they had fallen. He also rebutted "the legend that the jagunços had maltreated the cadavers"; burial squads apparently found that the bodies had no signs of postcombat cutting, etc. (93).

110. It seems reasonable to suppose that the reputation of Pedro Ruivo's men, who were serving with Captain Potyguara's unit, was known among the rebels and that they felt safer in Col. Cesar's hands. There is evidence that even after the fall of Santa Maria prisoners were mistreated and killed. See d'Assumpção, *Campanha do Contestado,* 2:402–3, 406. He cited two examples of prisoners entrusted to Potyguara's unit and to "Colonel" Fabrício's scouts being mutilated and murdered. Alcibiades Miranda also declared that they killed prisoners (see his *Contestado,* 95–96). In the post–Santa Maria mopping-up operations, death lists were used to determine which prisoners were to be killed. In Perdizinhas a mixed civilian-military force under Captain José Vieira da Rosa killed and burned the bodies of 248 prisoners. See Vinhas de Queiroz, *Messianismo e Conflicto Social,* 243.

111. Vinhas de Queiroz, *Messianismo e Conflicto Social,* 222–23.

112. 1st Lt. João Guedes da Fontoura [BAO no. 193; *DHBB,* 2:1313] to Col. Eduardo Arthur Socrates [BAO no. 134], Pôrto da União, Mar. 25, 1915 (Doc. 1599), Forças em Operações no Contestado, Caixa 12, Arquivo do Exército (Rio). A drawing shows that the plane landed on its nose after hitting the ground and bouncing, in an attempted emergency landing.

113. Faria to FSC, Rio, n.d., AFSC; editorial, *ADN,* Apr. 10, 1915, 197–98.

114. Manuel de Cerqueina Daltro Filho would become one of the army's top generals in the 1930s; "Daltro Filho," *DHBB,* 2:1043–46.

115. Manoel Fabrício Vieira was the Contestado's "king of *erva mate*" and one of the region's most powerful *coronéis,* who habitually organized local labor gangs. It appears that organizing an army scout detachment was a natural outgrowth of patrons using their clients as private paramilitary forces. For his labor organizing activities see Diacon, *Millenarian Vision,* 27–28, 104–5

116. Captain Alcibiades Miranda, *Contestado,* 97–105, provided an eyewitness account from his perspective as commander of point platoon of the Fifty-seventh.

117. d'Assumpção, *Campanha do Contestado,* 2:255–81; FSC to José Caetano de Faria, Curitiba, Mar. 13, 1915, Oficios Recibidos 20, Forças em Operações no Con-

testado, Caixa 12, Arquivo do Exército (Rio). The choice of music and dance shows the African influence on the culture of the common soldier; the *côco* was from the northeast, *mineiro* and *catopé* were from Minas Gerais; see Cascudo, *Dicionário do Folclore Brasileiro*, 195, 224–25, 479–80.

118. It is noteworthy that he cited Clausewitz, who believed that politics and the army were permanently linked; see Nunn, *Yesterday's Soldiers*, 78.

119. FSC to José Caetano de Faria, Curitiba, Mar. 13, 1915, Oficios Recibidos 20, Forças em Operações no Contestado, Caixa 12, Arquivo do Exército (Rio). Although Setembrino said that he wanted to reduce the "bandoleiros do Santa Maria" before cold weather set in, he could not be sure of success, so he requested funds and tents to get his troops through the winter. He reminded Faria that after the area was pacified, it would need "um policiamento moralisado e continuo." On Estillac's views see Miranda, *Contestado*, 105. Captain Miranda criticized the general's tendency to blame his subordinates (107).

120. See Manuel Onofre Moniz Ribeiro to Julio César, Canoinhas, Mar. 27, 1915; full text is in Miranda, *Contestado*, 326–28. There were no army regulations on how to write messages, orders, reports, or standards for map sketches to insure that all necessary information was transmitted; see FSC, *Relatório . . . Contestado*, 161.

121. d'Assumpção, *Campanha do Contestado*, 2:331–33. The Ninth eventually made contact with Onofre's troops and coordinated their blocking actions. On page 285 d'Assumpção said that the Ninth's prisoners were mostly women, children, the old, or the sick who had left the redoubt area while the males took up defensive positions. He also said that the Ninth treated the prisoners so well that they agreed to serve as guides for patrols searching out others hidden in the hills.

122. Vinhas de Queiroz, *Messianismo e Conflicto Social*, 231.

123. Potyguara's report in FSC, *Relatório . . . Contestado*, 250–51.

124. Ibid., 253.

125. Ibid., 254; Miranda, *Contestado*, 116.

126. FSC, *Relatório . . . Contestado*, 254.

127. The list of dead carried two named Marcellino Gonçalves, one with the Fifty-seventh Infantry Battalion and the other a civilian *vaqueano*. The first was killed near Santa Maria, the second in its taking. So the bugler here must have been the *vaqueano*. FSC, *Relatorio . . . Contestado*, Annexo 28, "Relação dos oficiaes, praças e civis, mortos em combate," pages unnumbered.

128. Text of note in d'Assumpção, *Campanha do Contestado*, 379–80.

129. I have relied here on Potyguara's own account in his after-action report to Setembrino, which the latter included in his report FSC, *Relatório . . . Contestado*, 249–59. On the Pacheco family involvement in the development of the crisis see Diacon, *Millenarian Vision*, 86–87.

130. Telegrams: Estillac to FSC, Santa Maria, Apr. 2, 1915 (8:40 A.M.); FSC to Estillac, Porto União, Apr. 2, 1915; Estillac to FSC, Santa Maria, Apr. 2, 1915 (2:20 P.M.); Estillac to FSC, Tapera, Apr. 2, 1915 (7:50 P.M.); FSC to Estillac, Porto União, Apr. 2, 1915; Estillac to FSC, Tapera, Apr. 3, 1915; full text in d'Assumpção, *Companha do Contestado*, 2:366–72.

131. Miranda, *Contestado*, 125. Throughout his account he kept careful track of casualties.

132. d'Assumpção, *Campanha do Contestado*, 2:390–91, 396; Potyguara's report in FSC, *Relatório . . . Contestado*, 258. Of his detachment's animals, 109 were killed. His troops expended 86,120 rounds from their Mauser rifles and machine guns, Winchesters, Parabellum and Nagant pistols, and revolvers. He commented that he intended his report to be an example of why orders should not be disputed and should be followed carefully to avoid disasters. Capt. T. de Albuquerque Potyguara to Senhor Colonel Manoel Onofre Muniz Ribeiro, Commandante da Columna Norte, Villa de Canoinhas, Apr. 20, 1915, "Tomada do Reducto de Santa Maria," Forças em Operações no Contestado, Caixa 12, Arquivo do Exército (Rio).

133. FSC to Estillac, Porto União, Apr. 4, 1915 (7 P.M.); Estillac to FSC, Tapera, Apr. 5, 1915; FSC to Estillac, Porto União, Apr. 5, 1915; full texts in d'Assumpção, *Campanha do Contestado*, 2:393–96.

134. d'Assumpção, *Campanha do Contestado*, 2:402–3. d'Assumpção said that he was with Col. Estillac, 1st Lt. Souza Reis, a Captain Pará, and a contingent of cavalry when they came on the body "desse bandoleiro todo mutilado: faltavam-lhes as orelhas, estava quasi inteiramente degollado." . . . "Bem desgraçada foi a sorte desse bandido. . . . O destacamento do norte, não sei porque motivo superior, não quiz levar o prisioneiro até á cidade de P. União" (see note, 402–3).

135. Felipe Schmidt to FSC, Florianópolis, Apr. 20, 1915, AFSC. Minister Faria wrote FSC congratulating him on the successful campaign and giving him a paid leave to rest. Faria to FSC, Rio, May 19, 1915, AFSC, CPDOC. Col. Antonio S. B. Pyrrho was at Canudos in July and August 1897 (see *Almanak . . . 1915*, 28). The Greek leader Pyrrhus (318–272 B.C.) won his costly victory over the Romans in 279 B.C. A force of scouts *(vaqueanos)* under army Captain José Vieira da Rosa of the Fifty-fourth Batt. Light Inf. of Florianópolis and local "Colonel" Maximino de Moraes conducted bloody operations—in Perdizinhas some 167 prisoners were executed; Vinhas de Queiroz, *Messianismo e Conflicto Social*, 230, 243; MG, *Relatório . . . Caetano de Faria . . . 1916*, 67–68, and *. . . 1918*, 34, 99. On "Colonel" Maximino see Diacon, *Millenarian Vision*, 108–9, 133. Capt. Alcibíades Miranda participated in the final stages and details army actions in his *Contestado* (143–64).

136. MG, *Relatório . . . Setembrino de Carvalho . . . 1915, Relatório* 137–80. Quotations from pages 130, 138, 141, 159, 160.

137. I found three officers from the German-trained "Young Turk" group among Contestado veterans: 1st Lt. (Inf.) Joaquim Sousa Reis Netto; 1st Lt. (Inf.) José Bento Thomaz Gonçalves, who was there from Mar. until June 1914 and from Feb. until May 1915; and 1st Lt. (Cav.) Euclydes de Oliveira Figueiredo, who commanded a courier platoon and was decorated for saving a soldier's life. Souza Reis and Figueiredo were among the founders of *A Defesa Nacional;* the latter later served on Gen. Setembrino's staff at the Fourth Military Region and when Setembrino was minister of war. He would reach Lt. Col. in 1924; in 1930 he opposed the revolution, and in 1932 he was a key leader of the paulista forces in the 1932 civil war. His son, João Figueiredo, was president of Brazil from 1979 to 1985. See MG, *Relatório . . . Setembrino de Carvalho . . . 1915*, 153; "Euclides Figueiredo," *DHBB*, 2:1270–74. By the early 1920s Souza Reis was a highly regarded officer on the general staff; he became so despondent on being relieved after failing to defeat the tenente rebels in 1924 that he shot himself in his Ministry of War office (see Chap. 7).

138. Mario Travassos, "Para a Frente, Custe o Que Custar!," *ADN,* Oct. 10, 1916, 15–17; he commanded the Brazilian Expeditionary Force's replacement depot in Italy in World War II and became brig. gen. in 1946 (BAO no. 264). Some other articles on the Contestado were Francisco de Paula Cidade, "Em Torno de Contestado," *ADN,* Jan. 10, 1915, 124–25; and *ADN,* Mar. 10, 1915, 179–82; "A campanha ingloria do Contestado . . . " Editorial, *ADN,* Apr. 10, 1915, 197– 198; [Col. Francisco Raul d'Estillac Leal] "Do Contestado, Observações colhidas nas operações da columna sul," *ADN,* Oct. 10, 1915, 27–30. On funds for heirs of those killed in the campaign see "Exemplo patriotico," *ADN,* May 10, 1915, 265; and "Subcripção em favor das victimas do Contestado," *ADN,* Nov. 10, 1916. They collected 14:781$670, which at 230.6 milreis to the U.S. dollar was about $64,268 in 1916 dollars.

139. "Relatório," *ADN,* Aug. 10, 1917, 356–58. Because this was an unsigned commentary, it was likely written by one of the editors.

140. *Almanak do Ministerio da Guerra para o anno de 1930* (Rio de Janeiro: Imprensa Militar, 1930), 7–17. Two stellar names were among the major generals of 1930: Nestor Sezefredo dos Passos and Tertuliano de A. Potyguara. They, along with all but one of the Contestado veterans, were among the twenty generals retired as a result of the Revolution of 1930. The one exception was José Luís Pereira de Vasconcellos, who as major general and commander of the Second Military Region in 1932, would join the paulista forces against the Vargas government; "Euclydes Hermes da Fonseca," *DHBB,* 2:1301–2; "Vasconcellos," *DHBB,* 4:3516. For Heitor Gonçalves see Setembrino, *Relatório . . . Setembrino de Carvalho . . . 1915,* 162. Numbers on campaign veterans still on active duty during the Revolution of 1930 were drawn from *Almanak do Ministerio da Guerra para o anno de 1931* (Rio de Janeiro: Imprensa Militar, 1931), 7–13 (Generals); 21–90 (Inf.); 191–218 (Cav.); 271–302 (Arty.); 371–86 (Eng.); 418–24 (Aviation); 443–60 (Med.); 499–506 (Pharmacy); 529–32 (Vet.). These figures indicate that the largest contingent were infantry officers: 65 out of 246 (for 26 percent), as compared to 12 cavalry officers out of 107 (for 11 percent) and 6 artillery officers out of 130 (for 4 percent).

The number of generals with Contestado experience came from my BAO project. Special thanks to Candace Kattar and Gus Lawlor for collecting and analyzing the data.

141. "Henrique Teixeira Lott," *DHBB,* 3:1937–43. Escola de Comando e Estado-Maior do Exército, Curso de Preparação, *Guerras Insurrecionais no Brasil (Canudos e Contestado)* (Rio de Janeiro: Imprensa Nacional, 1968); on lack of development of the Santa Maria area see Quatro Rodas, "98 Mapa Brasil," in *Guia Brasil 1998* (São Paulo: Ed. Abril, 1998). Today the Contestado region has a state university and is intent on using its history to attract tourism: see [http://www.contestado.com.br/roteiros/index.htm], accessed Jan. 10, 2003.

142. This last tidbit was from Miranda, *Contestado,* 126.

CHAPTER 4

1. Francisco Luiz Teixeira Vinhosa, *O Brasil e a Primeira Guerra Mundial* (Rio de Janeiro: Instituto Histórico e Geográfico Brasileiro, 1990), 31–36; see also his article "1914 ou escritores em guerra," *Jornal do Brasil* (Rio), Aug. 26, 1984, "Especial," 4; Dunshee de Abranches, *A Illusão Brasileira (Justificação Histórica de uma Attitude)* 5th ed. (Rio de Janeiro: Imprensa Nacional, 1917), 25, 28.

2. Campos Coelho, *Em Busca de Identidade,* 75–82.

3. 2d Lt. Francisco Paula Cidade, "Recrutamento de oficiaes," *ADN,* Nov. 10, 1914, 49–50. In 1919 Alfredo Malan d'Angrogne, while military attaché in Paris, prepared a report for President-elect Epítacio Pessôa, in which he presented a somewhat different division of the officer corps: (1) quality men with "book-learning" *(preparo livresco),* who had a real professional inclination that they actively cultivated; (2) officers who, despite ability, had been frozen in lower ranks and were too old for further professional development [he cited forty-five-year-old captains who should have been lieutenant colonels or colonels]; (3) those who were time-serving "public employees" rather than professional soldiers. Malan, *Uma Escolha, Um Destino,* 194.

4. The 1905 *Relatório* said that the time in Germany was to prepare them to become instructors in the army's schools. The following officers went:

Group 1—Capt. Emilio Sarmento (Inf.), Lt. Constancio Deschamps Cavalcanti (Inf.), 1st Lt. Cassiano da Silveira Mello Matos (Arty.), 2d Lt. Bento Marinho Alves (Arty.), 2d Lt. Manoel Bourgard de Castro e Silva (Arty.), Lt. Estellita Augusto Werner (Cav.); in MG, *Relatório . . . Argollo . . . 1905,* 17;

Group 2—1st Lt. Alexandre Galvão Bueno, 1st Lt. Leopoldo Itacoatiara de Senna, 2d Lt. Manoel Joaquim Pena, 2d Lt. Augusto da Silva Mendes, 2d Lt. Antonio Borba de Moura, 2d Lt. Amaro de Azambuja Villa Nova. Also sent to Europe to "improve themselves," but without a listed destination, were 2d LT. Mario Hermes da Fonseca, 2d Lt. Ignacio de Alencastro Guimarães Junior, 2d Lt. Pedro Carlos da Fonseca; in MG, *Relatório . . . Hermes . . . 1909,* 5.

Group 3—Capts. Luiz Furtado (Inf.), José Carlos Vital Filho (Inf.), Arnaldo Brandão (Cav.), Cesar Augusto Parga Rodrigues (Arty.), Epaminondas de Lima e Silva (Cav.), Francisco Jorge Pinheiro (Cav.), Emilio Rosauro de Almeida (Cav.); 1st Lts. José Antonio Coelho Ramalho, Luiz Gonzaga dos Santos Sarahyba, José Bento Thomaz Gonçalves, Joaquim de Souza Reis Netto, Julião Freire Esteves (all Inf.), Augusto de Lima Mendes, José Maria Franco Ferreira, Jeronymo Furtado do Nascimento, Euclydes de Oliveira Figueiredo (all Cav.), Olyntho de Meira (Mesquita) Vasconcellos, Bertholdo Klinger, Eduardo Cavalcanti de Albuquerque Sá (all Arty.), José Pinheiro de Ulhôa Cintra (Eng.); 2d Lts. Estevão Leitão de Carvalho (Inf.), Evaristo Marques da Silva (Cav.); in *Almanak . . . 1912,* 86; Leitão de Carvalho, *Dever Militar,* 34; and Aviso no. 683, Apr. 19, 1910, Boletim Especial no. 48 and Aviso no. 2846, Apr. 17, 1910, Boletim Especial no. 84, Arquivo do Exército, Rio de Janeiro.

5. On German-Turkish relations see Ulrich Trumpener, *Germany and the Ottoman Empire, 1914–1918* (Princeton, N.J.: Princeton University Press, 1968), esp. 69, 73, 105. German officers acted as Turkish chief of staff and held field commands during World War I, but they did not have complete control of the army.

6. See Estevão Leitão de Carvalho's account of the 1915 New Year's proclamation that he wrote for Minister of War Faria: Leitão de Carvalho, *Memórias,* 1:189–90.

7. Editorial, *ADN,* Oct. 10, 1913, 1–3.

8. Editorial, *ADN,* Nov. 10, 1914, 37–38.

9. Leitão de Carvalho, *Memórias,* 1:176.

10. Olavo Bilac, *A Defesa Nacional (Discursos)* (Rio de Janeiro: Editora Biblioteca do Exército, 1965), 25, 130, 27, 41 (in order of quotations). These are speeches that he gave in south-central Brazil in 1915 and 1916.

11. Ibid., quotations are from 61 and 68.

12. Ibid., 69.

13. See the interesting discussion in Barbosa Lima Sobrinho, *Presença de Alberto Tôrres (Sua Vida e Pensamento)* (Rio de Janeiro: Ed. Civilização Brasileira, 1968), 388–403.

14. Bilac, *A Defesa Nacional (Discursos)*, esp. text of São Paulo speech, "Em Marcha," 23–28 (quotations from 26–27).

15. Ibid.; and Lima Sobrinho, *Presença de Alberto Tôrres*, 393.

16. Bilac, *A Defesa Nacional (Discursos)*, 33–42; quotes are from "Ao Exército Nacional," a speech delivered at Clube Militar, Rio de Janeiro, Nov. 6, 1915.

17. Raymundo Magalhães Jr., *Olavo Bilac e sua época* (Rio de Janeiro: Editora Americana, 1974), 275.

18. Both works were reissued in 1933 by São Paulo's Companhia Editora Nacional in the famous "Brasiliana" collection and again in 1982 by the Editora Universidade de Brasília.

19. Alberto Tôrres, *A Organização Nacional* (1914; reprint, Brasília: Ed. Universidade de Brasília, 1982), 160.

20. Lima Sobrinho, *Presença de Alberto Tôrres*, 393–94.

21. Ibid., 395.

22. Ibid., 395–97.

23. Tôrres, *A Organização Nacional*, 330.

24. Lima Sobrinho, *Presença de Alberto Tôrres*, 399.

25. Decreto-Lei no. 1908, Dec. 26, 1939 (signed by G. Vargas, Eurico G. Dutra, and Henrique A. Guilhem); Decreto no. 58,222, Apr. 19, 1966 (signed by H. Castelo Branco, Zilmar de Araripe Macedo, Arthur da Costa e Silva, and Eduardo Gomes). Texts in Gen. Moacir Araujo Lopes, *Olavo Bilac, O Homen Cívico* (Rio de Janeiro: Liga da Defesa Nacional, 1968), 43–45.

26. MG, *Relatório . . . 1906 . . . Argolla* (Rio de Janeiro: Imprensa Nacional, 1906), 29. Career information is from various *Almanacs do Exército*. His BAO is no. 80.

27. *Almanac . . . 1915*, 562.

28. Estado-Maior do Exército, *História do Estado-Maior do Exército* (Rio de Janeiro: Biblioteca do Exército, 1984), 30. On the Chilean experience see Nunn, *Yesterday's Soldiers* 100–112.

29. MG, *Relatório . . . Faria . . . 1915*, 5–7.

30. MG, *Relatório . . . Faria . . . 1915*, 4–5. On European writers see Nunn cited above and Richard D. Challener, *The French Theory of the Nation in Arms, 1866–1939* (New York: Columbia University Press, 1952), 64. The most characteristic aspect of French military thinking from 1872 to 1914 was that the "army was a school and that, as such, it could perform an important social role in French life." Every citizen was to serve, thereby giving the army "the image of the nation." The Brazilians were borrowing heavily.

31. MG, *Relatório . . . Faria . . . 1915*, 14; Theodorico Lopes and Gentil Torres, *Ministros da Guerra do Brasil, 1808–1946* (Rio de Janeiro: n.p., 1947), 175–76. For a list of commanders and staff of strategic brigades and inspection districts see *Almanak . . . 1914* (Rio de Janeiro: Imprensa Militar, 1914), 603–12.

32. On strength see *Almanak . . . 1915*, 634–45. Each of the five divisions contained two infantry and one artillery brigade, a regiment of cavalry, and one battalion of engineers, plus appropriate trains, supply, and medical units (see 654–60).

33. Sir W. Haggard to Sir Edward Grey, Petrópolis, June 19, 1913, "Brazil, Annual Report, 1912," Confidential 10286, Foreign Office Confidential Print, 18–19.

34. MG, *Relatório . . . Faria . . . 1915,* 7–9.

35. Ibid., 10–11.

36. Leitão de Carvalho, *Memórias,* 1:189–90.

37. Ibid., 191.

38. Ibid., 210–11.

39. Mario Hermes da Fonseca and Ildefonso Escobar, *Primórdios da organização da defesa nacional* (Rio de Janeiro: Tipografia Glória, Pinho, & Manes, 1943), 139–56; "Liga da Defesa Nacional," *DHBB,* 3:1813. On ideology see Carone, *A República Velha,* 1:168–70.

40. Magalhães, *Olavo Bilac,* 399.

41. Ibid., 376–77. The banquet was organized by Generals Bento Ribeiro, Luís Barbedo, and Setembrino de Carvalho.

42. Ibid., 368–75. Division General Besouro was replaced on Dec. 2, 1916. His opposition was no small matter because he was a senior general who had been commandant of the general staff school from Sep. 1910 to May 1914 and would be assigned to the promotion board in Mar. 1917; *Almanak . . . 1914,* 554; and *Relatório . . . Faria . . . 1917,* 92.

43. Leitão de Carvalho, *Memórias,* 204, 213–15; David V. Fleischer, ed., *Carlos Peixoto Filho* (Brasília: Câmara dos Deputados, 1978), 523.

44. For a description of the day's events see Fonseca and Escobar, *Primórdios,* 157–60; Raymundo Magalhães Jr., *Olavo Bilac,* 398–402.

45. *O Estado de São Paulo,* Nov. 26, 1915, as in Carone, *A República Velha,* 2:306–7.

46. Carone, *A República Velha,* 2:307–8.

47. Abílio de Noronha, *Narrando a Verdade: Contribuição para a História da Revolução de S. Paulo* (São Paulo: Companhia Gráfica-Editora Monteiro Lobato, 1924); Col. Tobias Coelho, *O Exército Internamente, Reminiscencias Historicas* (Rio de Janeiro: Editorial Alba, [c. 1935?]), 186–89; Cidade, *Síntese de Três Séculos de Literatura Militar Brasileira,* 472–75.

48. The quotation regarding sympathy for the exiles is from *O Estado de São Paulo,* Apr. 10, 1916, as quoted in Carone, *A República Velha,* 2:308; Carone's comment is in note 113. None of the sources consulted indicated if any of the rebel sergeants had served in the Contestado, but, if they did, one could imagine that heightened responsibilities of sergeants in a combat zone could provoke dissatisfaction with their normal status.

49. MG, *Relatório . . . Faria . . . 1915,* 16–17; Câmara dos Deputados, *Mensagens Presidenciais, 1915–1918* (1921; reprint, Brasília: Câmara dos Deputados, 1978), 136–37.

50. Cidade, *Síntese de Três Séculos de Literatura Militar Brasileira,* 474–75.

51. Leitão de Carvalho, *Memórias,* 1:200–201. Sergeant Joaquim became a lieutenant in the Intendencia in 1916. That administrative service handled financial and quartermaster matters. He was born in 1886 and entered the army in 1903. By Nov. 1930 he was a captain. Administration provided an unknown number of sergeants a way into the officer corps. *Almanak . . . 1931,* 626.

52. MG, *Relatório . . . Faria . . . 1917,* 8.

53. Ibid., 6. Noting the large number who were unfit, Faria called for obligatory physical education to produce "strong and vigorous men." It is strange that he did

not first call for general obligatory public education to provide a venue for physical training.

54. Ibid., 22; and MG, *Relatório . . . Faria . . . 1918,* 16.

55. MG, *Relatório . . . Gen. Eurico Gaspar Dutra . . . 1940,* 22.

56. Albert Hale, *The South Americans* (Indianapolis: Bobbs-Merrill, 1907), 208–9.

57. MG, *Relatório . . . Setembrino de Carvalho . . . 1926,* 82–83.

58. In 1916–17 states without permanent garrisons, or with only small special-purpose detachments, were Amazonas, Piauí, Rio Grande do Norte, Alagoas, Sergipe, Espirito Santo, and Goiás. See MG, *Relatório . . . Faria . . . 1917,* 7–10. The 195 thousand contos constituted General Faria's ideal figure.

59. The army's purchasing power was reduced during the First World War by the country's financial situation. In 1914 Brazil's budget was 86,439 contos paper and 250 contos gold; the latter was used for foreign purchases. Over the next two years funding declined to 64,246 contos paper and 50 gold. See ibid., 24. On the condition of barracks see ibid., 15–17, 79–101. The commander of the Sixth Region cited the example of the unit in Santa Anna (SP) quartered in "um velho pardeiro que nos tempos primitivos da cidade foi construido com taipa, para um convento, sem ar, luz, accommodações e em pessimo estado de conservação." He was using troops to build a new one; ibid., 96–97. For war ministry budget figures 1910–16 see Câmara dos Deputados, *Mensagens Presidenciais, 1915–1918,* 137–38, 292–93, 482–83.

60. MG, *Relatório . . . Faria . . . 1917,* 18–20. On Brazil and World War I see Vinhosa, *O Brasil;* Otto Prazeres, *O Brasil na Guerra (Algumas Notas Para a História)* (Rio de Janeiro: Imprensa Nacional, 1918); and Pedro Cavalcanti, *A Presidência Wenceslau Braz, 1914–1918* (Brasília: Ed. Universidade de Brasília, 1981), 97–108. Thomas Skidmore discussed the war's effect on the development of nationalism in *Black into White,* 159–72.

61. Eurico Gaspar Dutra, *O Exército em Dez Anos de Governo do Presidente Vargas* (Rio de Janeiro: Ministério da Guerra, 1941), 27.

62. Murilo de Carvalho, "As Forças Armadas na Primeira República: O Poder Destabilizador," 141.

63. Alfred Stepan, *Military in Politics,* 26.

64. MG, *Relatório . . . Faria . . . 1918,* 21.

65. The government had ordered thirty batteries of 75 mm field guns from Krupp, which were in Hamburg ready for shipment when war broke out. Brig. Gen. João Candido Pereira de Castro Jr. (Diretor do Material Bellico) to Minister of War, Rio, Mar. 23, 1936, Directoria do Material Bellico, "Relatório do anno de 1935," 39. Carbon typescript copy in CDOC-EX, Brasília.

66. 1st Lt. Miguel de Castro Ayres, "Regimen das Massas," *ADN,* Nov. 10, 1915, 54–55; Editorial, "Plantar para o inimigo," *ADN,* July 10, 1916, 305–6. The quotations are from the latter.

67. MG, *Relatório . . . Aguiar . . . 1919,* 32.

68. MG, *Relatório . . . Mallet . . . 1899,* 60–65. The three 1899 arsenals were located in Rio de Janeiro, Rio Grande do Sul, and Cuiabá, Mato Grosso. The latter facility was constructed of mud and wattle *(taipa),* which suffered in the region's heavy rains, requiring that its detachments of military workers and teenage apprentice craftsmen spend as much time repairing the building as they did restoring arms.

69. Ibid., 65.

70. MG, *Relatório . . . Mallet . . . 1899,* 66–68; and *Relatório . . . Mallet . . . 1900,* 89.

71. MG, *Relatório . . . Gen. José Bernardino Bormann . . . 1910,* 129–30.

72. 1st Lt. Miguel de Castro Ayres, "Regimen das Masses," *ADN,* Nov. 10, 1915, 53–55.

73. Editorial, "Fabrica de cartuchos e artefactos de guerra do Realengo," *ADN,* May 10, 1914, 258–59.

74. Santos Dumont, who was from Minas Gerais, was a key figure in nonrigid airship development having constructed and flown the first gasoline-motored airship in 1898. He also built a successful monoplane in 1909.

75. Ed., *ADN,* Apr. 10, 1915, 197–98; Gen. Vespasiano de Albuquerque to Gen. Fernando Setembrino de Carvalho, Rio, Sep. 18, 27, 1914; and Gen. José Caetano de Faria to Gen. F. Setembrino de Carvalho, Rio, n.d., Arquivo F. Setembrino de Carvalho, CPDOC-Rio.

76. MG, *Relatório . . . Faria . . . 1916,* 19; MG, *Relatório . . . Faria . . . 1917,* 21; MG, *Relatório . . . Faria . . . 1918,* 31. The largest group went to France, but one army aviator went to Britain with a navy contingent; Keith Hart, "Brazilians in Britain, 1918," *Army Quarterly and Defence Journal* (Great Britain) 3, no. 4 (Oct. 1981): 475–78.

77. MG, *Relatório . . . Faria . . . 1918,* 31; 1st Lt. Marcos Evangelista da Costa Villela Jr., "A Aviação Militar no Brasil," *ADN,* Sep. 10, 1916, 379–80. The author was one of the aircraft's builders. The reader met him at Canudos as a gunnery sergeant.

78. Brig. Gen. João Candido Pereira de Castro Jr., "Relatório do Anno de 1935," Directoria do Material Bélico, Rio de Janeiro, Mar. 23, 1936, 39; carbon copy of typescript in CDOC-Ex, Brasília; MG, *Relatório . . . Faria . . . 1916,* 9.

79. MG, *Relatório . . . Faria . . . 1916,* 5; *Relatório . . . Faria . . . 1918,* 28, 32, 36–37.

80. On the Ipanema ironworks see Steven C. Topik, *Political Economy,* 130, 148–50.

81. *Jornal do Commércio* (Rio), Nov. 10, 1912, 13; quoted in Steven C. Topik, *Political Economy,* 149; Warren Dean, *The Industrialization of São Paulo, 1880–1945* (Austin: University of Texas Press, 1969), 147–48.

82. Editorial, *ADN,* June 10, 1917, 282–84; "A industria siderurgica como elemento da Defeza Nacional," *ADN,* Aug. 10, 1917, 395–96; "O problema siderúrgico," ibid., 361.

83. Editorial, "A industria nacional do aço," *ADN,* May 10, 1917, 250–51.

84. "O Exército e a Nação," *ADN,* June 10, 1916, 312. The general was Antonio Ilha Moreira.

85. MG, *Relatório . . . Faria . . . 1918,* 34–35; Malan, *Uma Escolha, Um Destino,* 166–67; and his, *Missão Militar Francesa de Instrução Junto ao Exército Brasileiro* (Rio de Janeiro: Biblioteca do Exército, 1988), 51–54.

86. Ambassador Edwin V. Morgan, Rio de Janeiro, Oct. 26, 1917, 9971K-5, and Nov. 6, 1917, 9971K-6; Col. P. D. Lochridge (Acting Chief of War College Division), memorandum for Chief of Staff, Washington, D.C., Nov. 22, 1917, 9971K-2; all Military Intelligence Division, General Staff, War Department, Record Group 165, National Archives, Washington, D.C. [indicated hereafter as MID, GS, WD, RG 165, NA]. See also Estevão Leitão de Carvalho, *Discursos, Conferências & Outros Escritos* (Rio de Janeiro: Imprensa do Exército, 1965), 215. Some American officers were suspicious that one of the mission's German-trained officers was a spy, but

there was no evidence that any of them were collecting information for other than Brazilian use.

87. On Brazil's military contribution in World War II see McCann, *Brazilian-American Alliance.*

88. João Cruz Costa, *Contribuição a História das Idéias no Brasil* (Rio de Janeiro: José Olympio Editora, 1967), 360–61. Costa used the expression "República dos Conselheiros." The nature of the system has been probed in a stimulating series of state-focused studies; see, e.g., Love, *Rio Grande do Sul;* Love, *São Paulo;* Levine, *Pernambuco;* and John D. Wirth, *Minas Gerais in the Brazilian Federation, 1889–1937* (Stanford, Calif.: Stanford University Press, 1977).

89. Nelson Werneck Sodré has argued that the new order saw the army as its enemy, that the politicians attacked militarism, sectarianism, and Jacobinism, which were associated with Florianismo because they were, he said, "national, popular, and democratic" qualities. "Militarism," he asserted, "was vigilance against class privilege, sectarianism was protection of democratic institutions, and jacobinism was the preservation of national sovereignty" (Sodré, *História Militar do Brasil,* 177, 183–84). There is some truth here, but remember that the army suffered from its own internal disorder and the weak financial status of the country's economy, which precluded large military expenditures, as much as from the desire of the states to keep the federal government weak. It is not any more likely that the oligarchies had a clear idea of the army as a threat than the army had of the need for social reform. It is possible that the civilian politicians saw little need for an army, and they believed that a pacific national image would be easier to project with a small, weak force. For a discussion of the use of military force in the political system see Henry H. Keith, "Armed Federal Interventions in the States During the Old Republic," in *Perspectives on Armed Politics in Brazil,* ed. Henry H. Keith and Robert A. Hayes (Tempe: Center for Latin American Studies, Arizona State University, 1976), 51–73.

90. A critic of the "Young Turks" claimed that when he served in the ministry's Central Department he ordered sold three tons of translated German regulations made obsolete by the new French regulations. He said that the poorly translated artillery regulations were for the German 77 cannon but that the Brazilian artillery was equipped with the Krupp 1908 campaign cannon so that when fired in a demonstration the shells fell up to 200 meters below the targets, one hitting a small house and destroying a pot of black beans. Col. José Tobias Coelho, *O Exército Internamente (Reminiscencias Historicas)* (Rio de Janeiro: Editora Alba, 1935), 67, 71–76.

91. *A República* (Recife), Jan. 9, 1912, as quoted in Levine, *Pernambuco,* 142.

92. Compiled from MG, *Relatórios . . . 1910–1918.* By comparison, the annual average for books in English was 105, and for items in Guarani, 2.25 a year. The average was for eight years, excluding 1913. Such data were apparently not reported after 1918, and the library was closed and its collection scattered in 1925.

93. Fonseca Filho, *Marechal Hermes,* 79.

94. Editorial, *ADN,* May 10, 1914, 241–44.

95. Major Raimundo Pinto Seidl, "Combatir o Analphabetismo é um Dever de Honra para o Official Brasileiro," *ADN,* Oct. 10, 1915, 44–47.

96. Editorial, "A Organisação Nacional," *ADN,* Mar. 10, 1916, 177–79.

97. Editorial, "Acima de Tudo Devemos Ser Brazileiros," *ADN,* June 10, 1916, 273–74.

98. Editorial, "Recuar Será uma Covardia," *ADN,* Sep. 10, 1916, 369–71.

99. Editorial, "Avante, Custe o Que Custar!" *ADN,* Oct. 10, 1916, 1–3.

100. Editorial, "A Grandeza Nacional e o Momento Militar," *ADN,* Nov. 10, 1915, 49– 51. *Bacharelismo,* as used here, was a derogatory term referring to the hollow intellectualizing of the graduates of the law and medical schools, who were found in large numbers in the government.

101. Editorial, "Avante, Custe o Que Custar!" *ADN,* Oct. 10, 1916, 1–3.

102. Mário Travassos, "Para a Frente, Custe o Que Custar!" *ADN,* Oct. 10, 1916, 15–17.

103. For a summary of the Faria–Bento Ribeiro years see Estado-Maior do Exército, *História do Estado-Maior do Exército,* 28–51.

104. Motta, *Formação do Oficial,* 302–3.

105. MG, *Relatório . . . Faria . . . 1918,* 25.

106. Ibid., 24–25, 44–45. Although there were only two hundred official *alumnos praças* in 1917–18, there were 13 lieutenants and aspirantes in artillery courses and 74 such officers in engineering. In addition there were 166 auditor *praças* in the basic course, the only time such a designation appeared; see ibid., 45. For enrollments see MG, *Relatório . . . Cardoso de Aguiar . . . May 1919,* 68; MG, *Relatório . . . Calógeras . . . June 1920,* 94. The latter noted that 51 second lieutenants and 146 aspirantes completed their studies in December 1919. These were the *turmas* or classes that formed the backbone of the tenente movement. For a description of the Escola Militar in 1917–18 see Juarez Távora, *Uma Vida e Muitas Lutas, Memórias* (Rio de Janeiro: José Olympio Editora, 1973), 1:84–95.

107. Tristão de Alencar Araripe, *A Coerência de Uma Vocação* (Rio de Janeiro: Imprensa do Exército, 1969), 94.

108. Motta, *Formação do Oficial,* 306.

109. Ibid., fly sheet between 306–7.

110. Odylio Denys, *Ciclo Revolucionário Brasileiro, Memórias* (Rio de Janeiro: Ed. Nova Fronteira, 1980), 173–74. The first group was designated on Dec. 5, 1918. This group and the various additions and replacements were upwardly mobile officers who left their mark on the army and the country. Of the nineteen Indigenous Mission officers who were at Realengo in 1920, at least eleven would later reach general's rank.

The 1920 group included Captain João Eduardo Pfeil; First Lieutenants Valentim Benicio da Silva (BAO no. 213), Eduardo Guedes Alcoforado (BAO no. 225), Renato Paquet (BAO no. 235), Arthur Joaquim Pamphiro, Newton de Andrade Cavalcanti (BAO no. 209), Dermeval Peixoto (BAO no. 242), João Barbosa Leite, Henrique Baptista Duffles Teixeira Lott (BAO no. 264), Penedo Pedra, Manoel Henrique Gomes, Orozimbo Martins Pereira, Antonio da Silva Rocha, Luiz de Araujo Corrêa Lima, Orestes da Rocha Lima (BAO no. 274), Alvaro Fuiza de Castro (BAO no. 236), Gustavo Cordeiro de Faria (BAO no. 239), Mario Ary Pires (BAO no. 230); and Second Lieutenant Odylio Denys (BAO no. 251). Names are from MG, *Almanaque do Exército, 1920* (Rio de Janeiro: Imprensa Militar, 1920), 554–55. The BAO numbers indicate generals identification code in my Brazilian Army Officer file of general officers.

111. A member of that turma, Oswaldo Cordeiro de Farias, recalled that "toda a minha geração de Escola Militar . . . teve participação destacada no movimento tenentista: Prestes, Sigueira Campos, Eduardo Gomes, Juarez saíram todos das mesmas turmas . . . os formados da turma de 1918 precisaram permanecer mais um ano para receber o mesmo treinamento. . . . Este é o segredo do êxito da Coluna Prestes. Éramos increivelmente unidos, como verdadeiros irmãos, e entre nós não havia ciúmes nem segredos. Existia uma união inseparável que nos ligava como membros de uma família" (Aspásia Camargo and Walder de Góes, *Meio século de combate: Diálogo com Cordeiro de Farias* [Rio de Janeiro: Nova Fronteira, 1981], 64–65).

For a discussion of *turma* see Frank D. McCann, "The Military," in *Modern Brazil: Elites and Masses in Historical Perspective,* ed. Michael L. Conniff and Frank D. Mc-Cann (Lincoln: University of Nebraska Press, 1989), 51–54.

112. Leitão de Carvalho, *Memórias,* 1:219–21.

CHAPTER 5

1. Major Fenton R. McCreery, Rio, Nov. 25, 1918, "Spanish Influenza Epidemic in Brazil," 2052-17, MID, GS, WD, NA; MG, *Relatório . . . Alberto Cardoso de Aguiar . . . 1919,* 67, 127; Melo Franco, *Um estadista da república,* 2:918–23; Távora, *Uma Vida e Muitas Lutas,* 1:89–90.

2. Gen. Caetano de Faria to Alfredo Malan d'Angrogne, Rio, Mar. 2, 1918, quoted in Malan, *Uma Escolha, Um Destino,* 174–75. Faria also argued that because foreigners could not serve in the army as soldiers, they certainly could not exercise command. He may have had the Chilean army in mind because there German officers had held command; see Frederick M. Nunn, *The Military in Chilean History: Essays on Civil-Military Relations, 1810–1973* (Albuquerque: University of New Mexico Press, 1976), 76.

3. Malan, *Uma Escolha, Um Destino,* 174.

4. On the paulista elite's French connections see Love, *São Paulo,* 62, 127, 168–69.

5. Fanneau de la Horie, "Note destiné e à expliquer et confirmer les télégrammes no. 135, 36, 37 bis," Rio de Janeiro, June 1918, Service Historique de l'Armée de Terre, as quoted in Manuel Domingos Neto, "L'Influence Etrangere dans la Modernization de L'Armee Bresilienne (1889–1930)" (thesis for Doctorat IIIéme Cycle, l'Institut des Hautes Etudes de l'Amerique Latine, Université de Paris III, 1979), 217–18.

6. Tasso Fragoso to Malan, Rio, Nov. 29, 1918, in Tristão de Alencar Araripe, *Tasso Fragoso, Um Pouco de História do Nosso Exército* (Rio de Janeiro: Ed. Biblioteca do Exército, 1960), 387; Pantaleão Pessôa, *Reminiscências e Imposições de Uma Vida (1885–1965)* (Rio de Janeiro: author published, 1972), 48, 54.

7. BAO no. 131; see note 9 below for detailed sources.

8. Major Fenton R. McCreery, Rio, Nov. 26, 1918, "President Elect, Vice President and Acting President, Minister of War," 2052-18, MID, GS, WD, RG 165, NA; Tasso Fragoso to Malan, Rio, Nov. 29, 1918, in Araripe, *Tasso Fragoso,* 388; Pessôa, *Reminiscências e Imposições,* 47. Pessôa said that he knew how to inspire confidence at first contact.

9. For his assignments see *Almanac . . . 1912,* 28; *Almanac . . . 1914,* 68; *Almanac . . . 1915,* 22, 240, 559. In 1915 Cardoso de Aguiar's merit position was fifteenth out of sixteen artillery colonels. For political links see Panaleão Pessôa, *Reminiscências e Imposições,* 50; Love, *São Paulo,* 114; Malan, *Uma Escolha, Um Destino,* 177.

10. Tasso Fragoso to Malan, Rio de Janeiro, Nov. 29, 1918, as quoted in Araripe, *Tasso Fragoso,* 385–87; Leitão de Carvalho, *Memórias,* 2:22; Pessôa, *Reminiscências e Imposições,* 54.

11. Araripe, *Tasso Fragoso,* 387–88; Malan, *Uma Escolha, Um Destino,* 177.

12. Maj. Fenton R. McCreery, Rio de Janeiro, Dec. 12, 1918, 2006/3, MID, GS, WD, RG 165, NA.

13. Ibid.

14. Leitão de Carvalho, *Memórias,* 2:22–23.

15. Ibid., 22; MG, *Almanaque . . . 1920,* 531–32.

16. Pessôa, *Reminiscências e Imposições,* 54. He and Mascarenhas went to the Escola de Aperfeiçaomento de Oficiais (Officers Advanced Course, hereafter EsAO), whereas Klinger and "other colleagues of *A Defesa Nacional* took the Review Course" (Leitão de Carvalho, *Memórias,* 2:25–26).

17. Malan, *Uma Escolha, Um Destino,* 178–82. Gamelin (1872–1958) spent 1919–23 in Brazil. In 1931 he was made chief of the French General Staff, commander of all French armies in 1939, and generalíssimo of allied forces at the start of World War II (Sep. 1939). In May 1940, with German forces smashing French defenses, he was relieved. Later arrested by the Vichy government, he spent the rest of the war as a prisoner in Germany. Memory of him is more positive in Brazil than it is in France.

18. Araripe, *Tasso Fragoso,* 382; Lawrence H. Hall, "João Pandiá Calógeras, Minister of War, 1919–1922: The Role of a Civilian in the Development of the Brazilian Army" (Ph.D. diss., New York University, 1983), 178–79.

19. Maj. Fenton R. McCreery, Rio de Janeiro, May 14, 1919, 2006-19, MID, GS, WD, RG 165, NA.

20. Maj. Fenton R. McCreery, Rio de Janeiro, Dec. 16, 1918, 2052-22; Jan. 3, 1919, 2006-8; Mar. 14, 1919, 2052-41; and Lt. Col. T. C. Cook (General Staff) to L. Lanier Winslow (Department of State), Washington, D.C., July 29, 1919, 2052-70, MID, GS, WD, RG 165, NA.

21. Col. R. H. Jordan to Director M[ilitary] I[ntelligence], Memo: "Effect of European War on Strength, Training and Military Policy of Brazilian Army," Sep. 1, 1919, 2006-30, MID, GS, WD, RG 165, NA.

22. President Delphim Moreira, "Mensagem 1919," in Câmara dos Deputados, *Mensagens Presidenciais, 1919–1922* (1922; reprint, Brasília: Câmara dos Deputados, 1978), 76; Maj. Fenton R. McCreery, Rio de Janeiro, May 13, 1919, 2006-18, "Specific Military Information," MID, GS, WD, RG 165, NA; Sir Ralph Paget to Earl Curzon, Rio de Janeiro, Apr. 5, 1920, "Brazil Annual Report, 1919," no. 11546, Foreign Office, 5.

23. MG, *Relatório . . . Cardoso de Aguiar . . . 1919,* 4–5.

24. Ibid., 5–12; Câmara dos Deputados, *Mensagens Presidenciais, 1919–1922,* 76; Major F. R. McCreery, Rio de Janeiro, Apr. 5, 1919, "German-Brazilian Recruits," 10987-524, and May 8, 1919, "President's Message (War Department)," 2052-62, MID, GS, WD, RG 165, NA.

25. Major F. R.McCreery, Rio de Janeiro, Dec. 28, 1918, 2006-3, MID, GS, WD, RG 165, NA. The officers complained that the buildings were not modern, but Major McCreery thought that they were well adapted to the tropical climate. MG, *Relatório . . . Dr. João Pandiá Calógeras . . . June 1920,* 153–58.

26. MG, *Relatório . . . Cardoso de Aguiar . . . 1919,* 87–88; Major F. R. McCreery, Rio de Janeiro, Dec. 28, 1918, 2006-3, MID, GS, WD, RG 165, NA. This sergeants school was partially a response to the discontent that noncommissioned officers displayed in the 1915 uprising.

27. MG, *Almanac . . . 1920,* 19–20, 211–12. The French Aviation Mission was contracted first and separately from the armywide mission, although once Gamelin was officially installed it was subject to him. The mission brought thirty aircraft with it to Campo de Afonsos. Maj. F. R. McCreery, Rio de Janeiro, Feb. 14, 1919, 2006-11, MID, GS, WD, RG 165, NA.

28. Cidade, *Síntese de Três Séculos de Literatura Militar Brasileira,* 361; Távora, *Memórias,* 1:86–91.

29. Araripe, *Tasso Fragoso,* 486.

30. *Jornal do Commércio,* Rio de Janeiro, June 9, 1919, as quoted in Major F. R. McCreery, Rio de Janeiro, June 17, 1919, 2006-65, MID, GS, WD, RG 165, NA.

31. Major F. R. McCreery, Rio de Janeiro, May 13, 1919, 2006-18, and June 17, 1919, 2006-25, MID, GS, WD, RG 165, NA.

32. Major F. R. McCreery, Rio de Janeiro, June 17, 1919, 2006-25, MID, GS, WD, RG 165, NA.

33. *O Jornal,* Rio de Janeiro, June 7, 1919, as quoted in Hall, "João Pandiá Calógeras," 183.

34. Hall, "João Pandiá Calógeras," 183.

35. Gamelin received sixty-five contos [1 conto = 1,000 milreis], or about U.S.$16,250, and an expense allowance of ten contos, or U.S.$2,500; his deputy got forty-five contos, whereas a low-ranked lieutenant received twenty-five contos, or U.S.$6,250. The officers' travel was first-class, with ample amounts for setting up their households. At the end of two years the officers were entitled to four months' home leave at full pay and appropriate per diem. Each officer was to have a Brazilian orderly and access to army horses.

36. Ten years later, when the Americans were interested in a possible aviation mission, the American attaché in Rio had a copy of the 1919 document stolen from Brazilian files. It is found in Major Lester Baker, Rio de Janeiro, Mar. 21, 1929, "Memo: Contracts Between Brazilian and French Governments for French Military Missions," 2006-44, MID, GS, WD, RG 165, NA. The two-year aviation contract was negotiated separately, even though it fell under Gamelin's command once he was installed. Text of the contracts are in Malan, *Missão Militar Francesa,* 207–11, 219–35. See also General A. de Lyra Tavares, *Brasil França ao Longo de 5 Séculos* (Rio de Janeiro: Biblioteca do Exército, 1979), 275–80.

37. Hall, "João Pandiá Calógeras," 187.

38. For the names of the French officers see MG, *Almanac . . . 1920,* 534; career data on some officers and assignments are in Malan, *Missão Militar Francesa,* 236–47.

39. MG, *Relatório . . . Calógeras . . . 1920,* 54–55.

40. Coelho, *Exército Internamente,* 66.

41. Cidade, *Síntese de Três Séculos de Literatura Militar Brasileira,* 407.

42. Capt. Raymundo da Silva Barros, *Sarilho d'Armas (Vida de Caserna)* (Rio de Janeiro: Ed. Calvino Filho, 1934), 59–68. He tells about the tricks a Brazilian orderly played on a French officer. The author was an "official de administração de intendencia" (quartermaster). The book has a rare glossary of army slang.

43. Editorial, "As Escolas da M.M.F.," *ADN,* May 10, 1920, 325–28.

44. Hall, "João Pandiá Calógeras," 195.

45. Quoted in ibid., 191–92.

46. Paul Kennedy, *The Rise and Fall of the Great Powers* (New York: Random House, 1987), 313.

47. Ibid.

48. Ibid., 201. Larry Hall is a retired U.S. Army colonel who studied at the Brazilian army's command and general staff school. Regarding French colonial experience, Gamelin served in Algeria early in the 1890s, and Col. Louis Buchalet, who set up the Quartermaster School, had served in Indochina, Senegal, Madagascar, and French West Africa. His experience in supplying troops in such areas was certainly relevant to the Brazilian army's needs. For Buchalet's career summary see Malan, *Missão Militar Francesa,* 75, 237–38.

49. Coelho, *Exército Internamente,* 66. He also argued that the French were distracting the Brazilians from their border with French Guiana in Amazonia by encouraging them in the view that Argentina was a future threat. He thought France a more probable adversary; see 68.

50. MG, *Relatório . . . Cardoso de Aguiar . . . 1919,* 33. This was from a section entitled "A Nossa Industria Militar," 32–40.

51. Ibid.

52. Ibid., 39.

53. For the activities of the Brazilian Purchasing Commission see File 9971K, MID, GS, WD, Old Navy and Army Branch, RG 165, NA. Most of these documents are from 1917 and 1918. The Brazilians were forced to consider domestic production because American factories could not meet the demands of the U.S. armed forces and their allies and, at the same time, supply the Brazilians with all that they desired.

54. Câmara dos Deputados, *Mensagens Presidenciais, 1919–1922,* 77–78; Maj. F. R. McCreery, Rio de Janeiro, May 8, 1919, "President's Message (War Department)," 2052-62, MID, GS, WD, RG 165, NA.

55. Araripe, *Tasso Fragoso,* 476.

56. Section on Directoria do Material Bellico in MG, *Relatório . . . Cardoso de Aguiar . . . 1919,* 111–22; quote from 113. This policy flowered in the late 1930s; see John D. Wirth, *The Politics of Brazilian Development* (Stanford, Calif.: Stanford University Press, 1970).

57. The arguments have centered on social and intellectual origins, with one group of scholars saying the tenentes represented the urban middle classes (Santa Rosa, Sodré, Jaguaribe, Ramos, Carone, Wirth) and another saying that they did not (Boris Fausto, Decio Saes). A third position is that they were middle class and members of the "military apparatus of the State" but that the lack of information on the urban middle classes makes it difficult to resolve the question of representativeness; Maria Cecila Spina Forjoz, *Tenentismo e Política* (Rio de Janeiro: Paz e Terra, 1977),

28. The standard essays in English are Robert J. Alexander, "Brazilian 'Tenentismo'," *Hispanic American Historical Review* 36 (May 1956): 229–42; John D. Wirth, "Tenentismo in the Brazilian Revolution of 1930," *Hispanic American Historical Review* 44 (May 1964): 161–79. Michael L. Conniff argued persuasively that the middle class supported the tenentes until they became dictatorial in 1931, whereas the lower middle class maintained an alliance until 1934; see his "The Tenentes in Power: A New Perspective on the Brazilian Revolution of 1930," *Journal of Latin American Studies* 10, no. 1 (1978): 61–82. Ilan Rachum's dissertation set the tenentes in the intellectual milieu of the 1920s; see Ilan Rachum, "Nationalism and Revolution in Brazil, 1922–1930: A Study of Intellectual, Military, and Political Protesters and of the Assault on the Old Republic" (Ph.D. diss., Columbia University, 1970).

58. Military Intelligence Division (War Dept.), Washington, D.C., Sep. 7, 1921, Memo: "Brazil's Military Participation in the War," 2006-52, MID, GS, WD, RG 165, ONA Branch, NA. Leitão de Carvalho referred to the secretary to the foreign minister as "meu ex-soldado do Tiro de Imprensa" in *Memórias,* 2:69.

59. Murilo de Carvalho, "As Forças Armadas na Primeira República: O Poder Desestablizador," 206. By comparison in the U.S. Army of 1920, 40 percent of officers were lieutenants.

60. For the history of military education in Brazil see Umberto Peregrino, *História e projeção das instituições CULTURAIS do Exército* (Rio de Janeiro: José Olympio Editora, 1967); and Motta, *Formação do Oficial.*

61. Alberto Tôrres, *O Problema Nacional Brasileiro* (1914; reprint, Brasília: Editora Universidade de Brasília, 1982), 113–33; quote from 133. John Wirth's pioneering article called attention to Tôrres's influence; see Wirth, "Tenentismo," 165. His ideas were given new life just prior to the 1930 Revolution by Francisco José de Oliveira Viana, *Problemas de política objetiva* (São Paulo: Ed. Nacional, 1930); see discussion of his work in Lúcia Lippi Oliveira, ed., *Elite Intelectual e Debate Político nos Anos 30* (Rio de Janeiro: Ed. Fundação Getúlio Vargas, 1980), 339–42.

62. It is worth observing that these two currents were not fixed; although a few officers, such as Leitão de Carvalho, pursued legalism religiously, others moved away from the legalist ranks in later crises. In 1930 the army was so split that even the high command turned against the government. In 1932 Young Turk leader Bertoldo Klinger would lead São Paulo's revolt. Eurico Dutra would assume an interventionist stance in 1937 and 1945, and board member Humberto de Castelo Branco would lead the 1964 coup. Given the apparent reemergence of many early *Defesa Nacional* ideas in the doctrines of the post–World War II Escola Superior de Guerra it would appear that during the Vargas years (1930–45) a synthesis took place that blended these ideas into the tenentes' revolutionary experience to create the more formal national security ideology.

63. Maj. F. R. McCreery, Rio de Janeiro, Feb. 5, 1919, "Maximalist Movement in Rio, November 18, 1918," 10987-499, MID, GS, WD, RG 165, ONA Branch, NA.

64. Col. R. H. Jordan, Rio de Janeiro, Sep. 9, 1919, "Maximalistic tendencies in Brazil; Rumors of discontent among armed forces," 2052-82, MID, GS, WD, RG 165, ONA Branch, NA; and Rio de Janeiro, Sep. 12, 1919, "Anarchistic demonstrations in Brazil," 2052-84, MID, GS, WD, RG 165, ONA Branch, NA. For labor strikes and movement of the era see Joel W. Wolfe, "Anarchist Ideology, Worker

Practice: The 1917 General Strike and the Formation of São Paulo's Working Class," *Hispanic American Historical Review* 71, no. 4 (Nov. 1991): 809–46.

65. See Murilo de Carvalho, "As Forças Armadas na Primeira República: O Poder Desestablizador," 232–33. That such an alliance had grown tighter by the 1930s seems evident from Stanley E. Hilton's *Brazil and the Great Powers, 1930–1939: The Politics of Trade Rivalry* (Austin: University of Texas Press, 1975). By the 1970s it was full blown as Brazil's active arms production and export program attested.

66. Col. R. H. Jordan, Rio de Janeiro, Sep. 1, 1919, "Effect of European War on strength, training and military policy of Brazilian Army," 2006-30, MID, GS, WD, RG 165, ONA Branch, NA.

67. Herculano Teixeira d'Assumpção, "Atividades Militares em Belo Horizonte," Belo Horizonte, Dec. 12, 1947, and his attached memorandum "Alistamento Militar (1875–1920)," Centro de Documentação do Exército, Quartel General do Exército, Brasília.

68. Office of the Military Attaché (likely prepared by Major F. L. Whitley, the then attaché), Rio de Janeiro, Oct. 5, 1921, 2006-56, MID, GS, WD, RG 165, ONA Branch, NA.

69. Col. R. H. Jordan, Rio de Janeiro, Sep. 1, 1919, "Effect of European War on strength, training, and military policy of Brazilian army," 2006-30, MID, GS, WD, RG 165, ONA Branch, NA.

70. Office of the Military Attache, Rio de Janeiro, Mar. 9, 1921, "Campaign Against French Military Mission—Munitions," 2006-44, MID, GS, WD, ONA Branch, NA.

71. Ibid.; MG, *Relatório . . . Dr. João Pandiá Calógeras . . . 1921,* 37–38. Calógeras wrote: "É crescido o martyrologio dos pilotos e dos alumnos, victimas de seu denodo, de sua audacia, por vezes imprudente, ou de circumstancias mal definidas, as que são objecto de continua investigação. De varios accidentes se pode affirmar serem filhos dos excesso de arrojo e impaciencias injustificados de suas victimas."

72. Capt. C. H. Woodward, United States Navy (U.S.N.), to Office of Naval Intelligence, Rio de Janeiro, July 27, 1920, copy attached to Capt. R. H. Jordan, United States Army (U.S.A.), Rio de Janeiro, July 28, 1920, "Activities of French Mission of Instruction," 2006-41, MID, GS, WD, RG 165, ONA Branch, NA.

73. Lt. Asdrubal Gwaier de Azevedo, *Discurso Pronunciado no Clube Militar no dia 25 de junho de 1922* (Recife: n.p., 1932), as reproduced in Sodré, *História Militar do Brasil,* 202–8. Lt. Gwaier accused Gen. Setembrino de Carvalho of falsifying receipts for foodstuffs during the Contestado campaign for personal gain. Col. Cláudio Moreira Bento, former director of the Arquivo Histórico do Exército, challenged the authenticity of Sodré's citation, saying that Gwaier de Azevedo had assumed a new post in Ipameri, Goiás, on June 23, 1922, and so could not have been at the meeting in Rio on June 25; moreover, he called into question the existence of the text cited. See C. Moreira Bento, "A Falsa Ata do Clube Militar," *ADN,* Jan.-Feb. 1989, 173–74. However, Lt. Gwaier, who died in 1970, did not contest Sodré's 1965 account. To make the matter more curious, Gwaier, while exiled in Portugal after taking part in the tenente revolt of 1924, published a book, *Os Militares e a Política* (Barcelos, Portugal: Companhia Editora do Minho, 1926), which totally ignores the affair. Trusting Sodré's honesty, I present this account, but the reader

should wonder where Gwaier was on June 25. Perhaps he had someone sign the record book in Goiás? Could Bento and Sodré both be right?

74. They were Senators Artur Lemos of Pará and Rivadávia Corrêa of Rio Grande do Sul, whom officers thought were likely to use the army for their own political purposes. Lawrence Hall, "To Create an Army: The Mission of Calógeras" (paper presented at American Historical Association, Chicago 1984, 10, n. 14).

75. *O Estado de São Paulo* (São Paulo), Aug. 1, 1919, as quoted in ibid.

76. Hall, "To Create an Army," 1–8.

77. Office of the Military Attaché, Rio de Janeiro, Feb. 21, 1921, 2006-44; Mar. 9, 1921, 2006-44/2; Mar. 28, 1921, 2006-44/3; Apr. 21, 1921, 2006-44/4; and Apr. 21, 1921, 2006-44/5, MID, GS, WD, RG 165, ONA Branch, NA. One of the detached officers was a *Defesa Nacional* founder, Capt. Bertoldo Klinger, who was sent to Peru, where the French also had a mission, as military attaché; Boletim, Estado-Maior do Exército, no. 9, Rio de Janeiro, Mar. 3, 1921, BK21.03.03, Arquivo Bertoldo Klinger, CPDOC.

78. The foregoing, including quotations, is based on Pantaleão Pessôa, *Reminiscências e Imposições,* 57–63.

79. Office of the Military Attaché, Rio de Janeiro, Apr. 25, 1921, "Relief of the Brazilian Chief of Staff," 2006-44/5, MID, GS, WD, RG 165, ONA Branch, NA.

80. Ibid.

81. Pessôa, *Reminiscências e Imposições,* 60.

82. Office of Military Attaché, Rio de Janeiro, Sep. 2, 1921, "Death of General Bento Ribeiro," 2006-44/7, MID, GS, WD, RG 165, ONA Branch, NA. The report described him as "one of the most efficient and experienced officers of the Brazilian Army." Possibly to avoid further demonstrations, or to express its disgust, the family dispensed with the usual military honors in favor of a private funeral.

83. Office of the Military Attaché, Rio de Janeiro, Mar. 28, 1921, 2006-44/3 and Apr. 25, 1921, 2006-44/5, MID, GS, WD, RG 165, ONA Branch, NA. The contract with Simonsen was signed Mar. 18, 1921. The objective was to complete the new posts before Sep. 7, 1922, the centennial of Brazilian independence.

In 1931 Roberto Simonsen published a book explaining and justifying his work: *A Construcção dos Quarteis Para o Exército* (São Paulo: n.p., 1931). See Hall, "João Pandiá Calógeras," 222–66.

84. Office of the Military Attaché, Rio de Janeiro, Sep. 16, 1921, 2006-54, MID, GS, WD, RG 165, ONA Branch, NA. The law specified that one-third of new majors were to be promoted on the basis of seniority and two-thirds by merit selection; one-half of new colonels would be by seniority and one-half by selection. Promotion to brigadier general and general of division would continue to be by presidential decision.

85. MG, *Relatório . . . Calógeras . . . 1920,* 70–71.

86. Delso Mendes da Fonseca interview, Oral History Collection, CPDOC, p. 20. Tasso Fragoso to Major Malan, Rio de Janeiro, Aug. 8, 1918, as quoted in Araripe, *Tasso Fragoso,* 386. "Creio que é temor de opisição da parte dos franceses daqui que receiam ver os Boches de perto." Gen. Araripe, from the vantage point of the late 1950s, thought Tasso unreasonable and alluded to the uselessness of such foreign adventures by pointing to the lack of benefits from Brazil's contribution in the Second

World War: "Sendo pequeno o pèso da balança, os vencedores não iriam dar à nossa cooperação, como aconteceu vinte e cinco anos depois, o devido valor" (386).

87. The attitude of Hermes regarding the French and Germans is a matter of some uncertainty. However, at this point he appeared more inclined toward the Germanic, Indigenous Mission wing than the Francophile wing of the Brazilian army. The U.S. attaché commented that Hermes was "anti-French and pro-German, he being unable to forget the overwhelming impression made by the general maneuvers of the German Army in 1908, which he witnessed as guest of the Kaiser." Office of the Military Attaché, Rio de Janeiro, Oct. 5, 1921, 2006-56, MID, GS, WD, RG 165, ONA Branch, NA; and Major F. L. Whitney, Rio de Janeiro, Oct. 9, 1922, 2006-64, MID, GS, WD, RG 165, ONA Branch, NA.

CHAPTER 6

1. Details from Fonseca Filho, *Marechal Hermes,* 270–73; reference to heart attack on 281.

2. José Augusto Drummond, *O Movimento Tenentista: A Intervenção Militar e Conflito Hierárquico (1922–1935)* (Rio de Janeiro: Ed. Graal, 1986), 72 and 172.

3. Major Lester Baker to Lt. Col. R. H. Williams (chief, Military Attaché Section, G-2), Rio, Oct. 2, 1928, "Population Data," 2054-114; Attaché's Report from Brazil to MID, Rio, Mar. 10, 1921, no. 67: "Animal Census of Brazil 1920," 2052-88; Major R. H. Jordan, Rio, Sep. 2, 1920, no. 53: "Initial Trip to States of São Paulo and Minas Gerais," 2052-86, MID, GS, WD, RG 165, NA.

4. Major Lester Baker, Rio, Oct. 2, 1928, 2052–114, MID, GS, WD, RG 165, NA.

5. Sir John Tilly to Marques Curzon of Kedleston, Rio, Feb. 22, 1923, "Brazil: Annual Report for 1922," Confidential 12147, p. 4.

6. Military Attaché, Brazil, Rio, Aug. 22, 1925, no. 486: "Brazil's Population," 2052-108, MID, GS, WD, RG 165, NA. Interestingly, blacks reportedly also had the highest birth rate (4.8 percent) as compared to whites (4 percent), Amerindians (4 percent), and mulattos (3.7 percent). For the effects of immigration on the state of São Paulo see Love, *São Paulo,* 1–36; and Thomas H. Holloway, "Migration and Mobility: Immigrants as Laborers and Landowners in the Coffee Zone of São Paulo, Brazil, 1886–1934" (Ph.D. diss., University of Wisconsin, 1974), and his "Immigration in the Rural South," in *Modern Brazil: Elites and Masses in Historical Perspective,* ed. Michael L. Conniff and Frank D. McCann (Lincoln: University of Nebraska Press, 1991), Table 1, 148. Sir W. Haggard to Sir Edward Grey, Petrópolis, Mar. 19, 1910, "Annual Report, 1909," Confidential 9690, p. 54.

7. Military Attaché, Brazil, Rio, Mar. 28, 1921, no. 602: "Inland Cities: São Paulo," 2052-93, MID, GS, WD, RG 165, NA. On the city's development in the preceding years see Warren Dean, *The Industrialization of São Paulo, 1880–1945* (Austin: University of Texas Press, 1969).

8. Military Attaché, Rio, Apr. 1, 1925, no. 439: "Chronology," 2052-96/15, MID, GS, WD, RG 165, NA.

9. Major F. L. Whitley, Rio, June 13, 1922, no. 143: "Reconnaissance of Southern Brazil," 2052-98, MID, GS, WD, RG 165, NA.

10. Ibid.; Paulo Prado, *Retrato do Brasil, Ensaio sôbre a Tristeza Brasileira* (Rio de Janeiro: José Olympio Editora, 1928), 3. He ended the book with the dark thought that the "future could not be worse than the past" (183).

11. Reported in Captain Hugh Barclay, Rio, Jan. 29, 1926, no. 526: "Influences Affecting Policy and Military System," 2006-85, MID, GS, WD, RG 165, NA.

12. Major F. L. Whitley, Rio, Aug. 4, 1923, no. 265: "Gendarmerie of Brazil," 2006-70, MID, GS, WD, RG 165, NA. By way of comparison the northern states of Pará and Amazonas had sixty officers and one thousand men for the first and sixteen officers and five hundred men for the second. Although the first was well quartered, uniformed, and armed, it was poorly trained and its officers were usually the governor's political protégés. The Manaus units were also badly trained and disciplined and "paid only at infrequent intervals." For other information on numbers see Heloisa Rodrigues Fernandes, *Política e Segurança, Fôrça Pública do Estado de São Paulo: Fundamentos Históricos-Sociais* (São Paulo: Editora Alfa-Omega, 1974), 219–21; Heloisa Rodrigues Fernandes, "A Força Pública do Estado de São Paulo," in *História Geral da Civilização Brasileira,* vol. 9, bk. 3, *O Brasil Republicano,* ed. Boris Fausto (Rio de Janeiro: DIFEL/Difusão, 1977), 237–56; Keith, "Armed Federal Interventions," 60; and Boris Fausto, ed., *História Geral da Civilização Brasileira,* vol. 9, bk. 3, *O Brasil Republicano.*

13. Captain Hugh Barclay, Rio, Mar. 18, 1926, no. 552: "Brazilian Organized Militia," 2006-70/6; and Captain Hugh Barclay, Rio, July 30, 1925, no. 476: "Combat Estimate for Brazil," 2006-61/5, MID, GS, WD, RG 165, NA. The federal army's strength authorization law for 1925 provided for 3,583 officers and 42,393 enlisted personnel. Throughout the 1920s a gap existed between authorized and actual strength.

14. Discussed in Barclay, Rio, Mar. 18, 1926, no. 552: "Brazilian Organized Militia," 2006-70/6, MID, GS, WD, RG 165, NA.

15. Estado-Maior do Exército, *Relatório dos Trabalhos do Estado-Maior . . . 1929 . . . pelo General de Divisão Alexandre Henriques Vieira Leal* (Rio de Janeiro: Imprensa Militar, Estado-Maior do Exército, 1930), 101. An example of error was that it gave the total of men called up as 557,863 rather than 619,753.

16. Capt. Hugh Barclay, Rio, Feb. 11, 1926, 6200a, 2006-87, GS, WD, RG 165, NA.

17. Capt. Hugh Barclay, Memo: "Recruiting Methods and Facilities," Rio, Feb. 22, 1926, 2006-81; and Maj. Lester Baker, Memo: "Defective Operation of Military Services Law," Rio, Nov. 30, 1928, 2006-81, GS, WD, RG 165, NA. *Correio da Manhã,* Rio, Nov. 29, 1928.

18. Col. Dr. Arthur Lobo da Silva, "A anthropologia no exército brasileiro," *Archivos do Museu Nacional* 30 (1928): 33, Quadro 7 and page 24. The average height of a soldier was 1.65 m. U.S. Army Capt. Hugh Barclay, visiting the army central hospital, reported that he was "impressed with the heavy proportion of venereal cases under treatment," although there had been notable improvement over the past four years. He used some of Col. Arthur Lobo's statistics. Barclay to Asst. Ch. of Staff (G2), Rio, June 17, 1924, no. 367, Brazil 6300, RG 165, NA.

19. Lobo da Silva, "A anthropologia no exército brasileiro," 36.

20. H. W. Brown, Q. M. Clerk (in absence of Col. R. H. Jordan) to Director, Military Intelligence, Rio, Feb. 3, 1920, 2006-37, GS, WD, RG 165, NA.

21. MG, Relatório . . . Gen. Div. Fernando Setembrino de Carvalho . . . 1926, 11.

22. Capt. Hugh Barclay, "Loyalty," Rio, Dec. 15, 1926, 2656-K-3, 6300; and Capt. Hugh Barclay, "Combat Training in the Brazilian Army," Rio, Dec. 17, 1926, 2006-97, 6700, RG 165, G-2 Regional Files, NA.

23. Capt. Hugh Barclay, "Brazil's Current Military Policy," Rio, Jan. 25, 1926, 2006-84, GS, WD, RG 165, NA. The closing of the army library is one of the explanations for the lack of systematic study of the army's history. The Biblioteca do Exército was restored and some of its old collection reunited in 1937. See Cidade, Síntese de Três Séculos de Literatura Militar Brasileira, 398–400. He says that Gen. Tasso Fragoso was not listened to in the decision to close the library. See also Umberto Peregrino, História e Projeção das Instituições Culturais do Exército (Rio de Janeiro: José Olympio Editora, 1967), 96–97.

24. Maj. Lester Baker, "Mental and Moral Traits of the Brazilian Soldier," no. 835, Rio, Oct. 19, 1928, 2006-108, GS, WD, RG 165, NA.

25. Capt. Hugh Barclay, "Commissioned Officers of Brazilian Army," no. 536, Rio, Feb. 18, 1926, 2006-88, GS, WD, RG 165, NA; and Capt. Hugh Barclay, "Combat Efficiency and Value of Brazilian Military Establishment," no. 655, Rio, Nov. 22, 1926, 2006-90, GS, WD, RG 165, NA.

26. Baker, "Mental and Moral Traits." It is suggestive that a modern Portuguese dictionary lists twenty-one synonyms for the word mentira (lie): Aurélio Buarque de Holanda Ferreira, Novo Dicionário da Língua Portuguesa, 1st ed. (Rio: Ed. Nova Fronteira, n.d.), 918. Regarding responsibility and stealing, several post commanders gave me similar explanations in the 1970s and 1980s.

27. Baker, "Mental and Moral Traits."

28. Brown to Director; Baker, "Defective Operation."

29. Capt. Hugh Barclay, Rio, Feb. 4, 1926, no. 529: "Brazilian War Department," 2006-86, MID, GS, WD, RG 165, NA.

30. For a career summary see "Setembrino de Carvalho," DHBB, 1:682–84.

31. Sketch based on DHBB, 3:2624–25. On Mato Grosso 1906 see Joaquim Ponce Leal, Os Homens e As Armas: Notícia de um Ciclo Revolucionário (Rio de Janeiro: Livraria Editora Cátedra, 1980), 233–96.

32. José Pereira da Graça Aranha (1868–1931) was also from Maranhão; his novel Canaan (Boston: Four Seas, 1920) examined the effects the interaction of immigrants and natives was having on Brazil. He contributed to growing nationalism by criticizing dependency and holding up the mulatto as the "true Brazilian."

33. Araripe, Tasso Fragoso; and DHBB, 2, 1343–45. His books are A Batalha do Passo do Rosário (Rio de Janeiro: Imprensa Militar, 1922); História da Guerra entre a Tríplice Aliança e o Paraguai, 5 vols. (Rio de Janeiro: Imprensa Militar, 1934); and A Revolução Farroupilha (1835–1845): Narrativa Sintétic a das Operações Militares (Rio de Janeiro: Imprensa Militar, 1938); A Paz com o Paraguai Depois da Guerra da Tríplice Aliança (Rio de Janeiro: Imprensa Militar, 1941).

34. The process of establishing the general staff had been slow. It was authorized in a law approved in October 1896 that indicated that it and a new general quartermaster (Intendencia Geral) would replace the adjutant general's and quartermaster

general's sections. They took until January 1899 to phase themselves out and for the general staff to begin to exist. Estado-Maior do Exército, *História do Estado-Maior do Exército* (Rio de Janeiro: Biblioteca do Exército, 1984), 12.

35. Tasso Fragoso had long been concerned with this problem. In 1918 he wrote Malan D'Angrogne, then in Paris, for information on the functioning and interaction of the French Ministry of War and general staff. He wrote that the "grupo Germanista" wanted to eliminate the ministry and put everything under the general staff. He feared that Gen. Alberto Cardoso de Aguiar would react by weakening the general staff to the point that it would return to being the equivalent of the old adjutant general's department. Tasso Fragoso to Major Malan, Rio, Nov. 29, 1918, in Araripe, *Tasso Fragoso,* 388.

36. Araripe, *Tasso Fragoso,* 520; Setembrino to Artur Bernardes, Rio, Aug. 29, 1922, FSC 22.08.29, Arquivo Fernando Setembrino de Carvalho, CPDOC, Rio de Janeiro.

37. Araripe, *Tasso Fragoso,* 520–23, 622.

38. Ibid., 523–24.

39. Ibid., 523–30. The quotation is from 526. In 1937 Tasso wrote about this in the essay "The Revolution of 1930," which was not published until 1951; see *Revista do Instituto Histórico e Geográfico Brasileiro,* vol. 211, Apr.-June 1951. Araripe reprinted it in full, 516–89. Tasso's report for 1927 (dated Apr. 1928) contained detailed recommendations for the new French contract; Estado-Maior do Exército, *Relatório dos Trabalhos do Estado-Maior . . . 1927 . . . Tasso Fragoso* (Rio de Janeiro: Imprensa Militar, 1928), 42–52.

40. Estado-Maior do Exército, *História do Estado-Maior do Exército* (Rio de Janeiro: Biblioteca do Exército Editora, 1984), 67–73; Estado-Maior do Exército, *Relatório dos Trabalhos do Estado-Maior . . . 1923 . . . Tasso Fragoso* (Rio: Imprensa Militar, 1924), 7.

41. MG, *Relatório . . . Setembrino de Carvalho . . . 1926,* 12; Military Attaché Office to MID, Rio, Sep. 16, 1921, 2006-54; and Capt. Hugh Barclay, Rio, Jan. 25, 1926, report 523, "Brazil's Current Military Policy," 2006-84, MID, GS, WD, RG 165, NA.

42. Laurita Pessôa Raja Gabaglia, *Epitácio Pessôa (1865–1942)* (Rio de Janeiro: José Olympio Editora, 1951), 2:593. For Epitácio's relationship with his older brother and with Deodoro see Lewin, *Politics and Parentela,* 169, 220–21, 363 n. 22. Epitácio owed his first political post to Deodoro.

43. Lewin, *Politics and Parentela,* 168; Lourival Coutinho, *O General Góes Depõe* (Rio de Janeiro: Livraria Editora Coelho Branco, 1956), 2; Murilo de Carvalho, "As Forças Armadas na Primeira República: O Poder Destabilizador," 120; Leitão de Carvalho, *Memórias,* 1:13. Gilberto Freyre, *Order and Progress,* 188.

44. Maj. F. L. Whitley to Asst. Chief of Staff (G-2), Rio, Aug. 22, 1923, no. 274, "Brazilian Army for 1924," 2006-73; and Whitley to ACS (G-2), Rio, Oct. 31, 1923, no. 306, "Sheets for Economic Monograph and for Combat Monograph," 2052-102, GS, WD, RG 165, NA.

45. Estado-Maior do Exército, *Relatório dos Trabalhos do Estado-Maior . . . 1923 . . . Tasso Fragoso,* 6; Arthur da Silva Bernardes, Rio, May 3, 1924, "Mensagem 1924," in Câmara dos Deputados, *Mensagens Presidenciais, 1923–1926* (1926; reprint, Brasília: Câmara dos Deputados, 1978), 234–35. Juarez Távora recalled that "due to the lack of officers, we exercised, as lieutenants, the command of the Companies" in the Fourth

Engineers Battalion in Itajubá, Minas Gerais, in 1921 (Távora, *Uma Vida e Muitas Lutas,* 1:105). The bill that would have funded the "authorized" numbers in Table 6.5 failed in Congress. The army had to face 1924 with the actual numbers in the table. See note 44 for the sources.

46. Maj. Lester Baker, "Commissioned Officers of Brazilian Army, 1928," no. 836, 2006-109, GS, WD, RG 165, NA; L. Baker, "Cadet Training in the Brazilian Army," no. 533, Rio, Feb. 13, 1926, 6740, 2277-K-6, RG 165, G-2 Regional Files, NA.

47. Capt. Hugh Barclay, "Discipline," no. 697, Rio, Jan. 25, 1927, 2006-102, Brazil 6300, RG 165, G-2 Regional Files, NA.

48. Ibid.; also Capt. Hugh Barclay, Rio, Nov. 22, 1926, no. 655, 2006-90, GS, WD, RG 165, NA.

49. Capt. Hugh Barclay, "Brazilian War Debt," no. 529, Rio, Feb. 4, 1926, 2006-86; and Capt. Hugh Barclay, "Chronology," no. 371, Rio, July 4, 1924, 2052-96/10, GS, WD, RG 165, NA.

50. MG, *Relatório . . . July 1921 . . . Calógeras* (Rio: Imprensa Militar, 1921), 47; Office of Military Attaché to Director MID, Rio, Oct. 5, 1921, no. 97, 2006-56, MID, GS, WD, RG 165, NA.

51. Távora, *Uma Vida e Muitas Lutas,* 1:100, 105.

52. Maj. F .L. Whitley, "Pay of the Army, Brazil," no. 477, Rio, July 31, 1925, 2006-65, GS, WD, RG 165, NA.

53. MG, *Almanak do Ministerio da Guerra para o anno de 1925* (Rio de Janeiro: Imprensa Militar, 1925), 15–16.

54. Maj. Lester Baker, "Brazil's New Retirement Law," no. 850, Rio, Jan. 7, 1929, and "Brazil's New Retirement Law Made Effective," no. 872, Rio, Apr. 30, 1929, 2006-110, GS, WD, RG 165, NA. The law extended benefits to enlisted men and their dependents but there were few "old soldiers" at that time. Perhaps it was intended to make an enlisted career more attractive. At any rate, the national treasury would not feel the effects for years to come.

55. Maj. Lester Baker, "Brazil's New Retirement Law," no. 850, Rio, Jan. 7, 1929, 2006-110, GS, WD, RG 165, NA.

56. Maj. F. L. Whitley to Asst. Ch. Staff (G2), Rio de Janeiro, May 13, 1924, 2277-K; idem, "Cadet Training in the Brazilian Army," Feb. 13, 1926, no. 533, 2277-K-6, 6740, G2 Regional, RG 165, NA.; Estado-Maior do Exército, *Relatório dos Trabalhos do Estado-Maior . . . 1927 . . . Tasso Fragoso,* 25–26; Estado-Maior do Exército, *Relatório dos Trabalhos do Estado-Maior . . . 1929 . . . Alexandre Henriques Vieira Leal,* 27.

57. Estado-Maior do Exército, *Relatório dos Trabalhos do Estado-Maior . . . 1927 . . . Tasso Fragoso,* 24. As noted elsewhere in this book, the title "cadet" had been proscribed in 1898, partly in response to the military school rebellion of 1897. Officially the students were called "alumnos" or sometimes "praças"; the name applied as well to soldiers. By the end of the 1920s sentiment to revive the title "cadet" seems to have been developing; in the 1927 relatório cited above Tasso Fragoso used "cadete de Realengo." In 1931 Col. José Pessôa Cavalcanti Albuquerque, who reorganized the military school and secured the new dress uniforms, also reestablished the tradition of calling the students "cadets." See Hiram de Freitas Câmara, *Marechal José Pessôa: A Força de um Ideal* (Rio de Janeiro: Biblioteca do Exército, 1985), 60–68. Juarez Távora mentioned the collar insignia; see Távora, *Uma Vida, Muitas Lutas,* 84.

The selection of the 1851–52 campaign uniforms may have been related to the series of eleven lectures that Capt. Genserico de Vasconcelos gave at the general staff school and EsAO in 1920 that were published as *História Militar do Brasil: Introdução da influencia do factor militar na organização da nacionalidade; A Campanha de 1851–1852* (Rio de Janeiro: Imprensa Militar, 1922).

58. Maj. F. L. Whitley, "Visit to Brazilian Military Academy at Realengo," Rio, May 13, 1924, no. 349, 2277-K-3, 6740, RG 165, G-2 Regional, NA; MG, *Relatório . . . Fernando Setembrino de Carvalho . . . Nov. 1924* (Rio: Imprensa Militar, 1924), 25; Estado-Maior do Exército, *Relatório dos Trabalhos do Estado-Maior . . . 1927 . . . Tasso Fragoso,* 21–26; Estado-Maior do Exército, *Relatório dos Trabalhos do Estado-Maior . . . 1929 . . . Alexandre Henriques Vieira Leal,* 23–24.

59. Motta, *Formação do Oficial,* 323–24. For grades see MG, *Relatório . . . Setembrino de Carvalho . . . Nov. 1924* (Rio: Imprensa Militar, 1924), 26–29. Estado-Maior do Exército, *Relatório dos Trabalhos do Estado-Maior . . . 1927 . . . Tasso Fragoso,* 22–23. The teaching staff was certainly carrying the dead weight of tenured faculty (twenty-seven out of an administrative and teaching staff of forty-five), who would appear "for an occasional lecture and leave the actual daily teaching to other instructors" (Capt. Hugh Barclay, "Cadet Training in the Brazilian Army," no. 533, Rio, Feb. 13, 1926, 2277-K-6, 6740, RG 165, G-2 Regional, NA).

60. Artilleryman Álvaro Fiúza de Castro [BAO no. 236; *DHBB,* 1:727–28] was chief of staff for six years, seven months in 1948–55; others who made general were Infantrymen Nile Horacio de Oliveira Sucupira [BAO no. 322; José Alves Magalhães [BAO no. 303; *DHBB,* 3:2024–25]; Euclides Zenóbio da Costa [BAO no. 240; *DHBB,* 2:988–89]; João Saraiva [BAO no. 551]; Aricles Gonçalves Pinto [BAO no. 398]; Alexandre Zacharias de Assumpção [BAO no. 253; later spelling Assunção, *DHBB,* 1:240–41]; and Engineer Benjamin Rodrigues Galhardo [BAO no. 335; *DHBB,* 2,1422–23]. MG, *Almanak . . . 1925,* 597–98.

61. Estado-Maior do Exército, *Relatório dos Trabalhos do Estado-Maior . . . 1923 . . . Tasso Fragoso,* 21; Estado-Maior do Exército, *Relatório dos Trabalhos do Estado-Maior . . . 1927 . . . Tasso Fragoso,* 23–25. Maj. F. L. Whitley, "Visit to Brazilian Military Academy at Realengo," no. 349, Rio, May 13, 1924, 2277-K-3, 6740, RG 165, G-2 Regional, NA. Perhaps for different reasons than Tasso Fragoso had in mind, during the Estado Novo (1937–45) the army would exclude Negroes, mulattoes, Jews, sons of immigrants from Poland or Russia, members of working-class families, sons of separated parents, and non-Catholics. The legal basis for such exclusions was the "Law of Social Conformism and Elimination of Nonconformists" that General Eurico Dutra wrote, which "formed the moral basis of the Army's disciplinary structure," and Article 177 of the Estado Novo Constitution, which permitted expulsions of officers when the high command considered such expulsions "in the interest of the public service or for convenience of the regime." MG, *Relatório . . . Gen. Eurico Gaspar Dutra . . . 1940* (Rio de Janeiro: Imprensa Militar, 1941), 22; Nelson Werneck Sodré, *Memórias de um Soldado* (Rio de Janeiro: Civilização Brasileira, 1967), 188–90; Murilo de Carvalho, "Armed Forces and Politics," 205–6.

62. Estado-Maior do Exército, *Relatório dos Trabalhos do Estado-Maior . . . 1929 . . . Alexandre Henriques Vieira Leal,* 23. Although the Brazilians were satisfied for most of the decade, in 1929 the French sent an infantry officer named Grancey, whose lack

of knowledge of Portuguese and of Brazil made it necessary to appoint a Brazilian as his adjutant. Ibid., 27.

63. MG, *Relatório . . . Calógeras . . . 1920,* 54

64. Marechal J. B. Mascarenhas de Moraes, *Memórias* (Rio de Janeiro: José Olympio Editora, 1969), 1:60–62; Pantaleão Pessôa, *Reminiscências e Imposições,* 54; Malan, *Missão Militar Francesa,* 101–3.

65. Estado-Maior do Exército, *Relatório dos Trabalhos do Estado-Maior . . . 1923 . . . Tasso Fragoso,* 18–19.

66. Ibid., 16–17. By 1929 a majority of those admitted to the Escola Estado-Maior (thirty-five out of thirty-eight captains and lieutenants) had *not* taken the exam. Estado-Maior do Exército, *Relatório dos Trabalhos do Estado-Maior . . . 1929 . . . Alexandre Henriques Vieira Leal,* 11.

67. Estado-Maior do Exército, *Relatório dos Trabalhos do Estado-Maior . . . 1929 . . . Alexandre Henriques Vieira Leal,* 81.

68. Estado-Maior do Exército, *Relatório dos Trabalhos do Estado-Maior . . . 1923 . . . Tasso Fragoso,* 33–35; Capt Hugh Barclay, Rio, Jan. 25, 1926, Rpt 523: "Brazil's Current Military Policy," 2006-84, GS, WD; Capt. Hugh Barclay to Lt. Col. N. E. Margetts (Chief MID, WD), Rio, Aug. 31, 1926, 2052-111, MID, GS, WD, RG 165, NA; Estado-Maior do Exército, *Relatório dos Trabalhos do Estado-Maior . . . 1929 . . . Alexandre Henriques Vieira Leal,* 13–14.

69. Estado-Maior do Exército, *Relatório dos Trabalhos Estado-Maior . . . 1923 . . . Tasso Fragoso,* 16, 40–42.

70. The French came in 1906, stayed until the outbreak of war in 1914, and returned in 1919. Fernandes, *Política e Segurança,* 157–63; H. W. Brown (Clerk), Rio, Dec. 12, 1925, 2006-70, MID, GS, WD, RG 165, NA. In 1924 the Força Pública totaled 14,200, which was nearly half the size of the federal army, which then had about 30,000 soldiers.

71. Estado-Maior do Exército, *Relatório dos Trabalhos do Estado-Maior . . . 1925 . . . Tasso Fragoso* (Rio de Janeiro: Imprensa Militar, 1926), 27–30.

72. Military Attaché, Rio, Jan. 16, 1925, no. 422: "Chief of French Military Mission in Brazil," 2006-44, MID, GS, WD, RG 165, NA. The attaché cited Gen. Abílio da Noronha as source of comment on inability to apply "the combat principles taught them by the French specialists."

73. Captain Hugh Barclay, Memo: "Combat Training in the Brazilian Army," Rio, Dec. 17, 1926, 2006-97, MID, GS, WD, RG 165, NA.

74. Estado-Maior do Exército, *Relatório do Trabalhos do Estado-Maior . . . 1925 . . . Tasso Fragoso,* 42–43.

75. Captain Hugh Barclay, Rio, Mar. 24, 1926, 2006-90, MID, GS, WD, RG 165, NA.

76. Estado-Maior do Exército, *Relatório do Trabalhos do Estado-Maior . . . 1925 . . . Tasso Fragoso,* 42–43. The Relatório was dated September 1926. His study "Reflexões sobre a Situação Militar do Brasil," Oct. 1927 (typed, bound) is in CDOC-EX, Brasília.

77. Estado-Maior do Exército, *Relatório dos Trabalhos do Estado-Maior . . . 1927 . . . Tasso Fragoso,* 4–5, 17–19, 42–47. Gen. Coffec had served as Chief of Artillery; see career summary, Military Attaché, Rio, Jan. 16, 1925, no. 422: "Chief of French Mil-

itary Mission in Brazil"; and H. W. Brown (Clerk), Rio, Sep. 5, 1927, "New Chief of the French Military Mission to Brazil," no. 743, both in 2006-44, MID, GS, WD, RG 165, NA.; for list of mission names see MG, *Alamanak . . . 1925, 571.*

78. Estado-Maior do Exército, *Relatório dos Trabalhos do Estado-Maior . . . 1927 . . . Tasso Fragoso,* 47–52. He made this point particularly in regard to aviation and the flight and mechanics training in France of Major Antonio Guedes Muniz and Captain Ivan Carpenter Ferreira. In 1931, however, both men were still in Europe, so any impact they would have had was delayed well beyond Tasso Fragoso's hopes of April 1928. *Almanak . . . 1931,* 420 and 423 gave their assignments.

79. Estado-Maior do Exército, *Relatório dos Trabalhos do Estado-Maior . . . 1929 . . . Alexandre Henriques Vieira Leal,* 45–49. See the chart on page 93 giving data on courses between 1920 and 1929.

80. Lieutenant Julio Schwenck (aide to General Ivo Soares) to Captain Hugh Barclay, Rio, Nov. 11, 1925; Harry W. Brown (Clerk) to Assistant Chief of Staff, G-2, Rio, Nov. 11, 1925; Captain Hugh Barclay to Assistant Chief of Staff, G-2; Secretary of State to Dr. Ivo Soares, Washington, n.d.; all 2257K-10, MID, GS, WD, RG 165, NA. Brown advised that the Brazilian medical service had received an appropriation of $670,000 for medical gear and that if the general visited the United States, the money would likely be spent there.

81. Maj. Aiden Simons (Military Sales Division, I. E. Dupont de Nemours & Co.) to Lt. Col. N. E. Margetts (Foreign Liaison Officer, General Staff), Wilmington, Del., Oct. 21, 1926, and attached correspondence, 2257K-12, MID, GS, WD, RG 165, NA.

82. Maj. Lester Baker to Lt. Col. R. H. Williams (Chief, Military Attaché Section, G-2), Rio, Aug. 9, 1928; and Williams to Baker, Washington, D.C., Sep. 1, 1928, 2257K-15, MID, GS, WD, RG 165, NA.

83. Captain Hugh Barclay, Memo: "Instruction with Foreign Armies," Rio, Dec. 3, 1926, 2257K-13, MID, GS, WD, RG 165, NA. Two who had trained in the United States were Alexandre Galvão Bueno and Marcolino Fagundes, who had spent three months at the Coast Artillery School at Fortress Monroe. Both also served on the purchasing commission to the United States during World War I. Galvão Bueno had been in the second group to go to Germany as well.

84. Major Lester Baker, Memo: "Contracts between Brazilian and French Governments for French Military Missions," Rio, Mar. 21, 1929, 2006-44, MID, GS, WD, RG 165, NA.

85. Major Lester Baker, Rio, May 29, 1930, 2006-44/13, MID, GS, WD, RG 165, NA; for a study of French cultural penetration see Gilles Matthieu, *Une Ambition Sud-Américaine: Politique culturelle (1914–1940)* (Paris: Ed. L. Harmattan, 1991).

86. Major Lester Baker, Rio, June 24, 1930, 2257K-16, MID, GS, WD, RG 165, NA. The critic hoped that President-elect Julio Prestes had gotten some reformist ideas during a 1930 visit to West Point.

87. Nunn, *Yesterday's Soldiers,* 192–200.

88. Lt. Col. Augusto Tasso Fragoso to Gen. Emygdio Dantas Barreto, Nov. 15, 1910: Memo—"Conjecturas sobre o plano de operações da Argentina contra Brasil," attached to 19ª Communicação do adido militar na República Argentina, Buenos Aires, Nov. 25, 1910, CDOC-EX, Brasília. For a lengthy quotation from this memo and a broader discussion of Brazilian strategic thought see Frank D. McCann, "The

Brazilian General Staff and Brazil's Military Situation, 1900–1945," *Journal of Inter-american Studies and World Affairs* 25, no. 3 (Aug. 1983): 299–324.

89. The two former attachés were Armando Duval and Genserico Vasconcellos. Duval was interested in the relationships among national organization, military power, and national prestige, and he wrote an analysis of the Argentine military that influenced Brazilian officers: *A Argentina, potência militar,* 2 vols. (Rio de Janeiro: Imprensa Nacional, 1922). And Vasconcellos wrote the *História Militar do Brasil* (1922), cited earlier, which dealt with the 1851–52 Brazilian intervention against the Rosas government.

90. Editorial, *ADN,* Apr. 10, 1915, 197–98; staff author, "Uma mobilisação," *ADN,* Aug. 10, 1914, 370; Francisco de Paula Cidade, "Os fanaticos, liame histórico," *ADN,* Oct. 10, 1914, 12–14; idem, "Em torno de contestado," *ADN,* Jan. 10, 1914, 124–25; Francisco Raul D'Estillac Leal, "Do contestado, observações colhidas nas operações da columna sul," *ADN,* Aug. 10, 1915, 357–61; idem, same title, *ADN,* Oct. 10, 1915, 27–30.

Decades later the campaign would still be an object of study for future staff officers preparing to enter the general staff school; Escola de Comando e Estado-Maior do Exército (Curso de Preparação), *Guerras Insurrecionais no Brasil (Canudos e Contestado)* (Rio de Janeiro: Imprensa Nacional, 1968).

91. The reader has already met many of these men. The list of participating officers included future chiefs of staff, ministers of war, many important commanders and political figures, and one president, as this selection will indicate: Lieutenants Pedro Aurélio de Góes Monteiro, Eduardo Gomes, Mario Travassos; Captains Valentim Benício da Silva, Francisco Gil Castelo Branco, Pedro de Alcantara Cavalcanti, Eurico Dutra, Euclides de Figueiredo, Álvaro Fiuza de Castro, Firmo Freire do Nascimento, Milton de Freitas Almeida, João Guedes da Fontoura, Estevão Leitão de Carvalho, Isauro Reguera, Anor Teixeira dos Santos, Genserico de Vasconcelos; Majors Manoel de Araripe and Armando Duval; Lieutenant-Colonel Alfredo Malan D'Angrogne; Colonels Nestor Sezefredo Passos and Tertuliano de Albuquerque Potyguara; and Generals Augusto Tasso Fragoso and Candido M. Rondon. General Maurice Gamelin (and Capt. Joaquim de Souza Reis Netto), *Manobra de Quardos de Exército de 1921–1922* (Rio de Janeiro: Imprensa Militar, 1922), 5, 18–20, 141–47. See also Leitão de Carvalho, *Memórias,* 2:46–49. The French wisely associated influential "Young Turks" with this and other activities. Gamelin seems to have taken Captain Souza Reis under his wing.

92. Augusto Tasso Fragoso, "Reflexões sobre a Situação militar do Brasil," Oct. 1927 (Carbon copy of document in CDOC-EX, Brasília).

93. João Pandiá Calógeras to Epitácio Pessôa, Rio, Nov. 15, 1922, in Câmara dos Deputados, *Mensagens Presidenciais, 1919–1922,* 631; MG, *Relatório . . . Calógeras . . . Junho de 1920,* 33. *Senzala* is the term used for slave quarters in Brazil. Its origin is Quimbundo, a language native to Angola. Calógeras must have chosen the term in a deliberate attempt to be shocking.

94. Editorial, *A Defeza Nacional* 8, no. 85 (Rio, Aug. 10, 1920): 1.

95. Major Egydio Moreira de Castro e Silva, *Á Margem do Ministério Calógeras (na pasta da guerra)* (Rio de Janeiro: Ed. Melso S.A., 1961), 89–115. The major was an engineer.

96. There are lists in MG, *Relatório . . . Calógeras . . . Outubro de 1922* (Rio de Janeiro: Imprensa Militar, 1922), 4–10; Calógeras to Epitácio Pessôa in the president's final report, Rio, Nov. 15, 1922, in Câmara dos Deputados, *Mensagens Presidenciais, 1919–1922* (Brasilia: Câmara dos Deputados, 1978), 632–34.

97. Hall, "João Pandiá Calógeras," 232.

98. MG, *Almanaque . . . 1891* (Rio de Janeiro: Imprensa Militar, 1891), xii. The Tenth Cav. Regiment was in São Paulo, and the Thirty-first Inf. Battalion was in Minas. MG, *Relatório . . . Jose Bernardino Bormann . . . Maio de 1910* (Rio de Janeiro: Imprensa Militar, 1910), pages following 166. *"Mappa da força do Exército em 1 de Abril de 1910."* There were a total of 62 officers and 821 soldiers in Minas and 63 officers and 437 soldiers in São Paulo in 1910. An artillery battalion was planned for Santos, but at the time of the *Relatório* it was not organized.

99. For 1918 paulista Força Pública numbers see Fernandes, *Política e Segurança,* 218–24. The 1926 figure is from Capt. Hugh Barclay, Rio, Mar. 18, 1926, no. 552: "Brazilian Organized Militia," 2006-70/6, MID, GS, WD, RG 165, NA. Fernandes cited the 1926 total as 9,216, but since she obtained that number from the authorization law, I decided that the contemporary U.S. military intelligence report is likely more accurate.

My interpretation here differs from that of Joseph Love, who wrote, "The Paulista's strategy of relying on state troops to offset the power of the army differed sharply from the strategy adopted by the Mineiros" (219). While I agree that Minas bargained support for federal policies in exchange for local autonomy, the mineiro leaders also took the precaution to insure that they had adequate firepower. See Love, *São Paulo,* 217–19.

The forces of both states were organized more like small armies than police units: Minas's were configured into five infantry battalions, one cavalry squadron, and one machine-gun company; São Paulo's more powerful force was grouped into ten infantry battalions, one school battalion, two cavalry regiments, one artillery battery, and one aviation section. See Barclay's Mar. 18 report above.

100. Hall, "João Pandiá Calógeras," 244–45.

101. Ibid., 252.

102. Castro e Silva, *Á Margem do Ministério Calógeras,* 42–43.

103. Ibid., 49–51. On a visit to São João del Rey in the 1970s I recall being awakened at dawn by artillery being fired just outside the town.

CHAPTER 7

1. The best study of the movement is Drummond, *O Movimento Tenentista.*

2. Sir John Tilley to Marquess Curzon of Kedleston, Rio, Feb. 22, 1923, Confidential 12147, "Brazil, Annual Report for 1922, Foreign Office Confidential Prints, 32. Hermes' wife, Nair de Teffé, suggested that his sons wanted him to be a candidate in the 1921 elections, that Ruy Barbosa, among others, tried to get him bitten again by the presidential "blue fly." Nair de Teffé Hermes da Fonseca, *A Verdade sobre a Revolução de 22* (Rio de Janeiro: Gráfica Portinho Cavalcanti, 1974), 94–95.

3. Odylio Denys, *Ciclo Revolucionário Brasileiro, Memórias* (Rio de Janeiro: Ed. Nova Fronteira, 1980), 173–74.

4. Delso Mendes da Fonseca, Oral History, CPDOC-Rio, 14 and 20. His BAO no. is 364. He thought that perhaps their preparation for, and frustrated desire to participate in, World War I might have influenced them to rebel. His career led to general's stars in 1952. For a biography see "Delso Mendes da Fonseca" *DHBB*, 2:1300–1301; Aspásia Camargo and Walder de Goes, *Meio seculo de combate: Diálogo com Cordeiro de Farias* (Rio de Janeiro: Ed. Nova Fronteira, 1981), 64–65. Cordeiro's BAO no. is 243. For a discussion of the role of turmas in the Brazilian officer corps see McCann, "The Military," 51–54.

5. Távora, *Uma Vida e Muitas Lutas*, 1:89–91. Regarding the Bangu strike see "Siqueira Campos," *DHBB*, 1:597.

6. See Chap. 6 for the French mission; and João Baptista de Magalhães, *A evolução militar do Brasil* (Rio de Janeiro: Biblioteca do Exército, 1958), 349–50; Sodré, *História Militar do Brasil*, 199–200; Rachum, "Nationalism and Revolution in Brazil," 120–21.

7. Frederick Nunn, "Military Professionalism and Professional Militarism in Brazil, 1870–1970: Historical Perspectives and Political Implications," *Journal of Latin American Studies* 4 (1972): 29–54; idem, "The Latin American Military Establishment: Some Thoughts on the Origins of Its Socio-political Role and an Illustrative Bibliographic Essay," *The Americas* 28 (1971): 135–41; idem, "Effects of European Military Training in Latin America: Origins and Nature of Professional Militarism in Argentina, Brazil, Chile, and Peru, 1890–1940," *Military Affairs* 39 (1975:, 1–7). Nunn has provided a fuller analysis in *Yesterday's Soldiers*. Samuel F. Huntington, *The Soldier and the State: The Theory and Politics of Civil-Military Relations* (Cambridge, Mass.: Harvard University Press, 1959) had argued that, based on the European experience, professionalism should have destroyed militarism. But in the Brazilian case it produced it.

8. On the tensions produced by the presence of the French mission see above Chaps. 5 and 6; see also McCann, "Influencia Estrangeira no Exército Brasileiro," 83–117. Sir Ralph Paget to Earl Curzon, Rio, Apr. 5, 1920, Confidential 11546, "Brazil, Annual Report, 1919," Foreign Office Confidential Prints, 5. Ambassador Paget observed that politicians feared that a properly functioning general staff would rob the president upon his assuming office of the privilege of appointing the chiefs. Further, he said that there appeared "to be no public opinion in favour of the formation of an efficient force, and Brazilians . . . always seem torn between the desire to introduce efficiency and the fear that an efficient army or navy might be subverted and used by a military dictator to overthrow the existing order" (5).

9. Edgard Carone in *O Tenentismo* (São Paulo: DIFEL, 1975) sees the tenentes as progressive and antioligarchic, but Maria do Carmo Campello de Souza, in *Estado e partidos políticos no Brasil (1930 a 1964)* (São Paulo: Alfa-Omega, 1976), 101–102, considers the movement ambiguous—reformist, but open to authoritarian political methods. Keith, "Armed Federal Interventions," 67–68, stresses professional impulses behind tenentismo, an interpretation that one of its more famous adherents, Juarez Távora, seems to support in *Á guisa de depoimento: Sobre a revolução brasileiro de 1924* (São Paulo: O Combate, 1927), 1:89–90. Drummond, *O Movimento Tenentista*, 50, 89, sees the tenentes as rebelling not against the "dominant classes" but against the "subordinate position of the army in the State apparatus," whereas their struggle with the military legalists was to determine which group acted in the army's name.

10. Hélio Silva, *1922: Sangue na areia de Copacabana* (Rio de Janeiro: Editora Civilização Brasileira, 1965), provides a documentary account of the rebellion. Hermes was confined for seventeen hours.

11. Campos Coelho, *Em Busca de Identidade,* 82–91.

12. Leitão de Carvalho, *Dever militar,* 91–93.

13. Delso Mendes da Fonseca, Oral History, CPDOC-Rio, 39; "Sigueira Campos" *DHBB,* 1:597–98; Hugo G. Borges Fortes, *Canhões Cruzados, Uma Síntese da História da Artilharia de Costa Brasileira* (Rio de Janeiro: Editora Biblioteca do Exército, 2001), 152–53.

14. Mascarenhas de Moraes, *Memórias,* 1:66–70. Filinto Müller and João Alberto were imprisoned for five months with other tenentes, giving them time for considerable conversation. Both men later participated in the revolt of 1924 and played major roles in the Vargas government of the 1930s. The commander of the regiment, João José de Lima (BAO no. 151), made general, and, of course, Mascarenhas became one of the major figures in Brazilian military history, commanding the expeditionary force to Italy during World War II.

15. Delso Mendes da Fonseca, Oral History, CPDOC-Rio, 13, 21, 23.

16. Távora, *Guisa de Depoimento,* 1:108.

17. The eleven were Captains Joaquim do Nascimento Fernandes Távora (*DHBB,* 4:3310–11), Juarez do Nascimento Távora (BAO no. 278; *DHBB,* 4:3311–25), Otávio Muniz Guimarães; Lieutenants Vitor César da Cunha Cruz (BAO no. 318), Estênio Caio de Albuquerque Lima (BAO no. 295; *DHBB,* 3:1828), Henrique Ricardo Hall (also Holl; *DHBB,* 2:1591–92), Eduardo Gomes (*DHBB,* 2:1477–86), José Coelho Valente do Couto, Lídio Gomes Barbosa, Rui da Cruz Almeida (*DHBB,* 1:88), and Ajudante Rômulo Fabrizzi. Names from Anna Maria Martinez Corrêa, *A Rebelião de 1924 em São Paulo* (São Paulo: HUCITEC, 1976), 64, n. 190.

18. Anna Maria Martinez Corrêa, *Rebelião de 1924,* 65. Newton Estallac Leal (BAO no. 252) was a graduate of Realengo in 1915 who supported the movement so discretely that he was promoted to captain of artillery in September 1922 and served on the staff of Gen. Abílio de Noronha, commander of the Second Military Region in São Paulo, until the outbreak of the 1924 rebellion; he would be Góes Monteiro's operations staff officer in the Revolution of 1930 and Vargas's minister of war 1951–54; see "Newton Estallac Leal," *DHBB,* 2:1751–58. Infantry officer Granville Belerofonte de Lima was commissioned aspirante from the military school when it was located in Porto Alegre in January 1910. He reached second lieutenant in October 1914 and first lieutenant in July 1919. His promotion to captain would be in November 1930, with a date of rank of September 1924. His promotion pattern was typical of those who sided with rebellion in 1922. MG, *Almanak . . . 1931,* 66.

19. Anna Maria Martinez Corrêa, *Rebelião de 1924,* 66.

20. Ibid., 67–69, 76–77; "Isidoro Dias Lopes," *DHBB,* 3:1918–19.

21. Drummond, *O Movimento Tenentista,* 103–4. That the tenentes were unwilling to act without this cover *(cobertura)* is shown in their use of Hermes in 1922, Isidoro in 1924, and Góes in 1930. In 1924 tenentes in Sergipe sought unsuccessfully the leadership of retired general José Calazans, and the desperation of those in the central-south, while Isidoro was making up his mind, was such that they discussed inviting General Abílio de Noronha, commander of the Second Military Region

headquartered in São Paulo, even though he had never shown the least inclination to rebel. For the tenentes a senior leader provided the possibility of "catalyzing last minute support among the officers of the Army, pulling into the rebellion close colleagues and/or hesitant ones" (103). Corrêa reviewed the tenente discussion regarding General Abílio in *Rebellião de 1924*, 89–90.

22. Corrêa, *Rebelião de 1924*, 76–77.

23. Ibid., 74–75; Távora, *Memórias*, 1:132–35; "Bertoldo Klinger," *DHBB*, 2:1686.

24. Anna Maria Martinez Corrêa, *Rebellião de 1924*, 77–80.

25. Hélio Silva, *1922*, 399–400; Corrêa, *Rebellião de 1924*, 93–94. For the past months the officers imprisoned at the general staff school in Rio not only had been kept appraised of the direction of events, but, because security at the school was so lax, they were able to sneak out for meetings. At least one of these meetings was in Barra do Piraí with officers from Minas and São Paulo. But a sudden inspection of their empty prison quarters led to the arrest of the officer of the day and the transfer, when they finally returned from their daily turn through the streets, of the tenente prisoners to a prison ship.

26. Joel W. Wolfe, "The Rise of Brazil's Industrial Working Class: Community, Work, and Politics in São Paulo, 1900–1955" (Ph.D. diss., University of Wisconsin, 1990), 93–95; Corrêa, *Rebelião de 1924*, 120–29.

27. Hélio Silva, *1922*, 396–99; Carone, *A primeira república*, 86–88; Neill Macaulay, *The Prestes Column; Revolution in Brazil* (New York: New Viewpoints, 1974), 14–15.

28. Setembrino de Carvalho to Firmiano Pinto, Mayor of São Paulo, Rio, July 12, 1924, as quoted in Corrêa, *Rebelião de 1924*, 141, fn. 451; the rest of this paragraph is based on 141–47.

29. Paulo Duarte, *Agora Nós* (São Paulo: n.p., 1927), 75–76, as quoted in Hélio Silva, *1922*, 377. Comment on Joaquim Távora is from Neill Macaulay, *Prestes Column*, 19. Corrêa cited a report by paulista mayor Firmiano Pinto that civilian deaths totaled five hundred; Corrêa, *Rebelião de 1924*, 151.

30. José Ibaré Costa Dantas, *O Tenentismo em Sergipe (Da Revolta de 1924 à Revolução de 1930)* (Petrópolis: Ed. Vozes, 1974), 91–143; Carone, *O Tenentismo*, 103–6; and idem, *República Velha*, 2:377–78; "José Calasans," *DHBB*, 1:537; "Augusto Maynard Gomes," *DHBB*, 2:1474–76; "Riograndino Kruel," *DHBB*, 2:1697–98. Maynard was promoted to captain by the revolutionary government in Nov. 1930 and then to major in Aug. 1931, lt. col. in 1936, and colonel in 1939. During the Vargas years he was twice interventor in Sergipe, and between 1947 and 1957 he was a federal senator. Kruel was eventually sent to a unit in Mato Grosso from which he deserted to Paraguay and Argentina, returning to Brazil only after the Revolution of 1930. He later served in various security posts and retired as a brigadier in 1944. He played a role in toppling President João Goulart in 1964.

31. Macaulay, *Prestes Column*, 15.

32. Ibid., 17–25. Quotation is from 17.

33. Dutra made this comment in a 1965 interview with Neill Macaulay; see Macaulay, *Prestes Column*, 91, 250 n. 62. Oswaldo Cordeiro de Farias said much the same in more detail. In later years he discussed these events with those on the other side, such as Góes Monteiro and Humberto de Castelo Branco, in whom he observed, as well as "em tantos outros o desinteresse em nos combater." He noted that

"o Exército não tinha, na época, quadros capazes de enfrentar a luta com a obstinação e a dureza com que a Coluna a enfrentou." See Camargo and Góes, *Meio século de combate,* 106.

34. Coutinho, *General Góes Depõe,* 12. Souza Reis committed suicide in the general staff offices in the Ministry of War in Rio de Janeiro.

35. Lourenço Moreira Lima, *A Coluna Prestes (Marchas e Combates)* 3d ed. (São Paulo: Ed. Alfa-Omega, 1979), 63–72. The author was the civilian secretary of the Prestes Column. Neill Macaulay called his book "by far the most valuable firsthand account of the march of the Prestes Column." Macaulay, *Prestes Column,* 252 n. 38. Góes Monteiro told of an officer on Colonel Mariante's staff, returning from combat in Paraná, who police attempted to arrest after he was heard, in the São Paulo railway station, criticizing the government. Only Mariante's "over my dead body" intervention prevented the officer from being seized. Coutinho, *General Góes Depõe,* 30–31.

36. Estado-Maior do Exército, *Relatório dos Trabalhos do Estado-Maior . . . 1925 . . . Tasso Fragoso,* 1, 4, 33–34; Estado-Maior do Exército, *Relatório dos Trabalhos do Estado-Maior . . . 1927 . . . Tasso Fragoso,* 53–55. There is a need for a study of the finances of the state and civl units during the 1920s and 1930s.

37. Estado-Maior do Exército, *Relatório dos Trabalhos do Estado-Maior . . . 1925 . . . Tasso Fragoso,* 5, 27, 29–30.

38. Góes's promotion from captain to major was unusually rapid, so much so that it later embarrassed him to the point that he described it as "an illicit promotion." He may well have been embarrassed because the promotion may have been compensation for spying on his fellow officers for President Bernardes. Góes to Bernardes, n.d., Góes Monteiro Papers (hereafter GMP); this is a draft or copy in Góes's handwriting. The letter was likely written between February and June 1926 because in it Góes referred to an incident at Joaseiro, and that was the only time he was there during operations against the Prestes Column.

Whatever the exact reasons for his promotion, in a system marked by patronage he clearly had powerful backers. Góes to Gen. Octávio de Azevedo Coutinho [Commander, First Division, Rio de Janeiro], July 5, 1929, GMP; for Góes's promotion dates see *Almanak . . . 1931,* 198. He was promoted to captain in January 1924 and to major in October 1926, a period of two years, ten months.

By comparison, contemporary legalists and fellow cavalry officers Eurico Dutra (captain in June 1921 and major in May 1927) spent five years eleven months, and Euclydes de Oliveira Figueiredo (captain in Mar. 1919 and major in Sep. 1922) waited three years, seven months; artillery officers Bertholdo Klinger (captain in Feb. 1918 and major in Dec. 1922) was three years, eleven months, and Armando Duval (captain, Nov. 1912 and major in May 1920) was seven years, six months; and infantry officer Estevão Leitão de Carvalho (captain, Jan. 1919 and major Feb. 1923) waited five years, one month. Clearly, Góes's promotion was fast by contemporary measure. Data were drawn from the above almanac.

39. Here Góes reflected the German writer Hans von Seeckt and the teachings of the French military mission. During World War I Von Seeckt had served on the Turkish front; from 1918 to 1926 he was commander in chief of the *Reichswehr;* and after retirement he reorganized Chiang Kai-shek's Chinese Nationalist Army. His most famous work, *Thoughts of a Soldier,* trans. Gilbert Waterhouse (London: Ernest

Benn, 1930), discussed many ideas that Góes echoed. He asserted that the army should be political but not in the sense of a political party. "The army serves the state and the state alone, for it is the state" (80).

In analyzing Seeckt and Frenchman Charles De Gaulle, Frederick Nunn noted that for the former "the army was *the* national institution, transcending the chronological confines of history, from the monarchy and empire of the past to the parliamentary republic"; but the latter thought that only officers could be "men of action . . . men of character." Nunn observed that there was a continuity of thought among the European officers and their South American counterparts that viewed civilian society as "self-destructive, fractious, without direction." The army in their view was "corporate, organic"; military training developed leaders (men of character); obligatory service made men into full citizens. Only in the army did men of all classes "rub shoulders." "Their ideas," Nunn wrote, " . . . were so similar as to constitute hard evidence of continuity in officer-class self-perception regardless of nationality" (Nunn, *Yesterday's Soldiers,* 226–30).

40. Brig. Gen. Clóvis Travassos, interview by Peter S. Smith, Rio de Janeiro, Nov. 10, 1974; "Clóvis Travassos," *DHBB,* 4:3373–74. He served on Góes's immediate staff during his second tour as minister of war, 1945–46; Travassos's father had been close to Góes, and the families were on good terms throughout Góes's life. Smith and I are writing a biography of Góes.

41. Henry H. Keith and Robert A. Hayes, eds., *Perspectives on Armed Politics in Brazil,* 69, 94, 121–22; Fernandes, *Política e Segurança,* 161–63.

42. Macaulay, *Prestes Column,* 227; Stanley E. Hilton, "The Armed Forces and Industrialists in Modern Brazil: The Drive for Military Autonomy, 1889–1954," *Hispanic American Historical Review* 62, no. 4 (Nov. 1982): 632–33.

43. Góes Monteiro, "O Destacamento Mariante no Paraná Occidental (Reminiscências)," Rio de Janeiro, Junho de 1925, 3–11, (typescript), Arquivo Histórico do Exército—Rio. This typescript also contains a single-page "explicação prévia," dated May 1936, perhaps when Góes considered publication. He lamented that the condition of the army had not changed.

44. "Resposta ao G[ener]al. Flores," 42; Fontoura, *O Globo* (Rio), Oct. 29, 1956; Coutinho, *General Góes Depõe,* 43–48.

45. *Diário Carioca* (Rio), July 18, 1928; *A Manhã* (Rio), Oct. 5, 1929; *Diário Carioca* (Rio), Aug. 21, 1928; *Diário Nacional* (São Paulo), May 30, 1929, as quoted in Rachum "Nationalism and Revolution in Brazil," 198, 199–200, 201, 207.

46. On the functioning of the pre-1930 electoral system see Michael L. Conniff, "The National Elite," in *Modern Brazil: Elites and Masses in Historical Perspective,* ed. Michael L. Conniff and Frank D. McCann (Lincoln: University of Nebraska Press, 1989), 29–31. Vargas represented Rio Grande do Sul in the federal Chamber of Deputies from 1922 to 1926, was minister of finance in the Washington Luís government from 1926 to 1928, and then president of Rio Grande do Sul, from which post he ran for federal president.

47. Washington Luís's first choice for minister of war, Brig. Gen. Alfred Malan d'Angrogne, turned down his offer because the president would not grant amnesty to the rebels; see Leitão de Carvalho, *Dever militar,* 169, and Chap. 8, n. 8, 520.

48. Leitão de Carvalho later charged that the war minister had been derelict in his duty, not alerting the administration to known dangers: ibid., 180–81. See also General Tasso Fragoso, "A revolução de 1930," *Revista do Instituto Histórico e Geográfico Brasileiro*, 211 (Apr.-June 1951): 30. The revolutionaries sounded Leitão out about leading the military revolt; he refused and led his troops in resistence, but significantly he did not turn in or arrest those who approached him.

49. Leitão de Carvalho in *Dever Militar* emphasized the role of those desiring amnesty in the formation of a "national *underground*"; see 174–75; Wirth, "Tenentismo," 161–79. On the second generation of tenentes see Drummond, *O Movimento Tenentista*, 171–73.

50. Coutinho, *General Góes Depõe*, 48–56.

51. Ibid., 57.

52. Ibid., 57–58; Pedro A. de Góes Monteiro, *A revolução de 30 e a finalidade política do exército* (Rio de Janeiro: Assis Cintra e Adersen, 1934), 38–39. Cícero was the youngest and Góes's favorite among his five brothers. The conversation with Aranha in January 1930 apparently occurred in the home of Góes's brother-in-law, Dr. Antonio de Saint-Pastous. Conspirators João Neves da Fontoura and João Alberto were there. João Neves da Fontoura, *Memórias* (Porto Alegre: Globo, 1963), 2:387. For dating see Góes's *Fé de ofício,* Arquivo do Exército—Rio.

53. Contemporaries disagreed over just when Góes received the offer and over how many others the rebel leadership had already approached. Indeed, it is likely that when he was first approached, the idea was not to make him military commander but to get him to join the revolutionary staff to be headed by another. Góes claimed the offer was "in his hands" by April, while the plotters were negotiating with Luís Carlos Prestes in Buenos Aires. Juarez Távora, however, said that Góes was the third choice, after Prestes and João Alberto Lins de Barros, and that the decision to approach Góes was a last-minute one in late August. There may even have been another name or two, in contention: in any event Góes was the last, because he accepted.

Góes's version may well be correct. In June he wrote to his friend Captain Aguinaldo Caiado de Castro on the General Staff in Rio, saying that he had turned the plotters down, preferring, he asserted, to work for change legally. Probably, Góes thought that his superiors would know that the conspirators had approached him and that his mail would be opened. He repeated his loyalist protestations to the same friend a month later. Mello Franco placed Góes in the center of events by July 26, so the decision was made before then. Leitão de Carvalho and Figueiredo both helped indirectly by not taking action against the conspirators and by keeping quiet about the approaches made to them. Leitão refused because he believed in preserving legality, Figueiredo because he felt bound by his personal loyalty to regional commander Gil de Almeida.

Coutinho, *General Góes Depõe*, 69–70, 147; Távora, *Uma Vida e Muitas Lutas,* 1:277–79; João Neves de Fontana, *Memórias,* 388; Robert M. Levine, *The Vargas Regime: The Critical Years, 1934–1938* (New York: Columbia University Press, 1970), 3; letters, Góes Monteiro to [Captain Aguinaldo] Caiado [de Castro], June 30, July 29, 1930, GMP; Virgilio de Mello Franco, *Outubro, 1930,* 2d ed. (Rio de Janeiro: Ed. Schmidt, 1931), 270, 277–80, 320–24; Estevão Leitão de Carvalho, *Na Revolução de*

30: A Attitude do 8º R.I. (Guarnição de Passo Fundo) (Rio de Janeiro: Ed. Schmidt, 1933), 170–76.

54. Lewin, *Politics and Parentela,* 364, 389, 406. In fact, he had gained a reputation as a "hard judge" because he continually demanded to review the decisions of lower military courts, which frequently gave minimum sentences of seven months. One such review of an officer-staffed court martial *(auditorias militares* or *conselhos)* was one aimed at Major Eurico Gaspar Dutra (later minister of war and president), who headed a court martial that had absolved a tenente deserter. "João Pessôa," *DHBB,* 4:2702.

55. Valentina da Rocha Lima, *Getúlio, uma história oral* (Rio de Janeiro: Ed. Record, 1986), 204.

56. Drummond, *O Movimento Tenentista,* 183–84.

57. Ibid., 185. The powerful state military police forces constituted the other strong arm.

58. Dênis de Moraes and Francisco Viana, *Prestes: Lutas e Autocríticas* (Petrópolis: Editora Vozes, 1982), 47–50.

59. Hélio Silva, *1930: A Revolução Traída* (Rio de Janeiro: Ed. Civilização Brasileira, 1966), 178–82; Ann Quiggins Tiller, "The Igniting Spark—Brazil 1930," *Hispanic American Historical Review* 35 (1965): 384–92; Jordan Young, *The Brazilian Revolution of 1930 and the Aftermath* (New Brunswick, N.J.: Rutgers University Press, 1967); Lewin, *Politics and Parentela,* 403–7. After the assassination the capital city of Paraíba was renamed João Pessôa.

60. Coutinho, *General Góes Depõe,* 74–75.

61. A. Saint-Pastous to Góes, P. Alegre, telegrams, Aug. 23, 26, 1930, GMP; Cícero de Góes Monteiro to Góes, telegrams, Pelotas, Sep. 1, 4, 7, 9, 1930, GMP.

62. Mello Franco, *Outubro, 1930,* 290, said that Antonio Carlos wanted to delay the revolt to make it Maciel's responsibility; on the codes and messages see 313–14. Mello Franco observed that later they found many of their messages and letters in Washington Luís's files, apparently undeciphered (see 313).

63. Coutinho, *General Góes Depõe,* 83–85; Mascarenhas de Moraes, *Memórias,* 1:84–87. Mascarenhas lamented the collapse of army unity, which he thought "ought to be the supreme objective sought by military chiefs" (87).

64. General Pedro Geraldo de Almeida, interview by Peter S. Smith, Rio de Janeiro, Dec. 16, 1974 (Almeida was one of Góes's aides in the 1940s. My thanks to him for sharing this information with me.); Paul Frischauer, *Presidente Vargas: Biografia* (São Paulo: Companhia Editora Nacional, 1944), 262–63.

65. *Fé de ofício* of Góes Monteiro, Arquivo do Exército—Rio.

66. General Gil Antonio Dias de Almeida, *Homens e factos de uma revolução* (Rio de Janeiro: Ed. Calvino Filho, n.d.), 149–54.

67. Leitão de Carvalho, *Na Revolução de 30,* 149–50.

68. Tasso Fragoso, "A Revolução de 1930," as quoted in Araripe, *Tasso Fragoso,* 546; Mello Franco, *Outubro, 1930,* 312.

69. For a discussion of elite attitudes toward the common people see Robert M. Levine, "Elite Perceptions of the Povo," in *Modern Brazil: Elites and Masses in Historical Perspective,* ed. Michael L. Conniff and Frank D. McCann (Lincoln: University of Nebraska Press, 1989), 209–24.

70. Pedro de Góes Monteiro, "Agosto de 1930" (typescript), GMP.

71. Ministério da Guerra, Inspetoria de 2° Grupo de Regiões Militares, "Plano geral de ação para a organização definitiva do Exército em vista de seu papel na hipótese de guerra. 1930" (typescript), GMP.

72. Jordan Young, "Military Aspects of the 1930 Brazilian Revolution," *Hispanic American Historical Review* 44 (1964): 180. Quotations are from "Agosto de 1930," GMP; this document is also in Manoel Luiz Lima Salgado Guimarães et al., eds., *A Revolução de 30: Textos e Documentos,* 2 vols. (Brasília: Editora Universidade de Brasília, 1982), 1:359. Góes's attitude reflects "the politics of the appetites" rather than a radical "politics of identity" as discussed in Chapter 3.

73. Coutinho, *General Góes Depõe,* 78, 82, 93–96. To avoid calling public attention to his presence in Porto Alegre, Góes did not see Vargas from January 1930 until October 1. Indeed, he did not even wear his uniform in the capital until the afternoon of the revolt. Alzira Vargas do Amaral Peixoto, *Getúlio Vargas, Meu Pai* (Rio de Janeiro: Ed. Globo, 1960), 36.

74. General Gil de Almeida, *Homens e Factos,* 223–34; Hélio Silva, *1930,* 185–98.

75. General Gil de Almeida, *Homens e Factos,* 231–36; Coutinho, *General Góes Depõe,* 106.

76. General Gil de Almeida, *Homens e Factos,* 231; Mello Franco, *Outubro, 1930,* 347.

77. Coutinho, *General Góes Depõe,* 99–100, 104–13; Carolina Nabuco, *A vida de Virgílio de Melo Franco* (Rio de Janeiro: José Olympio Editora, 1962), 21; Leitão de Carvalho, *Dever militar,* 183–90. Leitão saw the regional commander, General Gil, like the war minister, as irresolute and, despite ample warning of a coup, as not having taken sufficient precautions. The general believed Vargas's reassurances because of a long friendship and membership in his party, the *Partido Republicano* Rio-grandense. See also Virgílio de Mello Franco, *Outubro, 1930.* Mello Franco was secretary to Góes during the campaign. General Gil claimed that he had tried to prevent arms and munitions being sent to Rio Grande to keep them out of the wrong hands in case of rebellion; see his *Homens e Factos,* 293.

78. General Gil, *Homens e Factos,* 263–78; Leitão de Carvalho, *Na Revolução de 30,* 157–220; on side arms see 241.

79. Leitão de Carvalho, *Dever militar,* 183–99; Murilo de Carvalho, "Armed Forces and Politics," 194. Leitão was promoted for merit to colonel on Sept. 11, 1930; see MG, *Almanak . . . 1931,* 28.

80. Coutinho, *General Góes Depõe,* 102, 104, 117; see also "Afonso Henrique de Miranda Correia," *DHBB,* 2:934.

81. Coutinho, *General Góes Depõe,* 107–11; Mello Franco, *Outubro, 1930,* 347–52.

82. Camargo and Góes, *Meio século de combate,* 172, 177–85; Geraldo Tito Silveira, *Crônica da Polícia Militar de Minas* (Belo Horizonte: n.p., 1966), 113–32. Lt. Col. Aristarcho Pessôa was an aspirante of 1907; he served in the Contestado campaign in Oct. and Nov. 1912 and again in Dec. 1913–Feb. 1914. If it had not been for his brother's murder he likely would not have involved himself in the movement. He was promoted to colonel in 1931. See *Almanak . . . 1931,* 34; "Aristarco Pessôa Cavalcanti de Albuquerque," *DHBB,* 1:46.

83. Alexandre José Barbosa Lima Sobrinho, *A Verdade Sobre a Revolução de Outubro—1930,* 2d ed. (São Paulo: Alfa-Omega, 1975), 142–50. Tiro 333 was commanded

by a sergeant. The northeastern governors fled by sea, or tried to do so. Hélio Silva, *1930,* 280–92.

84. United States Department of State, *Foreign Relations of the United States, 1945,* 439; Young, *Brazilian Revolution,* 64–69.

85. Araripe, *Tasso Fragoso,* 547.

86. Malan, *Uma Escolha, Um Destino,* 304–5.

87. Araripe, *Tasso Fragoso,* 554.

88. Ibid., 555–57.

89. Ibid., 557–60.

90. Ibid., 557–61; Malan, *Uma Escolha, Um Destino,* 308; Jeneral [Bertoldo] Klinger, *Narrativas aotobiograficas,* vol. 5, *O Coronél* (Rio de Janeiro: "O Cruzeiro," 1950), 149–68; "João de Deus Mena Barreto," *DHBB,* 1:313–14.

91. Malan, *Uma Escolha, Um Destino,* 309–10. Among those at the meeting were Generals Octávio de Azeredo Coutinho, commander of First Military Region, Joao Gomes Ribeiro Filho (*DHBB,* 2:1488–89), in charge of the infantry brigade at Vila Militar, José Luiz Pereira de Vasconselos (*DHBB,* 4:3516), commander of another Rio infantry brigade, Álvaro Guilherme Mariante (*DHBB,* 3:2092–94), director of military aviation, and Alfredo Malan d'Angrogne (*DHBB,* 1:144–45), vice chief of the general staff.

92. Souto, *Uma Escolha, Um Destino,* 309–10.

93. Araripe, *Tasso Fragoso,* 561–62; "Sezefredo dos Passos," *DHBB,* 3:2624–25; Dialogue between Generals Nestor and Mena is from Jeneral [Bertoldo] Klinger, *Narrativas aotobiograficas,* 5:168–70, 206. There are photos of the fire in Ana Maria Brandão Murakami, ed., *A Revolução de 1930 e seus antecedentes* (Rio de Janeiro: Ed. Nova Fronteira, 1980), 182–83.

94. Lima Sobrinho, *A Verdade Sobre a Revolução,* 155–57; Araripe, *Tasso Fragoso,* 562–70. There was considerable mob action in São Paulo on October 24 and 25, where frustrated, angry workers burned the Cambuci prison, infamous for its mistreatment and torture of prisoners. When Vargas arrived there on October 29, striking workers pressed their case successfully for his intervention. See Wolfe, "Rise of Brazil's Industrial Working Class," 117–20.

95. See photos in Murakami, *Revolução de 1930,* 123–93.

96. Drummond, *O Movimento Tenentista,* 197–99.

97. Leitão de Carvalho, *Dever Militar,* 198.

CHAPTER 8

1. In April 1939 Aranha was foreign minister, negotiating with the United States regarding trade issues and the creation of a central bank that would restrict commerce with Germany, thereby limiting Brazil's ability to pay for German weapons. When an American asked what the army had to do with banking and trade, Aranha replied: "My dear fellow, you simply don't begin to know how much everything has to do with the army at the present time" (Norbert A. Bogdan to Laurence Duggan, Apr. 24, 1939, 033.3211 Aranha 71, NA; for full discussion see McCann, *Brazilian-American Alliance,* 131).

2. Góes Monteiro, *A Revolução,* 163.

3. Ministerio da Guerra, Estado-Maior do Exército, *Regulamento Interno e dos Serviços Geraes dos Corpos de Tropa do Exército* (R.I.S.G.) (Rio de Janeiro: Imprensa Militar, 1930), 9–10, 245, 250. Regulation 49 outlawed "authorizing, promoting, or signing collective petitions addressed to any civil or military authority" (243). It was also forbidden for soldiers to assemble publicly without permission (Articles 50, 51).

4. See Murilo de Carvalho, "Armed Forces and Politics," 193–223; and his more detailed "Forças Armadas e Política, 1930–1945," in CPDOC, *A Revolução de 30: Seminário Internacional,* 109–87. The Cuban sergeants revolt started as a protest against rumored pay cuts; restrictions on access to commissions as officers; and poor housing, uniforms, and meals. They had not set out to depose the government or remove the officer corps. But tactical alliance with antigovernment factions soon converted insubordination into a deeper rebellion. The causal complaints were remarkably similar to the situation in Brazil. Both armies had a large number of blacks in the enlisted and noncommissioned ranks. As Louis A. Pérez, the leading specialist on the Cuban army, commented: "[O]ne reason Batista enjoyed widespread popularity among the enlisted men was the social mobility he early infused into the hitherto predominantly all-white officer corps." See Louis A. Pérez, *Army Politics in Cuba, 1898–1958* (Pittsburgh: University of Pittsburgh Press, 1976), 81–85.

5. Campos Coelho, *Em Busca de Identidade,* 128–29.

6. For an interesting account of Getúlio's early years in the missions' region of Rio Grande's frontier see Rubens Vidal Araujo, *Os Vargas* (Porto Alegre: Editora Globo, 1985). On Madero's fateful mishandling of the federal army see John M. Hart, *Revolutionary Mexico: The Coming and Process of the Mexican Revolution* (Berkeley: University of California Press, 1987), 237–62. For the Mexican military more broadly see Roderic Ai Camp, *Generals in the Palacio: The Military in Modern Mexico* (New York: Oxford University Press, 1992).

7. Vargas, *Diário,* 1:29.

8. José Fernandes Leite de Castro, the son of an army marshal, was born October 5, 1871, in Cruz Alta, Rio Grande do Sul. He entered the School of Tactics and Marksmanship *(Tiro)* in Rio Pardo (RGS) in 1887, finishing the artillery course as an alferes in 1890. In the civil war he saw action both in Rio Grande and in the Rio de Janeiro area, where he distinguished himself in the battle for Niterói. After a stint as instructor in the Colégio Militar he joined the commission designing the coastal defenses for Santos (SP) and Rio, 1896–97, which brought him into contact with problems of heavy weapons procurement. Promoted to captain in 1901, he was in Europe from 1907 to 1909, studying the latest war material. In 1910 he commanded the bombardment of the marine barracks, ending the revolt on the Ilha das Cobras; the following year he was promoted to major and in 1916 to lieutenant colonel. He was part of the mission sent to France to observe war operations. Attached to the staff of artillery commander Gen. Charles M. E. Mangin he developed a plan that the French used for transporting allied forces. At French suggestion he was named to the League of Nations commission that redrew the boundaries of the Saar Basin. Raised to colonel in 1919, he was made chief of the commission responsible for studying war operations and for acquiring armaments, a post he held until 1928 that gave him much time in Europe. In 1922 he made general and was named director general of artillery in addition to his other jobs. In 1928 he was

inspector general of coastal defense. When the revolution broke out he was in Novo Friburgo (RGS) and returned to Rio to participate in the deposition of Washington Luís (see BAO no. 148; "José Fernandes Leite de Castro," *DHBB,* 1:731–32).

Alfred Malan d'Angrogne was born in Genoa, Italy, on June 25, 1873. His family brought him to Pelotas, RGS, in 1885; from there they moved to Rio de Janeiro, where in 1890 he entered the military school of Praia Vermelha. He was caught up in the school's disciplinary problems and sent to the ranks, where he became a sergeant before entering the preparatory school at Fortaleza, Ce. In December 1893 he was one of the 125 students sent aboard the *Andrada,* one of Flint's Fleet, to Rio to fight against the naval revolt. He saw action afloat and ashore in the south, where he was in Moreira César's detachment in Santa Catarina and Paraná until the end of the fighting in 1895. He spent two years at the military school in Rio Grande do Sul (1896–98) before obtaining his bachelor's degree in mathematics and physical sciences in 1902. From then until 1916, assigned to the cavalry and then to the engineers (in the latter he became a captain in 1905), he worked on mapping Rio Grande do Sul and demarcating the boundary with Uruguay. In 1914 he had been made major, now thoroughly familiar with the gaúcho state and the frontier regions. In May 1916 he went to Paris as military attaché, where he toured the Belgium front with Hermes da Fonseca, who was spending the war years in Europe. His articles on the war appeared in the *Correio do Povo* (Porto Alegre). In 1919 he handled the Paris side of the negotiations for the French military mission, including the selection of Gamelin as its first chief (see Chap. 5). He was Brazil's military delegate to the Versailles conference, after which he returned to Rio, where he became head of the personal staff of Minister of War Calógeras. In that position he took the general staff course and participated in the 1922 maneuvers in Rio Grande do Sul. In November that year he made full colonel and took command of the First Engineer Battalion at Vila Militar. With the rebellion in July 1924 he was given one of the detachments fighting the tenentes in São Paulo. Later that year he commanded the military district of Mato Grosso, in which post he received his Brig. General stars in December. He fought the Prestes Column, specifically the troops of Juarez Távora. In September 1926 he joined the general staff as Tasso Fragoso's first subchief. Washington Luís offered him the post of minister, which he refused because of his differences with the president's policies, especially regarding amnesty for the rebels of 1922 and 1924, which he favored. As Staff subchief he was twice head of the promotions commission. He asked to be relieved when Tasso resigned as chief, but the new chief, General Alexandre Leal, refused to let him go. With the Revolution of 1930 he participated in the deposition of Washington Luís. He served as chief of the general staff until January 1931, when a fatal illness forced him to step down. Although sick he was promoted to major general in October 1931. He died in Petrópolis in January 1932 (see BAO no. 161; "Alfred Malan d'Angrogne," *DHBB,* 1,144–45.)

Francisco Ramos de Andrade Neves was born in Rio Grande do Sul on May 31, 1874. At fifteen he entered the army and was a second lieutenant by nineteen. The sources do not make clear when he obtained his bachelors of mathematics and physical sciences, but likely it was in 1893. He fought for the government in the civil war of 1893–95. He was not at Canudos. In 1901 he made first lieutenant, in 1908 captain, and then he was promoted for merit to major in 1916 and was posted to Fort Copacabana. Raised to lieutenant colonel in 1919, he headed the second section of the general staff; he held various positions in the Brazilian delegation to the League of Nations and while there was made colonel in 1922. The next year he went to Belgium as military attaché. Returning to Brazil in 1925 he took over directorship of the arsenal in Rio de Janeiro. Winning his brigadier general's stars in 1926, he took over as director of War Material in 1927. It probably did not hurt his career that he married Zalda Vilela de Carvalho, daughter of Fernando Setembrino de Carvalho, minister of war, 1922–26. Washington Luís named him chief of his Casa Militar on Sep. 10, 1930. In that post Lindolfo Collor met with him about supporting the revolution. He was one of the generals in the pacification movement. Vargas kept him as his military adviser and promoted him to major general in April 1931 and sent him to Porto Alegre to command the Third Military Region. In that post he was involved in the crisis that led to the paulista civil war of 1932 (see BAO no. 167; "Francisco Ramos de Andrade Neves," *DHBB*, 3:2378–79).

9. Souto Malan, *Uma Escolha, Um Destino*, 312. He said this in the first meeting of the junta in the Catete on Oct. 24. Brig. Gen. Firmino Antônio Borba agreed with him. Borba was promoted to general of division and then retired, which was a way to reward him for his role on Oct. 24 and then to get him out of the army because of his attitude.

10. MG, *Almanak . . . 1931*, 683.

11. Vargas, *Diário*, 1:22.

12. MG, *Almanak . . . 1931*, 762–64; Conniff, "Tenentes in Power," 61–82.

13. The purged generals of division were Candido Mariano da Silva Rondon, Alexandre Henrique Vieira Leal, Antenor de Santa Cruz Pereira de Abreu, Hastimphilo de Moura, Nestor Sezefredo dos Passos, Tertuleano de Albuquerque Potyguara, João Nepomuceno da Costa, Octavio de Azeredo Coutinho, and João Alvares de Azevedo Costa. See MG, *Almanak . . . 1930*, 10–17. Potyguara also lost his seat as a federal deputy with the closing of the Congress. Rondon's case is curious; he does not appear on the 1931 list, but his biography has him staying on as inspector of frontiers (see "Cândido Rondon," *DHBB*, 4:3014). Alexandre Henrique Vieira Leal was also restored and made chief of staff.

The purge of brigadier generals, which cut deeper, included Eduardo Monteiro de Barros, Candido José Pamplona, Estanislau Viera Pamplona, Gil Antonio Dias de Almeida ("Gil de Almeida," *DHBB*, 1:77–78), Carlos Arlindo, Marçal Nonato de Farias, Francisco de Borba Pará da Silveira, Nicolas Antonio da Silva, Diogenes Monteiro Tourinho, Jorge França Wiedmann, José Victoriano Aranha da Silva, Augusto Limpo Teixeira de Freitas, João Baptisa Machado Vieira, Fernando de Medeiros, and Benedicto Olympio da Silveira. In addition, Brig. Gen. Alberto Lavenere Wanderley had been killed in the fighting in Alagoas. Lists compiled from *Almanak . . . 1930*, 7–10; and *Almanak . . . 1931*, 7–13.

14. Malan had been on the commission since June 1929 and was appointed chief of staff on Nov. 15, 1930. For a listing of general staff and commission see MG, *Almanak . . . 1931*, 675–76, 761. Souto Malan, *Uma Escolha, Um Destino*, 329–41; for his career see "Malan D'Angrogne" *DHBB*, 1:144–45; Vargas promoted Malan to general of division before his death. Borba was also promoted to general of division, but he turned on the regime in the paulista crisis of 1932 and tried unsuccessfully

to subvert the Fourth Military Region in Minas Gerais, was arrested and sent into exile, then was amnestied in May 1934 and returned to Brazil. See "Firmino Antônio Borba," *DHBB*, 1:411.

15. Góes Monteiro to Leite de Castro, Rio, Mar. 15, 1931, GMP; Juarez [do Nascimento Fernandes] Távora, learning of an effort to raise him from Major to Brigadier-General, demanded that the promoters halt. Távora, *Uma Vida e Muitas Lutas*, 2:27; "Juarez Távora," *DHBB*, 4:3311–25.

16. Cel. Olyntho de Mesquita Vasconcelos to G. Vargas, Rio (Vila Militar, First Mounted Artillery Regiment), May 12, 1931, 1931.05.12, Arquivo Getúlio Vargas (hereafter AGV), CPDOC. Young Turks can be identified in the *Almanak . . . 1931* by the notation *Serviu Exército Allemão* [Served in German army] (see 191, 272–75).

17. Capt. Heitor da Fontoura Rangel (Cav.) to Alcides Etchegoyen, Porto Alegre, Apr. 3, 1931, in Manoel Luiz Lima Salgado Guimarães et al., *Revolução de 30*, 2:179–192; quoted lines are on 180, 181, 189, 190.

18. See Chap. 4. The quotation is from an editorial: "A Grandeza Nacional e o Momento Militar," *ADN*, Nov. 10, 1915, 49–51. At least one group in the army, identified only as the "Revolutionary Committee of Rio de Janeiro," issued a proclamation containing more radical reform proposals that addressed civilian needs: limiting the work day; legislating a minimum salary; prevention of unemployment; equal pay for men and women; protection of children and women in the work place; freedom to form unions; government housing for workers; free obligatory education; allowing divorce; subdivision of latifundias and government lands; encouraging development of a steel industry by national or foreign firms; tax reform; etc. Comité Revolucionário do Rio de Janeiro, Apr. 22, 1931, "Proclamação ao Exército," GV 1931.04.22, AGV, CPDOC.

19. Harry W. Brown, QMC Clerk, U.S. Attaché's Office, Rio, Feb. 1, 1932: "Military Budget and expenditures for 1932," 1010, 2006-119, MID, GS, WD, RG 165, NA; numbers of officers are from the foregoing except for active duty officers of captain and below, which I took from *Almanak . . . 1931*.

20. For the 1930s the U.S. military attaché's reports provide considerable valuable detail. Harry W. Brown, a Quartermaster Corps clerk who had served with the attaché's office since 1919, was a particularly able and knowledgeable observer. See Brown, Rio, June 2, 1932: "Confusion and discipline," Brazil 6300-b, G-2 Regional, RG 165, NA. For Tasso's opposition to amnesty see Estado-Maior do Exército, *Relatório dos Trabalhos do Estado-Maior . . . 1925 . . . Tasso Fragoso*, 25. He called the rebels seeking amnesty "relapsos e retardatários." Drummond, *O Movimento Tenentista*, 245. During the popsicle and radish crisis Minister Leite e Castro repeatedly offered his resignation, which Vargas continued to refuse until he had a substitute ready. See Vargas, *Diário*, 1:106–13.

21. Vavy Pacheco Borges, *Tenentismo e Revolução Brasileira* (São Paulo: Editora Brasilense, 1992), 32–34.

22. Joel W. Wolfe, *Working Women, Working Men: São Paulo and the Rise of Brazil's Industrial Working Class, 1900–1955* (Durham, N.C.: Duke University Press, 1993), 50–53.

23. Stanley E. Hilton, *1932: A Guerra Civil Brasileira* (Rio de Janeiro: Editora Nova Fronteira, 1982), 27–38; for chronology see Hélio Silva, *1931: Os Tenentes no*

Poder (Rio de Janeiro: Editora Civilização Brasileira, 1966), 1–44; and Hélio Silva, *1932: A Guerra Paulista* (Rio de Janeiro: Editora Civilização Brasileira, 1967), 5–24.

24. Caludio Tavares, *Uma Rebelião Caluniada: O Levante do 21º BC em 1931* (Recife: Editora Guararapes, 1982), 11; he gave numbers of those arrested on page 14, and he mentioned Gen. José Sotero de Meneses' plotting prior to the revolt. Vargas, *Diário,* 1:120; entry for July 30 and 31 mentioned the complicity of Generals Mena Barreto and Sotero de Meneses in a plot in Rio. Hélio Silva, *1932, 263.* Harry W. Brown, Rio, Nov. 2, 1931, Rpt 994: "Pernambuco Mutiny of Oct 29th," 2006-118, MID, GS, WD, RG 165, NA; MG, *Almanak . . . 1931,* 160–86 (infantry), 257–65 (cavalry), 355–65 (artillery), 409–11 (engineers), 606–20 (quartermaster). There were 314 in the infantry, 77 in the cavalry, 86 in the artillery, 27 in the engineers, 151 paymasters *(contadores).* Brown's report said that most of these men had been commissioned in conjunction with the Revolution of 1930; however, the *Almanak . . . 1931* showed that most had earned that status in 1922 or 1924; in the four combat arms, out of a total of 504, it seems that only 111 were commissioned in October 1930. But the way the entries were made raised some doubt in my mind that even that figure was accurate. Five commissioned second lieutenants were assigned to the Twenty-first Light Infantry in 1931: José Dantas de Carvalho (commissioned 1924); Cantido das Neves Leal Ferreira (commissioned 1925); Elías Lopes da Trindade (commissioned 1925); and Sabino Firmino da Silva (commissioned 1925); see *Almanak . . . 1931,* 167, 175, 178, 182. So it could be that the U.S. attaché had been given false information, perhaps to downplay the significance of this revolt. Oddly, on Feb. 18, 1933, Vargas decreed that charges should be dropped *(arquivado)* against those involved in the Recife revolt. The Recife affair suggests that perhaps some of these so-called barracks revolts had greater ramifications and deserve to be reexamined in detail.

25. Lúcia Lahmeyer Lobo and Vanda M. Costa Aderaldo, "Movimentos Militares, 1930–1945," in CPDOC, *A Revolução de 30: Seminário Internacional,* 151–79.

26. Brown, Rio, June 2, 1932: "Confusion and discipline," Brazil 6300-b, G-2 Regional, RG 165, NA.

27. John W. F. Dulles, *Vargas of Brazil: A Political Biography* (Austin: University of Texas Press, 1967), 94–96; Glauco Carneiro, *Lusardo: O Último Caudilho* (Rio de Janeiro: Editora Nova Fronteira, 1978), 2:140–42. Considering that army regulations Articles 292 and 293 forbade officers and common soldiers from even playing sports or riding together, they could easily be seen as forbidding the sacking of a newspaper together; Ministério da Guerra, Estado-Maior do Exército, *R.I.S.G.* (Rio de Janeiro: Imprensa Militar, 1930), 203–4.

28. Vargas, *Diário,* 1:92.

29. Harry W. Brown, Office of the Military Attaché, Brazil, June 2, 1932: "Confusion and discipline," no. 1027, G-2 Regional, Brazil 6300-b, RG 165, NA

30. "Miguel Costa," *DHBB,* 2:981. On João Alberto and labor see Wolfe, *Working Women, Working Men,* 53. Shortly before these events a letter published in the newspapers from Luís Carlos Prestes in Buenos Aires to Brazil's common soldiers must have heightened Góes's disaffection from Isidoro. Prestes urged them to stop fighting the workers in their struggle for "a bit more bread." He charged that Góes and João Alberto cynically were preventing Isidoro from helping the workers. See typed report of a story in *Diário da Noite,* 27/3/31, AGV, CPDOC.

31. "Laudo Camargo," *DHBB*, 1:564; "João Alberto," *DHBB*, 1:39–42; and "Plínio Barreto," *DHBB*, 1:315–16.

32. Vargas, *Diário*, 1:73. Over the next five years Brazil would move away from the English pound toward the American dollar. Perhaps the first step was Vargas's decree making the dollar the official currency to be used in calculating coffee export taxes. At the same time Vargas extended federal control over coffee exports via the National Coffee Council and the Ministry of Treasury. "Otto Niemeyer," *DHBB*, 3:2389.

33. Vargas, *Diário*, 1:74–75, entries for Oct. 3–6 and 7–11. During these same days Vargas attended the dedication of the statue of Christ on Corcovado Mountain, during which he received the Pope's Apostolic Blessing. Clearly he needed all the help he could get.

34. Góes's BAO no. is 179. His career data came from *Almanak da Guerra*, especially *1931* and *1934*. An officer who served with Mariante and Góes through this period, Aguinaldo Caiado de Castro, worked with Góes to prepare a report on the pursuit of the Prestes Column. The two would be on opposite sides in the 1932 paulista civil war. "Góes Monteiro," *DHBB*, 3:2246–48; "Caiado de Castro," ibid., 1, 721–22. For the promotion rules and an analysis of their functioning see Harry Brown to MID, Rio, Sep. 16, 1921: "General outline . . . system of promotion for officers in Brazilian army," 2006-54, MID, GS, WD, RG 165, NA.

35. "João Gomes," *DHBB*, 2:1488–89; the first part of this report deals with Gen. Gomes: Harry W. Brown, Office of the Military Attaché, Brazil, June 2, 1932: "Confusion and discipline," no. 1027, G-2 Regional, Brazil, 6300-b, RG 165, NA.

36. "Bertoldo Klinger," *DHBB*, 2:1687. Mate Laranjeiras was an Argentine-owned company that held huge stretches of southern Mato Grosso. Two years later the general staff would warn that such "foreign establishments, notably Argentine, in that region, are a weak point in our national security." Gen. Francisco Ramos de Andrade Neves (Chief of General Staff) Relatório sobre o Reajustamento da Oranização do Exército (Rio de Janeiro: Imprensa Militar, Estado-Maior do Exército, 1934), 28–29.

37. Harry W. Brown, Office of the Military Attaché, Brazil, June 2, 1932: "Confusion and discipline," no. 1027,, G-2 Regional, Brazil, 6300-b, RG 165, NA. Brown described Klinger as an "erratic officer."

38. Oswaldo Aranha to Vargas, Rio, n.d., GV 1931.01.021, AGV, CPDOC.

39. "Augusto Inácio do Espírito Santo Cardoso" *DHBB*, 1:621–22; Vargas, *Diário*, 1:113. Vargas noted that Leite de Castro resigned out of "irritation with the revolutionary officers, principally Captain João Alberto, and disgust with his cabinet colleagues. He regarded himself abandoned and betrayed."

40. Gen. Bertholdo Klinger to Gen. Espirito Santo Cardoso, n.p., n.d., GV, 1932.07.01/3, AGV, CPDOC.

41. "Pantaleão da Silva Pessôa," *DHBB*, 4:2706–8; Pantaleão Pessôa, *Reminiscências e Imposições*, 87–90, 109; Klinger, *Narrativas Autobiográficas*, 6:307–8, 312–21.

42. Góes Monteiro to B. Klinger, n.p., n.d. [July 8, 1932], GV, 1932.07.08/2, AGV, CPDOC.

43. Klinger's successor was Col. Oscar Saturnino de Paiva, who was fifty-seven and had been in the army forty-one years. His career spanned the period of this study; as an enlisted man he fought for Floriano Peixoto in 1893–94, and as a cap-

tain he was in the Contestado in 1914–15; his promotions in the field-officer grades of major (1919), lieutenant colonel (1922), and colonel (1925) were based on merit; MG, *Almanak . . . 1931, 372.*

44. Euclydes Figueiredo, *Contribuição para a História da Revolução Constitucionalista de 1932* (São Paulo: Martins, 1977), 87–90.

45. Ibid., 85.

46. Mauro Renault Leite and Luiz Gonzaga Novelli Jr., eds., *Marechal Eurico Gaspar Dutra: O dever da verdade* (Rio de Janeiro: Editora Nova Fronteira, 1983), 31–36; Hélio Silva, *1932,* 91–93; his emissary must not have told Figueiredo exactly what Dutra had said because in his memoir he said Dutra did not define himself clearly; see Figueiredo, *Contribuição,* 157.

47. Figueiredo, *Contribuição,* 92.

48. Távora, *Uma Vida e Muitas Lutas,* 2:78–80.

49. Wolfe, *Working Women, Working Men,* 62.

50. General Burnod, *Napoleon's Maxims of War* (Philadelphia, Pa.: David McKay, 1902), maxim XIX, 50.

51. Vargas, *Diário,* 1:115–16; curiously, it would be July 28 before Vargas decreed the general's return to active duty (see 119); Coutinho, *General Góes Depõe,* 192–98; Pessôa, *Reminiscências e Imposições,* 110–14; Góes Monteiro, Barra Mansa (RJ), July 18, 1932: "Diretivas Gerais No. 1," GV 1932.07.18/1, AGV, CPDOC.

52. Nelson Lavenère-Wanderley, *História da Fôrça Aérea Brasileira* (Rio de Janeiro: Imprensa Nacional Ministério da Aeronáutica, 1967), 167–80. Lavenère-Wanderley flew for the federal forces.

53. Vargas, *Diário,* 1:116–17. On his deliberate calm appearance see entry for Aug. 3, 1932 (120).

54. Ibid., 119.

55. Capt. William Sackville, Oct. 26, 1932, Rio: "Active Operations of São Paulo revolt," 1045, 6670, MID, GS, WD, G-2 Regional, RG 165, NA.

56. Góes Monteiro to Vargas, Resende, Aug. 14, 1932, GV 1932.08.14/3, AGV, CPDOC.

57. Vargas, *Diário,* 1:122–25.

58. Vargas to B. Klinger, Rio, Sep. 29, 1932, GV 1932.09.29/3; Vargas to Góes Monteiro, Rio, Oct. 1, 1932, GV 1932.10.01/3, AGV, CPDOC.

59. Figueiredo, *Contribuição,* 300–302, calls his army "constitutionalist," and much of the literature applies the term to the paulista revolt.

60. Vargas, *Diário,* 1:416–17; 2:27 (meeting on Mar. 17); "Valdemar Ferreira," *DHBB,* 2:1265–66.

61. Hilton, *1932: A Guerra Civil Brasileira,* 329–30.

62. Wolfe, *Working Women, Working Men,* 62.

63. Capt. William Sackville, Oct. 26, 1932, Rio: "Manufacture of Military Equipment and its use by the Paulista forces," 1046, 6670; idem, "Active Operations of São Paulo revolt," 1045, 6670, MID, GS, WD, G-2 Regional, RG 165, NA. He toured the war zone Oct. 12 to Oct. 22, 1932.

64. See Sackville's report of Oct. 26, 1932, cited above.

65. Harry W. Brown for M[ilitary] A[ttaché], Rio, Mar. 1, 1932, 1013, "Brazil's tank company abolished," 2006-99, MID, GS, WD, RG 165, NA.

66. Góes Monteiro, "Memoria no. 3" (para o Governo), Q[uartel] G[eneral], Resende, Aug. 9, 1932, GV, 1932.08.09./1, AGV, CPDOC.

67. Vargas, *Diário,* 1:184–88, 193; see entries for Feb. 2, 6, 7, Mar. 9, 1933; curiously, the CPDOC editors misidentified Col. Gay as José Gay Cunha, who was a lieutenant commissionado, later involved in the communist uprising of 1935 and who fought in the Spanish Civil War; Góes Monteiro to Vargas, Rio Feb. 7, 1933, GV 1933.02.07/c and Feb. 10, 1933, GV 1933.02.10; J. F. Leite de Castro to Vargas, Rio, Feb. 7, 1933, GV 1933.02.07/1; A. I. do Espirito Santo Cardoso to Vargas, Rio, Feb. 8, 1933, GV 1933.02.08, all AGV, CPDOC.

68. MG, *Almanak . . . 1931;* the following gives the number of colonels promoted in the indicated years: 2 (1929), 3 (prior to Oct. 1930), 18 (1931), 17 (1932), 27 (1933), 16 (1934), 10 (1935), 10 (1936).

69. Pessôa, *Reminiscências e imposições de uma vida,* 126–27; I thank my colleague Peter Smith for sharing the interview he did with Pessôa, Apr. 17, 1975, in which the general said that he set the time and that Góes found the idea very amusing. *Jornal do Commercio* (Rio), Oct. 10–11, 1932, reported the return.

70. Coutinho, *General Góes Depõe,* 224–37; "Campanha de São Paulo; Operações do Destacamento de Exército de Leste de São Paulo," typewritten, MS, unfinished, n.d.; "Minha Missão em São Paulo," n.p., n.d., "Destacamento de Exército brazileiro [*sic*] do Leste de São Paulo (I) Despedida (II) Inimigos," n.d., GMP, AE.

71. Góes Monteiro favored stripping officers and sergeants of the vote to avoid having them active in political parties. Perhaps he had in mind Argentina's recent experience with the army backing partisan positions. Oddly, this meant that as their wives gained the vote, military officials lost theirs. See Alfred Stepan, *Military in Politics,* 75–79, for discussion of 1891, 1934, 1937, and 1946 Constitutions. For wording of 1988 Constitution see Título V, Capítulo II, Art. 142. Regarding the latter, Stepan discussed the drafting process and the military's objections to changes that would limit its ability to intervene; see Alfred Stepan, *Rethinking Military Politics, Brazil and the Southern Cone* (Princeton, N.J.: Princeton University Press, 1988), 111–14. When Stepan went to print, both President José Sarney and congressional leader Ulysses Guimarães advocated "retention of the traditional constitutional role of the military in domestic affairs" (114). For Góes Monteiro's argument regarding women in the army see Hélio Silva, *1934: A Constituinte* (Rio de Janeiro: Editora Civilização Brasileira, 1969), 450–51.

72. Major William Sackville, Rio, Nov. 9, 1933, "State Troops in Brazil," 6010a, G-2 Regional, RG 165, NA. He noted that the state troops were armed with Mauser 7 mm rifles, and all had machine guns, except São Paulo, which since the civil war had been denied the use of that weapon.

73. Coronel Y, "Os politicos e o Exército," Assumptos Militares, *Gazeta do Rio* (Rio de Janeiro), Nov. 24, 1933, in j/7, ACB. For a fuller discussion of the Coronel Y columns see John W. F. Dulles, *Castello Branco, The Making of a Brazilian President* (College Station: Texas A & M University Press, 1978), 42–45. I think Castelo may have chosen "Y" in honor of his wife Argentina, who was from Minas Gerais. Mineiros interject "Y" repeatedly in their normal conversation.

74. Vargas, *Diário,* 1:244–56.

75. See ibid., 254–62.

76. Ibid., 263. The difficulty of sorting out the interregime struggles lies in part in that opponents shifted with the political winds and that in face-to-face encounters and in correspondence they maintained the usages, tenses, and tone required of friends. The value of Vargas's *Diário* is that it reveals much that is hidden elsewhere.

77. Vargas, *Diário,* 1:262–64. Góes had already given Vargas a long document on the necessity of developing a national war plan in the face of obvious preparations by the powers of both hemispheres for a new conflict. He noted that the republicans had abolished the empire's war plan of intervention in neighboring countries, without replacing it with any plan to repel invasion. The republic's leaders were distracted by regional interests, and fearing the growth of military power, they let it stagnate as a lesser evil. He argued that "civilians, responsible for the destinies of Brazil, needed deeper knowledge of the country's military affairs so as not to make errors of conception and underestimation of our defense capacity." He wanted to eliminate the false presumptions and the inaccurate identification of the armed forces with "the different social classes." Góes Monteiro to G. Vargas, Rio, Jan. 4, 1934, AGV, CPDOC. In the letter of Jan. 18 he tried to set conditions before assuming the post—especially "credits and moneys, beyond the normal budgets, for the progressive, date targeted, equipping" of the army—and to put in practice suggested measures to "completely remodel and homogenize the officer corps and the troops" (Góes Monteiro to G. Vargas, Rio, Jan. 18, 1934, AGV, CPDOC).

78. G. Vargas to Flores da Cunha, Rio, Apr. 28, 30, 1934, GV 1934.05.28 and GV 1934.05.30; see also Flores da Cunha to G. Vargas, Rio, May 9, 1934, GV 1934.05.09/2; G. Vargas to Capt. Juracy Magalhães, Rio, Mar. 16, 1934, GV 1934.03.16; and G. Vargas to Capt. J. Magalhães, Bahia, May 2, 1924, GV 1934.05.02/2, all AGV, CPDOC.

An affable Cearense, Capt. Juracy adapted well to Bahia; he gave radio speeches regularly, assisted the archbishop, and made frequent visits to local chieftains, cutting out the middle men who formerly mediated between Salvador and the interior. Alzira Alves de Abreu, ed., *Juracy Magalhães: Minhas Memórias Provisórias* (Rio de Janeiro: Civilização Brasileira, 1982), 74–79.

79. Vargas, *Diário,* 1:219. For example, on June 19, 1933, he wrote, "I am not in good humor. Tiredness, disgust, disillusion . . . Brazil doesn't have money for as many purposes that they intend to devote it to. Will it be better if I leave!?"

80. Vargas, *Diário,* 1:276, 279, 285, 293, 298; Gen. Manoel Rabelo to Góes Monteiro, Rio, Mar. 18, 1934, GV 34.03.18, AGV, CPDOC.

81. Vargas sent Flores da Cunha this information in G. Vargas to Flores da Cunha, Rio, Apr. 29, 1934, GV 1934.04.29, AGV, CPDOC. Gen. Guedes is BAO no. 193. Born in Rio Grande do Sul, he had seen combat as a lieutenant in the Contestado, fought against the tenentes in the 1920s, and made lieutenant colonel in 1928. During 1929–30 he headed an inquiry aimed at expelling communists from the army; he was promoted to colonel in 1931, and he fought against the paulistas in 1932 and was given his general's stars. He served on the promotions board in 1934. See "João Guedes da Fontoura," *DHBB,* 2:1313. Gen. José Maria Franco Ferreira is BAO no. 180. He was born in Paraguay in 1876 during the Brazilian occupation. He was a distinguished cavalry officer who fought in the civil war of 1893–94; all of his promotions above first lieutenant (1908) were due to studies or merit, and he was one of those sent to Germany for training, so was a "Young Turk." As part of

the command changes of 1934 he moved from Porto Alegre (3rd Mil. Region) to Juiz de Fora, M.G. (4th Mil. Region), where he stayed until 1937. There is no biographical sketch in *DHBB.*

82. Vargas, *Diário,* 1:298. It is out of character for Aranha to have proposed this, but perhaps then he was fearful of a purely military movement. J. C. de Macedo Soares to G. Vargas, Rio, Apr. 11, 1934, GV 1934.04.11, AGV, CPDOC.

83. Vargas, *Diário,* 1:299; Pantaleão Pessôa, *Reminiscências e Imposições de uma Vida,* 164.

84. Góes Monteiro to G. Vargas, Rio, July 10, 1934, GV 1934.07.10, AGV, CPDOC; Vargas, *Diário,* 1:304–7.

85. Karl Loewenstein, *Brazil Under Vargas* (New York: Macmillan, 1942), 25–26; Ronald M. Schneider, *"Order and Progress": A Political History of Brazil* (Boulder, Colo.: Westview Press, 1991), 126–29.

86. Vargas, *Diário,* 1:304 (entry for May 27–31, 1934).

CHAPTER 9

1. Maj. William Sackville, Rio, Jan. 6, 1933, "Graduation Exercises at Military Academy," no. 1064, 2277-k-8, G-2 Regional, RG 165, NA; Rual Pedroso (Realengo, class of 1933), *Cadetes em Desfile (Escola Militar do Realengo)* (Rio de Janeiro: Editora Pongetti, 1969), 204–7, 228–29.

2. Pedroso, *Cadetes em Desfile,* on the top men of those years see 244–46; he also listed the training officers and professors, 11–14. Not all of these men were collected in my Brazilian Army Officer study; here I used Ministério do Exército, *Almanaque do Exército, 1970* (Rio de Janeiro: Estabelecimento General Gustavo Cordeiro de Farias, 1970).

3. "José Pessôa," *DHBB,* 4:2705–6; Câmara, *Marechal José Pessôa,* 27–41; *Almanak . . . 1931,* 193; [Brazilian Army], *Agulhas Negras,* 120–40.

4. Pedroso, *Cadetes em Desfile,* 35.

5. Câmara, *Marechal José Pessôa,* 60–90; Meira Mattos entered in Mar. 1933, see 89–90; "Meira Matos," *DHBB,* 3:2132– 2133; MG, *Almanak . . . 1970,* 15. He made colonel in August 1963 and brigadier general in March 1968.

6. For a cadet view of the maneuvers see Pedroso, *Cadetes em Desfile,* 194–203.

7. "Breno Borges Fortes," *DHBB,* 2:1336; "Amílcar Dutra de Menezes," *DHBB,* 3:2212. Travassos made brigadier general in May 1946; MG, *Almanak . . . 1952,* 33. Reis was general of division in November 1966, and Fortes reached the new top rank of general of the army in November 1969. He was chief of general staff from May 1972 to December 1973. MG, *Almanak . . . 1970,* 105.

8. Major William Sackville, Rio, May 15, 1933, "Brazil's Authorized Strength for 1933," no. 1112, 2006-105/6; and idem, Apr. 9, 1934, "Brazil's Authorized Army, 1934–1936," no. 1261, 2006-105, MID, GS, WD, RG 165, NA; Estado-Maior do Exército, *Relatório dos Trabalhos do Estado-Maior durante o ano de 1933 . . . pelo Gen. Div. Francisco Ramos de Andrade Neves* (Rio de Janeiro: Imprensa Militar, Estado-Maior do Exército, 1934), 5; Bryce Wood, *The United States and Latin American Wars, 1932–1942* (New York: Columbia University Press, 1966), 167–251; Robert Scheina,

"Chaco War," and Helen Delpar, "Leticia Dispute," both in *Encyclopedia of Latin American History and Culture,* ed. Barbara A. Tenenbaum et al. (New York: Charles Scribner's Sons, 1996), 2:70–72, 3:407; "Questão do Chaco" and "Conflito de Leticia," *DHBB,* 1:776, and 3, 1805.

9. G. Vargas to O. Aranha, n.p., Dec. 24, 1934, GV 1934.12.14/1, AGV, CPDOC; and O. Aranha to G. Vargas, Washington, D.C., Jan. 18, 1935, GV 1935.01.18/2, AGV, CPDOC.

10. Capt. Riograndense Kruel to G. Vargas, Buenos Aires, Sep. 28, 1932, GV 1932.09.28/5, and Aug. 29, 1932, GV 1932.09.29/1, AGV, CPDOC; 2d Secção Estado-Maior do Exército, "*Synthese das informações colhidas sobre a guerra boliviano-paraguaya no Chaco Boreal, e seus antecedentes,*" 12 de Março de 1935 (Rio de Janeiro: Estado-Maior do Exército, 1935), copy no. 4, CDOC-EX, Brasília. Nemo Canabarro Lucas graduated from Realengo in Jan. 1930; after the revolution he was active in tenentista organizations but came to believe that the provisional government was not interested in their reformist ideals. The biographical note in *DHBB* is silent about his Paraguayan adventure. He was active in the National Liberation Alliance and after the revolt in Nov. 1935 he was stripped of his commission and went into exile. He was in Spain in 1937 and served on a brigade staff in the Catalonian army against Franco. In April 1945 he benefited from the general amnesty and returned to the army, reaching the rank of colonel in 1956. "Nemo Canabarro Lucas," *DHBB,* 3:1947.

11. General de Divisão Francisco Ramos de Andrade Neves (Chief of Staff), Rio de Janeiro, Aug. 3, 1934: Estado-Maior do Exército, *Exame da Situação Militar do Brasil* (Rio de Janeiro: Imprensa do Estado-Maior do Exército, 1934), CDOC-EX, Brasília. Quotes are from pages 5–9.

12. See, e.g., Estado-Maior do Exército, 2a Grande Região Militar, Rio de Janeiro, n.d. Dec. 1936, Memo no. 1 (Situação do Paiz), Correspondência Pessoal, Acervo Pessoal Gen. Pedro de Góis Monteiro, Caixa 1, Arquivo do Exército (Rio). It noted (in sec. 4) that Brazil would not be able to maintain neutrality in event of a world conflict, that it would have to associate itself with one of the sides, and that because it lacked war materials, its mobilization would provide soldiers that would have to be equipped by another power, "which could not be other than the United States of America." Oswaldo Aranha to G. Vargas, Washington, D.C., Mar. 6, 1935, GV 1935.03.06/1, AGV, CPDOC. Aranha warned that Argentina was seeking to undermine Brazil's cordial relations with the United States and that "we must preserve our position so that in any eventuality we can count on this country."

13. Capt. Vernon A. Walters, Rio de Janeiro, Jan. 27, 1944, "The Plano Maximo," G-2 Regional Files, 5995, RG 165, NA.

14. Estado-Maior do Exército, *Relatório sôbre o Reajustamento da Organização do Exército,* Rio de Janeiro, Jan. 26, 1934, G[eneral de] D[ivisão] Francisco Ramos de Andrade Neves to Ministro de Guerra, 5–6, 29, 70.

15. Teixeira, quoted in T. Lynn Smith, *Brazil: People and Institutions* (Baton Rouge: Louisiana State University Press, 1963), 503; Daniel Levy, "O Estado e o Desenvolvimento das Universidades na América Latina: Um Panorama Comparativo (1920–1940)," CPDOC, *A Revolução de 30: Seminário Internacional,* 473–92; William L. Schurz, *Brazil: The Infinite Country* (New York: E. P. Dutton, 1961), 215.

16. See Norman Gall, "The Rise of Brazil," *Commentary* (Jan. 1977): 45–55.

17. MG, *Relatório . . . João Pandiá Calogéras . . . 1921*, 26–33; Report, Office of Military Attaché to Director MID, Rio, Oct. 5, 1921, no. 97, 2006-56, MID, GS, WD, RG 165, NA.

18. G[eneral de] B[rigada] João Candido Pereira de Castro Junior (Director of Ordnance), Rio, Mar. 23, 1936: "Relatório da Directoria do Material Bélico, 1935," and the Relatórios for 1934 and 1935, CDOC-EX, Brasília.

19. Major William Sackville, "Federal Active Operations, São Paulo revolt," Rio, Nov. 18, 1932, 1055, 6670, G-2 Regional, WD, RG 165, NA; on Vargas and aviation see Simon Schwartzman, *Estado Novo, um Auto-retrato* (Brasília: Editora Universidade de Brasília, 1982), 273; the aircraft were purchased from the United Air Craft Co. and the Waco Airplane Co. This source put the number at 137 craft, but Brazilian sources say 150; Nicolas E. Bates (E. I. du Pont de Nemours & Co. representative in Rio) to Major K.K.V. Casey (du Pont in Delaware), Rio de Janeiro, Apr. 28, 1933, copy attached to Sackville, "Brazilian Army Aviators sail for United States," Rio, Apr. 28, 1933, 1104, 2257-K-17, G-2 Regional, WD, RG 165, NA.

20. Based on conversations with him in August 1980. During the conflict he flew ninety-four missions that included attacking airfields and ground troops.

21. Nelson Freire Lavenère-Wanderley, *História da Fôrça Aérea Brasileira*, 196–201; three-year-old Pan American bought out the NYRBA (New York-Rio-Buenos Aires) and its five new Commodore flying boats in 1930 and organized Panair do Brasil (Sep. 1930). For details of early history see "Harvest in Brazil," *New Horizons, The Magazine of America's Merchant Marine of the Air* (NY), July 1942, 19–22.

22. Darci Vargas, the president's wife, christened the Pan Am clipper, see *Diário, 1930–1936*, 1:318; Major William Sackville, "Amazon River," Rio, June 27, 1933, 1126, 2052-116, MID, GS, WD, RG 165, NA; "President Vargas of Brazil on His March to the West . . . ," *New Horizons, The Magazine of America's Merchant Marine of the Air* (NY), Aug. 1941, 9–11. The PAA seaplanes could reach ninety-five miles per hour with their five-hundred-horse-power Pratt and Whitney engines. They could cruise at ten thousand feet and carry fourteen passengers, plus mail and baggage. Lavenère-Wanderley, *História da Fôrça Aérea Brasileira*, 200–201.

23. Nicolas E. Bates (E.I. du Pont de Nemours & Co. representative in Rio) to Major K. K. V. Casey (du Pont in Delaware), Rio de Janeiro, Apr. 28, 1933, copy attached to Sackville, "Brazilian Army Aviators sail for United States," Rio, Apr. 28, 1933, 1104, 2257-K-17, G-2 Regional, WD, RG 165, NA.

24. Col. C. Burnett (Foreign Liaison Officer) to Cyro de Freitas-Valle, Counselor, Brazilian Embassy, Washington, D.C., Oct. 10, 1934, 2257-K-18; Col. F. H. Lincoln (Acting Chief of Military Intelligence Division), Memo for Chief of Staff (MacArthur), Washington, D.C., Nov. 2, 1934, 2257-K-18/29, and Douglas MacArthur to Secretary of State, Washington, D.C., Nov. 3, 1934, 2257-K-18/30, MID, GS, WD, RG 165, NA. Both of these men returned to Brazil committed to American equipment and methods and great fans of the United States for the rest of their lives. Wanderley served with the Brazilian squadron attached to the Army Air Corps during the Italian campaign in World War II and served as minister of aeronautics (1964) and director of civil aviation.

25. "Leite de Castro," *DHBB*, 1:732.

26. McCann, *Brazilian-American Alliance*, 152–53.

27. Estado-Maior do Exército, *Relatório* . . . *1936* . . . *G[eneral] D[ivisão] Arnaldo de Souza Paes de Andrade* (Rio de Janeiro: Imprensa do Estado-Maior do Exército, 1937), 11–12. The second section also urged sending an attaché to Europe "in this moment of political instability" to follow the constant military changes. Significantly it wanted the attaché accredited in France so he could follow and guide the Brazilian officers training there (13).

28. Ibid., 4–5.

29. Vargas, *Diário*, 1:269.

30. Vargas, *Diário*, 1:293, 314, 316; Maj. Wm. Sackville, Rio, June 5, 1934 (apt. 1286: Rio Grande do Sul state troops), 2006-123, MID, GS, WD, RG 165, NA. Sackville noted that the Brigade had thirty-five hundred men in four infantry battalions, three cavalry regiments, and nuclei of eight provisional battalions. Many of those recruited for such units had a year of army training. These units were posted around Rio Grande near regular army units. In the previous months the state had heavily imported rifles, carbines, and machine guns from Czechoslovakia. It also had older weapons in storage, as well as some four million rounds of ammunition ready for use.

31. "João Guedes da Fontoura," *DHBB*, 2:1313. Gen. Guedes da Fontoura's career stretches across most of the years of this study. Born in Rio Grande do Sul in May 1879, at eighteen he enlisted in the army in 1897 and moved to the military school at Praia Vermelha (Rio), from which he was commissioned an alferes-aluno in 1904. Promoted to first lieutenant in 1913, he served in that rank through the Contestado campaign; 1919 saw him make captain, and in 1920 he was enrolled in the new French-run EsAO. In 1924 he stayed with the government against the tenente rebels who seized São Paulo, and he fought against the Prestes Column, being promoted to major in Oct. 1924. Rising securely now, he made lieutenant colonel in 1928, and in 1929 he headed a "political-military inquiry" (IPM) that aimed at expelling communists from the armed forces. Awarded his colonelcy in 1931, he fought against the paulistas the next year. In 1932 he received his brigadier general stars, and in 1934 he joined the ever important Promotions Commission. As seen in this chapter, he played a leading role in the drama leading up to the Estado Novo.

32. Vargas, *Diário*, 1:307 (entry for July 14–16, 1934), 321, 326, 328. On Sep. 25 Vargas noted, "The chief of police came to reiterate the warning about conspiring among the military, alleging that the government is opposed to raising pay" (330).

33. Pessôa, *Reminiscências e imposições*, 165–68. He noted Guedes threatened to parade his Vila Militar troops past the Congress and perhaps close it.

34. On Guedes Fontoura's statements see Flores da Cunha to Vargas, Mar. 29, 1935, AGV, CPDOC; Hélio Silva, *1935: A Revolta Vermelha* (Rio de Janeiro: Editora Civilização Brasileira, 1969), 113; Vargas, *Diário*, 1:348–51.

35. Frank D. McCann, "Brazilian Army Officers Biography Project" (panel on collective biography, Latin American Studies Association, Miami, Dec. 5, 1989).

36. Vargas, *Diário*, 1:314. On Aug. 11, 1934, the president noted: "Continuei assinando decretos fazendo mudanças nos altos comandos e procurando trazer, de preferência, para estas guarnições generais da minha confiança" (Leite and Novelli, *Marechal Eurico Gaspar Dutra*, 60–62); Hélio Silva, *1935*, 111, 131–47.

37. Vargas, *Diário*, 1:362–63. Presidential military aide General Pantaleão Pessôa had a major role in organizing the government's preventative measures against conspirators;

ibid., 363. Major William Sackville, "Brazil's military tempest," Rio, Apr. 23, 1935, 1438a, 2006-102, G-2 Regional, Brazil 6300, WD, RG 165, NA; on middle-class reaction to the economic climate see Brian P. Owensby, *Intimate Ironies: Modernity and the Making of Middle-Class Lives in Brazil* (Stanford, Calif.: Stanford University Press, 1999), 163–65.

38. Vargas followed these events closely; *Diário,* 1:378–79. Major William Sackville, "Brazilian Army's loyalty and discipline," Rio, Apr. 18, 1935, 1438, 2006-102, G-2 Regional, Brazil 6300, WD, RG 165, NA; Pessôa to Góes Monteiro, Apr. 4, 1935; Silva, *1935,* 135–37; Pessôa, *Reminiscências e imposições,* 168.

39. Pessôa, *Reminiscências e imposições,* 172–75. Captain Henrique Geisel went by Pessôa's house to bid his friend Captain Ciro farewell. Geisel's brother Orlando was at Cachoeira with Ciro and was one of the signers of the telegram. The three Geisel brothers, including Ernesto, were artillery officers who had been active supporters of the Revolution of 1930 and had stayed with the government in 1932. Henrique retired prior to 1964 but supported the coup vs. João Goulart. Orlando was minister of the army from 1969 to 1973, and Ernesto was president of Brazil 1974–79. See "Ernesto Geisel," *DHBB,* 2:1450–59; "Orlando Geisel," *DHBB,* 2:1459–60.

40. Major William Sackville, "Brazil's military tempest," Rio, Apr. 23, 1935, 1438a, 2006-102, G-2 Regional, Brazil 6300, WD, RG 165, NA; "Argemiro Dornelles," *DHBB,* 2:1114.

41. Silva, *1935,* 155–57.

42. Major William Sackville, "Brazilian Army's loyalty and discipline," Rio, Apr. 18, 1935, 1438, 2006-102, G-2 Regional, Brazil 6300, WD, RG 165, NA. Appended to this document was an intelligence estimate: "In the present situation, it appears that increased pay . . . will have little effect towards improving the morale or loyalty of the majority of army officers."

43. Vargas, *Diário,* 1:366–67. His words were "é preciso substituir os bois do arado" (literally "the plow oxen"). See entry for Mar. 11, 1935.

44. José Carlos de Macedo Soares to Getúlio Vargas, Rio, Apr. 11, 1934, AGV, CPDOC.

45. Major William Sackville, "Brazil's military tempest," Rio, Apr. 23, 1935, 1438a, 2006-102, G-2 Regional, Brazil 6300, WD, RG 165, NA; Vargas, *Diário,* 1:382–85 (entries are for Apr. 17 through 24). Leite and Novelli, *Marechal Eurico Gaspar Dutra,* 65–69. Leite and Novelli asserted that this was "a primeira tentativa séria para implantação de uma ditadura militar, no curso dos 44 anos da vida constitucional republicana" (69). Some details are from P. Pessôa, interview by Peter S. Smith, Rio, May 8, 1975.

46. Vargas, *Diário,* 1:385 (his words were "o Exército está fundamentalmente trabalhado por um espírito de indisciplina impressionante"); Major William Sackville, "Development of political issues," Rio, Apr. 12, 1935, 1434, 2607-K-103; and Sackville, "Monthly bonus for federal employees," Rio, Apr. 29, 1935, 1442, 2006-102, G-2 Regional, Brazil 6000a, WD, RG 165, NA. The milreis was 17$200 to the U.S. dollar on Apr. 29, a *conto* was a thousand milreis, written 1:000$. The last report gives the bonus amounts for each rank.

47. Major William Sackville, "Federal expenditures; Executive action on monthly bonus bill," Rio, May 16, 1935, 1451, 2006-102, G-2 Regional, Brazil 5020-b, MID, GS, WD, RG 165, NA.

48. Major William Sackville, "Strength of Active Commissioned Officers," Rio, Oct. 10, 1935, 1541, 2006-105, G-2 Regional, Brazil 6200-b, MID, GS, WD, RG 165, NA. See note 46 for Sackville's Apr. 29, 1935, report that contains the monthly bonus for cadets and privates up to generals of division. A captain's monthly pay was 1:500$000 to which was added a bonus of 600$000 for a total of 2:100$000, the monthly pay of 688 captains would be 1,444:800$000.

49. The figures here differ from those in Robert A. Hayes, *The Armed Nation: The Brazilian Corporate Mystique* (Tempe: Center for Latin American Studies, Arizona State University, 1989), 170.

50. Major William Sackville, "Agitation within Army to prevent reduction of effectives," Rio, Nov. 1, 1935, 1552, 2006-102, G-2 Regional, Brazil 6300-c, MID, GS, WD, RG 165, NA. Sackville could not have been more wrong when he concluded his report saying, "[T]here is not much probability of further agitation by officers."

51. The army does not seem to have paid close attention to the physical condition of its senior officers. Malan and Olimpio da Silveira died while chief of staff, Andrade Neves left the service because of ill health, and later even Góes Monteiro would be often sick. "Benedito Olimpio da Silveira," *DHBB,* 4:3187; Araripe, *Tasso Fragoso, 622;* MG, *Almanak . . . 1925,* 562. As chief he brought together planning that had been underway since the late 1920s to develop war plans and a compatible army structure; Capt. Francisco Ruas Santos (Adjunto da Subsec. de História Militar), "Resumo Histórico Período de Outubro de 1896 a Dezembro de 1950," Estado-Maior do Exército, 35–39, copy in CDOC-EX, Brasília; Estado-Maior do Exército, História do Estado-Maior do Exército (Rio de Janeiro: Biblioteca do Exército, 1984), 76–78.

52. Vargas, *Diário,* 1:399. The name of the presidential military staff had slightly different names during the 1930s. Popularly it was often referred to as the Casa Militar.

CHAPTER 10

1. Loewenstein, *Brazil Under Vargas,* 32–33.

2. "Plínio Salgado," *DHBB,* 4:3051–61, quotations from 3053–54; Lúcia Lippi Oliveira, ed., *Elite intelectual e debate político nos anos 30: Uma bibliografia comentada da Revolução de 1930* (Rio de Janeiro: Fundação Getúlio Vargas, 1980), 43; Owensby, *Intimate Ironies,* 135–39.

3. Lúcia Lippi Oliveira, introduction to *Elite intelectual e debate político nos anos 30,* 34–35.

4. Owensby, *Intimate Ironies,* 135; Loewenstein, *Brazil Under Vargas,* 32–34.

5. Vargas, *Diário,* 1:373 (entry for Mar. 28, 1935).

6. Ibid.

7. However, according to the leading student of the *AIB,* Hélio Trindade, the influence of European fascism and Nazism shaped "central aspects of its ideology, the form of its highly hierarchical organization, the charismatic style and autocratic power of its chief, and, even, the movement's rituals"; see Hélio Trindade, "Integralismo," *DHBB,* 2:1621–28; Lúcio José dos Santos, "Consulta sôbre o Integralismo," *Enciclopédia do Integralismo,* vol. 2, *Estudos e Depoimentos* (Rio de Janeiro: Livraria Clássica Brasileira, 1937), 30–32, 39–41; Hélio Trindade, *Integralismo (o fascismo Brasileiro na década de 30)* (São Paulo: Difusão Européia do Livro, 1974), 288–89; Frederico del

Villar, "Life and Death of Brazilian Fascism," *Inter-American Monthly,* June 1943, 16–19; Levine, *Vargas Regime,* 81–99; Frank D. McCann, "Vargas and the Destruction of the Brazilian Integralista and Nazi Parties," *The Americas* 26, no. 1 (July 1969): 15–34; and Stanley E. Hilton, "*Ação Integralista Brasileira*: Fascism in Brazil, 1932–1938," *Luso-Brazilian Review* 9, no. 2 (Dec. 1972): 3–29. For a useful analysis of Salgado's thinking see Ricardo Benzaquen de Araujo, "As Classificações de Plínio: Uma Análise do Pensamento de Plínio Salgado entre 1932 e 1938," *Revista de Ciência Política* 21, no. 3 (Sep. 1978): 161–79.

8. Pessôa, *Reminiscências e imposições,* 255–57.

9. Ibid., 229–37.

10. Brazilian journalist William Waack gained access to Comintern records in Moscow after the collapse of the Soviet Union; "Os papéis de Moscou: Documentos inéditos revelam a ação da Internacional Comunista em 1935," *Veja* (São Paulo), Sep. 8, 1993, 58–60; William Waack, *Camaradas: Nos Arquivos de Moscou; A história secreta da revolução brasileira de 1935* (Rio de Janeiro & São Paulo: co-edição Biblioteca do Exército Editora & Companhia das Letras, 1993), 206–12. He provided details on selection of agents, financial support, and decision making at the various levels.

11. Vargas stayed informed of communist agitation among workers on the Central do Brasil and the bus lines, as well as among taxi drivers and construction laborers. He noted that General Góes informed him about Red activities in the army ranks. Vargas, *Diário,* 1:321.

12. Stanley E. Hilton, *Brazil and the Soviet Challenge, 1917–1947* (Austin: University of Texas Press, 1991), 59–60.

13. Távora, *Uma Vida e Muitas Lutas,* 1:84–94, 159–75; Dênis de Moraes and Francisco Viana, *Prestes: Lutas e Autocríticas* (Petrópolis: Editora Vozes, 1982), 31–35; "Luís Carlos Prestes," *DHBB,* 4:2813–14.

14. Hélio Silva, *1935,* 43, 117.

15. The security law permitted investigations of the constant rumors of plots in the officer corps, particularly among senior officers. Vargas, *Diário,* 1:364; Major William Sackville, Rio, Apr. 9, 1935, rpt. 1430 "Brazil's National Security Law," 2657-K-103, RG 165, NA.

16. Hélio Silva, *1935,* 285–89; for biographical sketches of the two officers see Ronald M. Schneider, *The Political System of Brazil: Emergence of a "Modernizing" Authoritarian Regime, 1964–1970* (New York: Columbia University Press, 1971), 375–76; and *DHBB,* 3:1824–27, 2053–58.

17. Silva, *1935,* 299. As if Brazil did not have enough internal security problems with its state police and poorly disciplined army units, it also had bandit gangs roaming the interior of the northeast; see Billy J. Chandler, *The Bandit King: Lampião of Brazil* (College Station: Texas A & M University Press, 1978); Frederico Pernambucano de Mello, *Guerreiros do Sol: O banditismo no nordeste do Brasil* (Recife: Editora Massangana, 1985), 185–209.

18. Silva, *1935,* 280–84; João Café Filho, *Do Sindicato ao Catete: Memórias Políticas e Confissões Humanas,* 2 vols. (Rio de Janeiro: José Olympio Editora, 1966), 1:83–86; Levine, *Vargas Regime,* 104–12. After taking cash from federal and state fiscal offices, the three sergeants who led the mutiny commandeered a *Condor* (Brazilian subsidiary of *Lufthansa*) aircraft for their getaway. Their troops took over the Lloyd

Brasileiro Steamship *Santos* for their escape. Major William Sackville, "Military Revolt in Brazil," Rio, Nov. 28, 1935, no. 1572, G-2 Regional, Brazil 6300, RG 165, NA.

19. Hilton, *Brazil and the Soviet Challenge,* 79; "Gregório Bezerra," *DHBB,* 1:387–88; the offending Twenty-first and Twenty-ninth Light Infantry Battalions and the Third Infantry Regiment were dissolved and their numbers removed from the army's unit list. They were substituted by new units, the Thirtieth and Thirty-first Battalions and the Fourteenth Regiment. See Decreto 465 in MG, *Relatório . . . João Gomes Ribeiro Filho . . . 1936,* 236. Levine, *Vargas Regime,* 105, incorrectly labeled the Twenty-first as an "artillery battalion."

20. Pessôa, *Reminiscências e imposições,* 211–20. Gomes's refusal to accept the information uncovered by the general staff was a model of command blindness; it reached such intensity that Pessôa began to suspect that Gomes might be involved in the plot. His account gives the impression that the revolt was quickly suppressed, and after the isolation of the Third Inf. Reg. further violence was not necessary; they could wait until "thirst or hunger forced its submission" (219).

21. Paulo Sérgio Pinheiro, *Estratégias da Ilusão: A Revolução Mundial e o Brasil, 1922–1935* (São Paulo: Companhia das Letras, 1991), 300–301. There were seventeen hundred soldiers in the Third Infantry Regiment, of whom an estimated two-thirds adhered to the revolt. Apparently the rebel leaders told their troops that the reason for the rising was the prohibition against reenlistment and the reduction of troops in the army. Pinheiro also made the point that the choice of this barracks between "the mountains and the sea" was a poor one (302).

22. Major William Sackville, "Details of Military Revolt," Rio, Dec. 5, 1935, rpt. 1574, 6300, G-2 Regional, RG 165, NA. He said that Capt. Francisco Moésia Rolim and Lt. Paes Barreto had tried to incite the rebellion. Also that a number of noncommissioned officers had been arrested. Rolim had been active in protesting against the national security law a few months before. He had signed the founding document of the ANL. He was arrested but later released for lack of evidence. See "Moésia Rolim," *DHBB,* 4:3008. Testimony of Major Mariano de Oliveira, Inquérito Policial Militar, vol. 7, 1674–75, as quoted in Hélio Silva, *1935,* 324–25. Perhaps it was Dutra's order to shoot rebels that was the basis for the rumor about Gen. Gomes wanting to shoot the captured rebels at Praia Vermelha.

23. Silva, *1935,* 358. The resistance of the two companies made it impossible for the rebels to leave the barracks for the missions Prestes had assigned them. Thirty-nine years later General Fritz Manso would be chief of the general staff in the Geisel administration. See "Fritz Azevedo Manso," *DHBB,* 3:2074–75.

24. Leite and Novelli, *Marechal Eurico Gaspar Dutra,* 92–95.

25. I chose to recount the events from Vargas's point of view because his account sets the timing most clearly. Vargas, *Diário,* 1:446–47. The reader met Eduardo Gomes at Ft. Copacabana in July 1922. Ivo Borges was one of the army's first pilots in 1921; he commanded the paulista air force in 1932; after amnesty he returned to the army in January 1934 and in April 1935 took command of the aviation school, where he stayed until August 1939. With the creation of the independent air force in 1941 he transferred to the new arm and served as air attaché in Argentina and Uruguay from July 1941 to Aug. 1943; later he was zone commander in Belém from 1943 to 1944 and in Rio de Janeiro in 1945. See "Ivo Borges," *DHBB,* 1:413–14.

26. Mascarenhas de Moraes, *Memórias,* 1:93–96; Carlos Meira Mattos, *O Marechal Mascarenhas de Moraes e sua Época* (Rio de Janeiro: Editora Biblioteca do Exército, 1983), 1:64–67.

27. Camargo and Góes, *Meio século de combate,* 67. Note that this occurred before calls to Dutra's office from the Third announced the start of the revolt. Cordeiro was then studying at the general staff school, and the officers he gathered were likely from there. The level of intimacy among officers was displayed by Gomes's addressing Lt. Col. Cordeiro as "Menino" (Sonny, Kid, Little Boy).

28. Brig. Gen. Francisco José da Silva Jr. was born in Fortaleza in 1879, entered the army in August 1897, went through the preparatory school at Realengo, and graduated from Praia Vermelha in November 1904 as a second lieutenant. He joined the infantry in 1907, became first lieutenant in 1914 and captain in 1919, took the courses at the general staff school in the next year, and in 1922 was aide-de-camp to Minister Setembrino de Carvalho. He reached major in 1925 and lieutenant colonel in 1929. When the Revolution of 1930 broke out, he was subcommander of the Thirteenth Inf. Reg. in Ponta Grossa (PR). He joined the revolutionaries, commanding one of the detachments of the Miguel Costa Column heading toward Rio de Janeiro. He was at the head of the troops ready to attack Itararé (SP), when Washington Luís stepped down. In May 1931 he was made colonel and fought on the government side in 1932, this time taking Itararé. That October he was promoted to brigadier general and commanded the Third Infantry Brigade; he joined the generals in December 1935, demanding hard and fast punishments for the rebels of November. In 1938 he was made general of division and headed the Second Military Region (SP); in June 1939 he took over the First Military Region (RJ), which he headed until 1942. From 1943 until his death, in 1948, he was on the Supremo Tribunal Militar. See "Francisco José da Silva Júnior," *DHBB,* 4:3180–81; his testimony in the Political-Military Inquiry is quoted at length in Silva, *1935,* 361–64.

29. Camargo and Góes, *Meio século de combate,* 68. His father was Joaquim Barbosa Cordeiro de Faria, an alferes in Jan. 1889; he was a contemporary of Augusto Tasso Fragoso. Oswaldo Cordeiro de Farias would soon be the youngest general in the army at age forty-one, would serve as interventor in Rio Grande do Sul, command the FEB artillery in Italy, found the Escola Superior de Guerra after the war, be elected governor of Pernambuco, and play a role in establishing the military regime in 1964 and in ending it in the early 1980s. See "Cordeiro de Farias," *DHBB,* 2:1232–38.

30. This reconstruction is based on Dutra, Barata, & Vargas accounts: Leite and Novelli, *Marechal Eurico Gaspar Dutra,* 89–101; Dutra's aide was Capt. João Ribeiro Pinheiro. Agildo Barata told his story in *Vida de um Revolucionário (Memórias)* (Rio de Janeiro: Editora Melso, S.A., 1962), 253–300. Barata felt that Dutra had not played by the "rules" in refusing to speak with his representatives and in using tear gas: these two acts "showed the absolute lack of ethics and professional dignity of this general" (298–99). Barata spent ten years in jail for his mutiny. Vargas, *Diário,* 1:446–47. Minister of War Gomes, attempting to get closer to the barracks, accompanied by Dutra and several junior officers, was stopped by a burst of machine-gun fire that mortally wounded Dutra's aide and hit two of the minister's staff. He may have been angered by the experience, but there is no known evidence that he ordered the rebels shot.

Silva's account is clearest (see Hélio Silva, *1935*, 369–72). The regimental commander Col. José Fernando Afonso Ferreira was among the wounded, having suffered two wounds. One of the pilots who strafed and bombed was Captain Nero Moura, who would be Vargas's pilot between 1938 and 1943 and in the world war would command the Brazilian squadron in Italy; in the second Vargas government, 1951–54, he would be minister of aeronautics. See "Nero Moura," *DHBB*, 3:2311–13.

31. Luiz Vergara, *Fui Secretário de Getúlio Vargas* (Rio de Janeiro: Editôra Globo, 1960), 105, told the story, and General Dutra contested its truth. See Leite and Novelli, *Marechal Eurico Gaspar Dutra*, 101–102 n. 18. Stanley E. Hilton noted that Dutra told this to his old friend Vitorino de Brito Freire; see Hilton, *Brazil and the Soviet Challenge*, 71 n. 44. Freire was one of the second- or third-level politicians whose careers ran from 1930 to the 1970s; see "Vitoriano Freire," *DHBB*, 2:1378–80.

32. Miseal de Mendonça, born in 1885, had entered the army in 1903, was declared *aspirante* in 1910, and had reached captain in 1924. He was a legalist in the 1920s and fought against São Paulo in 1932. In 1933 he was made major and commander of the Third Battalion of the Third Inf. Reg. He was hit in the crossfire as he attempted to investigate the situation. "Miseal de Mendonça," *DHBB*, 3:2209. Hélio Silva provided the sad details about Meireles and Pereira in *1935*, 358–59. Ironically, Meireles is among the officers listed as killed by communists on the monument that now stands on the site of the barracks. Pereira had been among the Realengo cadets dismissed in 1922 and who returned to the army in the post-1930 amnesty.

33. Pessôa, *Reminiscências e imposições*, 211–15. Paulo Sérgio Pinheiro carefully examined the numbers and where they were killed in *Estratégias da Ilusão: A Revolução Mundial e o Brasil, 1922–1935* (São Paulo: Companhia das Letras, 1991), 302–6. The monument over their grave in Rio's São João Batista cemetery lists twenty-two names, seventeen killed in Rio, four in Natal, and one in Recife. Numbers were inflated in press and foreign intelligence accounts; the U.S. military attaché wrote, "The casualties at Praia Vermelha have not been announced officially. Best information obtainable places them at 4 officers (1 revolter and 3 loyal) and 150 enlisted men killed, the latter figure including casualties on both sides. This morning's press mentions 34 as being wounded, of these 6 being officers." Major William Sackville, "Military Revolt in Brazil," Rio, Nov. 28, 1935, rpt. 1572, Brazil 6300, G-2 Regional, RG 165, NA. The frequently cited fifty killed at Praia Vermelha, "mostly young rebel cadets," is an example of the precariousness of even contemporary sources; Levine, *Vargas Regime*, 120. More recently CPDOC follows José Campos de Aragão in summarizing the numbers for Rio as 19 killed and 159 wounded. "Eurico Gaspar Dutra," *DHBB*, 2:1129. The official army view that sleeping soldiers were killed seems to have softened. The recent "official" history takes pains to attribute to Glauco Carneiro: "Two loyalist officers . . . were killed . . . probably while still asleep." *História das Revoluções Brasileiras* (Rio de Janeiro: Edições O Cruzeiro, 1965), 2:429. With all deference, Carneiro wrote "diz-se que ainda dormindo" (it is said still sleeping). Luiz Paulo Macedo Cavalho, ed., *The Army in Brazilian History* (Rio de Janeiro & Salvador, Ba.: Biblioteca do Exército & Odebrecht, 1998), 3, 132. Murder is awful in any form, but to kill a helpless professional soldier adds insult to injury. At Campo dos Afonsos, Capt. Agilberto de Azevedo shot dead Lt. Benedito Lopes Bragança, who was a disarmed prisoner inside an automobile.

34. GetúlioVargas, *A Nova Política do Brasil* (Rio de Janeiro: José Olympio Editora, 1938–47), 4:141.

35. A full study of the undocumented sleeping murders, their symbolism and use, awaits an enterprising scholar. General Muricy mentioned Lieutenants Paladini and Bragança among those killed, but, of course, they were both awake and alert. General Antonio Carlos da Silva Muricy, *Palavras de Um Soldado* (Rio de Janeiro: Imprensa do Exército, 1971), 205.

36. Pedro Ernesto's arrest, trial, and imprisonment was and remains controversial. Some scholars have questioned whyVargas did not protect a longtime family friend (Levine in biography of Getúlio); others maintained his innocence. Deputado Adalberto Correia, chairman of the National Commission on Repression of Communism, was, according toVargas, "a tenacious persecutor" of Pedro Ernesto. The president became "disgusted, annoyed," by Correia's public criticism of the minister of justice and the police chief, but he agreed to the arrest of his doctor when Correia presented sufficient proof. When the arrest occurred on Apr. 3, 1936,Vargas wrote: "Although the circumstances forced me to consent to this arrest, I confess that I did it with sorrow. I had a crisis of conscience. I have doubts if this man is astray, or a traitor, misunderstood or a deceiver. Perhaps the future will tell" (Vargas, *Diário,* 1:492–94). Waack seems to accept the assertions in the captured Prestes papers and in the messages to Moscow of Pedro Ernesto's support, but the quotations and references he presents could be questioned. See *Camaradas,* 160–61, 181, 192, 200, 211, 224–25, 243, 287, 290, 310. Waack noted that the doctor kept Getúlio informed. I leave it to others to explore further the populist doctor's involvement.

37. Hilton, *Brazil and the Soviet Challenge,* 102–7; Waack, *Camaradas,* 289–300; Chateaubriand quote is from Levine, *Vargas Regime,* 124; see 125–37 for repression.

38. The question of institutional responsibility is complicated. For part of the time Müller's ability to use his federal police in the Federal District was, at least partially, checked by Mayor Pedro Ernesto's new municipal police force under the command of army major Euclides Zenóbio da Costa, who was an energetic, upwardly mobile officer, who would command the FEB infantry in Italy and serve as army minister in 1954. See "Zenóbio da Costa," *DHBB,* 2:988–92.

39. Vanda Maria Ribeiro Costa, "Com Rancor e Com Afeto: Rebeliões Militares na Década de 30," *Política e Estratégia* 4, no. 2 (Apr.–June 1986): 175–79, 183, 193.

40. MG, *Relatório . . . João Gomes Ribeiro Filho . . . 1936,* 7–8.

41. Vargas, *Diário,* 1:448–49.

42. *O Jornal* (Rio), Nov. 30, 1935; other quotations here are as quoted in Hilton, *Brazil and the Soviet Challenge,* 73–74.

43. Wolfe, *Working Women, Working Men,* 68.

44. Góes Monteiro opened his 1935 *Relatório* to the president with a forty-eight-page analysis of the army's problems that repeated many of his favorite themes. He listed the evils afflicting the army: (1) too many officers assigned outside its ranks; (2)undue involvement of officers in factious movements; (3)expressions of partisan concerns conflicting with army policy; (4) absence of a mentality capable of rejecting everything that is against, and accepting everything favorable to, the army's aims; (5) the general laissez-faire or laissez-passer, the irresponsibility of leaders, and the lack of moral authority that the "law of expending the least effort" generated. MG,

Relatório . . . Maio de 1935 . . . Góes Monteiro (Rio de Janeiro: Imprensa do Estado-Maior do Exército, 1935), 22–23.

45. Vargas, *Diário,* 1:450 n. 34.

46. For a summary of the generals' comments and Góes' statement see Hélio Silva, *1937: Todos os Golpes se Parecem* (Rio de Janeiro: Editora Civilização Brasileira, 1970), 87–97. His ending is especially striking because in the post–World War II era officers reacted heatedly if anyone suggested that the army was a militia, gendarme, or police force. His words: "A gendarmizá-las será preferível a dissolução."

47. Decreto no. 465, Dec. 3, 1935, appeared in the *Diário Official,* Dec. 11, 1935; MG, *Relatório . . . João Gomes Ribeiro Filho . . . 1936,* 236.

48. The Vargas diary provides a chronology at this stage. Vargas, *Diário,* 1:449–51. Summary of meeting in Silva, *1937,* 97–98. The generals were changing the rules and consequences of rebellion that had been in play during the previous four decades.

49. Vargas, *Diário,* 1:452–61. The text of the modifications in the security law (no. 38 of Apr. 4, 1935) is in MG, *Relatório . . . João Gomes Ribeiro Filho . . . 1936* (as Law 136, Dec. 14, 1935), 181–84. The entire cabinet signed Law 136.

50. Major William Sackville, "Political Issues and Problems, Communism in Brazil," Rio, Apr. 15, 1936, rpt. no. 1830, 2657-K-70, 6300a, G-2 Regional Brazil, RG 165, NA; there is a list of the names in Silva, *1937,* 126; on Col. Ferreira see Silva, *1937,* 135–36. Upward of twenty-five hundred military personnel had been arrested; see Hilton, *Brazil and the Soviet Challenge,* 79. The arrested Comintern agents were brutally tortured, one into insanity. Prestes seems to have been comparatively well treated.

51. Nelson Werneck Sodré, at that time a captain, called Correia *meio doido* [half-crazy] and noted that the deputy did not like Francisco Campos, whom he threatened publicly; see Sodré, *Memórias de um Soldado,* 55. Vargas commented on Deputy Correia: *Diário,* 1:492–93. For biography see "Adalberto Correia," *DHBB,* 2.934–35.

52. Elizabeth Cancelli, *O Mundo da Violência: A Polícia da Era Vargas* (Brasília: Editora Universidade de Brasília, 1993), 93–99; Vargas, *Diário,* 1:494 (entry for Apr. 3, 4, 1936). Also "Comissão Nacional de Repressão ao Communismo," *DHBB,* 1:854; and "Filipe Moreira Lima," *DHBB,* 3:1842–43. The most helpful analysis of Pedro Ernesto's arrest, trials, and release is Michael L. Conniff, *Urban Politics in Brazil: The Rise of Populism, 1925–45* (Pittsburgh, Pa.: University of Pittsburgh Press, 1981), 142–59.

53. Coutinho, *General Góes Depõe,* 274–75.

54. Vargas, *Diário,* 1:466; Carlos Lima Cavalcanti to Agamenon Magalhães, Recife, Dec. 12, 1935, as quoted in Silva, *1937,* 111.

55. Vargas, *Diário,* 1:506–8.

56. Góes Monteiro to Gen. Francisco José Pinto (Chief of President's military staff), Rio, May 1, 1936; Frederico Cristiano Buys to Góes, May 10, 1936, GMP. My thanks to Peter S. Smith for sharing this and other material on Góes Monteiro.

57. "João Gomes," *DHBB,* 2:1488–89; Vargas, *Diário,* 1:381–89; Panteleão Pessôa, *Reminiscências e Imposições,* 175–81. General P. Pessôa, interview by Peter S. Smith, Rio, May 8, 1975.

58. *Correio da Manhã* (Rio), May 23, 1936; Gen. Eurico Dutra, 1-a Região Militar, Estado-Maior, Quartel General, *Boletim reservado* no. 7, Rio, May 25, 1936, GMP.

59. Arnaldo de Sousa Pais de Andrade, who was chief from Mar. 16, 1936, until May 26, 1937, was seriously ill in the last months, but because of his respect and friendship Góes Monteiro refused to take over the general staff until Pais de Andrade decided of his own accord to step down. He died Aug. 8, 1937. "Pais de Andrade," *DHBB*, 1: 141. See Coutinho, *General Góes Depõe*, 286. Manoel de Cerqueira Daltro Filho (1938) fell mortally ill and was hospitalized Nov. 30, 1937, but did not die until January. Oswaldo Cordeiro de Farias to Eurico Dutra, Porto Alegre, Nov. 30, 1937, GV 37.11.30/4, AGV-CPDOC-Rio.

60. Leitão de Carvalho, *Memórias,* 3:273.

61. It is often difficult to ascribe exact meaning to command assignments. Many were more related to the ability, experience, and rank of available officers than to major political considerations. Because all of the generals had risen to that rank under Vargas, loyalty to the government was a given unless an individual demonstrated otherwise. The assignment of Estevão Leitão de Carvalho to Curitiba is a good example. He was one of the stellar officers of the twentieth century, professional, Young Turk, one of the *Defesa Nacional* founders; he had turned down the military leadership of the Revolution of 1930, survived the retirement purges of 1931, and was widely respected in the army. Even so, he had been passed over a dozen times for younger colonels who had demonstrated "revolutionary spirit." He played a leading role in the Chaco peace settlement, which earned him Foreign Minister Macedo Soares's recommendation to Vargas that he be promoted to brigadier general. In the interim even Col. José Joaquim de Andrade, who had commanded the resistance of the Twelfth Regimento de Infantaria in Belo Horizonte in October 1930, was elevated to brigadier general. On Nov. 14, 1935, Vargas and Gomes decided on Leitão de Carvalho's promotion, along with that of Newton de Andrade Cavalcanti (likely for his useful three-month interim service as interventor in the State of Rio de Janeiro, Aug.–Nov. 1935). Vargas, *Diário,* 1:441; Leitão de Carvalho, *Memórias,* 3:255–63. Minister Gomes named Leitão commander of the Ninth Inf. Brigade in Curitiba (Feb. 1936), his first unit command since the Eighth Inf. Reg. in Passo Fundo, RGS, down to Oct. 1930. After less than a month with the Ninth Brigade, he succeeded Gen. Paes de Andrade, who moved up to army chief of staff, as commander of the Fifth Military Region. Then in April Gomes notified him that he was to move back to the Ninth Inf. Brig. so that João Guedes da Fontoura, recently promoted to General de Divisão, could command the Fifth Military Region. This rapid little quadrille of changing commanders may have been an extreme case, but considering when it occurred and who was involved, its description illustrates the complexities of army administration as the Rio Grande crisis developed.

62. Vargas, *Diário,* 1:537. The *Ordem do Merito Militar* had been established in 1935. Its regulations are in MG, *Relatório . . . João Gomes Ribeiro Filho . . . Maio de 1936,* 291–93.

63. Major William Sackville, "Brazil's Authorized Army 1936–7–8," Rio, Mar. 4, 1936, rpt. no. 1609, 2006-105/11, 6010a; idem, "Budget for 1936," Rio, Mar. 7, 1936, Rpt no. 1612, 2006-142; Major Lawrence C. Mitchell, "Annual Maneuvers," Rio, Oct. 14, 1936, rpt. no. 1720, 2006-148, 6700g; idem, Oct. 29, 1936, rpt. no. 1732, 2006-148, 6700g, G-2 Regional Brazil, RG 165, NA. Sackville, Mar. 7, 1936, reported that the ministry appropriation was in milreis 475,201,357, or U.S.$37,933,446.

64. Major Lawrence C. Mitchell, "Postponement of Ministry of War Organization," Rio, Sep. 19, 1936, rpt. no. 1704, 2006-86, 6100c, G-2 Regional Brazil, RG 165, NA.

65. Leite and Novelli, *Marechal Eurico Gaspar Dutra,* 115. Gomes authorized the paulista purchases on Oct. 5, 1936; Dutra learned about them on Jan. 28, 1937 (with more detail on Feb. 25) and ordered their seizure on Mar. 1, 1937 (ibid., 158–63). Cardoso de Melo Neto, Armando Sales's successor as paulista governor, refused to sign the document ceding the weaponry to the army (ibid., 162–63).

66. Vargas, *Diário,* 1:564 (entry for Nov. 30, 1936): "Gente difícil estes militares, quando desconfiam que a força vale mais que a disciplina [Difficult people these military, when they suspect that force is worth more than discipline]."

67. Vargas, *Diário,* 1:559–63. Getúlio kept family crises from public view. For example, on the death of his mother, Candida Dornelles Vargas, he gathered his family in the isolation of Brocoió Island, which belonged to the Guinle family (see Leite and Novelli, *Marechal Eurico Gaspar Dutra,* 557).

68. Polícia Civil (RJ), "Relatório sobre o ambiente de hostilidade em torno do Ministro da Guerra, João Gomes Ribeiro Filho," GV 36.07.07/1, AGV, CPDOC-Rio; see comment in "João Gomes," *DHBB,* 2:1489; Vargas, *Diário,* 1:562.

69. Aranha said this to Getúlio on Feb. 3, 1937; Vargas, *Diário,* 2:19.

70. The link between the army and the Valladares–Antonio Carlos struggle was the mineiro military police. In early 1936 all of the state police forces in Brazil had been made reserve forces that could be federalized as need be. The supposed objective was to standardize training and equipment. But, of course, it satisfied an old army desire. Even so, the decision to accept federalization still rested with the state governors. Strategically, the army could not move against Rio Grande do Sul until the Minas flank was secure and São Paulo was neutralized. Valladares would not release any of his forces to federal control or action out of state until Antonio Carlos was subordinate. See Wirth, *Minas Gerais,* 186–92; Benedicto Valladares, *Tempos Idos e Vividos: Memórias* (Rio de Janeiro: Editora Civilização Brasileira, 1966), 109–21.

71. Vargas certainly understood the importance of Minas, and even though he had made Valladares the power in the state, he treated him very carefully. Interestingly, Vargas dated Valladares's commitment to the coup plot earlier in his diary than the governor did in his memoirs. Getúlio's entry for Nov. 19, 1936, reads, "I found him . . . very decided on the coup d'état, in the sense of dissolving Congress and declaring a new Constitution" (Vargas, *Diário,* 1:536); see also Valladares, *Tempos Idos e Vividos,* 122–41.

72. Dutra's career sketch is primarily based on "Eurico Gaspar Dutra," *DHBB,* 2:1126–29. On the anti-Bernardes crisis see Coelho, *Exército Internamente,* 11–27. Dutra was the 138th signer (15).

CHAPTER 11

1. Vargas, *Nova Política do Brasil,* 5:32; Estado-Maior do Exército, *Relatório dos Trabalhos do Estado-Maior . . . 1937 . . . pelo GD Pedro Aurélio de Góes Monteiro* (Rio de Janeiro: Imprensa do Estado-Maior do Exército, 1938), 4–5, 8–9.

2. Sodré, *Memórias de um Soldado,* 162. Sodré was describing an encounter with Dutra.

3. "Valdomiro Lima," *DHBB*, 3:1865–70.

4. Leite and Novelli, *Marechal Eurico Gaspar Dutra*, 131–36; the American attaché prepared a long report on the matter: Major Lawrence C. Mitchell, "Officers on Special Detail," Rio, Jan. 25, 1937, rpt. no. 1796, 2006-149, MMB, General and Special Staffs, WD, RG 165, NA. Fourteen states had detached army officers commanding their military police. Maj. Mitchell asserted that "in all cases, Army officers detailed to the service of a state governor are personal friends of the governor in question, detailed to that service at the request of the governor."

5. Vargas, *Diário*, 2:41–50 (entries for May 4, 14, 17, 28–29, 31, 1937); "Valdomiro Lima," *DHBB*, 3:1869; "José Pessôa," *DHBB*, 4:2706; Leite and Novelli, *Marechal Eurico Gaspar Dutra*, 195–96. Maj. Lawrence C. Mitchell, Rio, May 20, 1937: "Pre-election Activities, Army and Politics," rpt. no. 1869, 2657-K-74, 6000, G-2 Report, WD, RG 165, NA. The report contains the proclamation text. Major Mitchell expressed "wonderment . . . that it [was] considered necessary or even opportune."

6. The following generals replied: Pedro Cavalcanti, Constancio Deschamps Cavalcanti, Firmino Borba, José Osório, Brasílio Taborda, João Candido Pereira Castro Jr., Julio Caetano Horta Barbosa, José Antonio Coelho Neto, Francisco José Silva Jr., Manoel Rabelo, César Augusto Parga Rodrigues, Raymundo Barbosa, Collatino Marques, Penha, Paim Rodrigues, June 5–7, 1937, GMP, AE. The replies were dated June 7 or 8. Thanks to Peter M. Smith for calling this incident to my attention and sharing his documentation.

7. Coutinho, *General Góes Depõe*, 294–95. At this point in their careers Dutra and Góes were either highly motivated by conviction or by ambition. They had reached the thirty-fifth year of service and the army's highest ranks, and they could have taken their pensions and led less agitated lives. Maj. Lawrence C. Mitchell, Rio, June 16, 1937: "Army Feud," rpt. no. 1900; June 17, 1937: "Army Feud Developments," rpt. no 1901; June 24, 1937: "Further Developments in Army Feud," rpt. no. 1909, 2006-128, 6200d, MID, GS, WD, RG 165, NA.

8. Pessôa was promoted to general of division in 1940; he was inspector general of cavalry until 1945. Elected president of the Military Club in 1944, he was active in the events of October 1945 that led to the deposition of Vargas. See "José Pessôa," *DHBB*, 4:2705–6. Maj. Lawrence C. Mitchell, Rio, June 15, 1937: "Changes in High Command," rpt. no. 1897; July 1, 1937: "Army Feud Approaches Settlement," rpt. no. 1916, 2006-128, 6200d, MID, GS, WD, RG 165, NA.

9. José Américo de Almeida told his view of the campaign in *A Palavra e o Tempo (1937–1945–1950)* (Rio de Janeiro: José Olympio Editora, 1965), 5–83.

10. Vargas, *Diário*, 2:13 (entry for Jan. 18). Over the next months there are many references to arms shipments into Rio Grande do Sul and São Paulo.

11. Maj. Lawrence C. Mitchell, Rio, May 11, 1937: "Maneuvers, 3rd Region (Rio Grande do Sul)," rpt. no. 1858, 2006-151, 6700g, LCM/B, G-2 Regional, WD, RG 165, NA. A month later he reported that federal troops were being used to stop smuggling along the open borders with Argentina and Uruguay. They were not to have ordinary police duty but could be called on by customs agents for assistance. Maj. Mitchell noted that such nonmilitary duties were not unusual: "Soldiers always have been regarded as available for practically any service, subject to executive whim." Mitchell, Rio, June 21, 1937: "Employment of troops to repress smuggling," rpt. no. 1905, 2006-154, 6940c, G-2 Regional, WD, RG 165, NA.

12. Vargas, *Diário*, 2:13–32; Carlos E. Cortés, *Gaúcho Politics in Brazil: The Politics of Rio Grande do Sul, 1930–1964* (Albuquerque: University of New Mexico Press, 1974), 78–82; "Emílio Lúcio Esteves," *DHBB*, 2, 1205–6; Generals Esteves and Dutra discussed troop concentration via radio; 37.04.28/2, AGV, CPDOC-Rio.

13. General Esteves to Eurico Dutra, telegram, Porto Alegre, June 29, 1937, 37.06.29/1, AGV, CPDOC-Rio. The amount of documentation in the Vargas papers on the Rio Grande situation is enormous. It would be a mistake to assume that the whole affair had been merely trumped up against Flores da Cunha. See, e.g., the seventy-one pages of correspondence on the crisis in GV 37.05.01, AGV, CPDOC-Rio. Maj. Lawrence C. Mitchell, Rio, July 15, 1937: "Visit of Minister of War to Southern Brazil," rpt. no. 1929, 2657-k-74, 6940c; Aug. 17, 1937: "Displacement of Troops," rpt. no. 1951, 2657-K-74, 6180 LCM/B, both G-2 Regional, WD, RG 165, NA. He had reports that trenches had been constructed on the Santa Catarina–RGS border. Two battalions of light infantry, a cavalry regiment, a mountain artillery group, and engineering and communications companies had been moved to within striking distance of Rio Grande via the serra and coastal routes.

14. Ministro de Guerra to Commandantes de Regiões e Diretores de Serviços, circular, Rio de Janeiro, June 29, 1937, GMP, AE.

15. It is interesting that American military attaché Major Lawrence C. Mitchell assumed and reported to Washington that the delay in General Góes's taking the chief's position was because of the controversy with Gen. Waldomiro. But from the outset Góes and Dutra had agreed that he would wait until their sick friend General Pais de Andrade was ready to step down. Foreigners often had difficulty seeing, let alone accepting, the importance of friendship in Brazilian public life. L. C. Mitchell, Rio, Aug. 4, 1937: "Changes in High Commands," rpt. no. 1941, 2006-128, 6180a, MID, GS, WD, RG 165, NA. General Pais de Andrade died on Aug. 8, 1937; *DHBB*, 1:141.

16. *José Joaquim de Andrade* was born in Ceará in 1879. He passed through military schooling between 1896 and 1905, being declared alferes-aluno in that year. In 1907 he was promoted to second lieutenant of infantry and served in Rio's Fourth Infantry Regiment, where he helped suppress the Sailors' Revolt of 1910. In 1911 he was transferred to the Fifth Inf. Battalion in Ponta Grossa, Paraná, where in Oct. and Nov. 1912 he led troops in the Contestado campaign. In 1913 he was at the Escola de Estado-Maior in Rio and in 1914 was made first lieutenant in recognition of his studies. He served in Fortaleza, Ceará, before returning to Rio in 1915. Reaching captain in July 1919, he took the general staff review course and was assigned to work with the French military mission in 1920. After hours he studied medicine, earning his medical degree in 1923. In July 1924 he fought against the tenente rebels in São Paulo and in the next year was promoted to major for merit. In 1927 he was on the personal staff of Minister Nestor Sezefredo dos Passos, where he was promoted to lieutenant colonel for merit in 1928. The Revolution of 1930 found him in command of the Twelfth Infantry Regiment in Belo Horizonte, which became famous for its stubborn five-day resistance under fire, even though Lieutenant Colonel Andrade had been taken prisoner at the outset. Full colonel in October 1931, he commanded key units in the Paraíba valley against Góes Monteiro and Dutra in 1932. Proscribed and exiled to Portugal until the May 1934 amnesty, when he returned to active duty as chief of the general staff's Fourth Section. After a stint as head of the Second Infantry Regiment in Vila Militar, Rio, he was promoted to

brigadier general in July 1935 and command of the First Inf. Brigade and Vila Militar. As such, his troops suppressed the revolt of the air units in Campo dos Afonsos in Nov. 1935. In Oct. 1936 he took over the command of the Fifth Inf. Brigade and other units in Santa Maria (RGS). Then under the Estado Novo in Dec. 1937 he became head of army aviation and was promoted to general of division in Feb. 1938. For a short time in the next year he was Third Military Region commander, then took ill and died in Mar. 1940. "José Joaquim de Andrade," *DHBB,* 1:139–40.

17. Leite and Novelli, *Marechal Eurico Gaspar Dutra,* 199–202. The trip was from July 7 to July 19.

18. Maj. Lawrence C. Mitchell, Rio, Aug. 4, 1937: "Changes in High Commands," rpt. no. 1941, 2006-128, 6180a, MID, GS, WD, RG 165, NA.

19. The exchange of telegrams dated July 28, Aug. 2, 5, 9, 1937, are in Leite and Novelli, *Marechal Eurico Gaspar Dutra,* 199–202; Eurico Dutra to Flores da Cunha, telegram, Rio, Aug. 9, 1937, 37.08.09/2, AGV, CPDOC-Rio.

20. Leite and Novelli, *Marechal Eurico Gaspar Dutra,* 209–12. Dutra drew up orders for the regional commanders on where they should move their troops in the event of a clash in Rio Grande; see ibid., 213–20.

21. José Américo de Almeida, *Palavra e o Tempo,* 17–22; Hélio Silva, *1937,* 372. Vargas, *Diário,* 2:58–65. Col. Oswaldo Cordeiro de Farias, who was General Daltro's chief of staff, told how the suspected officers were removed from the regional staff: Camargo and Góes, *Meio século de combate,* 230–32. Daltro Filho to G. Vargas, Porto Alegre, Aug. 19, 1937, GV 37.08.19, AGV, CPDOC-Rio.

22. Alves de Abreu, Alzira (coordinatora), *Juacy Magalhães: Minhas Memórias Provisórias; Depoimento prestado ao CPDOC* (Rio de Janeiro: Editora Civilização Brasileira, 1982), 99.

23. On the destroyer deal, which would soon be torpedoed by Argentina and U.S. congressional objections see Naval Attaché's Report, Rio, Aug. 18, 1937: "Brazil-Navy; Ships, Destroyers," no. 912-800, Brazil 5900, G-2 Regional, MID, GS, WD, RG 165, NA; file GV 37.08.13, AGV, CPDOC-Rio; McCann, *Brazilian-American Alliance,* 113.

24. On his state of mind see Vargas, *Diário,* 2:64–67. Vargas committed suicide in the midst of another dark August crisis in 1954.

25. Vargas, *Diário,* 2:67 (entry for Aug. 27, 1937).

26. "O Dia do Soldado," *Revista Militar Brasileira,* Aug. 25, 1935, 3–4. On its opening page it stated that Caxias had been chosen as "patrono do Exército Brasileiro" and his birthday celebrated as Soldier's Day by virtue of aviso no. 366 of 1925. The reference to him as "guia espiritual" is on p. 4. Gen. Aurélio de Lyra Tavares, *Exército e Nação* (Recife: Imprensa Universitária, 1965), 13, 78–79. Celso Castro, "Entre Caxias e Osório: A Criação do Culto ao Patrono do Exército Brasileiro," *Estudos Históricos* 14, no. 25 (2000): 105–10; Murilo de Carvalho, *Formação das Almas,* 53–54. For a bibliography of articles see Francisco Ruas Santos, *Coleção Bibliográfica Militar* (Rio de Janeiro: Editora Biblioteca do Exército, 1960), 484–90.

27. The ceremony of passing the Caxias sabers was first held on Dec. 16, 1932, at the Caxias statue in the Largo do Machado in Rio; the following year it was on Aug. 25, and thereafter it was held at the military school. For Pessôa quote and the history of the "Espadim" see Câmara, *Marechal José Pessôa,* 73–77. The short sword

was modeled on the regulation one that Caxias gave to his wartime aide, Brig. Gen. João de Souza da Fonseca Costa (Baron and Visconde da Penha), whose son in turn gave it to the Instituto Geográfico e Histórica Brasileiro (Rio), where it is kept. The ceremony continues to be held at the military academy; see photos in *Agulhas Negras*, 135–39. While chief of coast artillery Gen. José Pessôa had the modernized Fort Vigia on top of Mt. Leme renamed Fort Duque de Caxias; Col. Annibal Barretto, *Fortificações do Brasil* (Rio de Janeiro: Editora Biblioteca do Exército, 1958), 247–49.

28. Murilo de Carvalho, *Formação das Almas*, 40–47 (photo of monument on 43); Renato Lemos, *Benjamin Constant: Vida e História* (Rio de Janeiro: Topbooks Editora, 1999), 531–42; the whole front of the park Campo Santana was moved back to make room for the widened avenue. On Caxias mausoleum see special issue of *Revista Militar Brasileira*, Aug. 25, 1949, 130–31.

29. João Gomes, "O Dia do Soldado," *Revista Militar Brasileira*, Aug. 25, 1935, 7–9; on 75 there is a photo of the statue in Largo do Machado.

30. Executive Decree No. 1899, Aug. 19, 1937. Maj. Lawrence C. Mitchell, Rio, Sep. 8, 1937: "New Discipline Regulations," rpt. no.1973, 2006-161, 6300b, MID, GS, WD, RG 165, NA.

31. O. Aranha to P. Góes Monteiro, Washington, D.C., Mar. 9, 1935, AOA, CP-DOC-Rio (italics added).

32. Ibid.

33. O. Aranha to Getúlio Vargas, Washington, D.C., June 4, 1937, AOA, CPDOC.

34. Vargas, *Diário*, 2:189 (Léticia crisis), 347 (Chaco War and "nosso complete falta de recursos para enfrentar uma situação"), 427 ("precariedade do nosso material belico").

35. Hilton, *Brazil and the Great Powers*, 117–29.

36. Estado-Maior do Exército, *Relatório dos Trabalhos do Estado-Maior . . . 1936 . . . pelo GD Arnaldo de Souza Paes de Andrade* (Rio de Janeiro: Imprensa do Estado-Maior do Exército, 1937), 4. MG, *Relatório . . . Eurico Dutra . . . Maio de 1937*, 37–38.

37. Vargas, *Diário*, 2:68–69 (entries for Sep. 7–13).

38. Conniff, *Urban Politics in Brazil*, 156–58.

39. Vargas, *Diário*, 2:70 (entry for Sep. 18, 1937). Dutra told Hélio Silva this version in 1959; Silva, *1937*, 390–91; Leite and Novelli, *Marechal Eurico Gaspar Dutra*, 228–29.

40. Valladares, *Tempos Idos e Vividos*, 157–66. The Constitution of 1934, Art. 167, made the military police forces of the states the reserve forces of the army. The enabling legislation that specified how this would work was Lei N. 192 of Jan. 17, 1936. It authorized the federal government to take control of the military police of the states in cases of foreign war or "grave commoção intestina." It provided for training and command by army officers, and it limited police arms to those used by army units in peacetime and forbade their possession of artillery, aircraft, and tanks. MG, *Relatório . . . Dutra . . . 1937*, Quarta Parte, 13–14.

41. Silva, *1937*, 455–56

42. Vargas, *Diário*, 2:71. Getúlio had just gotten Governor Valladares's commitment "to cooperate in a subversive movement to alter the situation caused by the presidential succession." "Newton Cavalcanti," *DHBB*, 1:749–51.

43. Aspásia Camargo et al., *O Golpe Silencioso: As origens da República Corporativa* (Rio de Janeiro: Rio Fundo Ed., 1989), 213.

44. Vargas, *Diário,* 2:71; "Venceram os aviadores militares," *A Nota* (Rio), Oct. 14, 1937; Ministerio da Viação e Obras Publicas, Dep. de Aeronautica Civil, *A Linha Aerea Internacional da America do Norte a Buenos Aires Através do Brasil e do Paraguay* (Rio de Janeiro: Officinas dos Correios e Telegraphos, 1937), 11–15.

45. The minutes of the meeting appear in both Silva, *1937,* 391–99, and Leite and Novelli, *Marechal Eurico Gaspar Dutra,* 231–38. The italics are mine.

46. Leite and Novelli, *Marechal Eurico Gaspar Dutra,* 231–38.

47. Vargas, *Diário,* 2:72

48. Dated Sep. 29, 1930, the text is in both Silva, *1937,* 403–9, and Leite and Novelli, *Marechal Eurico Gaspar Dutra,* 239–44. For various details see "José Carlos de Macedo Soares," *DHBB,* 4:3227–33. Macedo was the minister of justice, Mar. 6–Sep. 11, 1937, who formally sent the document to the Congress. On the twenty-eighth, according to what Dutra told Hélio Silva in 1959, Vargas told the service chiefs that if Macedo Soares did not agree with the request for a state of war, he would remove him (see Silva, *1937,* 403–9).

49. Vargas, *Diário,* 2:72

50. Camargo et al, *Golpe Silencioso,* 219.

51. Silva, *1937,* 414–25; Leite and Novelli, *Marechal Eurico Gaspar Dutra,* 246–56; Camargo and Góes, *Meio século de combate,* 232.

52. Vargas, *Diário* 2:75–76

53. On Oct. 15 Vargas commented, "The minister of war . . . is preparing decisively the march of events" (Vargas, *Diário,* 2:74); Paulo Brandi, *Vargas: Da Vida Para a História* (Rio de Janeiro: Zahar Editores, 1983), 119; Leite and Novelli, *Marechal Eurico Gaspar Dutra,* 257–58).

54. Vargas, *Diário,* 2:77–78. His words were "Caipira astuto e inteligente, mas entendemo-nos bem." This meeting was at the home of businessman Renato da Rocha Miranda, who acted as a go-between (see ibid., 574). John Dulles wrote that Vargas told Salgado that "the Armed Forces had decided to 'change the regime' and that he had agreed with them" (Dulles, *Vargas of Brazil,* 165). His source is not clear.

55. Valladares, *Tempos Idos e Vividos,* 174.

56. Leite and Novelli, *Marechal Eurico Gaspar Dutra,* 258–59; Vargas, *Diário,* 2:79.

57. Estimates of the number of green shirts taking part ranged from twenty thousand to fifty thousand. The lower figure is from Vargas, *Diário,* 2:79. Vargas's note gives the impression that Cavalcanti's appearance was not anticipated. But Vargas wrote that the integralistas marched by "in salute to the chief of the nation." While the parade was in progress, Dutra came by and was upset to see officers in the green shirt ranks. Dutra told his reaction to Hélio Silva in 1970; see Silva, *1937,* 457. Salgado's words are from Robert M. Scotten (U.S. Embassy), Rio, Nov. 6, 1937, 832.00/1083, Letter 126, RG 59, NA.

58. Vargas, *Diário,* 2:80; Carneiro, *Lusardo,* 2:208–10; "Artur Ferreira da Costa," *DHBB,* 2:962.

59. Vargas, *Diário,* 2:80–81; on the Negrão de Lima mission see Carneiro, *Lusardo,* 2:208–10. Lusardo was chair and Negrão was secretary of José Américo's election committee.

60. The manifesto's text appears in many places. I used Carneiro, *Lusardo,* 2:210–11; Scotten, Rio, Nov. 20, 832.00/1111 and /1106, RG 59, NA; on José Américo's refusal to sign see Leite and Novelli, *Marechal Eurico Gaspar Dutra,* 267.

61. "João Carlos Machado," *DHBB,* 3:1989–91; "Paulo de Morais Barros," *DHBB,* 1:331; see also Leite and Novelli, *Marechal Eurico Gaspar Dutra,* 269; Vargas, *Diário,* 2:82–83. Originally the plan was to stage the "reform" on Republic Day, November 15, but as tension built, it was changed to the eleventh and then with the manifesto to the tenth.

62. Vargas, *Diário,* 2:82–83; Carneiro, *Lusardo,* 2:211–12.

63. McCann, *Brazilian-American Alliance,* 46–47; Vargas, *Nova Política do Brasil,* 5:19–32, quotations from 28.

64. Quoted in Leite and Novelli, *Marechal Eurico Gaspar Dutra,* 271. Only Generals José Pompeu de Albuquerque Cavalcanti, commander of Coast Artillery, and Pantaleão Pessôa protested against the new regime; both were summarily retired. Pessôa's action stung Vargas, who wrote a lengthy passage in his diary saying how much he had done for his career, how Pessôa had allied himself with Flores da Cunha, and how he opposed the coup "of which earlier he was a partisan, counseling me more than once to dissolve the Congress" (Vargas, *Diário,* 2:86–87 [entry for Nov. 24]). Paulo Brandi said there were five generals who were relieved for protesting but only mentions the two above and General Guedes da Fontoura, who was likely marked for retirement in any case; Brandi, *Vargas,* 125.

65. Leitão de Carvalho, *Discursos, Conferências e Outros Escritos* (Rio de Janeiro: Imprensa do Exército, 1965), 274 (italics added).

66. Nélson de Mello, quoted in Valentina da Rocha Lima, ed., *Getúlio: Uma História Oral* (Rio de Janeiro: Editora Record, 1986), 204. "Nélson de Mello," *DHBB,* 3:2191–94. Vargas's daughter Alzira Vargas do Amaral Peixoto told me this in an interview on Aug. 10, 1969. There is a discussion of this question in my *Brazilian-American Alliance,* 43.

67. Getúlio Vargas to O. Aranha, Rio, Nov. 17, 1937, AOA, CPDOC. He also stressed that he wanted to use American capital "so that we would be able to avoid accepting offers from other countries, [read Germany?] that I have resisted and intend to resist."

68. Vargas, *Nova Política do Brasil,* 5:127–28 (New Year), 145 (Porto Alegre); the rest is from Robert M. Scotten, Rio, Jan. 19, 1938, dispatch 272, 832.001 Getúlio Vargas 10/47, RG 59, NA.

69. Estado-Maior do Exército, *Relatório dos Trabalhos do Estado-Maior . . . 1937 . . . pelo GD Pedro Aurélio de Góes Monteiro* (Rio de Janeiro: Imprensa do Estado-Maior do Exército, 1938), 4–5, 8–9. "Heredamos . . . um Exército quasi que apenas nominal, desprovido do essencial e, portanto, imprestável para o campo de batalha" (5).

70. The minutes of the meeting appear in both Silva, *1937,* 391–99, and Leite and Novelli, *Marechal Eurico Gaspar Dutra,* 231–38.

71. MG, *Relatório . . . Dutra . . . 1938,* 6–8.

72. Schneider, *"Order and Progress,"* 9.

73. Sumner Welles to F. D. Roosevelt, Washington, D.C., Jan. 26, 1937, President's Personal File 4473 (Vargas), FDRL. This contains Vargas's message, which said in the event of an attack on the United States "the vital interests of Brazil would necessarily be involved."

74. Oswaldo Aranha to Sumner Welles, Rio, Nov. 8, 1938, AOA, CPDOC.

75. Estado-Maior do Exército, *Relatório dos Trabalhos do Estado-Maior . . . 1937 . . . pelo GD Pedro Aurélio de Góes Monteiro,* 10–11. The United States Army had a coast

artillery mission working with that branch of the Brazilian army; consequently, there is a lot of detailed information in the National Archives about Brazilian port defenses. In September 1938 in some forts there was no powder for large caliber cannon and they had no antiaircraft guns. Brig. Gen. Allen Kimberly (chief of American Military Mission) to Eurico Dutra, Rio, Sep. 19, 1938: "Defense of Rio de Janeiro," 2667-K-4, Brazil 6800, G-2 Regional, RG 165, NA. Although General Kimberly's analysis was done for the Brazilians, he sent copies to the American War Department.

76. Vargas, *Diário,* 1:523–24. Interestingly, Vargas complained that Foreign Minister José Carlos de Macedo Soares was the one "continuously insisting" that the big purchases be made in Germany (525) and that the "publicity that he gave to the agreement, attributed to it an importance that it did not have, and were the principal reasons for American concerns" (525–26). I discussed the arms purchases and trade in *Brazilian-American Alliance,* 111–13, 148–75.

EPILOGUE

1. Murilo de Carvalho, "Armed Forces and Politics," 214. The professional officer quoted was Estevão Leitão de Carvalho, one of the German-influenced Young Turks and a founder of *A Defesa Nacional,* who had been offered the rebel command in 1930 but refused because it would violate his legalist principles. Author of several books, his attitudes are summarized in his *Dever Militar e Política Partidária* (São Paulo: Companhia Editora Nacional, 1959).

2. McCann, "The Military," 64–65; MG, *Relatório . . . Dutra . . . 1940,* 22; Sodré, *Memórias de um Soldado,* 188–90; Murilo de Carvalho, "Armed Forces and Politics," 205–7; for Decree-law 432 of May 19, 1938, see the summary in Major Lawrence C. Mitchell, Rio, June 17, 1938: "Law of Military Instruction," rpt. no. 2118, 2006-163, 6700, MID, GS, WD, G2 Regional, RG 165, NA.

3. Much of this was covered in McCann, *Brazilian-American Alliance,* and reconsidered in Frank D. McCann, "Brazil and World War II: The Forgotten Ally. What did you do in the war, *Zé Carioca?*" *Estudios Interdisciplinarios de America Latina y el Caribe* 6, no. 2 (July–Dec. 1995): 35–70.

4. Aspásia Camargo et al., *Golpe Silencioso,* 243.

5. Quotations from Dec. 1947 speech; American Embassy (Rio), Memo: "Speech by President Dutra at Army Maneuvers," Rio de Janeiro, Dec. 23, 1947, Dispatch 3252, 832.21/12-2347, RG 59, NA.

6. Ministério da Guerra, Estado-Maior do Exército, *O Éxodo Rural e o Exército* (Realengo, DF: Establecimento General Gustavo Cordeiro de Farias, 1955), 8–10. Copy in Centro de Documentação do Exército, Brasília.

7. Alfred Stepan, *Authoritarian Brazil,* 56.

8. See Thomas E. Skidmore, *Politics in Brazil, 1930–1964: An Experiment in Democracy* (New York: Oxford University Press, 1967). The Murilo de Carvalho quote is from his "Armed Forces and Politics," 223.

9. João Quartim de Moraes, *A Esquerda Militar no Brasil: Da conspiração republicana à guerrilha dos tenentes* (São Paulo: Edições Siciliano, 1991), 7. "Despite the evident differences in intellectual formation," he sees a "continuity of ethical-political inspi-

ration from the young abolitionist and republican officers, through the 'tenentes' of the 1920s, the anti-imperialist military of the 1950s, to the 'antigolpistas' of the 1960s." For the Korean War and U.S. military influence see Sonny B. Davis, *A Brotherhood of Arms: Brazil–United States Military Relations, 1945–1977* (Niwot: University Press of Colorado, 1996), 116–40.

10. General de Divisão Amauri Kruel (Ministro da Guerra), *Relatório Sucinto das Actividades do Ministerio da Guerra durante o ano de 1962, apresentado ao Excelentissimo Senhor Presidente da Republica* (Rio de Janeiro: SMG Imprensa do Exército, 1963), 4–8, 18–21, 23. Copy in CDOC-EX, Brasília. "Amauri Kruel," *DHBB*, 2:1694–97. He pointed to a steady decline in the army's percentage of the government's budget as follows:

Year	Army % of Govt. Budget
1958	14.1%
1959	13 %
1960	11 %
1961	10 %
1962	8 %
1963	7 %

11. "Amauri Kruel," *DHBB*, 2:1696. For the breakdown of the political system see Skidmore, *Politics in Brazil*, 253–302; Schneider, *Political System of Brazil*, 73–107; and Maria Celina D'Araujo, Gláucio Ary Dillon Soares, and Celso Castro, eds., *Visões do Golpe: A memória militar sobre 1964* (Rio de Janeiro: Relume-Dumará, 1994), 7–34.

12. See McCann, "The Brazilian Army and the Problem of Mission, 1939–1964," *Journal of Latin American Studies* 12, no. 1 (May 1980): 107–26. On ECEME's role in 1964 see Ana Lagôa, *SNI, Como Nasceu, Como Funciona* (São Paulo: Brasiliense, 1983), 86–87. My interviews with officers then at ECEME verified this type of activity. They believed that the left (Goulart's people in government, unions, communist party, and even favelados) was so well organized that the military conspiracy might well fail. They had plans to flee Brazil in such a case, and American officers had assured them that once outside Brazil they would receive U.S.A. training and logistical support to return to wage a guerrilla war inside the country.

13. Campos Coelho, *Em Busca de Identidade*, 169–70.

14. "Humberto Castelo Branco," *DHBB*, 1:698–717; "Costa e Silva," *DHBB*, 4:3144–49.

15. But paradoxically the officer corps believed that it was essentially democratic and committed to the development of democracy in Brazil. As General Aurélio de Lyra Tavares put it, "[I]n exceptional situations" when democratic processes were so threatened that the survival of national institutions and the sovereignty of the *Pátria* were endangered, it was the "legalist spirit of the army" that led it to invest itself in power for the sole purpose of "reestablishing democratic order." General Tavares graduated from the military school in Realengo in the 1925 Caxias turma and was minister of the army in that year of unhappy memory 1968. He believed and preached that the officer corps was a "priesthood" dedicated to the "defense of the *Pátria*." Further, as "soldiers of Caxias" the Brazilian army was to its very bones "democratic," faithful to its "popular roots." Many observers regarded such statements as cynical in face of

the replacement of stroke-stricken General Artur Costa e Silva in the presidency by General Emílio Garrastazú Médici, the choice of the "Cardinals of the military institution," that is to say the ranking officers. A. Lyra Tavares, *Nosso Exército: Essa Grande Escola* (Rio de Janeiro: Editora Biblioteca do Exército, 1985), 156–58, 165, 179; "Lira Tavares," *DHBB*, 4:3304–7; Thomas E. Skidmore, *The Politics of Military Rule in Brazil, 1964–85* (New York: Oxford University Press, 1988), 93–101; Schneider, *Political System of Brazil,* 290–96.

    16. Skidmore, *Politics of Military Rule,* 11–45, 306–10.

Select Bibliography

ARCHIVES

Arquivo Histórico do Exército, Rio de Janeiro

Arquivo Nacional, Rio de Janeiro.
—Papers of General Pedro de Góes Monteiro. (GMP)
Centro de Documentação do Exército (CDOC-EX), Quartel General do
Exército, Brasília.
Centro de Pesquisa e Documentação de História Contemporânea do Brasil,
Fundação Getúlio Vargas, Rio de Janeiro.
Collections
Arquivo Oswaldo Aranha.
Arquivo Bertoldo Klinger.
Arquivo Juracy Magalhães.
Arquivo Fernando Setembrino de Carvalho.
Arquivo Getúlio Vargas.

Programa de História Oral.
Depoimento Delso Mendes da Fonseca.

National Archives, Washington, D.C.

Department of State Records (Record Group [RG] 59).
Old Navy and Army Branch. (ONA)
Military Intelligence Division (MID), General Staff (GS), War Department
(WD)(RG 165).
U.S. Army Intelligence (G-2) Regional Files (Brazil)(RG 165).

Public Record Office, London

GOVERNMENT DOCUMENTS AND PUBLICATIONS

Associação dos Diplomados da Escola Superior de Guerra (ADESG). *Segurança Nacional e Segurança Interna*. Rio de Janeiro: Departmento de Ciclos de Estudos da ADESG, 1972.

Banha, Col. Paulo da Motta. Coordinator. *História do Estado-Maior do Exército.* Rio de Janeiro: Biblioteca do Exército, 1984.

Biblioteca Militar. *A República Brasileira.* Rio de Janeiro: Almanak Laeminert, 1939.

Câmara dos Deputados. *Mensagens Presidenciais, 1890–1910; Deodoro da Fonseca; Floriano Peixoto; Prudente de Moraes; Campo Salles; Rodrigues Alves; Affonso Penna; Nilo Peçanha.* Documentos Parlamentares 9. 1912. Reprint, Brasília: Câmara dos Deputados, 1978.

————. *Mensagens Presidenciais, 1910–1914; presidência Hermes da Fonseca.* Documentos Parlamentares 67. 1921. Reprint, Brasilia: Câmara dos Deputados, 1978.

————. *Mensagens Presidenciais, 1915–1918; presidência Wenceslau Braz.* Documentos Parlamentares 68. 1921. Reprint, Brasília: Câmara dos Deputados, 1978.

————. *Mensagens Presidenciais, 1919–1922; presidências Delphim Moreira and Epitácio Pessoa.* Documentos Parlamentares 71. 1922. Reprint, Brasília: Câmara dos Deputados, 1978.

————. *Mensagens Presidenciais, 1923–1926; presidência Arthur Bernardes.* Documentos Parlamentares 83. 1926. Reprint, Brasília: Câmara dos Deputados, 1978.

d'Assumpção, Herculano Teixeira. "Atividades Militares em Belo Horizonte." With attached memorandum "Alistamento Militar" (1875–1920). Typescript. December 12, 1947. Estado-Maior do Exército, CDOC-EX, Brasília.

A Defesa Nacional: Revista de Assuntos Militares. 1913–2002.

Directoria do Material Bellico. Relatórios, 1935–37. Carbon typescript copies in CDOC-EX, Brasília.

Escola de Comando e Estado-Maior do Exército. Curso de Preparação. *Guerras Insurrecionais no Brasil (Canudos e Contestado).* Rio de Janeiro: Imprensa Nacional, 1968.

Estado-Maior do Exército. *Relatório dos Trabalhos do Estado Maior Durante o Ano de 1923 apresentado ao Exmo. Sr. Marechal Fernando Setembrino de Carvalho pelo General de Divisão Augusto Tasso Fragoso Chefe do Estado-Maior do Exército.* Rio de Janeiro: Imprensa Militar, Estado-Maior do Exército, 1924.

————. *Relatório dos Trabalhos do Estado Maior Durante o Ano de 1925 apresentado ao Exmo. Sr. Marechal Fernando Setembrino de Carvalho pelo General de Divisão Augusto Tasso Fragoso Chefe do Estado-Maior do Exército.* Rio de Janeiro: Imprensa Militar, Estado-Maior do Exército, 1926.

————. *Relatorio dos Trabalhos do Estado-Maior durante o anno de 1927 apresentado ao Exmo. Sr. General de Divisão Nestor Sezefredo dos Passos Ministro da Guerra pelo General de Divisão Augusto Tasso Fragoso Chefe do Estado-Maior do Exército.* Rio de Janeiro: Imprensa Militar, Estado-Maior do Exército, 1928.

————. *Relatório dos Trabalhos do Estado-Maior durante o anno de 1929 apresentado ao Exmo. Sr. General de Divisão Nestor Sezefredo dos Passos pelo General de Divisão Alexandre Henriques Vieira Leal Chefe do Estado-Maior do Exército.* Rio de Janeiro: Imprensa Militar, Estado-Maior do Exército, 1930.

————. *O Êxodo Rural e o Exército.* Realengo, DF: Establecimento General Gustavo Cordeiro de Farias, 1955.

Gamelin, General Maurice, and Capt. Joaquim de Souza Reis Netto. *Manobra de Quardos de Exército de 1921–1922.* Rio de Janeiro: Imprensa Militar, 1922.

Góes Monteiro, (Capt.) Pedro A. de. "O Destacamento Mariante no Paraná Occidental (Reminiscências)." Rio de Janeiro. Junho de 1925. Typescript. Arquivo Histórico do Exército, Rio.

Kruel, Gen. de Div. Amaury (Ministro da Guerra). *Relatório Sucinto das Actividades do Ministerio da Guerra durante o ano de 1962, apresentado ao Excelentissimo Senhor Presidente da Republica.* Rio de Janeiro: SMG Imprensa do Exército, 1963.

Leite, Mauro Renault, and Luiz Gonzaga Novelli Jr., eds. *Marechal Eurico Gaspar Dutra: O dever da verdade.* Rio de Janeiro: Editora Nova Fronteira, 1983.

Ministerio da Guerra. *Relatórios* of the ministers of war. 1889–1945.

Ministerio da Guerra. *Almanak do Ministerio da Guerra.* 1889–1965.

Ministerio da Viação e Obras Publicas. Dep. de Aeronautica Civil. *A Linha Aerea Internacional da America do Norte a Buenos Aires Através do Brasil e do Paraguay.* Rio de Janeiro: Officinas dos Correios e Telegraphos, 1937.

Ruas Santos, (Capt.) Francisco. "Resumo Histórico, Periodo de Outubro de 1896 a Dezembro de 1950." Estado-Maior do Exército. Rio de Janeiro, November 5, 1951. CDOC-EX, Brasília.

Setembrino de Carvalho, Fernando. *Relatório apresentado ao General de Divisao José Caetano de Faria, Ministro de Guerra pelo General da Brigada Fernando Setembrino de Carvalho Commandante das Forças em operações de guerra no Contestado, 1915.* Rio de Janeiro: Imprensa Militar, Estado-Maior do Exército, 1916.

Tasso Fragoso, Augusto. "Reflexões sobre a Situação Militar do Brasil." October 1927. Typed and bound. CDOC-EX, Brasília.

United Kingdom. "Brazil, Annual Report." Foreign Office Confidential Prints, 1906–1929, 1937.

United States Department of State. *Foreign Relations of the United States 1945.* Washington, D.C.: Govt. Printing Office, 1969.

Vargas, Getúlio. *A Nova Política do Brasil.* 11 vols. Rio de Janeiro: José Olympio Editora, 1938–47.

———. *Diário.* Vol. 1, *1930–1936;* Vol. 2 *1937–1942.* São Paulo and Rio de Janeiro: Editoras Siciliano and Fundação Getúlio Vargas, 1995.

BOOKS AND DISSERTATIONS

Abrahamson, James L. *America Arms for a New Century: The Making of a Great Military Power.* New York: Free Press, 1981.

Abranches, João Dunshee de. *A Illusão Brasileira (Justificação Historica de uma Attitude).* 5th ed. Rio de Janeiro: Imprensa Nacional, 1917.

———. *Como se Faziam Presidentes: Homens e Fatos do Inicio da República.* Rio de Janeiro: José Olympio Editora, 1973.

Agulhas Negras: Tradição e Atualidade do Ensino Militar no Brasil. Rio de Janeiro: AC & M Editora, 1993.

Albuquerque, Manoel Maurício de. *Pequena História da Formação Social Brasileira.* Rio de Janeiro: Edições Graal, 1984.

Alden, Dauril, and Warren Dean, eds. *Essays Concerning the Socioeconomic History of Brazil and Portuguese India.* Gainesville: University Press of Florida, 1977.

Almeida, General Gil Antonio Dias de. *Homens e factos de uma revolução.* Rio de Janeiro: Ed. Calvino Filho, n.d.

Almeida, José Américo de. *A Palavra e o Tempo (1937–1945–1950).* Rio de Janeiro: José Olympio Editora, 1965.

Alves de Abreu, Alzira, coordinatora. *Juracy Magalhães: Minhas Memórias Provisórias; Depoimento prestado ao CPDOC.* Rio de Janeiro: Editora Civilização Brasileira, 1982.

Amaral, Antonio José do Azevedo. *O Estado Autoritário e a Realidade Nacional.* Brasília: Editora Universidade de Brasília, 1981.

Andrews, C. C. *Brazil: Its Condition and Prospects.* 3d ed. New York: D. Appleton, 1891.

Araripe, Tristão de Alencar. *Tasso Fragoso, Um Pouco de História do Nosso Exército.* Rio de Janeiro: Ed. Biblioteca do Exército, 1960.

———. *A Coerência de Uma Vocação.* Rio de Janeiro: Imprensa do Exército, 1969.

———. *Expedições Militares Contra Canudos: Seu Aspecto Marcial.* 2d ed. Rio de Janeiro: Biblioteca do Exército, 1985.

Araujo, Rubens Vidal. *Os Vargas.* Porto Alegre: Editora Globo, 1985.

Barata, Agildo. *Vida de um Revolucionário (Memórias).* Rio de Janeiro: Editora Melso, S.A., 1962.

Barbosa, Francisco de Assis. *A Vida de Lima Barreto.* 5th ed. Rio de Janeiro: José Olympio Editora, 1975.

Barbosa, Lívia. *O Jeitinho Brasileiro: A arte de ser mais igual que os outros.* Rio de Janeiro: Editora Campus, 1992.

Barman, Roderick J. *Brazil: The Forging of a Nation, 1789–1852.* Stanford, Calif.: Stanford University Press, 1988.

———. *Citizen Emperor: Pedro II and the Making of Brazil, 1825–1891.* Stanford, Calif.: Stanford University Press, 1999.

Barreto, Annibal. *Fortificações do Brasil.* Rio de Janeiro: Editora Biblioteca do Exército, 1958.

Bello, José Maria. *A History of Modern Brazil, 1889–1964.* Stanford, Calif.: Stanford University Press, 1966.

Beloch, Israel, and Alzira Alves de Abreu, eds. *Dicionário Histórico-Biografico Brasileiro, 1930–1983.* 4 vols. Rio de Janeiro: Forense-Universitária, 1984.

Bento, Cláudio Moreira. *O Exército na Proclamação da República.* Rio de Janeiro: SENAI, 1989.

———. *Academia Militar das Agulhas Negras (Jubileu de Ouro em Resende).* Resende: Soraaman, 1994.

Biblioteca Militar, *República Brasileira.* Rio de Janeiro: Almanak Laemmert, 1939.

Bilac, Olavo. *A Defesa Nacional (Discursos).* Rio de Janeiro: Editora Biblioteca do Exército, 1965.

Boehrer, George C. A. *Da Monarquia à República: História do Partido Republicano do Brasil (1870–1889).* Rio de Janeiro: Ministério de Educação e Cultura, 1954.

Bonalume Neto, Ricardo. *A Nussa Guerra: Os Brasileiros em Combate, 1942–1945.* Rio de Janeiro: Expressãoe Cultura, 1995.

Bonumá dos Santos, Cel. Newton, and Cel. Sergio Roberto Dentino Morgado. "Reflexões sobre a Cultura no Exército Brasileiro; Suas Dimensões, Objetivos, Estrutura, Instrumentos e Respostas." Monografia apresentada como Exigência curricular para a obtenção de Diploma do curso de Política, Estratégia e Alta Administração do Exército. Rio de Janeiro: Escola de Comando e Estado-Maior do Exército, 1990.

Brandi, Paulo. *Vargas: Da Vida Para a História*. Rio de Janeiro: Zahar Editores, 1983.

Brinton, Crane. *The Anatomy of Revolution*. New York: Vintage, 1957.

Brito, Ademar de. *O 52º batalhão de caçadores e a 3a companhia de metralhadoras pesadas.* Rio de Janeiro: Biblioteca do Exército, 1944.

Buarque de Hollanda, Sérgio. *Do Império à República.* Vol. 5 of *História Geral da Civilização Brasileira*. São Paulo: Difel/Difusão Editoral, 1972.

Burns, E. Bradford. *A Documentary History of Brazil*. New York: Knopf, 1966.

———. *The Unwritten Alliance: Rio-Branco and Brazilian-American Relations*. New York: Columbia University Press, 1966.

———. *Nationalism in Brazil; a Historical Survey*. New York: Praeger, 1968.

———. *A History of Brazil*. New York: Columbia University Press, 1970.

Calmon, Pedro. *História do Brasil.* Vol. 6. Rio de Janeiro: José Olympio Editora, 1959.

Calógeras, João Pandiá. *Problemas de Administração*. 2d ed. São Paulo: Companhia Editôra Nacional, 1938.

Câmara, (Lt. Col.) Hiram de Freitas. *Marechal José Pessôa: A Força de um Ideal*. Rio de Janeiro: Biblioteca do Exército, 1985.

Camargo, Aspásia, and Walder de Góes. *Meio século de combate: Diálogo com Cordeiro de Farias.* Rio de Janeiro: Editora Nova Fronteira, 1981.

Camargo, Aspásia, et al. *O Golpe Silencioso: As Origens da República Corporativa.* Rio de Janeiro: Rio Fundo Editora, 1989.

Camp, Roderic Ai. *Generals in the Palacio: The Military in Modern Mexico*. New York: Oxford University Press, 1992.

Campello de Souza, Maria do Carmo. *Estado e partidos políticos no Brasil (1930 a 1964).* São Paulo: Alfa-Omega, 1976.

Campos Coelho, Edmundo. *Em Busca de Identidade: O Exército e a Política na Sociedade Brasileira.* Rio de Janeiro: Forense-Universitária, 1976.

Canale, Dario, Francisco Viana, and José Nilo Tavares. *Novembro de 1935: Meio Século Depois.* Petrópolis: Editora Vozes, 1985.

Cancelli, Elizabeth. *O Mundo da Violência: A Polícia da Era Vargas.* Brasília: Editora Universidade de Brasília, 1993.

Carneiro, Glauco. *Historia da Revoluções Brasileiras.* 2 vols. Rio: Edições O Cruzeiro, 1965.

———. *Lusardo: O Último Caudilho.* 2 vols. Rio de Janeiro: Editora Nova Fronteira, 1978.

Carone, Edgard. *A primeira república (1889–1930) texto e contexto.* São Paulo: Difusão Européia do Livro, 1969.

———. *A República Velha.* Vol. 1, *Instituições e Classes Sociais*. São Paulo: Difusão Européia do Livro, 1971.

———. *A República Velha.* Vol. 2, *Evolução política*. São Paulo: Difusão Européia do Livro, 1972.

———. *A Segunda República (1930–1937).* São Paulo: Difusão Européia do Livro, 1973.

———. *O Tenentismo; Acontecimentos, Personagens, Programas.* São Paulo: Difusão Européia do Livro, 1975.

Cascudo, Luís da Câmara. *Dicionário do Folclore Brasileiro.* Rio de Janeiro: Instituto Nacional do Livro, 1962.

Castelo Branco, Col. Manoel Thomaz. *O Brasil na II Grande Guerra.* Rio de Janeiro: Biblioteca do Exército, 1960.

Castro, Celso. *O Espírito Militar: Um Estudo de Antropologia Social na Academia Militar das Agulhas Negras.* Rio de Janeiro: Jorge Zahar, 1990.

Castro, Sertório de. *A República que a Revolução Destruiu.* 1932. Reprint, Brasília: Editora Universidade de Brasília, 1982.

Castro e Silva, Major Egydio Moreira de. *Á Margem do Ministério Calógeras (na pasta da guerra).* Rio de Janeiro: Editora Melso S.A., 1961.

Cavalcanti, Pedro. *A Presidência Wenceslau Braz, 1914–1918.* Brasília: Editora Universidade de Brasília, 1981.

Celso, Alfonso. *Porque me Ufano do Meu Paiz.* Rio de Janeiro: Livaria Garnier, 1900.

Challenger, Richard D. *The French Theory of the Nation in Arms, 1866–1939.* New York: Columbia University Press, 1952.

Chandler, Billy Jaynes. *The Feitosas and the Sertão dos Inhamuns: The History of a Family and a Community in Northeast Brazil, 1700–1930.* Gainesville: University Press of Florida, 1972.

Cidade, Gen. Franciso de Paula. *Síntese de Três Séculos de Literatura Militar Brasileira.* Rio de Janeiro: Estabelecimento Gustavo Cordeiro de Faria, 1959.

Clifford, John G. *The Citizen Soldiers: The Plattsburg Training Camp Movement, 1913–1920.* Lexington: University Press of Kentucky, 1972.

Coelho, Col. José Tobias. *O Exército Internamente (Reminiscencias Historicas).* Rio de Janeiro: Editora Alba, 1935.

Coffman, Edward M. *The Old Army: A Portrait of the American Army in Peacetime, 1784–1898.* New York: Oxford University Press, 1986.

Conniff, Michael L. *Urban Politics in Brazil: The Rise of Populism, 1925–1945.* Pittsburgh: University of Pittsburgh Press, 1981.

Conniff, Michael L., and Frank D. McCann, eds. *Modern Brazil: Elites and Masses in Historical Perspective.* Lincoln: University of Nebraska Press, 1989.

Corrêa, Anna Maria Martinez. *A Rebelião de 1924 em São Paulo.* São Paulo: HUCITEC, 1976.

Corrêa, Carlos Humberto. *Militares e Civis num Governo sem Rumo: O Governo Provisório Revolucionário no sul do Brasil, 1893–1894.* Florianópolis: Ed. UFSC and Ed. Lunardelli, 1990.

Costa, João Cruz. *Contribuição a História das Idéias no Brasil.* Rio de Janeiro: José Olympio Editora, 1967.

Coutinho, Lourival. *O General Góes Depõe.* Rio de Janeiro: Livraria Editora Coelho Branco, 1956.

CPDOC. *A Revolução de 30: Seminário Internacional.* Brasília: Editora Universidade de Brasília, 1982.

d'Assumpção, Herculano Teixeira. *A Campanha do Contestado.* 2 vols. Belo Horizonte: Imprensa Oficial do Estado de Minas Gerais, 1917.

da Cunha, Euclydes. *Canudos, Diário de uma Expedição.* Rio de Janeiro: José Olympio Editora, 1939.

———. *Rebellion in the Backlands.* Trans. Samuel Putman. Chicago, Ill.: University of Chicago Press, 1944.

Danese, Sérgio. *Diplomacia Presidencial: História e crítica.* Rio de Janeiro: Topbooks Editora, 1999.

Dantas, José Ibaré Costa. *O Tenentismo em Sergipe (Da Revolta de 1924 à Revolução de 1930).* Petrópolis: Ed. Vozes, 1974.

D'Araujo, Maria Celina, and Celso Castro, eds. *Ernesto Geisel.* Rio de Janeiro: Fundacão Getúlio Vargas Editora, 1997.

Davis, Sonny B. *A Brotherhood of Arms: Brazil–United States Military Relations, 1945–1977.* Niwot: University Press of Colorado, 1996.

Dean, Warren. *The Industrialization of São Paulo, 1880–1945.* Austin: University of Texas Press, 1969.

Della Cava, Ralph. *Miracle at Joaseiro.* New York: Columbia University Press, 1970.

Denys, Odylio. *Ciclo Revolucionário Brasileiro, Memórias.* Rio de Janeiro: Editora Nova Fronteira, 1980.

Diacon, Todd A. *Millenarian Vision, Capitalist Reality: Brazil's Contestado Rebellion, 1912–1916.* Durham, N.C.: Duke University Press, 1991.

Domingos Neto, Manuel. "L'Influence Etrangere dans La Modernization de L'Armee Bresilienne (1889–1930)." Paris: Thése presentée a` l'Institut des Hautes Etudes de l'Amérique Latine, Université de Paris III, pour l'obtention du Doctorat IIIème Cycles, 1979.

Drummond, José Augusto. *O Movimento Tenentista: A Intervenção Militar e Conflito Hierárquico (1922–1935).* Rio de Janeiro: Editora Graal, 1986.

Dudley, William S. "Reform and Radicalism in the Brazilian Army, 1870–1889." Ph.D. diss., Columbia University, 1972.

Dulles, John W. F. *Vargas of Brazil: A Political Biography.* Austin: University of Texas Press, 1967.

———. *Castello Branco: The Making of a Brazilian President.* College Station: Texas A & M University Press, 1978.

Dutra, Eurico Gaspar. *O Exército em Dez Anos de Governo do Presidente Vargas.* Rio de Janeiro: Ministério da Guerra, 1941.

Duval, Armando. *Reorganisação do Exército.* Rio de Janeiro: Imprensa Nacional, 1901.

———. *A Argentina, potência militar.* 2 vols. Rio de Janeiro: Imprensa Nacional, 1922.

Facó, Rui. *Cangaçeiros e Fanáticos, Gênese e Lutos.* Rio de Janeiro: Editora Civilização Brasileira, 1976.

Faoro, Raymundo. *Os Donos do Poder, Formação do Patronato Político Brasileiro.* 2 vols. Porto Alegre and São Paulo: Ed. Globo and Ed. de Universidade de São Paulo, 1975.

Fernandes, Heloisa Rodrigues. *Política e Segurança, Fôrça Pública do Estado de São Paulo: Fundamentos Históricos-Sociais.* São Paulo: Editora Alfa-Omega, 1974.

Fifer, J. Valerie. *Bolivia: Land, Location, and Politics Since 1825.* Cambridge, U.K.: Cambridge University Press, 1972.

Fleischer, David V., ed. *Carlos Peixoto Filho.* Brasília: Câmara dos Deputados, 1978.

Flynn, Peter. *Brazil: A Political Analysis.* Boulder, Colo.: Westview Press, 1978.

Foch, Ferdinand. *The Principles of War.* New York: Henry Holt, 1920.

Fonseca Filho, Hermes da. *Marechal Hermes: Dados para uma biografia*. Rio de Janeiro: n.p., 1961.

Fonseca, Mario Hermes da, and Ildefonso Escobar, eds. *Primórdios da organização da defesa nacional*. Rio de Janeiro: Tipografia Glória, Pinho, and Manes, 1943.

Fonseca, Nair de Teffé Hermes da. *A Verdade sobre a Revolução de 22*. Rio de Janeiro: Gráfica Portinho Cavalcanti, 1974.

Fontoura, João Neves da. *Memórias*. Porto Alegre: Globo, 1963.

Forjoz, Maria Cecila Spina. *Tenentismo e Política*. Rio de Janeiro: Paz e Terra, 1977.

Fortes, Hugo G. Borges, *Canhões Cruzados, Uma Síntese da História da Artilharia de Costa Brasileira*. Rio de Janeiro: Editora Biblioteca do Exército, 2001.

Franck, Harry A. *Working North from Patagonia*. New York: Garden City Publishing, 1921.

Freixinho, Nilton. *Instituições em Crise: Dutra e Góes Monteiro, Duas Vidas Paralelas*. Rio de Janeiro: Biblioteca do Exército Editora, 1997.

Freyre, Gilberto. *Order and Progress: Brazil from Monarchy to Republic*. New York: Knopf, 1970.

Frischauer, Paul. *Presidente Vargas: Biografia*. São Paulo: Companhia Editora Nacional, 1944.

Gabaglia, Laurita Pessôa Raja. *Epitacio Pessôa (1865–1942)*. 2 vols. Rio de Janeiro: José Olympio Editora, 1951.

Galvão, Walnice Nogueira. *No Calor da Hora: A guerra de Canudos nos jornais, 4a expedição*. São Paulo: Ed. Ática, 1974.

Gauld, Charles A. *The Last Titan: Percival Farquhar, American Entrepreneur in Latin America*. Stanford, Calif.: Institute of Hispanic American and Luso-Brazilian Studies, 1964.

Globo, Editôra. *Vocabulário Sul-Rio-Grandense*. Porto Alegre: Editôra Globo, 1964.

Góes Monteiro, Gen. Pedro A. de. *A revolução de 30 e a finalidade política do exército*. Rio de Janeiro: Assis Cintra e Andersen, 1934.

Graça Aranha, José Pereira da. *Canaan*. Boston: Four Seas, 1920.

Guimarães, Carlos Eugênio de Andrada. *Arthur Oscar, Soldado do Império e da República*. Rio de Janeiro: Biblioteca do Exército, 1965.

Guimarães, Manoel Luiz Lima Salgado, et al., eds. *A Revolução de 30: Textos e Documentos*. 2 vols. Brasília: Editora Universidade de Brasília, 1982.

Hahner, June E. *Civilian-Military Relations in Brazil, 1889–1898*. Columbia, S.C.: University of South Carolina Press, 1969.

Hale, Albert. *The South Americans*. Indianapolis, Ind.: Bobbs-Merrill, 1907.

Hall, Lawrence H. "João Pandiá Calógeras, Minister of War, 1919–1922; The Role of a Civilian in the Development of the Brazilian Army." Ph.D. diss., New York University, 1983.

Harries, Meirion, and Susie Harries. *Soldiers of the Sun: The Rise and Fall of the Imperial Japanese Army*. New York: Random House, 1991.

Hart, John M. *Revolutionary Mexico: The Coming and Process of the Mexican Revolution*. Berkeley: University of California Press, 1987.

Hess, David J., and Roberto A. DaMatta, eds. *The Brazilian Puzzle: Culture on the Borderlands of the Western World*. New York: Columbia University Press, 1995.

Hilton, Stanley E. *Brazil and the Great Powers, 1930–1939: The Politics of Trade Rivalry*. Austin: University of Texas Press, 1975.

————. *1932: A Guerra Civil Brasileira (História da Revolução Constitucionalista de 1932)*. Rio de Janeiro: Editora Nova Fronteira, 1982.

————. *A Rebelião Vermelha*. Rio de Janeiro: Editora Record, 1986.

————. *Brazil and the Soviet Challenge, 1917–1947*. Austin: University of Texas Press, 1991.

Holloway, Thomas H. *Immigrants on the Land: Coffee and Society in São Paulo, 1886–1934*. Chapel Hill: University of North Carolina Press, 1980.

————. *Policing Rio de Janeiro: Repression and Resistance in a Nineteenth-Century City*. Stanford, Calif.: Stanford University Press, 1993.

Howard, Michael, and Peter Paret, eds. *Carl von Clausewitz on War*. Princeton, N.J.: Princeton University Press, 1976.

Huggins, Martha K. *Political Policing: The United States and Latin America*. Durham, N.C.: Duke University Press, 1998.

Huntington, Samuel F. *The Soldier and the State: The Theory and Politics of Civil-Military Relations*. Cambridge, Mass.: Harvard University Press, 1959.

Ikegami, Eiko. *The Taming of the Samurai: Honorific Individualism and the Making of Modern Japan*. Cambridge, Mass.: Harvard University Press, 1995.

Janotti, Maria de Lourdes Mônaco. *Os Subversivos da República*. São Paulo: Ed. Brasiliense, 1986.

Joffily, José. *O Caso Panther*. Rio de Janeiro: Paz e Terra, 1988.

Johnson, John J. *The Military and Society in Latin America*. Stanford, Calif.: Stanford University Press, 1964.

Jomini, Antoine Henri (Baron). *The Art of War*. 1862. Reprint, Westport, Conn.: Greenwood, 1971.

Keith, Henry H. *Soldados Salvadores: As Revoltas Militares Brasileiras de 1922 e 1924 Em Perpectiva Histórica*. Rio de Janeiro: Biblioteca do Exército, 1989.

Keith, Henry H., and Robert A. Hayes, eds. *Perspectives on Armed Politics in Brazil*. Tempe: Arizona State University, 1976.

Kennedy, Paul. *The Rise and Fall of the Great Powers*. New York: Random House, 1987.

Klinger, Jeneral [Bertoldo]. *Narrativas aotobiograficas*. 7 vols. Rio de Janeiro: O Cruzeiro, 1944–53.

Lagôa, Ana. *SNI, Como Nasceu, Como Funciona*. São Paulo: Brasiliense, 1983.

Lauerhass, Ludwig, Jr. *Getúlio Vargas e o Triunfo do Nacionalismo Brasileiro: Estudo do Advento da Geração Nacionalista de 1930*. São Paulo and Belo Horizonte: Editora da Universidade de São Paulo and Editora Itatiaia, 1986.

Leal, Joaquim Ponce. *Os Homens e As Armas: Notícia de um Ciclo Revolucionário*. Rio de Janeiro: Livraria Editora Cátedra, 1980.

Leitão de Carvalho, (Col.) Estevão. *Na Revolução de 30: A Attitude do 8º R.I. (Guarnição de Passo Fundo)*. Rio de Janeiro: Ed. Schmidt, 1933.

Leitão de Carvalho, (Gen.) Estevão. *Dever Militar e Polílitca Partidária*. São Paulo: Companhia Editora Nacional, 1959.

————. *Memórias de um soldado legalista*. 3 vols. Rio de Janeiro: SMG Imprensa do Exército, 1961, 1962, 1964.

————. *Discursos, Conferências & Outros Escritos*. Rio de Janeiro: Imprensa do Exército, 1965.

Lemos, Renato Luís do Couto Neto e. *Benjamin Constant: Vida e História.* Rio de Janeiro: Topbooks Editora, 1999.

Lessa, Renato. *A Invenção Republicana; Campos Sales, as Bases e a Decadência da Primeira República Brasileira.* São Paulo: Edições Vértice, 1988.

Leuchars, Christopher. "Brazilian Foreign Policy and the Great Powers, 1912–1930." D. Phil. diss., St. Antony's College, Oxford University, 1983.

Levine, Robert M. *The Vargas Regime: The Critical Years, 1934–1938.* New York: Columbia University Press, 1970.

———. *Pernambuco in the Brazilian Federation, 1889–1937.* Stanford, Calif.: Stanford University Press, 1978.

———. *Vale of Tears: Revisiting the Canudos Massacre in Northeastern Brazil, 1893–1897.* Berkeley: University of California Press, 1992.

———. *Father of the Poor? Vargas and his Era.* New York: Cambridge University Press, 1998.

Lewin, Linda. *Politics and Parentela in Paraíba: A Case Study of Family-Based Oligarchy in Brazil.* Princeton, N.J.: Princeton University Press, 1987.

Lieuwen, Edwin. *Arms and Politics in Latin America.* New York: Praeger, 1960.

Lima, Valentina da Rocha, coordinador. *Getúlio, uma história oral.* Rio de Janeiro: Editora Record, 1986.

Lima Sobrinho, Alexandre José Barbosa. *Presença de Alberto Tôrres (Sua Vida e Pensamento).* Rio de Janeiro: Ed. Civilização Brasileira, 1968.

———. *A Verdade Sobre a Revolução de Outubro–1930.* 2d ed. São Paulo: Alfa-Omega, 1975.

Lippi Oliveira, Lúcia, ed. *Elite Intelectual e Debate Político nos Anos 30.* Rio de Janeiro: Editora Fundação Getúlio Vargas, 1980.

Lippi Oliveira, Lúcia, Mônica Pimenta Velloso, and Ângela Maria Castro Gomes, *Estado Novo: Ideologia e Poder.* Rio de Janeiro: Zahar Editores, 1982.

Litrento, Oliveiros Lessa. *Canudos: Visões e Revisões.* Rio de Janeiro: Biblioteca do Exército Editora, 1998.

Lopes, Gen. Moacir Araujo. *Olavo Bilac, O Homem Cívico.* Rio de Janeiro: Liga da Defesa Nacional, 1968.

Lopes, Theodorico, and Gentil Torres. *Ministros da Guerra do Brasil, 1808–1946.* Rio de Janeiro: n.p., 1947.

Love, Joseph L. *Rio Grande do Sul and Brazilian Regionalism, 1882–1930.* Stanford, Calif.: Stanford University Press, 1971.

———. *São Paulo in the Brazilian Federation, 1889–1937.* Stanford, Calif.: Stanford University Press, 1980.

Loveman, Brian. *For la Pátria: Politics and the Armed Forces in Latin America.* Wilmington, Del.: SR Books, 1999.

Loveman, Brian, and Thomas M. Davies, eds. *The Politics of Anti-Politics: The Military in Latin America.* Wilmington, Del.: SR Books, 1997.

Lozoya, Jorge Alberto. *El Ejercito Mexicano, 1911–1965.* Mexico, D.F.: El Colegio de México, 1970.

Luttwak, Edward. *Coup d'Etat: A Practical Handbook.* New York: Knopf, 1968.

Lyra, Heitor. *História da Queda do Império.* 2 vols. São Paulo: Companhia Editora Nacional, 1964.

Lyra Tavares, *Exército e Nação.* Recife: Imprensa Universitária, 1965.

———. *O Brasil de Minha Geração.* Rio de Janeiro: Editora Biblioteca do Exército, 1976.

———. General Aurélio de. *Brasil França ao Longo de 5 Séculos.* Rio de Janeiro: Biblioteca do Exército, 1979.

Macaulay, Neill. *The Prestes Column; Revolution in Brazil.* New York: New Viewpoints, 1974.

Macedo Cavalho, Luiz Paulo, ed. *The Army in Brazilian History.* 4 vols. Rio de Janeiro and Salvador, Ba.: Biblioteca do Exército and Odebrecht, 1998.

Macedo Soares, Henrique Duque-Estrada de. *A Guerra de Canudos.* 1903. Reprint, Rio de Janeiro: Biblioteca do Exército, 1959.

Machado de Assis, Joaquim Maria. *Jacob and Esau.* Berkeley: University of California Press, 1965.

Magalhães, João Baptista de. *A evolução militar do Brasil.* Rio de Janeiro: Biblioteca do Exército, 1958.

Magalhães, Raimundo, Jr. *Deodoro: A Espada contra o Império.* Vol. 2, *O Galo na Tôrre.* São Paulo: Companhia Editora Nacional, 1957.

———. *Olavo Bilac e sua época.* Rio de Janeiro: Editora Americana, 1974.

Malan, Alfredo Souto. *Uma Escolha, Um Destino: Vida do Gen. Malan d'Angrogne.* Rio de Janeiro: Biblioteca do Exército, 1977.

———. *Missão Militar Francesa de Instrução Junto ao Exército Brasileiro.* Rio de Janeiro: Biblioteca do Exército, 1988.

Marinho, Fundação Roberto, *Contestado.* Rio de Janeiro: Editora Index, 1987.

Martins, Hélio Leôncio. *A Revolta da Armada.* Rio de Janeiro: Biblioteca do Exército Editora, 1997.

Mascarenhas de Moraes, Marechal João Baptisa. *Memórias.* 2 vols. Rio de Janeiro: José Olympio Editora, 1969.

Matthieu, Gilles. *Une Ambition Sud-Américaine: Politique culturelle (1914–1940).* Paris: Ed. L.Harmattan, 1991.

Maximiano, Cesar Campiani. *Onde Estão Nossos Heróis: Uma Breve História dos Brasileiros na 2a Guerra.* São Paulo: Editora Santuário, 1995.

McCann, Frank D. *The Brazilian-American Alliance, 1937–1945.* Princeton, N.J.: Princeton University Press, 1973.

———. *A Nação Armada: Ensaios Sobre a História do Exército Brasileiro.* Recife: Editora Guararapes, 1982.

Meade, Teresa A. *"Civilizing" Rio: Reform and Resistance in a Brazilian City, 1889–1930.* University Park: Pennsylvania State University Press, 1997.

Meira Mattos, Carlos. *O Marechal Mascarenhas de Moraes e sua Época.* Rio de Janeiro: Editora Biblioteca do Exército, 1983.

Mello Franco, Virgilio de. *Outubro, 1930.* 2d ed. Rio de Janeiro: Ed. Schimidt, 1931.

Melo, Hildebrando Bayard. *No Exército do Meu Tempo.* Rio de Janeiro: Biblioteca do Exército Editora, 1987.

Melo Franco, Afonso Arinos de. *Um estadista da república, Afranio de Melo Franco e seu tempo.* 2 vols. Rio de Janeiro: José Olympio Editora, 1955.

Mendes de Morais, General Luis. *Reforma do Ensino: Alterações no regulamento da Escola Militar do Brasil; Regulamento para a Escola Pratica do Exército; Resposta a um crítico.* Rio de Janeiro: Villas Boas, 1904.

Miranda, Alcibiades. *Contestado.* Curitiba: Lítero-Técnica, 1987.

Moniz, Edmundo. *A Guerra Social de Canudos.* Rio de Janeiro: Civilização Brasileira, 1978.

Moniz Bandeira, Luiz Alberto. *Presença dos EUA no Brasil.* Rio de Janeiro: Civilização Brasileira, 1973.

————. *Estado Nacional e Política Internacional na América Latina: O Continente nas Relações Argentina–Brazil (1930–1992).* São Paulo: Editora Ensaio, 1993.

————. *O Governo João Goulart: As lutas sociais no Brasil, 1961–1964.* Rio de Janeiro: Editora Revan, 2001.

Moraes, Dênis de, and Francisco Viana. *Prestes: Lutas e Autocríticas.* Petrópolis: Editora Vozes, 1982.

Moreira Lima, Lourenço. *A Coluna Prestes (Marchas e Combates).* 3d ed. São Paulo: Editora Alfa-Omega, 1979.

Morel, Edmar. *A Revolta da Chibata.* 3d ed. Rio de Janeiro: Editora Graal, 1979.

Motta, Jehovah. *Formação do Oficial do Exército: Currículos e regimes na Academia Militar, 1810–1944.* Rio de Janeiro: Ed. Companhia Brasileira de Artes Gráficas, 1976.

Murakami, Ana Maria Brandão, ed. *A Revolução de 1930 e seus antecedentes.* Rio de Janeiro: Editora Nova Fronteira, 1980.

Muricy, Antonio Carlos da Silva. *Palavras de Um Soldado.* Rio de Janeiro: Imprensa do Exército, 1971.

Murilo de Carvalho, José. *Os Bestializados: O Rio de Janeiro e a República que não foi.* São Paulo: Companhia das Letras, 1987.

————. *A Formação das Almas: O Imaginário da República no Brasil.* São Paulo: Companhia das Letras, 1990.

Nabuco, Carolina. *A vida de Virgílio de Melo Franco.* Rio de Janeiro: José Olympio Editora, 1962.

Nagle, Jorge. *Educação e sociedade na primeira república.* São Paulo: Editora da Universidade de São Paulo, 1974.

Needell, Jeffrey D. *A Tropcial Belle Epoque: Elite Culture and Society in Turn-of-the-Century Rio de Janeiro.* Cambridge, U.K.: Cambridge University Press, 1987.

Neves, Lúcia Maria Bastos Pereira das, and Humberto Fernandes Machado. *O Império do Brasil.* Rio de Janeiro: Editora Novo Fronteira, 1999.

Nogueira, Ataliba. *Antonio Conselheiro e Canudos: Revisão História.* São Paulo: Companhia Editora Nacional, 1974.

Noronha, Abílio de. *Narrando a Verdade: Contribuição para a História da Revolução de S. Paulo.* São Paulo: Companhia Gráfica-Editora Monteiro Lobato, 1924.

Nunes Leal, Victor. *Coronelismo, Enxada e Voto, O Municipio e O Regime Representativo no Brasil.* São Paulo: Ed. Alfa-Omega, 1976.

Nunn, Frederick M. *The Military in Chilean History: Essays on Civil-Military Relations, 1810–1973.* Albuquerque: University of New Mexico Press, 1976.

————. *Yesterday's Soldiers: European Military Professionalism in South America, 1890–1940.* Lincoln: University of Nebraska Press, 1983.

Oakenfull, J. C. *Brazil in 1911.* Frome, U.K.: Butler and Tanner, 1912.

————. *Brazil (1913).* Frome, U.K.: Butler and Tanner, 1914.

Oliveira, Eliézer Rizzo de, et al. *As Forças Armadas no Brasil*. Rio de Janeiro: Espaço e Tempo, 1987.

Oliveira Tôrres, João Camillo de. *História de Minas Gerais*. 5 vols. Belo Horizonte: Difusão Pan-Americana do Livro, 1961.

―――. *A Democracia Coroada, Teoria Política do Império do Brasil*. 2d ed. Petrópolis: Editora Vozes, 1964.

Oliveira Viana, Francisco José de. *Problemas de política objetiva*. São Paulo: Ed. Nacional, 1930.

Otaviano, Manuel. *A Coluna Prestes na Paraiba*. Joã Pessôa: Editora Acauã, 1979.

Owensby, Brian P. *Intimate Ironies: Modernity and the Making of Middle-Class Lives in Brazil*. Stanford, Calif.: Stanford University Press, 1999.

Paiva, Mário Garcia de. *A Grande Aventura de Rondon*. Rio de Janeiro: Instituto Nacional do Livro, 1971.

Pedrosa, José Fernando de Maya. *A Grande Barreira: Os Militares e a Esquerda Radical no Brasil, 1930–1968*. Rio de Janeiro: Biblioteca do Exército Editora, 1998.

Peixoto, Arthur Vieira. *Floriano, Biografia do Marechal Floriano Peixoto*. Rio de Janeiro: Ministerio da Educação, 1939.

Peixoto, Dermeval [pseudonym "Crivelaro Marcial"]. *A Campanha do Contestado—Episódios e Impressões*. Rio de Janeiro: 2° Milheiro, 1916.

Peixoto, General Dermeval. *Memórias de um velho soldado (Nomes, coisas e fatos militares de meio seculo atrás)*. Rio de Janeiro: Biblioteca do Exército, 1960.

Peregrino, Umberto. *"Os Sertões" Como História Militar*. Rio de Janeiro: Biblioteca do Exército, 1956.

―――. *História e Projeção das Instituições Culturais do Exército*. Rio de Janeiro: Biblioteca do Exército, 1967.

―――. *Euclides da Cunha e Outros Estudos*. Rio de Janeiro: Récord Editora, 1968.

Pérez, Louis A. *Army Politics in Cuba, 1898–1958*. Pittsburgh, Pa.: University of Pittsburgh Press, 1976.

Pessôa, Pantaleão. *Reminiscências e Imposições de Uma Vida (1885–1965)*. Rio de Janeiro: author published, 1972.

Pinheiro, Paulo Sérgio. *Estratégias da Ilusão: A Revolução e o Brasil, 1922–1935*. São Paulo: Companhia das Letras, 1991.

Prado, Paulo. *Retrato do Brasil, Ensaio sôbre a Tristeza Brasileira*. Rio de Janeiro: José Olympio Editora, 1928.

Prazeres, Otto. *O Brasil na Guerra (Algumas Notas Para a História)*. Rio de Janeiro: Imprensa Nacional, 1918.

Quartim de Morães, João. *A Esquerdo Militar no Brasil: Da Conspiração Republicana à Guerrilha dos Tenentes*. São Paulo: Edições Siciliano, 1991.

Queiroz, Maria Isaura Pereira de. *O Messianismo no Brasil e no Mundo*. São Paulo: Dominus Editora, 1965.

―――. *O Mandonismo local na Vida Política Brasileira e Outros Ensaios*. São Paulo: Ed. Alfa-Omega, 1976.

Queiroz, Suely Robles Reis de. *Os Radicais da República—Jacobinismo: Idelogia e Ação, 1893–1897*. São Paulo: Ed. Brasiliense, 1986.

Rachum, Ilan. "Nationalism and Revolution in Brazil, 1922–1930: A Study of Intellectual, Military, and Political Protesters and of the Assault on the Old Republic." Ph.D. diss., Columbia University, 1970.

Recalde, Pablo E. Tufari. *La Guerra del Chaco: Antecedentes Históricos y Conducción Político—Estratégica del Conflicto.* Asunción: Imprenta Militar, 1987.

Reed, John. *Insurgent Mexico.* New York: D. Appleton, 1914.

Roosevelt, Theodore, *Through the Brazilian Wilderness.* New York: Charles Scribner's Sons, 1919.

Rose, R. S. *One of the Forgotten Things: Getúlio Vargas and Brazilian Social Control, 1930–1945.* Westport, Conn.: Greenwood Press, 2000.

Rouquié, Alain. *The Military and the State in Latin America.* Berkeley: University of California Press, 1987.

Ruas Santos, Francisco. *Coleção Bibliográfica Militar.* Rio de Janeiro: Ed. Biblioteca do Exército, 1960.

Sá, Augusto. *Exércitos Regionaes ou O Problema de uma organisação para o nosso exército.* Porto Alegre: n.p., 1905.

Salas, Elizabeth. *Soldaderas in the Mexican Military: Myth and History.* Austin: University of Texas Press, 1990.

Schneider, Ronald M. *The Political System of Brazil: Emergence of a "Modernizing" Authoritarian Regime, 1964–1970.* New York: Columbia University Press, 1971.

———. *"Order and Progress": A Political History of Brazil.* Boulder, Colo.: Westview Press, 1991.

Schwarcz, Lilia Moritz. *As Barbas do Imperador: D. Pedro II, um Monarca nos Trópicos.* São Paulo: Companhia das Letras, 1998.

Schwartzman, Simon. *Bases do Autoritarismo Brasileiro.* Brasília: Editora Universidade de Brasília, 1982.

Senna, Ernesto. *Rascunhos e Perfis.* 1909. Reprint, Brasília: Editora Universidade de Brasília, 1982.

———. *Deodoro: Subsidios para a historia—Notas de um reporter.* Rio de Janeiro: Imprensa Nacional, 1913.

Silva, Alfredo Pretextato Maciel da. *Os Generais do Exército Brasileiro de 1822 a 1889 (Traços Biográficos).* 2d ed. Vol 2. Rio de Janeiro: Biblioteca Militar, 1940.

Silva, Ernani Ayrosa da. *Memórias de um Soldado.* Rio de Janeiro: Biblioteca do Exército Editora, 1985.

Silva, Hélio. *1922: Sangue na areia de Copacabana.* Rio de Janeiro: Editora Civilização Brasileira, 1965.

———. *1930: A Revolução Traída.* Rio de Janeiro: Editora Civilização Brasileira, 1966.

———. *1932: A Guerra Paulista.* Rio de Janeiro: Editora Civilização Brasileira, 1967.

———. *1933: A Crise do Tenentismo.* Rio de Janeiro: Editora Civilização Brasileira, 1968.

———. *1934: A Constituinte.* Rio de Janeiro: Editora Civilização Brasileira, 1969.

———. *1935: A Revolta Vermelha.* Rio de Janeiro: Editora Civilização Brasileira, 1969.

———. *1937: Todos os Golpes se Parecem.* Rio de Janeiro: Editora Civilização Brasileira, 1970.

————. *1889: A República não Esperou o Amanhecer.* Rio de Janeiro: Editora Civilização Brasileira, 1972.

————. *O Poder Militar.* Porto Alegre: L & PM Editores, 1984.

Silva Barros, Capt. Raymundo da. *Sarilho d'Armas (Vida de Caserna).* Rio de Janeiro: Ed. Calvino Filho, 1934.

Silveira, Geraldo Tito. *Crônica da Polícia Militar de Minas.* Belo Horizonte: n.p., 1966.

Simmons, Charles. *Marshal Deodoro and the Fall of Dom Pedro II.* Durham, N.C.: Duke University Press, 1966.

Simonsen, Roberto. *A Construcção dos Quarteis Para o Exército.* São Paulo: n.p., 1931.

Skidmore, Thomas E. *Politics in Brazil, 1930–1964: An Experiment in Democracy.* New York: Oxford University Press, 1967.

————. *Black into White: Race and Nationality in Brazilian Thought.* New York: Oxford University Press, 1974.

————. *The Politics of Military Rule in Brazil, 1964–85.* New York: Oxford University Press, 1988.

Smallman, Shawn C. "The Parting of the Waters: The Brazilian Army and Society, 1889–1954." Ph.D. diss., Yale University, 1995.

Sodré, Nelson Werneck. *História Militar do Brasil.* Rio de Janeiro: Editora Civilização Brasileira, 1965.

————. *Memórias de um soldado.* Rio de Janeiro: Civilização Brasileira, 1967.

————. *A Coluna Prestes: Análise e Depoimentos.* Rio de Janeiro: José Olympio Editora, 1985.

Stauffer, David H. "The Origin and Establishment of Brazil's Indian Service: 1889–1910." Ph.D. diss., University of Texas, Austin, 1955.

Stepan, Alfred. *The Military in Politics: Changing Patterns in Brazil.* Princeton, N.J.: Princeton University Press, 1971.

————. *Rethinking Military Politics: Brazil and the Southern Cone.* Princeton, N.J.: Princeton University Press, 1988.

————, ed. *Authoritarian Brazil: Origins, Policies, and Future.* New Haven, Conn.: Yale University Press, 1973.

Stepan, Nancy. *Beginnings of Brazilian Science: Oswaldo Cruz, Medical Research, and Policy, 1890–1920.* New York: Science History Publications, 1976.

Stokes, Charles E. "The Acre Revolutions, 1899–1903: A Study in Brazilian Expansion." Ph.D. diss., Tulane University, 1974.

Stumpf, Andre Gustavo, and Merval Pereira Filho. *A Segunda Guerra: Sucessão de Geisel.* São Paulo: Brasiliense, 1979.

Távora, Juarez. *Á guisa de depoimento: Sobre a revolução brasileiro de 1924.* São Paulo: O Combate, 1927.

————. *Uma Vida e Muitas Lutas, Memórias.* 3 vols. Rio de Janeiro: José Olympio Editora, 1973, 1976, 1977.

Teixeira Monteiro, Duglas. *Os Errantes do Novo Seculo, Um estudo sobre o surto Milenarista do Contestado.* São Paulo: Livraria Duas Cidades, 1974.

Thomé, Nilson. *Trem de Ferro, A Ferrovia no Contestado.* 1st ed. Caçador, Santa Catarina: Impressora Universal, 1980.

Thompson, Arthur. *Guerra Civil do Brasil de 1893–1895: Vida e Morte do Almirante Saldanha da Gama.* 3d ed. Rio de Janeiro: Editora Carioca, 1959.

Topik, Steven C. *The Political Economy of the Brazilian State, 1889–1930.* Austin: University of Texas Press, 1987.

———. *Trade and Gunboats: The United States and Brazil in the Age of Empire.* Stanford, Calif.: Stanford University Press, 1996.

Tôrres, Alberto. *A Organização Nacional.* 1914. Reprint, Brasília: Editora Universidade de Brasília, 1982.

———. *O Problema Nacional Brasileiro.* 1914. Reprint, Brasília: Editora Universidade de Brasília, 1982.

Tota, Antonio Pedro. *O Estado Novo.* São Paulo: Editora Brasiliense, 1987.

———. *O Imperialismo Sedutor: A Americanização do Brasil na Época da Segunda Guerra.* São Paulo: Companhia das Letras, 2000.

Trumpener, Ulrich. *Germany and the Ottoman Empire, 1914–1918.* Princeton, N.J.: Princeton University Press, 1968.

Valladares, Benedicto. *Tempos Idos e Vividos: Memórias.* Rio de Janeiro: Editora Civilização Brasileira, 1966.

Vargas do Amaral Peixoto, Alzira. *Getúlio Vargas, Meu Pai.* Rio de Janeiro: Editora Globo, 1960.

Vasconcelos, Capt. Genserico de. *História Militar do Brasil: Introdução da influencia do factor militar na organização da nacionalidade; A Campanha de 1851–1852.* Rio de Janeiro: Imprensa Militar, 1922.

Verissimo, Erico. *Time and the Wind.* New York: Macmillan, 1951.

Viana Filho, Luiz. *A Vida do Barão do Rio Branco.* Rio de Janeiro: José Olympio Editora, 1959.

Vianna, José Feliciano Lobo, ed. *Guia Militar para o Anno de 1898.* Rio de Janeiro: Imprensa Nacional, 1897.

———. *A Vida de Rui Barbosa.* 7th ed. São Paulo: Livraria Martins Editora, 1965.

Villela, Marcos Evangelista da Costa, Jr. *Canudos: Memórias de um Combatente.* São Paulo: Ed. Marco Zero, 1988.

Vinhas de Queiroz, Maurício. *Messianismo e Conflicto Social: A Guerra Sertaneja do Contestado, 1912–1916.* São Paulo: Editora Atica, 1977.

Vinhosa, Francisco Luiz Teixeira. *O Brasil e a Primeira Guerra Mundial.* Rio de Janeiro: Instituto Histórico e Geográfico Brasileiro, 1990.

Viotti da Costa, Emilia. *The Brazilian Empire: Myths and Histories.* Chicago, Ill.: University of Chicago Press, 1985.

von Seeckt, Hans. *Thoughts of a Soldier.* Trans. Gilbert Waterhouse. London: Ernest Benn, 1930.

Waack, William. *As duas faces da glória: A FEB vista pelos seus aliados e inimigos.* Rio de Janeiro: Editora Nova Fronteira, 1985.

———. *Camaradas: Nos Arquivos de Moscou; A história secreta da revolução brasileira de 1935.* Rio de Janeiro and São Paulo: Biblioteca do Exército Editora and Companhia das Letras, 1993.

Wagner, Arthur L. *Organization and Tactics.* Kansas City, Mo.: Franklin Hudson Publishing, 1906.

Wesson, Robert, and David V. Fleischer. *Brazil in Transition*. New York: Praeger, 1983.

Wheeler, Douglas L. *Republican Portugal: A Political History, 1910–1926*. Madison: University of Wisconsin Press, 1978.

Wirth, John D. *The Politics of Brazilian Development*. Stanford, Calif.: Stanford University Press, 1970.

———. *Minas Gerais in the Brazilian Federation, 1889–1937*. Stanford, Calif.: Stanford University Press, 1977.

Wolfe, Joel W. "The Rise of Brazil's Industrial Working Class: Community, Work, and Politics in São Paulo, 1900–1955." Ph.D. diss., University of Wisconsin, 1990.

———. *Working Women, Working Men: São Paulo and the Rise of Brazil's Industrial Working Class, 1900–1955*. Durham, N.C.: Duke University Press, 1993.

Wood, David L. "Abortive Panacea: Brazilian Military Settlements: 1850 to 1913." Ph.D. diss., University of Utah, 1972.

[Wright, Jaime, ed.] *Brasil: Nunca Mais*. Petrópolis: Editora Vozes, 1985.

Young, Jordan. *The Brazilian Revolution of 1930 and the Aftermath*. New Brunswick, N.J.: Rutgers University Press, 1967.

ARTICLES, CHAPTERS, AND CONFERENCE PAPERS

Alexander, Robert J. "Brazilian 'Tenentismo.'" *Hispanic American Historical Review* 36 (May 1956): 229–42.

Araujo, Ricardo Benzaquen de. "As Classificações de Plínio: Uma Análise do Pensamento de Plínio Salgado entre 1932 e 1938." *Revista de Ciência Política* 21, no. 3 (Sep. 1978): 161–79.

Bento, Cláudio Moreira. "Reunião no Clube Militar para a Fundação de *A Defesa Nacional*." *A Defesa Nacional*, Sep.-Oct. 1984, 163–68.

———. "Controvérsias sobre a Proclamação da República." *A Defesa Nacional*, July–Sep. 1990, 17–36.

———. "Uma Possível Explicação para a Violência na Revolução de 1893–95." *A Defesa Nacional*, Apr.–June 1995, 141–43.

Bittencourt, Capt. Dr. Liberato. "Pelo soldado Brazileiro." *Revista Academia Militar* 1, no. 9 (Jan. 27, 1904): 455–61.

"Bomba Oculta, Coronel doi chantageado no caso Riocentro." *Veja*, Oct. 16, 1985, 43.

Borges, Dain. "Salvador's 1890s: Paternalism and Its Discontents." *Luso-Brazilian Review* 30, no. 2 (winter 1993): 47–57.

Castro Ayres, 1st Lt. Miguel de. "Regimen das Massas." *A Defeza Nacional*. III, 26(Rio, 10 Nov 1915): 53–55.

Castro, Celso. "Entre Caxias e Osório: A criação do culto ao patrono do Exército brasileiro," *Estudos Históricos* 14, no. 25 (2000): 103–17.

Cavalcanti de Queiroz, Themistocles. "A Luta no Contestado," *Revista do Clube Militar* 31, no. 152 (1957): 49–57.

Cidade, Francisco de Paula. "Os Fanaticos, Liame Historico." *A Defesa Nacional*, Oct. 1914, 12–14.

———. "Recrutamento de Oficiaes." *A Defesa Nacional*, Nov. 1914, 49–50.

————. "Em Torno de Contestado." *A Defeza Nacional.* II, no. 16 (Jan 10, 1915): 124–25; and no. 18 (Mar.10, 1915): 179–82.

————. "O Exército em 1889: Resumo Histórico." In Biblioteca Militar, *A República Brasileira,* 232–304. Rio de Janeiro: Almanak Laemmert, 1939.

————. "Marechal Hermes Rodrigues da Fonseca." *Revista Militar Brasileira.* July–Dec. 1955, 229–42.

————. "Revivendo o Passado—Meio século mais tarde: A Escola de Guerra." *Revista do Clube Militar* 31, no. 152 (1958): 105–14.

Conniff, Michael L. "The Tenentes in Power: A New Perspective on the Brazilian Revolution of 1930." *Journal of Latin American Studies* 10, no. 1 (1978): 61–82.

————. "The National Elite." In *Modern Brazil: Elites and Masses in Historical Perspective,* ed. Michael L. Conniff and Frank D. McCann, 23–46. Lincoln: University of Nebraska Press, 1989.

Cordeiro de Farias, Ignez. "Um troupier na política: Entrevista com o general Antônio Carlos Muricy." In *Entre-vistas: Abordagens e usos da história oral,* coord. Marieta de Moraes Ferreira et al., 124–46. Rio de Janeiro: Editora da Fundação Getúlio Vargas, 1994.

Correia, Jonas. Introduction to *A Guerra de Canudos,* by Henrique Duque-Estrada de Macedo Soares, v–xxxviii. Rio de Janeiro: Biblioteca do Exército, 1959.

Costa, Octávio. "Os Militares na Sociedade Moderna." *Política e Estratégia* 4, no. 2 (Apr.–June 1986): 163–73.

Dassin, Joan. "Human Rights in Brazil: A Report as of March 1979." *Newsletter of Latin American Studies Association* 10, no. 3 (Sep. 1979): 24–36.

————. "The Culture of Fear." *Items and Issues* 40, no. 1 (Mar. 1986): 43.

della Cava, Ralph. "Brazilian Messianism and National Institutions: A Reappraisal of Canudos and Joaseiro." *Hispanic American Historical Review* 48, no. 3 (Aug. 1968): 402–20.

d'Estillac Leal, Col. Francisco Raul. "Do Contestado, Observações colhidos nas operações da columna sul." *A Defesa Nacional,* Aug. 1915, 357–61, and Oct. 1915, 27–30.

Dudley, William S. "Institutional Sources of Officer Discontent in the Brazilian Army, 1870–1889." *Hispanic American Historical Review* 55, no. 1 (Feb. 1975): 44–65.

————. "Professionalism and Politicization as Motivational Factors in the Brazilian Army Coup of 15 November 1889." *Journal of Latin American Studies* 8, no. 1 (May 1976): 101–24.

Editorial, "A campanha ingloria do Contestado." *A Defesa Nacional,* Apr. 1915, 197–98.

"Entrevista: Dickson Melges Grael, 'A nação quer a verdade's' (O coronel que investiga o Riocentro fala do terrorismo dos orgãos de segurança e seus efeitos sobre o prestigio das Forças Armadas)." *Veja,* Oct. 23, 1985, 5–8.

Fernandes, Heloisa Rodrigues. "A Força Pública do Estado de São Paulo." In *História Geral da Civilização Brasileira.* Vol. 9, bk. 3, *O Brasil Republicano,* ed. Boris Fausto, 237–56. Rio de Janeiro: DIFEL/Difusão, 1977.

Filho, Expedito. "Autópsia da sombra: O depoimento terrível de um ex-sargento que transitava no mundo clandestino da repressão militar resgata parte da história de uma guerra suja." *Veja,* Nov. 18, 1992, 20–32 [interview of ex-sergeant Marival Dias Chaves do Canto].

Flynn, Peter. "The Revolutionary Legion and the Brazilian Revolution of 1930." In *Latin American Affairs,* ed. Raymond Carr, 63–105. London: St. Anthony's Papers, 1970.

"Frestas na gaveta, Inquérito das bombas volta à Justiça Militar." *Isto É,* Oct. 9, 1985, 78.

Gomes, Angela Maria de Castro. "A Representção de Classes na Constituinte de 1934." *Revista de Ciência Política* 21, no. 3 (Sep. 1976): 53–115.

Guerra, Walter Pinheiro. "Euclides da Cunha, O Conselheiro e a Psiquiatria." *A Defesa Nacional,* July–Sep. 1990, 70–82.

Hall, Lawrence. "To Create an Army: The Mission of Calógeras." Paper presented at the annual meeting of the American Historical Association, Chicago, Ill., 1984.

Hart, Keith. "Brazilians in Britain 1918." *Army Quarterly and Defence Journal* (Great Britain) 3, no. 4 (Oct. 1981): 475–78.

Hermes, Mário Jorge da Fonseca. "Os Militares e os Políticos durante o Império." *A Defesa Nacional,* July–Sep. 1990, 83–105.

Hilton, Stanley E. "The Armed Forces and Industrialists in Modern Brazil: The Drive for Military Autonomy, 1889–1954." *Hispanic American Historical Review* 62, no. 4 (Nov. 1982): 629–73.

Holloway, Thomas H. "Immigration in the Rural South." In *Modern Brazil: Elites and Masses in Historical Perspective,* ed. Michael L. Conniff and Frank D. McCann, 140–60. Lincoln: University of Nebraska Press, 1991.

Keith, Henry H. "Armed Federal Interventions in the States during the Old Republic." In *Perspectives on Armed Politics in Brazil,* ed. Henry H. Keith and Robert A. Hayes. Tempe: Center for Latin American Studies, Arizona State University, 1976.

Levine, Robert M. "Mud-Hut Jerusalem: Canudos Revisited." *Hispanic American Historical Review* 68, no. 3 (Nov. 1988): 525–72.

———. "Elite Perceptions of the Povo." In *Modern Brazil: Elites and Masses in Historical Perspective,* ed. Michael L. Conniff and Frank D. McCann, 209–24. Lincoln: University of Nebraska Press, 1989.

"Lições de Terror." *Isto É,* Oct. 16, 1985, 18–23.

Lobo da Silva, Col. Dr. Arthur. "A Anthropologia no Exército Brasileiro." *Archivos do Museu Nacional* 30 (1928): 13–44, plus (unpaged) ten maps and thirty-one tables and graphs.

Macedo Carvalho, Luiz Paulo. "Repensando o General Góes." *A Defesa Nacional,* Apr.–June 1990, 7–18.

Martins da Silva, Alberto. "Cem Anos de Canudos (1896–1996)." *A Defesa Nacional,* 4 Trim. de 1996, 144–47.

McCann, Frank D. "The Nation in Arms: Obligatory Military Service During the Old Republic." In *Essays Concerning the Socioeconomic History of Brazil and Portuguese India,* ed. Dauril Alden and Warren Dean, 211–43. Gainesville: University Press of Florida, 1977.

———. "Origins of the 'New Professionalism' of the Brazilian Military." *Journal of Interamerican Studies and World Affairs* 21, no. 4 (Nov. 1979): 505–22.

————. "The Brazilian Army and the Problem of Mission, 1939–1964." *Journal of Latin American Studies* 12, no. 1 (May 1980): 107–26.

————. "The Brazilian General Staff and Brazil's Military Situation, 1900–1945." *Journal of Interamerican Studies and World Affairs* 25, no. 3 (August 1983): 299–324.

————. "Influencia Estrangeira no Exército Brasileiro." *A Defesa Nacional*, Jan.-Feb. 1985, 83–117.

————. "The Military." In *Modern Brazil: Elites and Masses in Historical Perspective*, ed. Michael L. Conniff and Frank D. McCann, 47–80. Lincoln: University of Nebraska Press, 1989.

————. "Brazilian Army Officers Biography Project." Panel on collective biography at the meeting of the Latin American Studies Association, Miami, Fla., Dec. 5, 1989.

————. "A Força Expedicionária Brasileira na Campanha Italiana, 1944–1945." In *A Luta dos Pracinhas: Força Expedicionária Brasileira na II Guerra Mundial*, ed. Joel Silveira and Thassilo Mitke, 267–87. Rio de Janeiro: Editora Record, 1993.

————. "Brazil and World War II: The Forgotten Ally. What did you do in the war, Zé Carioca?" *Estudios Interdisciplinarios de America Latina y El Caribe* 6, no. 2 (July–Dec. 1995): 36–70.

Meira Mattos, Carlos de. "Castello Branco—Oficial de Estado-Maior, Chefe Militar e Estadista." *A Defesa Nacional*, Jan.–Mar. 1990, 29–41.

Mello, Marco Antônio da Silva, and Arno Vogel. "Monarquia Contra República: A ideologia da terra e o paradigma do milênio na 'guerra santa' do Contestado." *Estudos Históricos* 2, no. 4 (1989): 190–13.

Mendes, Fábio Faria. "A 'Lei da Cumbuca': A revolta contra o sorteio militar." *Estudos Históricos* 13, no. 24 (1999): 267–93.

Meznar, Joan E. "The Ranks of the Poor: Military Service and Social Differentiation in Northeast Brazil, 1830–1875." *Hispanic American Historical Review* 72, no. 3 (Aug. 1992): 335–51.

Murilo de Carvalho, José. "As Forças Armadas na Primeira República: O Poder Destabilizador." *Cadernos do Departamento de Ciência Política*. Universidade Federal do Minas Gerais. No. 1 (Mar. 1974): 113–88.

————. "As Forças Armadas na Primeira República: O Poder Desestablizador." In *História Geral da Civilização Brasileira*. Vol. 9, bk. 3, *O Brasil Republicano*, ed. Boris Fausto, 183–234. Rio de Janeiro: DIFEL/Difusão, 1977.

————. "Forças Armadas e Política, 1930–1945." In *A Revolução de 30: Seminário Internacional*, by CPDOC, 109–87. Brasília: Editora Universidade de Brasília, 1982.

————. "Armed Forces and Politics in Brazil, 1930–45." *Hispanic American Historical Review* 62, no. 2 (May 1982): 193–223.

Nachman, Robert G. "Positivism and Revolution in Brazil's First Republic: The 1904 Revolt." *The Americas* 34, no. 1 (July 1977): 20–39.

Nunn, Frederick. "The Latin American Military Establishment: Some Thoughts on the Origins of Its Socio-Political Role and an Illustrative Bibliographic Essay." *The Americas* 28, no. 2 (Oct. 1971): 135–51.

————. "Military Professionalism and Professional Militarism in Brazil, 1870–1970: Historical Perspectives and Political Implications." *Journal of Latin American Studies* 4, no. 1 (1972): 29–54.

————. "Effects of European Military Training in Latin America: Origins and Nature of Professional Militarism in Argentina, Brazil, Chile, and Peru, 1890–1940." *Military Affairs* 39, no. 1 (1975): 1–7.

"O CIEx Meteu-se na Corrupção e no Terrorismo." *Veja,* Oct. 30, 1985, 46–47.

"O Porão Começa a Falar." *Veja,* Oct. 30, 1985, 42–47.

"O Tamanho do Porão: O Regime de 1985 Começa a Esercitar Uma Dificil Convivência com uma das Heranças Deixadas pelo Regime de 1964." *Veja,* Sep. 10, 1986, 43.

Parolini, Eulália, et al. "A Contribuição de Rondon para a Antropologia Brasileira." *Revista do Exército Brasileira* 119, no. 2 (Apr.–June 1982): 7–19.

Peregrino, Umberto. "Significação do Marechal Hermes." In *Euclides da Cunha e Outros Estudos,* by Umberto Peregrino, 111–48. Rio de Janeiro: Récord Editora, 1968.

Pinheiro, Ivan Cosme de Oliveira. "O Militar e a Política na República." *A Defesa Nacional,* Jan.–Mar. 1990, 58–95.

Powe, Major Marc B. "A Great Debate, The American General Staff (1903–16)." *Military Review* 55, no. 4 (Apr. 1976): 71–89.

Queiroz, Themistocles Cavalcanti de. "A Luta no Contestado" *Revista do Clube Militar* 31, no. 152 (1958): 49–57.

Ribeiro Costa, Vanda Maria. "Com Rancor e Com Afeto: Rebeliões Militares na Década de 30." *Política e Estratégia* 4, no. 2 (Apr.–June 1986): 173–200.

Ribeiro de Sena, Davis. "As Polícias Militares e Sua Destinação Legal." *A Defesa Nacional,* May-June 1980, 163–74.

————. "A Guerra das Caatingas." *A Defesa Nacional,* Jan.–Mar. 1990, 7–28.

————. "Serviço Militar Obrigatório e/ou Profissionalização do Exército." *A Defesa Nacional,* Apr.–June 1995, 23–37.

Sampaio, Consuelo Novais. "Repensando Canudos: Ojogo das Oligarquias." *Luso-Brazilian Review* 30, no. 2 (winter 1993): 92–113.

Schulz, John. "O Exército e o Império." In *História Geral da Civilização Brasileira,* ed. Sérgio Buarque de Holanda and Pedro Moacyr Campos, 6:235–58. São Paulo: Difusão do Livro, 1971.

Seidl, Major Raimundo Pinto. "Combatir o Analphabetismo é um Dever de Honra para o Official Brasileiro." *A Defeza Nacional.* III,25 (Rio, 10 October 1915): 44–47.

Tasso Fragoso, Gen. Augusto. "A revolução de 1930." *Revista do Instituto Histórico e Geográfico Brasileiro* 211 (Apr.–June 1951): 8–61.

Teixeira Monteiro, Duglas. "Um Confronto entre Juazeiro, Canudos e Contestado." In *História Geral da Civilização Brasileira,* ed. Boris Fausto, 9:58–71. Rio de Janeiro: DIFEL/Difusão, 1977.

Tiller, Ann Quiggins. "The Igniting Spark—Brazil 1930." *Hispanic American Historical Review* 35 (1965): 384–92.

Travassos, Mario. "Para a Frente, Custe o Que Custar!" *A Defeza Nacional.* IV, No. 38 (Oct. 10, 1916): 15–17.

Villela, 1st. Lt. Marcos Evangelista da Costa, Jr. "A Aviação Militar no Brasil." *A Defeza Nacional.* III, 36 (Rio, 10 Set 1916): 379–380.

Vinhosa, Francisco Luiz Teixeira. "1914 ou escritores em guerra." *Jornal do Brasil* (Rio de Janeiro). Aug. 26, 1984, "Especial," 4.

Wallace, Anthony F. C. "Identity and the Nature of Revolution." In *Latin America: The Dynamics of Social Change,* ed. Stefan A. Halper and John R. Sterling, 172–86. New York: St. Martin's, 1972.

Wirth, John D. "Tenentismo in the Brazilian Revolution of 1930." *Hispanic American Historical Review* 44, no. 2 (May 1964): 161–79.

Wolfe, Joel. "Anarchist Ideology, Worker Practice: The 1917 General Strike and the Formation of São Paulo's Working Class." *Hispanic American Historical Review* 71 no. 4 (Nov. 1991): 809–46.

Young, Jordan. "Military Aspects of the 1930 Brazilian Revolution." *Hispanic American Historical Review* 44, no. 2 (1964): 180–96

Index